Picking Up
the Pieces

Picking Up the Pieces

1971 War Babies' Odyssey from
Bangladesh to Canada

Mustafa Chowdhury

Rev. date: 09/30/2015

To order additional copies of this book, contact:
Xlibris
1-888-795-4274
www.Xlibris.com
Orders@Xlibris.com
622545

CONTENTS

I dedicate this book with love and appreciation to the women of Bangladesh who were "dishonored" in "Occupied Bangladesh" and to the babies who were born as a result of rape.

As well, to those extraordinary Canadian couples who, by taking responsibility for a few of the war babies, embraced them with filial love and provided them a safe and secure home in Canada.

FOREWORD

IN THIS BOOK, Mustafa Chowdhury presents the true story of the adoptive parents from the time they decided to adopt a number of war babies from Bangladesh. He describes the babies' odyssey to Canada, where, on their arrival in their new homes, the adoptive parents and other family members embraced them to raise them as their *own* children. Chowdhury's narrative impressively details the lives of the war babies through the years, with anecdotes of their rearing, nurturing, and becoming adults. We know of no other book with the depth of purpose, scope, and revelation of heretofore ignored historical facts. His work is an invaluable contribution to the story of adoption in Bangladesh and Canada.

It is a fascinating book for anyone interested in interracial adoption. Chowdhury investigated a wide range of topics including the importance of family and of tender loving care for each member of the family. We see both the adopters and the adoptees talk about their different experiences of courage, perseverance, and love, each from their own perspective.

He found that these adoptive parents as a group distinguished themselves by a greater psychical stability not often found in most couples. Following several rounds of discussions with the adoptive couples on parenting over a span of many years, he outlines how they have been able to cope with problems that might have been impossibly stressful for some other couples.

In the same way, having interviewed the adoptees several times with follow-up questions and clarifications, he has made excellent use of personal anecdotes. Having spent numerous absorbing hours with both the adoptive parents and their children, Chowdhury has intertwined the personal experiences of both sets of people with the legal, social, and moral complexities that shaped the social history of Canada and Bangladesh. In raising their children, Chowdhury has shown how the adoptive parents paid attention to ensuring that the child in question became independent – that the child learned how to relate to other people confidently and warmly.

The testimonies of the adoptive parents and the adoptees reveal a love that transcends all barriers, and that the most important thing is growing up as a family that loves and supports its children. One message that comes out loud and clear is that adopting orphans from other races and cultures is identical to the motivation of families who adopt of the same race: the love for children and the adoptive parents' commitment to having an eclectic family. Readers will find out for themselves how, through sharp analysis, Chowdhury has illustrated with poignant vignettes an important fact of life – that humans desire and need close relationships.

The inspirational efforts of the adoptive parents and the final outcome of their efforts outlined in the book may be seen as a springboard for talking about interracial adoption, having learned how these war babies came to Canada to be united with their families. As one leafs through the pages of this fascinating book, one will see how, following the war babies' odyssey and safe arrival in Canada, their traumatic life that began forty-three years ago became a life of dignity and accomplishment.

Mr. Chowdhury has spent years of research on this book, producing a truly amazing work and a remarkably enjoyable read. It was heartwarming to be able to "meet" these "babies" again. It was an emotionally rewarding read for us. We appreciate and commend Mr. Chowdhury's efforts. The book's only fault is his overgenerous depiction of the Cappuccinos.

Bonnie and Fred Cappuccino

They are Members of the Order of Canada
They live at 19014 Concession 7, Maxville, Ontario, Canada, K0C 1T0.
e-mail: fred@childhaven.ca

ACKNOWLEDGMENT

T HIS STUDY CHRONICLES the outcomes of the adoption of a number of Bangladeshi war babies into Canadian homes. It is based on an examination of primary documents pertaining to adoption observations pieced together, analyzed, and interpreted from historical records gathered both in Canada, where I live, and in Bangladesh, where I traveled to. Throughout the writing of this book, I have received valuable advice, assistance, and inspiration from several people who have offered astute and constructive criticism. Indeed, a great many people have contributed through sincere advice and encouragement in making this book possible; however, the responsibility for its content is absolutely my own. I stand on the firing line, for I lay no claim to comprehensiveness as the subject continues to challenge me.

While it is not practical to list all, there are a number of people to whom I owe a particular note of thanks. Among others whose help and encouragement I should like to acknowledge are the adoptive parents and the adoptees I have talked to. All of them welcomed me into their homes, gave generously their time, and provided me with their scrapbooks, "Bangladesh File," and other information they have collected over the years. I am perpetually grateful to those who had allowed me to quote them as I deemed appropriate; as well, for giving me full access to their correspondence with various officials during their quest for adoption from Bangladesh. I was blessed with many touching and informative letters/e-mails from the adoptive parents. Every time I went to their homes, their faces would expand in a smile of welcome that would raise my own comfort level.

This book is unique, because unlike other works on the war babies, it is largely based on insights from the point of view of the adoptive parents and the adoptees. Their support of my work acted as a pillar of strength during my moments of frustration. Indeed, the families I interviewed were major contributors to this book, and I will always remain grateful to them for their unwavering support, observations, and openness.

I am particularly grateful to the late Sr. Margaret Mary, then superior of the Missionaries of Charity, Dhaka, Bangladesh. I corresponded with her throughout the 1980s and 1990s when she was in Dhaka, Bangladesh, and later in Kolkata, West Bengal, India. Our correspondence gave me an opportunity to get a clear understanding of her role in the adoption of the war babies from Bangladesh's orphanages to Canadian homes.

I would also like to thank the following who read parts of the manuscript and made helpful comments and suggestions: Syed Tareque Rahman (Esty) Robert Mercier, Terry O'Donnell, Prof. Sirajul Islam Chowdhury, and Dr. Selim Sarwar. I owe a special debt of gratitude to Sadek Ali and Selina Chowdhury who contributed uniquely and invaluably and whose critical comments had been very useful. Both Ali and Chowdhury deserve special gratitude, as they stood by through the several phases of my work for donating hours of editing and proofreading; as well, always offering the best of professional help, support, and friendship from conception to fruition.

I am grateful to Jilhurain Jaigirdar for providing me his office to use computer facilities in Bangladesh while conducting research; as well, his marketing manager, Shubhasish Hossain, for scanning photographs and annexes for providing all other computer-related help. I am grateful to Rahul Datta and Nehar Ahmed (my daughter-in-law) for computer help; to Muhaimin Karim and Nazira Anher for helping me out with pictures, annexes, and other related work. I am greatly indebted to Ashfaque ur Rahman who deserves special thanks for his assistance in formatting the text. I am also indebted to Nabila Fairuz Rahman for frequently accessing Ottawa University library facilities for me; I am grateful to Khalid Raja for helping locate information. I am also indebted to Shahidul Islam Mitu of Sarban International Limited and his team member Azizur Rahman for allowing me office facilities in Dhaka.

Another set of thanks are also due to colleagues and friends who provided me with unique and invaluable encouragement necessary to complete the book. They frequently bounced off ideas all through my research; while some others, like Abdullahel Baqi, Saifullah Mahmud

Dulal, Jerome D'Costa, Fateh Ali Chowdhury, Mir Waliuzzaman, Amin Islam, Habia Zaman, Abdur Rahim, Zamil Zaman, Abdur Rahman Chowdhury, Mizan Rahman, Iqbal Sobhan Chowdhury, Nurul Ameen, Hasanat Murtaza, Luthful Kabir, Rahat Ahmed Chaudhuri, Mohammad Rafiquzzaman, Capt. Farid Zaman, Luthfur Rahman Chowdhury, Abdullahel Hadi, Yakub Ali, Syed Mesbahuddin Faruq, Mohammed Hannan, and Mohammad Zaman, had the instinct for applying pressure at the precise time. Again, many people read the earlier manuscript, each offering a particular perspective on the adoptive parents and the adoptees. While I have benefited greatly from everyone's advice and encouragement, I take responsibility for any errors, omissions, and shortcomings contained in this book.

I am indebted to Abdus Shahid, Member of Parliament and then Chief Whip, Bangladesh Parliament; and Shamim Iqbal, then Joint Secretary, Cabinet Division, Government of the People's Republic of Bangladesh, for their assistance in facilitating my access to the Library of Parliament and the National Archives of Bangladesh, respectively.

I am also grateful to Dr. Sadrul Amin, then dean, Faculty of Arts, Dhaka University, for his encouragement and assistance in using the University Library premises and the library's special collection in the *Muktojudho Cell* (research room); as well, to Prof. Abdur Rahim, Faculty of Business Administration, University of New Brunswick, for his encouragement in using the UNB library facilities every time I was in Fredericton. I am grateful to all of these persons.

I remain indebted to Kathy Santos, Lloyd Griffith and Bernadette Valdez for their assistance and cooperation all through the phase of publication.

Above all, thanks are due to my mother-in-law, Mahmuda Begum, for providing a private room for me at her place of residence in Dhaka, Bangladesh, for as long as I needed; my wife, Afroza, for her patience and forbearance with my frequent absences both in mind and body during the time of absorption in writing this book; as well, my children – Tarik, Seema, and Jaseem, for their unconditional support for my work and for supplying me with cups of tea. Without their love and support, it would have been impossible for me to complete the journey, which had been one of the most satisfying and enjoying experiences of my life.

PREFACE

THIS BOOK HAS been a work in progress for the last fifteen years. Having written about the 1971 war babies of Bangladesh in various Bengali journals during the past fifteen years or so, it occurred to me that it might be useful to integrate the evidence-based collective research work into a book chronicling an extraordinary story of fifteen abandoned war babies of Bangladesh that were sent to Canadian homes in the summer of 1972.

Needless to mention, one of the most widely talked about subjects of the Liberation War of 1971 is the "war babies," conceived in Occupied Bangladesh (March 1971–December 1971) while under the control of what is referred to as the Occupation Army (March 1971–December 1971) of Pakistan. These war babies are the products of one of the most outrageous crimes of the twentieth century. Within the context of Bangladesh, the term "war babies" specifically refers to babies conceived by Bangladeshi women and girls (as young as thirteen years old) who were the victims of rape committed by the Pakistani military personnel of the Occupation Army during the Occupation Period of the War of Independence. The Bangladeshi war babies were born between late October 1971 and early September 1972 and, due to the stigma surrounding rape, were abandoned upon birth by their birth mothers who had no choice but to do so.

Initially, Bangladeshis viewed these infants as "unwanted" because they had been abandoned by their birth mothers. The war babies have also been variously referred to as the "unwanted" or "unwelcome" children," the "enemy children," the "illegitimate children," the "children of mixed blood," the "throwaway" children, the "offspring of depravity," the "segregation of bad seeds," and more contemptuously, the "bastards." Another term that is often used to refer to the 1971 war babies is the "abandoned" babies of Bangladesh. In the same vein, their birth mothers have also been variously referred to as the "violated women," the "dishonored women," the "distressed women," the "rape victims," the "victims of military repression," the "affected women," and sometimes with an empathetic intonation, the "unfortunate" women of Bangladesh.

Characterizing them as "heroes," the International War Crimes Tribunal observed in December 2014 that it is the moral obligation of the nation to come forward to accept, recognize and honour the *Biranganas* (rape survivors of 1971, a title given by the Mujib administration in order to honour them as the nation's heroines by recognizing their sacrifices in the war of independence) and their babies (war babies) and to rehabilitate them.

Nevertheless, it is important to note that even today, the 1971 "war babies" are often confused with either the "war orphans" or the "abandoned children" of Bangladesh. People tend to use the terms "war babies" and "war orphans" interchangeably even though the "war babies" and "war orphans" are different. To ensure that the readers have no confusion, let us revisit the definition. Strictly speaking, the term "war orphans" refers to Bangladeshi children orphaned during the war due to the death or disappearance of their parents. In other words, they are called orphans because the war cost them their parents. The war orphans as a group are also referred to as the "abandoned children" of Bangladesh, or more generally, the victims of war. Historically speaking, in 1972, there were also many "abandoned children" because they were left behind (orphaned) by parents who were unable to care for them (due to physical injury, impoverishment, mental illness, or inability to adequately care for children with disabilities).

The war orphans and abandoned children were not necessarily born in 1971 or 1972. They were minors during the war, and they had lost their parents, which technically made them orphans. Their situation is quite different from those of the 1971 "war babies," which are the subject of the present book. All "war babies" (born as a result of rape by the Pakistani military personnel) are thus "war orphans," as they had been abandoned by their birth mothers, and their fathers (the men who fathered them; the term "father" not being really appropriate) never claimed them. The term "war orphans" (who became orphans because of abandonment by, or death of, their parents) should not be used for these "war babies," since they were not the product of rape by the Pakistani military personnel in Occupied Bangladesh.

By the third week of December 1971, the war babies' putative or alleged fathers had already surrendered to the Allied Forces, following which, at a later point, had gone to India as prisoners of war (POWs). The birth mothers, having abandoned their babies at birth, had also disappeared in anonymity. Because the birth mothers did not wish to conceive in the first place, these newborns were seen as "unwanted" or "disposable," and therefore, to some extent, "untouchable" in Bangladeshi society. Thanks to the personal efforts of Mother Teresa and her colleagues at the Dhaka-based Missionaries of Charity and the Montreal-based Families For Children (FFC), a nonprofit adoption agency for intercountry adoption, arrangements were made for the first time with the government of Bangladesh to allow the adoption of a number of war babies in Canadian homes. The present book is based on the documentary evidence available in Bangladesh, the United Kingdom, Switzerland, the United States of America, and Canada.

My objective is neither to describe the liberation war nor to establish a quantitative record to compare it with other tragedies of the last century. I have followed up on the first contingent of fifteen war babies that were sent off to Canada for adoption in Canadian homes. It is for this reason I have excluded Monowara Clark, a war baby who came to Canada in October 1972 during the second phase of the initiative undertaken by Robert and Helke Ferrie of Burlington, Ontario. I intended to explore the well-being of the first batch of 15 war babies who are now in their early forties and their personal views of their notion of identity in Canada where they grew up. They are the main subject of this book.

There are gaps in the history of the 1971 War of Liberation of Bangladesh in which tens of thousands of Bengali men, women, and children have lost their lives. Lack of documentation or knowledge of history with particular reference to sexual violence, commission of rape, and number of rape victims in the present case may be considered to have fallen under what is referred to as *historical relativism.* One may put it differently by saying that one's knowledge of the past is relative to a body of evidence actually in possession of historians.

As will be seen in the next few pages, the book grew out of an approach that is based on a combination of the official records of

Shishu Bhavan, the orphanage from where the infants were adopted, and records of the governments of Canada and Bangladesh and a variety of correspondences among provincial children's aid societies (CAS) with prospective adoptive parents through FFC (Families For Children), which made arrangements for the transfer of fifteen war babies from Bangladesh to Canada; as well, personal interviews of health professionals, social workers, and the adoptees and the adoptive parents. While I was working on the book, I became convinced that time has come for historians to agree on judgments of historical significance – what could be fully harmonized for all historians to agree on some object of ultimate value putting aside the culturally determined valuation that affects the language and judgment of historians.

To date, many freedom fighters and scholars alike have written about the history of liberation with rhetorical flourish and extraordinary language of passion and emotion. A great deal of such history seems "inspirational" or "triumphant" in that it romanticizes the War of Liberation by emphasizing the "heroism" of the *Mukti Bahini* (Freedom Fighters). Those who have written on Bangladesh are proud of the Bengalis' fight for independence. However, such pride, in turn, has colored much of one's work. To a lesser extent, some of such works simply expresses the rhapsodic hopes in *Shonar Bangla* (Golden Bengal) in light of the changed reality of the newly born country. Though based on meticulous research, most of the writers, however, have confined themselves to political subjects associated with "patriotism" and "nationalism."

It is a matter of profound regret that none of the histories written so far are all-inclusive history of the War of Liberation. By and large, the writers of Bangladeshi history have left out the tragic stories of the "dishonored" women and their abandoned children alleged to have been fathered by the Pakistani military personnel. So disproportionate is the work on the story of the violated women and their children that even today, it is as though a mere footnote in the historiography of the Bangladesh's history of the Liberation War; or, simply put, accounts of the war babies are hardly mentioned in the Bangladeshi history books.

The extent of rape, sexual slavery, enforced pregnancy, and the subsequent birth, death, abandonment, and adoption of the war babies remains a vital, unexplored area to be incorporated in the historical narrative of the War of Liberation of Bangladesh of which it is an integral part. It is indeed ironic that, although the library shelves in Bangladesh groan under the weight of books on the liberation of Bangladesh, no historical studies have been done on the war babies of Bangladesh or on the stories of their birth mothers who have been living and dying in anonymity since the independence of Bangladesh.

It may be safe to observe that there has hardly been any attempt made by the Bangladeshi historians or social scientists to say, "Let's tell the truth" about the war of independence in narrating the disparaging and denying results of rape at that time. This becomes more acutely painful when one recalls how, to this day, there is no monument to the unknown *Biranganas* at a time when there are countless monuments in every nook and cranny of Bangladesh to commemorate the unknown freedom fighters. This particular element of Bangladesh's history continually challenges anyone who attempts to deepen one's understanding of the victims – that is, the "dishonored" birth mothers and their "unwanted" babies.

Following the assassination of Sheikh Mujibur Rahman (Mujib), then president of Bangladesh, the successive governments considered the freedom movement and its events as a virtually closed chapter in Bangladesh's history. Far too long, the people of Bangladesh have ignored, neglected, or simply denied the horrific and damaging effect of sexual lunacy on the part of the Pakistan army on both victims and their families. It is as though there had been a conspiracy of silence on the part of the historical establishment in Bangladesh to suppress the truth in the historical narrative.

By distancing themselves from the darker side of the history of the War of Liberation of Bangladesh, no one has really gained anything except to hide significant facts from major Bangladeshi historical texts. Like the story of the Mi Lai massacre, which was first referred to as a "tragedy," and then began to be referred to only as an "incident," the story of rape, sodomy, and mutilations of Bengali women also came to be almost forgotten by everyone except for a few women writers and women's organizations. It might not be an overstatement to say that the story of the war babies has almost been erased from the national consciousness of the people of Bangladesh.

It is only recently that some writers and journalists in Pakistan have started to talk about the stories of rape and sexual violence perpetrated by the members of the Pakistani military personnel. Indeed, the first national discussion of these alleged crimes were arguably triggered from outside of both countries by the magazine *India Today,* which first published the excerpts of the Hamoodor Rahman Commission (HRC) Report. Later, Shehzad Amjad, a first-rate Pakistani journalist, made headlines with his thought-provoking article titled "Don't we owe a national apology to Bengalis?" This further opened up the topic to the people of Pakistan in a positive manner by making them put on their thinking cap that had made headlines.

Internationally, for the first time, Susan Brownmiller's groundbreaking work titled *Against Our Will: Men, Women and Rape* appeared in 1975 as a full-blown book in which she describes the *why* and the *how* of rape and violence in war, citing examples of such crimes in Bangladesh when it was still fighting for independence. Raunak Jahan, a distinguished and most prolific writer who writes on gender and development, has also written on the sexual violence during the Bengalis' struggle for independence. Again, journalists and writers like Robert Payne, Aubrey Menon, Tom Tied, Lee Patterson, and many others have written on the military brutality including rape of Bengali women in 1971. However, I am not aware of any study on the birth, abandonment, and adoption of the war babies of Bangladesh along with the adoption outcome in Bangladesh or anywhere in the world.

In Canada, Raymonde Provencher, a renowned Canadian journalist, wrote and directed a full-length documentary titled *War Babies* in 2003. It is on the fate of the children born to victims of wartime rape in various countries around the world. Painting the terrible picture of the ravages of war, Provencher depicted many of the women who, having survived wartime rape, are now living with a daily reminder of their ordeal; their children born of this crime are seen as the children of the enemy. Ryan Good, one of the Bangladeshi war babies discussed in the present book, is a character in the documentary, which has won critical acclaim and four Gémeneaux Awards. I am not aware of any other work in Canada on the outcome of the Bangladeshi war babies' adoption.

In Bangladesh, during the war, the military repression was most aptly expressed by Kamrul Hassan in one of his memorable paintings titled *Demons Are Rising Again,* which was distributed clandestinely among the supporters of the Bangladesh movement. Following the independence of Bangladesh, Dr. Nilima Ibrahim, in her *Ami Birangana Bolchi (Saying of a War Heroine, I),* narrated the stories of the victims of rape who were forced by the social circumstances surrounding rape in Bangladesh to remain silent and suffer in agony. She painstakingly described how, being forced, some of the rape victims, having disappeared from the society, had been living incognito since then. She did not write anything about the war babies of Bangladesh although she alluded to their birth in her book.

Very few of rape victims, who had the misfortune of being preyed upon by the military personnel, have ever come out in public. Ferdousi Priyobhashini is the first rape victim who had the courage to share in public her story of pain and agony at the hands of the Pakistani military personnel. In the 1990s, *Ekattorer Ghatak Dalal Nirmul Committee* (Committee to Exterminate the Killers and Collaborators), whose mission is to fight for justice, spearheaded by Jahanara Imam, Shahriar Kabir, Muntasir Mamun, and a few other prominent members of Bangladeshi society, had been successful in encouraging hitherto unknown rape victims to come out of the closet at a public hearing. The activities of the said committee were, however, deemed unlawful by the government of the day. The committee's fight continues to this day, and a great number Bangladeshis have been endorsing their support for the committee.

The two other prominent writers of India and Bangladesh, Nayanika Mookherjee and Bina D'Costa, respectively, have undertaken significant work on the disparaging and damaging effects of rape, rape victims, and their "undesirable" children referred to as the "war babies" of Bangladesh. Through their substantive work on sexual violence and rape victims and their tragic situations, both have made reference to the century-old traditions of marginalization of women, which is the focus of their research. They wrote about how women generally fall through the cracks despite every intention to glorify them. They have made only reference to the birth of the hapless war babies and adoption of some of these babies outside of Bangladesh; they have not written anything on the war babies themselves. D'Costa also made reference to furtive adoptions without writing anything further for lack of documentation.

Today these two writers are looked upon as eminent researchers having made significant contribution in the historiography of the Bengalis' struggle for independence and its fallout. Both of these distinguished scholars have been working laboriously in an attempt to fill in the gap in the historical narrative of the Bangladesh's War of Independence with reference to the untold story of the rape victims in a patriarchal society like Bangladesh. And yet, despite their pioneering work for which they became widely and favorably known, they have not been successful in bringing the issue to the forefront as Bangladesh's national agenda. This fact leaves one with the impression that the women of Bangladesh still need a concerted push to make any impact on the study of the war babies of Bangladesh.

Yasmin Saikia, another scholar of Indian origin, has also undertaken work on Bangladeshi rape victims of 1971. In her book *Women, War, and the Making of Bangladesh: Remembering 1971,* she has gathered first-person accounts of the gendered violence of the 1971 Bangladesh War of Independence. I remain impressed with the hard work, tireless efforts, and deep dedication of all three scholars: Mookherjee, D'Costa, and Saikia, in incorporating the missing pieces of the War of Independence that ought to become a part of the historical narrative in the history of Bangladeshis' struggle for independence.

To a lesser extent, I am aware of the work of the following: Sajid Hossain, A. S. M. Babar Ali, Khurshid Jahan Begum, and Shurma Jahid. Hossain, in his *Ekattorer Judhoshishu ('71 War Babies)*, addressed the pathetic situation of the rape victims in Bangladesh; as well, the *why* and the *how* of the war babies not only of Bangladesh but also of the war babies from around the world. Ali, in his *Muktijudhe Shoto Shoto Nari (Hundreds of Women in the Liberation War)*, has profiled many rape victims about whom he came to learn in the course of his investigation. Begum, in her *Ekattorer Judhoshishu ('71 War Babies)*, has given an account of the birth mothers and their abandoned babies based on her imagination by recalling those horrific days of military repression of 1971. Again, Jahid, in her *Ekattorer Nirjatito Narider Itihash (History of the Tortured Women of '71)*, has outlined the sordid stories of a number of rape victims discreetly obtained through their testimonies but no reference to the war babies.

Being impressed with the work of all of these writers, I started to think through more about the war babies, in particular, those who were adopted in Canada and for those there is documentary evidence in the Library and Archives Canada. By contrasting earlier and later works on the War of Liberation and its fallout, I quickly realized that historians of a given nation change over time and that history is being constantly reinterpreted – the same events judged, weighed, ordered, and generalized in different fashions. Though not a card-carrying historian, I was constantly reminded of K. N. Chitnis' remark that "a mere narration of facts is no real history, for it would be a mere catalogue of events and dates" (Chitnis, K. N., *Research Methodology in History*, Atlantic Publishers & Distributors, New Delhi, 1990, p. 1). With that in mind and in all seriousness, I have tried my best not to lose the thread of my discourse.

Not being a subscriber of *historical relativism*, which I understand to be a form of skepticism regarding our ability to make true statements about the past, I came to the conclusion that if no account of the war babies of Bangladesh is recorded now, it would otherwise pass into whispered history. I was convinced that historians of Bangladesh would be condemned for not writing about one of the sad realities of the struggle for the independence of Bangladesh. Throughout my investigation on this subject matter, I was guided by the notion of history as held by Theodor Mommsen (1817–1903), the famous jurist, epigrapher, and historian of all times: "History, after all, is nothing but the distinct knowledge of actual happenings, consisting, on the one hand, of the discovery and examination of the valuable testimony; and, on the other hand, of the weaving of this testimony into a narrative in accordance with one's understanding of the man who shaped the events and the conditions that prevailed" ("On the Training of Historians," by Theodor Mommsen in *The Varieties of History, From Voltaire to the Present*, ed. Fritz Stern, The World Publishing Co., Ohio, 1956, p. 192).

Given that there is no record of rape and violence other than statements and hearsay anecdotes and stories as observations, it is impossible to show a direct link between the sexual assaults of the Bengali women and the Pakistani military personnel in the field; as well, whether policy and administration of the military regime had condemned such actions during the Occupation Period. Recognizing that historical selectivity should be critically scrutinized, I had difficulty in posing balanced questions to put to the evidence. It has been one of the greatest challenges to my sense of fairness and justice because the evidence so clearly exposes the "crime." The lack of documentary evidence, whether in Bangladesh or Pakistan, soon acquainted me with the complexities and problems inherent in the study of the war babies in particular. Keeping in mind that the world community must not let this savage act fade from its memory, initially I started with some of the following broad questions: *What do the people of Bangladesh know about the war babies? Who are the war babies? Where are the women victims of 1971 today? What do they do for a living? Do the people of Bangladesh know their whereabouts?*

The hard and cruel fact is that Bangladeshis are sadly unaware, uninformed, or even misinformed about the war babies. Or one might ask: *Do they care?* Every year when December rolls by, numerous commemorative events take place in Bangladesh with wreaths and candles that include public gatherings, political rallies, peaceful marches, religious ceremonies, cultural events, academic symposiums, press conferences, as well as interviews of prominent Bangladeshis. Specifically, December 16 remains a national holiday, which is celebrated as the Victory Day throughout the length and breadth of Bangladesh mainly through commemoration of the martyrs of the war of independence.

The greatest problem that I had encountered was to find a starting point. The picture may remain clouded, as the story of rapes and sexual assaults by the military personnel during the Bengalis' struggle for independence is an area that is too delicate, too emotional, and much too complex to fully appreciate simply because of a lack of "official" disclosure. During my frequent visits to Bangladesh, I snooped around and met with many who remained closemouthed about what happened; some, apparently still furious, spoke with an ugly snarl; and some others had umpteen reasons for prompt response but were unable to direct me to original or primary sources. Being caught between the "denial of facts" and the "scarcity" of data, it is not difficult to recognize that it is not an untrammeled historical inquiry; I rummaged through official records in Bangladesh and Canada.

It is not known how many war babies had eventually made it to Canadian homes in the 1970s and 1980s, since there is a dearth of documentation. The present book, therefore, deals *only* with the first contingent of fifteen war babies based on the primary sources. Taking advantage of the documentary evidence mainly made available to me by the Dhaka-based Missionaries of Charity, the Geneva-based International Social Service (ISS), International Planned Parenthood Federation's Archives in London, United Kingdom, and Library and Archives Canada, I have reconstructed the story of adoption through the narratives of the war babies and the adoptive parents. Thus, the central cast of characters with whom I have interacted during the study is the adopters and the adoptees themselves now living in Canada. As mentioned, the subject matter of the present book, therefore, remains rather narrow in scope, since it does not deal with the 1971 war babies of Bangladesh in general but simply attempts to outline the *how* and the *why* of the adoption of the first contingent of fifteen war babies from Bangladesh to Canada back in July 1972 and its final outcome.

Though, to this day, I remain haunted by the complexity of the subject that often drove me to my wit's end, I decided to venture by sourcing original historical records. I had hoped to go further than just scratching the surface in recording the stories of the war babies who came to Canada – that their story of adoption and its outcome do not get lost in the mists of time. My hope, with all my heart, is that the publication of this will give the subject of war babies a new dimension in the historiography of the War of Liberation. Deep down in my heart, I also believe that if such events related to sexual violence and its aftermath are not recorded adequately, then opposite of the truth is likely to become the accepted version of the events surrounding the birth of the "war babies" of Bangladesh. Regrettably, the Bangladeshi establishment has remained silent on the question of the social acceptance of the war babies by the society as a whole.

It would be interesting to see how the Government of Bangladesh and various NGOs react to the observations of the International War Crimes Tribunal with reference to the war babies and their birth mothers who are to be honoured and rehabilitated.

I was encouraged by the saying of the great German historian and philosopher Ernst Troeltsch, who once said that there are times when it is more important to make a beginning than to produce the finished article. Given that there has been no attempt to write about the war babies of Bangladesh who made it to Canada, I was prompted by the age-old adage, "Nothing ventured, nothing gained."

I have strived to organize my findings into a cohesive collection, though within the limits set by limited documentary evidence. It has been an ongoing challenge to choose the manner in which to narrate the story from the evidence that exists in Bangladesh, the United Kingdom, Switzerland, the United States of America, and Canada. It is my intention that the adoption story of these war babies, though only a dot on the horizon, would not be seen as a mere recounting of events but instead a way to explore the underpinnings of the vital question of social acceptance of these "undesirable" children born under unusual circumstances. It is my hope that their story provides another lens through which to view interracial adoption on higher grounds of morality and justice. It is my grand hope that their story would be of interest to the extended circle of the people of Bangladesh, the people of Canada and, in general, to the social work and legal and medical professions in particular, each of which is concerned with many ramifications of interracial adoptions and their outcomes.

As the book progresses from one chapter to the next, readers will learn about the story of the war babies' journey from Bangladesh to Canadian homes, and their life in Canada that illustrates human relationships, which developed and matured into deeply satisfying experiences for both the adopters and the adoptees. As readers would flip through the pages, they would find fascinating anecdotes centering on the lives of the war babies in their country of adoption.

One note of caution is that, due to the sensitivity of the subject itself, any research on the war babies is bound to remain incomplete and unsatisfying as is the case with the present study. The present book is, therefore, my humble attempt to put something into record – a piece of history of the liberation of Bangladesh by providing a brief account of the infants born under pathetic circumstances but deemed "disposable" in their country of birth. It is written in the hope that it inspires public discussion and debate about adoption in general in Bangladesh and interracial adoption in Canada and given the backdrop of Canada's multiracial demographic composition. In fact, the subject of interracial adoption would be of interest to other countries around the world.

If the book has any merit, it is the story of the outcome of adoption in Canada that I have learned from the narratives of the adopters and the adoptees themselves – their versions of *what* is it like to *adopt* and *be adopted*.

Mustafa Chowdhury

May 20, 2015
448 Rougemount Crescent
Ottawa, Ontario, Canada K4A 2Y8
Mustafa.chowdhury49@gmail.com

A BRIEF NOTE ON SOURCES AND
RESEARCH METHODOLOGY

Historical sources

ALTHOUGH FREQUENT DISCOVERIES of *boydhobhumis* (a place of execution and slaughter in Occupied Bangladesh between March 1971 and December 1971 in small nooks and crannies of Bangladesh) assist us in learning about the stories of rape and murder during the war of independence, it does not, however, provide the precise number of victims or their "unwanted" infants. Lack of primary sources with regard to the number of rape victims gives rise to a series of questions: *How many women were murdered? How many had committed suicide? How many had died due to complications resulting from enforced pregnancies? How many war babies were born prior to, and how many following the independence of Bangladesh?* Most of the hearsay evidence is sketchy. For a while I felt as though I had run up against a brick wall. During the Occupation Period, people used to whisper about how abducted Bengali women of various ages used to become easy prey for the military and how, being confined in the premises, they were used for sexual services.

It was only after the surrender of the Pakistan army on December 16, 1971, that the rescue operation that went in full gear was able to free those who were abducted and sexually abused by the "Occupation Forces." By then many of them had become pregnant. The paucity of documentary evidence will soon acquaint the reader with the complexities inherent in the study of the babies born as a result of rape. Thus, what was needed was to develop an alternative research strategy that I undertook in Canada and Bangladesh. In Canada, official record of retention and destruction varies from province to province. In Bangladesh there is no policy of retaining government files on microfilm. Consequently, many valuable documents had been lost through the passage of forty-three years. Availability and accessibility of data remain an issue of serious concern among researchers in Bangladesh.

The greatest problem that I had encountered was to know where to begin, as the picture may remain lopsided, since the story of sexual violence on the part of the military personnel during the war is not recorded in any manner. It is not expected that such information would be recorded. Strongly discouraging throughout this long and difficult research work was the inability to find reference to the incidence of rape and sexual assault. Asked in varying tones of exasperation, there are endless questions: *Where are the birth mothers? Where are their babies whom they had abandoned? What happened to those war babies who made it to Canada through adoption?* The two most vital questions that I kept asking myself persistently throughout my research were : *What is the evidence for this? What is the documentation for this?* Having spent the first twenty-two years of my life in Bangladesh, where I witnessed the Bengalis' struggle for independence, I decided to complete the task to the best of my ability.

By posing the above-noted questions, my next attempt was to design the actual research proposal and gather evidence as much as obtainable to ensure that the materials gathered have been woven together in an attempt to answer the questions posed in the first place. The writing and reconstruction of the story of war babies thus amounted to a series of dialogue among the adoptive parents, their adopted children, and me in between them in an attempt to fill the historical information gap and to examine the documents that were available with penetrating questions that gave rise to new meaning to the material. This led to further questions, which, in turn, enabled me to obtain significant information resulting from interpretation of the collective body of knowledge from their own perspectives through dialogue, insight, and feelings. Looking at history as an inquiry, as well as an outcome, I pursued relentlessly taking nothing to be beyond the reach of a critical examination in Canada and Bangladesh, as I believed truth has had many shapes and values.

The primary sources for the reconstruction of the present story consist of governmental and nongovernmental records in Bangladesh, Switzerland, the United Kingdom, the United States of America, and Canada. The main records from both Bangladesh and Canada consist of volumes of cables, letters, minutes, summaries of discussions, decisions, reports, briefing notes and copies of memorandum of understanding of various governments and NGOs, and numerous press clippings and newspaper coverage of the day. In addition, historical records also include some home studies of applicants or potential adoptive parents conducted by the local children's aid societies (CAS) of the respective provinces of Canada that were deposited to the records office within the appropriate ministries, which made their way to the respective provincial archives. I was able to obtain relevant information through the *Freedom of Information and Protection of Privacy Act* and use them extensively as primary sources for the book.

In Canada the primary sources include papers of the Departments of External Affairs (now Department of Foreign Affairs and International Trade), Manpower and Immigration (now Citizenship and Immigration Canada), National Archives of Canada (now Library and Archives Canada), the records of the Archives of Ontario, Families For Children (FFC, the organization that conceived the project and formalized the joint venture), and the *Kuan-Yin Foundation* (which was also involved in the negotiations between the governments of Bangladesh and Canada) for the second contingent of war babies, the personal papers of some of the adoptive parents involved in the process, newspapers and media coverage, and interviews of the adoptive parents and the adoptees themselves. A few fragments of documents that have fortuitously survived, since they were in personal possession of adoptive parents, depict the bureaucratic barriers the adoptive couples had faced in bringing home their desired child from Bangladesh.

In Bangladesh the first set of valuable government sources are the records of two important ministries: Labour and Social Welfare and Law and Parliamentary Affairs, and various correspondences between the governments of Bangladesh and Canada. The original document signed by M. Sharafatullah, then deputy secretary, Ministry of Labour and Social Welfare, government of Bangladesh, is perhaps the single most important document that remains key to any historic inquiry and analysis of the subject at hand. When I looked at the document for the first time, I was at my wit's end being speechless – my flesh crept and my hair stood on end. I let it all hang out for minutes. This rare and historic document has been replicated **on page ... (appendix no.)** below with the actual names of the war babies as was given by the authority of the Missionaries of Charity in Dhaka along with the names of the adoptive parents with their full address who were at the airports to receive their designated child.

The second set of primary records permeates from the *Bangladesh Jatyo Nari Punarbashan Board* (translated in English as the National Board of Bangladesh Women's Rehabilitation Program [BWRP] and generally referred to as the *Board*) and the National Board for Bangladesh Women's Emancipation Program (BWEP). Needless to say, the microfilming technique, the modern technology of which enables a great deal of materials in the way of documentary evidence, is hardly applied in Bangladesh. Consequently, many important records have either been lost or discarded by the successive governments.

And yet from what little evidence we have, the more we probe, the more we realize that we, in fact, know very little. The local premises of the Board where sad stories were lived and tears were shed and where many of the war babies were born and abandoned remain a silent witness to a painful episode in Bangladesh's recent past that refuses to go away. Being challenged to be clear when presenting evidence on a sensitive topic like the present one, I needed to critically scrutinize all materials that I could lay my hands on. I needed to be doubly careful in addressing the lack of concern from the many smug and complacent individuals as well as many mass rape deniers despite much concrete material evidence to the contrary. I took it upon myself to present hard evidence and historical facts without seeking merely curious individuals who have heard and known about the murder, chaos, and sexual violence that had engulfed the Occupied Bangladesh.

Nongovernmental sources in Bangladesh are mainly the records of the Dhaka-based Missionaries of Charity's *Shishu Bhavan* (the orphanage from where the war babies were brought in to Canada, Europe, the United States of America, and Australia) and CORR (Christian Organization for Relief and Rehabilitation, now CARITAS) and correspondences with Fred and Bonnie Cappuccino of the Families For Children in Canada. Had it not been for the records of the Missionaries of Charity and the FFC that arranged for the adoption of these war babies brought from Bangladesh to Canada, it would have been impossible to track down the adoptive parents and their children in Canada.

The photos of the victims of rape and the newborn war babies that were flashed in the newspapers from time to time in 1972 did not remain in the minds of the people, as people generally have a very short memory. Ironically enough, it is as though the people of Bangladesh have collective amnesia even though there is considerable nondocumentary evidence of systemic rape and sexual slavery in Occupied Bangladesh.

Nevertheless, the newspaper coverage of the interviews of Sr. Margaret Mary, then superior, *Shishu Bhavan,* and a few other nuns who worked there in 1972 might be considered as prima facie evidence of the subject at hand to contextualize the birth and abandonment of the war babies. Reference to the pathetic situation of the rape victims, many of whom came to the orphanage premises as a last resort to give birth to their "unwanted" child, remains, to this day, one of the most reliable sources of information that also reveal the Bangladeshi society's attitudes and views on the war babies. From the information scattered in many interviews of foreign journalists who visited the various *Seva Sadans* (premises designed to serve the rape victims who needed care for having abortion or having the delivery of their babies), which were set up to handle the influx of the violated women who needed treatment, it is possible to reconstruct a pattern of birth and abandonment of the war babies following the liberation of Bangladesh.

The authorities of *Shishu Bhavan* have retained information on the war babies who were born in their premises and those who were brought to them for adoption after they were relinquished by their birth mothers. The information, considered highly confidential, and not generally accessible without special permission, is contained in a bounded book called the *Register Book.* This one single document is the most vital source of information on the war babies. I consider myself extremely lucky to have obtained full access to the *Register Book* only in the presence of the superior.

Again, going through Superior Sr. Margaret Mary's handwritten letters to prospective adoptive parents in Canada gave me a feeling of genuineness with respect to a matter of profound depth and history. I was touched by the critical situation Sr. Margaret Mary was in, something that, in a way, brought me closer to the problems. For me, it was an experience with many faces and places. I was intrigued every time I read or thought about my initiative, wondering how best I could meet my objectives.

I had the good fortune using both official records of the London-based International Planned Parenthood Federation (IPPF) and personal records of Dr. Geoffrey Davis, an Australian surgeon who was sent to Bangladesh through the IPPF to instruct the rape victims in practical methods for the termination of advanced pregnancies of particular importance. Working with a group of foreign nationals and Bangladeshi professionals such as social workers, psychiatrists, doctors, lawyers, NGO workers, and civil administrators, the IPPF representative Dr. Davis provided the required services to the violated women during February–August 1972.

Through a comprehensive examination of pertinent documents, it was possible to find other connected themes, such as resistance to abortion, the particular ways in which the victims were seen, and the thinking of the governments of the day with regard to the violated women, birth mothers, and their "throwaway" babies. The reports of the doctors' teamwork in collaboration with the deputy commissioners, the local civil surgeons, the local family planning officers, and nurses and midwives include description of the work with rape victims, the majority of whom chose to abort. It will be seen that some, however, had no choice but to carry their pregnancies to full term as they ran against the time. These records are the most authentic sources on the birth of the war babies.

Archival records of the American branch of the Geneva-based International Social Service (ISS, also was known as Travelers Aid-International Social Services of America [TAISSA] from 1972 to 1977) were used as primary sources. In fact, the Mujib administration heavily relied on the recommendations of the ISS, which it accepted. The government's *Intercountry Adoption Project Initiative* is the result of the recommendations of the ISS. The correspondences of the ISS with the government of Bangladesh form a significant part of the pertinent information on the war babies and adoption initiative that I have used extensively for my research.

An examination of the background papers, the internal memoranda, and the ministerial orders between the governments of Canada and Bangladesh that I have accessed and used indicate that there were many closed-door meetings in which confidential reports were discussed in an attempt to determine whether international adoption of the war babies was the best way to address the issue; and if so, *how could the government expedite the process of foreign adoption through enactment of a new legislation in Bangladesh?* It was through an examination of

MUSTAFA CHOWDHURY

the official records of these infants stored in the archives of Canada, London, Switzerland, and the United States of America that I was able to reconstruct their journey to Canada and record their subsequent life through testimonies of the adoptive parents and the adoptees in Canada. Had there been no available historical documentation, the true story of the same war babies would have probably remained shrouded in mystery, gossips, innuendoes, rumors, and exaggeration; I dare say, there would have been many, like the Holocaust deniers, who would have disavowed the entire tragic episode.

While working on the subject, I realized how historical research does not only consist in the pursuit of some particular evidence that will answer a particular question; instead, it consists of an exhausting reviewing of everything that may conceivably be germane to a given topic. This realization prompted me to meet with a great number of archivists and record administrators from the Library and Archives Canada, the Archives of Ontario, and record keepers in both governmental and nongovernmental organizations in Canada and Bangladesh. By that time, I had also realized that before all these materials could be used, of course, the component parts had to be carefully separated, a task that calls for a high degree of critical acumen.

Again, recognizing that it is incumbent upon me to reduce the uncertainties to a minimum, I examined them with an open and analytical mind. For me, it was a question of critically examining and comparing them with each and every relevant document on hand including the records of the Ministry of Community and Social Services of the Government of Ontario, housed at the Archives of Ontario, which were matched with the records from the government of Bangladesh along with the correspondences obtained from the adoptive parents in Canada. With due diligence, I compared the records that I had collected from the Ministry of Law and Parliamentary Affairs with the original records at Mother Teresa's *Shishu Bhavan*. As I leafed through the *Register Book* at *Shishu Bhavan,* I found my eyes blurred with tears, and I could not read through all the pages without finding my eyes welling from time to time. In fact, my frequent visits to the orphanage in the 1990s had brought back memories of those horrifying military brutality, of intense pain and immense sorrow.

The main objective for the comparison and cross-checking of documents and correspondences was to determine the authenticity of the records and assess their historic worth in conformity with the historical research at hand. Such exercise, though tedious, had enabled me to authenticate, following a close comparison of the content of the information included in the various correspondences among the governments of Canada and Bangladesh with Families For Children (FFC) and *Shishu Bhavan*. For me, going through the maze of records and information was an endurance test.

It was also imperative to speak to politicians, historians, archivists, lawyers, legal researchers, both in Bangladesh and Canada, in an attempt to understand the complex phenomena of adoption and, more importantly, intercountry and interracial adoption. Though an exclusively narrow empiricism in modern historical research, I realized that the evidence of the birth and relinquishment of the war babies can be made to yield relevant replies.

Interviews of the adoptive parents and the war babies

Immediately following the review of the evidence, I turned to the adoptive parents in Canada who have retained their correspondences with the governments of Canada and Bangladesh. To reconstruct the story of adoption, I needed to hear from both the adopters and the adoptees in Canada – their sides of the adoption equation. Putting on my best togs, I had traveled across Canada to meet the adoptive parents and the adoptees. The testimonies of the adoptive parents who opened their doors and hearts to talk to me in confidence are the most valuable form of primary evidence on the war babies adopted in Canada. Frequent telephone conversations and e-mail exchanges with the parents and their children both before and after interviews had allowed me to establish a more personal level of contact and their trust.

I started with the assumption that no one could speak with as much knowledge about such experience as those who had lived through it themselves. Over the years, I have interviewed both the adopters and the adoptees at their homes or at a designated place where I was welcome each time I had visited. Of the fourteen couples and fifteen war babies, it was possible to track twelve couples (one couple adopted two war babies) and fourteen war babies. I could not trace Kenneth and Mitzi McCoullough, who adopted a war baby and lived in Halifax, Nova Scotia, at the time of adoption. The closest information on the

McCoulloughs is that they are from the United States of America and that they had left for the States shortly after adoption of Probir (one of the fifteen war babies). Of the adoptees, seven are male and eight are female. Out of thirteen adoptees, ten had actively participated and cooperated.

Over the course of my research, I have learned firsthand from thirteen Canadian adoptive parents about the details of their experience with their children, more particularly about Bangladeshi-born abandoned war babies whom they have raised. From the outset, I worked on the premise that there was much to be gained through research interviews with the adoptive parents and the adoptees about what was involved in raising a racially different child adopted from Bangladesh. Their willingness to meet with me for follow-up questions had encouraged me a great deal to continue my ongoing liaison with them. It had also reinforced in my mind both the demonstrated evidence of the parent-children bond that I needed to see with my own eyes and the tremendous goodwill, warmth, and enthusiasm with which the parents had embraced the racially different war babies. For me, it a case of "seeing is believing." Having seen them in person and spoken with them on sundry occasions, I became more convinced of their genuine interest in my research initiative.

Due to the sensitivity of the events surrounding the birth of the war babies, it was particularly difficult to develop a set of standard questionnaire for them that would be acceptable to all. When I met the war babies individually for the first time for a face-to-face interview, they were then in their midtwenties. As soon as I met them, I recognized that each is different than the other, and yet they all seemed to have common manifestations. In fact, I also found that not only did they seem to be greatly different in their interest in and knowledge about their country of birth and birth history, but they had also grown up knowing different bits and pieces of history. As was the case, some took time to pursue their past history, while some others did not bother about it. Consequently, this, together with the varying degrees of differences within the adoptive families, has contributed to their differing personalities.

It became clear to me that, due to the differing knowledge of the circumstances surrounding their conception, birth, abandonment, and final adoption outside of their country of birth, it would remain an extremely difficult subject for them. Individually, each would have his or her own issues, and therefore, together, they will not have the same level of comfort, certainty, and interest to discuss the subject with me. Just as I started to interact with them with a view to gathering pertinent information, I also became convinced that one standard/ single technique to ask questions, or "one-size-fits-all" technique, is not going to work. It will not elicit appropriate and adequate answers. It would not be the right tool for them even though they were born about the same tumultuous time under the same tragic circumstances. I realized that I needed to modify the techniques of asking follow-up questions based on the nature of the answer they would provide, no matter how open-ended the questions are intended to be.

The research proposal, which began as a quasi-experimental study, thus had to be redesigned to focus on qualitative approach keeping in mind both the adoptees and the adoptive parents. Having modified the questionnaire, I went along with my gut feeling as to *how* to move forward especially in light of their initial responses.

My conversations with the adoptive parents were essentially two-pronged: parents' own version of adoption and their recollection of the rearing of their children. Specifically, for the parents, the questions centered upon: (1) the *why* and the *how* of adoption of transracial orphans especially from Bangladesh; (2) their own view of structuring their family mainly through adoption of racially different children; and, whether childlessness was an issue; (3) degree to which their adopted children have become self-supporting adults; (4) and finally, their relationships with their adopted children.

Over the years, I spoke with both parents (husband and wife) several times, allowing both father and mother a fuller recollection and exploration of their memories and experiences. There was an initial hurdle in speaking with them due to the very nature of the subject. Fortunately, I was successful to my satisfaction once I got them on a talking mode. Some spoke with certain reservations, while some spoke with openness. I let them speak as they wished – a technique that allowed me to help them raise their own comfort level. All through my interviews, I gave them the time and opportunity they needed to think through the questions most of which go back in years.

One of my interview strategies was to consciously avoid making quick judgments whether I talked to an adoptive parent or to an adoptee and forming instantly strong opinion on them. Instead, I made extra effort to allow what I gathered to sink in, unfold as they might, and let the facts of adoption and its fallout speak for them.

They needed some time to volunteer their knowledge, thoughts, emotions, and feelings about the subject, which is close to their hearts. Almost every adoptive couple I spoke with made available one's personal collection of files, photographs, films, videos, and other records. As well, those who went on a trip to Bangladesh in 1972 to pick out the said babies and those who went in 1989 with their children gave me full access to their scrappy notes, which they still have in their possession. Some have accumulated many types of valuable information over the years, while some had just basic information in their possession.

Depending on the response and the level of enthusiasm, or lack thereof, I had to continually paraphrase my follow-up questions; in some instances, I had to abandon many of the questions that I had intended to ask. Though unstructured in format, I had guided myself by an extensive and topical but flexible outline to suit each individual's sense and sensibility. In general, I have tried to refrain myself from asking too many personal questions, which I feared would shut them off. Reminding myself that the circumstances of the war were connected to horror and sexual violence that had, in fact, created them, I let them speak as they wished. Needless to say, given the sensitivity attached to the topic itself, it was a challenge to constantly reword and recraft my questions and statements or observations according to their visible reaction to the nature of my questions paused. Whether it was the parent or the adoptee, the dilemma is neatly summed up by the following aphorism: generally people don't like to see their private lives to be discussed in public by anyone.

Interview of the families, whether face-to-face or over the telephone, was both challenging as well as rewarding because it gave me an opportunity to "unlearn" some cultural oddities that I had picked up earlier while growing up in Bangladesh. This was particularly so with the use of many common words and expressions some of which often seemed like a breach of propriety in Canada. Never did I realize, even for a minute, how unknowingly I had continued to offend many parents by asking questions that were deemed inappropriate in the world of adoption. It never dawned on me until I was cautioned to pay extra attention to the use of words, terms, and terminologies while making inquiry.

When, for example, I asked Bonnie Cappuccino, an adoptive mother, about the number of children as her *own*, her quick retort took me aback: "They're all our children, some children are adopted, while some are biological." This quick and curt reply hit me as a red flag, cautioned me to be doubly careful in talking about a sensitive issue like adoption. It was a learning curve that literally forced me to both "unlearn" my particular ways of making an inquiry and learn on the fly as to what could be an offence against proprieties. Bonnie's sharp and single response also made me recognize my own naïvety – how inadvertently I was perpetuating the use of inappropriate (or offensive) terminologies, which must have offended them already. Reminding myself of the adage "Better late than never," I also recognized that such questions were not in good taste or ever asked.

My conversations with the war babies centered on their *own* version of their family relations, their world around them right from the time they were able to remember to the present time. I tried to achieve that by remaining focused on the following: (1) early years/peer relationships and school and community environment, (2) desire to know about their past and the country of birth, (3) family relationships/bonding with parents, (4) the war babies' first visit to their country of birth, (5) racial and Canadian identity, and (6) experience of racism. Along the same lines, there were also questions that centered on the broad concepts of their perception of ethnicity, personal preferences and ethnic awareness (including their knowledge of the country of birth), general interaction with the rest of the people around, and the extent to which they have integrated in Canadian society. An important feature of the research design is that both the adoptees and their adoptive parents were equal coparticipants in my project.

Since 1997, my discussions with the adoptees and their parents have been ongoing. In that sense, one may be inclined to characterize it as a longitudinal study. I have been going back and forth to them frequently with questions and comments. The process had enabled me to return to both parents and children again and again with further questions for better clarification from their perspectives.

To minimize their discomfort, I made sure that all interviews and meetings were informal and unstructured, hoping to allow the

MUSTAFA CHOWDHURY

interviewees to unwind, relax, open up, and be free totally. This gave both the interviewer and the interviewees greater leeway to be unobtrusive to the extent possible allowing free-flowing discursive conversation.

I was fortunate that, with the exception of two couples who were not very interested, all other participants were serious, interested, and cooperative even though many questions were of a personal nature. Every meeting I have had with the adoptive parents and the adoptees, I felt like it was a shot in the arm. All parents and adoptees I have talked to were enthusiastic in sharing their experiences, always finding time to respond to many follow-up questions with no hesitation. The discursive material that resulted from the interviews of both sets of participants was then placed under appropriate headings in each chapter.

Over the course of time, the evidence that I had collected had grown in the process of interpretation beyond the mere surface appearance. The response received from the adoptive parents, the adoptees and their siblings demonstrates an empirical level that neither of the families had any real problems with their racially different children, nor the children with their white adoptive parents. Needless to say, off the record, both parents and children were more comfortable without hype or whiff of trendiness. As I weaved together accounts of the adoptive parents and the adoptees themselves, it opened the door for further discussions on international and interracial adoptions, their pros and cons.

Having heard from the parents about *how* they had expanded their love across oceans and races, all the way from Canada to Bangladesh, the next step for me was to elicit maximum information gathered from the adoptive parents about the nature and result of adoption. In doing so, I had paid extra attention to ensure that there was no misrepresentation of truth or misinterpretation of what I had heard from the parents and/ or the children.

In chapters 5, 6, and 7, I have drawn heavily on extracts from my interviews the adopters and the adoptees and written correspondence with both the parents and their children. I then analyzed the wealth of information and discursive materials that I had obtained in order to compare the veracity of documentation on adoption of these babies that exists in various institutions in Switzerland, London, and Canada. Those who have had occasions to labor among records of history would recognize how the proper rules of evidence and reason severely limit not only in the interpretation of the scanty documentary evidence but also in his/her choice of the evidence on grounds of relevancy. The choice, in the present context, was made in seeking answer to questions on the *why* and the *how* the adoption of these babies. More importantly, how the *Bangladesh Project* was conceived and how it was negotiated through the efforts of the FFC. *What was its role in bringing the first contingent war babies to Canada in July 1972?*

Testimonies of Bangladeshi government officials, health professionals, and social workers

In the 1970s and 1980s, I had spent a great deal of time seeking the truth followed by every possible clue, such as looking up names in phonebooks of the 1970s, rummaging through old records in the Bangladeshi orphanages, scouring the pages of newspapers, and knocking on doors of old addresses hoping to find someone, anyone, out there who had seen or heard about the violated women and their babies. Testimonies of government officials, health professionals, and social workers, though disjointed and somewhat anomalous mainly due to the passage of time, remain, by far, one of the most valuable sources of information. Many years ago, when I first visited some of the orphanages and the Missionaries of Charity in Dhaka, Bangladesh, I was overwhelmed. One of my observations that impressed me was to see how the majority of the staff at *Shishu Bhavan,* who had worked long hours for a pittance, had a great sense of devotion and dedication.

For me it was a matter of getting a foot up in the first rung of a ladder while moving forward. I recall having sat there dejected and confused, often blurred by fatigue and anger. I tried to focus but found myself to be in a state of quandary. All through my interactions with a variety of people, I kept my eyes wide open and ears to the ground in an attempt to hear/overhear what one might say in an unguarded moment of revelation. From then on, every now and then, vivid images of *Shishu Bhavan* charge my heart and emotions that flash my mind.

I also recall having begun to reflect on the memories of military atrocities in Occupied Bangladesh percolated to the surface like a movie in a slow motion. It was as though the images of those nightmarish months came through with striking clarity: the tragic facts of military reprisal, kidnapping of women, forced confinement of them, and harrowing stories of sexual violence; they all seemed to have fallen into place, incapacitating me for a while.

In fact, it had made a lasting impression on me. Interviews of former and present staff, who gave me their time, having placed their trust on me, were very useful. The interviewees were not only friendly but also very forthcoming in their approach to my inquisitive questions. Amazingly enough, though not all, with some of the older staffers, those times have been etched indelibly in their minds. Some are able to recall in photographic details, especially the vigils at the bedside of dying infants at the orphanage. The Canadian team that visited the orphanages in July 1972 also recalls the same.

As I sprawled about in the government office premises, such as individual Ministries of Labour and Social Welfare and Law and Parliamentary Affairs in the Secretariat and the National Archives of Bangladesh, and snooped around for every bit of information that I could get my hands on, I found myself to be in rapport with many who had the firsthand knowledge of the rape victims. My follow-up visits to the orphanages in the late 1990s conveyed to me a sense of urgency and solemnity. I found myself reminding me of an often-cited Shakespearean quotation: "Time and tide wait for none." Many key players who had worked with large number of rape victims, such as doctors, health practitioners, and social workers in various capacities in the postindependent Bangladesh have already begun to leave for their eternal journey.

Fortunately, upon frequent revisits to the orphanage, I had found myself at ease with the surroundings and, without further delay, immersed in the examination of the documents on hand. I was able to snap right into the subject of writing with hammer and tongs. The idea of revisiting the orphanage premises was to bring the events of 1971 to closer. This was something that had helped me with my overweening self-confidence of the time (though not always desirable). In that sense, I did not pretend to play either the high priest or the clown on this subject matter.

My simple approach had been to explain with full clarity the bits and pieces of information I was able collect with which to reconstruct the past hitherto absent in the Bangladesh's historiography. I knew in my own mind that, for me, it was certainly not an illusion. Each visit had provided me the historical evidence of material kind that had helped me gain a fuller understanding of the magnitude of the crimes committed. I must admit, although I got into the swing of things, every time I reviewed the documents, my mind traveled back to the period reminiscent of the days of military repression from which I had tried to escape. Placed in a unique predicament, I reminded myself of an age-old adage: "We ain't seen nothing yet."

Interviews of two key government players of the day, Abdul Awal (then executive director, National Board of Bangladesh Women's Rehabilitation Program) and Abdur Rab Chaudhury (then secretary, Coordination Division for External Assistance for Relief and Rehabilitation, Prime Minister's Secretariat), were very informative. They had no lofty pretension. I found them enlightening seeing that both were rooted on the ground. During my long conversations at my second round of meeting with them in the summer of 2012, I found the topic mind-boggling again just like before. This was especially so, given the gravity of the matter at a time when the Mujib administration lurched from one crisis to another. Again, the testimonies of physicians and health practitioners, such as Drs. Geoffrey Davis, Mohammed Bashed, and Halida Hanum Akhter, had been extremely useful as that helped me deepen my own understanding of the medical and social challenges that they were faced with.

Sociologists, social workers, and counselors, such as Jahangeer Haider, Nurul Islam Khan, Mahmuda Begum, Fatema Kalam, Zeenat Ara Bhyuan, Nargis Akhter, Razia Haque, Taherennussa Abdullah, Hosne-Ara Kashem, Sajida Humayun Kabir, Ruby Ghaznavi, Shirin Jahangeer, and many others, willingly gave their time to be interviewed, having assured me of their unfailing support and encouragement.

My meetings and discussions with all of the above individuals have enabled me to cross-check the media report of the day and determine the veracity of the events and their consequences. As well, Father R. W. Timm, CSC, and Rev. Theotonious Gomes, CSC, Congregation of Holy Cross, have given me their valuable time every time I needed to meet with them to clarify my own understanding of the issues related to the birth, abandonment and adoption of the war babies, and the support of the Congregation of Holy Cross. It was through their reference and positive intervention that I had full access to the libraries of Caritas and the Christian Communications Center, which I have used extensively.

I am grateful to both Fr. Timm, CSC, and Rev. Theotonious Gomes, CSC.

To understand an important historical event or a phenomenon (in the present context, it is the sexual violence of the Pakistani army during the Bengalis' struggle for independence), one would need to see how the various pieces such as abduction, confinement, rape, and murder, forced pregnancies of Bengali women, and the birth and abandonment of their "unwanted" babies "fit together" to reveal their interconnectedness and the fallout of the liberation war.

All other reports and studies, together with a host of information, which I have used and found useful, are to be found in the bibliography, which is put together at the end of the book.

One final caution for the reader is that I have looked at the evidence through the prism of my own culture and time. All through my research endeavors, I have tried to know the difference between what I remembered, what I was told, and what I had learned. Therefore, I am aware that biases often are unacknowledged and unrecognized and influence the writer willy-nilly.

INTRODUCTION

WITH THE SUDDEN military crackdown on March 25, 1971, a contemporary tragedy began to unfold in what was then East Pakistan. Within days, the world media condemned the Pakistan government for the killing of Bengali civilians who had provoked the wrath of Pakistan's president Agha Muhammed Yahya Khan (Yahya) by demanding greater provincial autonomy for East Pakistan. Murderous forces were unleashed, and the country was thrown into a civil war, pitting the Bengali citizenry of East Pakistan versus the Pakistani military. Murder became massacre, and mutilation became a tool of repression and control. The death toll of civilians leaped from thousands to tens of thousands to hundreds of thousands in full view of international observers. Both commissioned and noncommissioned military officers, like packs of ravenous jungle beasts, pillaged cities and villages, indiscriminately destroying human lives and properties.

With the military forces were collaborators, such as *Razakars, Al-Badrs,* and *Al-Shams,* who not only remained loyal to the military regime but were also a party to the crimes committed by the Pakistani forces. Briefly, *Razakars* literally means "volunteers" who were a paramilitary group organized by the Pakistan army in East Pakistan; *Al-Badrs,* a paramilitary group of the West Pakistan Army that operated in East Pakistan; and *Al Shams*, also a paramilitary wing of several Islamist parties in East Pakistan. All three groups had worked against the Bengali nationalists during Bangladesh Liberation War in 1971.

Those spared still remained in constant fear of being arrested, imprisoned, tortured, or killed. For nine long months, the world media witnessed unrestrained brutality of the military regime. Having deemed them as unreliable, and therefore not worth living, the Yahya government's military personnel had continued to persecute Bengalis.

Yahya contended that the clandestine clampdown on innocent civilians was necessary to put down what he claimed to be a rebellion backed by India. Though apparently sudden to Bengalis, Yahya's military response appeared to be a premeditated plan by Yahya's strategic planners in Islamabad, Pakistan, to quell East Pakistan's (Bengalis') aspirations of autonomy by flexing West Pakistan's military muscle. The civil war, called the War of Independence, ended in Bengali nationalists declaring the independence of Bangladesh (formerly East Pakistan), throwing the Bengali-Pakistani union into the dustbin of history.

The story of the war babies of Bangladesh is somewhat reminiscent of the Vietnamese war babies fathered by both white and black Americans in the 1950s through mid-1970. They are also reminiscent of the Korean and Cambodian war babies, again fathered by American soldiers, often referred to as children of "mixed blood," "mixed race," or "Amerasian." While there has been a lot written about Amerasians in North America, unfortunately, almost nothing has been written about the war babies of Bangladesh with the exception of the material that I have referred to in Notes on Sources. To this day, both the "undesirable" war babies and their "dishonored" mothers, referred to as *biranganas,* remain largely unknown to the people of Bangladesh, and even less so to the outside world.

Nevertheless, the discomfort and disgust that tended to embroil the issue were that despite people's innate protective feelings toward the newborn infants, the war babies who were born as a result of rape by the members of the Occupation Army were viewed by people with derision. No one can say with any certainty how many Bangladeshi women and girls had given birth to babies conceived as a result of these rapes by Pakistani military personnel. The numbers are unknown because no one knows how many violated women took the first opportunity to commit suicide in Occupied Bangladesh; or how many, immediately after their release from the army barracks following the independence, had disappeared, having started to live incognito to avoid the shame and disgrace that they feared would come from their society. This book that deals with the journey of the first contingent fifteen war babies to Canada, their adoption in Canadian homes, and the outcome of inter-racial adoption, consists of eight interrelated chapters.

Chapter 1 sets the historical context, giving a short account of the War of Liberation in terms of the military atrocities and the ongoing repression of the Bengali citizenry, which included soldiers using sexual violence as a means of control. We attempt to "guesstimate" the number of *biranganas* based on evidentiary sources. We then review the documentary evidence of the birth of the war babies and their abandonment by their birth mothers.

In Bangladesh, the birth of the war babies, conceived as a result of rape, was seen as morally repugnant; hence, the infants thus born were "unwanted" in Bangladeshi society. Keeping in mind this social fact, it briefly discusses further how the problem with regard to the war babies became even more complicated due to the simple fact that they were not accepted by Bangladeshis, who remained both indifferent to and indignant toward such "disposable" babies. This fact had at once clearly categorized them as "undesirable;" as well, it also instantly subjected them to ostracism. It comments on the value, or lack thereof, attached by the people of Bangladesh to such babies who were abandoned by their helpless birth mothers immediately upon birth.

The chapter also highlights the lack of adequate data on the birth, death, abandonment, and adoption of the war babies, although there are several guesstimates available from various sources. It acknowledges that there might be instances of formal and/or informal adoption and foster care placements with Bangladeshi families and institutional placements for which no records are available.

As well, it discusses how the intense hatred by the Bengalis for Pakistani soldiers, who were alleged to have fathered these babies, might have been the additional reason for the decision to abandon and not to embrace the war babies. It also makes reference to the true and sad irony that, due to social stigma, many infertile Bengali couples longing to have a child for them could not or did not come forward to take a war baby into their homes. If they did, they do not share such news with anyone in Bangladesh.

Chapter 2 is a synopsis of the traditions and practices of adoption, and pertinent legislation governing adoption in Canada and Bangladesh, concentrating on the early 1970s, with a short account of orphanages and child-care institutions in the two countries. It provides a short description of *Shishu Bhavan* from where a few of the war babies were brought to Canada, the United States of America, Australia, and some European countries for adoption. It will be seen how the Mujib administration, immediately upon assumption of power, addressed the issue of adoption in a commendably deft manner at a time when it had many other hot-button issues to deal with. It will be seen how

Mujib himself was particularly sensitive to and mindful of the fact that negative attribute to the war babies (such as referring them as "unwanted") by the Bangladeshi society had made people see the war babies as "undesirable" and, therefore, "disposable" babies.

To the Mujib administration's way of thinking, the Bengalis' indignation for the newborns had displayed a more insidious form of bias of the part of the Bangladeshi society as a whole. People's attitude toward the war babies had been shaped by careful choice of word, the objective of which is to intentionally denigrate the status of the war babies in their country of birth. Right at the outset, the government encountered a serious problem, as there was no special legislation in Bangladesh governing adoption. The only applicable law at the time was the 1890 Guardian and Wards Act for the purpose of guardianship. At stake were two key concepts – Bangladeshi war babies and a group of Canadian couples' child quest that epitomizes story of parenting beyond genetic lines. Fearing that the political and religious leaders would play "hardball" politics, which could result in further stigmatization, the Mujib administration kept a low key but diligently worked with key players, such as the Geneva-based International Social Service (ISS) and national stakeholders, by keeping in mind "the best interest of the child."

It briefly discusses how, given the muddled and ambivalent attitude of Bengalis toward adoption, the government put the matters somewhat iconoclastically to counter social ostracism and alienation and moral and political dimensions of adoption. It was done in the hope that given the socioreligious feelings of the Bengalis, the ISS might see the issue from a broader perspective and recommend the right alignment to find a solution. Though the government was under tremendous pressure, it had no capacity to initiate any tenuous social, institutional, or administrative changes even though it was of the opinion that there was a need for a radical change.

It discusses how, following receipt of the recommendation of the ISS, the child welfare agencies of the Ministry of Labour and Social Welfare were assigned to draft appropriate legislation that would allow the infants to be sent to Canada and other countries where the prospective applicants for adoption (or the future adoptive parents) had agreed to an undertaking for adoption. The chapter reveals how, in the minds of Bangladeshi legislators, the linguistic juxtaposition had shown

MUSTAFA CHOWDHURY

the oscillation between reason and passion that had ultimately helped them come up with a special provision. By doing so, and being inspired by a new moral impetus, the Mujib administration wanted to construct a particular norm and the adoption of particular values in Bangladesh.

It will be seen how the government came up with a legislation that not only clarified but also strengthened the legal protection of children, removing deterrents to effective action in behalf of children that existed in Bangladesh. It describes the *Bangladesh Abandoned Children (Special Provisions) Order 1972*, which is a legislative response to the recommendations of the ISS. In clarifying the clauses within the Special Provisions Order, the government was careful, as it did not in any way want to get mired in confusion and controversy. We would see how the Government acceded to adoption to outside of Bangladesh, believing that it has made a thoughtful and informed final decision based on an ethical framework regarding interracial adoption. In doing so, it firmly believed that adoption should be an unfaltering commitment to providing families for children, rather than children for families.

It will be seen how, by allowing the birth mothers to abandon their child when the alleged father was nowhere to be found, the provision brought the law into more realistic correspondence with the actual circumstance in the newly independent country.

Chapter 3 describes the *Bangladesh Project* conceived by the Montreal's Families For Children (FFC), a nonprofit organization that advocate international and interracial adoption and welcomed by both the governments of Bangladesh and Canada. It outlines how, having fought the intransigent opposition or resistance, especially from certain officials in the government of Ontario, the adoptive parents worked through the strangling red tape of provincial and federal governments in Canada and the government of Bangladesh. It describes the experiences of the Ontario couples that were an emotionally grueling roller-coaster ride that had plunged them to uncertain future for days. Acting on the noblest of human virtues and compassion to save the relinquished war babies, the adoptive parents remain silent heroes. The spunk and determination of a group of Canadian couples were such that despite the difficulty, heartbreak, and almost insuperable barriers, they continued toward their heart's desire until they were given permission to adopt.

The persistent "fight" on the part of the prospective adoptive parents, who eventually forced the Ontario government to react positively, demonstrates one key point that the news media also picked up for public's consumption – their commitment to the adoptive parent identity, making it a core part of their overall identity. The project made it possible to arrange for a number of war babies to enter Canada for adoption at the invitation of the Bangladesh government through the proclamation of the *Bangladesh Abandoned Children (Special Provision) Order 1972*, which established legal guardianship of the war babies. Each couple had paid their own child's airfare, lawyer's fees, and other incidental expenses with no form of government assistance and fought each step of their way to provide a loving home for the war babies. In that sense, this chapter presents their fight for adoption as a story of unbridled optimism of a group of determined couples characterized by firmness. Having gone hell-bent, they made the adoption happen from Bangladesh to Canada.

While the government recognized that every prospective adoptive family offered potential opportunities, it, however, wanted to make sure that it had made an informed decision. In following the recommendation of the ISS, the government handed over fifteen war babies to the representatives of the FFC with a clear understanding that, following the transfer of the war babies, it was a requirement of the adoptive parents to legally firm up their adoption in appropriate courts in their place of residence in Canada. Once adopted, the children must be recognized as the children of the adoptive parents *as if begotten*, a status that is no different from a biological child born to his adoptive parents.

The inordinate delay that the prospective adoptive parents had to cope with, and the time lag between the decision to adopt and the actual arrival of the child, the process of which is usually referred to as "parental claiming," were unbearable. Nevertheless, delays were not enough to discourage them. Instead, encouraged by their faith and courage, they were able to overcome all insurmountable odds and opposition to achieve what they set out for – adoption of Bangladeshi war babies.

Chapter 4 describes the war babies' odyssey from Bangladesh to Canada, their arrival, their joyous reunion, and their formal adoption in Canada. It outlines behind-the-scenes work, logistics, and coordination with respect to the exact departure and arrival of the first batch of fifteen war babies from Bangladesh to Canada, via New Delhi and New York. The arrival of the war babies in Canadian homes instantly transformed the occasion into a cause for rejoicing. It outlines the concerns of the government of Bangladesh following the departure of the war babies, as there seemed to have been a disconnect between the government and the FFC officials who were obliged to keep the government posted on the status of the babies in their new homes. When both parties were reconnected after about three months, there was a sigh of relief for government officials, although the people of Bangladesh were oblivious of the entire episode.

It contrasts the media coverage of the historic odyssey of the war babies to Canada compared to the low-keyed coverage in Bangladesh, where the departure of the war babies was seen as a good riddance. By allowing foreign adoption of the war babies with the promulgation of the Special Ordinance, Bangladesh government breathed a sigh of relief having legitimized adoption of the war babies and orphans, collectively referred to as the "abandoned children."

Finally, it also describes how the war babies, who symbolized the dire human tragedy, were able to adjust to the new environment and accompanying problems that made parents worry about them due to a lack of adequate medical information. This is an area that raised a great deal of anxiety among the parents who sought advice and counsel in order to determine the next course of action given the medical information gap. In addition, it outlines various problems encountered by would-be parents of Ontario to complete the formalities for actual adoption in Canada according to the provincial requirements.

Chapter 5 presents profiles of the adoptive parents and their Bangladeshi child and describes the eclectic nature and the composition of their families that immediately sets them apart from other adoptive parents in Canada. The very fact that these couples, white middle-class Canadians who adopted children of a different race, had immediately made them different from the majority of white middle-class Canadian couples who usually choose to adopt and take the route for a white healthy baby. Their profiles collectively illustrate the complexity of adoption and, in particular, the many ways in which adoption, whether domestic or international, has always been, and continues to be, a part of the human experience. It argues that if the child's "best interest" is held to be the first consideration in a decision about adoption, as was the case in the present instance, the adoption of these war babies in Canada was undoubtedly in their "best interest." It describes how the adoptive parents had acted on the noblest of human virtues and compassion to save a few of the relinquished war babies of Bangladesh.

It also briefly discusses how these parents have had things to be proud of with respect to their children especially since none of whom had ever suffered from adopted child syndrome or ACS. This remains an illustration of the power of love, the ultimate raison d'être for adoption by a group of ordinary Canadian couples achieving extraordinary success. Theirs is an example of an achieved parenthood that does not necessarily de-emphasize blood descent and heredity, but, in a sense, preaches and interprets adoption as another means to making one's family.

The narrative includes the individual life of the war babies in their adoptive families; how, among their siblings from diverse backgrounds, they grew up together as "one big family," bonding with each member of the family in a very special way. Knowing from their parents how their lives had started in one of the most tragic possible circumstances from where they were rescued and what they had left behind, they remain ever grateful to their parents.

They also recognize that even though there were many tragic outcomes of the abandoned babies in Bangladesh, having been adopted and raised in Canada, they sure consider themselves to be extraordinarily lucky to have been adopted in Canada. Time and again, the adoptees mention how mindful they were of their parents' relentless fight with government officials to get through red tape to make their dream a reality. They recall how, with utmost frankness, the parents had explained to them the extraordinary circumstances during the war, incidence of sexual violence and its fallout, and other tragic circumstances surrounding their conception, birth, abandonment, and adoption in Canada.

It discusses how, being surrounded by diverse multiracial family members in a strong, supportive, and loving environment from childhood to adulthood, most of them had followed a similar developmental trajectory of self-awareness that had helped them to emerge from and evolve into multiracial and multicultural consciousness in the social milieu nuanced by environmental factors. It describes how the war babies grew up with human dignity they deserve, something for which today they are counted as citizens of the world.

Chapter 6 provides a vignette of the adoptive parents with accounts of their experience in parenting racially different children who were cherished and loved unconditionally. Their narratives reveal how they had formed their families in rather creative and insightful ways, having derived immense satisfaction from the enduring relationship and bonding attachment. It highlights the unique moments of the adoptive parents, the years when the children (both adopted and born to the family) grew up together in safe and caring homes of the adoptive parents. Though "unwanted" in their country of birth (Bangladesh), they were affectionately precious to the Canadian couples, who showered them with love, support, and every opportunity to blossom.

It will be seen through their individual narratives how they thought of the war babies as too precious to be wasted as "unwanted" children or homeless waifs. The couples that responded from their hearts to the needs of the "abandoned" babies saw them as casualties of the finale of the War of Liberation. It will be also seen how, in recounting their personal experiences, the adoptive parents in Ontario talked about the inflexibility of the Ontario government to the idea of interracial adoption. Such was the prejudice that they could not even get past officialdom in putting across the very important message: that it was not a matter of quality of life but the opportunity to life itself.

It outlines the parents' frank opinions on how they made sure that the "culture" their children grew up with was "Canadian" culture, which is embedded in multiculturalism with a new and added dimension in their outlook. The parents recognized this as a revealing feature of the identities of the war babies, which they had internalized as a social identity having a sense of belonging to the families that they were adopted into. In working out the identity, they don't recall their racially different children having any great difficulty in considering them as "Canadian." The parents talked about feeling reassured seeing how their child from Bangladesh had fitted into their homes where they were quick to *learn* having nothing to *unlearn*.

It will be seen through their testimonies how, by providing love and encouragement to ask question, they had allayed the fear and curiosity of their children and had strengthened the children/parent relationships. Their narratives will also show how they, with no atavistic fear, had always encouraged their child from Bangladesh to learn about the country and the people of Bangladesh. We will hear from a few adoptive parents who had accompanied the war babies in 1989 about their first trip to Bangladesh. Having developed a solid parent-child bond, which is a constant stimulus created through love and caring, the adoptive parents felt more entitled to parent.

They have heard many say, "Adoption is family building the easy way;" or they have often been asked, *Do you not have your own children?* Regardless of how or what was asked or said, they remained calm and courteous without reacting to such questions or comments. They talked freely and frankly about how they grew as parents (having learned to deal with pain and joy) and how their relationship with their children had also evolved over the years. They remember reaching a point where they had begun to feel good about themselves being in the midst of the warm and caring family environments. To the parents, it became evident that it is the *family environment* and not *biology* that largely helps one grow and *determines* as to *who* a particular person is.

Last, it will also be seen from the parents' narratives that love alone is not enough and that it takes unflagging commitment, inordinate endurance, and complete acceptance on the part of the family to form a family, whether through adoption, surrogacy, remarriage, or other combination, and to make it a success.

Chapter 7 explores the views of the war babies and analyzes the narratives of their lives through the years in Canada. It gives a short account of how they came to terms with their known and unknown past, circumstances surrounding their birth, abandonment, and adoption in Canadian homes. Each adoptee talked about his or her parents whom he or she calls Mom and Dad and knows of no other parents. It presents the adoptees' own views and their perceptions of themselves in relation to their background and family life in Canada by shedding some light on their adjustments in transracial families.

They talked about their integration in Canada and eventual participation in activities that are Canadian. It will show how many of the issues inherent in the adoptive experience had converged when the war babies reached adolescence; how freely they talked about three factors that intersected in their lives: (1) an awareness of the significance of being adopted in Canada, (2) a drive toward an effort to situate themselves among their Caucasian parents and siblings who are mostly of diverse backgrounds; and (3) psychosocial striving toward the development of an integrated identity in multiracial and multicultural Canada.

An analysis of their narratives would also demonstrate how they have developed and constructed a Canadian identity by embracing a gamut of feelings with respect to their lives; knowledge, or lack thereof, of their birth country; and historical and biological roots in the backdrop of the Bengalis' struggle for independence. It outlines how the war babies had sought to embrace a culture or an identity that had provided them with a proper "fit" in multicultural Canada while growing up in an ethnically diverse family headed by Caucasian parents. This was unique and rewarding experience for all of them.

Because multiculturalism encompassed their lives on a daily basis, they grew up being very conscious of the world around them and learned to celebrate diverse cultures, religions, and creeds that have been molded and shaped by everything Canadian. We shall see at the end how they became a part of the human landscape of Canada, the country they know to be their "home," by easily accepting their adoptive parents, who were deeply imbued with nothing but goodwill. It will be seen through their testimonies that they never had any ambiguity in situating them in the respective adoptive families and the Canadian society at large. Their own narratives will show how, unlike many children in the United States of America, where being black is often a special state of being, the Bangladeshi visible minority war babies in Canada have no such clear status, as they claim that they did not and/ or don't face any intense racial polarity.

The present chapter touches on a volley of questions that went around my head: *Is there, in the minds of the adoptees, a feeling of loss from their country of birth? Or while growing up in a multiracial family, did the adoptees fear a risk of losing a sense of how they present themselves to the world?* Such questions made me wonder what kinds of questions they might have in their minds as to *who* they are and *from whence* they came, including not only their race but also the politically unsettled question with regard to their Pakistani/Bangladeshi origin. It will also be seen how, for all practical purposes, the war babies, whose lives began in Canada, needed to know about their actual beginnings (culture and ethnicity) in order to have a complete sense of *who* they are and to feel connected to the world both genetically and environmentally.

Having received unequivocal and unconditional love from their parents, they recounted the richly rewarding feelings that grew from interactions among their siblings and parents back and forth. According to the adoptees, their parents have always treated each child, separated by age and/or opposite gender, as an individual while growing up. They have always felt that their parents were there all the time, "on their side," ready to help them meet their needs, whatever their needs might have been.

It would be found through their recount that the adoptees are content with what little they know about Bangladesh. As they grew, they recognized *how* there are many who believe that the most important thing in a child's life is *to have a family* – people who commit to *love* the child and take responsibility to *raise* and *care* for the child. Throughout their lives they adhered to this single belief that they carry with them to this day as to *who* they *are*.

The chapter ends with the revelation that, although expressed in different ways, the majority of the war babies view that being a part of a family with roots from different countries and races is something that has strengthened their identity and understanding of oneself in relation to others. In that sense, they do not see this as what many critics of transracial adoptions call the "denial of one's racial background." Instead, they see themselves as *Canadian* in an all-encompassing sense.

Chapter 8 attempts to summarize the findings and considers this incredible bringing-home-war babies initiative to be counted as a "success story" of a group of babies and sucklings who were badly in need of care and protection. It recognizes the fact that adoption has a lifelong impact and the issues are complex. It describes how, once sent to the safety of adoptive homes, they grew up with elements of happiness that are reflected in the sentiments expressed by both the adopters and the adoptees. It outlines how the adoptive parents had remained frank, transparent, and cooperative even though the abandoned babies were handed over to them without ever hoping and planning for a reunion of any kind anytime. Alluding to the parents' resolve to expand their families through adoption, it describes how they collectively went out of their way to overcome hurdles after hurdles in their determination to adopt the war babies in order not to meet their infertility but, instead, to meet the needs of the orphaned infants who needed a safe and secure home.

It also briefly describes the sentiments of the government of Bangladesh that Bangladesh was not just a faraway country tainted by the history of its abandonment of the war babies born as a result of rape. The Mujib administration made every attempt in all directions having firmly believed that the effort must be multiplied and expanded if the war babies were to be properly selected for adoption.

In outlining the most positive outcome, it points out that none of the war babies went through a sense of the "adoption trauma," unwitting deconstruction of the modern adoption practice that is often talked about in the adoption discourse. The adoptees' knowledge of "having been relinquished at birth" and their birth rights "having been compromised" through adoption to another country, away from their country of birth, did not obsess them in any way. In that sense, adoption, which was a household word in their families, came to mean for them nothing less than *endearment*. They consider their adoptive parents as "real" parents and see parenthood as "raising" rather than "giving birth" to children.

It is maintained that the FFC is to be solely credited for the entire *Bangladesh Project* right from its conception to the actual adoption of the war babies in Canada. All available records, though fragmentary in nature, show clearly how a group of dedicated volunteers, such as Lloyd and Sandra Simpson, Fred and Bonnie Cappuccino, Ray and Elisabeth Mowling, and Robert and Helke Ferrie, having sought assistance from various sources, fought persistently to adopt a few Bangladeshi war babies and succeeded in what they came to see as a challenge to their beliefs.

The chapter concludes with the statement that if one considers adoption as a means of providing a permanent relationship of parent and child between the adopting parents and the person adopted, the adoption of the war babies stands out as an outstanding story that illustrates complete adjustment of the Bangladeshi war babies brought to Canadian homes. In a sense, these extraordinary couples negate the observations of the famous sociologist H. David Kirk, who suggests that many people outside the adoptive family view adoption as a "second-best" way of becoming a family. It raises questions for a future discussion on international adoption, in particular, of racially different orphans.

CHAPTER ONE

Historical Context:
Birth of the War Babies
and the Aftermath

Rape in Occupied Bangladesh
(March 1971–December 1971)

T HE 1971 WAR of Independence remains an illustration of one of the most severe humanitarian crises of the previous century, involving massacres, torture, sexual violence, displacement, destruction, confiscation of property, and liquidation of Bengalis. There are far too many stories of Pakistani military personnel who looted, robbed, and shot people wantonly in both cities and outlying areas. Frequently did they go inside, smash people's possession, and molest the inhabitants in Occupied Bangladesh. As well, there are stories of frequent kidnapping of Bengali women, many of whom remained captive in military camps and barracks in the nook and cranny of Bangladesh until the occupied land was liberated after nine long months of struggle. Sadly enough, even a cursory look at the War of Independence of Bangladesh demonstrates that history is destined to be repeated. Since the beginning of time, as far back as one can recall, invading armies and occupation by foreign troops have always played havoc with the lives of the local inhabitants. The Pakistan army personnel, while reigning supreme, made no exception to this fact.

The greatest problem that one encounters is to find a starting point due to a lack of adequate documentary evidence, which will soon acquaint the reader with the complexities and problems inherent in the study of the war babies. To understand the story of the war babies, it is important that one has a clear knowledge of the extent of rape and sexual assault by the Pakistani military personnel in Occupied

Bangladesh; the subsequent and profound impact of these crimes on the victims and their family members. As a fallout, the birth of the war babies, seen as the "unwanted" babies of Bangladesh, since they were conceived as a result of rapes.

One also needs to keep in mind some of the following puzzling questions for which there does not seem to have an easy answer: *What does it mean, in terms of Bangladeshi social values, to be raped? How did the Bangladeshi society react to the birth of the babies conceived as a result of rapes? How did the government of the newly independent Bangladesh address the issue of rape and its victims who, like the rest of the Bangladeshis, dreamed of a Shonar Bangla (Golden Bengal)? Where are the women of Bangladesh who were dishonored? Where are the birth mothers who had to abandon the newborns? Where are the abandoned babies? How many had the good fortune of being adopted outside of Bangladesh? How many, if any, were adopted in Bangladesh?*

Raping of thousands of Bengali women by the Pakistani military personnel consisting of officers, soldiers, and *jawans* (foot soldiers) during the period the army was engaged in crushing the liberation movement would remain apparently meaningless unless one can demonstrate a causal relationship of rape and enforced pregnancy. One must bear in mind how sexuality and militarism of the Pakistani army were intertwined amid fear of guerilla attack, loneliness, and moral degradation among the lusty military men. One also needs to be mindful of how reliance on captive women became the standard measure for relieving the tension of guerilla war through the practice of rape, sodomy, and mutilation.

In fact, the large-scale raping of Bengali women by the Pakistani military personnel and anecdotal observations also strongly suggest a pattern of behavior of perpetrators consistent with brutalization that takes place in such protracted wars. "Tens of thousands of women had been raped as part of the Pakistani policy of intimidation, foreshadowing the approach taken by the Bosnian Serb army there decades later, and many became pregnant,"[1] wrote James Bartleman, first Canadian (resident) high commissioner to Bangladesh. One needs to move cautiously while approaching this particular subject. Needless to mention, lack of caution could easily lead one not to recognize the phenomena of rape and sexual assault. One is very likely to fail to piece together the various components, such as abduction, confinement, rape, murder, enforced pregnancy, birth, and consequent mass abandonment of the war babies that fit together in the historical narrative.

If historical research of this magnitude is not to be characterized by a form of imaginative reconstruction, commitment to objectivity and empirical method must remain firm. It is only when one looks at the incidences of pregnancy, abortion, and suicide on the part of the raped women and the birth and abandonment of the war babies from the known fact the actual circumstances surrounding sexual assaults of the Bengali women can one form a whole picture.

It is therefore important to put these events in proper historical perspective right at the outset. This means that the Liberation War and sexual violence during the reign of the military regime ought to be discussed first although, unfortunately, within the means provided by fragmented and, in many ways, insufficient documentary evidence. Naturally, it becomes a complex case, since there is hardly any documentary evidence of rape, sexual assault, and sexual servitude, which the victims were subjected to. While it is understandable why the military authority would not keep any such record even though it was aware of such occurrences, there are physical and material evidences of the birth, death, and abandonment of the war babies who were born in the government-established *Seva Sadan* (clinics and delivery centers that were set up to assist the rape victims), Baby Homes, and other orphanage premises across Bangladesh that give us a starting point.

Today the most popularly accepted figures within Bangladesh, and the one that has been reported in many external sources, are that up to three million people were killed or tortured to death; two hundred thousand women were raped in organized camps of which a large number of such rape victims were subjected to forced pregnancy, and more than ten million people were forced to flee to India. Since the focus of the book is clearly on the adoption of the war babies in Canadian homes and its outcome, the incidence of rape has been dealt with in a quick snapshot. The brief and inconclusive quantitative account below is only to contextualize sexual violence and its aftermath. The present chapter or any other chapter of the book does not address the validity of the cited numbers recently negated by many, including Sarmila Bose in her much-talked-about book titled *Dead Reckoning: Memories of the 1971 Bangladesh War*.

Since the scope of this book is strictly limited to the adoption of the first contingent of fifteen war babies in Canadian homes in 1972 and its outcome, the following headings are to assist readers to contextualize rape, enforced pregnancy, birth, abandonment, and adoption of the babies that were referred to as the "throwaway" babies of Bangladesh.

Incidence of rape, murder, suicide, death, pregnancy, and abortion

Rape

The first difficulty in reconstructing the events is that there is no data to move forward. One of the recurring problems in estimation and, perhaps the greatest challenge here, is to present just the facts (numbers). This, because of differing opinions, is often obfuscated by or exaggerated with arguments and commentaries passed off as facts. There is no consensus as to the number of women raped by the Pakistani military personnel, and the estimates vary quite widely.

Sporadic records support the view that the regime carried out a systematic pogrom of forced expulsions and torture, including terror, massacres, as well as rapes and sexual torture of Bengali women. The corroboration of these allegations is complicated by the incomplete and fragmentary nature of historical data for that period. Due to partial absence of data from all seventeen districts of Bangladesh at the time, one's capacity to quantify is severely limited to making simple assumptions on causal and arithmetical relations. The much-quoted exaggerated numbers are more of a hindrance to an objective study. Trying to estimate the number of rape victims is like searching a needle in a haystack.

An Italian medical survey that many talk about frequently, but without giving any appropriate or specific bibliographic citation, put the number of victims at four hundred thousand; the newspapers of the day also quoted numbers that are much higher than four hundred thousand. The London-based International Planned Parenthood Federation (IPPF) estimated the number at two hundred thousand.[2] Immediately following the liberation, due to apparent liberation, the government pf Bangladesh assigned the National Board of Bangladesh Women's Rehabilitation Program (BWRP, hereinafter referred to as the Board), set up in early 1972, with a view to looking after the rape victims and other disadvantaged women. The Board was also mandated to come up with estimation on the number of women who were raped by the Pakistani military personnel in Occupied Bangladesh between March 1971 and December 1971.

Initially, the Board members traveled extensively to villages across Bangladesh and estimated the number to be approximately 268,200. However, after a series of consultation with appropriate agencies and with those who had worked with the victims directly or indirectly, the Board did another round of estimation using the following methodology: that approximately two girls and women were reported missing daily in each *thana* (area of local police station authority) during the occupation period out of about 480 *thanas* at the time.

Based on the fact that the occupation army stayed for 270 days, the authority thus developed a formula for calculation in which the authority agreed that it is the reason that must preponderate. The formula was made in the following manner: 480 *thanas* x 270 (days) x 2 (females) = 268,200 (females). Allowing for exaggeration and for the fact that some women might have been missing for other reasons, the board rounded the figure to two hundred thousand, which since then became the official figure for citation.[3] Regardless of whether one accepts this estimation or not, in the face of formidable obstacle, one cannot make a substantial headway on this endlessly complex subject matter with any credibility.

Dr. Geoffrey Davis, an Australian surgeon, then IPPF director who came to Dhaka, was deeply touched and saddened by seeing the predicaments of the victims of sexual violence. He argued that the rape victims would "face lives of infertility and chronic disease."[4] After a review of the guesstimated numbers offered by various sources, and following his own observations in the field, he held the view that the number could go higher than what was estimated by the government of Bangladesh. Having worked with the rape victims and many health professionals, clearly Dr. Davis had certain reservations about the Board's estimation. He, along with his medical teams that consisted of Bangladeshi and Indian doctors, came to consider this to be an underestimation.

Speaking straight from the shoulder, Dr. Davis argued that the actual fieldwork by his team members in the remote areas at the district level had amounted between three hundred thousand and four hundred thousand Bengali women.[5] His team meticulously recorded the number of victims who were raped during the occupation period and those who were treated by them in early 1972 after the liberation of Bangladesh. Dr. Davis conducted his own analysis using the field reports obtained from his colleagues.

As about one-third of the country's villages were damaged, though not destroyed, the army activities included commission of sexual crime, such as rape, though the number of unwanted pregnancies would not necessarily be enormous; again, many women, who were heading for India, were separated from the refugee groups by elements of the army and *Razakar*[6] only to be subjected to gang rape by the military personnel. The total number of Bengalis who sought sanctuary in India was estimated at ten million of which approximately 1.5 million were adult women (based on family average of four children). Dr. Davis also maintained that although the official figures for the population of Occupied Bangladesh in mid-1971 was seventy-five million, it could easily have been as high as ninety million.

In any event, when the ten million who fled to India are deducted, the remaining population of Occupied Bangladesh was sixty-five million. Out of this, roughly 1.1 million were women of reproductive age. If a third of these were raped, argued Dr. Davis, then the number of victims would amount to three hundred thousand.[7] Justice Khalek Mohibus Sobhan, then chairperson of the National Board of Bangladesh Women's Rehabilitation Program (board), was inclined to agree with Dr. Davis' estimate. Nevertheless, the government of the day did not want to spend any more time in an academic dispute over these figures, as its priority was to rebuild the war-ravaged and resource-poor Bangladesh without any delay.

Again, comprehensive interviews of physicians and health and other subject specialists, such as Dr. Jahangeer Haider, then director (administration) of the Board, Fatema Kalam, Hosne-Ara Kashem, Razia Haque, who were involved in counseling many rape victims, also uncovered considerable evidence that direct to systematic rape and sexual slavery practiced by the military personnel. Jahangeer Haider, while working on the initial data that was deemed to be four hundred thousand women, presented his findings in the following manner: "Nearly four hundred thousand women have been violated of whom at least 20 per cent is social outcasts with their property or their male earning members lost."[8]

The first self-identified rape victim who came out in public to blow the gaff is Ferdousi Priyobhashini in November 1999. For the first time in Bangladesh, after twenty-eight long years of silence, Priyobhashini recounted her apocalyptic nightmare. She talked about how, day after day, many Bengali women were forcibly taken into designated camps. The people of Bangladesh were outraged and petrified having heard from Priyobhashini the sordid story of, on again and off again, forced confinement of her along with many other women who were kept naked so that they could neither escape nor commit suicide. Not only that, people also heard for the first time from an actual rape victim how the army personnel used to gang-rape and wantonly kill countless Bengali women.

Again, starting from the early 1990s, the *Ghatak Dalal Nirmul* Committee (committee to exterminate the killers and collaborators) made headway having encouraged rape victims to come out of the closet in public as a proof of sexual violence by the Pakistani soldiers who were assisted by many Bengali quislings. Unfortunately, the rape victims who responded to the call by appearing before the crowd as "dishonored" women found themselves in double jeopardy. Upon their return to their homes, people in the community subjected them to further pain and humiliation through social alienation. This single fact continues to discourage other victims to self-identify even though they have been living in torment. This does not help us in our estimation.

Murder

It is impossible to estimate the number of rape victims who were killed by the military personnel. The dead bodies of women (decomposed, unclad, half-clad, or nude) that were often found in many crannies of Occupied Bangladesh only remain as material evidence of the incidence of murder and suicide. "There were bodies in Jamuna right up to the distant parts of the country," observed Dr. Davis in an interview with Dr. Bina D'Costa.[9] Immediately following the liberation, such hearsay evidence had provided a stark example and a small token of the tragedy, although it does not assist us in determining or even approximating the number of such victims.

There is, however, a variety of accepted truth about the savage violence, murder, and lingering death by torture by the captors who committed these crimes with demonic pride and prowess. There are, again, different versions as to the treatment of the victim, the most common of which is that comparatively younger captives were kept for repeated use. This had continued until such time that they were found "unserviceable," a term that was used to indicate that the captives had either become pregnant or had shown overt sign of venereal diseases and, thereby, no longer "serviceable" to their clients. While there is no direct evidence for it, there are stories of what happened when one was found "unserviceable" while in captivity. The use of such terminology is also reflective of how the military force had used Bengali women as a commodity that gets devalued for repeated use. There is no number attached to the incidence of murder of women in Occupied Bangladesh.

Suicide

To understand *why* and *how* many rape victims had terminated their own lives and the lives of their fetuses, one has to understand the process of adhering to gender roles and the direct consequences of the imperatives of those rules – that the raped women had no choice but to perform abortions or to kill themselves. There exists among Bangladeshis a sentiment to blame the victim even though there might be signs of being battered and bruised while in captivity. The rules of femininity also demanded the victims to toe the social line.

Taken as whole, it is safe to assume that the women who were "dishonored" by the Pakistani military personnel must have gone into hiding immediately after their release from captivity. What is a known for a fact is that many rape victims had killed themselves, as dead bodies were found every now and then throughout 1972.

The reality on the ground was that because of inherent sexism in the Bangladeshi society, which is still riddled with myths and superstitions that thwart women's status on an equal footing, there were no immediate resources available to the victims who needed discrete measures to overcome the crisis. It took a while before the government was able to put its act together.

Having reached a crescendo, many depressed and heartbroken rape victims could not get out of the miasma of shame. Unable to cope with their situation, they saw themselves as though they were the proverbial fallen women of Bangladesh. Being in an excruciatingly painful and no-win situation, where the forlorn and unfulfilled rape victims had no way to stand on their feet in a society that offered no adequately satisfactory help, they found no meaning to their lives, since the society is inclined to victimize the victims.

Dr. Davis claims that just by talking to many rape victims whom he had treated, he has learned that they were "raped again and again and again" and that there were many who "did not get enough to eat."[10] As they received no treatment when they were sick, a "lot of them died in those camps. There was an air of disbelief about the whole thing. That nobody could credit that it really happened! But the evidence clearly showed that it did happen,"[11] observed Dr. Davis.

The only documented reference to the incidence of suicide between January and April 1972 puts the number at two hundred women. The figure two hundred again seems acceptable to Dr. Davis and his colleagues, who maintain that following the liberation, it was in the best interest of the families to discretely report the incidence of suicide. This was thought to be a safe way to avoid any murder investigation or further interrogation, which could potentially become public.

Dr. Davis had heard directly from the victims' family members about many young "girls of 12 and 13 [years old who] were found naked, stripped of their saris and roped together so that they couldn't run away or commit suicide."[12] What is even worse is that as soon as the military personnel "gave saris to them, a number of them hung themselves with them," and, observed Dr. Davis, many had "tied stones to themselves and jumped off bridges"[13] to end their lives. Understandably, the shame and isolation they felt in fear of degradation that lacerated their minds and hearts were not feelings they wanted to share with anyone at the time.

There is, however, no number that may be cited for the period prior to January 1972 (meaning there is no figure for the incidence of suicide from the entire period of military rule from March to December 1971). The ones that are known by a variety of innuendoes and hearsays tend to be exaggerated in nature. No one, not even journalists and reporters who came to Occupied Bangladesh while under the military regime, and even after the liberation of Bangladesh, attempted to cover the incidence of rape, sexual servitude, and forced prostitution, could come up with a hard number. Journalists and reporters always alluded to the fact that Bengali women were raped in large numbers, that's all.

Enforced pregnancies

With no definite number of rape victims, it is even harder to determine how many rape victims became pregnant – a possibility that remained certain as late as the first quarter of 1972. As the story goes, through hearsay and innuendoes, the captive Bengali women were allegedly forcefully impregnated, and many were held captive as sex slaves. Ferdousi Priyobhashini, the first rape victim to come out in public whom we have already alluded to, has testified to the news media the precarious conditions of the helpless captives. Speaking from her own experiences, according to Priyobhashini, being in the captivity of the ruthless military people, naturally the victims were forced to go all the way, willy-nilly.

The long and the short of it is that it *did happen* – in the nature of things. While in the camps, the rape victims would have no chance to slip out for a pregnancy test, although one could speculate that under the circumstances, such a victim would have tried to conceal her pregnancy at any cost. Any investigation along this line constantly reveals the nature of severe limitations, which one cannot overcome.

Following his visits to the remote areas of several districts including many clinics and rehabilitation centers in the Dhaka area, Dr. Davis was quite comfortable in guesstimating the incidence of pregnancies. He argued that the sexual violence was in the form of penile penetration. Having examined many of the rape victims, Dr. Davis concluded that of the approximately four hundred thousand women who were raped following the military crackdown, the report of approximately two hundred thousand becoming pregnant seemed an underestimation.[14] It is because, he argued, it took into account only those who were reported as missing. There were many families that did not dare to report for fear of persecution; as well, the same families also had tried to keep such incidences confidential.

"As about one third of the country's villages were molested, even though not destroyed, this army activity provides a huge number of cases of rape though the number of conceptions would not be enormous,"[15] argued Dr. Davis. It was also his observation that by the time he had arrived in Bangladesh in February 1972, many of the pregnant women he met and examined were already eight weeks pregnant. The media coverage of the day could not provide a verifiable number of pregnancies, although there were many allusions to sexual violence and its fallout.

Again, based on another estimation of three hundred thousand rape victims, who were as young as twelve or thirteen years of age, Dr. Davis maintained that with a population growth rate of 3 percent per annum, it was safe to assume that about half of these victims were pregnant – an assumption that would amount to 150,000 in this group. As mentioned, what had reinforced Dr. Davis' assumption was the known fact that the reason why many rape victims were let go by the military personnel was that they were deemed "unserviceable" due to pregnancy, overt sign of venereal diseases, or both. It is estimated that the incidence of pregnancy at the end of December 1971 was about 1,500 per district.[16] However, in most of the districts that Dr. Davis had visited, the numbers of unwanted pregnancies were lower than this figure. He further opines that "this figure would suggest and, taking into account the number already delivered and the suicides, the numbers available, usually about 10 per village cluster is low."[17]

Given the fact that the army had stayed longer in certain parts of towns and villages than others, the soldiers were likely to have committed more crimes over a longer period, thus increasing the probability of a greater number of pregnancies. For example, if the approximate figures of 1,500 per *thana* for half the 480 *thanas* (i.e., those afflicted by a high concentration of military for an extended period) are accepted, then one could come up with approximately 360,000 pregnancies, an argument with which Dr. Davis agreed at the time.[18]

Again, it was Dr. Davis' estimate that most of the victims were treated by the village *dais* (midwives), quacks, homeopaths, etc., leaving only a small number still pregnant. This was prior to his arrival in Bangladesh in February 1972. Not surprisingly, when he visited the remote villages, he had found that the number of unwanted pregnancies was lower than what he was led to believe after his first meeting with Bangladesh authorities in Dhaka.[19] Dr. Davis only came to Bangladesh in February 1972, whereas sexual violence had begun right from the night of March 25, 1971. The rape victims had started giving birth from as early as October 1971. Dr. Davis himself observed, "About 10% of all conceptions should have delivered before liberation."[20]

One must exercise caution and bear in mind that though Dr. Davis' observations were based on his personal visits to the premises where raped women were temporarily housed, he had no information with regard to the number of pregnancy of women who had killed themselves or were killed by the army. In addition, the information that Dr. Davis provides do not include information from all of the seventeen districts of Bangladesh at the time (1972). The actual number for the entire country could thus be potentially higher.

Death during childbirth

There is no record of such information, although there are references to the fact that many pregnant rape victims had died during childbirth. The medical teams remained busy looking after those who needed their immediate help. The closest description is again from Dr. Davis, who was alarmed at the existing situation at the time: "Throughout the country, there is a huge number of young attractive women (the army had no need to rape the plain ones) who have had early abortions in the villages and who now have short or long term complications as a result. Those with major complications have, by now, died and the number involved is not known."[21]

Given the workload of the medical team headed by the IPPF director, Malcolm Potts, who worked alongside Bangladeshi doctors, observed that there was no time or extra resources to focus on the number of death during the time babies were born. Not surprisingly, therefore, no one could come up even with an approximate figure of death of the birth mothers or their infants at birth.

Abortion

To understand the incidence of abortion, one must recognize at the outset that the Bangladeshi society regards sex outside of marriage, even consensual sex, as a sin and abortion an infanticide. The Bangladeshi society still frowns upon both unwed mother and the child. Therefore, the first choice of the pregnant rape victims was to abort the unborn. Though there is no reliable number for the incidence of abortion, evidence of abortion ties in quite well with the overall picture of enforced pregnancies.

In the newly independent Bangladesh, abortion had still continued to be governed by the provision of sections 312 and 313 of the *Penal Code of 1860,* which stated that whoever voluntarily causes a woman with a child to miscarry shall, if such miscarry be not caused in good faith for the purpose of saving the life of the woman, be punished. The vagueness of the law and the haphazard nature of its enforcement in the newly independent country had made it difficult to determine *what was* and *what was not* legal at the time.

To avoid the disruption of this service due to the resistance that was rising across Bangladesh, Dr. Davis met with a number of senior officials in the government, including Ruhul Quddus, then principal secretary to the prime minister. He persuaded the Mujib administration to amend the existing penal code. It was believed to be in the best interest of those raped women who desperately needed to terminate their pregnancy. Accordingly, in early 1972, the penal code was amended. From what Dr. Davis found through his fieldwork, he feared that although abortions performed by *dais,* and quacks were not in performed by *dais* and quacks were not in themselves very dangerous, nevertheless, the long-term complications and impact on the affected women's health was very serious.

Again, the Board persistently maintained that there should be no fear, as the government was supportive of abortion under these circumstances. Yet many doctors and nurses did not agree with what was being said. Many medical practitioners were wracked by ethical, legal, and moral questions. In fact, many were inextricably caught on the horns of a dilemma. The rape victims needed the help and cooperation of health community. It was expected of them to perform or assist in abortion, but the issue became problematic, to say the least.

Detailed field reports from each district, under the signature of the deputy commissioner, the civil surgeon, and the family planning officer of each city, are an important source of information with regard to abortion. Through contacts and interviews of Drs. Halima Hanum Akhter and Mohammed A. Bashed, it was as possible to cross-check the authenticity of these reports. As well, those who worked with Dr. Davis (and this includes a large number of NGO personnel, both Bengali and foreign nationals, members of the Bangladesh Medical Association, and its local chapters) reinforce the fact of abortion using traditional indigenous methods. But no one could assign a particular number to the incidence of abortions across Bangladesh performed (generally without the knowledge of anyone).

Another known fact about abortion by pregnant rape victims comes from many families that had slipped onto India to have abortions performed while Bangladesh was still under the occupation army. This was confirmed by the news reports from India and by members of the medical community who talked about it only discreetly upon their return to the newly independent Bangladesh from India. Following the liberation, this practice had continued by many families, though in utmost secret. Newspaper reports of the day, which included interviews of Justice K. M. Sobhan, chairperson of the board; Sr. Margaret Mary, superior, Missionaries of Charity; Dr. Geoffrey Davis; and the IPPF personnel, such as Odert von Shoultz, reveal different numbers with regard to the incidence of abortion that tend to be exaggerated. "Between 150,000 and 170,000 of the 200,000 who fell pregnant were aborted in highly undesirable but unavoidable conditions before the outside world even knew the problem existed,"[22] observed Dr. Davis.

This is perhaps the most comprehensive estimation on abortion in early 1972, following the arrival of the foreign doctors in Dhaka who worked with pregnant rape victims then placed in various abortion clinics and delivery centers referred to as *Seva Sedan.*

Incidence of birth, death, abandonment, and adoption of the war babies

Many abandoned babies were rescued by the sisters of the Missionaries of Charity in the hope that they could go to the homes of those who genuinely wanted to adopt some of these babies and were committed to raise them as their *own* children. Records of such information might be seen as *prima facie* evidence of sexual violence and its aftermath in Bangladesh. It is against this backdrop of social taboos surrounding the birth of the war babies born anywhere between October 1971 and September 1972 that one needs to seek information with respect to the birth, death, abandonment, and adoption of the war babies.

From the information found in many interviews of foreign journalists, it is possible to develop a pattern of birth and abandonment of the war babies immediately following the liberation of Bangladesh. As mentioned already, because of the deep-seated prejudice against these infants, they were seen as "unwanted" or "disposable" and therefore "untouchable." It was a case of enforced pregnancy through penile penetration against the will of the victims. As their bodies changed, many rape victims could not easily hide their pregnancies. Being scared to death, many were forced to carry their unwanted pregnancies to full term, give birth, and give the newborns up for adoption both in secret.

Despite limited resources, the staff at *Shishu Bhavan* and other delivery centers had recognized the increasingly urgent need to appreciate the unusual circumstances that had been quietly and tragically occurring on the doorstep. Upon their arrival, all mothers-to-be were simply asked their names. According to the staff of the orphanage, all incoming women were repeatedly assured of confidentiality with regard to their pregnancies as well as birth and abandonment of the newborns. It will be seen in the next chapter how the Mujib administration worked closely with the orphanage authority and other stakeholders in developing and implementing a policy of "don't ask, don't tell," whereby the pregnant women were not to be asked about the paternity of the child in question. The rape victims were also not expected or obliged to say anything about it.

Birth

The birth of the war babies under extraordinary circumstances remains an example of the resilience of these babies whose birth mothers, having failed to abort on time, had to carry their pregnancy to full term. Sr. Margaret Mary, then Superior of the Missionaries of Charity, went out looking for violated women who were expecting and encouraged them to bear the child. They were encouraged to abandon the baby if they wished to do so instead of resorting to terminating the life of the unborn. She spent quite a bit of time assuring all incoming clients at *Seva Sadan* that the Missionaries of Charity would take care of all babies who would survive the abortion attempts.

Within weeks after the independence of Bangladesh, the Mujib administration began to work closely with the Geneva-based International Social Service (ISS) in securing a safe place for pregnant rape victims who were then enticed to come in and give birth in confidence. After a desperate search for an appropriate place for the war babies in the Dhaka area, the ISS representatives found a place in Dhanmondi, Dhaka, for rent, which the ISS consultant described as "an absolutely ideal house on Road 32, Dhanmondi," a "two-story, with large rooms, two kitchens and five baths,"[23] to be used for pregnant rape victims.

Many expectant mothers had tried to abort but were unsuccessful. As well, there were some who were opposed to abortion. Fortunately, Mother Teresa was welcome by the government of Bangladesh when she came to Dhaka from Kolkata, West Bengal, India, to advocate her belief that the pregnant women should carry their pregnancies to term. Needless to say, although there was a difference in the viewpoint of the government of Bangladesh and that of Mother Teresa at the time, they were able to work together.

The government maintained that those who preferred abortion should have full access to such facility with complete confidentiality. In the event that abortion would be too late for an expectant mother, she should be encouraged to give birth and leave the newborn in the hands of the government should the birth mother wished to do so. At that time, there were also an undetermined number of makeshift shelters in addition to *Seva Sedan, Nari Punarbashan Board, Shishu Bhavan,* and baby home that had housed unknown number of violated women and their newborns in anonymity.

The Canadian team under the stewardship of Fred and Bonnie Cappuccino that visited Bangladesh in June 1972 to pick up a handful of war babies for adoption in Canadian homes is another source of information. Having visited the orphanage premises in Dhaka, the team maintains there were not as many infants as they had heard of while in Canada. "Early reporters had estimated that some 5000 war-babies would be born in 1972. From the statements of people about the widespread suffering at the hands of the Pakistanis, we had felt that 5000 was a reasonable conjecture,"[24] thus wrote Fred.

While visiting to the orphanages, clinics, *Seva Sadan,* Baby Homes, and rehabilitation centers for rape victims and pregnant women, they were advised by their escort Zerina Rashid, that the number of war babies was much lower than what was estimated earlier by various sources. This also ties in with Dr. Davis' direct observations. During their twenty-one-day stay in Dhaka, they were also able to network with missionaries in Chittagong, Barisal, and Padrishibpur through the Canadian Holy Cross Brothers and Sisters. Even Fr. Benjamin Labbé, then director of Christian Organization for Relief and Rehabilitation

(CORR), who was in the field all through the troubled months of 1971 having spent time with many rape victims, could not give any specific number of war babies born in Bangladesh.

Through their conversation with Sr. Margaret Mary, the team had also learned that many birth mothers were hiding their babies either to keep them or to abandon them secretly. It was disconcerting to the team members, as the orphanage personnel with whom they spoke made them cognizant of *how* and *what* was happening to both newborns and their birth mothers. Sr. Margaret Mary, who oversaw the birth of many war babies in her premises, also confirmed her own observation by saying that she was convinced that the newborn babies were being hidden by the families, and many were dying upon birth in large numbers.

After speaking to several orphanage personnel, the team members came to learn that even though it was estimated that about five thousand babies would be born, following the liberation, it became difficult to determine the number in exact term. This was later on confirmed by the International Social Service (ISS) consultant in the following manner: "The number of such babies [war babies] is not known and the socio cultural stigma attached to this particular issue provides a well ground for non-availability of the babies and their mothers in the present situation."[25]

Both Mother Teresa, who later years came to be known as the "Messenger of Love and Hope," and Sr. Margaret Mary, who came to be known as the "mother" of the "unwanted" children, remain important in estimating the number of war babies, as they directly dealt with those who worked in various orphanages and delivery centers at the time. Though they could not provide any hard number, the historical fact is that they had collected many dying newborns from clinics, slums, and remote areas by persuading the depressed birth mothers to leave their newborns behind, having given them assurance of confidentiality.

Again, there are many anecdotal stories of stillborn babies and the birth of very frail and prematurely born war babies, many of whom died shortly after the birth. Accounts of complications at delivery from those present at *Seva Sadan* and *Shishu Bhavan,* where these babies were born, include life-threatening instances of premature birth and associated complications arising from maternal hypertension. In examining the *Shishu Bhavan*'s records, extra caution must be used, as there are also records of those who are referred to as "orphans," "foundlings," "illegal" [probably meant to write "illegitimate"] who were not necessarily fathered by Pakistani soldiers. Newspaper reports indicate that between three thousand and four thousand babies were born in the premises of twenty-two *Seva Sadan,* which were established in 1972 by the *Jatyo Nari Punarbashan Board* across Bangladesh. Given that there is no hard number, based on the above analysis, it might be observed that the number of war babies born in Bangladesh would not be less than 2000 for certain.

Death

All through 1972, there were rumors, some exaggerated though not totally baseless, of babies secretly buried in bags or sacks by close relatives to avoid shame and disgrace. The news media relentlessly tried to cover the birth and death of the war babies. It is also rumored that under such circumstances, no standard or religious burial practices were followed and that many dead babies were wrapped in cloth and were simply dumped in holes or thrown into nearby canals and rivers.

Every now and then, partially or completely decomposed bodies of many little babies were discovered by people on the streets. Dr. Davis, who performed abortions on the pregnant women and assisted those who were too late for abortion and had to give birth in order to save their lives, found that ongoing psychological stress on the mothers during enforced pregnancy had produced negative outcomes for the babies – low birth weight being the main.[26]

According to medical professionals, there is no data for those born prematurely and/or with congenital defects or serious health problems. The orphanage personnel who had seen the victims and the horrors of the military repression in all its ghastliness had devoted their time to saving the lives of the newborn infants. Those who worked at *Shishu Bhavan* and other delivery centers recall in startling detail, vigils at the bedside of dying newborn infants at the orphanages as moments seared in their memories.

The Canadian team remains the firsthand observer of the grim situation in the orphanages' premises. In fact, the team would have failed to recognize the critical situation had it not been there in the premises. They were startled to see the challenges of trying to care for overwhelming number of infants, the majority of whom were underweight in the war-ravaged Bangladesh with far too few supplies, medicine, and human resources.

The illness of the newborns, such as ear infection, pneumonia, boils, fungal infections, etc., had overwhelmed the sisters and other staff, most of whom had no medical training except for the nurses. There were many who were so weak and so sick that they had perished immediately following their birth.

In the absence of any official figure, the general consensus based on the observation of those in the health field at the time is that the war babies born under the most unfavorable circumstances could not be provided with the minimum medical care they required; they had perished in course of time. While talking about the high incidence of death among the abandoned war babies, Sr. Margaret Mary opined back June 1972 that the newborn babies would "go on dying at least for a few more months."[27]

Due to the passage of time, even the intrusion of an inquiring mind fails to dredge up from obscurity, the number of war babies who did not survive. This remains a constant challenge to reconstruct the story of the birth and death of these babies. Simply put, many newborns did not survive. Ironically enough, what the desperate birth mothers had tried through abortion (termination of life) was eventually achieved in reality immediately after the birth of the infants through instant death. There is no hard number to associate or even to guesstimate the incidence of death.

Abandonment

Variously referred to as abandonment, relinquishment, surrender, or giving up of the "unwanted" babies who were being born right up to September 1972, there is again no quantitative information in this regard. Giving up of an infant by its birth mother in the absence of the child's natural father, who was neither physically present nor identifiable, meant that the birth mother had forsaken her child having no other choice. Legally, it also came to mean relinquishment of a child by the child's biological father (who was not around) and birth mother (who willingly gave up), hence the loss of parental rights. Under the circumstances, the orphanage authority became the caregiver/taker of such infants, while the government of Bangladesh became their "statutory guardian."

It was accepted by both the health professionals and the government authorities that under the circumstances, removing a newborn from its mother would necessarily be in "the best interest of the child" in question. In a sense, during the crisis, the abandonment of the babies metaphorically meant the helplessness of the birth mothers who could not resist the forces of social pressure in Bangladesh that had made it impossible for them to decide anything else at the time.

The intense hatred by the Bengalis of the Pakistani military, who were alleged to have fathered these babies, might have been an additional reason for the decision to abandon the child. Since there were no legal or social pressures on a birth mother to keep her baby, abandonment was the easiest option, which was seen to be rather normal at the time under the circumstance. Given the situation, the government of the day also did not believe in forcing the mother to care for a child who was the result of rape. In the absence of mandatory issuance of birth certificate and/or fear of social repercussion, all that a mother needed to do was to express an interest to relinquish one's baby and walk away.

Mahmuda Begum, then a social worker who joined the government following the liberation, recalled how she had found it "both tragic and ironic."[28] According to Begum, on the one hand, many rape victims became mothers through forced conception, which resulted in the birth of their babies; on the other hand, they had nothing to celebrate "motherhood" of such kind. "On seeing the newborn for the first time, the rape victims who became birth mothers had demonstrated no love for the newborns which is not only an emotional requirement but a biological necessity for a baby,"[29] recalled Hosne-Ara Kashem, one of the counselors at the Board. Because of the circumstances surrounding the conception and the ways in which the rape victims became mothers, their instinctive reaction was not to reach out to the newborns. Instead of love, cuddling, and hugging, which are natural responses of a birth mother, the first thought the birth mother had in mind was to abandon the child.

A volley of questions go around one's head: *How many war babies were abandoned at birth? How many birth mothers had looked after their child rather than giving them up for adoption?* There is no straight answer to such questions. In determining the incidence of abandonment, one runs into the same problems as the incidence of rape, enforced pregnancies, birth, and death of the war babies. What we know for a fact is that with the arrivals of new abandoned war babies, some of whom were left in baskets just outside the orphanage premises, the underresourced, overburdened, and understaffed orphanage personnel worked frenetically to get a handle on the workload and hoped for foreign intervention to rescue the newborns seen as "disposable" in the country in which they were born.

Adoption

We are aware of a variety of adoptions in Bangladesh, such as informal, formal, as well as adoption of older children and guardianship of orphans in various capacities. In the absence of any data, it stands to reason to maintain a position along the following line: that nobody is known to have come forward, not even social service agencies, hospitals, family physicians, or relatives of family friends, to adopt a war baby. If there were local adoptions, there are no records, since the families would still prefer not to talk about it.

Many infertile and fertile couples worldwide responded to the opportunity to adopt some of the Bangladeshi war babies in the hope that their wishes would be fulfilled. Through an examination of the archival records, it will be seen in chapter 3 how a group of ordinary Canadian couples took extraordinary steps to embrace some of the abandoned war babies and were successful in bringing them to Canada all the way from Bangladesh.

What is known through various documentary evidences is that by late fall (1972), there were very few war babies left for adoption, although there were war orphans still available for adoption. In one of her correspondences, Helke Ferrie, one of the Canadian team members, who was in Dhaka twice and who adopted two war babies from *Shishu Bhavan*, wrote about her findings based on her own observations to the immigration attaché in New Delhi following her visits to several orphanage premises. During the middle of July 1972, "some 25 babies, all between 1 week and 8 months [were] available for adoption."[30] Helke further advised him that only seventeen of them were available to FFC, as the rest were to go to families who had arranged private adoption.

Thus far we have learned this: in seeking quantitative information on the birth, death, abandonment, and adoption of these babies, we have no reliable record in Bangladesh other than the numbers generated by word of mouth.

To conclude, the commission of crime such as rape and murder by the cruel and diabolic military personnel having absolute power under the primordial law, "might is right," was a daily occurrence in Occupied Bangladesh. Given the nature of the crimes and the circumstances under which crimes were committed, it is problematic to determine the numbers out of tragic occurrences and the subsequent birth, abandonment, and adoption of the war babies born as a result of rapes.

Due to a lack of hard numbers, any number assigned would certainly stand up to historical scrutiny. Unfortunately, immediately following the liberation of Bangladesh, even the country's historians had also failed to record the specificities of the birth and abandonment of the war babies in 1972 and their subsequent adoption in foreign countries in appropriate interpretive context. We have seen various attempts to guesstimate. Nevertheless, these are, by no means, a shot in the dark; the guesstimates we have seen were carefully assigned, given the limitation with which the numbers had to be determined.

Having demonstrated a good understanding of their unique predicament, the government, however, did its best within its ability under the circumstances by putting in place an action program for both rape victims and the war babies. According to Justice Sobhan, due to the sensitivity of the subject, all pertinent documents had been destroyed by the Board upon advice from the government of the day.[31]

In the next few chapters, we shall explore the subject further through an examination of documentary evidence available on the first contingent of fifteen war babies.

Notes and References

[1]   James Bartleman, *On Six Continents: A Life in Canada's Foreign Service 1966–2002*, McClelland and Stewart Ltd., Toronto, 2004, p. 62.

[2]   International Planned Parenthood Federation (IPPF) is registered as a charity in the United Kingdom and is the largest voluntary

organization in the world to be concerned with family planning and sexual and reproductive health.

3   "The Changing Face of Genocide – Bangladesh," by Geoffrey Davis (1972). *Proceedings of the Medical Association for Prevention of War*, Volume 2, Part 7, June 1973, p. 176.

4   The *Toronto Star*, August 24, 1972.

5   *The Changing Face of Genocide-Bangladesh," opt. cited*, pp. 176–177.

6   Within the context of the Bangladesh-Pakistan War, a *Razakar* is a loyalist who was in favor of one Pakistan. More specifically, *Razakars* were a special force created by the Pakistani army consisting of members of the Bengali, Bihari, and other communities loyal to Pakistan.

7   *"The Changing Face of Genocide-Bangladesh," opt. cited*, pp. 176–177.

8   "Women's Rehabilitation towards Emancipation: Practice, Prospects and Problems for Family Planning," by S. Jahangeer Haider, *Proceedings of the Seminar on Family Planning*, November 21–25, 1972, Dhaka, Bangladesh. p. 535.

9   Bina D'Costa's interview of Dr. Geoffrey Davis, cited in her book titled *Nationbuilding, Gender and War-Crimes in South Asia*, New York, Routledge Contemporary South Asia Series, 2011, p. 197.

10 *Ibid.*, p. 198.

11 *Ibid.*, pp. 198–199.

12 The *Toronto Star*, August 24, 1972.

13 *Ibid.*

14 *"The Changing Face of Genocide-Bangladesh," opt. cited*, pp. 176–178.

15 *Ibid.*

16 *Ibid.*

17 *Ibid.*

18 *Ibid.*, 176–178.

19 This was expressed by Dr. Geoffrey Davis to the author in Sydney, Australia. Taking deep interest in the subject, Dr. Davis himself came over to the author's niece's house in Sydney where he was living at the time. By then Dr. Davis had retired from International Planned Parenthood Federation. The date of the meetings was February 17, 2002.

20 *"The Changing Face of Genocide-Bangladesh," opt. cited*, p. 177.

21 *"The Changing Face of Genocide-Bangladesh," opt. cited*, p. 185.

22 The *Toronto Star*, August 24, 1972.

23   Letter from Marie D. Levine, International Social Service, American branch, consultant in Dhaka, to Wells C. Klein, general director, International Social Service, American branch, June 19, 1972. The agreement between ISS and the government of Bangladesh was signed by the American Branch known at that time as Traveler's Aid-International Social Service (TAISSA from 1972 to 1977) with the understanding that all correspondences concerning this agreement should be in the hands of ISS American branch. Documents pertaining to the project of ISS in Bangladesh in 1972 are housed in the American branch office of ISS, reference # 1H5/ Bangladesh asg. per agreement.

24   Families For Children. *Bangladesh Project.* Part E, Chapter 32, *Bangladesh Babies,* 1982, p. 270.

25   *Inter-Country Adoption in Bangladesh,* under the heading *Importance of Publicity and Public Information.* Prepared by Wells C. Klein, General Director, International Social Service, American Branch, March 27, 1972, p. 1.

26   This was expressed by Dr. Geoffrey Davis to the author in Sydney in February, 2002, Australia, *opt. cited.*

27   Sr. Margaret Mary said this to the Canadian team during one of her meetings with the team members Fred and Bonnie Cappuccino and Elisabeth Mowling while visiting *Shishu Bhavan* immediately after their arrival in Dhaka.

28   This was expressed to the author on January 10, 2001, by Mahmuda Begum, who worked at the National Institute for Population and Research Training at the time.

29   This was expressed to the author by Hosne-Ara Kashem on January 15, 2001, a counselor at Bangladesh Women's Rehabilitation Board in 1972, now long retired.

30   Letter from Helke Ferrie to the immigration attaché in New Delhi, July 11, 1972. Helke Ferrie shared this letter with the author during his visit to her house in Alton, Ontario, on May 20, 2000.

31   This was said by Justice K. M. Sobhan to the author in an informal interview over a cup of tea at his house with the author in Dhaka, Bangladesh, on January 7, 2001.

CHAPTER TWO

Adoption Initiative in Bangladesh and Canada

A DOPTION, A PROCESS where a child is permanently cared for by parents other than the biological, is a widespread practice in many countries and cultures. Figuratively speaking, there is no difference in the use of the term "adoption" in Bangladesh and Canada. Both countries see adoption as a legally sanctioned procedure for ensuring that an adequate family life is provided to an orphan when parenting failure prevents the normal process. It is an axiomatic truth that for most orphans who cannot be with their biological families, adoptive placement offers the closest approximation of security that is available. The varying cultures, practices, legal systems, and agency networks of Canada and Bangladesh, however, provide quite different configuration of foster care, guardianship, and adoption placements in the two countries.

There are noticeable differences in policy and practices that reflect the differing traditions and religious and social values with regard to adoption among Bangladeshis and Canadians. In Canada, adoption is seen as a positive benefit that must be sought for an orphan in need of a family; whereas in Bangladesh, care within the child's extended family, fostering, or even institutional care in their own country is seen as a better alternative. In that sense, traditionally it is expected that some close next of kin assumes the responsibility instead of an unknown family. Thus upholding the child's right to be brought up by the child's own kith and kin, somewhat similar to long-term fostering.

Adoption and orphanages in Bangladesh

There are conflicting beliefs at the societal and cultural levels about adoption in Bangladesh. Some believe it as a good deed to adopt, while some view it as a providential gift from Almighty for childless couples. It is like getting a second chance to make a family, and yet a great bulk of people seems to prefer to have their "own" (biological) children to make a family. There was no legislation governing adoption in Pakistan or Bangladesh (then East Pakistan, being a part of a united Pakistan). Consequently adoption was not recognized in the penal law of Pakistan when Bangladesh was born out of East Pakistan in 1971.

Bangladesh shared with Pakistan the legislation promulgated prior to 1971, such as the 1890 *Guardian and Ward Act* and *the Muslim Family Ordinance of 1911*. Under this act, "guardianship" of a minor is permitted by a competent court if it is deemed to be "in the best interest of the child." Simply put, the Muslim law does not recognize adoption per se as it is understood in the western world. Death, illness, and economic hardship of natural parents are generally the precipitators of guardianship among extended family members and foster care placements in orphanages or institutions. Important to note, the 1982 Guardian and Ward Amendments Ordinances prohibit granting *guardianship* of Bangladeshi children to non-Bangladeshi parents.

In general, even in the case of divorce or separation of a couple, there seems to be a variation on the parents' right, philosophy, and the notion of custody of the children involved. In the absence of a court order, in reality, children are deemed not be overprotected. In such a case, parents have a right to follow their own child-rearing practices and tend to agree upon an arrangement mutually involving extended family members on the part of the couple. Again, socially speaking, an agreed-upon arrangement does not seem to present a flagrant problem in the eyes of the society either.

Historically speaking, adoption has been a matter of what is usually referred to as "informal" adoption whereby an orphan is taken into a home and raised as one's own child, except that it is never legalized. Informal adoptions occur when a relative or stepparent assumes permanent responsibilities without a court involvement. Such placements are seldom or never arranged by a social agency; instead, they are done informally by relatives. The rationale, clearly, is not to alienate the child totally from the child's own extended family in order to allow the child to satisfactorily meet his or her needs for his or her own emotional security with an assurance of protection in a milieu where there is a next of kin.

Although the law defines the exact moments when one set of parents ceases to have rights and responsibilities and the other set takes over in every respect, such certainty of law is not fully carried over in Bangladeshi tradition and customs. In a sense, Bangladeshis see such practice as sort of guardianship (as opposed to adoption) that provides the security and presence of adoption without cutting off extended family members who are important to the child. However, legally recognized adoptions require a court or other government agency to award permanent custody of a child to adoptive parents. The "formal" adoption of a child is generally considered to be rather exceptional even by involuntarily childless couples in Bangladesh where informal adoptions are part of the country's customs that date back to centuries.

Needless to point out, in Bangladesh, there is prejudice and/or discrimination against members of the adoption triad – biological parents, adoptive parents, and children. Therefore, the very landscape of adoption in Bangladesh is different in that adoption is seen as a "paper" kinship in the absence of conception, creation, gestation, and birth. In other words, being "chosen" or "selected for adoption" does not fit with cultural assumptions about parenthood in Bangladesh. Given the above social backdrop, naturally legal adoption, in the sense we understand it in Canada, is still relatively new in Bangladesh. For all practical purposes, guardianship of orphans had been rooted in the Bangladeshi tradition in which an adoptive family, which is usually an extended family, becomes the *guardian* of the child (generally an orphan).

By assuming responsibilities of an orphan, a relative thus simply becomes the guardian of that child. The said parents cease to be the guardian of the child in question *as* and *when* the said child reaches the age of majority. Assumption of such responsibility for raising an orphan by uncles, aunts, cousins, and distant relatives, however, may not fit the definition of "adoption" as it is understood in its legal sense in North America. As observed, traditionally in Bangladesh where kinship adoption (adoption by extended family members) is more prevalent, relatives don't necessarily "adopt" legally. As mentioned already, care within the child's extended family, fostering, or even institutional care in their own country is seen as better alternatives.

The appointment of guardians has thus been a method for providing care, protection, and supervision of the persons of minor age who are without natural guardians and for carrying on the administration of their estates. By bringing home a *yateem* (orphan), a couple may want to raise, educate, and treat him or her as the couple's own child having assumed his or her guardianship. Guardianship is a preferred custom in Bangladesh, as it does not legally impact on the relationship between child and family.

This would entail the responsible to protect, feed, clothe, teach, and love the child as the couple's own child. However, the point to note here is that the real lineal identity or paternity of the child has to be maintained. Most importantly, rights – that is, those rights reserved for one's natural (biological) children in the *Shari'ah* [1] – should not be granted. Foster care of orphaned children is encouraged, but it is not permitted to claim another person's child as one's own. In simple term, Islam emphasizes the rescue of abandoned children without permitting adoption. It is said that the Prophet Muhammad (peace be upon him) is known to have encouraged adoption as a social service and a humane act. The Prophet is esteemed to have said that the best house of Muslims is one where an orphan is cared for.[2]

The naming of the child after its natural father is obviously to avoid possible psychological trauma the said child might face at a later stage in his or her life. While Islam does not prohibit adoption, the Islamic concept of adoption is very different from that of its modern concept as it is understood and practiced in the western world, such as the USA and Canada. As observed, Islam's stance on adoption rests on the necessity of keeping the biological parents of the child always in the picture. In that sense, by adopting a child, Muslim parents assume guardianship of an orphan, a foundling, and a poor or needy child of known or unknown lineal identity. The key point to note here is that while raising an orphan, changing the child's identity and lineage for another untrue lineage is prohibited in Islam.

In other words, the cultural norm in Bangladesh is ingrained with the identity right at birth of a child. This is much unlike Canada, where, through formal adoption, the adoptive parents instantly *become parents without giving birth*. In the Bangladeshi society, "blood relationship" is an enduring and unbreakable bond by which the entire relationship is measured. Adopted children don't always fall into the same category, since they are seen as not having a sense of true belonging for their lack of relationship. The prevalence of the "ties of blood" is, therefore, of primordial importance in the Bangladeshi society. The concept of adoption thus exists in Bangladesh as a cultural belief that birth families should be preserved at all costs and under all circumstances. Since the cultural norm in Bangladesh is to know *who* one's parents are, the adoptive parents – that is, parents without giving birth – don't seem to be looked upon by people in general as parents. From both social and religious points of view, child bearing within marriage represents the *sine qua non* of psychological and physiological normalcy in Bangladesh.

During the early 1970s, there existed a long list of assumptions, principles, and values, most of which were negative surrounding adoption practice. In fact, there existed conflicting principles and practices as one looks at the history of formal adoption, traditional guardianship, and the socioreligious culture out of which it had grown. In that sense, in Bangladesh, the values, principles, assumptions, and practices with regard to adoption lack uniformity.

Again, in Bangladesh, one's status is assigned by family backgrounds. An individual's status seems to diminish when one learns that the same individual's family background is not known. The individual with an ambiguous family background seems to be of less social standing particularly if the individual's birth history is unknown. In a traditional society like Bangladesh, there are also strongly held moral attitudes of disapproval for acceptance of a child of unknown origin. In a country where often poor parents accept servitude and obedience on the part of their children in return for economic security or simple personal safety, it is not surprising why abandonment continues generation after generation, especially with regard to people who live in perpetual poverty. In western countries, an individual acquires his or her status from his or her job rather than from his parents, adoptive or biological.

To understand and appreciate the notion of adoption in the Bangladeshi society of the 1970s, when there was a sudden demand for adoption from abroad, it is important to be cognizant of what was happening around the world. The sexual revolution of the 1960s, changes in the social situation of women in relations to sex and parenthood, the changing attitudes toward illegitimacy, and the availability of contraceptives and abortion facilities that had created a climate of greater tolerance and of sexual change in the west did not make any inroad in the Pakistani society of the 1960s and/or the Bangladeshi society of the early 1970s. Even to this day, the Bangladeshi society emphasizes sexual norms that lead to goals of reproduction within marriage only – generally referred to as absolutist, insisting on abstinence from sexual relation except in marriage where life is seen as a thread of unbroken and evolving state of being.

There are many who argue that because adoption makes families from persons who are not related through biological procreation, it deconstructs naturalized versions of family separating biological procreation from nurture. Since the first thought of the child welfare people is to work with the immediate and extended family members, having come to a dead-end, one resorts to the court action only after all informal traditional avenues have been exhausted. To sum up, family members are encouraged to take responsibility of the child as opposed to allowing adoption of the child by a family unknown to the other party.

Adoption milieu in 1972

In pre-1970 Pakistan, due to poverty, illness, divorce, and separation, there were natural ebb and flow *if* and *when* any issue related to adoption had emerged from time to time. There is no record with regard to the number of orphans in East Pakistan prior to the liberation of Bangladesh. It is, however, a known fact that there were quite a few government-funded as well as private and semiprivate orphanages, generally referred to as orphans of Muslim, Hindu, and Christian faith, which conjure up a variety of images, some of which are negative. The child welfare agencies, which fell under the Ministry of Labor and Social Welfare, had suffered right from the Pakistani days from neglect and under-funding.

Consequently, following the liberation of Bangladesh in December 1971, the problem had simply compounded not only with the increase of orphaned children whose parents had either died or disappeared but also with the birth of the war babies. They were abandoned by their birth mothers at a time when their putative fathers, alleged to be Pakistani military personnel, had already been taken to India as prisoners of war (POWs). With the birth of the war babies together with the newly abandoned infants, the adoption issue resurfaced as one of the powerful sociopolitical crosscurrents that began to swirl among various stakeholders, advocacy organizations, and support groups across Bangladesh.

By and large, health-care professionals had retained a general framework of values that they shared among the major agencies that belonged to two schools of thought. One group looked upon the war babies as "unwelcome" infants, while another saw them as "children in need of love and care." Majority of the agencies, which differed from each other in interpreting their roles and responsibilities, were characterized by noncollaboration especially with respect to adoption because of the controversy surrounding the social acceptance of such babies. However, there was collaboration around more general issues in the larger field of child welfare. Their focus was on those children who were still with their own families and who had not reached the point of placement but in need of such services. They were comfortable in dealing with children whose parents were very poor and were divorced or separated from one another. In fact, those in charge looked upon placement (adoption) as a last resort, undertaken only after considerable effort, and many hours had gone into mobilizing community resources for keeping the child and the child's family together. It was not surprising to find children born as "undesirable" and seen as "disposable" were relinquished. War babies were not on the social workers' radar screen as "perfect" infant for consideration back in 1972. The foci of their major interest and concern due to a multitude of factors that led to insularity and unevenness of service did not direct their attention toward adoption either. In fact, given the local religious, social, economic, and cultural conditions, there existed a practice among social agencies where preference for the infants of unknown origin was on the back burner. In essence, it was a milieu in which a professional culture among social workers persisted through many generations where "unwelcome" children were not seen as their primary concern.

One particular attitude that persisted among Bangladeshis against the war babies, having the "badness" with which they were born, was so strong that it had continued to remain all through. For that matter, in Bangladesh, or in the entire Indian subcontinent, sentiment and tradition predominate over *rationality* and *personal choice* when it comes to sturdy parenthood. It might be observed with some exaggeration that Bangladeshis would continue to harbor the same sentiment toward adoption until the return of Halley's Comet. Although the people of Bangladesh were rigid in their view by putting on blinders, the government of the day, through the guidance of experienced legal and social science professionals, considered the issue as one of its serious misgivings that the occasion demanded a thorough review of various alternatives to guardianship and adoption under the circumstances.

Missionaries of Charity and Mother Teresa's *Shishu Bhavan*

Immediately after independence, Mother Teresa from Kolkata, West Bengal, India, came over to Dhaka on December 21, 1971, to meet Syed Nazrul Islam, then acting president of Bangladesh, to discuss her intention to help the violated women of Bangladesh. At that time, the newly formed government had no idea about what was happening to the interned leader of Bangladesh in Pakistani jail where he was still retained. Given the gravity of the matter, Islam welcomed Mother Teresa with warmth and met her with keen interest. She was thought by the government of the day to be ideally suited to work with the violated women and their babies in the war-ravaged Bangladesh. Placing complete trust on Mother Teresa who, by then, had already earned the respect of the world community for her selfless work, Islam gave her *carte blanche* to come up with an action plan for the distressed women in need of dire help.

At that time, a 350-year-old former Portuguese monastery located at 26 Islampur Road in the old section of Dhaka, which was run by eight nuns of the Missionaries of Charity, was used as a shelter for the rape victims. Within a matter of three weeks, Mother Teresa again returned to Dhaka, Bangladesh along with four Indian nuns and two nurses, to establish one of her homes that came to be called *Shishu Bhavan*.[3] It was at this premise that many victimized women were encouraged to come in and give birth in complete secrecy and full confidence. They were encouraged to relinquish the newborns if they wished to do so and to leave them with the orphanage authority for care and adoption. In addition, several *Seva Sadan* (premises designed to serve the rape victims who needed care for having abortion or having the delivery of their babies) were established across Bangladesh to render services to rape victims who needed shelter in full anonymity. The idea behind this was to find ways and means to encourage expectant mothers to come to the orphanage premises in confidence so that the lives of both the mother and the newborn could be saved. As mentioned in chapter 1, this was a time when many expectant mothers were committing suicide, and the stories of such instances were talked about in whispers.

Theotonius Amal Ganguly, CSC, then archbishop of the Archdiocese of Dhaka, who is referred to as a pillar of strength and empathy, and Fr. Benjamin Labbé, of the Canadian Holy Cross Order, then director of CORR (Christian Organization for Relief and Rehabilitation), were two lead persons who coordinated their work with Mother Teresa and other orphanage authorities and national partners. Having kept a low key in order not to bring the initiative to the public's notice, the two religious leaders in turn gathered strength by recruiting two other bishops, Joachim Rozario of Chittagong and Michael Atul D. Rozario of Khulna, to accompany them to meet the acting president in early January 1972. They discussed the level of relief work for CORR, which included various types of assistance to the rape victims across Bangladesh. Earlier Ganguly had also discussed the matter with Mother Teresa regarding assistance to both unwed mothers and violated women with a view to developing a work plan. Given the urgency of the matter, CORR by then had already received immediate approval of the Ministry of Relief and Rehabilitation for the proposed work plan. We shall see how soon they all got into the swing of things.

Initiatives of the Mujib administration

At a time when the government was committed to building a strong, vibrant, and independent *Shonar Bangla* (Golden Bengal), it was also faced with daunting challenges with respect to dependency, family breakups, personal poverty, and homelessness. In the postliberated Bangladesh, everything was in a flux, as violence was still surging in and around inner cities facing a growing plague of guns, gangs, and drugs. Amid intense political jockeying, where everything was in a helter-skelter, the newly formed embattled government lurched from crisis to crisis. To Mujib's way of thinking, a strong economy is fundamental and paramount to the kind of country and quality of life that Bangladeshis desire to build and sustain, although the uphill road to economic recovery might be long. The war-ravaged Bangladesh was experiencing an exploding population simultaneously with a decrease in economic capacity having been unable to take care of displaced persons.

While the government was concerned with the crisis of dislocation and rehabilitation, it also needed to turn its attention problems with respect to both the orphans and the "unwanted" war babies who were being born and relinquished in record numbers by their birth mothers. The long and the short of it was that given that the entire infrastructure had been shattered in Occupied Bangladesh, the Mujib administration needed to prioritize its nation building task at a time when it was also faced with the issue of war babies that fell in the vulnerable category of the population.

Having quickly recognized its national challenge that included not only ending corruption but also instituting true democratic governance, it forged inclusive national coherence with a view to allowing all Bangladeshi citizens to develop a feeling that they are equal members of a single country with a shared national purpose that was the dream of their national hero, Mujib. The government engaged itself in developing a vision for the future based on economic growth and diminishing disparity. Simultaneously, it also focused its attention on to the society's values on the children fathered by Pakistani military personnel.

Given the deep-seated societal stigma attached to the war babies' birth history, the government also recognized that adoption or acceptance of the war babies was an impossibility in Bangladesh. Unlike developed countries, the burden of caring for orphans in Bangladesh traditionally falls on the extended family, and very frequently on private philanthropy. Personally, Mujib was cognizant that the country was treading on a new ground and tackling a deep social issue. Anticipating such problems from the beginning, the government was concerned, as the war babies were being abandoned at the same rate they were being born in every nook and cranny of the country. Given that the Bangladeshi culture places tremendous emphasis on purity of lineage, and in the absence of their biological fathers, understandably, the birth mothers were relinquishing the newborns immediately upon birth.

The government recognized the situation of the hapless birth mothers and their family members who feared the violated women could be complete outcasts with little or no chance for a prospect of employment, marriage, education, or any of the necessary opportunities of life. From a practical and social point of view, the government was also aware of the potential future of these infants who, it believed, would likely be ostracized and therefore discriminated against in Bangladesh due to the "shameful" fact surrounding their birth. This, in turn, had immediately shifted the burden of dealing with the problem to the government, which needed to focus on both the war babies and the birth mothers. Any initiative the government undertook had to be a part of a comprehensive social service. It was Mujib's sincere hope that his proposed initiative would be viewed as part of a whole range of possibilities for the war babies who, otherwise, would have a bird-cage existence in a society that would frown upon such babies.

Intercountry adoption

From the outset, the government was sadly aware that several thousand babies who were conceived in rape of Bangladeshi women by Pakistani soldiers in Occupied Bangladesh were being born in Bangladesh anywhere between October 1971 and September 1972. It was one of the early challenges of the Mujib administration about which the government contemplated a great deal. It looked for ways to alleviate the suffering of the birth mothers and facilitate transition of the relinquished babies into the homes of those Bangladeshis who longed for children. With the increase in domestic tranquility as the local and regional administrations in the newly independent country had coalesced and begun to reestablish the social order lost in Occupied Bangladesh under the Yahya (Pres. Yahya Khan) regime, the government focused its attention to the issue at hand to provide new safeguard. As far as the government was concerned, Bangladesh was not just a faraway country to be tainted by the history of its abandonment of the war babies born as a result of rape.

The government strongly held the view that the newborns have had a right to survive, develop, and *be protected*. Unfortunately, the problem became so serious that it soon faced conflicting views regarding the prevailing values of the people and their sense of morality with respect to such babies though born under deplorable circumstances. The two most important unanswered questions were how to link the war waifs in need of a safe and secured home; and how the government could link its own accountability within the broad social environs in the newly created country. Socially speaking, changes with regard to adoption in Bangladesh might have been taking place in the minds of progressive citizens, although, by and large, the country was still anchored in a close matrix.

The government was aware that there were umpteen reasons for stalling the issue that are not far to seek. Being up the creek, the government's own awareness of the crosscurrents in adoption in the Bangladeshi society had made it very cautious in taking a major decision without consultation with the major stakeholders. Legislators and policy makers alike were of the opinion that the uncertainties of the like would always remain to be encountered as long as they lived. Some members of the Mujib Cabinet thought that there was definitely a need to reeducate the public with a more sensitive language. In general, it was also aware of a variety of domestic and transnational adoptions, such as informal and formal, of infant and older child with open and closed records, as well as the use of words and their variant meanings in the adoption discourse. It held the view that given the reality of ostracism associated with the birth of the war babies, in almost all localities and community and social groups, the chance of a war baby being accepted would, naturally without recrimination and social point of view, be virtually nil. Being fully aware of the sensitivity and vulnerability of its initiative on an issue involving foreign adoption, no matter what, the government knew it would be jeered and cheered. Nevertheless, the government remained resolute in its decision to seek counsel.

Amid many unanswered questions, the issue of adoption, both in country and international, had surfaced at a time when members of the public expected the government to pursue the issue with a wide-angled camera. Many responded with their own views on it. And yet there was another group of people who believed that although social workers and their professional colleagues in Bangladesh had looked increasingly toward the new government for policy direction to remedy the situation, they remained concerned that there was not a huge hue and cry on the public awareness of such tragedies. One of the conflicts was that, on the one hand, the government did not want to engage policy makers, social workers, social service managers, and other enlightened groups in a public discourse setting the issue of intercountry adoption in the wider context of adoption of war waifs; on the other hand, it wanted to go to the full monty, from consultation with stakeholders to a longer gamut of hoops in order to come up with a legal solution.

Under the circumstance, the government's next best choice was to secure an adoptive family either in Bangladesh or abroad after it had been satisfied that the child will go to a safe and secured home of a family that would want the child in question. Many of Mujib's core Cabinet members, who were on the same page, also knew that there would be many to give them the *heave-ho* but remained resolved to undertake the task of finding a way to raise the newborns.

A genuinely concerned government believed that the best way to comprehend the gravity of the matter and to make effective recommendations would be through consultation with stakeholders to gain a deeper understanding of the stigma attached to the notion of illegitimacy with regard to the adoption of the war babies and their particular needs. After giving it a high priority, Mujib formally requested International Social Service (ISS) to conduct a study for the purpose of intercountry adoption. Although ISS is not an intercountry adoption agency, it is called upon by clients to provide information on adoption and procedures in foreign countries, to act as an intermediary across countries, and to provide both home studies and follow-up reports.

To the extent possible, the government ignored flamboyant publicity or fierce campaign. Instead, it chose to play a quieter and a low-keyed role in raising the issue with the ISS, which was the first international nonprofit organization to come forward to advise the government in response to Mujib's personal request. Headquartered in Geneva with branches throughout many countries around the world, the ISS is mandated to facilitate inquiries and investigations between countries through a specialized staff to provide the technical advice that is often required. The government sought its advice at a time when there was no estimate of the number of abortions that were being performed, or the number of babies being born and abandoned across Bangladesh despite continued efforts of certain organizations to reach out to the birth mothers or the families concerned.

The government knew well that dealing with the war babies would be like skating on a thin ice simply because of the sensitivity of the subject and the mind-set of the people in general. The government did not wish to encourage or interpret to the community at large the scope and purpose of its adoption plan. It believed it would be worthwhile to deal with the entire issue with tact and diplomacy. A steadfast advocate of inclusiveness, Mujib also emphasized equality of participation and opportunity for all Bangladeshis. However, being determined to manage risks from all corners, he did not wish the adoption issue to be catapulted onto a national political stage. The government was not ready to ignite a raging debate and allow opposition to up the ante. In deference to a multitude of views, often conflicting with each other, the government was of the opinion that to understand the complexity, there was a particular merit in asking specialists in the field to hear from the different vantage points. It was left with no druthers but to engage the stakeholders with aplomb.

In fact, the government was counseled to note that for an issue of deep social magnitude, a shotgun approach would be hard to follow, as it was imperative to hold extensive consultation with both experts and stakeholders. The Mujib administration did not want to crank out a quick and dirty legislation through crystal gazing. In fact, even though it did not want too much publicity, it encouraged cross-fertilization of ideas through participation, having recognized that nothing could ever faithfully reflect all shades of emotional opinion in this agonizing question. Through cooperation and effort, the government wished to move closer to its common goal of ensuring the protection of the war babies temporarily housed in various orphanages. The government's objective was to rise above what might divide Bangladeshis irreparably and seek a common ground that would be acceptable to the majority. In doing that, the government's most dependable guideposts in this respect were tolerance, understanding, and maturity.

Personally, Mujib wanted to reach a final decision that could be deemed to be "in the best interest of the child." Having contemplated a great deal about the future of the war babies in Bangladesh, the Mujib administration recognized that the road ahead was long and beset with pitfalls. In a typical Mujibean debonair, he reminded his people that he was not just going to talk the talk but that his Cabinet was resolved to walk the talk. In saying this to his Cabinet colleagues, Mujib did not just mince the word but also said what he meant. "The best interest of the child" was front and center in his resolve to find a solution to the abandoned war babies. The government, however, needed to examine carefully its current legislation affecting children to make sure that the rights of both children and parents are protected.

Over the course of several weeks, representatives of the Ministries of Labor and Social Welfare and Law and Parliamentary Affairs gave the administration a thumbnail sketch on the government's initiatives touching on the full range of complexities in delineating with issues dealing with the war babies. Given the sensitivity of the issue, the government knew that there were no silver bullets. Drawing a pyramid of the administration's capabilities, Mujib tried to spark initiative, creativity, and passion from within. It was prepared not to give unrealistic hopes and expectations. Mujib was painfully aware of how poverty, illness, death, lack of social/family support, and religious and social stigma had separated the infants from their birth mothers. At the same time, he also believed, and acted accordingly, that laws should be codified and explicit, particularly in respect to provisions for guardianship, foster care, custody, and adoption. As well, he recognized the immediate need to write into the statute law specific provisions, which would empower the appropriate authority to terminate parental rights and make the orphans available for adoption where there was a clear evidence of relinquishment on the part of the parents.

While seeking counsel, the government needed to ensure that it had a mechanism in place to determine the protection and movement of these babies under the legal and social systems of countries where they were to be adopted. The government, however, felt unsure of its own position being apprehensive of the bureaucratic quagmire. It needed expert advice from the people who were in the profession of intercountry adoption due to the sensitivity of the emotionally laden subject. At the end, however, cooperation of a myriad of child-caring institutions and both governmental and nongovernmental organizations across Bangladesh had to be secured in order to make a concerted effort. This was a time when the government was still in the process of reengineering its administration but was trapped in the legacy of Pakistani military/bureaucracy. Thus, a cautious and practical Mujib remained passionate in not dousing the flames of the civil servant by being less rule driven than the Pakistani days.

The three representatives who came to Dhaka to examine the situation were Wells C. Klein, then general director, ISS/AB; Sidney Talisman, then associate director, ISS; and Marie D. Levine, ISS Geneva-based consultant. Two local voluntary agencies, the Dhaka-based Bangladesh Central Organization for Women Rehabilitation (generally referred to as the board) and the Bangladesh Family Planning Association had also worked with the ISS throughout the consultation and implementation phases. The primary objective of ISS in Bangladesh was to provide specialized services to the government of Bangladesh with regard to child protection, guardianship, and safeguard adoption.

Klein, who headed the consultation study with a view to coming up with a plan for the abandoned war babies, did not take long to find out the reasons for the apparent lack of interest in adoption of the newborns (foundlings) by Bangladeshis. Without having to delve further, Klein recognized how, due to stereotypes and stigmatization, it was out of the question on the part of Bangladeshis to adopt them in Bangladesh. Since these infants were rumored/known to have been conceived in repeated rapes, they were unacceptable to the society at large. Levine, who was assigned to liaise with the government, was primarily responsible for ensuring that the government was comfortable with the proposed institution of various measures and that it was also consistent in its approach to intercountry adoption. As well, she was also responsible for overseeing the program to ensure that the ISS had enough funding to run it to complete the project. To this effect, the Church World Service provided $50,000 to immediately begin the project. As the project got off the ground, the consultants immediately encountered many problems.

By then, of course, the government became afraid of wily baby snatchers seeking to make fortunes for fat wads of cash. Initially, senior bureaucrats in charge of the file did not think that baby trafficking would be an issue. It soon became evident that there was quite a bit of confusion and misinformation in this regard. The confusion, however, arose from the fact that the government's actual intention was to remove only the war babies (i.e., the babies fathered by the Pakistani soldiers), although the people in the field soon found themselves faced with not only the war babies but also a large number of older orphans who were left abandoned.

Identified by both the American branch of the Geneva-based ISS and Holt International Agency staff, the issue was soon brought to the attention of Abdur Rab Chaudhury, then coordinator of Relief and Rehabilitation and Rehabilitation, Prime Minister's Secretariat; and Abdul Awal, then executive secretary of the National Board of Bangladesh Women's Rehabilitation Program (BWRP); through Zerina

Rashid, then a social worker who worked closely with the Canadian team while in Dhaka. "Awal refused to believe it was happening and, although we urged that some stop be placed at the passport issuance level, he dragged his feet," wrote the international consultant who was examining the possibility of adoption.[4]

When foreign agencies attempted to adopt from those who were not necessarily the war babies but some orphaned older children from the baby home, they "were told by Awal that only the Pak-fathered children were approved."[5] By early summer (1972), of course, the greedy baby snatchers from around the world had started to come to Bangladesh in droves in the name of war babies and take away other orphans through third-party brokers. "There was considerable difficulty in stopping the grand scale operation of some of the adoption groups from lifting children out of the country,"[6] thus the government was cautioned by Levine. Government officials who were trying to assist soon found the matter to be far more complicated than they had anticipated.

While dealing with the issue, the government, however, had strict orders to the fellow countrymen that there be no shenanigan with regard to children and that there be no act of trafficking in the procurement, transplantation, forced movement, and/or selling and buying of child orphans within and/or across borders by fraudulent means. Ideally speaking, the government's preference was, and still is, to preserve and support the child in a biological family as the most natural environment. Given the prevailing negative sentiments against the "unwelcome" war babies, the government was convinced that adoption of the babies (preferably outside of Bangladesh) would be the perfect solution to a major socioeconomic problem in meeting the various needs, such as abandonment of the newborn war babies by birth mother right at birth, infertile couples who were longing for a child to fulfill their desires for a family, fecund couples who wished to enlarge their families through a different means, and more importantly, parents had to be found who would be willing to provide safe and secured homes for the war babies.

The ISS recognized the Bangladeshi tradition in which formal adoption outside of extended family was not (and still not) a form of child care. It is generally neither known nor used in old East Pakistan and/or the newly created Bangladesh. To develop a communication strategy, it needed to determine how exactly the government could address the level of communication. Given the prevalent social stigma in

Bangladesh against illegitimate children, the ISS staff was uncomfortable in suggesting a wide publicity for the proposed program.

Though pressed for time, they needed to be sure how to keep a low key with regard to its measures and at the same time how to disseminate this important initiative so that the birth mothers could come forward to relinquish the newborns. They needed to know how many babies had been placed for adoption instead of causing harm to both the mothers and the unborn. They worked closely with government personnel from relevant departments in their response to the crisis collectively. After three months of consultation with various nongovernmental organizations (NGOs) representing the diverse views of the people of Bangladesh, the long hours and hard work paid off. The ISS prepared a report titled *Inter-country Adoption – A Solution for Some Children in Bangladesh, March 27, 1972*.

Klein recognized the reasons why the war babies in Bangladesh were referred to as "unwanted" babies and why their birth mothers did not want them. Klein's familiarity with the circumstances surrounding the conception, birth, and abandonment of the war babies by their birth mothers and the helplessness of the said infants in Bangladesh had helped him address the issue from a humanitarian point of view with wider practical appeal. The thrust of the report was to highlight the option of adoption as a means to be utilized to find a solution for, at least, some of these babies in Bangladesh all of whom bear the stigma of illegitimacy in the eyes of the people of Bangladesh.

Below is the first observation of ISS by way of setting the context for recommendations: "Rape and the matter of children born out of wedlock are sensitive subjects in any society. As an outsider it is difficult to suggest what means should be utilized to advertise the availability of adoption as an alternative. It is none-the-less essential that the affected women and their families know that the Government cares and will find homes for these children, otherwise no *actual* alternative exist."[7] Earlier in his report, Klein outlined the necessity of adoption of war babies who were referred to as "ill-fated" and "unaccepted babies" from "strings of danger."[8] The ISS recommended intercountry adoption as an alternative in light of the prevalent socioreligious values of Bangladesh. It advocated intercountry adoption as a healthy and forward-looking alternative under the unusual circumstances: "In the aftermath of occupation and war, and in the emergency which faces Bangladesh today with limited available resources, inter-country adoption is clearly the best available alternative for some orphans or abandoned children, including those children born of distressed Bengali women."[9]

It argued that given that a sufficient number of good home existed in Western Europe and North America to meet the needs of Bangladeshi war waifs for prospective parents, intercountry adoption could be utilized for Bangladeshi orphans for whom other individualized forms of care were not available in the war-ravaged Bangladesh. Having worked in the area of intercountry adoption for many years, Klein was quick to observe how experience had "shown that trans-racial and trans-cultural adoption" had been "highly successful from the point of view of the child's welfare when handled professionally with appropriate safeguards."[10]

Klein was both cautious and firm in his recommendations: "Inter-country adoption is not a substitute for the development of national and local systems of child care. It is an alternative, to be utilized in those instances where other individualized forms of care are not available. Since the World War II, tens of thousands of orphaned or abandoned children and children facing the stigma of illegitimacy and mixed parentage have found homes outside their own countries."[11]

Recommending immediate adoption of the war babies, the ISS advocated quick action on the part of the government of Bangladesh with a cautionary note in the following manner: "If inter-country adoption is to be a realistic alternative to late term abortion and the termination of life, the government of Bangladesh, through the Directorate of Social Welfare, with co-operation from concerned voluntary agencies, should consider an immediate program to translate a theoretical alternative into a practical solution for Bengali women and their children."[12] Furthermore, it recommended, "It is physically and psychologically important that the children be removed from their mothers as quickly as possible to avoid unnecessary strain on the mother and her family."[13]

In making recommendations, the ISS based its suggestions on five key areas that relate to intercountry adoption: (1) administration, (2) operational requirements, (3) public information program, (4) establishment of reception centers and preadoption care, and (5) procedures and adoption practices.[14]

The government was counseled along the vein that although the stories of sexual violence and atrocities carried out by the Pakistani soldiers were tragically mind numbing and horrible, and that the people must not dwell on the past, instead, they ought to move forward being vigorously involved in the reconstruction of the newly independent country. It was, however, caught on the horns of a dilemma. On the one hand, Mujib's social-equality agenda seemed to have been in conflict with the reality on the ground; on the other hand, the administration was afraid of introducing measures that could be seen by the general population as a "radical agenda," a kind of political dynamite. Being aware of the stringent moral codes of "dos" and "don'ts" in Bangladesh, the government did not want to attempt to change public morality, which it feared would likely challenge the traditional social and cultural values of Bangladesh that the people had been adhering to.

Naturally, the government was left with no choice but to turn to adoption. After days of deliberation, Mujib formally gave an emphatic thumbs-up to the recommendations even though he was cognizant that many were opposed international adoption. Given the gravity of the matter that needed unbiased attention, the government held the view that if it was to face the music, so be it.

Interviews of those who were involved, such as the Canadian team, reveal that officials in Dhaka had serious misgivings: how to negate an existing perception of the rest of the world that in Bangladesh there was a wholesale removal of war babies to foreign countries. It came to consider the recommendation of ISS for international adoption as its *second-most-preferred solution* at a time when no demand for the war babies from within Bangladesh was forthcoming. The government was particularly mindful of ensuring that this was not a case of giving babies "up for grabs" even though the newborns were being abandoned by their birth mothers. Understandably, the government sought creative solutions – through programs that were future oriented and transformative in order to accomplish its desired goals. In a sense, even at this stage and having come thus far, the government was placed between the devil and the deep blue sea.

In accepting the recommendations of ISS, the government had tried to maintain its resolve to respect the wishes of the victims – that the stories of sexual sadism of the Pakistani military personnel perpetrated on them remain one of the most closely guarded secrets of their lives. In that sense, as mentioned, the government was caught between rock and a hard place. On the one hand, it was keen on reaching out to the victims; on the other hand, it had serious misgivings about bringing its programs to the attention of the general public who, it feared, might identify the victims and the newborns.

Accordingly, while implementing the recommendations of ISS, the government faced challenges in advertising the services of the reception centers and preadoption care. Social workers who worked in the facilities where the babies were born, such as *Seva Sedan, Shishu Bhavan, Nari Punarbashan Board,* and baby homes, had frequently found uninvited visitors in their premises. Having heard about the birth of the war babies through the grapevine, many curious visitors used to gather around to take a glance at the newborns.

In a sense, this had forced the government to recognize the curious alchemy of society and priorities and handle the issue with kid gloves. It was convinced that the negatively divergent viewpoints and indifference expressed by average Bangladeshis were an indication of the society's rules, for it was in the nature of human beings to desire what was held socially necessary and acceptable. *Does it bring a sense of shame and embarrassment to Bangladesh if the government allows adoption, which is an acknowledgment that it is not able to meet the needs of all of its children?* Evidently, people at higher echelon had wrestled with this question and many other questions along such vein. The government's think tank members finally found their own raison d'être having come to the conclusion that a war baby without any biological family ties had a right to grow up in the best adoptive home even if it is in another country, and at the home of a parent who is of a different racial background.

Once the decision was made to go ahead with the recommendations of ISS for international adoption, the government moved ahead, letting the chips fall where they might in the pursuit of a new legislative initiative. Within weeks, the Prime Minister's Secretariat had charged the Directorate of Social Welfare of the Ministry of Labor and Social Welfare with the responsibility of developing regulations relating to intercountry adoption. They were advised to the effect that the Directorate of Social Welfare would have the authority to coordinate and implement the entire process of intercountry adoption from the beginning of the process, such as documenting the child to selecting the international agency to permitting the child to leave Bangladesh for adoption. Fortunately for the government, there existed a collaborative relationship among all four ministries: Relief and Rehabilitation,

Labor and Social Welfare, Health and Family Planning, and Law and Parliamentary Affairs, with Mother Teresa's *Shishu Bhavan,* which was supportive of international adoption.

As those in charge tried to move forward, they faced yet another set of questions. Personally speaking, imbued with an impelling sense of social realities, Mujib is known to have made personal inquiry on this issue and had asked his Cabinet colleagues cautionary questions: *How is the adoption process going to be regulated? How would the birth mothers take the idea of relinquishing and its aftermath?* The government was counseled that to complete the transfer of the infants to adoptive parents, first and foremost, it needed to finalize the drafting of a new legislation and to get the ordinance off the ground soon. It needed a legal framework with which to legitimize adoption of the war babies and orphans, collectively referred to as the "abandoned children." The development of the desired legislation had to be proceeded cautiously and slowly.

The Bangladesh Abandoned Children (Special Provisions) Order, 1972

Given the complexity of the issue at hand, the government could not come up with a perfect solution – the one that would lay a golden egg. Between March and October 1972, policy wonks and legislators had spent an inordinate amount of time clarifying Bangladeshis' perception of where they stood on foreign adoption under the circumstances and assessing the dimension of the various risks associated with those limited choices with regard to the war babies in particular and orphans in general.

All were on the same wavelength in terms of desired changes to be affected legally in Bangladesh. Cabinet ministers were advised to take the time they needed; those in charge of writing the law were asked to reflect on the issue and craft the legislation with forethought than hindsight. The word came down from top also that legislators responsible for crafting the law must not be distracted by pressure, as there were still many more hoops to jump through before they could come up with the desired legislation. Fortunately, Mujib's Cabinet colleagues were solidly behind him and had at their disposal many experts to review the complicated process of foreign adoption and its applicability.

However, given the sensitivity of the issue at hand, the government still needed to clarify where it stood on the issue of transracial adoption outside of Bangladesh following receipt of the recommendations of ISS. It recognized that it was moving on a shaky ground; it certainly did not want to open a Pandora's box of opinions at the time, especially since it had already approved the recommendations. Considering it to be a done deal, the government took extra caution in assigning people with appropriate experience and responsibility to manage risk and anticipated political backlash. Ongoing consultation with the ISS personnel had, no doubt, helped key officials gather sufficient information about risks and develop mitigation strategies accordingly. Despite being in a quandary, those who worked on the drafting of the legislation believed that they could indeed deliver the product and achieve the objective through adherence to a basic consultation process.

While crafting the special provision, key government officials were acutely aware that adoption policy and practice around the world must serve the "best interest of the child," a common phrase in the formulation of children's rights. Not surprisingly, therefore, in developing the special provision order, they were guided by the stellar principle that the formation of it ought to be based on principle of what is in "the best interest of the child."

Throughout this period, the government was sadly aware of the values attached to adoption in Bangladesh, more particularly to the children of unknown parentage that are generally thought to be of inferior genetic stock. Given that in the Bangladeshi society, women are encouraged to do their "duty" to procreate where motherhood and maternal sacrifice are generally glorified, romanticized, and described as a woman's highest and truest calling and as the key to her female identity, the government recognized that it had come to a dramatic crisis and nearly insurmountable obstacles as it tried to push the adoption envelope.

It worked on the premise that the well-being of the war babies and children must be given priority if Bangladesh was to make any progress at all toward better tomorrows for the country. Many officials were aware how, despite the Bangladeshi society's tradition of extended family with its intricate system of obligations and supports, attitude toward adoption had not changed – not even for the war babies who needed to be loved and cared for rather than abandoned, rejected, or scapegoated. Within the Ministry of Law and Parliamentary Affairs, which was responsible for the drafting of the law that would make adoption procedures possible, there were, however, many who still held the orthodox view of adoption as sort of "being sold into slavery."

Officials were asked to conduct research but within the strict timelines. This became such a delicate issue with social and political implications that no one was able to prepare the draft for final review and signature when Mujib was out of the country in August and early September (1972) even though officials feared they would be upbraided should they fail produce the draft on time. No one in the government dared to float a trial balloon. This was despite the fact that earlier Mujib had delegated the task to the president himself. Upon his return from Europe when Mujib found out that there was hiatus of several weeks, he made sure that those in charge of drafting the legislation got their knuckles rapped. He insisted on having it ready to announce even though everyone who worked on it was hard-pressed.

Given the prevailing sentiments against the notion of being "unwanted," it recognized that placing a war baby with a Bengali family did not necessarily ensure a perfect match. Both the government and the adoption agencies of Bangladesh worked together firmly believing that adoption should always be *about finding families for children* and *not children for families*. Being caught on the horns of a dilemma, the government based its work on the premise that no legislation could be enacted without any compromise. Naturally, legislators were doubly careful in taking into account the ethical aspects of adoption having acknowledged that difference that would follow from being adopted could enhance and enrich the lives of all concerned.

At that time, adoption had still remained a controversial area and the controversy within social work and allied professions had reflected the general lack of consensus. A large swath of the public was not quite happy with the way in which the law was being drafted. As far as the government was concerned, even though there was a lack of social reform, the proposed special provisions order had to be drafted. It was not to be seen as a surprise initiative, since it was mainly in response to the "felt necessities" of the time – something that was already on the people's mental radar since this was an issue of national magnitude though there was no consensus.

This single document became all the more significant when one recognizes the fact that it was drafted under unusual and pressing circumstances where previously there had been no legislation governing adoption in Bangladesh. The primary objective of the presidential order was to establish "legal guardianship" of the abandoned infants and to provide certification of birth for children legally free for adoption both in and outside of Bangladesh.

The statutory guardian was mandated to authenticate the prospective adoptive parents from abroad who had already obtained clearance from the governments of their respective countries. The same person would then authorize those whose commitment had apparently transcended nationality for adoption of the orphans, *filius nullius* (nobody's child), who were in need of dependable parents. In doing so, the government was extra careful having recognized that adoption connotes a redefinition of parenthood, legal and/or formal establishment of a parental relationship that is not biological or genetic.

The key point that the government emphasized was that once adopted, the legal rights of the children be recognized as the children of the adoptive parents, *"as if begotten,"* a status that was no different from a *biological child* born to the child's adoptive parent. The spirit of the law was that the formal adoption in a given country would create a relationship that would invariably be considered as a relationship created in nature just as with genealogy as the prototype of kinship. In layperson's term, it established "guardianship" of such children with the social welfare director and gave him or her authority to set procedures for the adoptive placement of the children.

The directorate, in turn, designated then superior, Sr. Margaret Mary, of the Missionaries of Charity as the statutory guardian of the abandoned war babies in the following manner: "The statutory guardian may deliver an abandoned child for the purpose of adoption to any adoption agency in or outside of Bangladesh on such terms and conditions as may be prescribed and as such delivery shall constitute a valid adoption."[15] The proclamation also defined an abandoned child in the following: an "abandoned child" means a child, in the opinion of the government, is deserted or unclaimed or born out of wedlock.[16] The government paid attention to ensure that the abandoned war babies would retain neither natal status nor any legal relation to their biological parents once they had been abandoned. At that stage, they were therefore considered to have become the "ward" of the state. In doing so, the government ensured that the war orphans of Bangladesh were not thought of as chattels to be passed by deed from one family to another or one country to another. As the ordinance articulated, an abandoned child is declared abandoned in order to be legally available for adoption.

Upon assuming statutory guardianship, Sr. Margaret Mary's prime responsibility was to endeavor to lessen the stigmatization of these infants by making them available for adoption to couples who would assume their parenthood. The ordinance, as a whole, dealt with the social attitudes seeking opportunities to educate and liberalize the public's thinking having symbolized life and hope of better health and bearable condition for the war babies. The most important *sine qua non* of the legislation was, therefore, to guarantee that the child, upon reaching the age of majority, would obtain citizenship of the country in which the child was taken.

Another important point to note is that although originally it was intended for only Pakistani-fathered babies, the law in the final form was applied to all "abandoned" children. A society that is still riddled with myth and superstitions that inhibit the Bangladeshis' free and enlightened thinking thwarting the growth of mind, the proclamation, taking the long view, thus provided a new lens with which to view the predicament of the orphans and proposed solutions. The government saw adoption of the war babies by foreign parents, as a rescue operation by a group of long-serving dedicated people outside Bangladesh as their salvation.

And yet there were many who openly talked about the initiative for which there was a small but shrill chorus of criticism. Those with serious misgivings, saw the adoption initiative as a means to create a family for the "best interest" of the "undesirable" and "unwelcome" children who were being born at the time. At worst, some saw it as the government's callousness in passing the buck in the name of "foreign adoption" and an abandonment of its responsibility being enmeshed in its own political agenda and red tape.

Adoption in Canada

Adoption, which remains a provincial/territorial responsibility in Canada with varying laws and regulations in each province, is carried out by the local Children's Aid Societies (CAS) under the authority of the *Child Welfare Act* of the appropriate province or territory. Adoption statistics are difficult to compile because there is no central registry in Canada charged with keeping track of the total number of adoption orders completed in each province/territory.[17] In Canada, the provision of adoption in the provincial/territorial *Child Welfare Act* stemmed from the basic premise that adoption is the best and most desirable goal for children in need of parents.

In 1972, the year in which the war babies were brought to Canada through adoption, the federal government's then National Health and Welfare Canada was available to extend consultant help to the provinces/territories in participating and facilitating agreements. In addition, the Canada Welfare Council, a national planning agency, was also available for consultation services. Though primarily a provincial matter in Canada, the federal government's Immigration Department automatically gets involved when the child in question is not a Canadian. In such a case, the child may only be admitted as a sponsored dependent and must be under the age of thirteen and sponsored by the person who intends to adopt that child.

Generally speaking, in Canada adoption from foreign countries is done through the Geneva-based International Social Service (ISS), which works pretty well in every country with rare exception. Such adoptions are called private adoptions. Prospective adoptive applicants/parents who wish to adopt must fulfill the requirements set by the provincial/territorial governments of the province/territory in which the applicant lives and the country in which the child resides. In that sense, the most desirable method of foreign adoption from the point of view of both the protection of the child and the long-term well-being of the family is through channels recognized by both governments and the designation of a competent international agency agreed upon by both countries to carry on liaison activities.[18]

The prospective parents, however, must initially satisfy the provincial/territorial requirements through an acceptable home study conducted by an agent of the CAS representing the applicant's province/

territory.[19] Families wishing to adopt children whose identities are unknown are also usually interviewed by their local CAS and referred by the Child Welfare branch to the Canadian office of the ISS, which assists in intercountry adoption.

As a practice, the ISS would then locate an adoptable child in another country; once the identity of the child is known, the Department of Citizenship and Immigration Canada (CIC) is to be contacted. The same procedure outlined above for children whose identities are known are then followed. Legally speaking, the arrival of the child into the homes of the adoptive parents does not constitute adoption. It is only upon completion of the actual adoption – involving the solemn oath in front of the judge – that the parents assume full responsibility of the said child at which time adoption process is deemed to be complete.

Context for intercountry and transracial adoption

Historically speaking, international adoption is neither new nor rare in Canada, although by the beginning of the twenty-first century, international adoption had become a common practice in Canada. Intercountry adoption of transracial children was introduced in Canada to alleviate the surge of postwar illegitimate babies in Europe and Asia. Being a noble idea, this initiative proved to be one of the most suitable systems of adoption. About 1,200 orphaned refugee children came to Canada from Europe after Canadian government authorized their admission in 1947 and 1948. The first wave of children was orphans of the World War II, the Korean War, and the Vietnam War and/or children fathered by soldiers of occupying forces during these wars.

It is at that time that the families in the USA and Canada, for the first time in history, adopted children who were racially and culturally different from themselves, something that had produced mixed reactions, such as some called it, "a crazy social experiment," while some others worried about eventual integration of racially different minorities in America. Fortunately, Canada did not face any such concern perhaps due to the fact that the number of such type of adoption was very minimal. Many in the USA had watched with dismay the pathetic situations of the mixed-blood illegitimate infants who were often referred to as the "scar tissues of wounds of war." They followed with interest the initiatives of Harry Holt, an American philanthropist who, having gone to Korea, had formed an overseas group that came to be known as the Holt International Agency in the mid-1950.[20]

Around the same time, the Open Door Society (ODS), an association of adoptive families with children of mixed background that grew in North America, became active in playing advocacy role supporting international and interracial adoption in the USA and Canada. Particularly from the 1950s this autonomous organization had existed in Canada to find adoptive homes for the many unplaced children of minority ancestry. It was chartered in Montreal by three adoptive families who had already adopted transracial children.[21]

Looking back, since the formation of its first chapter in Montreal, Quebec, the ODS had been working closely with other partners in Canada and the USA since then through the Children's Service Center of Montreal, having raised awareness of mixed-race adoption. At that time, British Columbia was also very active in promoting intercountry and interracial adoption through the involvement with the Hong Kong–based International Social Service (ISS) in an intercountry adoption program with Hong Kong and Korea having received children from both these countries.

Although there is a direct nexus between availability of children and foreign-born adoptions, the main reason for such interest was the prospective parents' open-mindedness and broader outlook. True, the availability of children had decreased as a result of the loosening of conventions of sexual morality, gains from the women's liberation movement, and general acceptance of the notion of "permissive society." In fact, by early 1970s, although the liberalization of abortion laws had made an impact, it became obvious that each year there were more children born to single women; as well, there was a growing willingness of unmarried mothers to keep their children. This also meant that, relatively speaking, the supply of adoptable Canadian children was on the decrease.

Overall, in 1972, international adoption was still a new concept for Canada and Canadians, although adoption of international children was taking place at a slower pace across the country. Despite the moderate shortage of adoptable children in Canada, there were still opportunities for prospective parents to wait for a reasonable length of time to adopt Canadian children. North American or part-Indian orphans were also available in various provinces in the early 1972. Specifically, with regard to the native infants/children, records indicate that by the fall of 1972, only in the Province of Ontario there were "approximately 1,000 Crown Ward of Indian heritage," many of who were "school age and/or sibling groups."[22] Having seen the plight of Vietnamese war orphans and abandoned children fathered by American soldiers, many prospective adoptive parents became interested in interracial adoption.

No doubt, the motivation behind adoption during the first wave of intercountry adoption was largely humanitarian in nature. The prospective adoptive parents did not necessarily wish to adopt orphans that were available in Canada. Consequently, their desire to adopt internationally and the availability of children in Asian countries became the primary reason for intercountry adoption in Canada. It is also true that being unwilling to wait for an indefinite period for a child and impatient with the increasingly restrictive standards set by agencies in conducting home studies by the many local CAS offices, a large number of prospective adoptive parents were being forced to turn to private international adoption.

The two important organizations that were involved in intercountry adoption were *Terre des Hommes* (TDH), an international organization with its head office in Geneva and staffed in Montreal by a volunteer, and the Montreal-based volunteers who later formally established the Families For Children (FFC), having been in receipt of briefs from recognized welfare and professional for its role in international and interracial adoption. Though not yet formally established until 1971, the FFC had been playing a significant role since the late 1960s in bringing orphans especially from Vietnam, Cambodia, and Korea. During the mid-1970s and early 1980s, FFC expanded to several countries.

By the beginning of 1972, however, FFC had established itself in quick succession as a credible organization by becoming a part of an Interagency Adoption Committee, which was formed in June 1971. At that time, FFC consisted mainly of families that had previously adopted racially different children having worked closely with Holt Adoption Agency in Oregon, USA, for Korean orphans during the early 1970s. In addition, there is also the Council on Adoptable Children (COAC) that sprang up in the 1960s in Canada and the USA that had encouraged couples to adopt beyond racial boundaries – moving from in-racial to interracial adoption.

Interesting to note, of the provinces and territories, Quebec was way ahead of other jurisdictions in encouraging its own people to adopt internationally and transracially. Within a brief period, the FFC became one of the most important organizations in advancing the cause of intercountry adoption in Canada through its study groups and seminars by providing information on the need for cooperation and understanding between adoptive parents, the governments of the countries involved in adoption, and agencies in Canada.

Interesting to note, from 1970 onward, more and more couples in Canada had begun to see adoption as an acceptable way of creating or adding to the family. In fact, by the end of the 1970s, adoption had become a recognizable social pattern with an interest in interracial adoption in Canada, which occurred in two waves as a new phenomenon in the makeup of family life. While the first wave dates back to the period following the end of the Second World War, the second wave of international/interracial adoption began in 1975 with the fall of Saigon. It was triggered by a change in immigration policy, which allowed children whose adoptions had been finalized in the country of origin to enter Canada. Adoption of the war babies of Bangladesh in Canada in 1972, though not a sizable number at all, falls in between these two waves.

Adoption in Canada from Pakistan/Bangladesh

There is no record of large-scale adoption in Canada from Pakistan (both East and West Pakistan). Archival records indicate that the absence of any clear adoption law in Pakistan had, however, been a source of problem in Canada. Each time there was a request for adoption from Pakistan, Canadian officials were faced with problems associated with regard to the legality of adoption requiring more clarification on the process to follow. Archival records show how such inquiries were handled by Canadian officials through the Ottawa branch of the International Social Service (ISS) that wrote to the government of Canada in the following fashion: "There is no adoption law in Pakistan and the authorities are generally against having their children adopted in foreign countries by non-Moslem couples."[23]

The above is an actual citation of an ISS incumbent's response, taken as an example of many that are in the archives, to an inquiry made by a Canadian for adoption from Pakistan. Interesting to note, in one particular case, the Ottawa ISS office was also advised by the Geneva ISS office that it had handled "no case in East Pakistan where the Social Welfare resources seem to be less developed than in West Pakistan."[24] In its conclusion, the ISS had warned its client, saying that it would not take "any responsibility about a child going to Canada from there [i.e., East Pakistan],"[25] as it was not a common practice to request for adoption from Pakistan. The ISS was clear in its message that while it recognized that there might be "special reasons for a particular couple in Canada to adopt a child from Pakistan but, generally speaking," it would not, however, like to get involved in "in inter-country adoption cases with Pakistan."[26]

Available records, though very scanty, also indicate that if and when there was a request for adoption, it was basically left with the officer in Pakistan to assess the circumstances on a one-on-one basis. The visa officer "having knowledge of the situation" would "use his [or her] good judgment and decide whether a particular case is in fact a legal adoption or not."[27] If it is a borderline case, generally the visa officer would then "request the sponsor to provide documentary evidence that the adoption is one which is recognized by the province concerned."[28] This was the extent of information on adoption in Pakistan that was made available to those who had inquired about adoption in the 1960s and early 1970s. This information is available in the archives of ISS in Geneva.

However, the situation had drastically changed with the creation of Bangladesh as a separate and independent country. As the demand for adoption became more pronounced, the concept of adoption had also gained a new dimension in Canada that made the ISS involved actively in streamlining its process in Bangladesh. Although for all practical reasons, intercountry adoption of interracial babies had been more difficult and time-consuming than in-racial adoption in Canada; the adoption practices by 1970 had not yet adjusted to the new types of demand for interracial babies from abroad by Canadian parents. In that sense, request for adoption of Bangladeshi war babies came to represent a sharp break with traditional philosophy and practices opening the door to potential problems hitherto unknown to the authorities.

In sum, all through the 1960s, international and interracial adoptions had continued at a slow pace until the issue of interracial adoption came to the limelight through the national media coverage of

Helke Ferrie's hunger strike, the details of which is outlined in chapter 3. It will be seen in the next chapter that while it is true that there were more advocates for interracial adoption, especially in the case of the Bangladesh Project, there were also a fair number of detractors who held the view that adoption from Bangladesh was not the "best thing" to do. The typical argument against interracial adoption was (and continues to this day) that the adopted child is likely to be alienated from his or her culture and ethnicity, as the child in question would suffer from problems of identity in addition to being exposed to racist forces prevalent in many parts of Canada.

The next chapter outlines the ways in which the idea of adoption of the Bangladeshi war babies was conceived by a group of committed Canadian couples who successfully brought a number of war babies to their homes.

Notes and References

[1]   Islamic law derived from the Quran and Hadith.

[2]   The Quran has clearly directed the Muslims to maintain for the adopted children the names of their fathers; and if their fathers are not known, then they should be considered and called brethren in faith or the adopted children of the person concerned.

[3]   The *Bangladesh Observer,* February 9, 1972.

[4]   Letter from Marie D. Levine, International Social Service (ISS), American branch, consultant in Dhaka, to Wells C. Klein, general director, International Social Service, American branch, June 19, 1972, p. 3. The agreement between the ISS and the government of Bangladesh was signed by the American branch known at that time as Traveler's Aid International Social Service (TAISSA from 1972 to 1977) with the understanding that all correspondences concerning this agreement should be in the hands of ISS American branch. Documents pertaining to the project of ISS in Bangladesh are housed in the American branch office of ISS, reference # 1H5/ Bangladesh asg. per agreement.

[5]   *Ibid.,* p. 3.

[6]   Letter from Marie D. Levine, International Social Service (ISS), American branch, consultant in Dhaka, to Wells C. Klein, general director, International Social Service, American branch, July 5,

1972, p. 2. Marie Levine also liaised with Tahera Shafiq, who was named officer-in-charge of the project by the Social Welfare Department and served on a part-time basis. Levine found her professionally sound.

7   *Memorandum on Observations and Suggestions for Implementing Inter-Country Adoption* from Wells C. Klein, General Director, International Social Service, American Branch to M. Hassan-uj-Zaman, Secretary of Labor and Social Welfare, Government of the People's Republic of Bangladesh, May 9, 1972, p. 2.

8   *Inter-Country Adoption in Bangladesh* under the heading *Importance of Publicity and Public Information*. Prepared by Wells C. Klein, General Director, International Social Service, American Branch, March 27, 1972, p. 3.

9   *Ibid.,* p. 3.

10   *Memorandum on Inter-country Adoption: A Solution for Some Children,* p. 1.

11   *Ibid.,* p. 1.

12   *Memorandum on Observations and Suggestions for Implementing Inter-Country Adoption,* p. 2.

13   *Ibid.,* p. 3.

14   *Ibid.*

15   *Bangladesh Abandoned Children (Special Provision) Order,* 1972, Number 6, p. 2 in the *Bangladesh Gazette Extraordinary*, Wednesday, October 25, 1972.

16   *Ibid.,* p. 2.

17   Adoption is not a new idea in Canadian law. The earliest adoption legislation was in Nova Scotia and was passed in 1896. In 1924, and, again, in 1946, the Canadian Welfare Council published a comparative summary of the adoption laws of the nine provinces that were a part of Canada then, bearing witness to the fact that everywhere in Canada adoption is continually subject to amendment and improvement. For adoption in Canada, see *Child Adoption in the Modern World* by Margaret Kornitzer, Putnam, London, 1952.

18   Memorandum to E. D. Greathed, General Secretary, Intergovernmental Affairs, Ministry of Treasury, Economics, and Intergovernmental from Gordon McLellan, Executive Director, Children's Services Division, Ministry of Community and Social Services, Government of Ontario, February 26, 1973; also in the

Archives of Ontario, RG 29 -59, ACC 29612 TR 78-075, Box 6, File *Bangladesh Infants 1972–73.*

[19] Home study is a comprehensive document that describes a prospective adoptive applicant and the applicant's thoughts about adoption, ideas, and expectations about being a parent, and those things that are important to the applicant's life. The report is based on a combination of written documentation and a social worker's evaluation of a number of face-to-face interviews in the province of its applicants.

[20] The Holt Adoption Program Inc. in Crestwell, Oregon, is a Christian agency founded by an Oregon fundamentalist who felt impelled by God to "do something" about the mixed-race abandoned children in Korea in 1953.

[21] Madison Bernice Q. and Shapiro, Michael, "Black adoption-Issues and Policies: Review of Literature," *Social Service Review* XLV11, no. 4, 1973, pp. 531–560.

[22] Families For Children, *Newsletter,* March 13, 1973, p. 2 (Reprint of a letter written to Families For Children by C. B. H. Murphy, Director of Child Welfare, Department of Health, Welfare and Rehabilitation, Government of Yukon.

[23] Letter from A. River, Casework Division, International Social Service, Geneva, to Mrs. Ireland, ISS Canada, re: *Adoption in Pakistan*, reference # 1 H 5/Pak, December 13, 1962, Library and Archives Canada, RG 76 Vol. 1040, Box 141, *File*: 5020-1-606.

[24] *Ibid.*

[25] *Ibid.*

[26] *Ibid.*

[27] *Ibid.*

[28] Letter from Head, Directives Unit, Programs and Procedures Branch to Chief, Admission Section, Home Services Branch, Manpower and Immigration, Subject: *Selection of adopted children in Pakistan*, July 15, 1970. Library and Archives Canada, RG 76 Vol. 1040, Box 141, *File:* 5020-1-606.

CHAPTER THREE

A Move beyond Rhetoric: Bangladesh-Canada Joint Venture

THE CONCLUSION OF war in Bangladesh in December 1971 brought with it significant international attention to the plight of Bangladesh – a poor, war-ravaged nation of tens of millions of people trying to rebuild. Bangladesh covered an area of 147,570 km with a population of approximately seventy-five million people with a per capita GDP of about US$129 in 1970. In comparison to Bangladesh, Canada covered an area seventy times larger (9,985,000 km) with one-third of the population (twenty-one million) and a per capita GDP that was nearly forty times larger (over US$4,000 in 1970). However, the human tragedy in Bangladesh went beyond the numbers. For many international viewers, the headline story from Bangladesh in December 1971 was the story of the Bangladeshi war babies, children conceived in rape and, upon birth, summarily abandoned by their birth mothers.

On January 12, 1972, Sheikh Mujibur Rahman (Mujib) became the first prime minister of newly independent Bangladesh. His administration's top priority was to get Bangladesh on its feet. The nation was in ruins. The administration officially recognized the need for redress in the matter of the war babies and their violated mothers. However, Mujib had very little leeway to do much for either the women or the children. The government resources were very limited in 1972. Literally, millions of people across Bangladesh were in urgent need of government assistance. The government received numerous distressing but unverified reports that suggested the number of women raped and made pregnant during wartime. However, with further investigation, it was soon found that at least some of these reports were highly exaggerated and actually cover-ups for black market child-trafficking rings.

The government decided not to depend on these reports to form policy on the matter of the war babies because it felt that it needed reliable data to justify the resources to address the needs of the violated women and their abandoned children. It turned to the international community. Initially, the Mujib administration especially sought help from Canada because Canadian nongovernmental organizations (NGOs) demonstrated a genuine concern for war babies with their frontline work in the orphanages and reception centers for children who had been lost, abandoned, or orphaned during the war. To these ends, the Canadian and Bangladeshi governments of the day undertook the Bangladesh-Canada Joint Venture to allow foreign adoption of Bangladeshi war babies into Canadian families.

Both countries agreed that in adopting foreign children, the protection of the child and the long-term well-being of the adoptive family were the issues of paramount importance. The joint venture between Canada and Bangladesh involved designating an international agency, based in Canada, to act as a liaison between the two countries to facilitate foreign adoption to ensure that the outcomes of adoption would protect children (largely from traffickers) and the well-being of adoptive families in Canada. The designated agency was the Montreal-based nonprofit, nondenominational organization called Families For Children (FFC).[1]

Canadian initiatives under Families For Children (FFC)

FFC was the leading advocate of the Canadian NGOs for the adoption of the war babies. Formally established in 1971, FFC grew out of a strong desire of a handful of Canadian couples in the western suburb of Montreal, Quebec, to help prospective adoptive parents navigate through the formalities of adoption to adopt racially different children. The key objectives of FFC were, and still are, to help children in Canada and abroad who need a home, and families in Canada who would like to adopt such a child.

FFC specializes in adoptions where the children are generally hard to place in Canada (e.g., international interracial adoptions, the adoption of older children, and the adoption of mentally and psychiatrically challenged orphans). In the late 1960s and early 1970s, FFC volunteers worked closely with Rosemary Taylor, an Australian who operated an orphanage in Vietnam. She was instrumental in bringing hundreds of homeless children out of Vietnam and into adoptive homes in Europe and the USA through *Terre des Hommes (TDH)*. As already mentioned, by the beginning of 1972, FFC had established itself as a credible organization by becoming a member of the Interagency Adoption Committee, which was formed in June 1971.

The Mujib administration had been very impressed by the response to the war babies crisis made by major Canadian NGOs, such as Canadian UNICEF, Canadian Red Cross Society, Canadian Save the Children Fund, Oxfam Canada, World Vision of Canada, and CARE Canada. Canadian NGOs had expressed a strong desire to "do" something about the war babies. Their response, similar to Nigerian programs established following the Biafran Crisis in Nigeria (1967–1970), involved the setup of reception centers across Bangladesh to rehabilitate children who had been lost, abandoned, or orphaned. In late 1968, then prime minister Pierre Elliot Trudeau (Trudeau) appealed to Canadian families and aid organizations that represented children to "adopt orphans of the Nigerian conflict."[2] The people of Canada were still mindful of Trudeau's appeal three years later when civil war engulfed Bangladesh. While thinking about the war babies of Bangladesh, the adoptive parents had recalled Trudeau's assurance during the Biafran Crisis "that the Government would be prepared to use its relief aircrafts to transport the children to Canada."[3]

In 1971, prior to independence, representatives of Canadian NGOs visited Occupied Bangladesh (March 1971–December 1971) on a fact-finding-mission. They noted the gravity of the situation and "the particular problem of the raped mothers and children who [they believed] will not be accepted."[4] The government did not expect any serious initiatives from the NGOs because they are mandated to address the needs of refugees and displaced person, first and foremost, and not the victims of crimes and abandonment per se. However, the NGO community helped set up orphanages across Bangladesh, and they highlighted in their report that "considerable interest will be shown in Canada and North America as well as other countries for the placement of these children by inter-country adoption."[5]

FFC became aware of the war babies after the fact-finding mission to Occupied Bangladesh revealed the possibility that rape and unwanted pregnancies were a likely reality on the ground in Bangladesh. This was a time when there was not yet a Bangladeshi diplomatic mission in Canada, since the governments of Canada and Bangladesh were still negotiating the timing for establishing missions in both countries. However, since 1960, coinciding with the World Refugee Year, Canada had adopted a policy to allow orphaned refugee children to be admitted to Canada for adoption. Based on the urgent needs of Bangladesh and the ongoing interests of Canada regarding foreign adoptions of orphaned refugee children, FFC undertook the development of a proposal for possible adoption of the to-be-born war babies. By January 1972, Fred and Bonnie Cappuccino had investigated the *how* and the *why* of in-country and international adoption procedures including pertinent legislation, or lack thereof, in Bangladesh and also begun to think through the various phases for rolling out their proposed program for adopting war babies into Canadian families.

The most important person to facilitate and encourage the FFC volunteers to proceed with their proposal was Roberto Ribeiro, then head of NGO Division, Canadian International Development Agency (CIDA). Ribeiro was active in the exchange of information between various levels of the governments in both Canada and Bangladesh. He was also in contact with the NGO community. In particular, he wrote to World Vision Canada in an attempt to get Canadian NGOs to help postwar Bangladesh. He would eventually be one of the adoptive parents of the war babies. One of the main challenges with arranging aid for Bangladesh was the absence of a formal representative of the government of Bangladesh in Canada.

In lieu of a formal representative, the Cappuccinos turned to Prof. Muazzam Hussain (Hussain) of the Université de Sherbrooke in Quebec, a Canadian of Bangladeshi origin. In early 1972, the Cappuccinos "drove out there [Sherbrooke] to meet with him."[6] At that time, Hussain had assumed the role of an informal spokesperson for the Bangladeshi community in Canada. He had gained the attention of the Cappuccinos with his public advocacy work in favor of the independence of Bangladesh. Their discussions with Hussain centered upon the proposal of FFC to have interested Canadian couples adopt Bangladeshi war babies. Indicating that "inter-country adoption was undoubtedly the best solution for the war-babies who were expected to be born shortly,"[7] Hussain expressed his commitment to assisting them in every possible way.

By the first week of May 1972, Abdul Momin (Momin) had been appointed the new high commissioner for Bangladesh in Canada. Momin arrived in Ottawa shortly thereafter. Hussain arranged an interview with the FFC volunteers almost immediately. The meeting went very well, much to the satisfaction of the Cappuccinos. They were impressed with the high commissioner whom they described as a "neat, well-dressed, soft spoken gentleman."[8] One of the key issues that Momin and FFC discussed concerned the use of the term "war babies" and sensitivity surrounding it, especially in relation to the media. Momin suggested that a good term would be "war orphans," rather than "war babies."[9]

In our introduction, we make a distinction between the terms "war babies" and the "war orphans," being that war orphans is a more general term referring to all children left parentless by war. The FFC agreed with Momin that any publicity should be in good taste and inoffensive to the Bangladeshi people. Bonnie immediately communicated her observation and experience to all FFC members in the following manner: "all of them [that is, the high commission staff in Ottawa] have been most helpful and encouraging"[10] and that they had left his office feeling that the high commissioner "had been well briefed" about their effort "by the interim Bangladesh spokesman, Hussain."[11]

The high commissioner's positive response prompted the Cappuccinos to continue with the next step: to propose a three-prong strategy, which they sent to all FFC members via FFC's own newsletter. The first part of their proposed strategy was to affirm Hussain as a spokesperson for Bangladesh in Canada who would look into the number of babies that would be available in Bangladesh. The second part of their strategy would be to gauge how many parents in Canada would actually be interested in adopting Bangladeshi war babies. Finally, the FFC would seek clarification from the various levels of governments in Canada (i.e. federal, provincial, and municipal) to clarify each government's roles and responsibilities in the adoption and immigration of war babies.

The *raison d'être* for FFC undertaking the task was the following: "We started this project because we were horrified to read newspaper accounts of mass-rapes during the war."[12] In a simple matter-of-fact way, Bonnie referred to war babies as those who "would be born to Bangladesh[i] mothers and West Pakistani men . . . As we understand the situation, these babies will not be accepted by their mothers or their country and their only hope for a good life is to be adopted outside of Bangladesh."[13] It seems outdated today, but in 1972, it was important to emphasize to white Canadian families (who may not have ever seen people from the subcontinent) that the children coming over would look different: "There is no guarantee of how light or dark complexioned the child will be, so we feel they [the parents] should be able to accept a child of any color."[14] They were also warned that war babies have unknown heredity and medical history.

"Although we have had no official confirmation from the Bangladesh Government, we have heard through a Swedish source that Prime Minister Mujib has stated this as a possible solution,"[15] wrote Bonnie to her clients, giving them a heads-up. She then continues, "One or more babies have already been adopted in Sweden. Certainly in speaking to Bangladesh[i] people in North America, we have found them warmly sympathetic to the idea. They feel that Bangladesh would be willing to release these babies for adoption to Canadians and Americans. We have heard from various sources that it is difficult to find the babies of war victims, many mothers have been aborted, some babies have been killed at birth, and others are in hiding."[16]

The Cappuccinos worked behind the scene, lobbying the governments of both Bangladesh and Canada. In a letter to Mitchel Sharp, then minister of External Affairs (Canada), Bonnie wrote, "What we are asking in our letter to [the government of] Bangladesh, is whether Bangladesh would consider releasing for adoption by Canadian families, a number of homeless Bangladesh[i] children or babies. If this would be the case, we would need to clarify the fastest possible procedures here and in regard to the home-study and the immigration of these babies. We feel it would be advantageous all the way if they could enter as close to new-born as possible. The program for Korean and Vietnamese children is very good in most cases, but in this respect, if it is possible, we would like to be able to work even faster."[17] Bonnie then informed her clients how the minister had been "working with the federal Immigration Department in regard to expediting the visas into Canada for the children so that, if at all possible, some or all of the chosen babies will arrive in Canada with us."[18]

In the May 1972 issue of the FFC *Newsletter,* the Cappuccinos published short write-ups on the proposed Bangladesh Project to draw its readers' attention to the project. The write-up indicated how the core members of FFC had been working closely with the high commissioner of Bangladesh in Canada who had assured them that soon he would find out the actual position of the Bangladesh government regarding the proposed project. Over four hundred copies of the *Newsletter* were sent to adoption agencies across Canada, Canadian provincial and territorial governments, social workers, known adoptive parents, and other proadoption groups in an attempt to generate interest in the Bangladesh Project.

Within weeks, the Cappuccinos heard from the high commissioner of Bangladesh (Momin) that Abdur Rab Chaudhury, then secretary, Coordination Division for External Assistance for Relief and Rehabilitation, Prime Minister's Secretariat, government of Bangladesh, had responded in the following: "Our Prime Minister has approved the principle of inter-country adoption for some of the babies you have in mind."[19] Though a curt response, it meant a great deal to the Cappuccinos. By this time, the FFC had also received numerous requests from couples across Canada, from almost every province, wishing to adopt. These positive developments led the FFC to the next step – submitting a project proposal.

Bangladesh Project and dissemination of information

Conceived by Fred and Bonnie, the project proposed to bring about two dozen war babies to North America. The Bangladesh Project had two objectives: first, "to determine if any of babies born of Bengali women and West Pakistani men will be available for adoption by Canadian families;" and second, "to facilitate [the adoption] procedure, if possible."[20] The proposal required two teams under the stewardship of Fred Cappuccino, one from Montreal and one from Toronto. It also spelled out the costs to be borne by participating adoptive families: "The adoptive families would of course be responsible to pay transportation costs for their child, unless we find some Canadian agency willing to charter a plane to bring a group over. We *estimate* the cost will be between 3 to 5 hundred dollars."[21]

The Montreal team included Fred and Bonnie Cappuccino and another volunteer, Elisabeth Mowling. The Toronto team consisted of Dr. Robert Ferrie and his wife, Helke Ferrie, both of whom would pay for their own expenses themselves. As part of the project's task, the teams would "go to Bangladesh for the express purpose of exploring and opening up avenues of adoption for Canada and perhaps the U.S."[22] The team targeted to complete the entire negotiation with the Canadian and Bangladeshi governments within a matter of three weeks. The Cappuccinos also expressed their intention "to take dossiers of several dozen families who are all ready to take one or more of these babies, and bring back these babies"[23] by the third week of July 1972.

Needless to mention, the Cappuccinos' project proposal to go to Bangladesh for an exploratory visit was unanimously approved by the board of directors of the Lakeshore Unitarian Church in Pointe Claire, Quebec, in the following manner: "This board grants the Minister an opportunity to proceed on a journey with his wife to Bangladesh to set up arrangements to bring Bangladeshi babies to North America for adoption. In doing this, the Board is recognizing the right of the Minister to engage in such an activity which is in keeping with the aims of the Unitarian Universalist Movement."[24]

Fund-raising activities

Encouraged and assisted by Roberto Ribeiro of CIDA, FFC developed a fund-raising strategy and action plan for the Bangladesh Project. The project would require a substantial amount of money. They needed to arrange for their own airfare to visit Bangladesh and the expense of transporting a number of war babies to adoptive parents in Canada. They would also require the basic necessities for babies while the babies were in their care in transit to Canada. FFC solicited the support of the Canadian public. In its May *Newsletter,* FFC explained the Bangladesh Project in layperson's terms and included information on its fund-raising activities for the proposed project in cooperation with some relief and rehabilitation agencies.

The FFC raised money through charitable events, such as potluck dinners, get-togethers, and craft sales. By the end of May 1972, the

Bangladesh Project became well known to many church groups and social organizations, which came to appreciate the efforts of FFC volunteers. Individual and organizational pledges began to pour in. The Primate's World Relief and Development, Anglican Church of Canada ($2,000), Ottawa Unitarian Congregation ($200), Plan Nagua ($1,000) as well as private donations (from six individuals), who wished to remain anonymous, made pledged contributions totaling $5,000.[25] By the end of June 1972, when the FFC teams left for Bangladesh, FFC had already collected $5,105 from individuals and organizations. It was a "moral boost" for FFC volunteers who considered their fund-raising efforts as a successful initiative. The fund-raising for the Bangladesh Project had continued for quite some time even following the return of the team from Bangladesh through CFCF Radio, Place Bonaventure, Montreal, Quebec.

Initial reactions and hurdles

Many Canadians were touched by the situation of the abandoned war babies in Bangladesh. However, there were also many who reacted negatively to the idea of interracial adoption. FFC members took it as a challenge to expand the idea of family in Canada to one going beyond race and color. When Fred Cappuccino had raised the proposed Bangladesh Project at his congregation in Montreal, there were quite a few whispers among the people in the congregation. In fact, there were many among the longtime members of the congregation who were not only reluctant but also openly opposed to interracial adoption.

Following his presentation, there appeared a series of letters to the editor in the Montreal area newspapers and church newsletters about the rationale for the adoption of war babies from Bangladesh at a time when many believed in the adoption of Canadian children first. The debate centered on issues such as the quantity of adoptions and quality of life; availability of "Canadian babies," of "Natives and Eskimos," of older children, and of "hard-to-place children" (i.e., children with disabilities and special needs); and the need for modifying rules, regulations, and practices to facilitate adoption from one province to another within Canada.

Emphasizing the need to adopt local (Canadian) children, one particular member of the congregation argued that if her next-door neighbor needed help, she would not use her time and energy in driving to some community on the other end of the island to seek out someone in trouble: "In all honesty, I find the business of importing children from Bangladesh an exercise in futility,"[26] argued a Montrealer who was opposed to adoption from abroad. "India's problems will *never* improve until her own people try to do something about them,"[27] thus argued the same person.

As far as FFC was concerned, this particular individual had simply revealed her ignorance about the reality of Bangladesh, which was a newly independent country born out of erstwhile East Pakistan, which was a part of Pakistan that came into existence as a result of the partition of India way back in 1947. Many others also argued that international adoption would not provide a solution even though Canada had allowed it because of the anticipated large number of these babies – some five thousand or so, as anticipated to be born in Bangladesh. Strongly disagreeing with this line of argument, FFC counterargued by saying, "What's wrong with saving whatever number can be saved?"[28] The main thrust of the Cappuccinos' appeal was that Canada should not isolate herself from what was happening in Bangladesh.

Again, when the Bangladesh Project became known to the public, some would-be applicants began to face immediate resistance or indifference to the FFC's idea of bringing these babies to Canada. Evidently, throughout 1972, the Ottawa-based Canadian Council on Social Development (CCSD), a national association of individuals and organizations concerned with social welfare in Canada, had remained active in raising awareness of the children's plight in Bangladesh. As discussed in chapter 2, the Geneva-based International Social Service (ISS), which operates in Canada under the aegis of CCSD, had earlier recommended adoption of Bangladeshi war babies in response to the request of the government of Bangladesh. In fact, the ISS had maintained a close liaison in keeping the CCSD posted on issues pertaining to international adoption effort in assisting Bangladesh.

Furthermore, many bits and pieces of information on Canada's engagement in assisting Bangladesh in formulating child welfare services for distressed women and children were released by CCSD at that time. FFC saw this as a commendable work by CCSD, since it had helped sensitize the issue to the Canadian public. The areas of greatest needs, wrote CCSD, were "(a) clinics and counseling, (b) interim care of children for whom inter-country adoption may be a solution and, (c) procedures to safeguard the social and legal rights of children, their parents and the adopting parents."[29] Thus far, everyone was happy seeing the proactive role of CCSD. And yet, much to one's deep surprise, the FFC and some advocacy groups considered some of the messages emanated from CCSD not only unhelpful but also damaging to their cause.

Ironically enough, the very first opposition to intercountry adoption of mixed-race infants came from the director of CCSD himself who "warned sympathetic Canadian families against making hasty decisions to adopt these children [war babies]."[30] It stated further, "Some international adoption of children from Bangladesh now seems inevitable but families should keep in mind that adoption is a serious 'for-life' decision . . . Families should not feel guilty about not offering to adopt."[31] The proadoption groups found this both enigmatic and inexplicable given the mandated advocacy role of CCSD. They came to view this as ironic, negative, and somewhat patronizing. Seeing what was spelled out in its press release, it was difficult to determine the exact position of CCSD in a positive light especially given the fact that both the governments of Canada and Bangladesh had already agreed in principle. In any event, Fred and Bonnie chose to ignore such remarks, which they believed were based on prejudice, bigotry, and jealousy on the part of certain child welfare professionals, and remained committed to their project.

Problems encountered by Ontario couples

Opposition toward the initiative of FFC in the Ontario government was also somewhat negative. The leading government advocate against the Bangladesh Project was Betty Graham (Graham), then director of Child Welfare, Ministry of Community and Social Services. Instead of facilitating adoption and/or speeding up the home assessment part of the process, government social workers in her department deliberately stalled the adoption process. The director's preference was for domestic adoption, while international adoption was a second priority because of its risks, hazards, and volatility.

Ideally, Ontario should have been in a position to advise applicants seeking to adopt from Bangladesh on the modus operandi involved by the various governments of Canada and Bangladesh. Instead, the Ontario couples who wrote to their respective Children's Aid Societies (CAS) for conducting a home study experienced delays and uncertainties. Creating roadblocks for the applicants Ontario officials demanded more information from the couples, which confused them in relation to the roles and responsibilities of federal and provincial governments with respect to international adoptions. Applicants from other provinces were readily accepted and approved by having home studies completed privately or by the local CAS.

Ontario blamed Ottawa (the federal government) having maintained that it needed to hear from Ottawa whether or not Bangladesh would permit adoption abroad. Throughout spring and early summer of 1972, Ontario applicants continued to get runaround. No one in the appropriate CAS or in the Office of the Director of Child Welfare seemed to accept responsibility or give direction as to what the next step should be. Instead, there were delays in answering questions and phone calls on grounds of confidentiality. Indeed, the responsibility for any decision regarding the conducting of a home study was passed back and forth between the director of Child Welfare, the director of CAS, and the social worker in charge of a given file.

Upon further probing, and comparing notes with each other, the Ontario applicants became convinced that it was not the government of Ontario but Graham herself who was the root cause of the problem. She very positively tried to persuade them not to try foreign adoption. According to the Government, there were many children available for adoption in Ontario, and overseas children, particularly from Asia; but they were diseased, suffering from malnutrition, and louse ridden, said Fred Cappuccino when recalling some of Graham's arguments against interracial adoption.

Not surprisingly therefore, Graham's inaction and inappropriate response to the Goods (Dale and Doreen) was very confusing. They were in receipt of a few letters, which did not make any sense. In one of her letters to the Good family, Graham wrote, "Our sources that we have been able to contact indicate that there has been a considerable exaggeration in our press of the need for assistance for these children outside their own country. Major efforts are continuing within Bangladesh to rehabilitate the many families disrupted by recent conditions and the considerable Canadian aid that has been available has been invaluable in this process."[32] In the same letter, Graham suggested to the applicants that if they were "interested in the adoption of an Ontario child," then she was sure their "local Children's Aid Society would be glad to assist."[33]

Much to their shock and surprise, within a matter of weeks, the Goods were in receipt of a telegram from Graham, which stated, "I cannot provide any letter of approval until a favorable home-study from your local Children's Aid Society has been received."[34] While the Ontario couples appreciated Graham's growing feeling of Canadianism, patriotism, or placing of Canadian children in Canadian homes first, they, at the same time, also held the view that in their present situation, issues such as interprovincial, interracial, and international placements of orphans were both critical and urgent. According to the applicants, their case was just as valid and, therefore, ought to be considered "in the best interest of the children" in question. The Goods considered Graham's arguments as baseless.

In fact, Graham's hard-hitting response and ongoing cut-and-dried argument that she needed to hear from Ottawa (Department of Manpower and Immigration) whether the feds would allow the abandoned war babies to enter into Canada for the purpose of adoption was seen by all of the Ontario applicants as an excuse to delay the process.

True, having received numerous complaints and inquiries from applicants, Ontario had actually made an inquiry through External Affairs asking whether the Bangladesh government would release its war babies for adoption in Canada or other countries: "Is the Bangladesh Government interested and willing to have their citizens leaving the country? Are there health, immigration, or other problems that would impede the integration of such infants? We are not urging necessarily that such children be admitted to Canada but are seeking information in order to be better able to answer the enquiries that are coming to us."[35]

Implicit message in the letter of inquiry is that Ontario is not necessarily interested, nor is it seeking to adopt children from Bangladesh but only asking for clarification on behalf of a few Ontario couples. Being armed to the teeth, the Ontario couples counterargued against what they called Graham's tomfoolery and driveling demands. As far as they were concerned, there was no rhyme or reason why the minister would chose to write to federal government at a time when the minister's officials had already been informed by the FFC (having learned through the Office of the High Commissioner of Bangladesh in Canada) that an agreement in principle had been reached by the governments of Canada and Bangladesh. Being livid with anger, they pledged to continue their fight to bring home infants of *their* choice. In fact, with each day, each couple's resolve to bring their desired Bangladeshi war babies home became even stronger.

As late as June 8, 1972, René Brunelle, then minister of Community and Social Services of the government of Ontario, had continued to maintain that his ministry was not aware of the federal government's position on foreign adoption, particularly from Bangladesh. However, by the third week of June 1972, Brunelle and the other prospective adoptive parents had heard from Mitchell Sharp (minister of External Affairs), who responded on behalf of Prime Minister Pierre Elliott Trudeau in the following manner: "You will be happy to know that I have been informed by the Bangladesh authorities that approval in principle has now been given which would permit the adoption of Bengali children by foreign nationals."[36]

In his letter to the provincial governments, Sharp also explained the process that requires (with which the applicants had already become familiar having heard it repeatedly from different sources) a letter of approval that would have to be obtained from the provincial government, and that further compliance with certain Canadian immigration and health regulations would be necessary before a child would be permitted to enter Canada. Sharp's letter was a great relief, particularly to the Ontario couples, who, by then, had become anxious. Fortuitously, a press release titled "Statement of Brunelle, Minister of Community & Social Services, Respecting Adoption of Foreign Children by Ontario Citizens, June 19, 1972," appeared, which stated that adoption would be permitted. At the same time, they also learned from the Good family of a telegram, which stated that since the local CAS had not done the home study yet, the director of Child Welfare was unable to do anything at the time. To add further to the Ontario applicants' worries was a rumor that they were made privy to – that the local CAS offices had been asked to put on hold any home study for Bangladeshi infants until they were advised by Graham's office in Toronto. The rumor was soon established to be a fact. Ontario applicants, who were already very angry, were more resolved to continue their fight for the adoption of their choice.

To add to the confusion, despite Graham's demand for more information from the government of Bangladesh, Phil and Diane Rochefort of Espanola, Ontario, who had been waiting to hear about the status of their application, actually received an approval letter for adoption from Graham; whereas none of the other anxious applicants were given any update on the status of their applications. Note that the home studies for all of the applications should have been completed by this time. The FFC was nearly ready to leave for Bangladesh having received a positive response from the government of Bangladesh. In lieu of government-assigned home studies, the Ontario applicants turned to Christine Johnston, a well-known social worker in Ontario, to conduct home studies for them in the interim in an attempt to speed up the assessment process. There had been no response from Graham's office stating whether Johnston's home studies would be accepted or not, or how soon the ministry would complete its own assessment for the purpose of adoption.

The applicants became convinced that Ontario's noncooperation and dilatory techniques were deliberate. It was not until the first week of July 1972 that Ontario informed the applicants that Ottawa had been informed by the Bangladesh government that any couple interested in adoption of children from Bangladesh should direct its inquiries to Mr. Hasan uz Zaman, secretary, Ministry of Social Welfare, Dhaka, Bangladesh, in the following manner: "The Government of Bangladesh is currently drawing up guidelines as to the procedures and standards which they wish to have in operation in the country respecting the adoption of their citizens by foreign nationals."[37] Interesting to note, despite having the desired information at that stage in its possession, Ontario inquired again with the Immigration Department if it could "clarify the position of Bangladesh on this matter," and whether or not, under immigration regulations, "applying couples are required to undertake any form of guarantee in report with this eventuality."[38]

Ontario applicants were very anxious having been convinced that Ontario officials were deliberately delaying despite the minister's public assurance of cooperation. They were angered by Graham's dismissive attitude, her imperious manner, and her flippant remarks. They feared that any complaints against the ministry personnel could backfire and jeopardize any possibility they might have had for their adoptions. There was a general feeling of helplessness because none of the parents could do much to change the situation and had to just wait. And yet despite everything, neither the FFC nor its Ontario members had ever ceased their efforts in their fight to move ahead with the Bangladesh Project.

Roles and responsibilities of federal and provincial governments

The crux of the matter boiled down to questions along these lines: *What is the role of the federal government? What role must be played by the child welfare authority of the province of destination in cooperation with the child welfare authority of the child's country of origin?* Ontario applicants complained about runarounds, misleading and contradictory information from the Ontario government. The answers they received created confusion, which led to frustration, which in turn obscured the actual modus operandi for adoption in Ontario. Recognizing that interprovincial issues and conflicts were common, even the Office of the Prime Minister did not hesitate to admit the reality on the ground in his response to Fred's request to look into the province of Ontario's delay. In a very carefully worded letter, the jurisdictional role was explained in the following manner: that "the provinces are very jealous of their jurisdictional competences and federal 'interventions' are more often likely stiffen resistance to change than being about change."[39]

An examination of both federal and provincial government records revealed that the federal government had always remained straightforward and transparent in explaining the process of adoption from abroad by clarifying the roles and responsibilities of the two levels of governments where adoption is a provincial responsibility and immigration is a federal responsibility. Having recognized the importance of the Bangladesh Project, the federal government was very keen, positive, and helpful from the start. Correspondence on the subject of adoption from Bangladesh among the adoptive parents, FFC, members of Parliament (MPs) and members of Provincial Parliament (MPPs), government of Ontario, and the two federal departments, the Manpower and Immigration, and the External Affairs, reveals that Ottawa had been respectful and did not interfere with the different processes used for adoption in different provincial and territorial jurisdictions.

In fact, as early as March 1972, when the Cappuccinos (Reverend Fred and Bonnie Cappuccino) had made their initial inquiry regarding adoption from Bangladesh with Bryce Mackasey, then minister of Manpower and Immigration, he had indicated clearly that his office was "not yet aware of the law or the laws of adoption in the state of Bangladesh."[40] He further added that his officials were led to believe that "at last report, a fixed policy on adoption abroad of the unwanted children of Bangladesh has yet to be formulated."[41] Minister Mackasey had also clarified the process in an attempt to assure the Cappuccinos: "Although the processing necessary to secure a child's admission for adoption is complex because of the involvement of both the federal and provincial governments as well as the Canadian Council on Social Development (CCSD) and the International Social Service (ISS) abroad, the part of this process stemming from the immigration requirements is relatively simple. Once the adoptive parents have located a suitable child and secured provincial approval, there is little more involved than would be the case in securing the admission to Canada of any immigrant."[42] Mackasey commended the Cappuccinos for their "humanitarian and compassionate effort" in helping the homeless children of Bangladesh and other countries and wished the couple "every success" in their "endeavors." In fact, the minister ended his note by assuring Mrs. Cappuccino that "immigration officials will do everything possible to process any application received as quickly as possible."[43]

Again, in his response to similar questions to other applicants, Mackasey also took the time to explain clearly the process for sponsorship, immigration, and adoption. Specifically, he explained *how* his ministry gets involved *only* when it receives an application for sponsorship as it relates to *orphans*: "The children in question may only be admitted as sponsored dependents and they must be under the age of 13 and sponsored by the person who intends to adopt that child. The child must also be an orphan or a foundling, an illegitimate child placed with a welfare authority for adoption or alternatively a child whose parents are permanently separated and has been placed for adoption with the welfare authorities."[44] By this time, the prospective adoptive parents had already become familiar with the process. In dealing with adoption from outside of Canada, the main requirement, as they understood, is to ensure that legal requirements of Bangladesh and Canada had been met for the protection of the prospective adoptive parents, the biological children of the adoptive family, and the adopted child. Just so that there were no misunderstanding, the minister further explained, "The issuance of a visa and admission of such a child is dependent upon an officer providing a statement in writing that satisfactory arrangements have been made for them to supervise the adoption or that they will ensure that the child will be cared for if it is not adopted."[45]

Again, federal records also indicate that upon receipt of the long-awaited information from Bangladesh by early June, Department of External Affairs senior management briefed Mitchel Sharp (minister) in the following: "We have been advised by the Bangladesh High Commission, Ottawa, that Prime Minister Sheikh Mujibur Rahman has given agreement in principle to permit the adoption of Bangalee children by foreign nationals."[46] He was also informed that all necessary actions will be taken to move ahead with the next steps involved in the process. Both Sharp and Mackasey were careful in explaining the *modus operandi* to ensure that the applicants understand the roles and responsibilities of the respective governments. Both were frank, transparent, and cooperative.

According to the established procedure, Ontario did not even need to know this in order to conduct a home study, the objective of which is to determine eligibility and give permission for adoption if the prospective parent's home is found suitable. Instead, notwithstanding the fact that Ontario had all the information with regard to the government of Bangladesh's explicit interest, it continued to demand more information. At the same time, Ontario maintained that it was prepared to cooperate with the government of Canada, but in actual fact, it refused to allow the home studies the result of which is crucial to adoption.

The stalling tactics of the Ontario government become readily apparent when we look more closely at the correspondence between the federal government and its Ontario counterparts. The Ontario government had acknowledged that the adoptions were in fact allowable without further clarification from the federal government, and yet Ontario procrastinated in the name of further clarification. Clearly, unlike the Ontario government, federal ministers Sharp and Mackasey had kept the prospective parents fully informed. We have noted how the two ministers, in their correspondence, took their time to explain the modus operandi.

When during the first week of July (1972), Sharp and Mackasey were able to communicate to their clients about the positive response from the government of Bangladesh, t immediately informed the parents and the provincial governments of the final decision of the government of Bangladesh. However, Graham's office continued to stall in scheduling the home studies by maintaining that they were awaiting more information from Bangladesh through Ottawa. As we shall see, this situation came to a head and was only resolved as a result of persistent efforts of FFC and prospective parents who lobbied the top-most levels of government officials.

Lobbying and networking at governmental levels

FFC lobbied officials at both the federal and provincial levels. At the provincial level, FFC initially made a direct appeal to the Ontario minister of Community and Social Services to intervene on behalf of the parents. Its main argument was that the rest of Canada, namely the governments of Quebec, Nova Scotia, and Saskatchewan, had already provided the applicants with letters of approval. Director Graham, in charge of Ontario applicants, however, maintained that if such a placement, that is, adoption of infants from Bangladesh, was possible and met with the approval of the governments of Bangladesh and of Canada, Ontario would have no objection. But her remarks seemed disingenuous because she had already received assurances in writing from the Canadian and Bangladeshi governments that both countries had agreed on the matter, although the agreement's implementation was still to be fully determined.

The appeal of FFC was that, on the one hand, according to Ontario officials, they had been awaiting information from Bangladesh through Ottawa; on the other hand, evidently they had already been informed about the positive position of the government of Bangladesh. And yet Director Graham, despite being in possession of the same information sent by Ottawa and FFC, continued to maintain that home studies would be done *only* after she had been informed that Bangladesh would release its war babies. In fact, according to the established process, Ontario was supposed to initiate the adoption process by reporting accurate information about the suitability of prospective parents. Instead, Ontario remained uncooperative and continued to stall the processing of applications for adoption.

Seeing no other alternative, the FFC again asked the Ontario minister of Community and Social Services to intervene immediately on behalf of the Ontario couples in the following manner: "If Miss Graham is unwilling to sign the Provincial Agreement is there a possibility that, on humanitarian grounds, you could sign them personally? The monsoon season will be upon Bangladesh soon. We hope that these Canadian-bound infants and children are out before the worst of the monsoon and the expected epidemics, etc."[47]

In parallel, Bonnie Cappuccino also reached out to Prime Minister Sheikh Mujibur Rahman of Bangladesh. The FFC, encouraged by Professor Hussein of Sherbrooke and the Bangladeshi High Commissioner in Ottawa, wrote, "We are deeply concerned about the plight of the women affected by the war, and the babies now being born as a result of the war, and also other orphaned children. We would deem it a privilege to adopt some of the babies to love and cherish them as our own children."[48]

She then went on to say, "In addition to helping particular children, these adoptions also serve as a strong bond between nations. For example, when we adopted a mixed-race child from Japan 17 years ago, all of our friends and relatives became very interested in Japan, and they would make a point to call us when they heard that a Japanese student was in town. Our home became a gathering place for students from Japan."[49] Bonnie also wrote similar letters to A. H. M. Kamruzzaman and Abdus Samad Azad, then minister of Relief and Rehabilitation (Bangladesh) and minister of Foreign Affairs (Bangladesh), respectively. In their letters, the FFC outlined *who* exactly they represented in Canada and *what* FFC wanted to achieve.

To reinforce Bonnie's appeal, many wishing to adopt from Bangladesh also wrote directly to the government of Bangladesh, urging it to allow them to adopt its war babies. In a way, it may be observed that from the time the FFC started to lobby the government of Bangladesh, they also began "educating" the prospective adoptive parents about the need to demonstrate sensitivity in dealing with Bangladeshi government officials. In particular, the FFC emphasized to the potential applicants that it was very important to keep one's link with one's adopted child and advised them on *how* to write in the event they do write to Bangladeshi officials: "The letter saying you would be honored to adopt a Bangladesh[i] child . . . should not say anything about the under-developed situation there etc. But should stress the great privilege your family would be granted if you do find a child from Bangladesh to adopt. Assure them that your child would be informed of the heritage and culture of Bangladesh."[50]

Dr. Robin and Barbara Morrall of Saskatoon, Saskatchewan, were the first applicants who wrote to the government officials in Bangladesh expressing their desire to adopt a war baby from Bangladesh: "It remains for us to receive your permission to allow a child to leave your country and be entrusted to our care. If you grant us the favor of your permission, we shall, of course be highly honoured by the trust you place in us to bring up the child,"[51] thus wrote the Morralls. Continuing along the same vein, they wrote, "Such a child could share the happiness which good fortune has bestowed upon us."[52] They ended their letter by saying, "For our part, we can honestly say that we have given great thought to the matter. We have also discussed it with the authorities here. The fact that they are prepared to give this sanction to such an adoption, as you will see from the documents accompanying this letter, is an indication of the confidence they have in us as parents. We sincerely hope that you will be able to do us the honour of sharing their confidence."[53]

Although by May 1972, the FFC had successfully lobbied the Canadian federal government and the government of Bangladesh to allow the adoptions, it was unsuccessful to persuade Ontario provincial authorities to process the war baby adoption applications (this was even though the province had not officially disallowed the adoptions). Elisabeth Mowling, an active member of FFC (who also adopted a war baby from the first batch), sent out a handwritten note to all Ontario couples awaiting home study, urging them write to the minister of Community and Social Services. Elisabeth advised the couples to keep the pressure on by arguing that the children were in a life-and-death situation where time was of the essence. She warned that the minister "might try to pass the buck to Ottawa so let him know that his Department could open up the gates for these children if it would, and getting Ottawa to act might be too late."[54]

Around the same time, to keep the pressure on, Mary Jane Turner, then a liaison person for the Adoption Coordinator of the Ministry of

Community and Social Services; Rev. Marvin G. McDermott, a well-known personality in the religious community of the Toronto area; and Helke Ferrie, chairperson of Asian Adoption and secretary treasurer of the Ontario FFC branch, also held meetings among themselves. Both Turner and Reverend McDermott had a meeting with Minister Brunelle on May 31, 1972, that ended very well. They made a special request to the minister to speed up the conduct of home studies.

As part of its strategy, all through the month of June (1972), the FFC continued to recruit more couples interested in adoption. By this time, the Ontario couples had organized themselves, with Donna Wolsey leading the group, in a campaign of calling church ministers, federal MPs, and provincial MPPs to raise awareness and support for the adoptions given Ontario's "blocking techniques." One of the couples, Tony and Bonnie Boonstra of St. Thomas, Ontario, recalls returning from the immigration office in nearby London, Ontario, having been terribly upset because no one in the office would provide them any help. Sandra Simpson of Montreal, who had also applied for a war baby, convinced the Boonstras to go back to the same immigration officials again. "I remember the first clerk we met saying that what we were attempting to do would take at least a year. I told him that this did not help since the children would not be alive,"[55] recalled Tony. Other Ontario couples also reported similar experiences with Ontario immigration officials. The "unofficial" recalcitrant position of Ontario hardened the resolve of applicants. The group lobbied the government with the argument that further delay would mean more loss of lives.

The group demanded *transparency* and *fair assessment* in determining eligibility for adoption. They were extremely angry and upset. Tony Boonstra "became much more determined to continue with the process . . . [He] wasn't going to let some government officials stop [him]."[56] Even though many obstacles stood in the way, the relentless and courageous efforts of the group to obtain permission rested on the premise that it was their *right* to adopt a child from a country of *their choice* and that their choices were not to be dictated by the Ontario director of Child Welfare.

John and Dorothy Morris of Brantford, Ontario, became well known in the news media, following their application for adoption of two orphans from Vietnam and Bangladesh. From the start, they had asserted their *right* to adopt from *any country of their choice*.

They were particularly concerned that children from places such as Vietnam and Bangladesh "don't even have a chance to live in most instances."[57] By midsummer 1972, they had already written to all three levels of government arguing that they "feel that this [adoption from Bangladesh] is something that we have to do."[58] When the Morrises specifically inquired about the process of adoption from Bangladesh, Graham, not surprisingly, attempted to dissuade the couple.

They were informed that "the babies were very sickly, with diarrhea, lice, etc., etc."[59] So determined were Ontario officials in favor of children other than Bangladeshis that a week before the arrival of the war babies, a representative from the local CAS visited the Morrises and offered them an eighteen-month-old multiracial Canadian child in place of their chosen child from Bangladesh. The couple's immediate reaction was to not accept the offer. The Morrises respectfully declined on the ground that they still felt that they "had to go where the need was the greatest."[60] Having made up their minds already, they stated that their next move would be to continue their "fight to the bitter end."[61] The Morrises learned soon after this incident that this "mythical" child was also offered to other applicants.

"It would appear that your concern is with the quality of life of Canadian orphans. We maintain that in most cases these Canadian children have the basic necessities of life, such as housing, clothing, food, education and health care. We do agree with you however that they lack the love, safety and security of a family which is a large part of the quality of life,"[62] wrote the Morrises. "Our main concern at this time is not the quality of life of Canadian orphans or the quality of life of Vietnamese or Bangladesh[i] orphans. Our main concern is the very life of the Vietnamese or Bangladesh[i] orphans,"[63] wrote John with striking clarity and continued further in the following manner: "We would indeed hate to go through the whole procedure of finding and arranging only to have to abandon our plans through a rejection of our application by the Province."[64] The Morrises, like other couples, recognized that it was *not* Ontario officials per se but Betty Graham (director in charge) who had serious reservations about the adoption of racially different children in Ontario.

By the third week of June (1972), the Canadian FFC team was scheduled to leave for Bangladesh to pick out a number of war babies for adoption. And yet despite every effort, nobody even at that time really knew what was going on with regard to home study for the Ontario couples. Applicants were told that home studies for adoption of Bangladeshi babies were put on hold for an indefinite period by the local CAS upon instruction from Toronto. This prompted Dale and Doreen Good also to write directly to Prime Minister Trudeau urging him for his *personal* intervention because they felt that they had *no one* to turn to. Seeking his *immediate* and *positive* intervention, they appealed that "time is limited" and that "it is essential that" the government works "quickly for the welfare of the children."[65] They explained that, thus far, they had done everything that they needed to do, including having a home study completed by a private social worker (because the local CAS would not conduct the home study). They asked the prime minister to "give" the matter his "most urgent consideration and reply by return mail."[66]

Collective and individual efforts

In general, FFC avoided the media. Their position was that adoptions are a sensitive issue for everyone involved, so the best approach is to keep a low profile. FFC had deliberately avoided going to the press to defend the adoption of mixed-race children in Canada. Moreover, they believed that the government of Bangladesh preferred to keep publicity to a minimum. But in the end, while lobbying the government of Ontario in particular, FFC was forced to go public in order to expose Ontario officials and demand prompt action without further delay. However, they were very careful in their press releases to make the distinction that they were not going to Bangladesh in the name of social or political action; instead, they were going on purely humanitarian grounds "because human beings are suffering to a degree that is unimaginable in Canada."[67]

During the course of their interaction with Ontario officials, the applicants were repeatedly warned that foreign children could be "high-risk" adoptions because of their unknown background. Moreover, it would be fast and easy to verify the backgrounds of local orphans. The message that came across to the applicants was clear: home studies by the local CAS could be conducted much faster for a local child than they would be able to do one for a "foreign" child. Being frustrated and seeing her racist attitude, the Ontario couples neither understood nor appreciated Director Graham's seemingly unprofessional behavior. They deemed her behavior repulsive, disgraceful, and morally unacceptable. Having been convinced of Graham's ulterior motives and apparent procrastination, the majority of Ontario applicants came to believe that the resistance to adoption by Graham must have stemmed from racism of some sort.

Naturally, by then, feelings of uncertainty had frustrated the applicants almost beyond endurance. Behind the scene, of course, Ontario's main concern was that foreign adoption, if allowed to take place, might come to mean one less space for a Canadian adoption. Neither the FFC nor the prospective adopters ever thought along this vein. However, because of the federal government's assurance that it would welcome infants from Bangladesh, the anxious couples awaiting home studies decided to go public in their accusation of racist behavior on the part of Ontario officials. As mentioned, other provinces had not only conducted home studies but also already given approval for adoption from Bangladesh.[68]

They blamed Graham personally for her derogatory comments about adoption of racially different children. Taking a lead role, Lloyd and Sandra Simpson (of Montreal) offered to help the Ontario couples organize their efforts. They contrived a campaign according to which all prospective parents would simultaneously call the Office of the Minister. Each caller would deliver a prepared media line to the minister with examples of the misleading and contradictory information doled out by Graham and her office. The parents' argument was that no matter how cooperative the ministry claimed to have been, the need for would-be adoptive parents could not be met unless prompt service was given by the local CAS. Their early June (1972) campaign completely tied up the ministry's telephone lines with inquiries, directed to the minister's office, regarding the status of their home studies. Under the circumstances, they thought of this to be the only way to force clarification from the province as to *what* was needed to be done and what was *not being done* by Ontario.

Their plan worked. The local news media picked up the story, which caught the ministry by surprise. Putting even more pressure into the situation was that, by this time, the FFC team had already left for Bangladesh. Robert Kertsen (a bureaucrat in the Ministry of Community and Social Services) is on record as having been in charge of briefing the minister on the concerns of the FFC regarding the delays in the war baby adoptions. The minister was informed that the delay was being caused by Graham's demand for documentation, which she did not require in order to conduct home studies. Kertsen further informed the minister in the following manner: "Evidently, we are demanding birth certificates and also Form 1009, an Immigration Sponsor Form, and the insistence that we have the last name of the child . . . The Delhi High Commission's office is retaining the birth certificates. Immigration officials are evidently satisfied about Form 1009 . . . The Province of Quebec, Monique Peron (tel. 418-643-3016), approves the children destined for that Province without the red-tape we are imposing. Mrs. Simpson feels we are making this unnecessarily complicated."[69]

The Ontario government still refused to proceed with processing the adoption applications even though they were fully aware of the risks to the children and the efforts that everyone involved had taken to make the adoptions possible. The applicants went to the media a second time. This time they shared with the news media the details of how the Ontario government had not been cooperating with them and, more importantly, the absurd reasons for the delay of their responses to the applications from Graham's office. They pointed out the director's stated view that it was wrong to uproot the war babies from their country of origin: that it was wrong to adopt from abroad when there were many babies in Canada who could just as well be adopted. The director was of the view that it would be difficult for the racially different babies from Bangladesh to adjust to Canadian life. This time the director's office was inundated with calls not from parents but instead from television and radio reporters with hard-hitting inquiries such as "We understand that you're not going to allow these little babies into Canada, is that true? Is it true that you're actually prohibiting the 15 Bangladeshi orphans to come to Canada?"[70]

The lack of an immediate response and the noble cause of the adoptive parents prompted the media to conclude that the government should simply do the long-overdue home studies. One of the parents, Helke Ferrie of Burlington, Ontario, openly accused Graham of being a racist. Helke demanded three points of clarification from Graham. First, she wanted to know why Graham's response to the adoptions differed so much with Graham's counterparts in Quebec, Nova Scotia, and Saskatchewan, who had already conducted home studies; by the end of May 1972, they had been advised by their respective governments of their findings (and had allowed the adoptions).

Second, all of the prospective adoptive parents had already been assured by the federal government that it had worked out an arrangement with the government of Bangladesh, having agreed in principle to allow a number of the Bangladeshi war babies to be brought to Canada for adoption. *So why did Ontario require more documentation?* thus asked an outraged Helke. Third, provincial governments are required to conduct home studies in order *only* to determine the suitability of prospective parents and not to allow or disallow adoptions. Having claimed that Ontario had already had the information it required, Helke pointedly asked Graham, *Exactly what* was *causing the delay*?

Graham's insistence that Ontario needed to hear from Ottawa *if* Bangladesh would release its war babies was nothing but a *red herring,* argued Helke. Helke was not prepared to take no for an answer. She went to the highest level of government to solicit support and cooperation from both the federal and provincial governments. Helke fired off a series of letters on behalf of all of the Ontario applicants, first to Minister René Brunelle of Ontario and then to Prime Minister Pierre Elliott Trudeau. Her appeal to Brunelle was to do "anything" he was able to do on behalf of the Ontario couples and the infants and children of Bangladesh who might come into the adoptive homes in Ontario.

In her letter to Prime Minister Trudeau, Helke appealed for his *immediate* and *personal* intervention. She wrote, "Sir, forgive my urgent tone, but I am writing to you as a frustrated mother of two natural born children. Both my husband and I are praying for the two children we wish to adopt from Vietnam and the two also from Bangladesh. I am also a frustrated representative of those families for whom I am appealing to you, who wish to adopt some of the children from Bangladesh to be released for adoption. I am of German origin and know only too well from the two World Wars what war means for children, and how millions starved. Through my 12-year experience in India, I also dread the monsoon season in July. I am supported in this by the representative of International Social Service in Ottawa and by Father Labbé, who is the head of C.O.R.R. [Christian Organization for Relief and Rehabilitation], the UN financed organization in Dacca, taking care of all relief activities."[71]

Helke emphasized that there was indeed a prima facie case on humanitarian grounds for expediting the home study so that the FFC, which had made progress in arranging for the babies to be flown to Canada, could go to Bangladesh as planned. However, Helke ended her letter with a warning that she would go on a hunger strike: "I would like to announce that in the event of either a refusal on your part to comply with our requests for all couples mentioned above or any further delay, *I am going to go on a hunger-strike, beginning Saturday, June 17th, if I have not heard from you* either by phone (confirming that the permissions have been sent out) or received news from Mrs. Bonnie Cappuccino, President of QUEBEC FAMILIES FOR CHILDREN, 10 Bowling Green, Pointe Claire, 720, Quebec, that she has received the permissions granted by you in the mail.

The most important national and international news agencies will receive a copy of this letter and a history of our efforts by express mail on Saturday and will also be informed of *my hunger-strike which I shall not terminate until these couples have received their lawful right to adopt children from Bangladesh,* so that these children, they wish to sponsor will be able to come to Canada by July, as planned."[72] Helke sent copies of her letter to William Davis, then premier of Ontario; René Brunelle, minister of Community and Social Services of the government of Ontario; Lincoln Alexander, member of Parliament, for Hamilton West (although a letter directly addressed to him was sent to him already); and Jack McNie, member of the Legislative Assembly of Ontario. She also invited all of the major newspapers in Canada and the Canadian Press Syndicate in Toronto for a press conference on the morning of Saturday, June 17, 1972, in the likely event that she would indeed go on a hunger strike.

Helke also hand-delivered a separate letter to Graham's office in Toronto in which she wrote, "I sincerely regret having to write in this urgent and demanding tone, but I am speaking for those children we wish to adopt. Bangladesh, a new nation, founded on the heroic resistance to oppression, is in the same plight that Europe was after the two World Wars and is hoping for the help of kind-hearted people and understanding governments who will undertake such adoptions."[73]

As planned, on Saturday, June 17, at 9:00 a.m., Helke began her hunger strike at her Burlington residence. She protested against what she considered an endless delay in completing home studies by the director of Child Welfare in the Ontario Ministry of Community and Social Services. She had hired a private security firm to act as an independent witness. The guard remained by her side right from the moment she commenced her hunger strike. Helke vowed to drink only one glass of milk per day – a total of only 160 calories – until her case was resolved. Helke was visited by her family physician, Dr. Vivian MacKrell, who reported that Helke was in good health. Helke took the unusual step (especially back in 1972 in Canada) of a hunger strike because she feared for the children's lives and she wanted the people of Canada to see for themselves the racism of Ontario officials.

Helke was quoted in the paper that she would maintain her strike "until I get what I want."[74] The news media covered the story in its entirety. Her hunger strike made national headlines on TV, in print, and over radio. Describing Helke as a courageous woman, the print media wrote, "A 24 year-old mother of two has begun a hunger-strike to protest what she claims is deliberate stalling on the part of Betty Graham, Ontario, Director of Child Welfare, to permit the adoption of foreign children," wrote the *Globe and Mail*.[75] "For the last six months, we've had nothing but stalling from Miss Graham. She has no right to put us off. Whether we're trying to adopt from Bangladesh or Timbuktu, her job is to advise Children's Aid Society to do a home-study,"[76] said an angry Robert Ferrie (her husband) in a media interview. Expressing his shock and disgust at the inordinate delay, he summed up the situation, "We feel like we're trying and someone has thrown sand in our faces."[77]

"My husband and I have been trying since January to get a statement from Queen's Park [premises where government departments are located] as to whether or not we are suitable to adopt,"[78] complained an angry Helke to a news reporter. "Try as we might, we've had no luck. But we're not giving up, despite the endless delays. We intend to bring these children to Canada come hell or high water," said a determined Helke to a news reporter.[79] The massive media coverage exposed the Ontario government and put both the feds and the province in an awkward position. However, even at that time, Graham still insisted that there had been no wrongdoing.[80] She argued that there had been no undue delay in the Ferries' case. Graham said this knowing that it was her department that would not conduct the "official" home study.

Gordon McLellan, then executive assistant to the deputy minister of Family and Social Planning for Ontario, said in a media interview that his ministry had received no official word from Ottawa indicating that Bangladesh had agreed to let its orphans be adopted outside the country and that he was not aware of any applications for home studies being held up. Needless to say, McLellan's statement regarding the position of the Bangladesh government is simply incorrect. The Ferries vehemently refuted the claim that home studies were not being unduly delayed.

The matter thus boiled down to one single question: *What is the process?* Time and again, Helke pointed out to news reporters the adoption process requires the local CAS staff to conduct the home study first to determine the applicant's suitability and eligibility to adopt. The child in question, explained Helke, could come from anywhere. Ontario officials did not need to know whether the government of Bangladesh or a particular country would release its babies. In the case in point, Helke feared that if "the adoption process [was not] expedited, the children [would fall] victim to the cholera epidemics that often accompany the July monsoons."[81] Most reporters found both Helke and the other Ontario couples more credible than the Ontario government. The sole reason for the delays, according to Graham, was that "it was unlikely the countries involved would let children leave."[82] However, the applications should have been processed *in a timely manner, either way*. In fact, as reporters noted, Graham had no rationale to explain the inaction.

Helke's hunger strike (and all of the media coverage) made an impact in top political circles. Her key message to the Canadian public and Ontario officials was that the social workers whom they were dealing with were not only unhelpful but also disparaging in regard to interracial adoption. While government officials were embarrassed by Helke's much-publicized hunger strike, this was the straw that broke the camel's back. Within forty eight hours, Helke was in receipt of written assurance from the minister of Community and Social Services who, in an interview with the media, made it clear that international adoption is *legal* and that home studies would commence immediately. For the minister, it was an attempt to put a lid on.

Everyone was surprised and relieved with the result – especially the promptness with which Ontario officials responded. The media reported that Ontario officials had started "to do everything possible to cut through the red tape."[83] Seeing the media coverage and the positive reaction of the government, on the third day of her hunger strike,

Helke broke her fast at 8:00 p.m. after a deluge of positive publicity. Dr. Gordon Askewith, then executive director of the Halton CAS, who had previously denied interaction with the Ferries since January 1972, immediately spoke with the media as though nothing untoward had happened. He indicated that "as far as policy went, there was nothing to prevent foreign children from being adopted in Halton."[84] This was in sharp contrast to what Graham had intuited by seeking "more documentation."

Helke then thanked the minister in writing for his prompt intervention: "My husband and I very much want to thank you for the two statements you made to the press which we received in their complete originals as soon as they had been released to the press. I consequently terminated my hunger-strike at 8 p.m. on Tuesday, as I felt that the two statements were the official reply from your Ministry to the issue we had raised and brought to the attention of the public."[85]

On July 5, 1972, the director of Child Welfare was able to formally advise the presidents and local directors of CAS in writing in the following manner: that "the Bangladesh government has agreed in principle to the adoption by foreign nationals of Bangladesh[i] children."[86] After months of disappointment and frustration, the couples awaiting home studies felt some relief; however, they did not stop putting the pressure on. They pledged to continue their efforts until the adoptive parents had all exercised their *right* to *pick* and *choose* a child from wherever they want. A go-getter Helke remained resolved to leave no stone unturned until she got what she wanted.

Documents required by Canadian government

It took several rounds of consultation with the representatives of the governments of Canada, Bangladesh, and provincial ministries for the FFC to collect an exhaustive list of forms required from all of the applicants from across Canada. For the applicants, undoubtedly the most confusing forms were for application/sponsorship (#1009) required by the Department of Manpower and Immigration. The forms required that the applicants provide the name, date and place of birth of the child, identity of sex, along with the child's address in Bangladesh. It was difficult to obtain original records in the postwar Bangladesh especially when some of the babies had not yet been chosen by the FFC. Again, in some cases, babies had not even been born.

Naturally, for many babies, birth certificates had not yet been issued by the orphanage authority in Bangladesh. As observed, in spite of the lack of information, the governments of Quebec, Nova Scotia, and Saskatchewan were amenable to the information gaps. They advised the applicants that their applications had been forwarded to the federal Department of Manpower and Immigration for further consideration with the stipulation that all outstanding and pertinent information on the child would have to be submitted as soon as available. To the frustration of the Ontario couples, their provincial government was still uncooperative. It demanded the particulars of the infants even though earlier the minister had given apodictic assurance of his full cooperation. In particular, the Ontario government continued to ask for the last name of the child when even the first name of the child was not known to anyone.

Fortunately, since the federal government was very cooperative and keen on the Bangladesh Project, it proactively informed the FFC team exactly which documents were required to obtain exit permit/visa for the children. After weeks of exhaustive search and having liaised with the federal government, the FFC team was able to obtain the required information to submit in order to complete the formalities. So that the adoptive parents were not taken by surprise or intimidated by seeing the formidable list of items needed to be filled out, Ottawa carefully cited each specific form for the sponsored immigrant applications that had to be filled out by each prospective adoptive couple.

In no time did the Cappuccinos send the entire information package with accompanying guides and instructions to the applicants asking them to collect the following thirteen documents to support their case: (1) home study from adoption agency, (2) birth certificates of parents, (3) marriage certificate, (4) health certificates, (5) letter of credit from bank, (6) letter of provincial approval, (7) power of attorney, (8) letters of reference, (9) pictures of family, (10) Canadian immigration papers for child, and (11) medical report on the to-be-adopted child. As well, to obtain and complete the following: (12) Immigration Form OS 8, in compliance with medical requirements, procuring of valid national travel documents, and (13) completion of sponsorship form, IMM 1009, along with evidence of approval of the appropriate child welfare authority. The provision of documentation and federal assurance for visas was a great relief to the Ontario applicants who had thus far no support from the provincial authorities.

Preparation to leave for Bangladesh

The FFC team consisted of Robert and Helke Ferrie, Fred and Bonnie Cappuccino, and Elisabeth Mowling. The team was led by Fred Cappuccino. The team had four main concerns: (1) to have no *objection* certificates issued to applicants, (2) to streamline communications between parties representing Canada and Bangladesh so that the FFC counsel would be the sole person responsible for coordination, (3) to arrange logistics of travel from overseas with infants, and (4) to procure the needed baby clothes, food, and medicines while the babies were en route to Canada.

By the time the team was ready to leave for Bangladesh, they were confident that the adoption applications and their intergovernmental communication strategy through counsel were in order. But they had still not fully reckoned the logistics of *how* to bring two dozen infants at the same time on the same flight home to Canada. According to the airline requirements, there had to be one adult for every two babies on the trip. The in-flight arrangements for caring for the babies would be critical to success because the undernourished newborns would be prone to dehydration (and possible death) during the long overseas flight. Thankfully, the needed supplies for the trip appeared just in time in the form of donations of clothes, medicine, and cash. Canadians who had heard in the media of the project gave generously and just in time for the FFC team.

The reluctance of the airlines to bring so many babies back on a single flight meant hiring at least one more stewardess. The travel agent of FFC, Agnes Henchey, took a personal interest in the Bangladesh Project having spent long hours of negotiation with various airlines to get the least expensive and most direct flights in midsummer during peak season. Eventually, Air India agreed to carry the babies on the condition that there would be at least one adult (including the stewardess) for every three babies. They needed to bring seventeen babies, which meant that they needed one more adult for their team. As mentioned already, Elisabeth Mowling also an applicant for adoption, volunteered to accompany the team in Bangladesh at her own expense.

Helke Ferrie represented the Ontario couples. She kept the couples informed on the team's progress. Helke also acted as an emotional support for the families. In one of her letters to the Ontario families, written just a few days before leaving for India and Bangladesh, Helke addressed them as "Dear Expectant Parents," which generated a lot of laughter at a time when they were down in spirit (because of the Ontario government's delays in processing their adoption applications). Assuring them that they were close to getting their babies, Helke wrote that they were at the "last phases of adoptive pregnancies" where "[it] is absolutely necessary that Mr. Copeland [lawyer retained by the FFC to represent its members] handles all affairs over here, so the fastest possible way of doing things can be done."[87]

She warned the adoptive parents that on the team's way back to Canada, the infants would require extra attention. She provided them an exhaustive list of items they should buy and keep them handy for the baby-to-arrive. "On the airplane it will be cool, and we don't need pneumonia on top of dysentery and malnutrition."[88] Advising them to do their shopping for the soon-to-arrive babies, she informed them that she herself had gone "shopping for their babies-to-be to bring to Bangladesh diapers, plastic pants and feeding bottles."[89]

The five-member FFC team left in two separate groups. The Ferries left Toronto on June 25, 1972, for India where they planned to spend a few days in Mussoorie, Uttar Pradesh, before joining the Cappuccinos in Dhaka, Bangladesh. The Cappuccinos and Elisabeth Mowling left for Bangladesh on June 28, 1972, via New York to New Delhi to Dhaka, Bangladesh. Their return flight was scheduled for July 19, 1972, with a reservation for seventeen infant passengers. The team arrived in Dhaka, Bangladesh, on June 29, carrying with them a great load of luggage full of diapers, baby clothes, medicines, and other necessities for bringing the babies home.

Twenty-one hectic days in Dhaka (June 29–July 19, 1972)

Prior to their arrival in Dhaka, the FFC team had been briefed by Jean Pelletier, then Canada's first CUSO (Canadian University Services Overseas) representative in Bangladesh, about the chaotic situation in Bangladesh. The team was made aware that the Mujib administration was particularly keen on adoption, which it believed to be the most appropriate way of saving the war babies from an uncertain future in Bangladesh. In the eyes of the Bangladeshis, the team was told that birth of the war babies was associated with "shame" and "dishonor."

Their team's first contact was Fr. Benjamin Labbé, then regional director of Christian Organization for Relief and Rehabilitation (CORR). The team had first met Fr. Labbé two months ago in Montreal, Quebec, in May. He had spent many years working in Bangladesh, including the nine long months during the war of liberation. Father Labbé had a good relationship with the country's top officials. He gave the team his personal address and provided office premises, his typewriter, photocopy machine, and telex facilities to exchange correspondence with their partners in Canada.

Their second contact was Emile Baron of the Canadian International Development Agency then attached to the Canadian High Commission in Dhaka. Baron was at the team's disposal, following the instruction of then Canadian High commissioner, Jim Bartleman, who was interested in seeing a smooth transfer of the babies into Canadian homes. The High Commission staff quickly gave them a short briefing on the roles and responsibilities of the various ministries within the Mujib administration. Having identified some key players in the Cabinet, Baron cautioned the team to take extra care in dealing with government officials, as the team would be discussing a subject requiring tact and diplomacy. Since they would be skating on a thin ice in a different cultural milieu, they are bound to face a new challenge, so they were warned. The team was also reminded that though the liberation was supposed to have washed away the old forces, there were many quislings still around and very much present in the government. Using Baron's letter of introduction on the high commissioner's letterhead, the team was able to arrange a series of meetings with a number of senior mandarins in the Departments of Labor and Social Welfare and Law and Parliamentary Affairs almost immediately.

Their third contact was Zerina Rashid, a volunteer social worker at the time involved in assisting disadvantaged women in Bangladesh. She had been recommended to the team by the high commissioner of Bangladesh in Ottawa. Apart from being a dedicated social worker, Zerina was also the sister-in-law of the high commissioner. When the team met Zerina in Dhaka, she immediately introduced the team to her husband, Abdur Rashid, who had retired as secretary of

Communications, government of Pakistan, only two years ago (1970). Initially, the team stayed at Hotel Intercontinental (now *Rupashi Bangla*). However, with the help of the Rashids, they found two rooms at Hotel Purabani for the rest of their stay in Dhaka. Known to a close coterie of friends in high places, the Rashids were indispensable in helping the team.

Zerina explained the team exactly *when, where,* and *how* to draw the line in their interactions with Bangladeshi authorities. She gave them a good idea about the types of officials the team would be dealing with – a mix of overenthusiastic, cynical, vulgar, and apathetic bureaucrats. After giving them a roster of local experts for the team to meet with, she also counseled them – how to meet the formidable but not insurmountable challenge of interpreting and reacting to Bangladeshi cultural norms. She cautioned the Canadian team to notice and respect how people in Bangladesh interact with each other (which can be quite confusing for non-Bangladeshis). This was particularly important because of the sensitive nature of foreign adoptions at that time. They were counseled not to try to ride roughshod over officials.

The team recognized that the Rashids were not only close to the corridors of power but also well informed on issues surrounding adoption of the war babies. Being utterly frank and candid with the team, Zerina told them that they might also have to do some unexpected things while negotiating with government officials. The explicit message in her cautionary admonition was that if the team members upset any of the bureaucrats, then they would risk the success of their entire mission. The Rashids also gave the team a behind-the-scene briefing as to where the Mujib administration was going with its economic plan, its mission and vision.

The team's game plan was as follows. First, having done some arm-twisting and hand-wringing, they would finalize the negotiations with the government of Bangladesh for the transfer of a number of war babies to Canadian parents. Then they would locate, identify, and pick out the war babies that were available for adoption from the designated Dhaka-based orphanages. Both tasks required persuading government officials and orphanage authorities in Dhaka to assist the team. The Rashids reviewed the team's game plan to ensure that the team was not barking up the wrong tree while meeting the top mandarins.

The team assigned Dr. Robert Ferrie (a medical doctor) to obtain permission of the Department of Manpower and Immigration to conduct the medical examinations of the infants. His wife, Helke, was made responsible for liaising with the Immigration authorities and the New Delhi-based Canadian High Commission personnel in India. Fred and Bonnie Cappuccino were responsible for communication with political leaders, social workers, senior bureaucrats, and the ISS and orphanage personnel in Dhaka; while Elisabeth Mowling was like a free agent to assist the Cappuccinos on anything that needed to be done. In the evenings, the team would meet together to do a reality check, debrief, and strategize accordingly.

The two most powerful members of the Mujib administration with whom the team also met in Dhaka were Dr. Kamal Hussain, then minister of Law and Parliamentary Affairs, and Abdur Rab Chaudhury, then coordinator of Relief and Rehabilitation, Prime Minister's Secretariat. Both men welcomed the team with open arms and great enthusiasm. Momin, the Bangladeshi high commissioner in Canada, had earlier written to Chowdhury to meet the team upon its arrival in Dhaka. Both Hussain and Chowdhury intimated that Mujib himself believed that the war babies should be seen as a matter of national concern. However, war babies were neither his *only* nor his *most* important concern at that time.

The team was impressed with the politeness, generosity, and sophistication of both Hussain and Chaudhury. During the next few days, they met many other prominent members of the Bangladeshi society. To their utmost relief, they noted that their mission was viewed in a positive light. Chowdhury, along with other senior officials, was impressed with the team members seeing how well versed they were in matters of international adoption and the compassionate approach that they took to the entire project. Again, Chaudhury was also impressed with the team's *can-do attitude* and the way in which Fred was so forthright in presenting his strict timeframes and tight travel plans.

The team was glad to see that the Mujib administration gave the issue of the international adoption of the war babies its full backing. However, there remained a quagmire of due process. Given the newly formed government, officials were uncertain about which ministries were responsible for which tasks. They could not figure out whether the release and adoption of the war babies fell within the purview of the Ministry of Relief and Rehabilitation or the Ministry of Labor and Social Welfare or the Ministry of Law and Parliamentary Affairs.

As the days passed, the team (and their well-wishers) felt that the government was dragging its feet. However, Chaudhury pointed out to them that in actual fact, they were making very tangible progress. Most significantly, they would be enacting a new law to ensure "the best interest of the children." It is only through the cooperation and mutual understanding of social workers, adoption agency personnel, doctors, lawyers, and government officials of Canada and Bangladesh that the task at hand would come to fruition, reminded Chaudhury. The government held the view that it could not rush through the process without proper consultation with its own legal services, the ISS, and the orphanage personnel it had designated earlier as the statutory guardian to work with foreign adoption agencies.

The government also needed to ensure that due process has been followed within established legal rules and that all local and international requirements be met before the babies would be transferred to the adoptive couples. It did not wish to exercise plenary authority in its decision to allow foreign adoption. In particular, it wanted work within the ISS guidelines and ensure that all ISS requirements were fulfilled. In a sense, there was an irony in taking such a position to ensure the safety of the war babies. It is in that many were fearful that the babies might not survive to go through the "due process." Chaudhury appealed to the team to stay calm and implored them, "Please don't leave without taking the children."[90] The team's brief interaction with some of the key people in the Mujib Cabinet and their supportive gestures gave them some hope. They recognized that both Chaudhury and the entire Mujib cabinet genuinely wanted to bring about a true and positive change for the newly born country.

Feeling hopeful, the team met with Marie Levine of the ISS. Unfortunately, their discussion with Levine and the ISS had an undertone of hostility and resentment. They asked how long she thought "it would take for [Levine] to organize things so that the babies would actually leave for adoptive homes abroad."[91] The team members did not like what they heard from Levine: "It will be months."[92] Levine did not disguise her feelings. She had a litany of complaints. To her, the government was procrastinating. It was nowhere close to having the proposed draft paperwork ready. The ISS was still engaged in an initial exploratory research to provide a framework before it could make recommendations about the international adoptions. Levine did not just stop at that. She did not even "have a copy-machine which would take months to arrive from the State,"[93] thus continued Levine. Her response caught the team off guard. The Cappuccinos feared that perhaps their visit to Dhaka was premature. Though government officials had tried to convey a feeling of implicit reassurance, the team recognized that it was unlikely that an acceptable and an all-inclusive legislation on adoption could be drafted within such a short time.

The team became a bit apprehensive upon realizing that neither the government nor the ISS would likely be able to fulfill the team's short-term needs in the legal immigration and adoption of the war babies. As far as the Cappuccinos were concerned, the adoptive parents had waited long enough having already invested much too emotion, time, and money. Most importantly, the delays would put the war babies at risk of nothing less than death. The sooner the war babies were released, the better it would be for all. They decided that they would simply go ahead – try to find and choose the babies for adoption. They prayed that the government would let the team return to Canada with the babies of *their choice* for adoption. The team did not let the ISS personnel with their blunt manners and lack of cooperation deter them.

Meanwhile, the Ministry of Law and Parliamentary Affairs, which was mandated to lead the file to craft the proposed legislation on adoption, was engaged in a comprehensive consultation with experts from the ISS, Terre des Hommes (TDH), *Gono Unnayan Prochesta* (a joint effort with Quaker Peace Service [QPS], an arm of the international Quaker movement, Quaker Service of Bangladesh [QSB],) Christian Organization for Relief and Rehabilitation (CORR), and other grassroots organizations dealing with social welfare and community development. The Bangladesh Quaker Service (BQS)[94] had also worked closely with both the orphanage staff at the Missionaries of Charity and government officials to lobby the release of the babies.

On a daily basis, the team would first meet high government officials during mornings, generally chaperoned by Zerina who would then also take them to various orphanages in Dhaka. The superior of the home, as well as the statutory guardian, Sr. Margaret Mary, personally welcomed the team. She offered to assist them after meticulously explaining her position vis-à-vis the "process" – from the availability of the war babies to the transfer of guardianship through the to-be-proclaimed legislation.

They were impressed with Sr. Margaret Mary especially for her deep understanding of the complexity of intercountry adoption in which she had been involved in India since 1965. However, they were deeply moved by the challenges of trying to care for an overwhelming number of newborns, the majority of whom were grossly underweight, in the war-ravaged Bangladesh with too few supplies and too little medicine. The harsh reality on the ground was that resources were never enough to meet the ongoing needs of the people.

One of the first observations of the team was that the infants' rooms, where the babies slept, were overcrowded with cribs and boxes (storage of sundry items) and piles of toys. The majority of furniture consisted of old beds, cribs, and coarse floor mats made of date leaves or palm leaves. As well, in most cases, the same dishes were reused at meal time for all children. The babies lay in the cribs most of the time, wet and crying where the smell of feces made no difference. They always had the time to hold the babies – something that is so vital to the lives and development of babies. Though humbled by the devotion of the staff on duty, volunteers in the orphanages and *Seva Sadan* (premises designed to serve the rape victims who needed care for having abortion or having the delivery of their babies) spent enormous amount of time in doing their bit.

The team members would have never believed the reality of the situation had they not been in the orphanages. They were impressed to see how the *ayas* (midwives and/or nurse maids), attendant nurses, and doctors were not just working perfunctorily but also working with a dedication and commitment that went above and beyond the call of duty. Although the smell of feces and stale urine permeated the surroundings, there was no shortage of love for the infants on the part of the *ayas* and staffers who worked without complaint and remained busy in giving medication and shots.

With the help of the Rashids, the team was able to hand-walk the files every day from one desk to the next. They continued on day after day with an unrelenting pressure. Beyond expectation, having plugged away for weeks, the news came to them that the exit papers were ready and that the team could leave as scheduled with a number of war babies *only* if they were found medically fit. Grabbing the release letter that was hand-delivered to the Cappuccinos, Fred immediately reconnected with Sandra Simpson back in Montreal.

Requirements of the government of Bangladesh

The first legal requirement of the government was to have the *Bangladesh Abandoned Children (Special Provision) Order 1972* proclaimed in order to enable the transfer of guardianship leading to adoption (see chapter 2). The actual proclamation, however, did not come until October 1972. But due to the extraordinary circumstances, the government was willing to allow the request of the Canadian team, under the aegis of the draft proclamation, to release fifteen war babies selected to be adopted in Canada. The government's immediate response may be seen as an instance of its flexibility and reasonable accommodation for the war babies who, it believed, deserved *safe homes,* first and foremost.

The next important legal requirement was an approval letter based on the home study done on the suitability of the prospective adoptive parents in Canada. The letter, generally sent by a local Children's Aid Society (CAS) office, constitutes the first requirement in a legal adoption. It is variously referred to as a *No Objection Certificate, Letter of Approval, Okay Paper,* etc., that must clearly state whether the applicant has been found eligible/suitable for adoption. It was imperative for officials in Dhaka to review this particular document to *verify* full and complete facts about the applicants or to-be-adoptive parents in Canada. Further, officials needed to review the Canadian home study reports to determine that no information was withheld to increase the likelihood of adoption.

One of the challenges was to ensure that adopted babies in Canada would form a *secure* and *trusting* relationship between the child and the parent who had applied for adoption. As part of the requirement while reviewing the home study report, officials were required to look for information that stated whether the couples were well-functioning happy/stable couples who must be able to provide the child with emotional and physical security as well as with acceptance and demonstrated love. Since there were no ways to go for a trial placement for a limited period, the government had to be doubly sure to determine the eligibility and qualifications of the prospective adoptive parents based on the reports from Canada. In the absence of any direct contact with them or socials workers in Canada, officials in Dhaka also had to ensure that they had not simply jumped on a band wagon or they were not caught in the emotion of the moment.

Officials had to be satisfied that the applicants *did* indeed have the noted qualifications. Bangladeshi officials had to take their time to be convinced that they had no further question or any doubt whatsoever about the information on the applicants whose profiles were only outlined (and not deeply explored in the studies). In their insistence on examination of necessary papers, Bangladeshi officials were clear that they would not only review the provincial approval letters but also all other accompanying documentation, such as reference letters, letters of approval, profiles of the adoptive parents, medical examination reports of the infants, etc., even though the team was pressed for time. Officials worked on the premise that without proper examination of documentations, they would be unable to ensure that the child in question would indeed be *wanted* and *legally adopted* when the child arrived in Canada.

A document titled *International Adoptions – Some Essential Principles* was a key booklet that the provincial governments and government agencies had adhered to throughout the selection process in the first and successive waves of foreign adoptions from Bangladesh of the adoptive parent. The document outlined how exactly both countries were involved and how the various levels of their governments would seek assurances. Time and again, both Canada and Bangladesh had made reference to the following: "Both countries must be accepting of the standards recognized by one another in the gathering and evaluation of the data required and in the means of channeling it between countries. Each should reserve the right to withdraw from such arrangements if they are not compatible with their own child welfare standards."[95]

Selection of adoptive parents

As statutory guardian of the war babies, Sr. Margaret Mary was assigned to assess the applicants. Fortunately, her personal reputation was such that health professionals and representatives from various international organizations with which she had worked did not see her only as an agent of the state but also a compassionate woman of action who was known for her commitment to the idea that every child deserves a home. She appreciated the difference between *helping* a child and *rescuing* a child who was, by and large, not "wanted" in the child's birth country. Prior to the selection of the adoptive parents, Sr. Margaret Mary had already met the Cappuccinos, the Ferries, and Elisabeth Mowling, who, in addition to being the team members, were also prospective adoptive parents under consideration.

To complete the work of adoption, three things had to happen. Sister Mary needed to determine (1) that the war babies in question were adoptable, (2) that adoption outside of Bangladesh was "in the best interest of the war babies," and (3) that respective provincial governments in Canada had deemed the racially different applicants both eligible and suitable to adopt a Bangladeshi war baby. Put it in another way, she was responsible to assess the documentary evidence from the Canadian provincial child welfare authorities and verify the information to the effect that the province concerned had *no objection* to the proposed adoption. As well, she was required to ensure that all provincial laws and regulations governing adoption had been met.

The process of selection was very much unlike the systematic process that is strictly followed by social workers in Canada to match a particular child with adoptive parents. The Canadian process takes into consideration a host of available information beyond the documentation from home studies. Sr. Margaret Mary was primarily occupied in verifying the information on the proposed adoptive parents whom she thought would be the best match. She was aware that there was (and is) a fundamental principle and practice that children should be placed whenever possible with adoptive parents of the same racial backgrounds as themselves.

It may be an important point to note that although there was a fairly large number of Canadians of Pakistani and Bangladeshi origin, not a single family of Pakistani or Bangladeshi origin in Canada had applied for adoption of these war babies. Therefore, from the outset, given the combination of circumstances, Sr. Margaret Mary did not take into consideration factors such as physical resemblance to the child; level of intelligence and intellectual potentiality; cultural, educational, religious, racial, and nationality background; temperamental needs; geographical separation from natural parents; and other physical characteristics of the child's family. Instead, she was primarily involved in reviewing whether the files of the prospective parents appeared sufficient and accurate.

She reflected a great deal just to ensure that she was not opening the gateway to adoption or putting the war babies in the market place for mass adoption or for that matter placing a war baby in any available crib. Recognizing that this was in response to the *felt* necessities of the time, she spent some time scrutinizing by seeking a distinction between altruistically "rescuing" a child and selfishly "having" a child. Deep down, she knew that not even the most experienced social worker could expect to make infallible judgment in selection of parents and babies in the face of the uncertainties of human nature and the complexities of the relationships involved due to racial differences.

Sr. Margaret Mary spent considerable time with the Cappuccinos to make sure that there were no misunderstandings in the legal responsibilities of the adoptive parents. In assessing the Canadian couples' capacity for parenting, she kept in mind things like how long the couple had been married, how they earned their living and the kind of child they envisioned adopting from Bangladesh. She revisited the files again and again to see whether she had sufficient evidence of psychological stability, a stable marital relationship (no longer mandatory nowadays), and economic stability. She was made aware by the team that the FFC had earlier advised the prospective adoptive parents of the poor physical conditions of the infants. She was glad to hear that such forewarnings had been made. It was an important reality that would help the couples prepares themselves for the adoptions.

Again, Sr. Margaret Mary also felt that the *needs of the child* and *the needs of the adoptive parents* should be weighed in order to assure as much as it was humanly possible that the family unit in Canada could evolve and adapt with the adoption. To her, this assessment was unlike any of the other adoptions that she had dealt with in the past. It was a unique and difficult challenge that she faced: how could she determine the quality of the prospective adoptive parents who were thousands of kilometers away in Canada, were ostensibly unreachable in the short term for in-depth assessment, and were awaiting the news that they had been selected? The daily evening visits of the Canadian team members and their ongoing "dialogue" with Sr. Margaret Mary had helped her greatly in gaining insight into the objective of the FFC and the adoptive parents.

Throughout the review period, Sr. Margaret Mary asked herself: how careful could she be in taking a rational approach in understanding the internal family dynamics of the applicants some of whom had already adopted across racial boundaries? How much does she know about the interaction and relationships between the adopted child and members of their family? How enlightened would they be in ignoring the stigma of illegitimacy? In fact, she had asked these questions many times all throughout while reviewing the dossiers. She went over and over again through the files in an attempt to determine whether the prospective adoptive parents had made a thoughtful and informed final decision.

She asked herself if it was in the "best interest of the babies" to be raised in *Shishu Bhavan* or to be brought up in a foreign family with no other motive but to give them a *chance to live.* She also believed that the government was responsible to "safeguard the child" against what is often referred to as baby trafficking. Seeing the passions with which the Canadian team was approaching the matter and having read the profiles of the other applicants in Canada, Sr. Margaret Mary was satisfied that the applicants' intentions were pure, their homes in Canada prepared, and emotionally, they had accepted the war babies as one of their *own.* Following a detailed examination of all pertinent papers, Sr. Margaret Mary selected fourteen couples.

Selection of the war babies

By the time Sister Mary had completed her assessments of the parents' dossiers, the team had spent almost three weeks in Dhaka. In the meantime, many infants who were born prematurely did not survive for long. Having been in the premises, the team witnessed how the sisters in *Shishu Bhavan* and *Seva Sadan* would attempt to save the newborns.

In selecting the war babies, the FFC team did not use the usual practice – where prospective parents decide on the individual child after learning the child's background history. The Cappuccinos simply chose the children they thought would survive the journey and were best matched with each couple. Having been in the field of adoption, the Cappuccinos had considerable experience in assessing the war babies. Sr. Margaret Mary left the choice of war babies largely in the hands of the team. The FFC team visited many orphanages and *Seva Sadan* in Dhaka to compare the health conditions of the war babies. In a way, the team's visits to various orphanages and meetings with orphanage authorities might be described as, to use the Canadian vocabulary, "preplacement meetings" generally arranged in order to allow representatives from both sides of the adoption to get acquainted with each other. Once the selection was made, Margaret Mary reassessed the suitability of the proposed parents.

She found herself in a conflicted situation and under tremendous pressure to move forward. The ISS had recommended that the Bangladeshi orphanage authorities "ship out" the "unwanted" newborns as fast as possible. She appreciated the lasting benefits in the early mothering of infants, which establishes a deep connection between parents and child. This meant for her early placement of the war babies. However, she vowed to herself to keep the babies for as long as necessary to ensure that the parties selected were deemed the most "ideal" parents. This was a precarious position because the newborns were dying within weeks of birth.

Moreover, institutionalization of orphans, especially the length of time a child is kept, can greatly affect the physical, emotional, and psychological development of children. In other words, such child often becomes much less desirable for adoption. In retrospect, it becomes clear that Sr. Margaret Mary was really assessing whether the adoptive parents were committed to raising the children. She believed that "a living family is better than even the very best institution."[96] The Cappuccinos chose fifteen war babies for fourteen couples, one for each couple with the exception of Robert and Helke Ferrie who picked out two war babies for adoption.

Having done the final selection of the adoptive parents and matched their babies with their parents for each other, an emotional Sr. Margaret Mary informed the team that though undernourished and underweight, these babies could be made available for foreign adoption per the government's commitment and the requirements that had been set out by the Canadian and Bangladeshi authorities. The team was very happy with Sr. Margaret Mary, who demonstrated a rare type of compassion that no one around could match, recalls Fred.

Mandatory medical examination of the war babies

The Canadian federal Department of Manpower and Immigration officials were flexible in their approach to the medical examination given the stringent requirements that it usually entails. We have noted already how, earlier, Mackasey, minister of Manpower and Immigration, had assured them of his full support. However, the FFC team feared delays because Canada had not yet established a presence in Bangladesh. All matters pertaining to Bangladesh were handled by Canada's embassy in Bangkok, Thailand. Moreover, even though the Canadian government was aware of the poor physical condition of the babies, having seen the infants in undernourished conditions, the team had serious reservations regarding the outcome of the medical examination fearing that the underweight infants would perhaps not get a clean bill of health.

Back in Canada, many people joined in lobbying all levels of government to expedite the process. Immigration Canada suggested that the infants be medically examined right in the orphanage premises so that they would not have to be sent away to Hong Kong or Kuala Lumpur or even India. To speed up the process, the director of Operations, Foreign Services, bent over backward in assessing "how these children could be processed for immigration with the least possible administrative delay." The Cappuccinos were relieved to hear directly from the ministry: "Due to the problem you would encounter in taking these small children to Hong Kong, and your statement that you would have no particular difficulty in taking them to Delhi, it has been decided, on humanitarian ground, to have this group dealt with by Delhi." They were informed that the minister's officials would offer their "utmost cooperation" in the matter, which was a great relief to the Cappuccinos.

Regardless of where the test is conducted, the team's fear was that the test itself was critical and cumbersome, since it could either qualify or disqualify an infant with regard to its entry into Canada. Apparently, earlier, Lincoln Alexander, then a conservative Member of Parliament (MP) for Hamilton West, had made inquiries on behalf of a group of prospective adoptive parents of Ontario. Mackasey advised him in the following: "We have taken measures designed to simplify the normal immigration examination of the children. Medical assessment of the children will be done through the New Delhi office, or if it is more convenient to the organizers, through Kuala Lumpur . . . It is hoped that this will eliminate the need for any of the children to be taken personally to New Delhi or to Kuala Lumpur for examination . . . Additionally, assuming that the Bangladesh Government has no objection to Dr. Ferrie carrying out medical examinations, the Immigration Medical Service will accept the results of his examination for consideration."[97] The team also felt greatly relieved upon learning that Dr. Robert Ferrie, a fellow of the Royal College of Surgeons and a qualified surgeon at Joseph Brant Memorial Hospital in Burlington, Ontario, one of the team members, would be allowed to conduct the official examination for the war babies.

Dr. Ferrie was advised that after completing medical examinations, he should present medical reports, x-rays, or tuberculin tests to the medical officer in New Delhi for review and assessment. He was also informed that as soon as the medical requirements would be met and the IMM 1009 form (main application form for sponsorship) received from Canada, visas would be issued subject to the approval and issuance of passport by Bangladesh authorities.

Dr. Ferrie immediately accepted the offer and prepared for the medical examinations of the infants in the orphanage premises, which he described as a tiny building on a cramped, cluttered street in downtown Dhaka. He established contact with Dr. Leclerc, a temporary medical officer from the Department of National Health and Welfare then attached to the Canadian High Commission in New Delhi. Dr. Ferrie examined fifteen infants at *Shishu Bhavan* and prepared a separate report for each child. Because Dr. Ferrie had no knowledge of prenatal events or birth experience, he prepared the reports with scant information. All medical reports were immediately sent to the authorized National Health and Welfare personnel in New Delhi.

Under normal circumstances, the initial medical examination would have been considered as only part of the *prescreening* process to ensure that the infants could be taken to New Delhi for further examination with a reasonable chance of meeting normal medical requirements. However, given the urgency of the situation, another exception was made by the Canadian federal government in exempting the second round of medical tests. Immigration officials accepted Dr. Ferrie's professional assessment of the war babies as final. The medical report of Dr. Ferrie was accepted without any comment, however, with a caveat that the test results would remain valid for six months and that the babies would have to be taken to Canada within that period.

Issuance of travel permit

With the medical examinations completed, the team next had to obtain passports and travel papers for all fifteen infants. The Bangladesh government, having obtained the names of the adoptive parents selected by Sr. Margaret Mary and positive medical reports for the fifteen war babies, needed to make a decision on whether to allow the war babies to leave for Canada. Guided by the principle that it would be in the "best interest" of the war babies, the government issued release papers for all fifteen war babies under the auspice of the Special Provision Order, which would not be passed until some months later. The goal was to have the FFC team and infants leave discreetly so as to avoid publicity and possible unrest due to the exceptional circumstances. The risk was real because the country had just recently come out of a bitter civil war and became an independent country but had still not come anywhere close to terms with issues like the war babies.

The travel permit for the war babies came directly from the Ministry of Labor and Social Welfare on July 17, 1972, in the form of a letter. To prepare the travel permit, the government needed to assign a name to each selected abandoned child and then to register the name of the baby to produce a "birth certificate" for each child issued by the orphanage authority. In general, upon birth at *Shishu Bhavan,* the sisters named the newborns because the birth mothers would leave quickly in secret, taking no interest in the babies.

Again, as mentioned in chapter 1, when the abandoned newborns were brought to the orphanages by relatives, acquaintances, or neighbors saying that either the mother had died or given up the baby, the orphanage authority used to give the baby a name and register its existence on its *Register Book.* The orphanage authority would then issue a birth certificate without the name of the birth mother and alleged father. This would "prove" the child's existence, give the child a legal identity, and establish the child's orphan status and the child's eligibility for adoption.

The approval letter signed by M. Sharafatullah, then deputy secretary, Ministry of Labor and Social Welfare, government of

Bangladesh, is a meticulous document that restates the position of the government of Bangladesh in the letter itself. Approval for release of all fifteen war babies was given on a single legal-size (8 1/2 by 14 inches) sheet of paper. The letter contained the names of the babies, their date of birth, gender, and the names and addresses of the proposed adoptive parents in Canada.[98] Although this document was not a passport, it was variously referred to as *group passport, travel document, travel permit, release paper/order, exit permit,* etc. This was the *only* document for the war babies to travel out of Bangladesh. The government issued the letter to expedite the departure of the war babies believing that it would be faster to issue than a formal passport or any other travel permit for individual war babies.

As statutory guardian of the abandoned war babies of Bangladesh, the deputy secretary again reminded Mother Teresa, from whose *Home* these children were allowed to be taken away, in the following manner: that permission had been given to take these children "to Canada for adoption under Canadian Law with full rights of Canadian citizenship in due course and with no liability in regard to the children in the future to the Government of the People's Republic of Bangladesh."[99] Again, the responsibility of the provincial governments of Canada to follow up on individual cases of adoption in the respective provinces was also reiterated. It was reminded that the release orders were granted in the hope that postplacement services provided by each province would help the families in the adoption of the Bangladeshi infants.

The key point emphasized here was that under no circumstances would the government of the People's Republic of Bangladesh have any liability with regard to the war babies in the future. In that sense, the Ministries of Labor and Social Welfare and Law and Parliamentary Affairs had the responsibility to ensure that the *legal commitment* of the adoptive parents remained paramount even under the changed circumstances. Sharafatullah further advised Mother Teresa that all fifteen war babies were being allowed to leave for Canada under the guidance of Fred and Bonnie Cappuccino along with three team members – Robert and Helke Ferrie, and Elisabeth Mowling. If evidence can be described as "the surviving deposit of an historical event," as discussed by G. R. Elton,[100] this travel document (or the *release paper/ group passport* as often referred to*)* with names of the infants remains as prime facie evidence of the birth, abandonment, and subsequent adoption of fifteen war babies in Canada in 1972 that immediately became an important part of Bangladesh's historical narrative.

Fred Cappuccino made fifteen photocopies of the same document and attached fifteen photos of the infant passengers, one on each sheet, in order to make fifteen separate distinguishable travel permit (i.e., one for each child). He also prepared name tags for each child and organized the medical records and identification data. The team recognized that Bangladeshi officials took more time than they expected but were engaged in the work and remained committed throughout to help them achieve their task. An overjoyed Fred considered this to be "an extraordinary instance of human beings taking precedence over paper work."[101] With travel permit in hand, amid tears of joy, relief, and gratitude, the last item on the list for the team members was to get their hands on the copies of the medical reports of the infants and fly back to Canada ASAP.

Final departure from Bangladesh

As soon as the final release paper was received by the team, just two days before their scheduled departure, Fred contacted Indian Airlines to confirm their flight arrangements and ensure that the airline would be prepared for transporting the fifteen war babies. Since almost all selected war babies were born prematurely, the team members worried that many of them might not be able to make the overseas trip. While negotiating the airfare and services, they asked *how to make the trip less exhausting for the weak and underweight babies.*

Next, they contacted the US consul in Dhaka and the Canadian High Commission in New Delhi. The High Commission officials in both Dhaka and New Delhi worked closely to ensure that all formalities were met, paperwork filed (by the governments of Bangladesh and Canada and the respective provincial governments of Canada), and adoptive parents were contacted to inform them of team's plan for the return journey to Canada.

The New Delhi office of the Canadian High Commission then sent a telex to Sandra Simpson, the main contact of FFC in Montreal, to coordinate the team's return back home. Throughout the mission, Sandra had kept the would-be parents informed with the latest developments of the team on a daily basis. An excited Sandra immediately informed all prospective adoptive parents within hours that the team would return to Canada with fifteen war babies on July 20, 1972.

The same office also informed Ottawa of the details of *how* the baby passengers would arrive in Canada. En route the war babies would be escorted by volunteers from Air Canada and that National Health and Welfare's medical officers would be on board to provide medical assistance if required. As well, National Health and Welfare's staff who were designated to act as emergency nurses for the babies upon landing would be at each airport to assist the team. The team would be split into two groups in New York. One would head for Toronto and the other for Montreal. The details of the historic journey of the war babies are retold in the next chapter.

Notes and References

[1] Though the Families For Children (FFC) was officially founded in 1971, its history goes back to the late 1960s. It started with three Montreal couples, Lloyd and Sandra Simpson, Fred and Bonnie Cappuccino, and Herb and Naomi Bronstein, who became very concerned about the deteriorating situation in Vietnam and wanted to do their best in whatever way they could to alleviate the situation. By contacting the Phu My Orphanage in Saigon (now Ho Chi Minh City) in the late 1960s, these courageously determined couples had arranged to adopt Vietnamese children in their own homes.

Due to positive media coverage of the stories of adoption of needy children, the Montreal couples started to receive phone call from Canadians across the country expressing their desire to do likewise. Being encouraged by unusual demands for adoption of mixed-race children from overseas, the three couples thus responded to the demands of the Canadians by forming the said FFC.

[2] The *Toronto Star,* October 29, 1968.

[3] *Ibid.*

[4] The Minutes of the Eighteenth Combined Appeal for Pakistani Relief, May 25, 1972, p. 2 Library and Archives Canada, MG 28 1 270, Vol. 18, *File:* CAPR.

[5] *Ibid.* p. 2. It is interesting to note here that of the fourteen Canadian couples who adopted fifteen war babies from Bangladesh, there is one couple, both of whom were employees of the Canadian

International Development Agency (CIDA), who had worked closely with the Canadian NGOs and had been aware of the tragic situation in Bangladesh to a greater extent. They are Roberto Ribeiro and Margo-Carr Ribeiro. For details, see chapter 5.

6   Families For Children, *Bangladesh Project*. Part E, Chapter 32, *Bangladesh Babies*, 1982, p. 255. Hereinafter, referred to as, *Bangladesh Project*. A large bulk of documents in the form of correspondence is still with Fred and Bonnie Cappuccino in their personal home library collection on *Bangladesh File*.

7   *Ibid.*, p. 255.

8   *Ibid.*, p. 262, Fred and Bonnie Cappuccino also repeated the same to the author on several occasions during their ongoing discussion between 1999 and 2005 on their project initiative.

9   Letter from Bonnie Cappuccino, President, Families For Children, addressed to all members as "Dear Friends," June 25, 1972.

10   Families For Children. *Newsletter.* Vol.11, No.1, May 15, 1972.

11   Letter from Bonnie Cappuccino, President, Families For Children, addressed to all members as "Dear Friends," May 16, 1972.

12   Bonnie Cappuccino said this in an interview with Jane Finlayson of the *Citizen,* January 22, 1973.

13   Letter from Bonnie Cappuccino, President, Families For Children, addressed to all members as "Dear Friends," April 13, 1972.

14   *Bangladesh Project,* pp. 264–265.

15   Letter from Bonnie Cappuccino, President, Families For Children, addressed to all members as "Dear Friends," May 16, 1972.

16   *Ibid.*

17   Letter from Bonnie Cappuccino, President, Families For Children, to Mitchell Sharp, Minister of External Affairs, March 24, 1972. This document is retained in the Department of External Affairs' Archives, No. 38-11-11 *Bangla,* 001786.

18   Letter from Bonnie Cappuccino, President, Families For Children, addressed to all members as "Dear Friends, May 16, 1972.

19   Letter from His Excellency Abdul Momin, high commissioner to Canada, to Fred Cappuccino, secretary, Families For Children, June 7, 1972.

20   Families For Children. *Newsletter.* Vol.11, No.1, May 15, 1972.

21   Letter from Bonnie Cappuccino, president, Families For Children, addressed to all members as "Dear Friends," April 13, 1972.

22 Families For Children. *Newsletter.* Vol.11, No.1, May 15, 1972.
23 *Ibid.*
24 *Bangladesh Project.* 1972, p. 262.
25 *Ibid.,* p. 263.
26 *Ibid.,* p. 258.
27 *Ibid.*
28 *Ibid.*
29 Canadian Council on Social Development, *Press Release,* from Reuben C. Baetz, Executive Director, May 27, 1972, p. 2. Library and Archives Canada. RG 76, Vol. 1040, *File* 5020-1-710, Pt. 1.
30 *Ibid.,* p. 1.
31 *Ibid.*
32 Letter from Betty Graham, Director of Child Welfare to Mr. and Mrs. Dale and Doreen Good, May 31, 1972. Archives of Ontario, RG 29-59, Acc 15296/2 TR78-075, Box 6, *File: Bangladesh Infants* 1972–1973.
33 *Ibid.*
34 Telegram from Betty Graham, Director of Child Welfare, Ministry of Community and Social Services, Government of Ontario to Mr. and Mrs. Dale Good; the telegram is dated June 19, 1972.
35 Letter from René Brunelle, Minister of Community and Social Services, Government of Ontario, to Mitchell Sharp, Secretary of State for External Affairs, May 15, 1972. Library and Archives Canada, RG 76, Vol. 1040, Box 141 *File* 5020-1-710, Pt. 1.
36 Letter from Mitchell Sharp, Secretary of State for External Affairs to Mr. Dale and Doreen Good, June 23, 1972. Library and Archives Canada, RG 76, Vol. 1040, Box 141, *File* 5020-1-710, Pt. 1.
37 Letter from Betty Graham, Director of Child Welfare, to Mr. and Mrs. Dale and Doreen Good, July 4, 1972. Archives of Ontario, RG 29-59, Acc 15296/2 TR78-075, Box 6, *File: Bangladesh Infants* 1972–1973.
38 Letter from Gordon McLellan, Executive Director, Children's Services Division, to J. E. Cardwell, Executive Director, Immigration and Appeals Section Division, July, 12, 1972, Library and Archives Canada. RG 76, Vol. Box 141, 1040, *Box 141 File* 5020-1-710, Pt. 1.
39 Letter from Henry Alan Lawless, Correspondence Secretary, Prime Minister's Office, to Fred Cappuccino, Secretary, Families For

Children, May 31, 1972. Library and Archives Canada, RG 26, Series 08, Vol. 275, *File* 2125, 1972.

[40] Letter from Bryce Mackasey, Minister of Manpower and Immigration to Mrs. Bonnie Cappuccino, President, Families For Children, April 20, 1972. Library and Archives Canada, RG 76, Vol. 1040, Box 141, *File* 5020-1-710, pt.1.

[41] *Ibid.*

[42] *Ibid.*

[43] *Ibid.*

[44] Letter from Bryce Mackasey, Minister of Manpower and Immigration, to Lincoln Alexander, Member of Parliament for Hamilton West, July 7, 1972. Library and Archives Canada, RG 76, Vol. 1040 Box 141, *File* 5020-1-710, pt.1. Evidently Alexander made an inquiry on behalf of Dr. Robert Ferrie and Helke Ferrie of Burlington, Ontario.

[45] *Ibid.*

[46] Memorandum to the Minister of External Affairs written by South Asia Division, Department of External Affairs, June 21, 1972. Library and Archives Canada, RG 76, Vol. 1040, *File* 5020-1-710, Pt. 1.

[47] Letter from Bonnie Cappuccino, President, Families For Children to René Brunelle, Minister of Community and Social Services, Government of Ontario. June 9, 1972. Archives of Ontario, RG 29-59, Minister's Correspondence, ACC 15296/2, TR 75-875-Box 6, *File: Bangladesh Infants* 1972–73.

[48] Letter from Bonnie Cappuccino, President, Families For Children to Sheikh Mujibur Rahman, Prime Minister, People's Republic of Bangladesh. June 12, 1972. This letter is now in the Cappuccinos' personal library collection on *Bangladesh File.*

[49] *Ibid.*

[50] Letter from Bonnie Cappuccino, President, Families For Children addressed to all members as "Dear Friends," June 7, 1972. This letter is now in the Cappuccinos' Library collection.

[51] Letter from Dr. Robin Morrall, to Sheikh Mujibur Rahman, Prime Minister of Bangladesh, May 13, 1972. The letter is in the form of TO WHOM IT MAY CONCERN sent as a package of information to Bonnie Cappuccino, president, Families For Children, who in turn had sent the entire package to the government of Bangladesh.

This letter is now in the Cappuccinos' personal library collection on *Bangladesh File*.

52 *Ibid.*

53 *Ibid.*

54 Letter from Elisabeth Mowling, Secretary, Families For Children, to Bonnie Cappuccino, President, Families For Children, April 20, 1972. This letter is now in the Cappuccinos' personal library collection on *Bangladesh File*.

55 E-mail from Tony Boonstra to Mustafa Chowdhury, April 20, 2012. The Boonstras had several meetings with the author since the 1990s. They are in regular touch with each other.

56 *Ibid.*

57 The Morrises said that in an interview with a reporter for the *Expositor*, June 20, 1972 [published in Brantford, Ontario].

58 An open letter from John and Dorothy Morris, addressed as "To Whom It May Concern" in which they outlined their grievances. They had given a copy of the letter to the author. They claim that they had hand-delivered the original letter to the Ontario minister of Community and Social Services and a photocopy of the letter to the Member of the Legislative Assembly of Ontario as well as the federal Member of Parliament for their constituency. This is in John and Dorothy Morris's personal collection on *Bangladesh File*.

59 *Ibid.*

60 *Ibid.*

61 *Ibid.*

62 Letter from John and Dorothy Morris to Betty Graham, Director of Child Welfare, Child Welfare Branch, Ministry of Community and Social Services, Government of Ontario, June 19, 1972. Archives of Ontario, RG 29-59, Acc. 15296/2 TR. 75-875, Box 6, *File: Bangladesh Infants* 1972–73.

63 *Ibid.*

64 *Ibid.*

65 Letter from Dale and Doreen Good, to Pierre Elliott Trudeau, Prime Minister of Canada, June 16, 1972, Library and Archives Canada, RG 76, Vol. 1040, Box 141, *File* 5020-1-710, pt. 1.

66 *Ibid.*

67 *Bangladesh Project*, p. 259.

68   As observed, fortunately, applicants from other provinces had no problems in approaching for the home studies. Indeed the Quebec's position was that the Cappuccinos had "worked very closely" with the Children's Service Centre of Montreal, and Quebec officials felt that the Cappuccinos had "enhanced" the work of the agency, which in turn had contributed to their "endeavours." This was in a letter from Elizabeth Bissett, head, Adoption Services, Children's Service Centre addressed as *To Whom It May Concern*. The letter is dated June 23, 1972. This letter is now in the Cappuccinos' personal library collection on *Bangladesh File*.

In fact, Elizabeth Bissett was very supportive of the *Bangladesh Project*. She made herself available for any kind of assistance that the FFC might be needed. In a letter of commendation, she stated that the families "proposing to adopt children from Bangladesh" were "all pioneer of this group themselves and in addition to adopting children who have demonstrated a great deal of sensitivity to the other families who" were "considering" the adoption of a child. She also indicated that the Cappuccinos, the Mowlings, and the Simpsons had "helped families over the initial adjustment period and "had been able to do this because of their own experience and very great capacity to parent children as well as assist children to become part of their own families at a later stage in their development" (*ibid.*).

69   Memorandum to René Brunelle, Minister, Community and Social Services, Government of Ontario, by Robert Kertsen, July 12, 1972. Archives of Ontario, RG 29-59, Minister's Correspondence. ACC 15296/2, TR 75-875-Box 6, *File: Bangladesh Infants* 1972–73.

70   *Bangladesh Project*, p. 276.

71   Letter from Helke Ferrie, chairperson of Asian Adoptions, Ontario Branch, Families For Children to Pierre Elliott Trudeau, Prime Minister of Canada, June 15, 1972. Library and Archives Canada, RG 76, Vol. 1040, Box 141, *File* 5020-1-710, Pt. 1.

72   *Ibid.*

73   Letter from Helke Ferrie, chairperson of Asian Adoptions, Ontario Branch, Families For Children, to Betty Graham, director of Child Welfare, Ministry of Community and Social Services, government of Ontario; the letter is dated 14, June, 1972, p. 2. Helke has given the author a copy of this letter. She maintains that a copy of this

letter was hand-delivered to Betty Graham's assistant. When Helke Ferrie went to the office, she was informed that Betty Graham was away in St. John's, Newfoundland, attending a meeting of the directors of Child Welfare. Upon Helke Ferrie's insistence, Graham's assistant phoned Graham and read the letter to her over the phone.

74 The *Globe and Mail,* June 20, 1972. Helke's hunger strike, however, was not supported by all the members of the FFC. In fact, the day Helke went on a hunger strike, FFC put out a press release signed by its Public Relations Department in which it stated that FFC would support Helke Ferrie's right as an individual to protest in any way she felt she must; nevertheless, Helke, at that time, did not speak for Families For Children, nor did Families For Children necessarily agree with all she said.

75 The *Globe and Mail,* June 20, 1972.

76 *Ibid.*

77 *Ibid.*

78 The *Spectator* [Hamilton, Ontario], June 19, 1972.

79 *Ibid.*

80 *Ibid.*

81 *Burlington Gazette,* Vol. 7, No 36, July 27, 1972.

82 The *Globe and Mail,* June 20, 1972.

83 The *Globe and Mail,* July 21, 1972.

84 *Ibid.*

85 Letter from Helke Ferrie, Chairperson of Asian Adoption, Ontario Branch, Families For Children to René Brunelle, Minister of Community and Social Services, June 22, 1972. Archives of Ontario RG 29-59, Minister's Correspondence, ACC 15296/2, TR 75-875-Box 6, *File:* Bangladesh Infants 1972–73.

86 Memorandum to: Presidents and Local Directors of Children's Aid Societies re: *Applications for the Admission to Canada of Foreign Born Children for Purposes of Adoption,* from Betty Graham, Director of Child Welfare, Ontario Ministry of Community and Social Services, July 5, 1972. Archives of Ontario. RG 29-59, Minister's Correspondence. ACC 15296/2, TR 75-875-Box 6, *File: Bangladesh Infants* 1972–73.

Copies of the particular sections of the federal *Immigration Regulations* were also sent. They contained the requirement of the regulations insofar as the provincial child welfare authority was concerned for the entry of children who have been adopted by the applicants, or who were to be adopted following admission to Canada.

[87] Letter from Helke Ferrie, Chairperson of Asian Adoption, Ontario Branch, Families For Children, to all six Ontario applicants for adoption, June 23, 1972. Helke has given a photocopy of the letter to the author. This and all other documents pertaining to Helke and Robert Ferries that I have used in the book are in their personal collection on *Bangladesh File.*

[88] *Ibid.*

[89] *Ibid.*

[90] *Bangladesh Project,* p. 273.

[91] *Ibid.,* p. 274.

[92] *Ibid.*

[93] *Ibid.*

[94] The Quakers' offer of their services as mediators before or during the conflicts is rooted in the Quaker belief that there is something of God in everybody, therefore, no one should be debased, exploited, or killed.

[95] Archives of Ontario, RG 29-59, ACC 15296/2, TR78-075-Box 6, *File: Bangladesh Infants* 1972–73.

[96] Families For Children, *Bangladesh Project Report,* August 2, 1972, p. 4.

[97] Letter from G. M. Mitchell, Acting Director of Operations, Foreign Services, to Fred Cappuccino, May 25, 1972. Library and Archives Canada, RG 76, Vol. 1040, Box 141, *File:* 5020-1-710, Pt. 1.

[98] Letter of Approval addressed to Mother Teresa by M. Sharafatullah, Deputy Secretary, Ministry of Labor & Social Welfare, People's Republic of Bangladesh; the letter is dated 17 July 1972. Library and Archives Canada, RG 76, Vol. 1040, Box 141, *File:* 5020-1-710, Pt. 1. Library and Archives Canada, RG 76, Vol. 1040, Box 141, *File:* 5020-1-710, Pt. 1.

[99] *Ibid.*

[100] Elton, G. R. *The Practice of History,* Fontana Press, London, 1990, p. 109.

[101] *Bangladesh Project,* p. 278.

CHAPTER FOUR

War Babies' Odyssey from Bangladesh to Canada

HAVING OVERCOME THE bureaucratic delays and red tape of the various levels of governments, finally the first contingent of fifteen war babies of Bangladesh left for Canada on July 19, 1972. Needless to mention, the impetus for this was the Bangladesh Project initiated by the Families For Children (FFC) was made possible mainly under the terms of a policy adopted by the Canadian government in 1960, which marked the World Refugee Year.[1] The story of the war babies' odyssey, when placed in historical perspective, may be seen as an informal small-scale save-the-children mission by a group of ordinary Canadians. Looking back, their arrival in Canada from halfway around the world is a slice of history in the making. It was the culmination of a year of hope and planning and tireless efforts of a group of dedicated Canadians. Viewed from that angle, the war babies' arrival in Canada, miraculously in good health, may be termed as both human salvage operation and journey to freedom. It is a matter of cause célèbre for all those who were involved in the initiative, including the staff of the Dhaka-based Canadian High Commission.

Behind-the-scene preparations at the governmental level

The federal government played an important role in order to facilitate the process. The two federal departments, the Manpower and Immigration, and External Affairs, were cognizant and supportive of the Bangladesh Project from its inception. They were kept posted ever since the Canadian team had left for Bangladesh at the end of June 1972. It coordinated and assumed overall responsibility for the administration of departure operation from Bangladesh, specifically the identification process, the release of the babies, the medical assistance on board, the volunteers and escorts, the records, the governmental communication, etc. Behind the scene, immigration officials in Ottawa and Canadian High Commissioners in New Delhi and Dhaka worked hard to ensure a smooth journey for the infants all the way from Dhaka to Toronto and Montreal via New Delhi and New York. Since the plane was scheduled to stop in New York, the team had to make sure that they get a helping hand there so that they could easily split into two groups to make "the New York transfer with a minimum of fuss"[2] while carrying all fifteen frail babies in precarious health conditions.

The federal government's interest was so deep that John Munro, then minister of Health and Welfare, had earlier expressed interest in looking into getting a plane that could provide for transporting the war babies from Bangladesh. Ottawa officials were aware of the poor health conditions of the prematurely born and severely undernourished and underweight infants. As soon as the team's arrival was firmed up, telexes were sent to both departments from the office of the Canadian High Commission in New Delhi. Officials in the two said ministries remained busy preparing briefing packages for their ministers with respect to *when* and *how* the team was to return to two different cities, Montreal and Toronto, under the supervision of two team leaders. "The first to arrive in Canada, the orphans are part of a group of 15, ranging in age from three weeks to eight months, who will arrive in separate groups, Thursday at Toronto and Montreal,"[3] thus was informed Mitchel Sharp, then minister of External Affairs.

In arranging the flight from Bangladesh to Canada, the first challenge was to conform to the North American air regulations that infants be escorted by sufficient number of adults. Since it was an expensive proposition to purchase tickets for the escorts/attendants, the FFC desperately looked for volunteers to assist them in their project to overcome the last hurdle. Apart from the five team members, there were offers from both Air India and Air Canada officials to assist the team. Some Air Canada staff came forward to volunteer their time and money to accompany the team from New York to Montreal and Toronto. The initial flight by Air India was from Dhaka to New Delhi portion. From there, upon completion of immigration matters, the team would fly to New York.

Special arrangements were thus made with Air India jumbo jet to carry the infant passengers from New Delhi to New York en route to

Canada (Toronto and Montreal). This included two air hostesses who looked after the infant passengers by rotation all through the flight from New Delhi to New York. It was a feat of logistics to coordinate the feeding of the babies on board. So that no one was to be caught by surprise at the sudden arrival of the war babies, Canadian officials in New Delhi and Dhaka coordinated all telex messages and facilitated the Canadian team in establishing their contact with all adoptive parents through Sandra Simpson of Montreal, Quebec, who was holding the fort while the team was away.

The last official telegram immediately prior to the Canadian team's departure outlined the entire travel plan, including *how many* infants were coming and how many *attendants* were escorting them, along with the flight information stating clearly the *when, how,* and *where* of their arrival in Toronto and Montreal. It was sent by the Immigration Office in the New Delhi High Commission informing Ottawa that all fifteen war babies would be leaving Bangladesh accompanied by Fred and Bonnie Cappuccino, Robert and Helke Ferries, and Elisabeth Mowling, all of whom had already picked out four out of the fifteen babies for themselves for adoption. It also contained information that in compliance with air regulations, babies would be accompanied by Air Canada volunteers who had flown from Dhaka and that a National Health and Welfare Canada medical officer would be on board and that nurses would be at airports to assist the passengers, if needed.

Though by nature brief, the telegram also described *how* the group from New York would split into two – one destined for Montreal (with seven war babies) and another for Toronto (with eight war babies). It was announced that Bryce Mackasey, then minister of Manpower and Immigration, would also be at the Mirabel Airport to receive and welcome the couples. In fact, based on this information, and knowing that there was an interest in seeing the arrival of the war babies, External Affairs immediately put out a press release for the news media before their actual arrival. However, even though Canadian officials in Dhaka took care of the travel plan, Fred, the representative of FFC in Dhaka, did not want to rely on the government's telegram only but wanted a more direct communication with his contact person. An overjoyed Fred immediately sent a personal telegram to Sandra with whom he was in constant touch. Just as the team's telegram, saying, "Mazel tov bringing 15 babies as scheduled July 19 hallelujah,"[4] reached an excited Sandra, she immediately started to spread the news among the adoption community in Canada.

This rare photo of 21 war-babies was taken during the second week of July 1972 at Mother Teresa's *Shishu Bhavan*, 26 Islampur Road, Dhaka Bangladesh. Out of 21 babies, 15 were allowed for adoption in Canadian homes. Six other prematurely-born frail babies were found medically unsuitable to sustain an overseas trip. Some had died within days.

Source: Missionaries of Charity gave each adoptive family a copy of this picture.

Departure from Dhaka

There was a dramatic moment at the orphanage as the babies were about to leave their caregivers. Sadness and excitement were mixed. It was a sad occasion because there were nuns and a few *dais* (midwife/milk nurse) also interchangeably referred to in Bengali as *ayas* (midwife/nurse maid) who were the ones who took care of the newborns from their birth. Naturally, they stood speechless with tears in their eyes gazed through the windows as the babies were brought out one after another who were about to be loaded onto two vans. It was also a scene of excitement because, just as the babies were brought out to the front yard of the premises to embark on the vans, the *ayas* and nuns kissed each and every infant with all of their love and tears of joy in their cheeks before turning away to the team members in frightful silence. "There were also tearful goodbye at the orphanage as the Sisters and their helpers bade farewell to the babies they had cared for so well,"[5] wrote Fred, describing their farewell or good-bye, which was a mixture of joy, tears, anticipation, and fear. All those who had warily watched and took care of the frail babies until then gathered once again to say good-bye for the last time before they were to be put onto the parked vans to be whisked away to the airport.

As soon as the vans drove off the premises, they began to inch their way through the dense Dhaka traffic, slowly heading to the airport. Soon the team members began to worry about the lack of access to the supply of boiled water for the babies while inside the van. They were worried that the babies could become dehydrated in the oppressive heat of the van. To make the matter worse, there was an incredible traffic jam on their way to the airport. Fred recalls, having been inside the van for quite some time, he realized that being clogged with rickshaws and other vehicles, their vans were not moving. It was as though both the vehicles and the people on the street were running over each other in order to move forward. Slowly, much to the team's relief, the two vans made their way toward the airport on time.

The moment the vans stopped at the airport entrance, the team immediately sprang into action. With the help of the airport staff, one by one, all the babies were unloaded from the vans. Being jittery, the team members still wondered if their plane would leave the airport without any delay or any unforeseen troubles. One can imagine how any miscalculation on the part of the team or its escorts could have affected the caring of fifteen baby passengers on three different and long flights. Right from the time the babies were brought to the airport, volunteers and social workers attempted to clear the immigration counter to load them onto the plane. The designated escorts and flight crews quickly carried them into the plane. Fortunately, everything went smooth as though the escorts and volunteers were well acquainted with the needs of each child.

At the airport starting from Dhaka to New Delhi, India, leg of the journey prior to each flight, the airplane needed to be stocked with diapers, formula, milk, and plastic garbage bags, which were plentiful – an exercise that they conducted on each flight. Once on board, the flight crews and escorts hurried through the aisles in an attempt to get proper seat for everyone without any delay so that the plane could take off on time.

According to Fred, had the team not received this support, chaos would have ensued without attendants who were in a marathon of feeding and changing diapers, among other things. Everyone around was aware of the urgency with which one needed to act. Just as the preparation for taking off began, so did the sound of the engine roar nearly deafening everyone on board.

Logistically, to care for the infant passengers, the escorts had divided up the rows and had spent the entire time on board attending to the infants' varied needs on a rotational basis. Fred recalled, there was a great sense of relief and satisfaction that they were finally airborne. The first thing that both Fred and Bonnie would do was to carefully check the tag of each baby passenger against the master list in their hands to make sure that all fifteen babies are property boarded and settled. And yet a nervous and apprehensive Bonnie recalled how she and Fred kept counting the babies again and again, making 100 percent sure that all fifteen baby passengers were in with the assigned escorts.

In terms of numbers, the flight carried fifteen baby passengers, a fourteen-flight-member crew for the infants, two sets of to-be-adoptive parents (Fred and Bonnie Cappuccino and Robert and Helke Ferrie), and one to-be-adoptive mother (Elisabeth Mowling). The drawing up of guidelines for escorts, flight crews, and team members was a phenomenal task, recalled Elisabeth. She also recalled the behind-the-scene work by all, which was a great relief to the team. Per schedule, the Air India flight took off on time Wednesday afternoon, July 19, 1972, for New Delhi, arriving at 6:00 p.m. To make the journey smooth and tension-free, a special pressurized cabin was fitted with hanging baby cots. The motion of the plane lulled the baby passengers to near silence. Dr. Ferrie asked the pilot to turn down the air conditioning, which was done. But it was comfortable. Fortunately, no problem arose on this leg of the journey, but they realized that there were still more flights ahead of them before they finally reached home. Naturally, they were afraid that any of the babies on board could take turn for the worse.

At New Delhi

Landing in New Delhi, the team was received by James George, then Canadian high commissioner in New Delhi, his wife, and the spouses of the High Commission officials. As well, the federal National Health and Welfare medical officer and his associates were also present there to look after the baby passengers, if and when needed. Having taken a personal interest in ensuring that the team did not run into any hassle with immigration authority at the airport, George had earlier instructed his staff, especially Van Staalduinen, the immigration attaché in New Delhi, to extend their cooperation to the team on an urgent basis for a safe and comfortable journey. High Commission staff prepared the necessary documentation for the baby passengers to enable the team to travel problem-free to Canada via New York. Since the officers in charge were already briefed by the high commissioner prior to the team's arrival, there was practically no problem at the airport.

Both the immigration staff on duty and the volunteers, having offered their help, laboriously checked the documents and assisted them with escort visas, loading and unloading buses, and getting Canadian exit stamps. While the immigration officials checked the travel documents, the Canadian High Commission staff and their spouses looked after the babies and gave the Cappuccinos and their team a welcome respite. Such spontaneous offer of help restored the team's confidence. Soon the Canadian immigration officials were able to clear the documents, such as birth certificate, release form, government travel permit, etc. Earlier, George had also spent some time in assisting the team members who were still awaiting immigration formalities for the two babies picked out by Dr. Robert and Helke Ferrie. As mentioned in chapter 3, Ontario government had continued to create roadblocks especially for the Ferries despite its public assurance of cooperation and prompt service. Fortunately for the Ferries, George had successfully worked out a ministerial permit for entry into Canada for their two babies who were a part of this contingent.

After being awake for twenty-four hours following the flight from Dhaka to New Delhi, naturally some of the escorts were dusty, sweaty, and exhausted. They needed to fight off an overwhelming desire to sleep. Realizing that the hum of the engine had already made them drowsy during the flight to New Delhi, they felt that coping with the next leg to New York and then on to Canada required some sleep. Interestingly enough, despite the commotion surrounding the loading and transporting of the babies, some were still sleeping, some awake, while some others crying. They did not bother these happy volunteers. There was no dearth of volunteers who were always at the team leaders' disposal. Occasional assistance also came from the flight crews. It resembled one large family traveling on the air.

Even forty-three years later, Elisabeth recalled how the flight attendants and volunteer parents had tried hard to shake off the fatigue and remained focused on the needs of the babies. All were committed to making it a journey of care and comfort. Happily for the team, since everyone around was extending a helping hand, all of the paperwork for the flight to New York was completed quickly. Much to the relief of the team, and after a break of a few hours, the same night, July 19, 1972, the team boarded a huge Air India Boeing 747 plane for a fourteen-hour journey to New York. Canadian officials at New Delhi airport gave a warm farewell embrace for the team bound for New York.

From New Delhi to New York

The long night went on as the team worked almost unceasingly feeding, changing diapers, and comforting the crying babies. During the period they were on board, the Toronto team leader, Dr. Robert Ferrie, also had to wear his other hat as the medical surgeon responsible to examine the babies. Happily, he found them in good health. However, he recalled having to remain ever ready with his medical kit at his disposal in case he was called to check out any of the mini passengers. He did not fail to notice how, during the long flight, some babies were swaddled in blankets and some slept; some wept while some stared solemnly up at the attendants.

Again, many of the restless babies were carried up and down the aisle on comforting shoulder. Not surprisingly, throughout the flight, the aisles were congested with the crew members and escorts rushing back and forth. Again, there were times when it seemed almost all of the fifteen infants were awake and crying simultaneously in the stifling heat. Given that newborns vary enormously in such things as levels of irritability, muscular tension, and length of crying periods, the team had to take extra caution.

There were times when Elisabeth was stressed out to the point that, at one stage, she "suddenly felt like the floor [was] moving under" her and that "there was an earthquake."[6] She noticed, all through the hustle and bustle, the babies had slept in the arms of the escorts or cried, screamed, or squirmed unaware of the drama surrounding the historic flight and the central stage they occupied. All of a sudden, she recognized that it was the low blood sugar that she immediately fixed with a Coke and a package of sugar. Throughout the period, the babies did what babies will do, and at any given time, some infants were wet, hungry, or just wanted to get attention to be held. Some attendants cradled them on their folded legs and coaxed them to eat or drink; while some infants responded instantly drinking the formula down at a time when some others needed more tender and care. The Cappuccinos recall, when fed, some babies stopped crying and smiled.

Amid continued sounds of crying, some humorous comments were also made by passengers that often provoked laughter despite the worries. "To our joy, many passengers offered to hold and feed the babies, some of whom were so tiny they needed to be fed every two hours,"[7] recalled Elisabeth. The designated escorts, having remembered some cautionary remarks of the doctors and nurses, had also checked for signs of dehydration and respiratory disasters. Interesting to note, despite fear and nervousness, the team had some fun in carrying the babies. They were, to say the least, a spectacle to the passengers on board. Every time there was a mess, as the babies soiled diapers, the attendants expertly diapered, fed, changed, and neatly dressed them as many times as needed throughout the overseas journey.

Having picked a baby boy for herself and her husband, Elisabeth recalled how, in a fit of excitement, she asked a fellow passenger if he would be interested in holding one of the infants. No sooner had she asked than there begun a lineup of adult passengers who wanted to hold the babies. Many could not refrain themselves as they found the tiny adorable babies just like cuddly kittens. Without making a fuss, Bonnie would give them one baby at a time, saying, "Bring him back if he needs to be changed."[8] Fred described it as a "mobile baby library."[9] Within minutes, the crew began to loan out stronger babies to passengers while the escorts attended the weaker ones, fondly recalled Fred. At one point, Fred noticed the babies were all over the plane, being "loaned" out to interested passengers. This was happening at a time when the odors of vomit and soiled diapers permeated the cabin. And yet no one complained it. Like a circulation librarian, Fred kept track of who was "loaned" out and who was returned, making sure that the total number fifteen had always matched. Prior to landing, stewardesses handed out embarkation cards, which Fred patiently filled out along with other necessary forms for each baby passenger while the escorts looked after the babies.

At NY John F. Kennedy Airport

All went smoothly at JFK Airport in New York. The US consulate was briefed about the arrival of the babies well in advance by New Delhi office. Papers were checked and OK'd almost right away without any delay. As scheduled, the team was divided into two groups – the Cappuccinos and Elisabeth Mowling headed for Montreal, Quebec, carrying seven war babies; while Robert and Helke Ferrie headed for Toronto, Ontario, carrying eight war babies aboard Air Canada. Again, several Air Canada volunteers who came from Toronto and Montreal to help accompanied the groups to give the team a hand – helping to carry the babies and equipment up the steps of the planes and travel to Toronto and Montreal.

Arrival of the babies at Toronto and Montreal airports

After long hours of exhausting flights from Dhaka to New Delhi to New York, the two teams finally reached separately at Toronto and Dorval airport on July 20, 1972. The arrival of the first contingent carrying fifteen war babies of Bangladesh in Toronto and Montreal amid the film crews, bright lights, camera cables, and curious bystanders was perhaps one of the most bewildering spectacles of the year. It was as though the people of Canada saw the arrival of these babies as reliving disruption in the war-torn Bangladesh and deep longing at home. Immediately prior to landing at both airports, the escorts dressed the babies cutely, putting *bindi* (a little black dot) on each of their foreheads adorning them with an exotic appearance. As the saying goes, this *bindi,* a cosmetic mark, is used by people in the subcontinent to ward off the evil eye for babies and young children.

At the time, some babies began to cry as they were awakened from their sound sleep, and the commotion of getting ready frightened them even more. There were onlookers at both airports who impatiently waited to have a glimpse of these babies about whom they have heard in recent months. They stood at the gate impatiently wishing they could elbow their way through the crowd to get close to the babies. At both airports, relatives and family members waited in a VIP room.

At the Toronto International Airport (now Pearson), among the anxiously awaiting Ontario adoptive parents were John and Dorothy Morris of Brantford, Dale and Doreen Good of Copetown, Del and Donna Wolsey of Komoka, Tony and Bonnie Boonstra of St. Thomas, Phil and Diane Rochefort of Espanola, and Barbara Morrall of Saskatoon, Saskatchewan. The Toronto flight was supposed to arrive at 9:30 p.m. When the couples arrived at the airport, they and their family members learned that the flight was delayed by about two hours. The families were asked to attend a meeting with John Munro, then minister of Health and Welfare, and to meet the press prior to the arrival of the war babies. It turned out that the minister could not make it at the end due to circumstances beyond his control.

The couples brought not only pictures of their to-be sons and daughters, whom they had not seen yet, but also a handful of bottles, diapers, and other paraphernalia. While awaiting the babies' arrival, many parents remained tight-lipped, as an element of anxiety still persisted in their minds until they had their child in their own arms. As they waited for the team to get off the plane with their babies, their hearts throbbed with excitement. Holding their breaths, they awaited the arrival of Robert and Helke Ferrie, the couple responsible for carrying the babies.

All waiting family members were then directed to a large room where the airport authority had also laid out a large buffet table supplied with sandwiches, doughnuts, juices, and coffee/tea for the families. The festivity and the hospitality on the part of the airport authority made the parents feel "great" and "important" at the time. Having waited for three long hours, everyone was excited when the flight finally arrived at 11:00 p.m. As soon as the door opened, the Ferries and stewardesses came out the door carrying the babies. Each baby's wrist had a bracelet on with the names of the adoptive parents, and two little bangle bracelets for each girl to identify each baby separately. Instantly, as the lights sprang up to focus on the war babies who were coming to join their awaiting parents to go to their new "homes," people were able to see a glimpse of the babies.

All babies wore a little undershirt, a nightie, and a diaper. Just as the cherubic-looking babies were brought through immigration, much to the excitement of the awaiting adoptive parents, the airport nursery area had immediately turned into a bedlam. There was plenty of support for Robert and Helke who had already caused waves only a month ago when Helke Ferrie went on a hunger strike for a three-and-a-half-day protest (described in chapter 3) for what she claimed, stalling by Ontario officials in processing the necessary papers permitting the adoption.

News reporters, who had covered her story only four weeks ago, had stood at the gate impatiently. They remembered Helke's demand, which was to speed up the process, as she feared the summer monsoon in the Indian subcontinent in July could cause cholera outbreaks that could potentially kill the infants the Canadians were trying to adopt. Naturally, the news reporters were just as excited to see how Helke's persistent demand was being realized and were waiting with eager avidity to write an exemplary story of a strong will and determination. At that time, all to-be-adoptive parents were taken to the immigration counter where they had to wait for some more time for the babies to be cleared first.

To this day, the adoptive parents' memories of that day are filled with an overwhelming feeling of emotion and elation. Just as the Ferries carried War Baby B and Orun, the following names of the baby passengers were announced through the PA system one after another when they were bustling about cheerfully: Amina, Omar, Jorina, Rija Ruphea, Rani, and Bathol. With the help of an escort, the name tags of the babies were cross-checked with the names of the parents-to-be before they were allowed to get their hands on their child. Amid tears when they held their underweight babies the first time, they knew it to be true moments – perhaps one of the most unforgettable moments of their lives. The situation with the Ferries, however, was very critical. The frail ten-day-old War Baby B's (one of the war babies, a girl) health was so bad that she looked like a skeleton covered by a thin layer of skin. Because of her high fever, she needed immediate medical attention. After leaving the Toronto airport, Helke went straight to a local hospital, while her husband took Orun (another war baby, a boy they picked out) home.

For Del and Donna Wolsey, particularly Donna, it was "like a dream came true" feeling when they laid their hands on the girl they had been waiting for months. While waiting at the airport, she ruminated over how, ever since her childhood, she had dreamed of adopting twins long before she knew what life is all about. To say the least, the two-hour drive to the Toronto airport to receive their first child, three-and-a-half-month-old Amina, was both scary and exciting at the same time. The fear, the tension, and yet the excitement of picking up their child together gave them an indescribable feeling – the thrill of a lifetime, a thrill mixed with an element of apprehension. Sixteen years later, Donna recalled her feelings of that day to a reporter in the following: "There was fear the plane wasn't going to land, then there was the thrill when she came out and the disbelief . . . I had bonded with a name and a picture, then there she was."[10] Seeing that the babies had made it finally, the Wolseys could not wait any longer. Having grabbed their daughter, an excited couple rushed out of the airport, smiling and waving good-byes to the people around.

Both Tony and Bonnie Boonstra treasure the memory of the arrival of their two-and-a-half-month-old son, then named Omar, from Bangladesh and their preparation to head to the airport well in advance to pick up the boy for whom they had been passionately waiting. "It was a very hot evening. Government officials had put together a place where we could meet. Looking back on this, I realize it was their chance to have a good photo opportunity. There was a feeling of relief and joy that this day had finally arrived after such an intense 'roller coaster ride' to get clearance from Government authorities to have the children come to Canada."[11] Speaking on behalf of his wife, Bonnie, Tony says jokingly, "Perhaps the struggle beforehand was a little like pregnancy in that there was anticipation but also a real struggle for new life to enter into the world."[12] The little boy they picked up "was not a happy camper," recalls Bonnie. The couple also remembers "how the frail little boy cried most of the way home, a two hour ride from the Toronto airport to St. Thomas,"[13] their home at the time. "His cry was very loud with his mouth opened wide,"[14] recalled Tony. Amazingly enough, even though little boy cried on and off on their way home, he clung to Bonnie, his new mother, in a way as if he had known her for a long time, recalls Tony.

The arrival of the war babies has remained engraved in the minds of John and Dorothy Morris forever as the best, long-awaited summer present, something they still see happening just the other day despite the passage of time. They distinctly recall the name of the stewardess, Dorothy Young, who handed over nine-month-old Jorina to them. "She was the most beautiful sight to us and a few tears were shed looking at her fast asleep in the little carrier. She woke up and gazed up at her new Dad with her large black eyes and fell asleep,"[15] recalls Dorothy. To this day, Dorothy remembers every minute from the time she and her husband had arrived at the airport when all adoptive couples were taken to immigration counter where they had to wait for some more time for the babies to be cleared first. As they picked up the puny little baby, they could not believe their eyes, thinking how soon the cuddly infant would be nestled in their nursery. The arrival of Jorina, along with other war babies, seemed surreal. It was an amazing experience of being together with their long-awaited daughter from Bangladesh. On their way home, they thanked their stars believing in their hearts' hearts that they had received the most amazing gift anyone could ever receive.

Phil and Diane Rochefort headed to the airport early enough just so that they could meet other couples who would also be there to pick up their own babies. Even though the Toronto-bound flight from New York was delayed by a couple of hours, the Rocheforts' time at the airport went pretty quickly. They soon met five other couples, all of whom were impatiently waiting for the Toronto-bound flight. Just before eleven, that is, prior to the landing of the plane, the couple began to be a bit nervous and queasy, unable to gather any more strength. They had been in stress for months prior to the arrival of their baby. Everything started to change for them as the hours of their daughter's arrival came closer, thinking that she was to arrive anytime. Even though there were no more barriers to overcome at that stage, there were still both nervousness and anticipation in their minds.

As soon as their name was announced, Diane moved forward to pick up their daughter with a sigh of relief. Nothing, not even the chaos, bright lights, microphones, cameras, news reporters, and crowds of people, could have intimidated an excited couple. Instantly, the five-month-old little girl, Ruphea Rita[16] was handed over to Diane. Just as she grabbed the little girl, she was told that at five months, she was still underweight. Cuddling the little girl, an ecstatic Diane, who already had one adopted and one biological child, said they were expecting to add two more babies from Vietnam in their family by Christmas. "We want a large family. It's exciting and scary,"[17] said an exuberant Diane as she and her husband headed to the parking lot.

Robin and Barbara Morrall recalled, having been a bit leery, they had tried not to get themselves too excited ahead of time, as they had heard of other prospective parents who were devastated when the adoption process had broken down. Barbara recollects the day she picked up the three-and-a-half-month-old Rani in the following manner: "The wait at the airport was difficult in some ways but it gave me a chance to connect with some of the other parents. This was very important to me as I didn't know anyone else who had adopted internationally."[18] However, right from the time they received a card from Bonnie saying that she had picked out a baby girl for them, they were thrilled! "We couldn't believe our good fortune,"[19] said Barbara recalling that period. On the day of their daughter's arrival, Barbara flew to Toronto from Saskatoon to pick up the baby, having left Robin to look after their son. When an overexcited Barbara picked up her daughter from the Ferries, having checked the name tag, she could not believe her eyes. "It was so surreal," recalled Barbara. Even forty three years later, her feelings of having Rani in her arm first time has remained etched in her mind.

"It was a tremendous feeling to hold Rani for the first time. She had black curly hair and lovely big dark eyes and chubby cheeks. However, when I got her back to the hotel room and took the blanket off, I was surprised to see how skinny and short her legs were. I do remember not sleeping that night as I kept looking at her and trying to feed her. I was worried about her becoming dehydrated,"[20] recalled Barbara. Though Barbara had missed having Robin with her to pick up Rani, she knew it was the right decision for him to stay with John (their son) and prepare him for the arrival of his sister. Barbara also remembers how, as soon as she got back to the hotel, she had called her husband. Robin remembers what Barbara had said to him about the little girl, although his recollection of the details of the wait is rather poor now: "that Rani was so beautiful I couldn't help crying. I was very glad to have had Joy [Barbara's friend who lived in Toronto] at the airport to support me. I had no idea I would feel so emotional."[21] "I got a lot of help from John's grandma [Barb's mom, living in Saskatoon] on the day Barb flew to Toronto and I recall walking a lot in the neighborhood with John and talking to him about having a sister and her being adopted,"[22] recalled Robin. As the couple revisits that day, they remember how a sense of anxious anticipation had prevailed in their minds throughout the day.

Having experienced many delays and bureaucratic stonewalling in the process of seeking to adopt a child from another country, Dale and Doreen were afraid to be too hopeful that this was actually going to happen. On the day of their three-week-old son Bathol's arrival in Canada, they were excited with a curious mixture of fearfulness and eagerness as they headed for the airport fairly early. The first thing they did was to check the notice board where they saw the actual flight number posted. They were ecstatic, daring to believe that their dream child would actually arrive! Dale remembers they met other anxious couples in a private area arranged by the media where there were sandwiches and drinks. This is when they met Donna and Del Wolsey, another couple who was there to pick up their daughter. As mentioned, the plane was late. When they heard through the PA system that the parents' names would be called to present them their baby, an overexcited couple immediately swarmed the attendants and soon found their own "little bundle of joy!"[23]

Both Doreen and Donna Wolsey, the two adoptive mothers she just met, became so emotional that they ran to the escorts. Doreen remembers that precise moment when the beautiful babies, Bathol and Amina, among others, were carried by the escorts one after another to the awaiting couples. She also remembers being speechless. Doreen admits the special feelings of that particular occasion are beyond her ability to describe in words. Despite the passage of time, the couple remembers, funnily enough, how Bathol (a boy) came in a pink infant carrier and Amina (a girl) in a blue one. Their husbands, Dale and Del, wondered if they should trade their babies. "Both Donna and I were aghast!! Trade babies? No way!!"[24] The guys had meant baby carriers – not babies! Thus, recalled Doreen. "How amazingly instinctive the 'Mother Bear' reaction was – after only 5-10 minutes of motherhood at the airport,"[25] said Doreen, recalling those memorable moments of their son's arrival.

There were, however, a few other couples whose hopes of getting their children were dashed. The original plan for the FFC was to bring about twenty-four war babies from Bangladesh. They were initially disappointed, but at the end, they were not so unhappy. On the one hand, they were sad, as the team was unable to find sufficient babies for everyone on the list; on the other hand, they were thrilled to see how the war babies picked out by the team were handed over to their designated parents.

Dorval Airport

Fred, Bonnie, and Elisabeth became overjoyed just as the Montreal-bound Air Canada flight was about to land in Dorval Airport (now Pierre Elliott Trudeau Airport). Within a matter of few minutes, they bottled up all the infants with the help of volunteers. Among the anxiously awaiting couples filled with a mixture of anxiety and breathless anticipation were Joel and Trudy Hartt of Beaconsfield, Quebec; Lloyd and Sandra Simpson of Pointe Claire, Quebec; Roberto and Margo Carr-Ribeiro of Hull, Quebec; Pierre and Lise Hogue of Arvida, Quebec; Mitzi McCullough of Halifax, Nova Scotia; Ray Mowling (husband of Elisabeth Mowling) of Beaconsfield, Quebec; and many members of the Cappuccino family. Excitement reached its highest pitch when the day finally arrived for the families to take their child into their homes. Carrying pictures of their boys and girls they had never met, they felt like they were running out of patience as the felt from New York was delayed. It seemed like they had been waiting forever in the room 401, the couples recall. It was as though each couple was holding their breath and every second felt like hours in great expectation.

Upon arrival, the overexcited parents also learned that Bryce Mackasey, then minister of Manpower and Immigration who was supposed to be at the Dorval Airport, was unable to make it. As the time approached and the arrival of the flight from New York was announced, the would-be parents could wait no longer. Friends and acquaintances who could not be at the airport on time at the airport took advantage of the delay. They rushed to the airport to witness what they considered to be a historic event in Canada. When the Air Canada flight finally pulled up, a mass of people pushed up against the glass window of the airport.

The passengers slowly came out of the plane through the front door, at a time when there was quite a bit of commotion at the reception area where parents had gathered to meet and greet. When a second door was opened, the baby passengers and their escorts, following a long and exhaustive trip, were asked to disembark slowly, while the parents-to-be were anxiously waiting for their Bangladeshi child they had not seen yet. With a triumphant grin on their faces that were bedewed with tears of happiness, Fred, Bonnie, Elisabeth, and Air Canada attendants slowly came out of the plane carrying seven babies. There was a Royal Canadian Mounted Police (RCMP) car with red and blue lights and three limousines with yellow lights flashing to take them to an airport lounge amid reporters, spotlight television camera crews, and video recorders aimed at the plane in the presence of the representatives from the RCMP. One of the limousines had been sent by then prime minister Pierre Elliott Trudeau to drive the babies and their escorts to the terminal, recalled Elisabeth. Like the Toronto airport, there were also numerous onlookers and members of the public, only to have a glimpse of the war babies.

As the names of the parents were announced, the nervous and yet excited parents-to-be quickly came forward to accept their new child having cross-checked the name tags. Amid tears of joy, many who were overcome with excitement at that special moment tried to reach out to the infants and take them in their arms. They thanked God that the babies were safe. The feeling was one of great relief for other family members who also came with the couples. They marveled at the strength of the babies who barely had the stamina to sustain an overseas trip. The adoptive parents were so thrilled that they were momentarily speechless as the dark-eyed infants landed in their laps. Having gone through so many emotions, for a minute, they were not sure if it was really true. All over the exit areas, the proud couples held their newly found babies up, admired them, and exchanged greetings with friends and families. For them, like the couples in Toronto, it was also a moment of "dream came true" after months of waiting, as though the God had whispered comforting words to their ears.

Ray Mowling, who stayed back in Montreal, while his wife, Elisabeth, went to Bangladesh with the team to pick out the babies, had prepared himself well to wait longer than usual, as he was already familiar with flight from the overseas. He knew that such overseas flights are often delayed. However, he recalls arriving earlier than many other parents as he wished to meet up with the rest of the parents. Though he met a few couples and exchanged greetings, his mind was set on the seven-week-old boy named Onil to arrive soon. When the Cappuccinos stepped out of the plane and touched their feet on the ground, an excited Ray could not wait any longer to see his wife, Elisabeth, with Onil in her arms. An excited Ray reportedly said, "I think there should be more projects like this. I hope this is the first of many."[26]

To this day, he still remembers his intense feelings of joy and happiness of those precise moments at the airport as he saw all seven war babies for the first time. He recalled how the camera crews and newspaper reporters had followed them, attempting to capture their thoughts, feelings, and emotions. What he also remembers is how he and his wife tried to dash off as fast as they could in order to avoid the news reporters.[27]

Fred and Bonnie Cappuccino, who were in charge of the entire project, were almost at the end of their rope by the time the plane landed. And yet in addition to holding on to the four-month-old Shikha (a girl they picked out for themselves) in her arms, Bonnie remained anxious to make sure that all adoptive parents get to pick up their own child without any confusion. Fred remained busy ensuring that each couple picked the right child so that he could check off the name on his list. They were so busy that for the first few minutes, they had no time meet their own family members who were waiting to see Shikha. As soon as the babies were handed over to their parents, they took the first opportunity to meet their family members. They immediately left the airport to avoid the media personnel who were looking for them.

Roberto and Margo-Carr Ribeiro, who prefer to keep their story to themselves, remain reticent to talk about their inmost feelings during the arrival of their three-month-old son, then named Shomor. Despite having feelings of joy at the arrival of their dream child, they chose to remain quiet about it. Years later Margo, still resolved to keep matters related to adoption to themselves within their own family, frankly said that the arrival of Shomor from Bangladesh was "one of the memorable events"[28] in their lives. The family was greatly relieved to have their little son in their own arms, although the boy's arrival to Canada in their home in Hull, Quebec, took a long time that had caused angst in their lives. Margo does not wish to describe her feelings of the day, nor does she want to "talk about her labor pain in public."[29] Echoing the same sentiment as his wife, Roberto, also a private person, expects people to respect their privacy. He recalled the arrival of their boy as being perhaps the most "unforgettable day of their lives."[30]

Joel and Trudy Hartt had a busy day, having to tie up loose ends at home, as they had three other children at the time. The first thing that came to their minds while they recalled the arrival of their two-and-a-half-month-old daughter, then named Molly, is the rush they were in on that particular day. Trudy's parents came to the airport to look after their children all of whom were also there to greet their new sister. The grandparents took care of all the children, while the Hartts remained busy signing immigration papers and mingling with other adoptive parents. As soon as Trudy grabbed little Molly, she was transported with indescribable joy and excitement: "I thought I had never seen anyone so beautiful! I was grateful, in love with feelings I'd never experienced before," recalled Trudy."[31] In fact, for minutes, both Joel and Trudy had continued to look at Molly who was "so small and yet so wonderful."[32] They rushed to the lobby where they were flagged for a photo shoot. They then tried to run away from the crowd to introduce Molly to her grandparents and siblings who had been waiting to see this "tiny wonderful person."[33]

Mitzi McCoulough came to Montreal alone from Halifax, Nova Scotia, leaving her husband, Ken, behind, as the couple could not afford two airfares. A nervous and yet terribly excited twenty-three-year-old Mitzi remained speechless for minutes even though she was surrounded by reporters. While waiting for her three-and-a-half-month-old son, then named Prodip, Mitzi went through the entire gamut of feelings, from the time they filled out the application forms for adoption to the day of their child's arrival from Bangladesh. Given the complexities involved in adoption process, Mitzi recalled how she and her husband had been on tenterhooks, as they had no surety whether the team would be successful in locating a baby for them; and if so, what would the child look like? Holding Prodip with both a feeling of joy and nervousness, she reportedly cried out, "This is the second time I've ever even held a baby, I'm terrified."[34] Prodip was the couple's first child. She felt a connection with him the minute she took him in her arms. All of her fears and apprehension melted away in a flood of maternal feelings. As she proudly took her baby in her arms, she said to a news reporter who approached her, "We can always have a baby of our own but it's not every day we get a chance to have a special baby like this."[35] Mitzi said this to a reporter just as she was getting ready to take the next flight to Halifax with her son.

Though excited to have another child in their home, Lloyd and Sandra Simpson of Beaconsfield, Montreal, were veteran parents well known to the news media for their unique work in raising awareness among Canadians in favor of both in-country and international adoption. In embracing the twenty-day-old Rajib, the couple was just as excited as they were in having other children into their family. Because Sandra was in direct contact with the Cappuccinos all through the team's "child quest" in Dhaka, she was aware of the barriers they had to overcome to make the trip back with the war babies. Naturally, she and her husband were apprehensive about their timely departure from Bangladesh. She could not believe that the team would indeed be able to leave with the babies at the scheduled time. "It's incredible that they were able to get over so quickly,"[36] said an astonished Sandra. She was given a twenty-four-hour advanced notice by the team as soon as the date was firmed up for the team's arrival.

While heading for the airport, Lise and Pierre Hogue of Arvida, Quebec, could hardly contain themselves. "We, in the car and her, in a plane, were getting closer and closer to a new destiny,"[37] recalled Pierre. They picked up their eight-month-old daughter, then named Rajina, the minute the names were announced. Just as they came out through the gates, mixing into the stream of people surging everywhere, they were flagged by curious news reporters. "The expectation proved to very exciting and the feeling was similar to the one I had when my son was born, apart from the physical pain, of course. When the hostess gave me Rajina in my arms, immediately I felt that she was already my daughter,"[38] recalled Lise those unforgettable moments of their child's arrival. Trembling with joy, they wanted to scoop their child up and whisk away in silence straight to the parking lot to hold the child in their arms and rejoice. For a while, it was as though the overjoyed Hogues had completely forgotten their four-year-old son Benoit, who was impatiently waiting at home for them to arrive with his sister. When they returned home, Benoit was looking out the window to welcome his little sister with open arms.

It was one of the most exciting, if scary, times for the parents given the uncertainty surrounding the safe arrival and handing over of the babies to their respective parents for the first time following their continuous journey of two days. Having received their sons and daughters, naturally, the parents wanted to head home straight. They had no time to "stand and stare." Flagging them on their way out of the airport, a throng of reporters tried to talk to them while taking pictures until the parents discreetly ducked out of sight.

The joy and bewilderment shone on the faces of these happy new parents reflected the intensely dramatic reality of these poignant moments. As far as the parents were concerned, having crossed the Atlantic, their long-awaited children had landed in Canadian soil, which would be known as their "homeland" for the rest of their lives. "Each of the parents felt their baby was the most special and most beautiful baby. We were all happy and so grateful to all those who helped us in Canada, in Bangladesh, in India. So many people have played their part well,"[39] wrote Fred in his report.

As the parents drove off and headed home, they considered them lucky to be able to pick up the babies of their *choice* and hoped that their innocent lives in Canada would start with a clean slate with none of the stereotypes of Bangladesh. As things turned out, the war babies who came to an unknown world, little did they know that their life would all be wrapped up in constant change – change for the betterment of their lives. We shall explore this in the next three chapters. In the meantime, let us explore the immediate reactions in Canada and Bangladesh in the next few pages of the present chapter.

Table 1
Original names of the war babies and designated adoptive parents in Canada

Original name	Date of birth	Adoptive parents in Canada with original address
Shikha	12/3/1972	Fred and Bonnie Cappuccino 10 Bowling Green, Pointe Claire, Quebec, Canada
Rani	30/3/1972	Dr. Robin and Barbara Morrall 910, 9th Avenue Saskatoon, Saskatchewan, Canada
Omar	29/4/1972	Reverend Tony and Bonnie Boonstra 80 Baily Avenue St. Thomas, Ontario, Canada

War Baby B	8/7/1972	Dr. Robert and Mrs. Helke Ferrie 3139 Princes Boulevard Burlington, Ontario, Canada
Orun	27/5/1972	Dr. Robert and Mrs. Helke Ferrie 3139 Princes Boulevard Burlington, Ontario, Canada
Rajib	1/7/1972	Lloyd and Sandra Simpson 10 Bowling Green, Pointe Claire, Quebec, Canada
Molly	4/5/1972	Joel and Trudy Hartt 302 Acadia Drive Beaconsfield, Quebec, Canada
Prodip	25/3/1972	Kenneth and Mitzi McCoulough 3647 Windsor Street Halifax, Nova Scotia, Canada
Shomor	7/4/1972	Roberto and Margo-Carr Ribeiro 68 Doucet Hull, Quebec, Canada
Onil	23/5/1972	Ray and Liz Mowling 191 Creswell Drive Beaconsfield, Quebec, Canada
Bathol	27/6/1972	Dale and Doreen Good Box 69 Copetown, Ontario, Canada
Amina	3/4/1972	Del and Donna Wolsey RR # 3 Komoka, Ontario, Canada
Regina (Rajina)	24/11/1971	Pierre and Lise Hogue 1254 Buiers Street St. Bruno, Quebec, Canada
Ruphea Rita	15/2/1972	Phillipe and Diane Rochefort Box 1445 Espanola, Ontario, Canada
Jorina	23/10/1971	John and Dorothy Morris 3 Acorn Lane, Brantford, Canada

Source: Letter from M. Sharafatullah, Deputy Secretary, Ministry of Labor and Social Welfare, Bangladesh Secretariat, Government of the People's Republic of Bangladesh to Mother Teresa, 26 Islampur Road,

Dacca [sic], July, 17, 1972. Library and Archives Canada, RG 76, Vol. 1040, Box 141, *File* 5020-1-710, Pt. 1.

Media coverage in Canada

The safe arrival of the war babies in Canadian homes may be considered to be a milestone in the history of interracial adoption in Canada. It is a historic event to reckon with especially when one considers the fact that the babies were not "wanted" in their country of birth. Naturally, having been given up, they were not sought after for adoption in Bangladesh. These were infants that could be termed, using the adoption vocabulary, "hard to place," almost certainly doomed to a life spent in Bangladeshi orphanages. Their arrival was the culmination of the collective effort initiated by a group of enthusiastic and altruistic Canadian couples. Describing the war babies as the "children of despair," the media came to focus them as a subject of profound interest to the people of Canada.

On the day of their arrival, even outside the airport at the arrival zone, headlights flashed and horns blared, joining the cheers of curious onlookers, many with tear-filled eyes. Gone were the stigmas with which the babies were born in Bangladesh. As the team landed in Canada with the babies, the team members and escorts were hugged by the respective families. It was as though the frail war babies were reborn upon arrival in Canada – born of the adoptive parents' kindness. The next day, on July 21, 1972, the major newspapers, especially of Ontario and Quebec, carried headline articles on their arrival, congratulating the adoptive parents and welcoming the infants in Canada.

To the news media, the arrival of the war babies was the "most newsworthy" item of the day in Canada. Had it been only one or two babies, perhaps there would have been a different scene. Since there was a planeload of babies, their arrival became a spectacular scene for both the general public and the media. Naturally, since the coverage was widespread, one might assume that everyone had read, listened to, or viewed the same coverage of events. For days together, people talked about it – on the subways and in the parks and at tables at many outdoor cafés. These adoptions took on a whole new meaning to Canadians who saw for themselves how television cameras and dozens of still photographers recorded the historic moment. The major dailies published the photos in full-page articles showing how the curious and exhausted parents anxiously waited for hours until the plane landed. They described the chaotic first encounter of the adoptive parents with their never-seen-before babies as truly touching. The fascinating narrative that unfolded depicted the passionate feelings of the families with which they had embraced these war babies unconditionally.

Unlike Bangladesh where the war babies' departure was a low-keyed event, their arrival in Canada was just the opposite. "Bangladesh Orphans en route to Canada" was the most common newspaper headline. The general public was able to learn for the first time how fifteen war babies had been rescued by Canadian parents and adopted into their families as their *own* children. Below are a few of these headlines:

- "Love at First Sight: 15 Bangladesh Orphans Find Canadian Homes." The *Ottawa Citizen,* July 21, 1972.
- "15 Bangladesh Babies Our Newest Immigrants." The *Toronto Star,* July 21, 1972.
- "Bangladesh Babies Arrive, Here Is Rajib, Where's Mom?" The *Gazette,* July 21, 1972.
- "Bienvenue Chez Nous!" *le journal de Montréal, vol. 1X, no 38,* 22 Juillet, 1972.
- "Delighted Parents Finally United with Their Bangladesh Babies." *Ottawa Journal,* July 21, 1972.
- "Six familles du Québec adoptent des Bengalis." *la Presse,* 21 Juillet, 1972.
- "Oohs and Ahs Greet Babies." The *Montreal Star,* July 21, 1972.
- . . . babies "with coarse hair, dark skin and caste marks painted on their tiny foreheads." The *Gazette,* July 21, 1972.
- ". . . suddenly the tension broke, and the new Canadian parents pressed forward to touch this country's newest citizens." The *Gazette,* July 21, 1972.
- "Dry Diapers and Love as New Parents Greet Bangladesh Babies." The *Globe and Mail,* July 21, 1972.
- "First Bangladesh Babies Delight Adopting Parents." *Kitchener Waterloo Record*, July 21, 1972.

- "Bangladesh War Orphans Thriving and Happy in Ontario." The *London Free Press*, July 23, 1973.
- "Victims of the Bangladesh War of Independence." The *London Free Press,* July 23, 1973.
- "An outcast in his own country;" "the offspring resulting from the mass rape which occurred during the war in which Bangladesh won its independence." *Mennonite Reporters*, April 14, 1972.
- "Most were fathered by Pakistani soldiers during hostilities between Pakistan and Bangladesh and were without families." *Montreal Star,* November 29, 1972.

Description of the war babies

- Under the news caption, "Delighted Parents Finally United with Their Bangladesh Babies," one Ottawa-based newsaper wrote, the "cries of hunger and weariness from much-traveled babies mingled with the delighted exclamation" of new parents who received their babies at the airports. The *Ottawa Journal,* July 21, 1972.
- "Some of the children were the offspring of women raped by West Pakistani soldiers during the civil war. Others were abandoned by their families." *Montreal Star*, November 28, 1972.
- "All had been orphaned in the recent Pakistan-Bangladesh war." The *Gazette*, July 21, 1972.
- ". . . these unwanted infants to be brought to Canada." The *Gazette,* July 21, 1972.
- ". . . the children of rape." Letter from Reverend R. D. MacRae, secretary, Anglican Church of Canada to Reverend Fred Cappuccino, September 19, 1972.
- ". . . the orphans of West Pakistani rapes." The *Globe and Mail,* September 12, 1972.
- Once Rani was settled into the house of Robin and Barbara Morrall in Saskatoon, Saskatchewan, the local newspaper described her as "an orphan baptized by its war of independence and burdened by inherited poverty." John Hay of the Ottawa Staff of the Canadian Press, titled "World's

Most Expensive Charity Case," *Star-Phoenix*, Saskatoon, October 14, 1972.
- The "distressed children." *Press Release*, May 25, 1972, Canadian Council on Social Development.
- The "infants born as a result of the raping of Bangladesh women by Pakistani soldiers." Letter from René Brunelle, Minister of Community and Social Services, government of Ontario to Mitchell Sharp, minister of External Affairs, May 15, 1972.
- "Ryan was an outcast in his own country because he was one of thousands of offspring resulting from the mass rape which occurred during the war in which Bangladesh won its independence." *Mennonite Reporter*, April 14, 1975.

The arrival of the war babies in Canada in 1972, however, did not accompany any controversy the like of which had surfaced in the USA following the dramatic airlift and adoption of Vietnamese orphans in 1975. As well known, during the time of Operation Baby Lift, more than two thousand babies and children were flown out of South Vietnam by military and private planes to be adopted by families in the USA. The war babies' arrival three years before the Vietnamese orphan flights in 1975 was a much lower keyed event, although the event was covered extensively by the news media. Comparatively, of course, the number of children involved in the Canadian operation was greatly insignificant.

One undisputed fact of the adoption of the war babies is that none of the war babies was adopted against the will of the birth mothers who had given them up immediately upon birth. Earlier, the news media had described *how* birth mothers were violated, *how* they had conceived their babies, and under *what* circumstances birth mothers had relinquished the newborns. This is much unlike the war orphans of Vietnam taken out through Operation Baby Lift, many of whom were alleged to have taken forcibly from South Vietnam from the birth mothers or parents, suggesting a murkier legal status.

Immediate reaction in Canada

Upon their arrival, the FFC team expressed its gratitude to all those who had assisted them in bringing the Bangladesh Project to fruition. It also received numerous congratulatory notes. Abdul Momin, then Bangladeshi high commissioner in Ottawa, was the first one to congratulate the team followed by a note from Bryce Mackasey, then minister of Manpower and Immigration, and Pierre Elliott Trudeau, then prime minister of Canada. As mentioned in chapter 3, Momin, who had earlier worked with the FFC team, had encouraged the team members to continue their efforts by conveying his government's key message that it was the conviction of the Mujib administration that adoption of the war babies in Canadian homes would give them the best chance for a better life they might not otherwise have in their country of birth. He took personal interest in their safe arrival and transfer to the selected adoptive parents. Recognizing the sensitivities surrounding the adoption of interracial babies in general and, more particularly, the war babies of Bangladesh, he expressed his desire to the Cappuccinos that he would very much like to meet the adoptive parents to hear from them about their varied experiences with their child from Bangladesh unless they wished to remain anonymous.

Archival records also indicate that Bryce Mackasey had wished the Cappuccinos twice. In April while explaining the process of immigration and roles and responsibilities, he wished them "every success" in their "endeavors" and wrote in the following manner: "May I take this opportunity of commending you on your humanitarian and compassionate efforts in respect to the homeless children of Bangladesh."[40] Again after the arrival of the babies in Canada, he wrote to the Cappuccinos expressing his gratitude "on the successful completion"[41] of their project. Mackasey thanked the team once again for their initiative in bringing the hapless babies from Bangladesh and regretted that he was unable to be at the airport to welcome the babies at such a short notice.

Again, having welcomed the arrival of the war babies in Canada, in his letter of praise and appreciation of the volunteers, Prime Minister Trudeau congratulated the team and its volunteers for their trip to Bangladesh, which he saw as a "heart-warming odyssey indeed."[42] Trudeau thanked them profusely for bringing "the babies to Canadian families" that had "brought much happiness," which all could "share in a measure."[43]

The key message, whether it was from individuals or from the news media, was that interracial adoption programs are a positive initiative and that Canadians of diverse backgrounds should endorse such initiative. Interesting to note, although the people of Canada saw adoption from Bangladesh as a positive step, there were, however, a few who had reacted rather negatively when the war babies were discussed. Soon it became clear that across the country, there were a growing number of families that wished to adopt war orphans of Bangladesh, irrespective of their culture, nationality, and races.

The strongest appeal to the government to respond to the needs of the moment was made by the *Toronto Star* at a time when as many war orphans were dying as were being born and abandoned. Congratulating the Families For Children for its initiative, the paper asked, "Why should salvation for these children depend on the initiative of private citizen?"[44] Alluding to the fact that there was an unfulfilled demand for infants to adopt in Canada, the paper commended the private individuals who had taken upon themselves to speed up the process as the situation became more precarious: ". . . before any more babies die in Bangladesh why not have the Children's Aid Societies step in and actively recruit parents here?"[45] Again, calling this "an opportunity . . . to serve human happiness in a lasting way," the same newspaper argued, "When there are eligible adults here who want babies, and babies in Bangladesh who desperately need parents and support, they should be brought together."[46]

As there was no dearth of prospective adoptive parents, such arguments increased the project's credibility with the wider public. It soon became evident through Helke Ferrie's efforts that maintaining a balance was the key to determining how this could be achieved in Canada. From the beginning of the War of Liberation of Bangladesh, Canadians had a soft corner for the Bengalis who were seen as the victims of military reprisal. Canadians were stirred by frequent reports of atrocities and devastation during the Bengalis' fight for independence. Bangladesh had seventy-five million people squeezed into an area about the size of the Maritimes and was then the eighth-most populous country in the world. Comprehensive news reports of adoption had immediately triggered an interest in the war babies among a large number of Canadians. They saw it as an attempt to rescue at least a few abandoned babies from Bangladesh, as well as from other underdeveloped and war-torn countries.

Since the Ferries took a stand against Ontario's prevarication and went ahead to form their own organization, they soon became known to the general public who supported this initiative. In one of his interviews with the news media, Dr. Robert Ferrie expressed his hope that "the 15 infants who came to Canada on Tuesday will set a precedent for intergovernmental cooperation, and assure Ontario child welfare authorities that Bangladesh adoption can be carried out successfully."[47] Continuing along the same vein, the Ferries argued that there was no future for the war babies in their country of birth both socially and economically. Many saw the Ferries' involvement in this initiative as a "humanitarian effort" that had the potential to allow them to bring a few war babies to Canada "to give them a new life in a new country."[48] Collectively, the initiative of FFC was seen by the news media as an instance that represented "not just fundamental human goodness" but also "the ideals that Canada had always stood for."[49]

The newspaper coverage of the accounts of the initiative of FFC had also generated an interest hitherto unknown not only among the members of the public but also the dominant religious groups. Reverend R. D. MacRae, then secretary of the Anglican Church of Canada, for example, wrote to the Cappuccinos, congratulating the adoptive parents and expressed his desire to hear about "the current actual state of the children"[50] that were brought to Canada. Wishing them the best for the newly adopted babies, he requested them to fill him in with more information about the babies and the parents' "perspectives" on "international adoption." In fact, Reverend MacRae had raised some deeper questions about the circumstances surrounding the birth of the war babies and the status of the birth mothers in a country that generally blames the victim: "What are the conditions within Bangladesh with respect to the mother, potential institutional care in Bangladesh or other alternatives? What does the Canadian Pakistani or Bangladesh community have to say about children being adopted in Canada? Has consideration been given to protecting the children of rape from having their past known?"[51]

Despite publicity of great magnitude, no single Pakistani or Bangladeshi Canadian living in Canada is known to have shown any interest in adopting these ("undesirable") war babies. In fact, ironically enough, it was just the opposite. Our research indicates that there is at least one instance in which contrary view had been recorded. The position of Dr. Arshad Majeed, then a psychiatrist in the Burlington area, Ontario, spoke his mind with regard to interracial adoption. It is worth alluding to in our discussion. As a Canadian of Pakistani origin, he openly took an issue with interracial adoption and questioned whether "anyone, anywhere, has the right to make a decision regarding a child that will change his life style completely – when the child, himself, has no say in the matter."[52] An apparently angry Majeed asked, "Is it nobler to live a lesser life in dignity, than one of great convenience and comfort, but with less dignity?"[53] Dr. Majeed did not just stop there. In fact, having continued along the same vein, he further remarked, "The people of Bangladesh felt as if they were being taken out of the country. They were angered – they felt they were being aggressed upon."[54] Nevertheless, no evidence of any feelings or reactions was found in Bangladesh while conducting the study.

Demand for more babies

One of the snowball effects of positive media coverage was that people had turned attention further for more war babies in Canada for the purpose of adoption. Many parents immediately began to express their interest in bringing home war babies from Bangladesh. The news media continued to keep the momentum going in favor of interracial adoption for days together. Volunteers at FFC were deluged with phone calls from people across Canada seeking counsel to adopt war babies from Bangladesh. Many Canadians believed that unless the newborns were immediately removed from the orphanages and temporary makeshift homes where they had been warehoused, they would continue to die. By fall 1972, the Cappuccinos were able to make contacts with a large number of couples who, having been encouraged directly by the news reports, had seriously sought their counsel.

Recognizing the sensitivity surrounding the birth of the war babies, the newspapers had been careful to focus on the widespread raping of Bengali women by the Pakistani soldiers during the Liberation War and consequently how it had left the new state of Bangladesh with many orphaned infants. Within days, Helke Ferrie, then also chairperson of

Asian Adoption and secretary-treasurer of the Ontario chapter of the Families For Children, came to be known nationally. Even though she had already adopted two war babies in July (1972), by fall, she was ready for more. She appeared on the national news as an advocate of interracial adoption. Soon she was swarmed with applications for adoption. It was at that time that she and her husband decided to create their own adoption foundation. Within weeks of their arrival from Bangladesh, the Ferries established the *Kuan-Yin Foundation* [55] with a view to finding homes for orphans from around the world. Between July and August 1972, the Ferries alone received over one hundred applications from Ontario couples. So eager were they that out of these, fifty-four families had already managed to complete the necessary formalities for provincial approval with the Child Welfare Departments of the seven provinces involved.

Seeing that Canadians had taken interest in the war babies, Momin (Bangladeshi high commissioner in Canada) had kept in touch with the FFC members. He made use of his contacts and began his public relations job. Expressing his sheer delight and pleasure in their success in their first venture for which they had to overcome many bureaucratic stumbling blocks, he wrote, "We have read about your earlier trip to Bangladesh and your return to Toronto with an armful of babies, war-orphans, whom kind Canadian homes wanted to adopt."[56] Needless to say, Momin, like many other Bengali officials, believed that though the Bangladesh Project did not get a high profile in Bangladesh, it had been one of the greatest initiatives under the Mujib administration in the war-ravaged Bangladesh within six months of its creation: "What you have been doing speaks of a noble trait of character – love of children – on your part and on the part of those who have offered their homes for the adoption of war orphans from Bangladesh,"[57] wrote Momin.

In a sense, by retelling the stories of international adoption, the media had transformed the minds of the Canadian public. Just as the interest for the war babies was expressed from various countries, including Canada, some rumors were going around that the Mujib administration was not going to release any more children as the government was interested in in-country adoption by establishing more orphanages. Meanwhile, the Cappuccinos' phone was ringing off the hook for days from calls from potential parents for adoption from Bangladesh. The Cappuccinos needed to be sure whether this was a fact or just a rumor.

MUSTAFA CHOWDHURY

To assist those who wanted to adopt from Bangladesh, they remained in touch with them both organizationally and individually.

Seeking frank and sincere opinion of his friends at the Bangladesh Quakers Service (BQS) and Missionaries of Charity, Fred inquired the status of the newborn and sought their personal advice on this matter. Knowing that the BQS personnel were very busy, the Cappuccinos wrote that "even a few lines would be nice"[58] by way of their response. Both the Quakers and Sr. Margaret Mary wrote back confirming the rumor and giving their personal take on the availability of babies: that the government's program was going well and that they were "feeding about 16,000 children [i.e., orphans]" at the time and were "well into the rehabilitation work."[59] He then added, "You ask about making another trip to adopt more children, and maintain your feelings of pessimism about it. I share your doubts but from a positive point of view perhaps. The system for inter-country is now working. The law is passed, the home is set and the government is functioning. Children will be adopted through this system."[60] What the Quaker was referring to was that they were hopeful that the *Bangladesh Abandoned Children (Special Provision) Order of 1972* (we have discussed in chapter 2) would be applied to in-country adoption and would meet its objectives.

Earlier, Sr. Margaret Mary had been quite upfront in saying that there were not enough war babies left for adoption. In fact, she had warned all interested parties about unavailability of the war babies in Bangladesh particularly in response to Helke Ferrie's request through the Cappuccinos. At that time, Helke was ready to go to Bangladesh for another trip for about fifty or so war babies. Sr. Margaret Mary wrote to Fred in the following manner: "Please tell Dr. Ferrie and others that there will be no babies just now for adoption – we have 9 more babies who are booked now. We do have some older children but that we have to wait for legal adoption to come."[61] In the same letter, Sister Mary also indicated that she was deluged with requests from people from around the world "who wanted children [war babies] from" her, but she had "refused"[62] them, since there were no more war babies left other than nine babies that had already been committed.

The ones who were available were older children in need of caring parents and safe homes but not necessarily "war babies" for whom she was flooded with request. As the statutory guardian of the abandoned children" vested under the aegis of the *Bangladesh Abandoned Children*

(Special Provision) Order of 1972, Sr. Margaret Mary had different sets of orphans, such as "war babies," "baby orphans," and "older orphans." The reality of the situation, explained Sr. Margaret Mary, was that the war babies had continued to die due to poor health conditions. She informed all those concerned that, technically speaking, from September onward, no new war baby can be expected to be born.

Regardless of what had been happening in Bangladesh with respect to its new initiatives for orphans, a dashing Helke remained resolved in continuing her endeavors in transporting orphans from Bangladesh through her newly established organization. Helke made her second trip back to Dhaka, Bangladesh, in the fall (October) of 1972. This time around, she met with the prime minister of the day, Sheikh Mujibur Rahman, and a few key players who gladly assisted her in collecting eight babies from *Shishu Bhavan*. Their age ranged from six months to almost six years. During this time, her goal was to have both war babies as well as a number of homeless, orphan, and poor and abandoned children who were not necessarily "war babies."

Media coverage in Bangladesh

Even though the departure of the war babies destined for Canadian families is an unprecedented historic event for both Bangladesh and Canada, the evacuation did not get any effective media coverage in Bangladesh. The departure of the war babies from their country of birth was, at best, a low-keyed event that did not hit the news media the way it did in Canada. Ironically, the people of Bangladesh were oblivious of this milestone in the life of the war babies at a time when history was unfolding right in Bangladesh's own backyard. At Dhaka Airport, the babies were quietly whisking custom. Though the Dhaka Airport was its usual crowded self, a bevy of people did not seem to know anything about what was going on. Even though there was a large group of "baby passengers," no one took any interest. It was as though the war babies' odyssey out of their country of birth was not newsworthy.

Of the approximately twenty Bangladeshi national dailies at the time, only one newspaper, the *Bangladesh Observer* (July 20, 1972), carried the news of the war babies' journey to Canada. It carried the news in the front page. The story, headlined "War-Babies Leave for New Homes," written by the *Bangladesh Observer*'s staff correspondent, had adequately described the *who, how, why,* and *where* of the war babies and the initiative of the Montreal-based Families For Children (FFC). The report contained the names of all fifteen war babies who were destined for Canada along with the names and addresses of their adoptive parents in Canada. It also reported that out of fifteen war babies, twelve were born in the Dhaka-based Mother Theresa's *Shishu Bhavan,* while three others were brought there from another "home" run by the government for adoption. The report commended the FFC, which was the first organization in the world that came to Bangladesh with a concrete project initiative that became successful. Many other organizations were simply talking the talk; while the FCC had successfully walked the talk.

True, back then, Canada was still a far distant country in the north as far as an average Bangladeshi was concerned. To them, Canada conjured up an image of a vast frozen wasteland of scurrying Eskimos and polar bears where Mom's apple pie could stay fresh forever. It was not until the 1980s and 1990s that a large number of Bangladeshis started to immigrate to Canada. Bangladeshi's lack of adequate knowledge about Canada, coupled with the low-keyed news coverage of the "undesirable" war babies, did not trigger any interest even among researchers to seek more information about the war babies. The only interested person, as already mentioned, was the Bangladeshi high commissioner in Canada who was appreciative of the Bangladesh Project.

As we have noted already, he had sent a congratulatory note to each set of adoptive parents wishing them the best with their babies. The parents in Canada also recall receiving congratulatory notes from Rev. Paulinus Costa, then acting national director of Christian Organization for Relief and Rehabilitation (CORR). Again, writing on behalf of the Canadian Holy Cross father, Benjamin Labbé, who was of great assistance to the Canadian team in Dhaka, Reverend Costa expressed the hope of the Canadian Holy Cross father in the following manner: "The babies will soon find that they are no strangers to the new parents."[63]

Attempts of monitor

The babies soon adjusted to the new environments, while the people of Bangladesh had remained unaware of the war babies' journey to safe homes in Canada. Although the people of Bangladesh did not seem to care much about the birth, deaths, and shipment of the war babies, the government of Bangladesh and Sr. Margaret Mary, the statutory guardian of the war babies, were concerned about their status. They were eager to hear back from the adoptive couples. Having arrived home, the Cappuccinos were so involved with their tasks that they did not get a chance to contact Sr. Margaret Mary right away regarding *how* the war babies were doing after they were handed over to their adoptive parents. Sr. Margaret Mary, who loved these babies, had serious misgivings from the time the babies had left Dhaka. Her anxiety had increased with the passage of time and lack of information.

Given Sr. Margaret Mary's responsibility and accountability as statutory guardian of the orphans entrusted under the *Bangladesh Abandoned Children (Special Provisions) Order of 1972*, it was only natural that she would be anxious and that she would worry about the "disappearance" of the Canadian team that was supposed to send her a biweekly update. Each adoptive family became busier than before in putting things in place and adjusting to the new member of the family. No one took any time to contact Sr. Margaret Mary at a time when she was also being pressured by Abdul Awal, then executive secretary of the National Board of Bangladesh Women's Rehabilitation Program (BWRP), to provide a biweekly update on the babies.

When weeks went by without hearing from the FFC, government officials became quite concerned. They considered the long silence on the part of the adoptive parents in Canada to be unusual. "I am anxiously awaiting information from you about the babies you are nourishing with care, love and sympathy. Are they all happy? Are they living together still in your residence? Please write few sentences on them. Convey my best wishes to Mrs. Cappuccino and Mrs. Mowling,"[64] thus wrote K. M. Islam, then assistant director of the Coordination Division for the Ministry of Relief and Rehabilitation, Prime Minister's Secretariat, directly to the FFC team leader who represented the FFC in Dhaka.

Even though Sr. Margaret Mary was aware that government officials would be contacting the Cappuccinos, personally she could not just wait without doing something about the unexpected delay. Her anxiety for "her babies" was triggered again upon receipt of a cable about the safe arrival of 132 babies destined for Europe that had left Bangladesh around the same time of the Cappuccinos' departure. This had caused the sister to worry about the rumor she heard that some of the babies destined for Canada had died during their voyage. Knowing about the fragile health of the war babies that were sent off to Canada, an angry and frustrated Sr. Margaret Mary immediately fired off a letter to Fred. She reminded him that the adoptive families must conform to the postadoption requirements and forward a biweekly update on the babies taken from the Bangladesh orphanage. "I have been a big fool to be so soft in giving 15 children to Canada when so many individual families wanted children. I hear some of them died on the way. What mistake I made, I can't forgive myself. If some of them died, well they are in Heaven, and I ought to know,"[65] wrote an extremely angry and upset sister.

Despite the physical distance between Canada and Bangladesh, Sr. Margaret Mary expected more communication and collaboration than she had experienced at the beginning. Her approach was more like "Let's get together over issues." Remoteness, as far as Sr. Mary was concerned, must not be promoted as an excuse. An enraged Sr. Margaret Mary wondered, "Perhaps all these are alive, they are not welcomed in Canadian families or does [sic] these Canadian families treat them as parcels or as human children for whom we gave all our time and pleasure to serve them to bring them from death's door for them to be loved in families."[66]

Not knowing how the babies were adapting to everyday life in their new homes and how they were developing, she remained quite concerned. She reminded the adoptive parents of the requirement in the letter of understanding that stipulates that even though the parents were responsible for the child's maintenance and safety, "guardianship" rights had still remained in the hands of the statutory guardian until Canadian citizenship had been obtained. Knowing that the war babies had varying states of health, Sr. Margaret Mary feared that probably the adopting families too would have their own strengths and weaknesses in dealing with their child's needs. Personally, she considered international adoption to be an excellent parenting choice, although moving a child to an entirely different country is a significant undertaking.

In her attempt to point out their responsibilities and obligations, she stressed a simple point: that no matter what, whether warm or cool the beginnings might be, the adoptive parents remain absolutely responsible for the new child and for fulfilling all necessary roles and functions according to the Canadian laws and social norms. Deep down, Sr. Margaret Mary had always believed that both the director of Social Welfare of the government of Bangladesh and the *Shishu Bhavan* authority had acted in "good faith" in handing over the babies to the FFC long before the proclamation of the ordinance by bending over backward. Naturally, until Sr. Margaret Mary heard from the Cappuccinos, she remained so concerned that within a matter of three weeks, she felt obliged to connect with the Cappuccinos regardless. She therefore wrote again, referring to a rumor that several of the war babies had died on their way to Canada and that she was desperate to ascertain the rumor. As far as she was concerned, she considered these babies as her "own" and wrote to the Cappuccinos that any mother would be anxious about her children.

Upon receipt of her letter, the Cappuccinos immediately advised each parents to personally write to Sr. Margaret Mary describing the progress their child had made thus far. In addition, the Cappuccinos also sent her a telegram, which read, "All babies arrived safely as scheduled and were met at airport by happy parents. Thank you and all your helpers on behalf of all the families. Letter will follow. Fred and Bonnie Cappuccino."[67]

The Cappuccinos' immediate response came as a great relief to a frustrated Sr. Margaret Mary who right away dashed off the following few lines: "Many thanks for your kind letter and also the telegram. I write this letter for all those families who wrote to us about their new babies. Please thank or circulate this letter which I mean for everyone. We were really very anxious about the children."[68]

Saying that she trusted the sincerity and dedication of the adoptive parents, Sister Mary advised, through Bonnie, that the babies in question would require extra attention and care. Speaking from her own experience of dealing for many years with premature babies, she advised them that "a premature child will take longer to catch up with things, they will be more delicate – whether a normal child may be small yet can resist better."[69] She also requested them to keep her posted on the activities of the children who were still very close to her heart.

Between July and the first week of September (1972), letters were exchanged among Sr. Margaret Mary, the Cappuccinos, and the adoptive parents in an attempt to share the latest since the arrival of the war babies in Canada. Describing their own activities that included their move from Montreal to Avida within four weeks since the arrival of their child Rajina into their family, the Hogues (Pierre and Lise Hogue) wrote, "Rajina is just marvelous; she seems to have adapted herself very easily. She is smiling all the time; she now stands up (with our help of course) but it is a great improvement since when she arrived she could hardly stay seated by herself for more than a few minutes. She eats and eats and eats. She now weighs 18 pounds (4 pounds more than when she arrived). She seems to be happy with us as we are with her."[70] The orphanage authority was delighted to receive letters from the adoptive parents with updates and snapshots of the babies. Both Sr. Margaret Mary and Bangladeshi officials believed that, over time, each family would make its own adjustments. Sr. Margaret Mary was able to overcome her frustration, and gone were her anger and exasperation. In fact, from then on, she was able to establish a cordial relationship with the adoptive families.

In the meantime, like Sr. Margaret Mary, Fred also turned his attention to catch up with and express his gratitude to all those who had assisted the team while in Dhaka. The Cappuccinos wrote to Emile Baran, of the Canadian High Commission in Bangladesh, thanking him and his staff for their help and giving them an update. They sure would be "pleased to know," the Cappuccinos wrote, "that the fifteen babies had no difficulties on the plane trip to Canada and were all greeted by their very pleased new parents."[71] Furthermore, "they are getting fat and chubby. Still very lovely," wrote the Cappuccinos.[72] Without the "openness," "willingness," and "encouragement" of the people of Bangladesh, "it would have been much harder to obtain their [war babies] release; without their [High Commission officials'] help," it would have been "probably impossible"[73] to accomplish their mission, thus wrote Fred.

Having alerted the parents, Fred also fired off letters of acknowledgment with updates to a few key players in the government of Bangladesh. In one such letter to Abdul Awal, then executive director for the National Board of Bangladesh Women's Rehabilitation Program (BWRP), Fred wrote, "You will be very pleased to know all the babies came to Canada are in good health and were met at the airport in Toronto and Montreal by their happy and very exciting new parents. They were each taken to their new homes by their new parents that same evening. We have heard often from each couple and they tell us very good things about each of the babies. They are growing and learning very quickly. Each of the parents thinks that his baby is the most intelligent baby ever born."[74]

Meanwhile, after the initial euphoria of becoming adoptive parents, although some had already gone through the adoption process with other children, they realized how badly they needed information on their child's medical checkups. Though the babies were not critically ill, there were a number of medical concerns, so medical follow-up upon their arrival was essential. Even though the parents were told that there was no medical information on the file, they still contacted the orphanage authority in Bangladesh through Bonnie to hear from Dhaka if, by any chance, any (whatever little that might be) information on their child was available at all. They thought they would take a chance just in case there was any information available per chance.

Evidently some of the adoptive parents had already been in touch with the *Shishu Bhavan* and corresponded with at least two other nurses in addition to Sr. Margaret Mary. They remembered a while ago they had learned through Sister Shobha of *Shishu Bhavan* whether their particular child had already DPT shots or not. Apart from Sister Shobha, who was quite popular, there was Sister Vincentia, a nurse who came to the *Shishu Bhavan* from India with whom some of the adoptive parents had corresponded. Because of their earlier correspondence with the *Shishu Bhavan* authority (or personnel, such as individual nurses), they felt encouraged to write again, hoping against hope for any additional information that might still be there in their possession.

For the first few years, this was almost a routine like activity for the adoptive parents to remain in touch with orphanage staff. Understandably, because these babies were pitifully frail at the time of their departure, the orphanage authority had remained apprehensive about their health conditions, which they feared would deteriorate at least for the first few years or so. To the orphanage people's way of thinking, even though the babies were away from them, they were not out of minds and hearts, at least for a while. Receipt of the latest pictures of these babies from Canada used to be a great source of joy and delight to the staff at *Shishu Bhavan*. "Sometimes they send photographs from Canada," recalled Sister Vincentia in one of her media interviews while taking delight in seeing see how the babies were settling into their new homes in Canada who, by then, had "grown so big and pretty."[75] Regular correspondences between the orphanage authority and the adoptive parents in Canada had, in fact, bonded them well. This had allowed the staff to gradually come to appreciate the fact that these prematurely born babies, having left the orphanage, were growing up healthy.

Problems encountered in doing the actual adoption

Following their arrival in Canada, the parents were required to go to the family court in their area of residence and complete the adoption process by formally accepting the child into the parents' family. This is generally done in the form of a formal sworn-in ceremony in front of a judge who presides over the ceremony of adoption. The adoptive parents of Ontario had retained Irving Copeland as their counsel to assist them in completing the formal adoption. Ideally speaking, it was then a matter of filing a legal document ordinarily known as a petition. This paper, which forms the legal basis for proceeding, generally contains pertinent information on the child, the child's birth mother, the adoptive parents, and the formal demand for the issuance by the court of the adoption order. In the present case, the document originating from the Ministry of Labor and Social Welfare, government of Bangladesh, signed by M. Sharafatullah, then deputy secretary, dated July 17, 1972, addressed to Mother Teresa had the effect of an adoption decree terminating the relationship between the rights of the statutory guardian, then Sr. Margaret Mary, and the war babies who had been released for adoption in Canada

All of the adoptive parents had the required papers, such as photocopies of the child's original birth certificate, the consent and release order from the orphanage for adoption, and letters from the government of Bangladesh allowing the children to leave Bangladesh for Canada for the purpose of adoption. The pertinent information package (or adoption decree that has been referred to) stated that citizenship would have to be given to the children upon reaching the age of majority and that it would absolve the government of Bangladesh of any further responsibility for these children. As mentioned, it also included a photocopy of names of the child's adoptive parents in Canada issued by the government of Bangladesh. Despite having all these documents, Ontario's demand for more information was in stark contrast with the governments of Quebec, Saskatchewan, and Nova Scotia, the three provinces that had received the same information package. Having known the circumstances surrounding the birth and the arrival of the war babies, provincial courts in Halifax, Montreal, and Saskatoon had accepted them without any question in order to effect the formal adoption. Unfortunately the adoptive parents in Ontario again began to face the same problems as before discussed in the previous chapter.

Upon hearing about the difficult experience of the Ontario couples, many supportive international organizations and individuals began to pull together to voice their concerns. Joining forces with the Ontario couples' cause, the Anglican Church of Canada's Primate's World Relief and Development Fund and the Ottawa Unitarian Congregation wrote, "While bureaucratic and inter-governmental relations need to be respected, we feel that a minimum of bureaucratic complications should be a priority when it comes to the life or death of matter such as the one you have been involved in."[76] Joint letters to politicians, local members of Parliament (MPs), through a collective approach to the problem were sent, pointing fingers at individuals in the Ontario Ministry of Community and Social Welfare who were dragging their feet just like before with regard to home study, which we have seen in chapter 3. They were asked to unmistakably spell out exactly *what* documents were required individually or collectively insofar as to be consistent with other provinces across the country.

In chapter 2, we have briefly touched on the process of adoption and have explained how legislations governing adoption existed in every province and territory. We have noted that there is no one uniform approach. Since the Ontario government had set its own requirements, it created additional problems that continued to delay the process for the same couples who had fought hard just to get their home studies done by the government. Applicants were confused, frustrated, and enraged. Fortunately, Helke Ferrie who, by then, had also brought another bunch of war orphans (including a few war babies), became more familiar not only with the complex issue of birth certificate but also with how to get around to such problems and bypass the bureaucratic red tape. The nature of the problem, explained Helke, was that the government of Bangladesh could not and would not authenticate all the birth certificates issued by *Shishu Bhavan* where the babies were born under the supervision of the orphanage staff: "these birth certificates can only be authenticated if a doctor, licensed to practice in Bangladesh, sees the child and testifies to the approximate age of the child in comparison to the certificate given out by the orphanage director,"[77] explained Helke.

Given the fact that the war babies were being born and abandoned both in secret immediately upon birth, there was no way one could have obtained government-issued birth certificate. Therefore, Helke's advice to the Ontario couples was to engage the Bangladeshi high commissioner in Ottawa in seeking his counsel with respect to the problem at hand.

It will be seen in chapter 5 that these infants were released from the orphanage with no formal birth certificate as such, although they had documents that stated the date of birth of the child in question. Because of the unusual constraint of the government of Bangladesh, it was unable to produce/authenticate official birth certificates for the children born in the orphanage under the circumstances. In certain cases such as Jorina's and a few others, the certificates were signed by Sr. Margaret Mary in order to facilitate the release of the said war babies.

Due to the sensitivity of the subject matter, the government of Bangladesh deemed it important to respect the wishes of the birth mothers who did not want their identities revealed. As far as the government was concerned, it was therefore preferable to get the orphanage authority to produce a document stating the date of birth of those who were born there under certain surreptitious circumstances. The government felt comfortable that this would ensure the release of the children ASAP, with documents stating the date of birth produced by the orphanage authority so that more lives could be saved. Naturally, each adoptive couple had thus the same types of information and papers received from the federal government and the government of Bangladesh in order for their child to be brought to Canada for the purpose of adoption.

The frustration level of the Ontario couple, however, had reached a point that they were forced to seek the intervention of their riding MPPs and the premier of Ontario and the federal members of Parliaments (MPs) of their respective constituencies just the way they had engaged them earlier in order to get the home studies done only four months ago. Taking a lead role in their fight for the formal adoption of their babies from Bangladesh, John and Dorothy Morris directed their appeal personally to William Davis, then premier of Ontario. In a letter addressed to the premier, the Morrises commended the work of the employees of the federal Manpower and Immigration who had earlier extended their cooperation on "humanitarian grounds" and had expedited their "daughter's immigration papers in a very short time"[78] following receipt of permission from the Child Welfare branch after obtaining a positive assessment of a home to study done by the local Children's Aid Society (CAS).

Describing the hurdles the couples had been encountering, and having exhausted all avenues to cut through the red tape, the couple made a desperate plea to the premier of Ontario: "Mr. Davis, what we are down to is a little orphan girl who, because of the length of time spent at *Shishu Bhavan,* was loved by the good sisters but unwanted and unloved by anyone else, who has now arrived in Canada and is with people who love and want her. This is beautiful, let's not lose sight of this in a mass of bureaucratic red tape."[79] The Morrises emphasized the point that the papers duly submitted were "well within the spirit of the law provided common sense, and discretion are exercised in the spirit of humanity."[80] "A place to stand and a place to grow. This is exactly what we are trying to give to a little girl nobody wanted in the country of her birth. Let's not get lost in red tape,"[81] wrote a forlorn helpless couple expressing their utter frustration.

In their personal appeal to the premier, the Morrises also alluded to the fact that in Ontario, they not only had to pay for the private home study (which was not conducted by the local children's aid society that generally conducts such study free of cost) but also were being asked to submit more papers than were necessary at a time when neither the governments of Saskatchewan, Nova Scotia, and Quebec sought additional information nor charged any fee for the home study conducted by them. "In the name of humanity we are trying to help another human being and in the name of humanity we are asking the Province of Ontario through you, Mr. Davis, to help another human being,"[82] thus appealed the Morrises.

Stubborn as it may seem, Ontario officials maintained that important papers were still missing in order to complete the process of adoption. "Proper consents to adoption, medical consents and birth certificates are not yet available,"[83] thus wrote Betty Graham, then director Child Welfare, to the Ontario couples. As it turned out, despite her repeated assurance of cooperation, she continued on in her own way showing a complete lack of compassion and sensitivity at a time when they were needed the most: "We are informed that the Director of Social Welfare in Bangladesh will be the legal guardian designate. We understand the law provides, at present, only for the release of infants of raped Bangladesh[i] women. When further information is received as to the documents that will be available to regularize the status of these children in Ontario, we will be informing the solicitors concerned and your Society . . . Meanwhile, we shall look forward to receiving your customary reports for such a placement."[84] Information along such vein was not at all helpful to the couples who wanted to move forward and complete the formal adoption. Clearly, the Ontario couples were caught in the toils of unnecessary and rigid regulations.

After some time, however, Ontario officials gradually paid attention to what was being sought. The applicants were eventually allowed to formally adopt the children of their *choice*. Interesting to note, since international adoption is primarily a federal immigration matter, it was alleged that Graham was acting outside her jurisdiction. When this was brought to the attention of Stephen Lewis, then the NDP leader of the opposition in Ontario, it was subsequently revealed along with many more recorded outrageous prejudices over a two-day exposition in the Legislative Assembly of Ontario (see *Hansard,* October 22 and 23, 1973). Helke's three-and-a-half-day hunger strike then broke the logjam, and the following year, Betty Graham was fired. While formally adopting the war babies, the adoptive parents were cognizant of the general effect of the adoption decree, which is to terminate all rights and duties between the child and its natural parents/statutory guardian, and to make the child legally the child of the adopting parents.

Since the original birth certificates had no information other than a single name, which could well be one's first or last name, some adoptive parents believed that any Canadian who is not familiar with typical Bangladeshi names might have difficulty figuring out their meanings. They came up with their own ideas in keeping or modifying their child's first and/or middle names and registered them according to their wishes. Each war baby's profile in chapter 5 addresses this. In the next chapter, we shall hear from the adoptive parents their firsthand experience in raising racially different children.

Table 2
War babies' weight chart

Name (original)	Date of birth	Weight at birth
Shikha	12/3/1972	2.7 kg
Rani	30/3/1972	1 kg
Omar	29/4/1972	2.5 kg
War Baby B	8/7/1972	2.5 kg
Orun	27/5/1972	2.4 kg
Rajib	1/7/1972	3 kg
Molly	4/5/1972	1.2 kg
Prodip	25/3/1972	2.5 kg
Shomor	7/4/1972	1 kg
Onil	23/5/1972	3 kg
Bathol	27/6/1972	2.2 kg
Amina	3/4/1972	2 kg
Regina (Rajina)	24/11/1971	4 kg
Ruphea Rita	15/2/1972	2 kg
Jorina	23/10/1971	2.7 kg

Source: *Register Book, Shishu Bhavan,* Missionaries of Charity, 26 Islampur Road, Dhaka, Bangladesh, housed at *Shishu Bhavan's* collection of records.

Notes and References

1   Memorandum to the Minister of External Affairs, Mitchell Sharp: Subject: *News Release – Bangladesh War Orphans,* July 18, 1972. Library and Archives Canada, RG 76, Vol. 1040, Box 141, *File* 5020-1-710 Pt. 1. In the past years, 1947–1948, however, approximately 1,200 orphaned Europeans were brought to Canada. The 1960 Policy had also allowed immigration of orphaned refugees in Canada with prior approval of provincial child welfare authorities that assess the prospective adoptive parents' eligibility and suitability.

2   *Ibid.*

3   *Ibid.*

4   Families For Children, *Bangladesh Project.* Part E, Chapter 32, *Bangladesh Babies.* 1982. p. 278. Hereinafter, referred to as the *Bangladesh Project.* Families For Children (FFC) also used to publish information on its project in Bangladesh in its in-house newsletter in 1972 and 1973. This will be referred to as the *Bangladesh Project Report.* There is also a large bulk of documents that is still with Fred and Bonnie Cappuccino in Cappuccinos' personal collection called *Bangladesh File.*

5   *Bangladesh Project Report,* Families For Children, August 1972, p. 4.

6   E-mail from Elisabeth Mowling to Mustafa Chowdhury, February 20, 2001. Also, prior to her e-mail, Elisabeth stated this to the author during one of her interviews with the author on May 23, 1999, at her house in Mississauga, Ontario.

7   *Ibid.*

8   *Bangladesh Project,* 1982, p. 280.

9   *Ibid.* p. 281.

10 The *London Free Press,* January 28, 1989.

11 E-mail from Rev. Tony Boonstra to Mustafa Chowdhury, July 27, 2010. Prior to confirming this in writing, Tony had mentioned this to the author during the interview with members of the Boonstra family on June 21, 1998.

12 *Ibid.*

13 *Ibid.*

14 *Ibid.*

15 Letter from Dorothy Morris to Mustafa Chowdhury, November 23, 1999. The same letter also contains few pages of handwritten notes that Dorothy wrote following the arrival of Jorina. Dorothy meticulously recorded her own experiences and observations as the little girl started to grow. Dorothy presented the same notes to Jorina when she became an adult. Dorothy made a copy of that note for the author. Hereinafter, referred to as *Dorothy's note.*

16 Interesting to note, although the documents from Bangladesh state the name of the baby girl as Ruphea Rita, somehow in the Canadian media she was referred to as Rija instead of Rita.

17 *Kitchener-Waterloo Record,* July 21, 1972.

18 E-mail from Robin and Barbara Morrall to Mustafa Chowdhury, March 18, 2012. In addition to meeting having a face-to-face interview with the couple in Saskatoon, Saskatchewan, on August 10, 1998, the author has been in touch with the couple on a regular basis.

19 *Ibid.*

20 *Ibid.*

21 *Ibid.*

22 *Ibid.*

23 E-mail from Doreen Good to Mustafa Chowdhury, April 29, 2009. Over the years, the author has been in regular touch with the couple.

24 *Ibid.*

25 *Ibid.*

26 The *Montreal Star,* July 21, 1972.

27 E-mail from Ray Mowling to Mustafa Chowdhury, June 23, 2012.

28 Margo-Carr Ribeiro said this in an interview with the author at Place du Portage, Hull, Quebec, her place of work. She was working for the Canadian International Development Agency (CIDA) at the time. The author, too, worked for the Department of Human Resources Development Canada (HRDC) in the same premises during the same years. They met at one of the food courts of the office premises on May 25, 1997. Again, the author also met Margo's husband, Roberto Ribeiro. He also worked for CIDA at

the time. They met at food court on several occasions between 1997 and 2007. The author tried to broach the subject (adoption of Shomor who is known as Martin) but had no luck. Information on their profile in chapter 5 was collected in bits and pieces over the years.

[29] *Ibid.*

[30] *Ibid.*

[31] E-mail from Trudy Hartt to Mustafa Chowdhury on November 1, 1998. Following this, the couple and their daughter Shama came to Ottawa to meet with the author on June 23, 2000. Together, they met at a restaurant in downtown Ottawa and discussed the project over lunch. Since then they have been in touch with each other and corresponded regularly. Shama Hartt and the author are Facebook friends.

[32] *Ibid.*

[33] *Ibid.*

[34] *Kitchener-Waterloo Record*, July 21, 1972.

[35] *Ibid.*

[36] The *Montreal Star*, July 21, 1972.

[37] E-mail from Pierre Hogue to Mustafa Chowdhury, May 12, 2012. Over the years, author has corresponded with both Pierre Hogue and Lise Bertrand and talked over the phone on a regular basis.

[38] E-mail from Lise Bertrand to Mustafa Chowdhury, April 10, 2012. Over the years, author has corresponded with both Lise Bertrand and Pierre Hogue and talked to them separately over the phone on a regular basis. They took great interest in the project and provided feedback to the author especially with reference to chapters 5, 6, and 7.

[39] *The Bangladesh Project*, p. 284.

[40] Letter from Bryce Mackasey, Minister of Manpower and Immigration, to Fred and Bonnie Cappuccino, Families For Children, April 20, 1972. Library and Archives Canada, RG 76, Vol. 1040, *File* 50201-710, Pt. 1.

[41] Letter from Bryce Mackasey, Minister of Manpower and Immigration, to Mr. Fred Cappuccino and Mrs. Bonnie Cappuccino, Families For Children, August 25, 1972. Library and Archives Canada, RG 76, Vol. 1040, *File* 50201-710, Pt. 1.

42   Letter from Pierre Elliott Trudeau, Prime Minister of Canada, to Mr. Fred Cappuccino and Mrs. Bonnie Cappuccino, Families For Children, September 1, 1972. Library and Archives Canada, MG 26, Series 8, Vol. 297.

43   *Ibid.*

44   The *Toronto Star* November 4, 1972.

45   *Ibid.*

46   *Ibid.*

47   *Burlington Gazette,* Vol. 7, No. 36, July 27, 1972.

48   *Ibid.*

49   *Ibid.*

50   Letter from Reverend R. D. MacRae, secretary, Anglican Church of Canada, to Rev. Fred Cappuccino and Bonnie Cappuccino, Families For Children, September 19, 1972. This letter and all other personal letters addressed to the Cappuccinos along with other information from the Cappuccinos that have been used in this book are also in the Cappuccinos' personal library collection on *Bangladesh File.*

51   *Ibid.*

52   *Homemaker's* November 1975. p. 8.

53   *Ibid.*

54   *Ibid.*

55   *Kuan-Yin Foundation, Report on Bangladesh Project.* October 2, 1972, p. 3. The *Report* and other letters addressed to Helke Ferrie by those who were involved in the project and that have been used in this book are in the Ferries' personal collection on file titled *Bangladesh Project* on *Bangladesh File.*

56   Letter from His Excellency Abdul Momin, High Commissioner of Bangladesh, to Helke Ferrie, Chairperson of Asian Adoptions, Ontario Branch, Families For Children, September 27, 1972.

57   *Ibid.* This was in response to Helke's new project to bring another batch of war-orphans from Bangladesh in October 1972.

58   Letter from Fred Cappuccino, Secretary, Families For Children to the Bangladesh Quakers Service, August 23, 1972. The present letter, along with all other correspondences that have been used for this book, is in the Cappuccinos' personal collection on *Bangladesh File.*

59   Letter from the Quaker Service of Bangladesh to Rev. Fred Cappuccino, October 13, 1972.

60   *Ibid.*

61   Letter from Sister Margaret Mary, Superior, Missionaries of Charity, to Mrs. Bonnie Cappuccino, President, Families For Children, September 4, 1972.

62   *Ibid.*

63   Letter to from Paulinus Costa, Acting National Director, Christian Organization for Relief and Rehabilitation to Fred Cappuccino, Secretary, Families For Children. September 11, 1972.

64   Letter from K. M. Islam, Assistant Director, Coordination Division, Ministry of Relief and Rehabilitation, Government of the People's Republic of Bangladesh to Fred Cappuccino, Secretary, Families For Children, August 32, 1972.

65   Letter from Sister Margaret Mary, Superior, Missionaries of Charity to Fred Cappuccino, Secretary, Families For Children. August 13, 1972.

66   *Ibid.*

67   Letter from Bonnie Cappuccino, president, Families For Children, addressed to all adoptive parents. There is no date in the said letter, although it is evident that this letter was in response to the letter of Sr. Margaret Mary, which she wrote to Bonnie on September 4, 1972.

68   Letter from Sister Margaret Mary, Superior, Missionaries of Charity to Bonnie Cappuccino, President, Families For Children, no date.

69   *Ibid.*

70   Letter from Lise Hogue to Fred and Bonnie Cappuccino, Secretary and President, Families For Children. August 22, 1972.

71   Letter from Fred Cappuccino, Secretary, Families For Children to Emile and Rosemarie Baran, Canadian High Commission in Bangladesh. August 27, 1972.

72   *Ibid.*

73   *Ibid.*

74   Letter from Fred Cappuccino, *Families For Children,* to Abdul Awal, Executive Director, National Board of Bangladesh Women's Rehabilitation Program, Ministry of Labor and Social Welfare, Government of the People's Republic of Bangladesh, September 23, 1972.

75 Sister Vincentia's interview with Samuel Abt titled "Venereal Disease Rampant, Bangladesh Women Suffer Still from Wartime Rapes" published in the *International Herald Tribune,* Tuesday, October 2, 1973.

76 Letter from Reverend R. D. MacRae, Secretary, Anglican Church of Canada, to Rev. Fred Cappuccino, Secretary, Families For Children. September 19, 1972.

77 Letter from Helke Ferrie, Chairperson of Asian Adoptions, Ontario Branch, Families For Children, to John and Dorothy Morris, Phil and Diane Rochefort, Del and Donna Wolsey, Tony and Bonnie Boonstra, Fred and Bonnie Cappuccino, August 31, 1972.

78 Letter from John and Dorothy Morris to William Davis, Premier of Ontario. There is no date in the letter. The couple claims that this letter was hand-delivered to the premier's office due to the urgency of the matter. The Morrises gave the author a copy of the letter. The couple has kept all their correspondences with government officials in a file titled *Bangladesh File.*

79 *Ibid.*

80 *Ibid.*

81 *Ibid.*

82 *Ibid.*

83 Memorandum to Mr. T. W. A. van Overdijk, Children's Aid Society, Brantford, Ontario, from Children's Welfare Branch, signed by Betty Graham, director, September 13, 1972, to be sent to all applicants for home studies. Archives of Ontario, RG 29-59, Acc 15296/2 TR 78-075, Box 6, *File*: *Bangladesh Infants 1972–1973.* According to Helke Ferrie, Betty Graham then director of Child Welfare in the Ministry of Community and Social Services, government of Ontario, said to her, "It is God's will that they [the orphans] die over there." Helke said that in an interview with the author on July 31, 1998, at her house (R.R. # 2) in Alton, Ontario. Helke also maintains that Graham also made it clear to her and other Ontario couples, saying, "As long as you ask for an international adoption we will not cooperate."

84 *Ibid.*

CHAPTER FIVE

Adoptive Parents and War Babies: A Vignette

TYPICALLY, ALL FOURTEEN marital couples who adopted Bangladeshi war babies were in their thirties, homogeneously middle class, and with a secure and healthy income; some were dual-career couples, while some were stay-home mothers, but all with middle-class values. Despite part-time jobs on the part of some mothers, most mothers had fulfilled the traditional role of homemaker and main caretaker of the children, while their husbands concentrated on their full-time employment/business. Overall, they were ordinary run-of-the-mill people of Canada having neither exaggerated missionary zeal nor condescending attitude with a paternalistic idea of "civilizing" or "Canadianizing" the children. They were keen on seeing in their children the development of their talents and formation of strong self-esteem and other values and ethics that would prepare them as honest, kind, and compassionate Canadian for the future. Nevertheless, despite many commonalities, one must not paint them with too broad a brush. All families, with the exception of one who was Jewish, were Christians although their denominations varied in many instances.

There are two common features of the adoptive parents that are worth mentioning: first, they were a group of strong-willed Caucasian couples the majority of whom had no problem with fertility. That being the case, for the would-be-adoptive parents, coping with infertility as a man or woman, or letting go of dreams of being a biological parent was never an issue with them. The adoptive parents held an expanded view of parenthood, the social construction of the family, and the significance of consanguinity especially when it was not a matter of negotiation of infertility through adoption. It was also not a question of going through a transition, from expecting to be a biological parent to becoming an adoptive parent that usually involves a process of resocialization in which the prospective adoptive parents unlearn elements of biological parenthood and learn the aspects of parenthood associated with adoption.

In that sense, this simple fact makes the present group of parents different from other adoptive couples. To them, adhering to strong value for and attachment to the family had always been, and still is, a priority. Briefly, the families had the following characteristics of being atypical: truly diverse and deeply interested in various areas of transracial adoption. There were no divorces with the exception of two couples. The adoptive fathers who left their homes had continued to carry on their responsibilities, both financial and familial, toward their children. And the particular children in question had remained in touch with both their parents, something they continue to this day. Two families adopted more than one child from Bangladesh. With the exception of one family, the rest of the families had adopted white, black, mulatto, Korean, Vietnamese, Cambodian, Haitian, Indian, and Aboriginal babies as well.

In every home, the word "adoption" had been a household word, as the fact of adoption was much too apparent to the adoptees that came from different countries. One notable similarity in each of the family history is the parents' willingness to pursue an alternative way to create a family with no particular concern regarding the ethnic or racial attributes of children available for adoption from a country of their choice. Without being opposed to creating a family in the traditional way only, they wished to expand their families through using other routes of parenting. This is significant in that, even in those days, there were a variety of alternatives of ways and means to bring a child into the lives of a couple – apart from direct adoption to high-tech medical procedures through in vitro fertilization to surrogacy with increased success.

It will be seen how these couples, who turned to Families For Children (FFC) in their quest for parenthood, went through considerable emotional struggle even before they approached the FFC. The story of adoption from Bangladesh takes on a special meaning when one considers the fact that during the time of adoption, they were aware of how many child welfare professionals in the USA had publicly warned of the risks involved in interracial adoption. Although the authorities in the USA had challenged the advisability of removing children from their native lands, this particular group had remained resolved in its desire to adopt from Bangladesh. As far as they were concerned, no negative stories or reports could ever deter them in pursuing their goal.

The first contingent of fifteen Bangladeshi war babies, eight girls and seven boys, who came to Canada on July 20, 1972, through an adoption initiative of the FFC (we have seen in the previous chapter), was also the first set of war babies to be released by the government of Bangladesh.

It will be seen under individual profile how the adoptive parents, while formally adopting them in Canada, chose to amend the names of their child according to their wishes. The birth certificates of the war babies contained only the place, the day and the year of birth of the infant, as well as the first name of the infant, and in some instances, the infant's mother's first name only if the said mother had provided the name. In majority of the cases, the birth mothers chose not to give their names. All birth certificates and relevant documents were signed by Sr. Margaret Mary, then superior of the Missionaries of Charity and statutory guardian of the war babies. Upon arriving in Canada, these documents were then attested by the high commissioner of Bangladesh in Ottawa to facilitate formal adoption in Canadian courts.

The adoptive parents were aware that the orphanage authority was particularly respectful of the wishes of the distraught birth mothers." Without exception, all adoptive parents from this bunch believed that the issue of naming one's child deserved careful and well-informed thought and action on their part. In doing so, they had reflected a great deal on the notion that one is identified by one's name and that one's name is part of one's own self and identity.

Moving forward, it will also be seen how carefully the adoptive parents chose the name for each of their adopted child recognizing the significance of their own family and sociocultural background in Canada. This may be referred to as an attempt to "Canadianize" their names at a time when they had to add the family's surname (last name) as mandatory requirement in Canada. In "Canadianizing" the name of the child, they paid attention to what sounded pleasing to their ears, which was an important way to "claim" their child. At the same time, they were respectful of the child's original Bengali name that was already given by the orphanage authority upon birth. In claiming their child, they tried to proceed with caution to offer a name that they believed would be valuable within their family and culture keeping in mind the name that was given by the nuns. The chart below show their original name given by the nuns at *Shishu Bhavan* (the name with which they traveled) and their amended names in Canada.

Table 3
Original and amended names of the war babies

Original names given in Bangladesh	Names added by parents in Canada
Shikha	Shikha Deepa Margaret Cappuccino
Orun	Ashoka Ferrie
Amina	Amina Lynn Wolsey
Rani	Rani Joy Morrall
Omar	Christopher Omar Boonstra
Bathol	Ryan Bathol Good
Jorina	Lara Jorina Morris
Ruphea Rita	Ruphea Rija Rochefort
Onil	Mark Onil Mowling
Rajib	Rajib Cappuccino Simpson
Prodip	Mathew McCullough
Ragina	Rajina Josée Hogue

	War Baby B
Shomor	Martin Ribeiro
Molly	Shama Jameela Mollie Hartt

Source: *Taken from the individual birth records of the war babies provided by their parents and final names given by them in Canada.*

By and large, the parents were confident that the general environment, the multicultural values, and the lifestyle that their children were being exposed to would help the children become successful in their personal adjustments as adults. They were more concerned about instilling within their children a strong sense of human identity believing that the young child, whether it was their Bangladeshi war baby or any other orphan from anywhere else, *needs the feeling of belonging, having a secure home and family.* A look at their individual profiles would give us yet another interesting aspect of the adoptive parents. Below are brief sketches of the couples and their Bangladeshi babies in alphabetical order.

Tony Boonstra and Bonnie Boonstra

The life story of the Boonstras is at once interesting and, in many ways, full of ups and downs, mystery, and drama. Tony, originally from Holland, came to Canada at the age of eight and grew up in British Columbia; while a wonderfully warmhearted and soft-spoken Bonnie is originally from Grand Rapid, Michigan, USA. Tony and Bonnie met during the time Tony did his undergraduate studies at Calvin College in Grand Rapids. After graduating in 1967, Tony accepted a teaching position in Aylmer, Ontario, where the couple moved with their first son, Anthony William, who was only one month old at the time.

Both Bonnie and Tony looked forward to having more children, and a little over a year and a half, their second child, Vonda, was born. It was a real trauma to them when this beautiful child died at seven months from sudden infant death syndrome. At the time, Bonnie was pregnant, but due to complications and poor medical care, the little boy Timothy was born prematurely and did not survive.

During this time, the Boonstras had been involved in social services and adopted a little girl, Jodi, born on September 22, 1969. People in the social service area drew their attention to the possibility of international adoptions. As the Boonstras continued to work with the social service agencies, they also provided a temporary home for a teenager for some time in the early 1970s. They recall those tough times when Bonnie was again experiencing difficulty with another pregnancy. This time around, Annette Duursma, their nineteen-year-old niece from British Columbia, came to live with them to help them out around the house. Their third son, Luke, was born prematurely on June 1, 1971. Not only that but he also had hyaline membrane disorder and had breathing problems for the first two years of his life. The Boonstras thought for a while that he had cystic fibrosis.

It was at that time that they made inquiries with a number of social service agencies specifically about adoption from overseas and were put in touch with Rev. Fred Cappuccino and his wife, Bonnie Cappuccino, who were heading the Montreal-based Families For children (FFC) at the time. Within months, they joined the Cappuccinos in lobbying the government and drummed up support for the adoption of the war babies from Bangladesh. It was at this time that they also met Del and Donna Wolsey of Komoka, Ontario, another adoptive couple who lobbied the government from the very beginning, and worked together with them.

Even though they had three children at the time, they were still interested and firm in their decision to adopt a war baby from Bangladesh who would be their fourth child. It did not matter to them if the child was a boy or a girl, as they were well in control of their emotions. Adoption of a Bangladeshi war baby was thus conceived while the war was still going on in Occupied Bangladesh back in late 1971.

Despite the passage of time, the inordinate delay in doing the paperwork through various levels of governments, including the hard time they were subjected to while dealing with immigration officials in London, Ontario, still lingers in their memory. In fact, even to this day, Tony can't seem to forget the miserable time he and other prospective adoptive parents were subjected to in going through the process of getting the home studies done and meeting other formalities. They still can't understand why on earth some Ontario officials were giving the applicants runaround for nothing for a noble cause like providing a safe home to an orphan. In an attempt to head-start, they worked closely also with Sandra Simpson (FFC, Montreal) and the Wolseys to whip up public interest in international and interracial adoption.

What remains embedded in their minds is the day on which they picked up their long-awaited son who arrived with fourteen other war babies. It was only when they held the baby with their own hands at the airport that they felt relieved for the first time after months of stress and strain.

Within a very short time after the arrival of their son, Omar, later named Christopher, from Bangladesh, the family contracted dysentery. For a while, Bonnie was hospitalized, and Tony took care of the children, three of them still in diapers. Chris was the carrier of the dysentery. For a while, the family was quarantined, and their eldest son, Tony, was not able to go to school. But in time they all recovered.

The following year, in 1973, the couple adopted an eight-year-old boy, Brian. Then came Kara, born in Ottawa on February 12, 1976, who was adopted at the age of four months. Five years later in 1981, the Boonstras became legal guardian of two brothers: Todd and Tommy were then ten and five year old respectively. For eight years, they raised them as *their* children until they decided to return to their natural father. Three years later in 1984, they adopted their last son, Joshua, born February 22, 1984. With the final adoption of Joshua, the number of Boonstra children (both adopted and biological) stood at seven without Todd and Tommy who by then had left them the Boonstra family..

All through their lives, the Boonstras had been flexible while raising their children, at least during the initial periods. Out of their family of seven children, Christopher and Kara have Bangladeshi parentage – the difference being Christopher, a war baby born in Bangladesh; while Kara born in Ottawa of Bangladeshi parentage. Their last son, Joshua, is an aboriginal, born in Vancouver, while the others are white Canadians. Like other adoptive families, the Boonstras are a truly multiracial family where cultural differences were valued and respected by each and every member.

In 1973 when Tony became a principal at the Ottawa Christian School in Ottawa, Ontario, the family moved to Ashton. This was a busy period for the family when Bonnie remained focused on the children who were growing up having t spend most of her time with the children. As parents, both of them grew too, having learned new ways to develop greater parenting skills. According to the children, their parents had reared their children using their own knowledge of "do's" and "don'ts." The family lived together in Ashton for two years until Tony left for Montreal to attend Presbyterian College at McGill University campus.

For one year, Bonnie and the children stayed back in Ashton, while Tony began his studies in theology and divinity. In 1977, however, the entire family moved to Scotstown in the Eastern Townships of Quebec. Needless to mention, by then Bonnie had assumed greater family responsibility in order to make sure that the diverse needs of the growing children were met both individually and collectively especially when the father of the children was away for an extended period of time coming home only on weekends. While Bonnie looked after the children, Tony had to dedicate himself to his studies.

One of the strongest points that sticks out about the Boonstras is the way in which the family remained united despite long periods of separation between Tony and Bonnie along with the children during the three years Tony studied at McGill. In fact, even though the family frequently moved from one city to another, the Boonstras made sure that the children's needs were prioritized so that they would have no disruption in their studies. Happily for the Boonstra children, all of them had enjoyed the moves and had made friendship with the people they had encountered in each successive school.

By early 1978 Tony had completed a bachelor's degree in theology and master's degree in divinity. He was ordained at St. Andrew's Presbyterian Church in Carleton Place in June (1978). Following his graduation and ordination, Tony became a minister at St. Columbia Presbyterian Church in Parksville, Vancouver Island, British Columbia.

Having stayed in British Columbia for eight years, another big move came in 1986 when Tony responded to a call to become minister at St. Andrew's Presbyterian Church, an inner city church in Edmonton. This time, again, the family moved and settled quickly to allow their children to continue their studies and choose their own extracurricular activities.

By late 1980s, not only were the Boonstra children involved in studies, but by then many of them had also part-time jobs and were involved in seasonal sports; again some children became involved in other spheres of activities in and around where they lived. In 1994 the

Boonstras moved to Richmond, Ontario, a suburb of Ottawa, where Tony became a minister at St. Andrews Presbyterian Church. Needless to say, within a short period following the family's move to Richmond, some of the older Boonstra children began to move to Ottawa and other cities to pursue their own lives. Those who moved out, however, remained close to their parents and siblings.

The Boonstras gave their children a sense of independence to pursue their own interest without any interference. Not surprisingly, therefore, although the couple had always been quite religious, they never imposed their own beliefs on their children. Instead, the children were taught to be loving, kind, and compassionate to each other and recognize the value of a close-knit family. The Boonstras made sure that they practiced what they preached, such as respect for others, tolerance of other people's views, sincerity, and open-mindedness. Like other adoptive parents under discussion, the Boonstras are atypical representing, in a way, the characteristics of Canadian multiculturalism, multiracialism, and broader social values.

As far as the Boonstra children are concerned – both natural and adopted – they grew up in a multiracial family in which there was no dearth of love and affection from their parents. Because the family inculcated on the notion of pluralism and diversity, having encouraged greater interaction among people of different races, the children became comfortable with these concepts right from the beginning. Thus, through the parents' special efforts, and despite the racial difference among the Boonstra children, all siblings were taught how to be affectionate and friendly to each other, adhering to the values their parents had instilled in them during their early years.

Every Boonstra child, whether adopted or born to the family, grew up knowing the meaning of adoption and how the Boonstra children with different racial background became sibling to each other. As parents of the children of diverse racial backgrounds, the Boonstras had always been open with their children with regard to their children's birth history and other information to the extent they themselves were cognizant of. The parents always attempted to make sure that each child was also made aware of his or her roots and anecdotes relating to adoption.

They also taught the children the importance of sensitivity to issues surrounding adoption and abandonment as well as the demonstration of respect for people's privacy from an early age. Consequently, when the children were growing up, having heard about the stories of adoption, they too had endless questions about the *why* and *how* of adoption. As far as the children are concerned, they never hesitated to ask any question that they might have had with regard to adoption, and were happy to have their parents' responses to their questions that were asked on sundry occasions over the years when they were growing up. As for the parents, they too had exercised infinite patience in responding to their children's questions and queries at any given time.

The Boonstras' collection of information on each child had helped their children who wished to pursue further. As adults, each adopted child had full access to their child's family files, which Bonnie had kept with great care for posterity. In a sense, the documentation, which might be called the *Boonstra File,* is a small archive of the family that contains collection of photographs, letters, correspondences, birth records, home study approval letters, adoption papers, and newspaper clippings.

Some Boonstra children took interest in delving into their past, while some other children remained unenthusiastic about their family background. In fact, the latter group never made any attempt to pursue the subject at all. Upon reaching the age of majority, some of the adopted children had spent hours together in their parents' home library/archives where information on all of their siblings was kept. It was up to the children to take that bit of information and do the necessary digging, which they had encouraged.

The Boonstras are still living in Ashton although now in an empty nest. They remain thankful to God for giving them all these children whose fault and follies they have always ignored especially when the children were growing up. They recognized early in their life that every child is a mixture of many different attributes and there are many gradations within each child. Having raised them in their own way, they have full confidence in their children who are now on their own.

Today the Boonstras have nine grandchildren scattered across the country. Every now and then, the Boonstras try to arrange family reunions, which are a great opportunity for the Boonstra children to spend some quality time together. Bonnie is in touch with the Wolseys, who have been organizing annual reunions of the war babies and other Bengali adoptees in and around Ontario. In 2010, Bonnie attended the reunion with Chris (their child from Bangladesh) who had enjoyed the gathering a great deal and seemed to have taken greater interest in the war babies than before.

Omar

Born on April 29, 1972, in Dhaka, Bangladesh, at Mother Teresa's *Shishu Bhavan,* then named Omar weighed 2.5 kg at birth. When he arrived at the age of two and half months, he weighed 2.7 kg, having gained only 0.2 kg in six weeks. At a later time, when his parents took him to Sears to get a picture taken, he was still the size of a newborn, but he used to give great big smiles. "It surprised all the people nearby who also had to smile to see such a small person with such a big smile," recalled the Boonstras.[1]

Like other prematurely born war babies, the said infant was so frail that those who took care of him feared that he would not make it. Fortunately, soon the baby began to show signs of progress, and during the time of selection of the babies, the same baby looked promising to the Canadian doctor who examined him for the purpose of adoption. He was, therefore, picked out for adoption. He arrived in Canada with the rest of the war babies. During his formal adoption in Canada, his parents named him Christopher (his first name), retained Omar as his middle name, and added their surname (Boonstra). Omar thus grew up as Christopher Omar Boonstra.

In September 1976, the family moved to Scotstown, Quebec. The children were enrolled in an English school, since they were not permanent residents of the province of Quebec. At that time, the *Partie Quebecois,* which was in power in Quebec, had insisted that all children were to attend French school. Since the Boonstras were English speaking and temporarily living in Quebec, they were allowed to send their children to English school with a proviso that they would provide a recognized birth certificate for the child in question. Unfortunately, they could not could not provide any documentation with regard to Chris' birth parents' citizenship, their country of residence, their first language or the language they speak at home, and other pertinent information.

Having adopted Chris with a mere handwritten birth certificate issued by the Dhaka-based Missionaries of Charity, and no other information on him or his biological parents, the adoptive parents then living in Quebec felt helpless. The school board had refused to take into consideration any other factor. At that time, they had no choice but to put Chris in a French medium school upon advice from the school board. This was even though the adoptive parents in Canada were English speaking and all their other children were placed in English school. Despite the stretch of time, Tony recalls with anger and resentment all the runarounds and hassles that they were subjected to and the process they had to go through against their wishes at the time just to put Chris through the Quebec school system. The unpleasant memory of the emotionally disturbing experiences in their attempt to put Chris through the school system still lingers on in their minds.

For whatever reason, Chris never picked up the French language. Starting with what the Quebec school board called the "inappropriate" birth record or documentation, "Chris became a victim of circumstances," says Bonnie while recalling those days (e-mail from Tony and Bonnie Boonstra to the author). Right from the time Chris started his first schooling in Scotstown, Chris had faced one after another barrier, adding only disappointments and frustrations in his parents' minds. In fact, with respect to Chris, there were many disruptive events that ranged over a wide spectrum of issues. In a sense, when the couple looked back to narrate their experience of the time, they felt as though such recollection gave them a way to ventilate their pent-up feelings.

Though putting Chris to French school was the only choice they were left with, they maintain that this had caused Chris more harm than good. From the start, Chris seemed like a misfit at the particular school environment. For one thing, he was a tiny boy. Chris "was so small for his age that he was a kind of curiosity to the people around. He would often hide in little cubby holes and did not participate in the class since he did not understand French," recalls Tony (e-mail from Tony and Bonnie Boonstra to the author). However, as it turned out, since Chris' parents were English speaking, he learned English as his first language at home. Naturally, he was prompt and responsive in English as opposed to French with which he had much less familiarity. Consequently, being at a French medium school, Chris was at a disadvantageous situation and had lagged behind having lost some time at school. "As far as I am concerned this was a complete wasted year for him," said Tony with a kind of anger and regret (e-mail from Tony and Bonnie Boonstra to the author).

What is even more maddening for the couple is that Chris lost his school years not only in Quebec but also in Vancouver Island when the family moved to the province of British Columbia. Much to the family's shock and surprise, Chris had to be hospitalized all of a sudden on an urgent basis. The doctor in charge discovered that Chris' "passage from the kidney to the bladder was somewhat blocked" (e-mail from Tony and Bonnie Boonstra to the author). The couple shuddered at the thought of not diagnosing the boy's illness earlier: "If they had not discovered this, Chris would have probably lost one of his kidneys," maintain his parents (e-mail from Tony and Bonnie Boonstra to the author). Naturally, they went ahead with the doctor's advice and had the surgery done right away. For Chris, this meant again more loss of time at school and repetition of class at a later time. Nevertheless, the good thing about the entire family is that Chris regained his health and became a completely healthy boy. The parents were relieved to see how he was back on track with both studies and sports.

Over the years, however, things turned out quite differently for Chris who became less and less interested in pursuing studies in a formal educational institution. Chris is frank in admitting the fact that he was no longer interested in following any formal education, something that had never attracted him. As far as Chris is concerned, if it sounds bad, so be it. That's the truth with regard to his personal view on formal education. Despite lack of interest, Chris had successfully attended both elementary and middle school at Parksville Elementary School and Parksville Middle School in Vancouver Island. When the family moved to Edmonton, Alberta, Chris went to the East Wood Community School to complete grades 6–8. He then went to Victoria Composite High School to work toward his final high school diploma. There were many things that he did not like about school and the environment, said Chris.[2]

Not surprisingly, therefore, Chris simply dropped out of high school like many other young adults of his age. Needless to say, initially the Boonstras were disappointed with Chris' decision but did not come down on him like many parents who cannot control their anger. In fact, his parents had always refrained from picking at him or, for that matter, at any of their children. According to Chris, his parents had always treated their children with deference. They, however, encouraged him to become a responsible adult in life following the dictates of his conscience. After leaving his studies, Chris took up a series of odd jobs but determined to move forward with his life.

Naturally, his first few jobs were at various restaurants in and around the Edmonton city, such as Bullwinkle Family Food at Bonnie Doon Shopping Centre, Grande Lees Bakery and Eating Place, and New York Fries at the Kingsway Garden Mall. In those years during summer months, he used to work for Kannawin, a Presbyterian summer camp in Silver Lake, Alberta. Within few years, Chris had gained enough experience to become a camp cook. Having joined the workforce at an early age, Chris continued to work without any break and had remained focused on his work. This was between 1988 and early 1995. In a sense, Chris became more mature with his recently gained valuable life experiences mainly through an exposure to a world of reality. In fact, as he buckled down to work, he learned the trick of the trade in course of his years of work.

Over the years, he held various positions, both full time and part time, from busboy to a head cook. In 1996, he became assistant cook at Gracefield Camp and Conference Centre, Gracefield, Quebec. Like the Kannawin Camp in Sylvan Lake, this camp is also a Presbyterian camp whose director/owner took a special liking for Chris, as they became close to each other while at the resort. Indeed, one of Chris' skills is that he can instantly break the ice and develop a kind of rapport with people around. It is his overweening self-confidence that never makes him feel like a new kid on the block even in a new environment.

It was at this camp that Chris met the camp director's daughter, Linda Herbert, his future wife. Linda and Chris went through periods of romance, love, and serious commitment. Both Linda's mother, who is originally from Texas, USA, and father, who is from England, had been naturalized Canadians for many years and were supportive of their daughter's marriage with Chris. By 1997, they were already engaged with a big plan for the wedding in 1999. Chris looked forward to the dawn of happier days with his wife. This was perhaps the most exhilarating news of the year for the entire family. Sure enough, the wedding of his son was an exciting day, recalls Tony.

Within a short period of time at the Gracefield Camp, Chris moved up from the position of assistant cook to head cook, assuming greater responsibility, a job that he accepted with alacrity. Chris remained busy at work, keeping his nose to the grindstone. Looking back, Chris believes he has progressed through jobs quite satisfactorily given his qualifications. His job kept him busy during the summers of 1997 and 1998, which made it impossible for him to visit his parents as frequently as he used to. After doing some serious thinking, however, Chris left his job. By fall 1998, Chris moved back again to the Ottawa area with Linda, his fiancée, and he immediately found a small apartment in Nepean, Ontario. It also did not take him long to land a job at one of the Wendy's fast restaurants in Ottawa.

A hardnosed Chris tried to move ahead with great effort and hope even in the face of obstacle and extenuating circumstances. A quick reality check made Chris recognize that the likelihood of getting a proper job was exceedingly small. Technically speaking, there were times when he was unemployed; again there were times when he felt that he was just going in circles. And yet Chris never gave up though felt a bit disappointed as though he was in a funk, but not deeply frustrated. Never giving up, Chris always took the bull by the horn. He continued to look for employment in his areas of interest and expertise with some glimmer of hope.

Despite frequent setbacks, his interest in cooking led him to curb out his future area of work in which he felt sure to excel in course of time. Having thought about various options, he and his betrothed wife then decided to return to school as early as possible considering the potential expenses that lay ahead. By then Linda had already started to take specialized courses in bakery at Algonquin College of Applied Arts and Technology in Ottawa, while Chris seriously thought about studying culinary management, a two-year diploma program, at the same college. At the end, however, this plan did not materialize for them.

As 1999 began to roll by, Linda and Chris started to prepare themselves for their grand wedding they had been dreaming about. It was held at Gracefield Camp and attended by many of the people that worked at the camp over the years. It actually took place outdoors in a beautiful camp setting with wooden benches in between the tall pine trees overlooking the lake. It was Chris' dad (Tony) who performed the marriage. After the wedding, there was an evening of food and celebration right at the camp. The date was early September, the Labor Day weekend, 1999.

Chris loves music with a passion. Apart from work and family, and despite busy schedule and heavy workload, Chris had always been fond of music, which had been a great source of joy for him. During the years he was growing up, he regularly played music to entertain people of all ages. As a matter of fact, Chris loved music so much that he used to jump at every opportunity to play music even after he had left home. According to his parents, there were times when Chris used to be deadbeat, and yet he would find extra time and energy for music. At that time, having joined the church choir, Chris used to sing both at St. Andrew's in Edmonton and St. Andrew's in Richmond. He was part of the bass selection and was good at it.

Like Shikha, Ruphea Rija, Martin, and some of the other war babies who came to Canada together in July 1972, Chris did not take any interest in his own birth history and family background. He speaks with candor without any pretense to having no interest in knowing about his putative father or his birth mother who abandoned him at birth. Chris does not say anything about his lack of interest with respect to Bangladesh, although he might have umpteen reasons for being nonchalant. Perhaps the most disturbing fact about Chris' life in Canada is obtaining of Canadian citizenship upon reaching the age of majority. This might have contributed to his disinterest in a country that did not want him in the first place. Fortunately, none of the other war babies had any such problem, since the birth certificates produced by the Bangladesh orphanage authority were deemed acceptable to all other provinces.

It was only in Chris' case that certain immigration officials were not satisfied with his birth certificate. Chris grew up in Canada, considering him to be Canadian like any other child who was raised in Canada. Chris' application for citizenship was turned down on the ground that he neither had a formal Canadian birth certificate nor adequate documentation (official papers from his country of birth) to be considered for citizenship. The family was in absolute shock when Citizenship and Immigration Canada refused on the ground of inadequate documentation. It is almost unbelievable that to this day, Chris is not a citizen of Canada even though he has been living in Canada for over last forty years. The issue has not been resolved yet.

Despite everything, Chris remains cheerful having shown his gratitude and admiration for his parents in Canada. He recognizes that probing into one's birth history may well be very palatable to someone who would not mind digging up one's past. He believes that there might be some who may do so only to reconfirm that so-and-so was abandoned and was deemed "unwanted" in one's country of birth. This, however, is not his cup of tea. Having chosen to be a nonsearcher, Chris considers him to be lucky to have been adopted by loving and caring parents.

As far as Chris is concerned, he had known from his early adulthood from his parents that there is no record available with respect to his birth mother and his alleged father neither in Canada where he was adopted nor in Bangladesh where he was born and abandoned. This single fact had convinced him from the beginning of his adult life that any attempt to look for his birth history would only go in vain.

Again, like all other war babies, having been in Canada from as far back as Chris remembers as a child, he sees himself as nothing but a Canadian who was born in Bangladesh. Chris does recognize his own racial background, which is different than that of his parents in Canada, and that he was born in Bangladesh of unknown parentage. Nevertheless, this single fact does not negate his feelings of identification with Canada and his Canadian parents and siblings.

Circumstances surrounding his schooling and the hurdles in obtaining Canadian citizenship due to a lack of documentation (even though this was not the case with other war babies who came to Canada with him with the same documentation package) are, however, long-forgotten past that hardly cross his mind at a time when he has many things going on in life, which center on his own family. Today a happily married Chris is the father of his daughter Christian, who turned thirteen on July 4, 2014.

Chris now works for an upscale coffee shop, Bridgehead, in Ottawa, while Linda works for a local Bank in downtown Ottawa. Both keep themselves busy. Having no quest for additional information, Chris does not seem to have any time to look back to subject himself to a common fear of his unknown past. Counting his blessings for being in Canada, he spends most of his time with his own family, wife and his daughter, who are a source of joyous energy for the entire Boonstra family.

Reverend Fred and Bonnie Cappuccino

For the Cappuccinos, one of the most celebrated couples in Canada, nothing could be more enjoyable than offering their home to adoptable children from all over the world. Before they were married, they together had decided to have a maximum of two children born to them, believing in "zero population growth," and if they wanted more, they would adopt one or two. Fred was a Methodist minister in Chicago. His wife, Bonnie, received training in nursing. They married in 1953.

In 1954, right after their first child was born to them, Bonnie wrote letters to 103 adoption agencies within a day's drive of their home in Chicago, asking to adopt a child who, for some reason, was "hard to place," either because of racial mixture or physical disability, although they could not take a child who required expensive treatment.

Only a third of the 103 agencies bothered to reply, and they all said, in effect, "Our agency has a policy of not giving a child to couples who can have children by natural means."[3] At that time, the couple came to learn that there was an agency that was gathering babies that were fathered by American soldiers (generally referred to as the GI babies) in Japan. Fred and Bonnie's first adopted child was a five-year-old girl from Japan. Her mother was Japanese; her father was a black American soldier. This little girl created quite a storm in the Methodist church where Fred was a minister. One-third of the congregation left. They disapproved, perhaps because they were afraid "blacks will move into our community" (e-mail from Fred Cappuccino to Mustafa Chowdhury, February 19, 2013). Interestingly, the rest of the congregation supported the adoption, and church finances remained at the same level. But a few months later, Fred and Bonnie were told they could stay at that church if they "did not adopt any more controversial children" (e-mail from Fred Cappuccino to the author).

Of course they could not agree to that and, in 1956, accepted a call to another Methodist church, which had an entirely different attitude. They *wanted* to integrate. Soon another black Japanese child was adopted from Japan; a second child was born to them, followed by a GI toddler from Korea. While in this congregation, Bonnie operated an informal soup kitchen in their home for homeless men in Chicago.

After reading about many black babies abandoned in Cook County Hospital in Chicago, Bonnie and Fred applied to adopt one of them. A social worker came to visit and announced to them, "You don't realize it, but you both have 'inverted prejudice' much to our surprise" (e-mail from Fred Cappucino to the author). The Cappuccinos asked, "What is that?" "Since you want to limit the number of natural-born children, you are prejudiced against them. I talked this over with my supervisor, who is a Negro, and he agrees with this assessment" (e-mail from Fred Cappuccino to the author). Bonnie and Fred were totally dumbfounded! There was no recourse. The social worker and her supervisor apparently had never heard of the population explosion in the world, which Bonnie and Fred wanted to alleviate and chose to limit their birth children to two.

At that point, the adoption gates opened up. One of the 103 agencies wrote to them: "We understand that you have one child born to you and would like to adopt a child. Would you be interested in a six-month-old boy?" (e-mail from Fred Cappuccino to the author). Bonnie wrote back, "We now have five children – three of them adopted, but we would still be very much interested in adopting another child" (e-mail from Fred Cappuccino to the author). They acquired their sixth child a week later, for a total of six.

After a third Methodist appointment, Fred transferred to the Unitarian ministry and was called to the Unitarian Church in Silver Spring, Maryland. This congregation was very interested in racial justice, and virtually every one of them was present to hear Martin Luther King's "I Have a Dream" speech. Of course, Fred and Bonnie were present with their six children – and two hundred thousand other people enthusiastically cheering with tears in their eyes. Bonnie and Fred adopted their seventh child, a six-day-old baby boy of Sri Lankan heritage. In 1965 Fred's friend and colleague, the Rev. James Reeb, was fatally beaten in Selma, Alabama. Fred and went to Selma, where he participated in the five-day Gandhian standoff between the protesters and the police, which ended successfully when President Johnson pledged that he would send a voting rights bill to Congress.

In 1967 the Cappuccinos began a new chapter in their lives, which demonstrates their strong desire and tenacity to help the helpless that to this day remains paramount in their scheme of things. Between 1967 and 1974, the Cappuccinos lived in Pointe Claire, Quebec, Canada, and with a few friends founded the Families For Children (FFC), a nonprofit and nonsectarian organization that advocates international adoption. They spent every bit of their spare time in volunteering for the FFC all through their stay in Quebec. In fact, Bonnie was president of FFC, while Fred was its secretary. The couple continued to help potential families find and adopt orphan children from abroad. At Lakeshore Unitarian Church where Fred worked, they held regular meetings and discussions on topics of general and specific interests, such as parenting children of mixed parentage, transracial adoption, human rights, etc.

In the early 1970s, the couple worked closely with Rosemary Taylor, an Australian teacher and a social worker who ran an orphanage in Saigon, Vietnam, and had found homes in Europe and North America for hundreds of mixed black Vietnamese and handicapped orphans. During that time, the Cappuccinos also became well known to the media both locally and nationally. Encouraged by the positive coverage of the news media, the Cappuccinos had continued multitasking and proving to be "doers."

They relentlessly pushed the adoption of racially different orphans' envelope among both government officials and individual families. The media coverage with respect to the Cappuccinos' initiatives thus became an important avenue for awareness, promotion, and sensitization of adoption of handicapped and hard-to-place orphans. Pretty well everyone in the community came to know the Cappuccinos as a wonderful couple who kept themselves busy in pursuing their commitment to facilitate adoption of handicapped and older children – both Canadian and foreign. This fact was a natural phenomenon in the Cappuccino residence.

In 1974 the Cappuccinos moved to a farm on a one-hundred-acre land, a pioneer log cabin six miles east of Maxville, a small rural community in eastern Ontario where most of their children grew up. While in Maxville, Fred worked as a remotivational therapist with the elderly at Mcdonell Memorial Hospital in Cornwall, Ontario. As well, he was a minister of the Unitarian Fellowship of Ottawa. Bonnie, though trained in nursing, was a full-time stay-at-home mom. In 1976, for a year and a half, the couple went with their seven young children to Sri Lanka and then to India. With the help of the Indian Council of Welfare, the FFC opened two homes for destitute children.

The family, however, moved back to Maxville, Canada, after eighteen months upon insistence of their children. Followers of the teachings of Mahatma Gandhi, the Cappuccinos, with the help of Dr. Nathubhai Shah and his wife, Kala Shah, of Cornwall, founded the Child Haven International (*www.childhaven.ca*) in 1985. It is a nonsectarian organization that follows a Gandhian philosophy for children and women in India, Bangladesh, Nepal, and Tibet. They operate two training centers for women. Fred and Bonnie are the main persons involved. Bonnie visits all eleven projects four times a year. Operating on a Gandhian philosophy means no change of religion, boys and girls equal, simple living, vegetarianism, nonviolence. It was established in the wake of the Union Carbide Chemical accident in Bhopal, India, which left scores of children blind and maimed.

The Cappuccinos' fascination for the Indian subcontinent, however, goes way back to the 1960s when they adopted two of their sons from the Indian subcontinent. One of them is named Mohan, after Mohandas Karamchand Gandhi (1868–1948), whose teachings inspired nonviolent movements around the world; and the other one is named Kahlil, after the renowned Lebanese American artist, poet, and writer Kahlil Gibran (1883–1931). Naturally, it was not surprising that the Cappuccinos' admiration for Martin Luther King and Mahatma Gandhi had led them to choose India as the site for their eventual charity work. Bonnie now visits their nine homes for destitute children in India, Nepal, Tibet, and Bangladesh four times a year, which are run by the Child Haven International.

The Cappuccinos agreed they did not want to bring a lot of children into the world because they thought the world was already populated. With two biological children, they thought they would adopt two or three more. As the years rolled by, the Cappuccino family began to grow by leaps and bounds. When Shikha, a Bangladeshi war baby, arrived in the Cappuccino family in July 1972, she became their tenth child. In a sense, taking the Yuletide message of giving and sharing, between 1954 and 1982, the Cappuccinos expanded their family to twenty-one children, only two of whom were biological, or what they call "home made."

In addition, the family had two St. Bernard dogs, Buttercup and Pansy, both of whom were their children's favorite. The rest of the nineteen children came from different parts of the world, representing a total of eleven nationalities, such as Indian, Japanese, Korean, Pakistani, Bangladeshi, to name a few. A number of children they adopted were what could be termed "hard-to-place" orphans; for they were victims of war overseas who would perhaps have been doomed to orphanages with no definite future they enjoyed in Canada. Specifically, in addition to having mental and other anxieties, three of their children have visible handicaps – the first one had polio and needed corrective foot surgery, the second one has 30 percent hearing loss in both ears, and the third one has dyslexia. This is what makes the Cappuccinos a unique and atypical family that consists of international cross section of races.

With regard to the *why* and the *how* of the adoption of so many children, Fred's humble answer was . . . "We were never looking for any of the children. Specifically, it is just what we saw the need. When a baby is put on your doorstep, you learn to love it as your own."[4] In fact, in one of their interviews following Shikha's arrival, the Cappuccinos observed how strongly they felt about the "population explosion" around the world. Such feelings had convinced them to seek an alternate way to raise family. The Cappuccinos, therefore, decided to adopt "rather than having such a big family themselves."[5]

Every time the couple is asked why they do/did adopt so many children, they essentially have/had the same type of reply, implying their strong desire to be surrounded by children: "We feel privileged to be able to be around all our children who have such tremendous potential," said Fred in one his interviews **(The** *Montreal Star,* November 29, 1972). Bonnie too admits, "We never dreamed we'd someday have so many children" (The *Montreal Star,* November 29, 1972), and yet in a way, it seemed so natural for them to adopt one after another to fulfill their dream of having children all around them.

Not surprisingly, Fred's answers to questions along these lines are always rather philosophical: "Knowing how other parts of the world think is important, we made a conscious effort to give the neediest children a home – those who were handicapped or of a mixed race. We're all in the same boat. If part of the world dies, we rise and fall together." (*The Ottawa Citizen,* March 26, 1990)

When the children were growing up in the Cappuccinos' old two-story farmhouse in Maxville with its thirteen sleeping places (not bedrooms) and some bunk beds and two bathrooms, to many people, the house was a mini United Nations. At that time, one common practice in the family that continues to this day is to show respect for each other; accordingly each is/was to be treated as equal to the other.

For example, when they adopted a child of a new nationality, the Cappuccinos used to make sure that they had books, food, music, and pictures of that child's native homeland. In the case of the Bangladeshi war baby, for example, the Cappuccinos had always made extra effort to find ways and means to meet students, visitors, and Canadians of Bangladeshi origin, taking advantages of opportunities to better "educate" themselves and their child of Bangladeshi background. As the Cappuccinos recall, this was the best way to keep the family united and respectful of each other.

All through the 1970s and 1980s, when the children were younger, news reporters from various parts of Canada used to visit the couple just to get a sense of their unique family life. When asked by the *Ottawa Citizen* reporter, Julia Elliott, what it was like to be around so many children of different ages, Bonnie recalled they had "pre-school children" in their "family for an uninterrupted period of 26 years until Vodinh started Kindergarten. What a glorious day that was!" (*The Ottawa Citizen,* March 26, 1990)

News reporters and journalists who had met this extraordinary couple also wrote about their personal impressions in glowing terms especially seeing the ways in which the couple had found joys of sharing that outweighed a few sacrifices. Even when the family had ten children back in 1972 during Shikha's arrival from Bangladesh, the Cappuccino house was described as a bedlam filled with worn but cheery paraphernalia of children: "with piles of laundry, toys, bikes, pictures, mitts, over-coats and semi broken-down furniture strewn all over" (The *Montreal Star,* November 29, 1972). Naturally, many would ask Bonnie how she managed the culinary and household chores. For many news reporters, it was a matter of "seeing is believing" Bonnie who struck them as a "bionic" or a "wonder" woman of the day.

The Cappuccinos also proved that a couple does not necessarily have to be rich to raise a large family, but the parent does have to be a good money manager. Come to think of it, just the logistics of the large adoptive family is staggering – the need to have enough flexibilities and yet to maintain some order just for daily household chores, such as cooking, laundry, homework, etc.

In the days when the children were growing up, a typical breakfast consisted of dozens of eggs, three loaves of bread, two or three gallons of milk, and mounds of bacon. What about supper? Bonnie recalls, generally supper used to be spaghetti from a huge cauldron or an oriental dish, such as chop suey or chow mein, and four or five pounds of rice. The family members still remember how they used to eat strawberries, plums, and apples from their own garden on the farm all through summer where they also used to consume home-grown vegetables. In fact, the family also had a vegetable garden that served them with the year-round supply.

They were always happy with what they had, although the family had to scrape through with Fred's humble salary from his work as a therapist helping depressed patients at Mcdonell Memorial Hospital and the monthly family allowance payment. Of course, what had helped the family was the way in which the family had arranged to buy food in quantity, which Bonnie used to pick up from a food co-op in nearby Alexandria once a week, while Fred used to stop by to buy extras on his way home from work at night. Again, they also raised their own animals – three cows that used to give them all the milk they needed as well as butter. This was assigned to their children who would to make butter every night by shaking cream in a gallon glass jar often while watching television. They also used to freeze vegetables in big piles. Just organizing her bustling household had been a gigantic task, quite herculean, one might say.

As for the division of labor, by and large, the daily chores consisted of teamwork and a variety of tasks, such as chopping woods, washing dishes, hanging laundry, sweeping floors, and feeding to dogs. Fred recalls, with so many helping hands and having so many young adults around, it was not hard to divvy up the work: "We divide up into teams and the older children are the leaders. Some might go off to split and pile up wood; others might clear the barn and so on" (*Ottawa Journal,* December 12, 1979). In a way, everyone in the family had a job, an assigned task. This had helped the Cappuccinos encourage and practice teamwork that also facilitated the development of a healthy rapport among the siblings and their parents.

One of the most persistent themes in the Cappuccino family, especially when the children were growing up, was to foster a "do all you can" attitude – to assist each other in the family. In their own home, the Cappuccinos created a nurturing haven where equality of treatment and opportunity became the most important aspect of the family life. Interesting to note, often they had to treat their children "differently" in order to get the same result, for sometimes the level playing field had not been the same for all children.

Not surprisingly, therefore, the diverse array of adoptees (both able-bodied and challenged) grew up together knowing and respecting the notion of unity that had brought them close to each other just like friends. With so many kids at home, the Cappuccinos needed to be around and present especially when they were growing up – being involved in both unobtrusive and visible ways. They loved them with all their hearts.

The Cappuccinos' simply decorated and clean but somewhat cluttered house is something that is noticeable just as anyone steps in. Among the items of interests are the couple's research library, photo collection, newspaper clippings, and sundry artifacts from India and Bangladesh, etc. The family library contains more than five thousand titles, and individual country files, especially country files based on the countries in which the orphans were born. The Cappuccinos children knew well that their parents' collection of photographs, scrap books, testimonials, and numerous letters written back and forth between the representatives of the governments of Bangladesh, India, Vietnam, etc., and the FFC are a fascinating source of firsthand information on international adoption.

As well, there are displays, survey records, and studies on children and adoption contained in the library's cabinet drawers and individualized pamphlet boxes, which the children were always welcome to browse through and consult. The children had (and still have) complete access to any and all information they required to fulfill their desire for information. Years seem to have gone by fast for the Cappuccinos.

Over the years, however, as the children grew up, many also began to live away from home to successfully pursue professional careers and attend colleges and universities in Canada and the United States. With the help of loans, financial aid, and their own savings through hard work, the Cappuccinos were able to send some of their children to colleges and universities. In their journey as a large family, they approached with a feeling of abundance, meaning that they were people-rich, having no sense of deprivation.

The Cappuccinos, having earned credibility in advocating interracial adoption, had lobbied the governments of many countries with confidence all through their active lives. By the end of 1970, the

Cappuccinos had demonstrably earned a name for themselves for their passion for children of mixed race whether they come from Canada or from overseas. Having been in the field of adoption for so long, they have attracted the attention of many, including those in the Quebec Department of Social Welfare.

At every opportunity, Quebec officials commended them for their tireless work: "They have helped families over the initial adjustment period and have been able to do this because of their own experience and very great capacity to parent children as well as assist children to become part of their own families at a later stage in their development,"[6] thus wrote Elizabeth Bissett, then head of Adoption Services, about the Cappuccinos.

Such letter of commendation had helped the Cappuccinos raise their own status to other governments who came to regard them as avant-garde in interracial adoption. By the time they began to lobby the governments of Bangladesh and Canada to allow adoption of certain number of war babies, they were seen as representatives of a credible organization committed to reaching out to orphans around the world. In fact, it would not be an exaggeration to state that, at that time, they were regarded as trailblazers committed to finding ways to embrace the war babies of Bangladesh. Fortunately, this was a time when the government of Bangladesh was also contemplating various options with regard to its war waifs. Much to their credit, the prime minister of Canada and Labor and Social Welfare minister of Bangladesh were impressed with the Cappuccinos' initiatives and responded to their requests positively.

Though a huge family by its sheer size, consisting of twenty-one children, all of them now live on their own. The most remarkable aspect of the Cappuccinos is that they remain committed to what they have been doing all along – having maintained their connection with each other. Though their nest is empty, the Cappuccinos are still reaching out to the marginalized children around the world. Friends and neighbors around the Maxville area marvel at the deep commitment and selflessness of the Cappuccinos who had devoted themselves to the complete care of their children who come from different countries of the world and had made their lifelong dream a reality.

Although the Cappuccinos preferred to enlarge their families through adoption instead of having "home-made" children and are highly regarded by people in general, as far as the Cappuccinos are concerned, their life goes on in their own ways as they see fit. Over the years, the Cappuccinos, generally referred to as "a unique couple," have earned numerous awards and accolades, such as Friends of Peace Award, Ottawa Mayor (2004); Friend of Children Award (2004); the Order of Canada (1996); North American Council on Adoptive Children (1992); South Asian of the Year Award, Ontario Federation of South Asian Studies (1992); UNESCO Honor for Teaching Human Rights (1989); the Canada Volunteer Award for Contributions to Children (1986); and Ontario Medal for Good Citizenship (1985).

As the mementos of these honors fill the wall of their home, they are variously characterized as "courageous," "intelligent," "social activist," "atypical family," "extra-ordinary family," and the "exceptionally wonderful family." For them, "reaching out" to the marginalized is a way of life and a passion. The Cappuccinos illustrate a kind of "international togetherness" within a family makeup created by a couple who could never say *no* to an orphan who needed a home. It would not be an exaggeration to say that it was as though the couple is imbued with a humanistic spirit.

In sharing their life experiences, knowledge and skills, and pains and joys of parenting, the Cappuccinos believe they have learned from each other a great deal and have empowered their children to their satisfaction. By equipping them with skills, explanations, and responses to face the real world, which is sometimes cruel and is not always kind to people with disabilities, they have helped them evolve. When the children were growing up, each family member or child was taught to be to be protective, confident, and a source of happiness for others. While Bonnie struggled to cope with motherhood and household chores, the children did not take long to appreciate the family rules, disciplines, values, and most importantly, the family's unique cultural ethos. In particular, they looked for, and succeeded in developing to a great extent, the ability of each individual child to stimulate the creativity of the other siblings at home.

Today, the Cappuccinos are still living in the same farmhouse, which they have converted into their home-cum-office. They have a total of twenty-seven grandchildren and five great-grandchildren. They have tied an invisible string to their children to whom they gave love and warmth, which they had lacked when they were abandoned. One might wonder what else could be more important than finding home for orphans from around the world. The Cappuccinos usually arrange family get-togethers on special occasions, such as Easter, Canada Day, Thanksgiving, and Christmas. While every Cappuccino family member cannot attend each get-together, many are able to attend such get-togethers to meet and share one's stories with family members present.

The Cappuccinos continue to promote the theme of "reaching out" to the needy people even on each family reunion. The Cappuccinos' children in various orphanages under the protection of the Child Haven International amount to hundreds. Usually referred to as the couple's "other children," they live in the homes in Hyderabad, Joshi Farm, and Kaliyampoodi who are abandoned at birth, older orphans, or whose parents are sick and/or too poor to provide them even one meal a day.

Though the couple became well known, they have retained their modesty. They did not wish to rest on their laurels; instead, they remain engaged. Cappuccinos continue to work on many projects through their own network. Again, through both formal and informal get-togethers, they provide information on international adoption of racially different orphans and, more importantly, hard-to-place orphans. In fact even to this day, they are occupied with one thing or another devoting most of their time for a cause the family believes in – adoption of orphans from around the world with the strength of youth and the wisdom of age. The most important legacy of the Cappuccinos is that they have steadfastly promoted the social integration of people of diverse race in both their profession and personal lives.

Needless to say, the media coverage with respect to the Cappuccinos thus also became an important avenue for awareness, promotion, and sensitization of adoption of racially different orphans.

Shikha

Born after a seven-month pregnancy, on March 12, 1972, in Dhaka, Bangladesh, Shikha weighed 2.7 kg at birth. She was immediately brought to Mother Teresa's *Shishu Bhavan* premises by someone who wished to remain anonymous. The record does not identify if it was the birth mother or someone else who brought the baby girl in the orphanage. She was brought there to be left with the orphanage authority for adoption. Sr. Margaret Mary gave the name Shikha and immediately began to take care of her, as the baby girl was pitifully frail. She seemed like she was not going to make it. She was picked out by the Cappuccinos who went to Dhaka, Bangladesh, to seal the deal with respect to the Bangladesh Project initiative.

When asked why they chose a frail girl like Shikha from the orphanages where there might have been other babies stronger than Shikha, the Cappuccinos replied, "She was absolutely the loveliest in all creation with delicate facial features. Her miniature hands and feet were brown on top and white underneath."[7] Of all the babies in the orphanage, Shikha was obviously, and without question, "the most beautiful baby" they had picked out from among other war babies, said the Cappuccinos (Bangladesh Project, 275).

Looking back, the Cappuccinos said, for them, it was a matter of instantly falling in love with the baby girl. Having picked the frail baby, the Cappuccinos recall their next worry was about the long flight back home with the baby in good health. They worried a lot because the baby looked awfully weak, giving them the jitters lest anything might happen during the long overseas trip. Fortunately, having passed the medical test, the baby Shikha proved to be resilient enough to sustain an overseas trip to Canada all the way from Bangladesh. As Bonnie recalls, being so little, she slept most of the time during the first few weeks. Much to their relief and anxiety, Shikha recovered gradually and turned out to be as beautiful as ever, said Bonnie.

While doing the formal adoption in Montreal, the Cappuccinos gave Shikha the following name: Shikha Deepa Margaret Cappuccino. The parents take pride in Shikha's first and only name given by the nuns at *Shishu Bhavan,* where she was brought in and taken care of. They were told, in Bengali, "Shikha" means "flame" to which the Cappuccinos added Deepa and Margaret in honor of the Sisters Deepa and Margaret Mary, the two nuns who nursed the baby so lovingly and painstakingly and had saved Shikha's life when she was frightfully sick and frail. As well, according to the Cappuccinos, Shikha is named after her great-aunt Margaret Trevis, who took care of the Cappuccino children while they were in Bangladesh to pick out the babies from there. Naturally, Shikha got her last name, Cappuccino, from her adoptive parents.

Like many typical young Canadian adults, Shikha did not finish her high school diploma on time. After successfully completing elementary school from Maxville Elementary School Maxville, Ontario, Shikha attended Glengarry District High School but chose to drop out before completion. Being on her own, Shikha realized that she would have to finish her high school degree in order for her to move ahead in life. She began to take adult courses, which allowed her to obtain the high school equivalency. Shikha then started to work and, over the years, had gained the experience of the real life. From then on, Shikha took many jobs working in a number of places on and off while expanding her horizon.

Shikha grew up at a home where she, along with her siblings, had the warmth and assurance of steady devotion as well as the stimulation of undemanding affection – everything that a diverse and well-knit family circle could supply. Shikha grew up knowing her parents had always recognized the validity and desirability of differences and had encouraged their children to make every attempt to resolve them harmoniously. According to Shikha, her parents had given each of their children a true identity as a child. All through her school years, Shikha was well liked by those who came across her due to her pleasant and attractive personality. She was known for being charming, social, friendly and, therefore, popular among friends and acquaintances.

Shikha's mother recalls how her elementary teacher, Claire Bezner, once described little Shikha as "small but mighty." Implicit in the teacher's succinct description was Shikha's sense of fairness, decency, and sincerity that she exuded even when she was a child. As Shikha grew up to be an adult, she expanded her horizon and cultivated friendship with a great number of people and moved on with her life. Today Shikha is admired by many who had always found her to be appropriately expressive and self-assuring.

Comparatively speaking, Shikha tends to be quite different from some of the other war babies of her age who came to Canada with her. Her parents' efforts to connect her to her own historical or biological past somehow did not appeal to her to the extent it did to Rani or Ryan, for example. She is at ease and quite content with what little she knows about her birth story. She does not recall having any unbearably disturbing feelings after she learned about the circumstances surrounding her birth and adoption. She is aware that some of the war babies had been to Bangladesh first in 1989 and later on in the 1990s. Like Josée, Shama, Chris, and others (about whom we shall read in the next few pages), Shikha never felt any sense of urgency in her mind to find out more about her birth mother and putative father in her attempt to further identify herself.

However, the years had brought an altered emphasis in her mind – having found herself with a changed attitude. The story of adoption had always been so natural in her family that it was like having toast and coffee for breakfast. While growing up, Shikha never felt alienated or detached like many adoptees who feel as though they do/did not have a family of their "own" or they were people with no "origin." Shikha has bonded herself with her (adoptive) parents, whom she knew as her *only* parents in her life, along with her siblings of diverse origin. She never felt, nor does she feel now, that there is a void in her life. Shikha lacks some basic information, such as the knowledge of her birth mother and alleged father. But that does not bother her.

In fact, Shikha grew up knowing full well the story of adoption and appreciating the fact that the Cappuccinos are her *only* parents as far back as she remembers. She did not feel terribly inclined to do any research on *where* she came from or on her past. All through her young adult life, Shikha seemed very content to live without searching her roots with which she is not very familiar. She is quite comfortable in stating the fact of her life that she was adopted from Bangladesh. No matter how the subject is broached to her, she seems to be in complete contentment with her situation – the story surrounding her birth and adoption. In a sense, Shikha illustrates how sheer filial affection can go a very long way to make up for any missing genealogical or personal information.

While, on the one hand, Shikha considers herself Canadian, on the other hand, she is also aware of other people's perception of her. She fully recognizes that someone on the street, regardless of what she thinks of herself, might see her as being different and, therefore, depending on the person's knowledge and levels of awareness, might or might not see a visible minority Shikha as "Canadian" in the same spirit and manner one would look upon a white Canadian. This seems to be the least of Shikha's concern. Throughout her life, Shikha had never cared to reflect along such lines as she always considers herself to be "Canadian." Thus, having had the opportunity to grow up in a truly multiracial environment representing eleven nationalities within a single family, Shikha along with her siblings has learned, sustained, and reinforced a sense of belonging to the multiracial aspect of Canada.

This has allowed Shikha to look at herself first as Canadian and then as a Canadian with an ethnic background at the same time, although the latter part of her identity is very minimal.

Not surprisingly, therefore, Shikha does not have an emotional attachment to her country of birth. Instead, her emotions are tied closer at home in Canada where she grew up. For that matter, Shikha does not have a strong desire to visit to her country of birth to learn more about Bangladesh and Bangladeshis even at the present time. She also maintains that if she ever does visit Bangladesh, she would certainly like to spend some time at Mother Teresa's Home from where she was brought to Canada. In that sense, she feels connected to her country of birth and remains grateful to the orphanage authority but not to the extent of calling her country of birth her "home." As far as Shikha is concerned, Canada is her home where she grew up.

Shikha contends that she has never experienced any kind of racism that many encounter in their day to day life. As such, she is not aware of any anecdote to relate to. She does not see this as a barrier in her case, although she is aware that this is often the case with many people.

Over the years, Shikha has worked on and off for the Child Haven International, her parents' charitable organization, and managed office work and public relations providing administrative support. On many other occasions, she has engaged herself in fund-raising activities and various other events that were undertaken by the same organization, such as the benefit dinner for the Ottawa Friends of Tibet. The knowledge, inner strength, and wisdom Shikha has developed and nurtured have prepared her for what life has to offer. However, a pragmatic Shikha also recognized that she must take the initiative to create and seek opportunities and not wait around for favors.

Shikha has had many ups and downs in her personal life. When she was left alone with her first daughter, following her boyfriend's accidental death, she quickly came to grips with the burdensome aspect of her life. Shikha has had her parents and siblings to fall back on. Following her boyfriend's death, Shikha was married again for couple of years, She is now a single mom who is happily raising her children. She has moved on with her life, taking a forward-looking approach. With her two daughters, twenty-one-year-old Katarina and nine-year-old Karma, Shikha remains pretty occupied taking care of them at home and managing the household chores at the same time. Shikha's both daughters are doing well. Karma is in grade fuve. Katarina has finished her fourth year of school at Carleton University, Ottawa, majoring in international development and political science, with a minor in French. She will go on to get her master's degree.

All of Shikha's difficulties seem to have smoothed out with the passage of years. On-and-off part-time jobs help her supplement her income, although she would prefer to have a steady job. Given her situation, she does not have any time to conjure up Bangladesh and/or Bangladeshis – something that neither was her past-time passion in her younger years nor is now in her present life. At present, with dogged determination as a single mom, Shikha's life centers about her family, her two daughters.

Interesting to note, although Shikha has not been very interested in knowing about Bangladesh or meeting Bangladeshi Canadians, she was very keen on attending the 2012 *Iftar Mahfeel* (breaking of fast) ceremony organized by the Ottawa-based Canada Bangladesh Muslim Community where her father, Fred Cappuccino, was the keynote speaker. Both Katarina and Karma enjoyed the gathering and expressed their interest to attend such occasions in the future.

Dr. Robert and Helke Ferrie

The story of Dr. Robert Ferrie and his wife, Helke, is one not only of complete compassion but also of their unique ability to change the rigid government behavior in striving to achieve their personal beliefs and goals. In 1972, Dr. Robert Ferrie, a surgeon and urologist at Joseph Brant Hospital in Burlington, Ontario, Canada, and his wife, Helke Ferrie, were approached by the Montreal-based Families For Children (FFC), an organization that advocates international adoption. They were asked to assist in some of its work.

Helke Ferrie was born in Germany and grew up in India where she had studied Indian philosophy and culture at Benares Hindu University. Her link with the third world was strengthened as a result of her own personal research into Asian studies and Indology in particular. Being influenced by her father, Helke herself became interested in studying Hinduism and Buddhism. In 1969 Helke and Robert met at Benares Hindu University in Varanasi, India, where Helke was studying and Robert taught surgery. They were married in 1970 in Canada.

The socially conscientious couple had always thought beyond racial boundaries. When it came to adoption, they were not concerned with the traditional "matching" concept in adoption. Rather, they believed in trying to bring orphans and families together and not to drive them apart. The foremost consideration in all matters of child welfare could not and must not be the culture of the child in question, but rather the child's survival, said Helke.[8] They believed that while raising their multiracial children, the most important ingredient for the mental development of a child is the presence of a parental figure devoted to the child's well-being and needs. "If we worry about cultural ties, we are likely to ignore the more fundamental needs of a human being," maintained Helke Ferrie (this was said by Helke Ferrie to Mustafa Chowdhury at an interview at the Ferries' residence in Alton, Ontario, on May 20, 2000).

One of the most interesting and somewhat intriguing manifestations of the couple is their desire to rehabilitate hard-to-place orphans who were generally ignored by both social workers as well as prospective adoptive parents while placing an orphan. Seeing that such orphans were practically bypassed or stashed aside when it came to picking out a child, the Ferries took it upon themselves to look for children who might have difficulties in finding an adoptive home because of their age or a disability.

When asked *why* they were interested in hard-to-place children, an affectionate and courageous Helke's quick response was "We believed that it'd be easy for the regular orphans to be picked up. We worried about orphans with disabilities who might end up in various institutions for good unless we did something about them" (Helke's interview with the author). A social activist and gravely concerned Helke used to ask, "Do we want to continue setting up such barriers for children who are already discarded by societies?" (Helke's interview with the author). The Ferries, therefore, did not look for children with blue eyes and blond hair (i.e., a "blue-ribbon" baby); rather they sought children, regardless of race and gender, whose chances of being adopted were demonstrably less.

Prompted by the many news reports on the plight of children in Bangladesh following its independence, Helke and Robert joined the efforts of the FFC. While the provincial government of Quebec and the Canadian federal government were most helpful with regard to adoption from Bangladesh and agreed to streamline the immigration of orphans destined for adoption by Canadians, the province of Ontario deliberately stalled the process – something that we have already noted in chapter 3. Prospective applicants for home studies expected a prompt and empathetic approach on the part of the director of Children's Services for the Province of Ontario at that time, Ms. Betty Graham. Within weeks, however, they came to realize that they could not be certain about Betty's true position. Helke's immediate reaction was one of anger. Betty's every action seemed to counter to further the process for parents trying to adopt, especially with regard to conducting the mandatory home studies, which were a part of the process.

To Helke and the Ontario applicants, Betty's immature behavior was nothing short of pure nonsense, especially since it came from someone in high ranks. Whatever rationale Betty might have had, the prospective adoptive parents found it frivolous, sardonic, and unacceptable. They came to regard Betty as an epitome of the top Ontario bureaucrat guilty of levity. Helke relentlessly continued her fight while Ontario officials continued to procrastinate in carrying out the home studies. Helke wrote to high-level federal and provincial government officials against those who were delaying the process, whom she did not hesitate to brand as "racists." A determined Helke never chose to quit her struggle. Believing that "a quitter never wins" and "a winner never quits," she continued her fight having her husband with her all the time by her side. She is known to have said to herself that she was not going to let anyone "jerk" her "around" especially when she was convinced that Ontario officials were merely talking the talk.

Taking a lead role and standing on the firing line, Helke moved heaven and earth together with the other applicants, who were fully supportive of her, having gathered in unison to raise their collective voice. They became furious at the frequent and acerbic remarks made by Betty. They saw Betty as not only a control freak without a vestige of sensitivity but also, unfortunately, someone who was very close to the corridors of power in the Ontario government. Helke was clear that until her demands were met, the battle was far from being over. Helke worked in close collaboration with many other groups and individuals, some of whom were also livid with anger.

Helke caused waves when she went on a nationally televised three-and-a-half-day hunger strike to put her point across to Canadians at large

– that Ontario officials were resistant to the adoption of racially different orphans from outside of Canada. The whirlwind that had become her life accelerated even more. This resulted in drawing attention through the news media toward the nonresponsive Ontario government officials and their refusal to carry out the home study, which is a prerequisite for adoption. This forced Ontario government officials to finally cooperate with the rest of the parties involved in the process. Her hunger strike was based on her admiration for Mahatma Gandhi.

The pith of her argument for adoption was that international adoptions were not only humane but also necessary in a world that was already an international arena of multiple races and cultures. The Ferries and other Ontario applicants saw Betty as someone who had a knack for offending people. They could never be sure of the government's equivocal response. Pointing fingers at Betty, she said that willful delay had already produced a palpable wave of disgust toward Ontario officials for their unnecessary indifference to the adoption position and process.

Helke began to receive letters of support from communities and from many charities she had championed. The minister of Community and Social Services, already embarrassed by the negative publicity, was forced to give her assurance publicly for immediate approval for adoption from overseas. Within hours, Helke, an eternal optimist, proved her point. The details of Helke's three and a half days of hunger strike and the long-haul fight against government officials, which we have seen in chapter 3, are a rare example in Canada.

In June 1972, once the arrangements for adoption was firmed up between the government of Bangladesh and the FFC, the Ferries opted to go to Bangladesh at their own expense to join the Canadian team led by Fred Cappuccino and his wife, Bonnie, who departed from Montreal. Canada's Manpower and Immigration Department requested Dr. Ferrie to conduct the medical examination of those war babies who were to be released for adoption in Canada. (We have seen the details of the teamwork in chapter 3.)

Dr. Ferrie determined the suitability and sustainability of the infants, many of whom were prematurely born and deemed to be at high risk. They also picked out two war babies, the weakest boy and girl that they could find for adoption for themselves. We shall call them war babies A and B, as they did not wish to be identified by their real names. Dr. Ferrie also remembers one of the great concerns of the government of Bangladesh – which was the fact that the newborns were dying just as fast as they were being born at the time. In tandem, the Canadian team was concerned as to how many infants would actually pass the medical test and then sustain the long overseas trip given their precarious health conditions.

Between 1972 and 1985, the Ferries adopted a total of ten children. The Ferries also had three biological children of their own. They raised thirteen children. In 1972 the family moved from their home in Burlington to a large 140-year-old stone farmhouse also in Burlington. It had to be completely renovated with further additional rooms and spaces to accommodate all the children and pets. In the early years when the children were growing up, the family had many cats and dogs, a monkey, and a tame chicken. Both the size and the nature of the family were constantly changing, creating an ethnically diverse family. Five of their adoptive children had physical disabilities.

For Robert and Helke, their human endurance never reached its breaking point. Their thinking was influenced by their belief that all individuals deserve the opportunity to develop to their maximum potential. The news of bringing the two weakest war babies of all had attracted the attention of the news media. Once they were in the Ferries' home and received appropriate care, the couple caught the public's attention while they grew and thrived and became healthy children. Within six months of their arrival, they were described by the news media as "blue-eyed babies" with "sweet auras about them" (*The Toronto Star*, February 1, 1973).

Though years have gave gone by since the adoption of A and B from Bangladesh, the unpleasant experience with Ontario officials while seeking permission for home studies still lingers on in the couple's minds. As far as the Ferries are concerned, they had endured their fair share of wait and uncertainty during the process of adoption itself. A humorous Helke facetiously compares the inordinate delays in adoption proceedings, in some aspects, with the endurance of a pregnancy, which she had experienced shortly after bringing A and B all the way from Bangladesh to their new home in Canada.

The Ferries still remember that first Canadopt (network of Ontario adoptive parents) get-together that took place at the couple's home where many Ontario parents gathered and talked about their initial experience of adoptive parenting. "It was indeed a pleasure to have had you all at our house and to have seen your babies fat and round and healthy with lusty yells and normal bowl movements,"[9] thus wrote Helke to all those who frequently attended the get-together parties and shared their stories of exuberance and worries about their babies' food habits, sleeping patterns, and other itsy-bitsy items and compared notes.

In sharing their own opinion about how the Bangladesh Project was pulled off so quickly, they were frank and candid with the rest of the team members: "This particular trip to Bangladesh [June 23–July 19, 1972] was a kind of emergency mission which should not and would not be the regular way of doing this sort of a thing. It was a crazy adventure that worked out wonderfully in the end and we feel as gratified as you do, that these 15 lives were saved against some overwhelming odds."[10]

Perhaps the most commendable aspect of the Ferries is the way in which the couple has instilled in their children valuable life skills that had helped them become more independent and self-confident. They worked diligently with each child in order to make sure that each had an opportunity to be always supervised at least by one parent at the required or desired level and being sensitive to the child's individual suffering. In raising their children, the couple always looked for their intellectual capacity no matter how challenged some of the children were in many obvious ways.

Helke considers her husband, Robert, to be a strong asset, and vice-versa. Robert, who was sometimes very outspoken, spent his life dedicated to his family and profession, and succeeded in both. All through the years, Robert and Helke always operated like a team, not as traditional father-and-mother type. Robert would joke that Helke was the "commander of our family troops," while he always wanted to adopt more children. Helke often had the task of pointing out that the family was big enough. Believing strongly that everyone deserves to live with dignity, the couple continued to work toward what they had set out to achieve: a balance in their lives by defining and redefining family kinship through adoption of racially different orphans who had difficulty in finding adoptive parents.

Following their return from Bangladesh, the team received positive publicity in the news media. Many couples contacted the Ferries not only from across Canada but also from the USA and offered their homes for international adoption. Hoping that they could do more to save orphans, the same year they established their own organization named the Kuan-Yin Foundation.[11]

Between August and September of 1972, Helke worked tirelessly in an attempt to bring over more orphans from Bangladesh. In October Helke went to Bangladesh again at the invitation of then prime minister Sheikh Mujibur Rahman (Mujib). This time she met members of the Mujib administration including the prime minister himself with whom she discussed the issue of adoption with admirable lucidity and insight. Having seen how people were living in abysmal conditions at a time of rampant patronage, political favoritism, and influence peddling, Helke expressed her heartache for the sufferings of the people. Both Robert and Helke claimed that they felt duty bound and, therefore, took it upon them to initiate the dialogue with Mujib himself.

Personally, Mujib is known to have been impressed with Helke's knowledge of orphans and sense of true compassion for them. They met at a time when it was believed that a high expectancy of change and sense of a new era for the newly born country existed at a deep psychological level as just a start. Accordingly, the Ferries thoughtfully drew their plan taking a step-by-step approach to find homes for Bangladeshi war orphans.

In October, Helke brought eight war orphans from Bangladesh. Some of them were war babies abandoned by their birth mothers, while some were war orphans – parentless following the liberation of Bangladesh. These children ranged from eight months to six years old. Monowara Clark, a war baby now living in Vancouver, is known to have been brought to Canada by Helke Ferrie along with this group.

The couple has embraced many "unwanted" orphans with love and affection who were left behind in their respective countries, as there was no one to adopt them. The couple's dedication and commitment illustrate perhaps the greatest characteristic of the family values that the couple had fostered. Victoria Leach, adoption coordinator of the Ontario government's Ministry of Community and Social Services in the 1970s, had met some of the orphans who were originally from South Vietnamese orphanages and later brought to Canada. Having visited the Ferries on a few occasions to see the outcome of the placement of two orphans from Vietnam, Leach was extremely pleased. She had nothing but praise for the Ferries.

During her visit to the Ferries' house, the family consisted of seven children. The first thing that Leach recalled was the ease and comfort with which the two Vietnamese orphans were interacting with the rest of the family. She was impressed to notice the notable positive difference in the boys. "I stayed several hours and watched the interaction and felt quite comfortable and confident that this is a family with unusual dedication and warmth,"[12] wrote Leach as part of her recommendation to the Ministry of Community and Social Services about the Ferries. Having worked jointly, the Ferries proved something in which they always firmly believe: that the greatest power on earth is the power of the human will.

However, not all of their children were entirely happy in that two of their children had left home whose whereabouts are not known to them. "Adoptions are as varied in their results as the relationship to biological children," remarked Helke (e-mail from Helke Ferrie to the author, May 25, 2012). The key message that the Ferries put across is that through such adoptions, one could solve at least some problems. By 1999, all their children were grown up and had left home to pursue their individual careers. Nevertheless, the parent-children bond that had been created from the start of their lives remains strong to this day with most of them. Several of them now have their own families, and the Ferries now have eight grandchildren and one great-grandchild.

Having retired from child welfare work, Helke is now a medical science writer, while Robert practices psychotherapy and EMDR (eye movement desensitization and repressing) specifically for people with post-traumatic stress disorder. They keep busy in pursuing their own varied interests, both professionally and socially. The Ferries are still not without the visits from their children and grandchildren and great-grandchild who keep them on their toes. To the Ferries, this is a whole new world of fulfillment.

When the couple read the author's draft on their profile, Helke's reaction was that they are not extraordinary but just ordinary Canadians with a commitment. Their children turned out like all other families – some did better than others, although they have proved how, through sheer love, one could create an indissoluble parent-child bond with one's child. "It is embarrassing to me to have so much praise and admiration heaped on me. Your intentions are excellent but maybe you should consider my feelings too. I do not believe that we did anything

MUSTAFA CHOWDHURY

praiseworthy at all. We were struck by the suffering of children and that there is nothing amazing about taking a few kids into one's home. I come from Germany – so what? They came from Bangladesh – so what? The story you wish to tell is hair-raising, no doubt and worth telling. But the underlying humanity is basic stuff. People feel for people," wrote Helke to the author in her own humble way (e-mail from Helke Ferrie to the author, May 25, 2012).

War Baby A

Born prematurely on May 27, 1972, in Dhaka at *Shishu Bhavan*, Orun weighed 2.4 kg at birth. At three months of age, he became even thinner and weighed 1.8 kg due to extreme malnutrition. The circumstances surrounding his birth at the orphanage are the same as all the other war babies. His biological mother is known to have secretly come to the orphanage to deliver the baby without anybody knowing about it and had left the orphanage soon after the delivery. The orphanage authority named the boy Orun. The nuns and *ayas* (midwives) nursed the infant and looked after him to the best of their abilities under the circumstance. Unfortunately, there was never enough food, no baby formula or even milk, plus no medicines, which resulted in the death of many prematurely born war babies. The nuns had nothing to feed the babies except rice water.

Upon his arrival in Canada, the Ferries changed the boy's name. We shall call him A. Growing up in Burlington, Ontario, as a child of the Ferries was very natural to A as he had several siblings who also grew up at the same time in the same home. It was the only life he had ever known. One of A's early memories include the strong awareness of his parents' good reputation; that both his mother and father were well known and respected in the community. A attended Fairview Elementary School in Burlington, Ontario, and then went to India for two years of schooling. His school years from elementary to high school had been years of fun, joy, and pleasure. His mother was very keen on having her children, especially A and B, exposed to the diverse cultures of the Indian subcontinent. The Ferries thus sent them to Woodstock International High School, a boarding school in Mussoorie, Utter Pradesh, India, in order for them to learn more about the Indian subcontinent.

Both parents considered A to be a bright and perceptive child who had won several awards during his early years at school. It was around 1977, at the age of five, that he came to know from his parents about *how* and *when* he and his sibling B were born in Bangladesh and were brought to Canada. He was not old enough to fully understand the word "adoption." He could see his family was distinctly multiracial. His family was known to most families in the neighborhood. A believes that if it was not for his parents' encouragement in everything to help him stay active and stimulated, he could not have been involved in many of the activities to the extent he did. Children's get-togethers, picnics, barbecues, and games, where A used to have a lot of fun, were a common practice at the Ferries residence. A treasures these memories fondly.

Immediately upon arrival in Utter Pradesh, A fell in love with the place which is one of the most famous places in India. At school A soon became very active, and among other things, he was also interested in sports and games. It was there in Mussoorie where A met a few students from Bangladesh. He stayed in India for two years (1987–1989).

Though only seventeen, A started to reflect on his own identity against a slew of questions that he was faced with. He needed to find answers to the many questions that ran through his mind to understand the true concepts of "belongingness" and "interracial adoption." He needed to situate himself in terms of his identity that he had known in Canada versus his own biological background, and the respective positions of his siblings of diverse backgrounds in relation to Canada, the country they call "home."

A did not have the same skin color as the majority Canadians, nor was he like the students at school who came from Bangladesh. His identity crisis and belongingness continued to wrestle around in his mind during this year. Soon, A became so homesick that he frequently longed for Canada, the country where his family was and the country with which he closely identified. He continued to grow and become more mature in dealing with his personal identity. After a bit of reflection, he did not seem to have any doubt about *who* he is; he came to see the entire situation in the following: that it was in *Canada* where he grew up, learned to talk, and began his school. The first seven weeks of his life in Bangladesh had remained only a topic of interest.

A returned to Canada from India in 1987 to complete his high school. In September 1989, he attended Lester B. Pearson High School in Burlington. The following year, he moved to Orangeville to attend grade 12 at Orangeville Secondary School. This time again, A's sense of "belongingness" had developed even more as he became matured in his mind. He was able to reflect a great deal. This time, A came to terms with the reality of his situation in Canada. It did not make him feel ashamed or terribly proud. He remembered how, upon learning the circumstances surrounding his birth, he considered the matter closed and did not wish to pursue it. He also remembered that whenever he had any question, his parents had always been there, ready to answer. He did not see himself as being any different from the rest of the students who were mainly white. Never feeling "different" from his white friends, A continued to grow up considering himself to be "Canadian" by all definition.

During his late teen years, A became involved in construction work. He spent eight months working to build houses for the less fortunate and low-income group of people. He worked hard with a strong determination not to join the rank of the unemployed. At that time, he also volunteered in a number of projects on the Indian reserve in Chapleau in northern Canada, close to Timmins, Ontario. There were times when he received only subsistence allowance, but he had continued to work in whatever capacity he could. Naturally, soon he came to be recognized by the community at large. It was only natural for him to volunteer, since he grew up seeing his parents and siblings who had spent inordinate amounts of time doing charity work. Needless to say, A is able to accommodate his own schedule with voluntary work just the same way his parents and family did.

During the summer of 1992, A decided to pursue a career in hospitality. He left home and moved to Toronto where he attended George Brown College. Being away from home was initially difficult, but he adjusted himself well with the passage of time. While at school, he also took up a series of odd jobs mostly at restaurants to support himself during the school yearsThough initially determined to complete his diploma, A found himself changing his career aspirations. Now he wanted to pursue nursing. Switching the field of study every now and then became a pattern due to one obstacle or another. He recognized that time had gone by and that he was falling through the cracks.

At one point, his first target was to become debt-free by paying off his Ontario Students Assistance Program (OSAP) loan first and then continue with his studies. During this period, he also switched from one job to another, something else that became a common practice with A. Neither unemployment nor underemployment had ever corroded his self-esteem.

Disruptions of this kind had, however, hampered his continuing education. But he quickly learned that regardless of his plans for his study, he needed to work part time simultaneously to support himself. He must try to pay off his loan. Unfortunately, A's plan fell through again, and he succumbed to other competing priorities at the cost of his studies. Socially speaking, A is quite comfortable with his friends and acquaintances, the majority of whom are white. Being content with his Canadian identity, he finds himself in a position where he cannot further identify with Bangladeshis or easily relate to them.

A remains close to his parents, siblings, nieces, and nephews. As far as he is concerned, the Ferries are his *only* parents, having known no other in his entire life. He echoes the same sentiment as all of the war babies of the present bunch who grew up in Canada under the love and care of their respective Canadian (adoptive) parents. He is grateful to his parents for everything – especially for their affectionate love toward their children. There was no dearth of love in the family. He remembers his mother who was never overprotective or a mother hen over her brood. Instead, he sees his parents with deep respect who have raised their children with unconditional love, enabling them to use their own sense of judgment. He also recognizes with admiration his mother's enthusiasm and years of dedication in advancing the cause of adoption, especially of hard-to-place children.

Interesting aspect of A's character is that, over the years, he has met and interacted with many Bangladeshis. He recalls having liked them as well as their company, but that's it. Although he had never been to Bangladesh, he does not want to disregard the possibility for a trip to Bangladesh. He believes he could possibly to do some voluntary work there.

Currently he works for a recycling company in Burlington, Ontario, and is enjoying his job and his time with his numerous friends most of whom are white. Still single, A believes there is no rush to get married. He would rather find a permanent job first before he shifts his focus on marriage. At the moment, he does not seem to have any inclination to tie the knot, or noose, as he sees it. He seems content with what he has been doing, although he says he would like to win a jackpot to pay off his loans.

War Baby B

Born prematurely on July 8, 1972, at *Shishu Bhavan* in Dhaka, Bangladesh, the baby girl weighed only 2.2 kg at birth. She was born when the Canadian team was already in Dhaka to negotiate with the government of Bangladesh to bring back to Canada a dozen or two war babies from the various orphanages of Bangladesh. War Baby B does not wish to participate in this project.

Dale and Doreen Good

In 1972 when Dale and Doreen Good adopted Bathol, a war baby from Bangladesh, Dale was a manager at Master Feeds, Copetown Branch near Hamilton, Ontario, while his wife, Doreen, a registered nurse, worked part time as a teaching assistant at St. Joseph's Hospital in Hamilton. Their desire to adopt started with Doreen's experience as a student nurse while working in the nursery. Many babies were frequently left in hospital premises by their birth mothers for adoption. The idea of adoption as a way to have their family had been in the couple's mind from the beginning of their married life. "*Why not give a home to a child who would otherwise not have one?*"[13] Doreen wondered and asked her husband.

When the Goods first inquired about adoption through the local Children's Aid Society (CAS), they were informed that they would have to be deemed infertile by the medical profession before they would be considered eligible to adopt. As well, they were warned that there was a long waiting list of would-be-adoptive parents in Ontario. Around the same time, the Goods also learned from an article in the local weekend magazine about the possibility of adopting a Vietnamese orphan through the Montreal-based Families For Children (FFC). The FFC workers' faith and dedication in their work with underprivileged children around the world inspired the Goods to open their eyes to a new realm of possibilities. The Goods contacted Helke Ferrie of

Burlington, Ontario, who was the spokesperson for the Ontario branch of FFC. Helke worked closely with the Goods and other couples in lobbying the Ontario government to speed up the adoption process.

The Goods' two children, Ryan (changed from Bathol) and Rachona, both came from Bangladesh. Twenty-two-day-old Ryan came to Canada in July 1972, while Rachona came in 1975 at the age of ten weeks. Doreen instantly felt so bonded with her son that she "cannot imagine that one would be any more bonded to a child that we gave birth to" (letter from Doreen Good to the author, cited in the notes and references). Having Ryan and Rachona within a span of three years, the Goods became so busy with their children that they did not wish to expand their family any more. Consequently, they never got around to doing a fertility test either. The couple was so occupied with their new son, and later on daughter, that for a while, all else in their lives had paled into insignificance.

The couple recalls the long and uncertain time they had while waiting for Ryan to arrive from Bangladesh. Interracial adoption was still a new phenomenon in Ontario. The Ministry of Community and Social Services, responsible for approving home studies intended for adoptions, did not seem to be wholeheartedly supportive of the concept of interracial adoption. To counter such views, and to show a united front to gain support from those interested in interracial adoption, the Goods became one of a group of seven families who banded together to lobby for adoption of *their* choice. When Ryan finally arrived, the Goods were a very relieved couple.

Perhaps the most important aspect of the conjugal life of this Caucasian couple is that, deep down, the Goods had always wanted to have a child from a different country and background than their own. The racially different Ryan was the right fit to their passionate desire to bring home the first child of their dreams. "That is the least we can do for the world situation,"[14] said Doreen in an interview two months after Ryan came to their home.

Having learned about the couple's desire for a racially different child, a local news reporter visited the Goods and was impressed with what he saw – nine-week-old Ryan in the arms of his adoptive mother Doreen, who seemed completely happy in his new home in Canada. "It's not the most difficult thing in the world to love a baby and there is a beauty about the soft contours of a dark skin that makes an infant from the Far East most appealing," wrote the reporter (*Wentworth Marketplace*, September 6, 1972).

The Goods recall they often they used to run into people who would tell them that they had their family "the easy way," meaning that Doreen did not have to give birth to the child (letter from Doreen Good to the author). On every such occasion, they were quick to point out that the process was never easy – what they might have missed in physical discomfort, pain, and inconvenience, they more than made up for in emotional stress, anxiety, and uncertainty. "Anyone can give birth – but not just anyone can adopt," observed the Goods (letter from Doreen Good to the author). In the case of Ryan, the interminable wait felt much longer than nine months of pregnancy. The Goods had to wade through cumbersome and voluminous paperwork and a lengthy approval process that had to be completed.

Being a part of Canadopt, a group of parents with mixed-race children (the details of which are described in chapter 6), the Goods were introduced to other families in southwestern Ontario, where adoption of the racially different children had just begun. The Goods have a particular way of describing that feeling of ownership and belonging relating to the adoption of their second child from Bangladesh. Upon receipt of the first picture of their prospective second child, a girl from Bangladesh, they instantly bonded with the child though she was thousands of miles away.

However, before the adoption and immigration formalities could be completed, that child became sick and died. "There was a feeling of loss and grief," maintain the Goods even though they neither saw nor ever physically hugged the child (letter from Doreen Good to the author). It was after the loss of the "unseen" child that Rachona arrived later to replace the dead child earlier assigned to the Good family. As far as the Goods were concerned, this was a unique experience that was hard to describe or even discuss. According to Doreen, bonding does not just occur by holding one's child a certain way so many minutes after birth. "For us bonding started when we received a picture of the child that had been chosen for us," says a proud Doreen (letter from Doreen Good to the author). From that moment on, that child belonged to them.

There was considerable interest and curiosity among people in the neighborhood as well as the broader public for their racially different children, especially when Ryan was very little. This was perhaps heightened, since Doreen is a blonde, fair-skinned woman who was seen carrying a beautiful brown infant. Often she used to be stopped in the grocery store, drugstore, etc., by some stranger to admire Ryan who, to the Goods, "was a real cutie!" (letter from Doreen Good to the author, cited in notes and references). Many would instantly fall in love with Ryan. Given that the Goods lived in a small community where the majority was white, Doreen remembers many would ask questions such as "What color is the father?" "Who will he marry?" and "What language will he speak?" (letter from Doreen Good to the author).

From the start, the Goods were frank and open with their children about their birth history and past. They told the children "how they loved their brown skin, dark hair and dark eyes that make the difference in their appearance and their parents" – a fact of life for families with racially different children (letter from Doreen Good to the author, cited in notes and references). They attempted to give the children basic information on and exposure to Bengali heritage. However, as it turned out, the children grew up, by and large, with a strong "Canadian" culture, which, of course, encompassed multiculturalism. When the children became adults, they came to know more precisely that Ryan was a Bangladeshi war baby and Rachona an orphan but not a war baby. The couple saved newspaper articles about their adoption and the political climate in their birth country at the time of their adoption.

According to Doreen, when Ryan grew up, he very much needed to return to his country of birth. Rachona, however, had much less enthusiasm and curiosity about her country of birth than Ryan. Evidently, Rachona had an issue with self-esteem as well. "Fortunately, that is no longer the case with Rachona as she has changed over the years. Now that she is married and living in a more international community, she seems more comfortable in her own skin," observed Doreen (letter from Doreen Good to the author). Taking initiatives in finding about their children's country of birth, the Goods gradually learned more about their children's background and birth. This had helped them relate to their children better.

In many ways, the Goods remain atypical. Unlike many adoptive parents who continue to feel threatened by the phenomenon of adoptee searching, the Goods encouraged Ryan in his drive to discover his birth history while he was in Bangladesh. They believed that this was the right thing to do. Having no atavistic fear, they were in constant

MUSTAFA CHOWDHURY

touch with Ryan always encouraging him to pursue his endeavors to "discover" his country of birth to the fullest extent possible.

In 1989 when Canadopt arranged for a trip for the adoptees from Bangladesh, the Goods volunteered to join them along with their children. For the family, it was a wonderful opportunity to take advantage of the initiative undertaken by Canadopt. (The details of the hectic weeklong trip are discussed under subtitle "The war babies' first visit to their country of birth" in chapter 7.) What they remember from their trip is that Bangladesh is a country that is about the size of New Brunswick, Canada, where there were over ten million people only in the capital city of Dhaka at the time. The Goods also remember how enchanted they were by the sheer natural beauty of Bangladesh and the warmth of the people they met during their one-week stay in Dhaka.

However, the most rewarding thing for the Goods was to see the reactions of Ryan and Rachona who were both excited and frightened by the thought of going to their country of birth. It was the look on their children that had touched them more than anything else. They could "see" how their children felt to be so lucky to be in Canada as they *could have* been part of these children in the orphanage or, for that matter, on the street begging or stealing. It gave them "a chance to get a true taste of what their lives would have been like if they had remained in Bangladesh."[15] In summing up the experiences of the Goods' whirlwind visit to Bangladesh, Yvonne Reynolds, a reporter, observed how, following their trip, they had returned "with a heightened awareness of the strengths and the needs of fellow humans living on the other side of the world" (*Focus*, May 30, 1989).

Following their return, the Goods reflected for days on what "they saw and experienced in Bangladesh during their trip" (*Focus*, May 30, 1989). In a sense, the Goods admitted to having pangs of guilt seeing how lucky they were in Canada. Dale says for weeks he felt utterly frustrated not knowing what the future would hold for Bangladesh or for those on the streets or for those at the shacks made from scraps and burlap, displaying gaunt bodies and protruding bones and hopelessness. In a 1975 interview with the *Mennonite Reporter,* the Goods said that they "wanted to give someone a home that didn't have a home."[16]

As time went by, and upon reflection, the Goods realized that the children they had adopted "did them a favor" in that those children filled their lives with joy giving them "a new sense of purpose and meaning in life" (letter from Doreen Good to the author. For the Goods, nothing, no medal or commendation, could ever equal the gift of a son and a daughter. The joy and happiness that their children brought to them far outweighed anything they *could* give them.

Having raised their children with rewarding experience and seeing that both Ryan and Rachona have turned out to be exceptionally kind and loving people, who are making a positive contribution to society, the retired couple remains very proud. Today, both of their children are married (the details of Ryan are below). Rachona, a confident psychiatric nurse, is married to Mark Meza, of Mexican descent, and has a teenage stepson, Zak, and is now living in Los Angeles, California.

Dale and Doreen continue to live in Exeter today though in an empty nest. Due to close proximity, Ryan and his children spend more time with the Goods than Rachona. They look forward to their regular visits to California to spend time with Rachona and her family. Every visit by their children and grandchildren is a great source of enjoyment for the family.

Bathol

Born on June 27, 1972, at Mother Teresa's *Shishu Bhavan* in Dhaka, Bangladesh, the baby boy weighed 2.5 kg at birth. When the infant arrived in Canada at the age of three weeks, he weighed 2.9 kg. The orphanage authority named the boy Bathol, which is also mentioned in his certificate and travel documents. The boy was abandoned by his birth mother who did not wish to provide any more information, since it was an enforced pregnancy. She immediately left the orphanage premises in secret following the birth of the baby.

His adoptive parents in Canada changed his name to Ryan having added the family's surname, Good. Bathol thus came to be called Ryan Bathol Good. Ryan grew up in the small town of Copetown, Ontario, and attended Walpole North Elementary School, Hagersville (1978–1982); South Perth Centennial School, Kirkton (1982–1986); and South Huron District High School (1986–1991). He then went to University of Waterloo from 1992 to 1996 and completed an honor's degree in environmental and resource studies. While still in high school, Ryan had an opportunity to go on a trip to Bangladesh in 1989 with his parents. (The details have been discussed in chapter 7 under "The war babies' first visit to their country of birth.") In fact, this visit, or homecoming, had a positive impact on his life, triggering further interest about Bangladesh and Bangladeshis.

While at Waterloo and still very young, Ryan decided on a future visit to Bangladesh to fulfill the interest that he had developed during his first visit. Ryan took a year off and returned to Bangladesh again for a short visit with his friend Brent Gingerich. At nineteen, his blood was teaming with vigor with an inmost yearning to reconnect to his birth mother who, according to the staff at *Shishu Bhavan,* was from the district of Barisal, Bangladesh. Instantly, Ryan was driven by an overwhelming desire to find out about his birth mother, wherever she is.

For Ryan, it was as though this call to adventure became a call to self. With all the enthusiasm in the world, Ryan headed for Barisal, a city about two hundred kilometers south of Dhaka. He had no luck, as he had no other information to follow. This was a time when some extraordinary emotions were brought on by encountering a new reality that seemed to have surfaced with incredible intensity. He then went to the headquarters of the Missionaries of Charity in Kolkata, West Bengal, India. In every place his questions were left unanswered. Having tossed back and forth between the past and the present, it dawned on the nineteen-year-old Ryan that his undertaking was neither practical nor achievable.

A reality check brought Ryan back to the actual world with a thud – the impossibility of ever finding his birth mother. A smart but emotionally fatigued Ryan quickly realized that he would *never* find the anonymous woman who brought him into this world but had to abandon him. Ryan concluded his search by saying to himself that even though he would not be successful in his mission to find his birth mother, he could *still* find out more about his birth country, Bangladesh. After much reflection on *who* he is, *where* he came from, or *who* was the mother who gave him up upon birth, Ryan came to grips with it all in an amazingly straightforward way.

Of the first fifteen war babies who were brought to Canada in July 1972, Ryan is the only one who has made three visits to Bangladesh thus far. The purpose of his third visit to Bangladesh was to "discover" the country and the people of Bangladesh. He had been asking himself the question *Where is Bangladesh?,*[17] with no answer to his satisfaction. At twenty-six, a courageous Ryan showed no worry about heading toward an unknown edge from his secure Canadian life to a new and unpredictable life in Bangladesh. Eager to learn and aware that his knowledge of Bangladesh and Bangladeshi was woefully inadequate; he realized that he must interact with a large number of people all through his stay in Bangladesh. He hoped to enhance his knowledge base through interactions with a variety of people.

Actuated by the best of intentions, a vibrant Ryan was full of new dreams and possibilities having been genuinely interested in learning more about the "motherland" he came to see. In fact, at that time, Ryan felt encouraged and reassured, as he believed he had experiences of his last two trips in his back pocket as "lessons learned." Imagining that he had the whole world "by the tail," he was ready to take the bull by the horn and confront them. In his attempt to grapple with the problems in Dhaka, during the first few months, Ryan wondered aimlessly with all of his senses in keen focus – excited, nervous, scared, and yet curious. The more he saw and learned, the prouder he felt to be a Canadian with roots in Bangladesh.

Right from the beginning of his stay in Dhaka, Ryan had established a communication mechanism with his folks back "home" in Canada to keep them in the loop. In fact, all through his stay, Ryan kept his parents posted on his activities on a regular basis through e-mails. Typically, an e-mail would highlight his activities in Dhaka. As well, it would contain many itsy-bitsy items of interest on sundry topics. At the outset, Ryan wrote to his friends and family saying that his missives might be considered to be his "humble and, sometimes, feeble attempts at summarizing the events and experiences of the previous 30 days" – a kind of infotainment containing both information and entertainment (Ryan's e-mail, October 31, 1997, cited in notes and references).

His stay in Bangladesh helped him observe Bangladeshi culture up close – at its best and at its worst. His frequent e-mails on the highs and lows and exchanges on sundry items made Ryan feel like he was having an ongoing *conversation* with his parents as though they were within earshot. For Ryan's parents, his missives became not only an authentic source of information on their son's adventure but also a source of fun, the reading of which often made them laugh and reminded them of what they saw for themselves in 1989 when they visited Bangladesh.

"It wasn't until I typed the date that I realized today is Halloween. A mere 30 days into this crazy adventure, and already my sense of western trick-or-treating begins to vanish," wrote Ryan who got into the "swing of things" in an attempt to make himself a part of the community (Ryan's e-mail, October 31, 1997). They might consider his e-mails "a spontaneous and violent gastric expulsion of a month long feast," wrote Ryan with his usual wit and humor (Ryan's e-mail, October 31, 1997). Having progressed through several trips with a kind of joyous energy, Ryan was able to "discover" the beauty of Bangladesh during the first few weeks following his arrival. This made him hope for more fun and substantive work. As time went by, Ryan helped his parents familiarize them with his hectic life in Dhaka.

Ryan shared his apartment with another Bangladeshi whom he called a "friend." Using his natural humor, Ryan described his rooms in his apartment: "To give a summary illustration, our kitchen is a shelf with a camp stove on top; accompanied by a single faucet overtop and a cement reservoir on the floor for a sink. Our washing machine is the bathroom floor" (Ryan's e-mail, May 8, 1998). He then described how he used to go about doing his daily rituals of going to bed, "tucking all except one edge underneath" his mattress and then "spending five to ten minutes killing all the mosquitoes that generally used to remain inside the net" (Ryan's e-mail, May 8, 1998), as he did not want to compromise his sleep by giving mosquitoes any opportunity to bite him.

So detailed were Ryan's descriptions that one could visualize him as if confined to a cage in an attempt to save him from mosquito bites. "I must smack my bedding all about so as to round up all the smarter creatures who are hiding under the covers" (Ryan's e-mail, May 8, 1998). Ryan reminded his parents that this was not the end of the daily ritual yet. He had more to do by "sitting still and looking all around for a minimum of one minute" before he would "slip out of the mosquito net very carefully so as not to permit any unlawful entries" (Ryan's e-mail, May 8, 1998). He would then shut off the light and reenter in the same manner, tuck the entrance side in, and then go to bed. Ryan's picturesque description of his nightly ritual before going to bed had attracted readers in Canada who thoroughly enjoyed reading them and visualizing Ryan sleeping like a king. Those not familiar with mosquitoes soon became engaged in reading and enjoying his descriptive missives.

In no time did Ryan begin to follow the adage, "When in Rome do as the Romans do." It did not take him long to adapt himself to disruptions, detours, and longer travel times. In describing the city and the people of Dhaka, Ryan told his parents how he became a part of the crowd, never hesitating to do what many others do: "About a week or so ago, I was taking a pee in the sewer at the side of the street. It was about 9:00 pm. At once, there were frantic shrieks, and I turned to see a woman running. Before I could pull up my fly, a deafening blast was heard followed by two more blasts, and what felt like stones grazed my face. What followed was some serious commotion" (Ryan's e-mail, October 31, 1997).

Within weeks of his arrival, the news media learned about Ryan and started to follow him. By the first week of December 1997, Ryan was all over the newspapers as the first ever known war baby of Bangladesh. Ryan was impressed with the glaring and sensational headlines thinking that they would awaken public consciousness. In fact, he felt greatly encouraged by the sudden publicity and attention recognizing his potential in Bangladesh for making an impact in the minds of Bangladeshis. On second thought, however, he felt that he should not be too enthused with the idea that he would be getting extra attention and become a bit of a celebrity. As he started to interact with the news media, he came to learn about people's take on 1971, something that he did not know much about when in Canada: "The issue of liberation and war-babies is very serious and very important," wrote Ryan (Ryan's e-mail, December 7, 1997).

Considering this as an area with a lot of potential, he saw a role for himself in this matter. "It would seem that I may have the power (by sheer coincidence of my birth) to make or at least start the process of these changes. In the coming months I will explain this in more detail" (Ryan's e-mail, December 7, 1997). Ryan thus gave his parents a head's-up. Despite Ryan's seemingly bright future, he, nevertheless, had a gut feeling that there would be bumps ahead.

The people of Bangladesh have grown up "sharing and living with a maximum amount of people in a minimum amount of space. It is as though the over-crowded Dhaka City people, a scraggly band of impoverished Bengalis, were bursting at the seams. One double bed will typically house up to four people. Of course, this form of nurturing extends itself to societal affections," wrote Ryan to his parents describing the underlying realities (Ryan's e-mail, January 3, 1998).

MUSTAFA CHOWDHURY

Ryan's observations on the religious and political lives of the Bengalis were both interesting and educational for his readers in Canada. Claiming that he does not know the "warp and woof" of Bengali culture, he wrote about *what* he saw, *how* he saw, and *what* he thought about the people of Bangladesh. Ryan started off by explaining the call for prayers for Muslims: "The *Azan,* if I have not mentioned before, is the pervasive call to prayer in the Muslim universe. It is inescapable. Indeed it has permanently secured a position in the top five shocks on the culture-shock parade. It seems to go without saying that every unsuspecting visitor inevitably falls victim to the mesmerizing glow of *Azan"* (Ryan's e-mail, July 3, 1998).

At the beginning of the holy month of Ramadan, "when the Muslims all around the world begin to fast," wrote Ryan, "Bangladeshi Muslims practice religious obligations" (Ryan's e-mail, July 3, 1998) with noticeable seriousness. Without any pretense to intellectuality, Ryan shared what he had learned about Ramadan, in simple English: "During Ramadan, the people get up at 5:00 am or so and begin to eat as this will be their last chance until sunset. Just before sunrise, the siren is sound over the mosque loudspeaker and people are told to stop eating (If) it happens that food is being lifted from hand to mouth when the warning is heard – the hand must be lowered and the morsel never makes it to the stomach. So it goes" (Ryan's e-mail, July 3, 1998).

At the end of Ramadan when Bangladeshis (Muslims) were ready to celebrate the *Eid-ul-Fitr,* (marks the end of the month of Ramadan; festival of breaking of the fast by Muslims), without wishing to mischaracterize the occasion, Ryan described *what* it is and *what* it means to Muslims. "Although I have not yet experienced it, I can make a *priori* description of this special day. It seems to be like Christmas for us. The same sort of spirit is flowing in the community. All shops are packed. Vast amounts of money are being spent. Joy is in the air. Indeed, I am being enveloped by all this fun and frolic. This past Christmas I felt nothing. Now, at the time of *Eid,* I am feeling the same sort of spirit that I should have felt at Christmas. Crisscross, crisscross!" (Ryan's e-mail, July 3, 1998).

Implicit in Ryan's description is his recognition of the difference between Muslim tradition, centering their religious festivals, and the Christian traditions back "home" with which he is more familiar – something that made him feel that these customs and traditions of

Bangladesh were not *his,* for he is "Canadian," and for sure, he *feels* like a "foreigner" in Bangladesh. And yet what remains paramount in Ryan's mind is his view that he was born in Bangladesh for which he is proud.

At twenty-six, Ryan's quick, keen, and comprehensive intellect also made him recognize how the political leaders of Bangladesh were divided on almost every issue. He did not fail to notice the unusually blunt and spiky manner of the politicians of the 1990s and the enormity of their insidious behavior. Ryan, of course, saw the political climate of Bangladesh through a different lens. He was alarmed to see how the streams of violent controversies that were swirling in the political arena gave rise to patriotic hysteria, cheap shots, arm-twisting, and opportunism on the part of politicos.

The term "hartal," wrote Ryan, in general, means strike that is called by one or more of the political opposition parties every now and then in protest against the government. Ryan also painted a vivid picture of Bangladesh for those not familiar with its power and politics. *"Hartal* is a common phenomenon which is a major personal annoyance not to mention a serious societal disruption," wrote Ryan (Ryan's e-mail, February 10, 1998). He then explained *when, how,* and under *what* circumstances such *hartals* occur in the major cities of the country, as well as the frequency of *hartals* in Dhaka, something that happens every few weeks, followed by mass demonstrations. He was alarmed to notice intractable conflicts that were plagued by irreconcilable differences. There was no dearth of turncoats. He was disgusted at the political chicanery, pettifogging, and gerrymandering of the leaders who, he believed, had excelled only in circumlocutory speeches, the majority of which he found to be full of sound and fury signifying nothing. Ryan was filled with anger and resentment, seeing the extent of unscrupulous activity among the leaders throughout the country.

With his eyes wide open, Ryan also began to see social confusion that, he believed, in turn had given rise to rancorous and unjust actions by politicians. In search of ideal values, a somewhat naïve Ryan interpreted the current political events of the day as the result of ethical anarchy and moral ambivalence. "Drug addiction is very much a problem in Dhaka and it is definitely on the rise. This seems almost understandable as the environment and opportunities for young people are bleak, to say the least," wrote Ryan (Ryan's e-mail, May 8, 1998).

MUSTAFA CHOWDHURY

He was dismayed to see how arrogantly the ruling party remained determined to cling to power, while the opposition parties squabbled over everything with hysterical intensity harboring nothing but resentment and contempt for each other. He also saw with his own eyes the totality of Bangladeshi politics of the late 1990s – including the long-standing practice of dichotomizing individuals politically as "friends" or "enemies." The role of the national political leaders of Bangladesh must have contributed to Ryan's frustrations. Every politician seemed busy trying to up the ante for oneself. He took a scunner against those he considered simply scums of the earth.

As Ryan mulled over the hypocritical and pervasive corruption among the Bangladeshi politicians, he felt only repugnance. Though a neophyte, he recognized the jiggery-pokery of the unsavory Bangladeshi politicians – a different kettle of fish altogether. Politicians, observed Ryan, were only interested in cheating the poor out of every penny with no consideration for the aspirations of the people who had fought for equality and justice and had won the country's independence. He concluded that he needed more time to comprehend the complex politics of Bangladesh. Meantime, he wanted to see the political zaniness come to an end.

Ryan was turned off by the prevalence and depth of corruption in Bangladesh, which seemed to be embedded in every sector of the country. To him, this was a particular factor attributable to the economic misfortunes of the impoverished Bangladesh. "I am convinced of this evil and it has surely affected my sense of mission and resulting existence here in Bangladesh" (Ryan's e-mail, May 30, 1998). Blinded by his idealism, Ryan expected to find bureaucrats and politicians with a spirit of give and take, and with a readiness for cooperation rather than confrontation. His thoughts, ideas, and actions that were coming in spurts and gushes too often created a kind of tidal wave in his wake. At times Ryan keenly felt his intellectual limits. At other times, he felt that his ability to work and concentrate, and his mood and temper were being resolved, at least in part.

As Ryan traveled to other districts of Bangladesh, he warily watched the waves of unrest, looting and banditry, having no doubt that the problems would continue to bedevil. "After arriving in the early morning at Dhaka airport, I was trapped inside of a baby taxi by two hoodlums. I kicked the one guy in the crown jewels and escaped, very pissed, but thankfully unharmed" (Ryan's e-mail, September 20, 1998). This is how he described one of his experiences when he was attacked by a group of miscreants.

Ryan also talked about extortionists, or *mustans,* as they are known in Bangladesh. "The Mafia in Bangladesh is called *Mustan.* They are everywhere and they exist at all levels from the street on up. They can be highly dangerous. Every day, I read about *Mustans* and their actions in the newspaper. They use crude homemade bombs of sharp objects or acid; sharp instruments and more and more guns" (Ryan's e-mail, October 31, 1997).

Seeing that no one in the government took any interest in national issues, Ryan questioned the Bangladeshis' notion of liberation. He became convinced that it was nothing but an illusion. As Ryan saw it, Bangladesh is not liberated and will not be liberated until it resolves the tragic disparity between the unvanquished and the vanquished.

Ryan had many occasions to speak at formal gatherings in his capacity as the "first ever known war baby" in Bangladesh. In such instances, an enthusiastic Ryan would feel a surge of encouragement and would take pride in his own situation in speaking about himself and other war babies of Bangladesh. Ryan once introduced himself to a group of Bangladeshis by reading a short poem he had written:

You don't know me,
But you know of me.
I don't know you
But I know of you.
I am here,
When for so many years,
I have not
You are here,
When for so many years,
you have,
You were born from
blood,
I was born from blood.

You are a war baby,
I too, am a war baby.
You yearn for truth,
I also yearn for truth
Together we shall shine
light on this disguise.
Together we shall break
these walls.
Together we shall
reconcile.
This is our challenge,
This is our task.

Tumra Bangladesher (you are of Bangladesh)
Ami Bangladesher (I'm of Bangladesh)

MUSTAFA CHOWDHURY

Amra Bangladesher (we are of Bangladesh).

Calmly but firmly Ryan expressed his innermost feelings while stating the facts of his life, however tragic. Ryan realized that the people of Bangladesh knew of him only because his birth was associated with the birth of Bangladesh, but they really did not know him as a person. Ryan continued to learn from and share with others about the war babies and the birth of his country, both born of a ferocious bloodbath. Ryan told the audience that questions regarding his origins and roots became complex as he evolved. Ryan alternately felt both closeness to and distance with Bengalis and Bangladeshis. "I did not understand what it meant to be a war-baby until late in my teenage years. As my understanding of war in general and the atrocities that occur began to increase, so did my realization that I was a result of the Liberation War of Bangladesh. My birth mother was raped by a Pakistani soldier," said Ryan candidly (Ryan's e-mail, November 7, 1997). Ryan, nevertheless, felt propelled to move forward.

For the first time in their lives, the people of Bangladesh heard from Ryan, an actual war baby born on the sacred soil of the newly born Bangladesh. Feeling heroically honored to associate his birth with that of his nation, he expressed a deep and steadfast love toward Bangladesh, the birth of which he proudly linked to his own humble beginnings. An emotional Ryan then succinctly spelled out how Bangladesh and the war babies were both born of blood from "a very tragic but important war" (Ryan's e-mail, November 7, 1997). Setting the context of the Bengalis' struggle for independence and the bloodbath that they were subjected to, a passionate Ryan delivered his barnburner speech for the crowd: "Out of this ferocious bath, you and I were born. Let us not forget those who sacrificed their lives and livelihoods for our Independence" (Ryan's e-mail, November 7, 1997). Ryan then appealed directly to his audience: "Let us grow together as we both struggle to answer the question, where is Bangladesh?" (Ryan's e-mail, November 7, 1997).

The audience took note of the emphasis with which Ryan narrated the tragic and historic story of his birth and that of the other war babies. As the audience listened, they recognized Ryan's dichotomy – how he was torn between his love for his country of birth and his "home" country, Canada, where he was raised. Many who hugged and greeted him told him how thrilled they were to meet a war baby for the first time about whom they had only heard. They empathized with his loneliness seeing that he was going through a bumpy road in Bangladesh.

The next few days, the news media in Dhaka provided an extensive coverage on Ryan. Prof. Monwara Islam, a renowned Rotarian, invited Ryan to her house for a home-cooked dinner, which Ryan enjoyed immensely. Islam remembers how Ryan thanked her profusely for having him over at her place. She was so excited that she instantly wrote a poem about Ryan, dedicating it to all the war babies and their birth mothers, embracing them all in bewildering profusion. It was published in a local newspaper. Harun Habib, a freedom fighter and a journalist, met Ryan and wrote an interesting piece on him, which was published in one of Habib's selected prose collection. As well, Saifullah Mahmud Dulal and a few others also followed suit by writing poems, songs, and plays on Ryan.

Within weeks, however, the initial excitement frizzled out. Since nothing had yet happened with regard to the trials of the perpetrators, Ryan wondered if Bangladesh had truly become liberated. He reasoned that "if one's oppressor had not been vanquished or punished, then the oppressor has not been conquered" (Ryan's e-mail, November 9, 1997). He believed that the perpetrators had been allowed to escape punishment. To Ryan's way of thinking, in the absence of a trial for the perpetrators, Bangladeshis were, in effect, saying that the oppressive actions of the Yahya regime (military repression under the direction of then president Yahya Khan) were acceptable. A frustrated Ryan came to believe that only a very few paid attention to this issue of national importance.

By 2010, however, things had changed in the political arena as the government of the day belatedly set up an International War Crimes Tribunal to address crimes against humanity in Occupied Bangladesh. Although approached by the tribunal, Ryan did not wish to participate, as he did not see any direct role that he could play.

Apart from the trial of the perpetrators, back then in 1998, Ryan remained pessimistic about Bangladesh's prospects. "Indeed, the tunnel is dark, and the end remains unseen. The age demography of Bangladesh is pyramid shaped. This means that there are many young people who will very soon grow up only to find a society which has nothing to accommodate them. No jobs, no chances, no scope for real leisure.

They will have grown up in a globalized Bangladesh – cable TV and other cultural imports are at work, and believe me, they are working overtime" (Ryan's e-mail, May 8, 1998).

Not surprisingly, within months, Ryan faltered in his desire to live in Bangladesh. His dissatisfaction and frustration increased continually. Initial barriers and roadblocks paled in comparison to the later problems. "Bangladesh. So much to tell, so little time, so little patience, so little ability! It is questionable whether it is possible for me to understand, let alone express, what has happened, what is happening and what will happen to Ryan in this crazy place called Bangladesh," wrote Ryan to his folks in Canada (Ryan's e-mail, June 19, 1998).

Having traveled to Bangladesh with a newly cultivated understanding and love for his country of birth, Ryan had hoped to know and discover him in a new light, as well as to develop a fresh vision on how to continue his work in Bangladesh. Ryan tried to "regroup" in light of the newly revealed reality, wondering if he had the strength to help poor children break the thrall of dependence to emerge from poverty and obscurity. In his attempt at "getting to know his roots," and having spent some time in Bangladesh, he became dissatisfied as he experienced a hard and different reality. In the midst of frenetic absorption, he found it daunting to move around even on a day-to-day basis. Feelings of dissatisfaction soon turned into anxiety and depression as he tried to correlate his experiences with his expectations. He became disenchanted with a life that he found to be of different and confusing social mores. Ryan never got used to the kerfuffle all around him.

Day after day, dejection and hopelessness invaded Ryan, making him more disturbed and disheartened. He continually racked his brain. Although he had intended to use his "vast knowledge and 'western' expertise to aid" his native country . . . "to give something back, to make a difference . . ." (Ryan's e-mail, September 20, 1998), Ryan's efforts seemed fruitless. Caught in the middle, the events that unfolded only provoked irritation. One part of his self was telling him, "But Ryan, you know that life is but an endless series of storms and calms. You have weathered before – why not again? Oh, but every storm is different. Sometimes, the boats don't come back" (Ryan's e-mail, September 20, 1998). But at a moment of frustration, another part of his cynical mind led him to rethink, "I do not know if my conscience can muster all the reasons and things that I want to change about myself, but my intentions are all good. I strive for the ultimate ethical, humanitarian and environmental value set" (Ryan's e-mail, September 20, 1998).

Practically, during his entire year in Bangladesh, Ryan felt conflicted in spite of his intentions to do something worthwhile for Bangladesh. Unfortunately, he did not have any knowledge or strength to carry out a plan of action. In truth, he was unable to formulate any manageable steps toward realistic and concrete humanitarian goals. His heart and mind burst with desire to do well – yet he always collided with the metaphorical wall. Hence his frustration: the clash of dreams versus reality, with harsh reality holding the upper hand.

Ryan simply could not conceptualize *what* he dreamed for Bangladesh – and *what* he would like it to become. He had a kind of happy, feel-good vision for his country of birth, but the "dream" was maddeningly short on specifics! His own mission and his vision for Bangladesh simply did not crystallize – thereby leaving Ryan prone to inaction and procrastination as he waited vaguely for something to happen.

Although surrounded by many well-meaning people, Ryan felt conflicted, since these individuals – whom he resembled physically – were worlds apart psychologically and culturally. "In the crowd I was no different than anyone else. Indeed, in Bangladesh, I am no different in appearance than the locals. The problem is that while my genes are Bengali, my brain is Canadian. I am barricaded against the Bengali and I am barricaded against the Western. This fact is tough to bear," wrote Ryan (Ryan's e-mail, June 20, 1998). At first glance, they appeared to be kindred spirits; however, the reality was frustratingly at variance with appearances, and Ryan felt himself drifting as an outsider. Instead of peace and serenity, he experienced inner turmoil. At times he felt he was losing his own western abilities and culture. On such occasions, he would try ever harder to immerse himself in Bangladeshi culture.

As if Ryan did not have enough on his plate, it seemed that each month resulted in further physical and psychological deterioration. As Ryan approached his one-year anniversary in Bangladesh, the twenty-six-year-old once again informed his parents about his precarious health: "Every month, I have had something to combat. If it isn't a cold, it is strange bumps on my skin. Anyways, I don't think you want to hear all about my health problems" (Ryan's e-mail, March 1, 1998).

More and more, Ryan saw himself as a kind of Shakespearian tragic figure "strutting and fretting his hour upon the stage" but accomplishing little or nothing at all. Ryan asked himself, "What am I doing here? I think I am losing sight. I am searching for romantic peace. I feel like a tragic hero. My world is a stage; and I'm the only actor. I feel so alone" (Ryan's e-mail, July 12, 1998). Time and again, Ryan felt acute loneliness even while countless people teamed around him.

Again, the more he applied himself to understanding the reality of Bangladesh, the more elusive it became. Having soldiered on for some time with compulsive over commitment, it dawned on Ryan that no matter what he did, it would cut no ice. He was at his wit's end. He tried with great effort and hopes to buckle down and often delivered "pep talks" to himself – but with little success. While he knew that the longest journey "begins with a single step," it seems he could not even do that.

Throughout his year in Bangladesh, Ryan continually experienced the persistent tension between his Canadian "can-do" self and the self he tried to become as the son born of a Bangladeshi mother raped during their struggle for independence in 1971. Occasionally, Ryan recognized with clarity and humility that he might never fully grasp the reality of Bangladesh no matter how much he struggled.

Ryan tried vainly to apply his Canadian-learned western knowledge and experience to the harsh realities of Bangladesh. Still, Ryan felt he had failed miserably. The more Ryan reflected on what was happening to himself and within Bangladesh, the more alienated he became from the people of Bangladesh. "My knowledge and expertise is so little, and the problem is so big. My plan is constantly changing. I run. I hide. Retreat to school. Retreat to more experience. Retreat to the fountain of knowledge" (Ryan's e-mail, October 10, 1997).

Speaking from his own accumulated experience of a year's stay in Bangladesh, Ryan acknowledged the reality of the predicament that paralyzed him, leaving him hopeless in spite of his intentions to the contrary: "I am sick with contradictions and hypocrisies. I am so sick. The world is sick" (Ryan's e-mail, September 20, 1998). A resolved but terribly dissatisfied Ryan sensed what was in the offing: "I have seen the future. And, I don't like what I see. It is a nightmare yet to come. Or, has it already come?" (Ryan's e-mail, September 20, 1998).

While he had visions of "doing things" he had neither the means nor the know-how, in his own mind, Ryan believed he was clear as to *what* he wanted. In reality, he recognized that his plans were perhaps airy-fairy, since he could not see the forest for the trees. *Was he barking up the wrong tree?* thus asked an uncertain Ryan. As a neophyte, he recognized his inability to outline his vision or mission with lucidity and precision. He spelled out the price of failing to follow through his plan. Understandably, a rookie Ryan needed to be more circumspect, cautious, and therefore, less spontaneous. Caught between a rock and a hard place, an immensely talented but hapless Ryan could not decide which part to follow.

Paradoxically, although Ryan often expressed hopelessness, even despair, that he might never succeed in integrating himself into Bangladeshi culture and contribute positively, he resolutely soldiered on. He continued his struggle to rise above the ordinary – to do the best he could under the circumstances he encountered.

Ryan's e-mail "conversations" with his parents and friends reflect how Ryan, though resolved, had suffered at every step of the way, always feeling unsure of himself in a country he found stranger than fiction. He tried to remind himself that his birth mother came from Bangladesh, a land rich with history, language, and culture. Yet deep down, he seemed to recognize he was psychologically situated far from the madding crowd of Bangladesh. Seeing the entire situation from a Canadian perspective, Ryan had persistently asked how he could craft a purposeful role in Bangladesh.

Reading his letters, one is left with the impression that, in spite of his frustration, Ryan would hold on to his *can-do* attitude with determination. Even at the very end, a devastated Ryan could only dramatize his own sense of self-pity. On the one hand, Ryan was unbearably frustrated with the situation he was placed in; on the other hand, he felt that he must never give up. Despite setback after setback, Ryan never quit.

In summarizing his struggle to come to terms with his Bangladeshi roots and his Canadian upbringing, the writer finds that Ryan's life hinges on several huge anchors, the first and strongest of which is the unstinting love and nurturing provided by Doreen and Dale Good – particularly their unconditional love in treating Ryan and his sister, Rachona, as their very *own* children. At no point is Ryan left in doubt with their vast love and support, a bond so strong that it sustains him in his darkest hours in Bangladesh – a quarter century after his birth. The fact that the Goods were fully integrated within Canadian society made that same integration a virtual "slam dunk" for Ryan. Finally, because the Goods had always allowed Ryan to explore and celebrate his roots in Bangladesh, he was able to embark on his own journey to discover his "real self."

The fact that Ryan was unable to find a specific niche for himself in the complex and daunting reality found in contemporary Bangladesh in no way diminishes his love for the country of his birth. Ryan demonstrated that love and commitment by securing Bangladeshi citizenship during his one-year stay – something that he did by going out of his way. It was at that time that he was told that the spelling of his middle name, Bathol, was wrong and that it should have been "Badol." While taking out Bangladeshi citizenship, Ryan corrected the spelling accordingly.

As to his efforts to integrate himself in Bengali society and his experiences in Bangladesh, in a certain sense, Ryan is no worse off than the most dedicated statesman in that burgeoning nation – which is still attempting to find its way in a challenging, often unfair, modern world.

In Raymonde Provencher's famous 2003 documentary titled *War Babies*, Ryan is a character. Today Ryan is married to Martine, a Caucasian of French background. They have two children, Calin, twelve, and Cadelle, nine, all of whom live in Kitchener, Ontario. Over the years, Ryan has successfully established himself in Kitchener, Ontario, where he owns a bar called Chainsaw and a property management company with over forty employees. Given Martine's francophone roots, the Caucasian Martine brings her own uniqueness to their union. Ryan, doubtless, welcomes her unique contributions to their union.

One also imagines that Ryan will continue to share within his own family and his community his humanitarian values, his work ethic, his "can-do" approach, and his "never say die" approach to every situation.

Joel and Trudy Hartt

One of the fascinating couples with stories of international adoption, Joel and Trudy Hartt, have been known to the people of Quebec from the beginning of the couple's active life. In 1972 when the couple adopted a Bangladeshi war baby, Joel was chairman of the Humanities Department, John Abbott College, and lecturer in philosophy at what was then Sir George College (now Concordia University); while Trudy, his wife, was a teacher. At that time, the couple lived in Beaconsfield, Quebec, with their four children all of whom were adopted. Shama became their fifth child. The Hartts were so committed to finding homes for the orphans that over the years, they had continued to adopt one after another orphan – all with one purpose, to embrace them as their *own* children.

By 1976 the Hartt family came to consist of nine children (six sons and three daughters) of which only the last child was born to the family. Of the six sons, five were born in Canada, while one was born in Vietnam. Again, of the three daughters, one was born in Canada, one in Bangladesh, and one in Haiti. Throughout 1970s and 1980s, the couple remained active in a variety of professional and voluntary work in addition to raising a family of nine children. Working closely with the Families For Children (FFC), a nonprofit organization that advances the cause of intercountry adoption, they were involved in both formal and informal gatherings, such as seminars and workshops, as well as potluck dinners, coffee, and play.

Whether it was the Citizen Adoption Coalition or the local chapter of the Open Door Society, the Hartts were active in both raising funds and awareness among Canadians. In fact, through the Montreal chapter of the Open Door Society, the Hartts also lobbied for immigration from the third world. So deep was their commitment for open immigration that, in advocating immigration in general, and more particularly of the Ugandan immigrants in 1972, Joel passionately argued for what he believed to be important for Canada. The local newspapers carried his name portraying him as a Canadian greatly concerned about Canada's obligation to deal with the issue.

Joel had a particular style to appeal to Canadians of European backgrounds who came to Canada a few generations ago. In fact, Joel is known to have reminded Canadians that their "own parents and grandparents have entered Canada under somewhat similar circumstances,"[18] and, therefore, people should open their doors now to the needy people. Despite their busy schedule, at every opportunity, the couple liaised with advocacy groups and organizations that voiced their concerns and became involved in facilitating adoption for the disadvantaged children/orphans whether in Canada or anywhere else in the world.

This brave and selfless couple believed that many children in the third world were in great need and something had to be done. Trudy, being the secretary/recorder of FFC, then headed by Bonnie and Fred Cappuccino, president and secretary, respectively, had also her hands full in addition to the household chores in a house that had nine children. Given their interest in interracial adoption at a time when Canada was still lagging behind the USA, the Hartts had always found time to initiate discussions and dialogues on issues such as adoption legislation, civil rights, public education, and other issues that had a bearing on international adoption.

When they decided to have another child back in 1972, they also decided that the said child would be through adoption. The situation of the war babies in Bangladesh came to their knowledge (consciousness) through a radio broadcast about the war in what was then East Pakistan, which had made an immediate impact in their minds, recalls Trudy. "Listening to the broadcast, I knew there was a baby in Bangladesh for us,"[19] said a soft-spoken Trudy. Being members and supportive of the various initiatives of FFC, it was simply a matter of confirming with Fred and Bonnie Cappuccino of the FFC their interest in adopting a war baby from Bangladesh when the Cappuccinos were gathering names of interested couples for adoption from Bangladesh.

When Shama came to the Hartts' home in 1972, the family did not need any preparation to welcome Shama, since all the other four children were not only adopted but also of racially different backgrounds from their Caucasian parents. "We already had children of different race and culture," say the Hartts (letter from Trudy Hartt to the author, cited in notes and references). Addition of Shama in the Hartt family simply meant that there was another adoption in the family. Although Shama was the Hartts' fifth child, her arrival in 1972 remains engraved in their minds even to this day. "My parents came with us to greet Shama and to take care of her brothers and sisters at the airport. This was when we signed the necessary immigration papers," recalls Trudy (letter from Trudy Hartt to the author). When the couple saw their two-month-old daughter for the first time, Trudy, to use her own words, was "transported" with joy and excitement. At that moment, she recalls, all she "wanted [was] only to look at her" (letter from Trudy Hartts to the author). And she did just that. "I thought I had never seen anyone so beautiful; I was grateful and was in love." (Letter from Trudy Hartt to the author)

Such was their delight that it was as though the Hartts had never experienced such feelings of joy and euphoria before until they had embraced the baby girl that was handed over to Trudy by Bonnie who picked out this particular girl for them. This is how Trudy remembers those precious moments.

The next thing they recall is the way in which they rushed out, having posed for photographs at the request of news reporters, to the lobby to introduce the baby girl to her grandparents and siblings who were equally excited and amazed. The children were thrilled to see their sister who had finally made it to Canada having come all the way from Bangladesh to join them in their happy home.

To the Hartts, adoption is a natural phenomenon. "We considered and consider adoption as a normal way to create and expand one's family,"[20] said the Hartts. This view distinguishes the Hartts and some of the other adoptive parents under discussion from the ordinary but generally infertile Canadian couples who make a family mainly through adoption as a second choice.

Perhaps for this reason, the Hartts would shrug off the suggestion that there is anything exceptional about them. In fact, such is their sense of humility that they insist others to look upon them as any other ordinary Canadian couple with nothing extraordinary about them or about the composition of their family. Like the Good family (Dale and Doreen Good) that have adopted two children from Bangladesh, the Hartts too consider them to be "fortunate" to have been able to adopt. They are very happy to have children of diverse backgrounds whom they were able to raise with the love and care they needed most at a time when they were abandoned. "We have done nothing particularly 'commendable' through adoption," observes Trudy humbly (letter from Trudy Hartt to the author).

When someone tried to see their children through a different lens, the Hartts would point out that *their* children are *their* children, "whether born in Canada or elsewhere," and that they are not "children of despair," as was reported by some Canadian newspapers at the time of their arrival in Canada (letter from Trudy Hartt to the author). As far back as the couple remembers, often they were looked at or frowned upon, not for having racially different children, but instead for having a large family. They have "experienced more difficulties because of biases against large families and adoption," said Trudy (letter from Trudy Hartt to the author).

Again, the Hartts are relatively private persons who never really wanted any publicity or news coverage about them or their family. Trudy was utterly frank in stating their feelings: "I am not comfortable with any of this being published or attributed. If I have a story to tell, I would prefer to tell it myself and for it to explore the issue that are important to me. Your objectives are as valid as any I would have, but they are not mine,"[21] wrote Trudy to the author (letter from Trudy Hartt to the author).

The Hartts were aware that there were many in Canada as well as outside of Canada who did not (and even to this day, they do not) support interracial adoption, which they see as the destruction of ethnicity and identity. Those opposed to transracial adoption believe that it is important for a child to be parented by people of the same race. They think that, otherwise, the child would be racially and culturally deprived; some even go to the extent of labeling such adoption as racial genocide.

Trudy attempted to react to such views in the following manner: "There is no way to respond to this. However, much we learned about other cultures, we could not make a home steeped in the cultures into which we were born. Our job was to love our children and convey the values we lived by (one has no choice but to do that); we would not pretend to be other than what we were. We could expose our children to people who, presumably, shared their racial and cultural heritage *(this is difficult: is one's culture racial? Is it based in the larger or smaller community? It is naïve to think that all Black people share one single culture; beyond that, if a child has parents from two different cultures, which is the child's?)* At one time, we did try, but the children considered it just something more they 'had to do' and resisted it. One does not learn culture on a hothouse" (Letter from Trudy Hartt to the author).

Continuing along the same vein, the couple even went further to state their position: "We had already decided that we wanted to be parents, that we wanted a large family, and that at least part of our family would be by adoption" (letter from Trudy Hartt to the author). One important point to note here is that the Hartts have raised their children as individuals, above all, as "Canadian" in multiracial Canada. They have remained committed to their dearly held view having ignored criticisms of all kinds. The Hartts recalled their thinking of the time by saying, "What were we thinking?" asked Trudy. She then responds in the following manner: "We wanted another child; that a baby needed a family. We were overjoyed at the prospect of a new baby," recalled the Hartts (letter from Trudy Hartt to the author). The key point, or their rationale, for additional children had been their very strong desire to bring a baby who needed a family.

Immediately after the arrival of the war babies in Canada, a nasty rumor centering on the babies was fast spreading around, saying that the recently arrived babies from Bangladesh were being neglected by their adoptive parents. We have seen this in chapter 4 the rumor that the newly arrived war babies were not being loved and cared for. The adoptive parents, including the Hartts, were shocked since such rumors were far from truth. It was distressing for them all to hear from many that the babies brought from Bangladesh were not being loved and cared for. Having taken such baseless rumor/allegation seriously, the Hartts immediately wrote to Sr. Margaret Mary, then statutory guardian of the war babies in Bangladesh. "I wanted to reassure the sisters that the babies were in homes and loved. I did this by talking about our family and baby and sent photos, etc.," said Trudy (letter from Trudy Hartt to the author).

While raising their children, the couple did not chose to have a "special" story line that is often made/used by many adoptive parents in order to give their adopted children a sense of extra love and security. Even though Shama is a war baby, the Hartts had followed the same practice of treating all their children the same way as *their* children. Therefore, they considered Shama as *their* "baby" (just a baby) and not a "war baby." By this, the couple meant to say that referring to Shama as a "war baby" would mean attachment of a "special" label onto Shama. They did not wish to distinguish their children one from another. "Adoption was part of our family culture; it is assumed," said Trudy (letter from Trudy Hartt to the author). The children had known about their adoption from an early age, and they had nothing to "find out," as the fact of adoption was never suppressed. Again, this was the norm in the family, "not something special," according to the couple (letter from Trudy Hartt to the author).

People in the neighborhood, or people who came to know them, had always considered adoption to be a natural and integral part of the Hartt family. No one wondered about the children or their parents. In that sense, everything about them seemed natural to the people around having known and accepted the fact of adoption. The Hartts gratefully acknowledge the association with their friends and acquaintances who had always been very supportive of their needs as they relate to their children of diverse background.

Unfortunately, Joel passed away in July 2009, leaving behind his wife, children, and grandchildren. Joel had always given generously of himself and his spirit when he was alive. His former students spoke of him with special reverence for his long involvement with many organizations and groups, including the Lakeshore Unitarian Church. His activities bear testimony to the couple's commitment to the principles of individual freedom of belief. Those who knew Joel would recognize how much desire and determination grew in him out of his deeply held commitment in human welfare at large. Calling him a man of extraordinary courage, determination, and spirit, many paid tribute to a quiet and graceful man who was an inspiration to all who knew him and whose sparkle continues to live on among all those who are around.

Trudy continues to work in her teaching job. Having raised nine children successfully, today they have eleven grandchildren. Trudy alone manages the family tradition of get-togethers with assistance from her children.

Molly

Born on prematurely on May 4, 1972, at Mother Teresa's *Shishu Bhavan*, Dhaka, Bangladesh, the baby girl weighed 1.2 kg at birth. She was named Molly by sisters from the Missionaries of Charity. As was the case with the rest of the war babies, having abandoned the baby, her birth mother left her with the orphanage authority for adoption. Upon arrival in Canada, the baby girl went through a name change just like all other war babies. Unlike all other adoptive parents of the war babies who "Canadianized" their children's names, the Hartts did just the opposite.

In fact, during the formal adoption in Montreal, the couple retained the name Molly that was given in Bangladesh but changed the spelling to "Mollie" and added two more names, Shama and Jameela, because of their distinct meanings, in addition to the family's surname, Hartt. As the Hartts understood, Shama, a Hindu name often used in Hindi poetry, means "the flame of the candle;" again, Jameela, a Muslim name, means "beautiful." The final name that appears in the official documents in Canada stands as the following: Shama Jameela Mollie Hartt. The couple believed in their hearts that the naming of their child in such a manner would seem progressive that would offer their child a mutual identity – a Canadian of Bangladeshi origin. "Most parents choose the names of their children and I don't see why this should be different for parents by adoption, unless the child is old enough to be accustomed to a name," argues Trudy (letter from Trudy Hartt to the author).

After finishing high school at Beaconsfield High School and CEGEP (Collège d'enseignement général et professionnel) at John Abbott College, Montreal, Shama attended York University in Toronto where she completed a bachelor of arts in English literature; she then went to Concordia University in Montreal where she obtained a bachelor of education with specialization in teaching English as a second language. She also earned a masters of arts in educational studies with a concentration in adult education from Concordia University. In the late 1990s, Shama taught English (language arts) as well as a variety of optional courses in the adult education sector.

From the beginning of her university life, Shama had visualized her own line of work early enough – a step-by-step mental rehearsal had thus helped her create a blueprint for action. Following the footsteps of her father and mother, Shama also became a full-time teacher/educator and began to teach from early on. Specifically, she taught in an alternative center for students in grades ten and eleven who are not necessarily disadvantaged or challenged, yet bright and often frustrated with a system that has either given up on them or labeled them negatively. By being involved early, Shama has learned a lot, which she, in turn, is able to offer to her students.

Shama had always been at ease with regard to her past. It will be seen in chapter 7 under the heading "Desire to know about their past and their country of birth," the word "adoption" had been a part of a common vocabulary not only in Shama's family but also in the families of the rest of the war babies. Not surprisingly, therefore, it seemed quite natural to Shama that while growing up, there was nothing to "find out" about her background. Shama never took any interest in finding or knowing any more than what she was told by her parents about her birth history and the story of her adoption.

Again, unlike many adoptees that often spend an inordinate amount of time in searching for their roots especially during their teen years, a coolheaded Shama never had an issue with it at all. It was only when she was at the university in her early twenties that Shama remembers how she began to "wonder" about her background. Only after watching a show on adopted children in search of their biological roots that she felt that it had caused her much angst. The feeling was so intense that it made her think about it more with a view to learning about her medical history through genealogy.

Looking back, Shama sees this simply as an urge that did not expand to learn about her putative father or birth mother who she knew had no choice but to abandon her at birth. All she was interested in was to fill in the genealogical information gap that had existed in her file. This, recalls Shama, made her contact the orphanage authority in Bangladesh only to learn that there is no information available given the circumstances surrounding her birth. Since then, having heard from the orphanage authority, Shama has remained content with whatever she knew about her background. She never became interested in probing the subject any further.

Personally speaking, since Shama grew up in a house that had nine children many of whom were of different racial backgrounds, she never felt isolated. Instead, she enjoyed being part of a large family surrounded by siblings of diverse origin. Having done research on the issue of race and race relations, Shama can comfortably situate herself and her family in Canada. She empathizes with other adoptees who express feelings of void and loss or alienation and isolation.

At the same time, she also believes that dwelling on these feelings might be a hindrance to self-growth: "I do not remember ever feeling a sense of loss or void concerning my birth mother and putative father or feeling alienated or isolated because I am adopted,"[22] observes Shama calmly. She goes on to explain why she feels that way: "In these respects, I try to deal with what is and what isn't or could have been. I see there are many children out there who are with parents who don't want them, who are abandoned or are in foster care waiting to be adopted and would give anything to have a parent and sibling to call a family (letter from Shama Hartt to the author).

Growing up in a multiracial family was so natural to Shama that she never felt that her family was "different" or "special." Even though Shama's parents were white, the children claim that they did not grow up in a white family in that they grew up in a truly multiracial family in a primarily white neighborhood in Beaconsfield, Quebec. This is not inexplicable, says Shama, when one comes to think of her (Shama's) age when she came to join her adoptive parents and how she grew up with siblings of diverse backgrounds: "Living in a multi-racial family is all I've ever known," says Shama (letter from Shama Hartt to the author). Furthermore, she adds, "Perhaps because I was so young when I was adopted and because of my character/personality and outlook on life, and perhaps because of my parents and siblings, I feel the way I do" (letter from Shama Hartt to the author).

Having studied cultural anthropology, Shama has always found the questions of ethnicity, culture, and race interesting and yet, at the same time, rather complex. A well-versed Shama is fully cognizant of *how* she looks and *how*, because of her look or the color of her skin, other people are likely to *see* her in relations to race and identity. Shama can draw numerous illustrations from many anecdotes in her own life having recognized *how* so many people often do not see her as "Canadian." To their way of seeing, she looks like a "foreigner."

We shall see in chapter 7 her most favorite example from York University where one of her professors assumed that English was not her first language for obvious reasons. A coolheaded Shama was neither surprised nor shocked. Shama needs no one to remind her that there are far too many instances that demonstrate that people's perception of a visible minority as a "foreigner" is something that is neither new nor rare in Canada. In fact, over the years, Shama has had many such experiences that remind her that others *do not* see her as "Canadian" simply because her skin is not white.

For the last few years, a high-achiever Shama, who is blessed with a quick mind and keen eye, has been working in a number of areas. As a teacher, and especially one who is a female and visible minority, Shama has taken it upon herself to "educate" people to differences, histories, and acceptance. She is aware of how frequently the news media stereotypes or makes an issue of acts committed by a visible minority.

Shama is also conscious of the fact that many would include her and her siblings in the negative stereotypes depicted and reinforced by the news media because they too are a product of this society. Shama's conclusion is that such propensities are inherent in human nature, and, therefore, it is easy to "classify and generalize people – it is easy and comfortable" (letter from Shama Hartt to the author).

In such a case, she says she sees it for what it is: a product of the ever-growing and accepting racist society. When minorities are stereotyped, Shama does not see herself portrayed in such coverage (positive or negative) because she knows herself as well as her personal ethics and values she grew up with. Regardless of what others do, Shama does not tell, laugh at, or in any way, acquiesce to racial, ethnic, religious, or gender jokes; or, for that matter, she does not condone any practice that she deems is intended to demean rather than enhance another human being. Shama seems to know always what to say, how to say, and just when to insert a joke to lighten the mood.

With a strong sense of self-esteem and a positive sense of her identity in Canada, Shama feels positive about how she grew up in a happy and nurturing home. Her very strong sense of being nothing but "Canadian" does not, however, negate her Bangladeshi origin. In a sense, deep down, Shama also knows that she does have a link with Bangladesh – her country of birth. There does not seem to be a conflict in Shama's mind with regard to her sense of identity in Canada.

She is utterly frank in saying that she would not mind to visit Bangladesh if an opportunity presents itself. The fact that to this day Shama has not ruled out any possibility of visiting Bangladesh is an indication of her desire that she continues to cherish in her mind. It may be a latent desire. Who knows, someday, something might trigger that desire that someday might become a reality! At the moment, an unpretentious Shama, like everyone else, has competing priorities. For an honest and upfront Shama, visiting her country of birth is probably not one of her top priorities, which keep shifting with the changes in personal circumstances.

Over the years, she has earned recognition awards even from the time she was a student. Shama has an honorable mention in the *Homemaker's Magazine* in the summer of 1995 edition for an essay contest. Today Shama is a successful teacher and employed by Sir Wilfrid Laurier School Board. Shama was in a common-law relationship with Mike

Bonnell, a French-Canadian whom she met in university and is also a teacher. Together, they have a beautiful daughter they named Savannah Bonnell. The couple, however, separated. Shama and Savannah live in Joliette, northeast of Montreal, Quebec.

Pierre and Lise Hogue

Born and raised in Montreal, Quebec, Pierre and Lise Bertrand have lived in Quebec all their lives with a short break for two years from 1970 to 1972 when they lived in Lynemouth, north of New Castle, United Kingdom, while on an assignment with Alcan UK for training manager for the start-up of an aluminum smelter. Having started with the Montreal-based Alcan Aluminum Ltd., Pierre later on specialized in human resources and worked for a number of reputed organizations in Quebec until he retired in 2000 as audit consultant with Bombardier. His wife, Lise, had been in the federal public service mostly in the Quebec region until she retired in 2006 as director of policy and program, Department of Justice. While the war was going on, the couple could not escape the media coverage of the events in Occupied Bangladesh especially with reference to military repression and sexual violence. Like many other people in Great Britain, they were shocked and outraged by the news of rape, enforced pregnancy, and birth of the war babies.

This was a time when the couple was also thinking about adopting a child, a brother or a sister for Benoît, their biological child. While in Great Britain, the couple learned that they could not do much about international adoption because of their temporary status there.. In 1972 when they returned home, the idea of adoption began to take shape in their minds as they became more serious about it. Initially, just as they started to make inquiries, they were disappointed. They were told that as fertile couple, they "would be considered a low priority on the eligibility list,"[23] especially in the municipality they were living in at the time.

Following a careful planning and after doing a great deal of thinking, they decided to expand their family through international adoption. Once they decided to have their second child through adoption, preferably interracial adoption, they remained on the lookout. It was a matter of connecting with the right agency to facilitate the process. When they

MUSTAFA CHOWDHURY

learned about the possibility of having a war baby from Bangladesh through the Families For Children (FFC), they immediately contacted Fred and Bonnie Cappuccino, who were secretary and president of the FFC, respectively. There was no hesitation, as they had thought about the pros and cons and had already decided to go ahead quite some time ago. At the same time, they also began to prepare themselves mentally to receive a war baby from Bangladesh.

The process was facilitated by the fact that while asking for a child, they were open about the gender, age, and health condition of the child. This meant that the Cappuccinos, who went to Bangladesh to pick out the babies for them, had some flexibility in making a selection based on their *own* judgment. When the Hogues received a cable from the Cappuccinos indicating that they had chosen a baby girl for them and that a photo of the child was in the mail, they instantly believed as though they already have a child living in Bangladesh. Her name was Rajina, an eight-month-old girl. Emotion ran so high that they right away felt connected to the baby girl though she was far away from them at the time. "We were charmed, attracted and anxious to hold her in our arms,"[24] recalled Pierre following receipt of a photo of the selected little girl.

The Hogues remember spending quite a bit of time with their four-year-old son Benoît, talking about his sister who was to arrive any time from Bangladesh. Together, they had decorated their soon-to-arrive daughter's bedroom, engaging future big brother Benoît all throughout. They contacted the local medical resources alerting the imminent arrival of their daughter all the way from Bangladesh who might be in need of medical assistance upon landing in Montreal due to the generally poor health conditions of all of the babies. Looking back, Pierre said, "Above all, we did have the same attitude and expectations of a normal pregnancy and future delivery" (e-mail from Pierre Hogue to the author). The baby girl arrived in Montreal on July 20, 1972, along with six other war babies while the rest of the babies landed in Toronto.

Prior to the arrival of their daughter, then named Rajina, the Hogues lived in St. Bruno on the south shore of Montreal. Within a month following Rajina's arrival in the family, the Hogues moved to Arvida, a small town in the Saguenay/Lac St. Jean region (now part of Jonquiere, about five hundred kilometers northeast of Montreal) where they lived for about three years. This was inhabited predominantly by

French Canadian Catholic community where there was hardly any visible minority family. Pierre recalled, many neighbors thought their daughter was from Africa, as they were not familiar with the Indian subcontinent.

"Curiosity was such that many of them, especially children, wanted to touch 'the little dark skinned girl' who looked so pretty," recalled Pierre, having always reacted positively with good humor to such innocuous occasions (e-mail from Pierre Hogue to the author). In a sense, the couple was seen as precursor at the time given the fact that local people in the Saguenay region of Quebec were still unfamiliar with overseas adoption involving racially different orphans especially from an unknown country like Bangladesh. When Rajina was about four and a half years old, the family moved back to the Montreal region in Longueuil.

The couple remembers vividly how immediately after the arrival of their daughter from Bangladesh, the little girl was not used to solid food at all. Once they figured out the diet, they noticed how rapidly she had begun to improve her health, recalled Lise. As the child began to gain weight and improve overall, both Pierre and Lise became very happy having enjoyed every bit of time in getting used to a new baby in the family especially at a time when their four-year-old son was also sticking around his new sister all the time. The couple could not wait to share their feelings of joy and happiness with Bonnie and Fred. Pierre and Lise are grateful to the Cappuccinos for having chosen, as far as they are concerned, the "prettiest" child of the group.

When the Hogues learned that, back in Bangladesh, Sr. Margaret Mary, having never heard from the adoptive parents, was worried about the war babies who were sent to Canada, they were the first couple who wrote to her. Expressing the family's gratitude to her for giving them an opportunity to adopt Rajina, they described how well the little girl had adjusted to the new environment in her new home much to the satisfaction of the parents. They also sent Sr. Margaret Mary a family picture to show her how happy the little girl was in their arms.

Like other parents, they too needed to add their family name to the child's name. They liked the name Rajina given by the orphanage authority. "We had kept her [Rajina's] name because it suited her so well, but we had registered her as Rajina Josée, so that she could have both – a common name originating from her country of origin and another common name reflecting her country of adoption" (letter from Lise Bertrand to the author). However, years later, Rajina herself switched her first and middle name, which has been mentioned under individual profile below.

The couple does not remember when the word "adoption" was broached first. What they recalled is that an intelligent Josée must have known from early on that she was adopted, a fact that all other adoptees under discussion had also known from the start of their lives. The Hogues also did not have a fairy-tale story for Josée, like other adoptive couples from the present group. They wanted to, and they did, raise their daughter the same way as Benoît with no favoritism of any kind.

As Josée began to mature over the years, pretty well the entire story of war and violence, a very sensitive topic no doubt, was gradually described to her to the satisfaction of the mother and the child: "Subsequently, I answered her questions as they were asked in relations with her age and ability to understand," observed Lise (letter from Lise Bertrand to the author). They recall having remained prepared to answer with age-appropriate content any question that she might have had about the *why* and *how* of adoption. They had answered from time The couple does not recall being ever confronted with a question that they could not respond to.

Josée was very young when, for the first time, she became aware of the color of her skin being different than her mother. Lise describes the circumstances in the following: "Josée made this observation while I was putting her mittens on before driving her to babysitter's. I was late and in hurry, and she looked at her hand and said to me: 'Mom, look my hand is not the same color as yours.' Taking a deep breath, I explained that indeed, her skin was brown, mine was white, because her birth mother had brown skin and my mother's was white and that in her country of origin, all people were like her. And that was all; she was satisfied with that answer" (e-mail from Lise Bertrand to the author). She also remembers Josée never broached the topic again.

A strong-willed couple, however, was quite aware of problems often associated with interracial adoption. They were glad to see that a cheerful Josée with a happy demeanor had always remained grounded in her factual history having never felt insubstantial like many adoptees who grieve over being relinquished by their birth mothers. Josée never seemed to have been attached to her "never-known" birth mother, recalled Lise. And yet Lise had always encouraged Josée to visit her country of birth and had even offered to come along with her. With no atavistic fear, the Hogues, therefore, never felt that continuity of their family with their two children, Benoît and Josée, would be threatened if Josée ever tries to search for her biological roots. Josée's observations in Bangladesh have been outlined below under her profile.

According to the Hogues, ever since a mature Josée learned about her background and the context of her adoption into the Hogue family, the entire episode surrounding her birth, though very tragic, became a closed chapter. They were amazed to notice how a mature and level heared Josée, having heard the tragic story of war, sexual violence, enforced pregnancies, birth, and relinquishment, did not react negatively at all. The parents recall how easily without any resentment Josée had moved forward with her life in Canada she calls "home." They always believed that they had provided their daughter a positive context for her birth mother and the permanency of her relationship with her parents and sibling in Canada.

One of the most persistent themes in the Hogue family, especially when the children were growing up, was to foster a "do-all-you-can" attitude to assist each other in the family. In their own home, the Hogues created a nurturing environment where equality of treatment and opportunity became the most important aspect of the family life. They tried to give their children feelings of autonomy and self-determination. While raising their children, the Hogues paid particular attention to ensure that there was no difference in treatment of their children.

They did not treat their daughter from Bangladesh as a "special" or a "queen" child because she had been adopted. The Hogues also made sure that their extended family members were also appreciative of their position with regard to their children. The couple taught the children to be protective and be confident, and remain a source of happiness for each other. Not surprisingly, both Benoit and Josée got along very well, just like any brother and sister, a relationship that they have sustained to this day. Benoît was excited to have a sister who became his friend and playmate. Benoît was always proud to remind people that he too has adopted Josée, a sister who came all the way from Bangladesh.

Their love for their children remained paramount even when the couple divorced back in 1982. Among other things, they committed to carry out their filial responsibilities while opting for a divorce. Both Pierre and Lise had thought through their situation to work out an arrangement that was deemed to be "in the best interest" of Benoît and Josée. Both were on the same page in their thinking that filial responsibility was of prime importance in their case. "My divorce was amicable. The father of my children and I have lived in the same neighborhood so that the children could go from one place to the other as they wanted. We communicated easily on issues pertaining to our children and they knew they had [and still have] two parents who loved them and were on good terms with each other," says Lise (e-mail from Lise Bertrand to the author).

As things turned out, although Pierre lived with Benoît and Josée with Lise, both liked the arrangement that worked well for all even though the couple had lived apart. Josée was only eleven at that time, and it took her some time to adjust to the situation. As she grew up and became mature, she came to appreciate the reality of it and adjusted well to the new set of circumstances. Both have proved that they have had an innate skill in handling children. A divorce is never an easy thing, and when it happens, it destabilizes children to a certain extent, says Pierre. Josée does not recall any negative impact because of the separation of her parents whom she considers as loving and nurturing parents above all.

Those who have known the Hogues since the 1970s, back in the Saguenay region where interracial adoption was very rare, used to look upon the couple as avant-garde. Pierre is of the opinion that the Bangladesh Project initiative has benefited both the adopters and the adoptees. "Let's not forget that it was also in response to our profound desire and need," says Pierre humbly (e-mail from Pierre Hogue to the author).

With the passage of time, their love for their child grew just as Josée grew successfully into an accomplished Canadian citizen. Today, they feel privileged to have raised their children having accomplished their own goals as parents. When Lise says, "I am very proud of her," she feels utterly content and natural (e-mail from Lise Bertrand to the author).

With one grandchild, both Lise and Pierre remain busy spending time with their children according to their individual and separate schedules. Josée, now an adult with her own life, always finds time to remain in touch with them and her brother's family and regularly visits them in between her hectic work schedules and frequent travels. It is the family bond that is their strength that helps them and their children continue with life with all its ups and downs.

Rajina

Born on November 24, 1971, Rajina was the second-oldest war baby that came to Canada through the Bangladesh Project initiative. She was brought to *Shishu Bhavan* surreptitiously and was left with Sr. Margaret Mary, then superior, for the purpose of adoption. Sr. Margaret Mary, who named the baby Rajina, recalled how weak and frail the baby was when she was left with her. At birth she weighed four kilograms. Fred and Bonnie Cappuccino, who were in charge of matching the babies with the adoptive parents in Canada, selected her for the Hogues, as they thought she looked attractive despite her light weight. They were convinced that the little frail baby girl would make it to Canada and would turn out to be a pretty good choice. They were right in their thinking.

As mentioned, the couple liked the name of the child given by the orphanage authority in Bangladesh. However, they also thought that when their daughter would get older, she might want a different (common) name. She was thus formally registered as Rajina Josée Hogue at register civil du Québec. While she was growing up in a small town in Quebec, she also began to realize that it was not a very common name and that "it didn't reflect" *who* she is.[25] She recalled how the coach, whether at soccer, softball, or field hockey, often did not bother to ask her name; instead with a quick look at her face, the coach would say, "You must be Rajina," instantly associating her skin color with her "strange" name (e-mail from Josée to the author, cited in notes and references). This was something that, Josée recalled, "used to get on my nerves" (e-mail from Josée to the author).

Gradually she began to use her middle name (Josée) as her first name. By the time she was fourteen, she began to be known as Josée, although Pierre and her brother were not very keen on the idea of switching her first name. Pierre had preferred to call her Rajina, always much to the teenager's anger. Occasionally, she would tell him that she would not respond if he called her Rajina, a mild warning that did not always seem to work. However, gradually, over the years, Pierre also became used to her name and began to call her Josée.

Having been raised in a small town in Quebec in the 1970s and 1980s, Josée went to St. Clair and Rabeau Elementary Schools in Longueuil and St. Lambert, and then to the Collège and Durocher private high school also in St. Lambert. Josée successfully completed CEGEP (Collège d'enseignement general et professionnel) in human sciences with mathematics in 1992. Josée started her first job at the age of sixteen and has never stopped working even while in school just as her brother before her. Following her graduation, she took up a professional job and has been working since then. Over the years, she has worked for a number of organizations assuming greater responsibility. Currently she is with the federal public service in the Department of Public Safety. She is holding a position that requires her to travel nationally and internationally. She is passionate about her job.

Josée does not remember ever being told that she was adopted. She recalls if and when a stranger would ask her about her origin, she would tell that she is from Bangladesh and that she was adopted. Obviously, when she was very young, she had questions about her origin or skin color and she wondered *why* she was different than the rest of the family. Her parents, she recalls, had always answered her questions that used to come up while she was growing up.

Josée considers her parents as "great people" who, she came to learn, had begun to love her even before she had arrived in Canada. According to Josée, it is as though she finds many similarities with her (adoptive) parents: "I have black hair like my Dad, my hair is curly like my mother. I'm pig headed like my father. I have my mother's sensitivity and, just like her, I am a good listener. And the list of similarities between my parents and me goes on and on. But most of all, I am my parents' daughter because part of them has become part of me" (e-mail from Josée to the author).

As an adult, Josée did not yearn to visit Bangladesh, nor did she feel any ties to it except to acknowledge the fact that she was born there. Even when growing up, she seemed to have a very good understanding of the circumstances of her birth in the aftermath of a war, for it was clear to her that her birth mother, or for that matter, all other birth mothers, had no choice at the time. The stigma of rape was such that keeping a baby born out of such circumstance would be unbearable for the birth mother. In a sense, Josée understood that the greatest gift a birth mother could give her was to abandon the baby she could not take care of in the hope that the same baby would have a better survival chance, if adopted.

One of Josée's early and very common observations are that those who don't know her immediately look upon her as someone from outside of Canada. In fact, many people she came across saw her as a kind of enigma especially when she lived in the small neighborhood: "They find that the way I speak and the way I look don't match. But when I tell them that I was adopted they understand that I am exactly like them. They very often forget that I am a visible minority. And to me, that is a real proof that there is no question that I am Canadian" (letter from Josée Hogue to the author).

Josée sees herself as a Canadian born in Bangladesh, something that other war babies we have looked at say also. To Josée's way of looking at it, she is Canadian, a child of her (Canadian) francophone parents; or a Quebecor, because of her parents' French background; she is what she has inherited from her family. This is even though she had always been very consciously proud of *where* she was *born*. "At a very early age, I knew I was different than everybody else because I was adopted and also because of my skin" (letter from Josée Hogue to the author). Knowing that she was born in Bangladesh did not bother her at all, nor did it generate any interest in her mind to delve into her past. With Josée, *where* she was *raised* and *who* raised her define *who* she is.

From very early on, Josée used to tell people *where* and *how* she was born during the war of independence in Occupied Bangladesh. "As early as in kindergarten, she had a globe and could explain where she was born and how people were in her country," recalled her mom (e-mail from Lise Bertrand to the author). The parents, of course, remember the time when they had obtained basic information on Bangladesh from the Bangladesh High Commission in Ottawa around 1977 or so. Josée remembers often she would be asked, "What's it like to be adopted?" or "Do you consider your parents as your 'real' parents?" Since such questions are of very personal nature, Josée answered them as when she felt like. At one point, she would stop answering when she judged them inappropriate and obtrusive.

Though not keen on delving into any background history in any detail, Josée had always been very much aware of the political identity of Bangladesh. When people often use Pakistan, India, and Bangladesh interchangeably, Josée does not hesitate to point out *how* and *when*

Bangladesh became independent following nine long grueling months of bloodbath: "Bangladesh is an independent country, [and] that the people of Bangladesh [have] earned it through hard way" is Josée's usual answer (letter from Josée Hogue to the author). In doing so, Josée humbly tries to point out the Bengalis' struggle for independence and their ultimate victory even though no further interest in Bangladesh is triggered in her mind.

Josée does not remember ever feeling deprived of love and attention of her either parent. This was even though Josée's parents were divorced and had lived apart since she was eleven years old. She remains attached to her family having a true family bond. Her brother, Benoît, asked Josée to be his daughter's godmother when she was baptized, an offer Josée gladly accepted without any hesitation. They have a relationship just like any other godmother and godchild. "I'm sure she [her niece] realizes even at an early age that we are not the same color but to her I am her aunt and she loves me just as I love her" (letter from Josée Hogue to the author).

There was a time when the entire family had the intention to visit Bangladesh. But as years went by and the family situation changed, interest in such matter also dwindled. They thought it is important to visit their child's birthplace. As it turned out, Josée ended up going to Bangladesh twice in the last few years. In September 2004 she went on a business trip to Bangladesh only for a forty-eight-hour stay. "Of course going to Bangladesh is not a short journey and upon my arrival, I contacted my colleagues' station in Dhaka," recalled Josée (e-mail from Josée Hogue to the author).

There were ongoing demonstrations and agitations on the streets of Dhaka for quite some time prior to her arrival. Naturally, Josée's mother was quite nervous about Josée being alone all by herself in a strange land. "She thought it might be hard emotionally and, as a mother, she wanted to be with me to make sure I would be OK," said Josée (e-mail from Josée Hogue to the author). Unfortunately, it was not a very pleasant trip for her, to say the least.

Although she was supposed to contact someone whose name was given to her by her colleague to arrange for a tour of the city, Josée did not even bother to call him. Being somewhat deadbeat and having been at the end of her tether, she remained inside the premises where she was staying. Josée sums up her two-day trip to her country of birth in the following: "Just walking outside the hotel was a nightmare. I had not walked a whole block that already I was overwhelmed by the people trying to get my attention, desperately trying to sell me something or service. I was insulted a few times; I was dressed with pants, long sleeve shirt tied all the way up to the neck and wrists to be respectful. But still the North American style did not seem agreeable. To them it was obvious that I was a stranger in a strange land. Since I was there for less than 48 hours, I left it at that knowing I would be returning soon." (e-mail from Josée Hogue to the author)

However, Josée did not get totally turned off despite the initial unpleasant experiences. Her intention to return to Bangladesh was still there in her mind. She was told by some people she met that she would have a place to stay with them who thought her "story" was extraordinary. The next year in January 2005, she went back to Bangladesh for a week again, this time with her mother. She was also told that there were many who were interested in her "story." Naturally both mom and daughter were excited about it.

Having traveled extensively to many countries, "seeing armed guards or military is not very uncommon," remarked Josée (e-mail from Josée Hogue to the author). But her mother, born and raised in Montreal, Canada, was taken aback immediately upon their arrival especially after seeing armed guards all around and even in the exclusive diplomatic zone where they were residing. "We were told that even in that district, we should never go on foot, always by car for safety reasons. Talk about culture shock!" recalled Josée (e-mail from Josée Hogue to the author).

They had plans to do sightseeing and meeting people, which they did, but due to political unrest and ongoing demonstrations, it was cut short. They were quarantined during the last three consecutive days due to *hartal* (protest demonstration by the opposition party or parties) when the Dhaka City was completely paralyzed. "Sadly, we were then unable to visit the orphanage where I was kept as a baby because it was unsafe," recalled Josée with a sense of regret and disappointment that she could neither visit the orphanage nor meet the people who work there (e-mail from Josée Hogue to the author).

"I wanted to see them in their premises, to tell them that what they do has good results and that I am living the proof of that. I wanted to tell them that I was grateful that their devotion gave me the chance to survive and meet my family in Canada," said Josée (e-mail from Josée Hogue to the author).

During the first four days, they were able to meet certain Bengali people of higher social status. Josée, however, found this rather irritable when she noticed that to them, she was more like an object of "curiosity" – born in Bangladesh but raised outside. Their tour guide was only five years old during the liberation war (1971), but he told them that he still remembers how "the soldiers were shooting their guns while they were running and hiding all the time and not knowing where his father was or if he was even alive," wrote Josée, quoting the driver (e-mail from Josée Hogue to the author).

While on this subject, Josée explained to the guide that she was born as a result of sexual violence during the Bengalis' struggle for independence and that is why she was adopted in Canada. Both Josée and her mother found it somewhat interesting that even though he acknowledged the fact that many women were raped during that time, he did not seem to be able to connect Josée with that part of the history. He did not have the slightest notion that Josée was the result of an enforced pregnancy. "To him, it seemed unreal that I was raised in Canada by a white family. It did not register with him that the woman traveling with me was my mother" (e-mail from Josée Hogue to the author). This was a strange encounter, recalled Josée.

Josée and her mom found this rather ironic that many people they met and talked to had heard about the war, sexual violence in Occupied Bangladesh, and its aftermath, and yet never for a minute did it dawn on any of them that the woman they had been talking to was the result of that war – that she had to be sent away for adoption in Canada. "I don't think they realised that the reason why I was raised outside of Bangladesh; that I was rejected by Bangladesh," said Josée (e-mail from Josée Hogue to the author, cited in notes and references). Both the mother and the daughter never ceased to wonder how they were stunned to see Josée who puzzled them more than anything else having failed to connect Josée with sexual violence about and enforced pregnancy and its aftermath. Many people they ran into could not get over the fact that she was raised in Canada by a white family.

Interesting to note, as the people's curiosity grew more and more about Josée, especially when they learned that she was born in Bangladesh during the war, many began to ask if, after all, she has any knowledge of Bengali culture and heritage. "They were eager to tell me all about Bengali culture. I don't know how many times I was asked if I had read anything written by Rabindranath Tagore who won the Nobel Prize for literature in 1913," said Josée (e-mail from Josée Hogue to the author).

She remembers that all she could do was to keep her cool, stay calm, smile, and keep her my mouth shut but inside very angry and disgusted.

"In a sense, I wanted to shout! What a bunch of hypocrite you all make. How dare you? You want to bathe me in a culture that rejected me and all the other babies and their mothers? We had to be sent away to have the right to live; and now, you want to make me a part of you? What about the ones who never made it? Did they ever care about that? I don't think they ever did" (e-mail from Josée Hogue to the author).

Josée returned "home" (Canada) with no doubts in her mind that she is Canadian, for Canada is her home where she grew up. Before going to Bangladesh, she never felt close to Bangladesh even though it is her country of birth; following her return, she continues to remain the same with no feeling of attachment. The short encounters that she had with a few people in Bangladesh were enough to confirm her belief in her own mind that she is truly Canadian and that she has nothing in common with the people of Bangladesh except for the fact that she was born there.

Josée's father, Pierre's, remark, having heard from Josée about her not-too-pleasant experience in Bangladesh, is interesting and somewhat thought provoking. Seeing it from a different perspective, Pierre observed: Josée's "strange" experiences, unbearable encounters, almost offensive inquisitiveness of those she interacted with, and the negative impression about Bangladesh are, in a sense, perhaps, "an indication of her deep-rooted integration in Canada" (e-mail from Pierre Hogue to the author). The more Josée felt about her being "Canadian," the more detached she felt in Bangladesh, a land to which she believes she does not belong. She feels more at home when in Canada.

Every member of the Hogue family has a very busy schedule, but each is able to make time to get together. It is important to the Hogues to stay in touch and be there for one another just like any other family. Despite her own busy schedule at work, Josée tries to find time to visit her family.

Kenneth and Mitzi McCullough

Unfortunately, this is the only couple that could not be located despite many efforts. The author has spent an inordinate amount of time in an attempt to trace the couple but had no luck. The social service agencies of Nova Scotia had interacted with the couple back in 1972 when they had lived in Halifax, Nova Scotia. They have no forwarding address for the couple.

Those who have known the McCulloughs believe that since they are originally from the USA, they must have gone to the States. The couple had never been a part of the adoptive couples' network.

What is known for a fact is that when Kenneth and Mitzi McCullough adopted Probir in 1972, they lived in Halifax, Nova Scotia. Before even they had the boy in their arms, they named him Mathew McCullough. While carrying her new son, just when Mitzi was about to board her flight to Halifax, she responded to a reporter's query about the name of her child: "We thought Prodip sounded like some kind of snack food, and since it sounded funny even to us, we figured he'd be laughed at all through his life. So we decided on Mathew" (the *Gazette,* July 21, 1971).

Apparently, the McCulloughs had remained in touch with the Cappuccinos at least for some time following the arrival of their son. They had written to the Cappuccinos about their feelings of joy and excitement having embraced Probir, whom they named Mathew, as their own son. They wrote about the little boy's alertness, curiosity, growing confidence, and ability to interact in the new home with new family members. In fact, the couple was so overwhelmed with joy that they shared their happiness through the Cappuccinos with other adoptive families in the same network and talked about how they felt intensely connected since the baby was thriving on frequent interactions. Gradually the couple just drifted apart, and none of the adoptive parents know their whereabouts.

While the McCulloughs were still living in Halifax, their correspondence with the Cappuccinos (Fred and Bonnie) is available in the Cappuccinos' personal collection. It still remains as a rare documentary evidence following the adoption of Probir. Since the McCulloughs could not be traced, no additional information is available about the outcome of this particular adoption.

Dr. Robin and Barbara Morrall

By 1972, the Morralls had been married for eight years and had a son named John Morrall, born in 1969. Robin Morrall was a professor of biology at the University of Saskatchewan, Saskatoon. His wife, Barbara, homemaker, was mostly occupied with their son. This was a time when they were thinking about having a second child, a sibling for John. They thought about having their next child by way of adoption – not an uncommon practice altogether for fertile parents at the time. In the late 1960s, Canada was going through a social change where adoption was viewed as a new way to make a family. This was a time when the popular understanding of parenthood, especially motherhood, was also undergoing a transformation.

By chance, the couple had read an article titled "A Family Is a Child's Best Gift" by Lolly Golt in the *Weekend Magazine* of November 20, 1971. It was an article about Vietnamese orphans adopted into Canadian homes that raised their own awareness about adoption of orphans born outside of Canada. The passage in the article that touched the Morralls most, and which they remember to this day, was the following: "In Vietnam, children have only a 50 percent chance of living until their third birthday. For the thousands of orphans there, the situation is worse. But something can be done for them, and Canadians are doing it – adoption."[26]

Like many other Canadian couples in the 1970s, the Morralls had been greatly influenced by a campaign, initiated by a number of Canadian social organizations working in the third world, to encourage adoption. In Barbara's own words, "We were very much concerned about overpopulation and the numbers of children we would read about in orphanages who had no families."[27]

What could we do? This was a question that the Morralls had asked themselves for several days after reading Lolly Golt's article. This single article appealed to their emotions so much so that it acted as the trigger in their minds to pursue international adoption. As days went by, the Morralls' desire to adopt a child grew stronger and stronger to the point where they needed to simply "do something" about it. With the intention of adoption firmly in their hearts, the Morralls began their search: "We felt that we could provide a good home for another child and felt very open about the possibility of adoption," recalls Barbara (letter from Barbara Morrall to the author).

Late in 1971, the Morralls had heard about the possibility of adoption of war babies from East Pakistan where the Bengali East Pakistanis had already declared independence. In December they contacted Fred and Bonnie Cappuccino, who were then president and secretary, respectively, of the Families For Children (FFC), a nonprofit adoption agency in Montreal that was involved in interracial adoption of children from Asian countries for Canadian couples interested in adopting racially different orphans. The Morralls wrote to the Cappuccinos inquiring about the possibility of adopting a child. From then on, recalls the Morralls, one thing then led to another in quick succession toward adopting a child.

By late December 1971, the FFC had already been in touch with the newly established government in Bangladesh. Upon learning about the pathetic situation there, the Morralls recall their initial reaction of deep sympathy. With the assistance of the government of Canada, the FFC had begun serious bilateral discussions with the government of Bangladesh on the possibility of Canadian couples adopting war babies who would be born in 1972. Within days the Cappuccinos replied to the Morralls' initial inquiry on behalf of the FFC. In their response, the FFC indicated that this was a very good opportunity for the Morralls. The correspondence from the Cappuccinos seemed so encouraging to the Morralls that it was an instant decision for them to proceed with adopting a war baby from Bangladesh, although they were still in correspondence with the authorities in Vietnam from where they had earlier considered adopting a child.

The Morralls did not express any particular preference for a boy or a girl in their application for adoption even though they already had a son. From the start, the Morralls were very open and flexible in their search for adoption, especially with respect to the gender of the child – it did not matter to them whether the child was a boy or a girl. Following their decision to adopt, the Morralls recall how they went through a period of doubting themselves, questioning whether they would be fit parents for a foreign-born child.

By May 1972, the Morralls had joined the FFC in its appeal to the government of Bangladesh to allow adoption of certain number of war babies to parents outside of Bangladesh. By this time, the Morralls felt emotionally ready, without any reservations, to receive their second child – to begin their hope of raising a Bangladeshi war baby. In the previous chapter, we read about the Cappuccinos' trip to Bangladesh in July 1972 to pick out a number of war babies from local orphanages in Bangladesh for would-be-adoptive parents in Canada. The girl the Cappuccinos picked out for the Morralls from *Shishu Bhavan*, an orphanage in Dhaka, was one of the fifteen war babies who were adopted into Canadian homes.

From Dhaka, Bonnie Cappuccino hastily sent the Morralls a handwritten postcard giving the good news that they had found a baby girl for them. In her note, Bonnie described the three-and-a-half-month-old child as "a lovely baby girl with crisp black hair and a cute face."[28] Both Barbara and Robin were thrilled to receive the news and were excited that they would soon have a sister for their son, John. From the moment they received the mail from the Cappuccinos, the Morralls began to feel in their hearts that the baby who was to arrive in Canada was their *dear* daughter. Amid joy, hope, and anticipation that came along with the news, they recall how they began to conjure up fanciful images of the arrival of their daughter-to-be and her joining their family. In the same air mail, Bonnie wrote, "The girls watching her say she is naughty because they want her to stay" (letter from Barbara Morrall to the author). The couple began making regular contributions to *Shishu Bhavan* where their daughter had been born, housed, and looked after by *ayas* (midwives, women who take care of babies) until she was sent away. Though a humble contribution, they continued this for many years following their daughter's arrival in Canada.

The next thing the Morralls recall was the brief period (of a few days) of preparation for the arrival of their daughter. Between the time they had been informed about the child and her actual arrival in Canada, they worried that there could be long delays and that she might not survive the journey, given the high incidence of infant mortality among the undernourished war babies. Prior to the baby's arrival, Robin had refused to be interviewed by the local Saskatoon daily, the *Star-Phoenix,* about their decision to adopt. The Morralls wanted to keep the news to themselves. They viewed the adoption of their daughter from Bangladesh as a family occasion that should remain a matter of private celebration. By nature, the Morralls shunned any kind of publicity, even though the arrival would be one of the most memorable days of their lives. Both Robin and Barbara wanted this to be a private family matter of a personal nature. Were they successful? Not quite.

On July 20, 1972, their daughter-to-be finally arrived. Robin recalls how he stayed home all day with their two-and-a-half-year-old son, John, and made elaborate arrangements to welcome the daughter and the mother home. Barbara had flown alone to Toronto to pick up their daughter at the Toronto airport. She was scheduled to bring home the baby by taking a late flight back to Saskatoon the same night. They had hoped that the late-night return to Saskatoon would keep the reporters away from Barbara and the baby. Their baby along with fourteen other war babies traveled from Dhaka to Toronto and Montreal via New Delhi and New York that day.

The flight from New York to Toronto arrived late. As soon as the babies were off the plane, the news of the arrival of the war babies in Canada hit the media airwaves across the country. Barbara and the baby ended up having to stay overnight at a hotel in Toronto. The next evening, somewhat to the dismay of the Morralls, the local daily, the *Star-Phoenix,* which the family had avoided thus far, ran a short news item under News Summary titled "Babies Canada-bound." Despite efforts to keep a low profile, the arrival of their daughter, whose given name was Rani, had been feted across local and national media.

Within days of arriving in Saskatoon, Barbara wrote to Bonnie Cappuccino describing how "thoroughly delighted" they were and how "tremendously lucky [they have been] in having her [their daughter Rani]."[29] The Morralls were concerned about Rani's medical needs because they had limited prior knowledge of her medical history.

However, Rani was underweight when she first arrived in Canada. Barbara still remembers how she used to pass days without having an appetite for any type of food – something that naturally worries every parent. Barbara also recalls how Rani needed time to adjust to the time differences between Dhaka and Saskatoon. Although the difference tends to affect people of all ages, for Rani the adjustment seemed to take longer than expected. In recalling their early years with Rani, the couple took pride in saying how their instincts had told them that their daughter would respond to the new environment before long; and sure enough, Rani responded and grew to be a healthy young girl.

In Rani's early years (1972 to 1987), the circumstances surrounding her birth were a known fact in the family from the start. Rani became a part of the Morrall family with no outward signs of being bothered by her special past. At home, no attempt was ever made to pretend otherwise, nor was there any other story fabricated to replace Rani's birth history. What the Morralls don't remember is *when* Rani came to understand the implications of her background. They find it hard to pinpoint the exact time period.

As far back as they can remember, her adoption had always been a fact of life about which they had been very frank and open to everyone. According to Barbara, Rani must have known about her story of adoption, almost from day one, although she believes Rani was too young to understand the true meaning of adoption. The family believes that Rani grew up knowing the scanty nature of information on her birth record. The recorded information simply stated that she was born in Bangladesh, had been adopted, and was brought to Canada through adoption, and that the orphanage authority in Dhaka had no knowledge of her biological father or mother.

The Morralls describe Rani, while she was growing up, as having been a friendly girl who was both active and outgoing. "Rani used to make friends in no time because she was a very likable person," observe the Morralls (Barbara said this to the author in an interview with him at a hotel in Saskatoon, Saskatchewan, on March 23, 1997). The Morralls committed themselves to expose their daughter to Indian subcontinental culture to the extent possible. This commitment led them to actively seek out Bangladeshi and Indian community in Saskatoon. However, there were only a handful of Bangladeshi families in Saskatoon in the early 1970s. The Morralls had known and mingled with the Sarkars frequently. Dr. Asit Sarkar, a Canadian of Bangladeshi origin, was a colleague of Robin at the university; while his wife, Ila Sarkar, was a social worker. The Sarkar's daughter, Tanya, who was a little older, would become one of Rani's early childhood friends. Because it was rare to find Bangladeshis in the Saskatoon area, the family turned to the East Indian community in Saskatoon for greater opportunities to interact with subcontinental cultural community.

Rani involved herself in some typical *Indian* activities hings. For instance, Barbara remembers how excited Rani used to be about the private dance lesson that she took at Mrs. Lal's home. Barbara does not recall her first name, as the dance teacher was commonly known as Mrs. Lal. Herself a Canadian of Indian origin, Mrs. Lal taught children classical Indian dances. Rani picked up dance very quickly. Through Mrs. Lal's lessons, Rani formed an interest in the performing arts and Indian classical dance in particular.

Every time Rani performed a dance or participated in a cultural show, she would wear any jewelry that she could get her hands on, often borrowing Indian jewelry from her friends' mothers, and she would still complain for not having enough jewelry: "How come my mother doesn't have the kind of jewellery my friends' mothers have?" recalls Barbara (letter from Barbara Morrall to the author). This was one of Rani's common complaints every time she was involved in a show. On sundry occasions, Rani enjoyed dressing up as an Indian girl, wearing a typical Indian *sari* and Indian jewelry. For special occasions, to encourage Rani in her cultural explorations, the Morralls would buy her gorgeous Indian dresses. It was through the Indian community that both Rani and her parents developed a shared taste for Indian food and culture.

Aside from cultural exposure, Barbara made sure that Rani also received formal religious teaching during her formative years. She started by taking Rani to Knox United Church on Sundays and other Christian occasions to develop church attendance as a habit. Rani was baptized at Grosvenor Park United Church in 1984 at the age of twelve. The Morralls also felt it is important to ensure that they maintained a connection with the other Bangladeshi war babies who arrived at the same time as Rani.

For the first few years after Rani's arrival, they continued to keep in touch with adoptive families in Ontario as well as the Cappuccinos and Sandra Simpson (Families For Children) in Montreal. The adoptive parents, under the leadership of Donna Wolsey (discussed under Del and Donna Wolsey later in the present chapter), had formed an informal support group, Canadopt, for each other. The group exchanged letters, spoke on the phone, and visited each other as and when opportunities arose. Thus far, Rani had experienced no major problems. She seemed a normal, active young girl.

However, by 1987 (when Rani turned fifteen or so), the Morralls recall how Rani began to exhibit signs of a disturbed mind. This remains as one of the most shocking experiences for the Morralls, one that they have never been able to forget. They recall a marked sudden change in Rani's personality. They observed how the outgoing Rani rapidly became introspective and isolated at a time when most of her friends were out enjoying their teenage years. Rani became somewhat aloof – a sudden shift from an active happy girl to a withdrawn one, as though in search of something unsaid.

They made attempts to help her, but Rani's reticence neither helped them to *understand* the situation nor helped them to *prescribe* measures to help Rani's depression. Barbara felt that Rani's mental state was deteriorating so fast that Rani herself was incapable of fathoming the situation. This was an obvious red flag for the parents. Barbara was eventually able to convince Rani to see a psychologist at this time. Later after a suicide attempt, she was seen by a psychiatrist and attended a youth services facility on a weekly basis. Rani was very secretive about her inner thoughts, which made it difficult for health professions to help her.

Is it an identity crisis? Barbara asked herself repeatedly with no answer as Rani continued to keep herself withdrawn. Reflecting on a smart, independent, and competent young girl, Barbara remembers picturing to herself in her mind's eye whether Rani was imagining a whole slew of utterly new things: *Is it possible that Rani was asking, "Where do I come from? How did it all happen?"* Despite his good knowledge of parenting, Robin too was at an utter loss with regard to Rani's deteriorating mental state. The couple reckoned that after much conjecture, Rani was struggling to come to terms with her adoption and her special personal history as a war baby.

With the benefit of hindsight, they have realized that they only *became fully aware* of Rani's mental health problems in the late 1980s. In retrospect, they recognize that Rani's problems went back much further. Barbara believed that one of the problems (which have been observed in many adoptees) related to Rani who was *not coming to terms with* her roots. Robin and Barbara felt that perhaps a visit to Bangladesh, Rani's country of birth, might help her come to terms with her origins, although they were not certain about it. Without a past, Rani would have no future. It was this belief that prompted the Morralls to propose to Rani to visit Bangladesh.

When offered a trip to Bangladesh, Rani jumped at the opportunity ecstatically, which made her parents happy for the time being. The Morralls hoped that this trip would give them a chance to show Rani her native land and might allow her to resolve the disquiet in her mind. Barbara remembers how the very idea of going to Bangladesh rejuvenated Rani. She became more talkative again after her yearlong period of confusion and lack of spirit and vitality.

Coincidentally, at that time, Donna Wolsey, the mother of war baby Amina, was making arrangements for a grand trip to Bangladesh with a number of war babies and orphans who had also come from Bangladesh. The Morralls decided to be a part of the 1989 trip initiated by the Wolseys, the details of which are described in chapter 7 under the "War babies' first trip to their country of birth."

After weeks of preparation, the group arrived in Dhaka, Bangladesh. The first thing the Morralls noticed was Rani's mental state – excitement and enthusiasm. Every day they had outings and activities with the orphans in three orphanages in or near Dhaka. A few of the original staff members of *Shishu Bhavan* who were still around at the time were thrilled to see Rani after sixteen long years. That trip to Bangladesh, the parents recall, was perhaps the happiest thing that happened to Rani in her teenage years.

It was only following her visit to Bangladesh, or specifically having been at the orphanage premises that Rani began to show outwardly her strong feelings about her relationship with her birth mother, observes Barbara (this was said to the author by the Morralls on March 23, 1997, during a meeting at a hotel in Saskatoon, Saskatchewan). However, unlike many adoptees that tend to believe that their parents had taken them from their birth mothers, a sense being kidnapped, Rani had no such illusion. Rani's knowledge that her birth mother had given her up at birth did not seem to prompt her to hold anything against her adoptive parents whose unconditional love for her had always led her to accept them as her *only* true parents.

By age seventeen, having gained new knowledge about herself, Rani seemed ready to tell the world what it *meant* to *be adopted* in Canada and to have been *given up* by the mother who *gave* her life. However, the Morralls could also see *how* Rani had recognized what it was like to have *no* biological connection with her adoptive family even though they *embraced* her with love and affection and that they were ever-ready to assist her to understand the *truth* about the *reality* of Rani's situation. She had a loving, secure parent-child relationship with her parents. However, sometime after her return from Bangladesh, depression set in again. Over the intervening years into adulthood, the Morralls witnessed their daughter descend into a complete mental breakdown. With flexibility and calmness, Robin and Barbara did their best to cope with Rani's constantly changing reality.

A variety of forces operate in an individual's mental development and crystallization of self, especially during the crucial years of adolescence. The Morralls understood Rani's struggle for authenticity, her desire to be close to the birth mother whom she never knew and could never know. The Morralls had known about the research outcome of many writers on adoption who maintain that one of the ominous themes of adoption that adoptees have to deal with all their lives is a sense of being "unwanted," rejected, or abandoned by birth parents. Having deep empathy for Rani, and having recognized the depression and anxiety that Rani was suffering from, they turned to every possible professional help they could.

Evidently, of all of the war babies, Rani had the most disturbed mind. She seemed to struggle with two mothers – the mother she had never "known" and the mother who had raised her. We cannot tell whether Rani was waiting for her "real" mother to return, as many adoptees do for their "guardian angel." As Rani saw it, her adoptive mother was "real," since she had always been around to raise Rani. Given her situation, Rani was challenged with reconciling her feelings for her biological mother who also seemed "real" after having visited Bangladesh. Nevertheless, it is speculative that the root problem was the two-mother issue; it is equally possible that the primary cause was Rani's mental illness.

Barbara felt that Rani was looking for self-worth, identity, and a sense of self. But despite their love and affection, the parents could not fully understand Rani's internal struggle. As Rani came of age, they believe that she felt the need to finally come to terms with *who* she was. Thus, even though Rani felt assured of trust and permanency in her home in Canada, still she had to deal with relinquishment and its related losses against a background of a mental illness. However, her parents could never figure out whether tracing her own connections was really Rani's principal source of anguish.

After visiting Bangladesh in February 1989, Rani completed her high school in 1990 and entered in nursing program at Queen's University in Kingston, Ontario. She completed the first year and appeared to be enjoying student life. However, the second year did not go so well, and by June 1992, Rani was hospitalized for depression. Barbara flew to Kingston and arranged to transfer her to a psychiatric ward in Saskatoon. The Morralls recall 1992 as a dreadful year with Rani having to return to Saskatoon and leave her studies behind.

At one point, they were still hopeful that Rani would recover and that she would return to the school of nursing to complete her studies. But as Rani's depression deepened and psychotic episodes became more frequent, the hope for a change eventually dimmed. Rani and the family were on a roller coaster for the next seven years. Rani seemed to respond to new approaches (activities, psychotherapy, medication, living accommodation, etc.) to alleviate her symptoms for a certain length of time. Unfortunately, the improvement didn't last, and she would become severely depressed again. From a fairly early age, Rani had gone through periods when she became elated, hyperactive, and very talkative and would take unnecessary risks.

These periods of elation would always be followed by a depressive period. This type of behavior continued and led some psychiatrists to believe she had bipolar disorder. Rani needed to be admitted to the psychiatric ward many times over the years when she became suicidal. It wasn't safe for her to remain with her parents or in a personal care home. Creative writing and songwriting played an important role in Rani's life as mechanisms to express her inner feelings, but they were not enough to help her deal with her mental health successfully. Nothing, no therapy of any kind, seemed to help Rani in the end.

In Rani's early adulthood, the Morralls witnessed Rani's search for her roots and how the circumstances surrounding her birth and relinquishment appeared to contribute to her state of depression. Rani's condition tended to become progressive and insidious. Her parents helplessly watched how she was being gripped by a cauldron of confusion and anger. On the one hand, her visit to Bangladesh had satisfied her need for factual information and touched the deepest level of the heart and soul. On the other hand, it had given rise to inner trepidation in her mind about the complexities and ambiguities of the situation and eventually contributed in her adulthood to deep depression, despondency, hopelessness, and helplessness.

Despite the heartache of seeing the continuing devastation in Rani, the Morralls never called into question their own sense of being her parents. They were mindful of the feelings of rejection and identity confusion that happen to be common to all adoptees to some degree. They believed that Rani could not survive simply by being *understood*.

She also had to be *loved* and *cared for* demonstrably. Barbara made herself Rani's partner throughout these troubled times. Both parents worried about the turbulence of a tempestuous life filled with feelings of sadness, rejection, disappointment, and loss of control. They neither ignored nor denied the complexity of Rani's background, as this would mean denying the reality of Rani's loss. They had confidence in their open and loving connection with Rani.

Having been with her daughter throughout her life, Barbara felt that Rani's relationship with her had been strengthened as she had tried to help her cope with her illness. She recognized that Rani did not have any ambivalence toward them even though at times she seemed to be focused on the "unknown" mother who gave birth to her. The Morralls maintain that all along, Rani had considered Barbara as her *only* "mom" from whom she had received unconditional love. They know for sure that Rani had never pictured in her mind anyone else but Barbara as her mother. Nevertheless, it was also their understanding that over the years, Rani became preoccupied with a sense of rejection having developed from a recurring fear of abandonment rather than from any kind of deprivation on the part of the adoptive family.

As time went by, the Morralls became convinced that perhaps there was no cure for her illness. In fact, it had generated a particular type of thought patterns toward self-harm and suicide. Rani did not appear to have the inner strength and natural resilience necessary to overcome her condition. Yet to the end, the Morralls kept hoping against hope, as though searching for light in the darkness. However, Rani never returned to school and eventually departed from a world in which she could no longer live.

The funeral was attended by a large number of people: relatives, friends of Rani, friends and colleagues of Barbara and Robin including some from many years ago, and members of Rani's tae kwon do club. The service was officiated by Reverends Ron McConnell and Bill Shank. Words of remembrance were presented by Robin, Barbara, John, and Kim Morrall (daughter-in-law). The musical part consisted of some of Rani's favorite pieces. "Here I Am, Lord;' "In the Bulb There Is A Flower;" and "Precious Lord, Take My Hand" were all hymns that had provided Rani with a great deal of comfort in the seven years before she died.

A grieved Robin who read about Rani's short life (1972–1999) at the funeral service described her life as follows: "Rani's tragic and premature death was something that we had feared many times before. May we all try to take comfort in the fact that Rani's memory will always be with us."[30] Robin and other members of the family talked about the somberness with which the family was filled, yet touched on some of the treasured joyful memories of the life they had had together. They recalled when Rani reached a dangerous level of despondency, they remained firm in their belief that she might respond to some new intervention. At the reception later, many people talked about the happy remembrances they had of Rani.

The family is grateful to many who stood by them throughout Rani's illness. Reverends Ron McConnell, Ken Moen, and Bill Shank, in particular, gave spiritual counsel to Rani and provided considerable support to the family. The Morralls were touched by and surprised at the number of people who attended Rani's funeral, especially by the number of messages of sympathy they received and visits to their home. All of this was definitely very helpful. To this day, the Morralls remember their dear Rani in the same spirit of love and affection with which they had embraced her upon her arrival in Canada. The family intended to take Rani's ashes to Bangladesh. However, regrettably, this has not yet happened. Recently they have been discussing scattering them in a special place on the riverbank in Saskatoon.

For the Morralls, life has never been the same without Rani. The normal grieving process lasted a very long time for Barbara, but she was fortunate to have a supportive husband, close friends, and a counselor to help her through the worst periods. Despite the trauma of Rani's death, Robin and Barbara's life together goes on. Their other child, John, and his wife, Kim, live in Prince Albert and enjoy a very active life with four children, aged from twelve to eighteen years. Seeing their grandchildren grow up and become involved in numerous activities provides the Morralls a great deal of pleasure.

Rani

Rani was born prematurely on March 30, 1972, at Mother Teresa's *Shishu Bhavan.* She weighed one kilogram at birth. She was registered as "Rani" with no other name. Her biological mother had left the baby in the hands of the orphanage authority immediately after giving birth. Rani came to Canada on July 20, 1972, to join the Morrall family. Rani's adoptive parents changed her name to Rani Joy Morrall. According to the family, Rani's middle name, Joy, carries a double meaning: in English "joy" means "happiness;" whereas in Bengali, they were told, it means "victory." To the Morralls, Rani's escape to Canada from the war-torn Bangladesh held in it a great victory while bringing to them all of the happiness in the world. To this day, Rani's middle name, Joy, remains very important to the Morralls both symbolically and otherwise, as Rani was a joy to them.

Rani grew up in Saskatoon, Saskatchewan. The city had a population of approximately 120,000 people in the early 1970s. Between 1974 and 1975, when Rani was about two years old, her father, who was a professor at the University of Saskatchewan, went on sabbatical and moved his family to Dijon, France. Upon returning from sabbatical, the family continued to live in Saskatoon where they lived before. From an early age, Rani was interested in music. She began attending Suzuki violin classes at the age of three.

In 1976, Rani began attending the Saskatoon French School – a French immersion elementary school. There, she met children of mixed races and cultures, which exposed her to Canadian multiculturalism from a very early age. Barbara recalls Rani being a bright child, full of life and vigor. Rani had a close relationship with her older brother, John, both of whom played and quarreled together like other children of their age. The Morralls returned to France for a subsequent sabbatical in 1981 and lived there for one year. Like many Canadian children, Rani learned to speak and spell competently in French again. However, in later years, her French language skills waned from disuse.

In 1986, Rani attended Bishop James Mahoney High School. Rani was now fourteen years old and pursued many interests, especially in the creative arts. Throughout her high school years, she played violin for the Saskatoon Youth Orchestra. She also taught herself how to play flute and excelled at it. Rani wrote songs and came to be known in high school as a bit of a rhymester. She developed a passion for creative writing, which included her writing numerous poems and songs on a variety of subjects expressing her innermost feelings.

Rani's friends were from diverse backgrounds – European, African, Chinese, and Indian, to name only a few. The 1980s was a time when the concept of Canadian multiculturalism was at its peak. Being surrounded by many ethnoculturally diverse groups of friends, Rani was able to enrich her own knowledge of the world and the world around her. She played an active part in enhancing the Canadian cultural mosaic of Saskatoon. Looking back, Barbara remembers Rani's hectic high school years as largely an exciting and joyful time in Rani's life. The biggest challenge for Rani came at the age of fifteen when Rani first began to openly question her identity as an adopted child. For a time at age sixteen, as mentioned in her parent's narrative, Rani became despondent and withdrew from the people around her. She fell into a deep funk and perhaps, in retrospect, a full-blown depression.

According to Barbara, even though they accompanied Rani to Bangladesh, they could not fully appreciate what it meant to Rani, in terms of wonder, awe, silence, and brooding, to be in her country of birth. Rani longed to know her birth mother. Her parents witnessed her ecstatic mood when they visited Rani's first home, the orphanage *Shishu Bhavan*.

At the instant of seeing her own name in the register book, her emotion reached a new height of intensity. Seeing her own name, date, and place of birth with her own eyes gave Rani a sense of awareness and of truly being connected to Bangladesh – her country of birth. It is a kind of experience that is referred to in Buddhist tradition as *satori*, meaning "sudden enlightenment" or "awakening." Rani came to know *how* and under *what* circumstances she was born, abandoned, and adopted. From that moment, Rani had validated the story of her birth, as told to her by her adoptive parents, and felt as though she had "seen" and made a connection to her birth mother.

On her return to Canada from her first and only trip to Bangladesh in February 1989, Rani seemed renewed as if she had come to terms with her own background and was ready to take on the challenges of adulthood. However, it appeared that Rani was continuing to seek peace with the balance of her Bangladeshi and Canadian identities. Rani attempted to incorporate the best of both worlds – the world of Canada where she lived and had been raised, and the world of Bangladesh where she was born and abandoned. When she evaluated her relationship with her adoptive parents, she came to believe that although abandoned, she was still a "wanted" child. Her parents in Canada never hesitated to reinforce and support their "wanted" child.

Discovering of her origin, her adoptive parents believe, did give her a renewed sense of identity. It seemed to replace her rearing mother, her feelings of emptiness, confusion, and pain with love when thinking about her birth mother. Instead of anger and resentment toward her birth mother, as is sometimes the case with many adoptees, Rani was able to embrace her with *love, sympathy,* and *forgiveness*. Adoptees often feel ashamed because of the way secrets are embedded into their identity records. For Rani, she did not seem to exhibit this shame. She was able to connect the thread in her mind that had been left dangling in Bangladesh to weave the bits and pieces of her story into a single narrative of her birth, including relinquishment by her birth mother in Bangladesh and adoption by her parents in Canada.

However, Rani was still torn between Canada and Bangladesh. Rani's parents did their best to help Rani work through this inner conflict. Being unable to contain her anger and frustration, there were times when Rani used to explode into a tremendous rage, which would generally manifest itself by her acting out and exhibiting self-destructive behavior. Also an emotional Rani articulated her intensely emotional and complex state of mind certainly in more positive ways. Poetry and songwriting were an example, especially at a time when her parents were there to give her the requisite emotional backup she was in need of. She wrote a poem, "Child of the Rivers," in which epitomized her sense of belonging to both her country of birth and her adopted country.

Child of the Rivers

You gave me up, when I was young
I don't know why, I never will
But mom I'll always think of you
And love you, like I do still.
I was sad, I cried for you
I felt the pain, so many nights
And I thought it'd never go away
Till I felt you, hold me tight.

Child of the rivers
Is what they call this land, so lush and green

With water all around, and people's honest faces
It's the most gorgeous land, I've ever seen.

When I went to the orphanage
I held the children, in my arms
All they wanted was to be held tight
To be kept safe, from any harm.
I saw my name, in the record book
Met my first mothers, I ever knew
I saw where I was kept so warm

To save the life, I got from you.

Is what they call this land, so lush
and green
With water all around, and people's
honest faces
It's the most gorgeous land, I've ever
seen.
I'll always love, and think of you
But don't feel the pain, I always knew
Cause I saw my name, and have a
family now
And they keep me safe, for you.

I know the day, I must have changed
When I felt peace, and happiness
It was the day I saw the red sunrise

Over the green, of Bangladesh.

Child of the rivers
Is what they call this land, so lush
and green
With water all around, and people's
honest faces
It's the most gorgeous land, I've ever
seen.

Child of the rivers
You calmed the stormy waves, I
always knew
You turned them into rivers, of peace
and love
So for the rest of life, I'll sail with
you.[31]

At once moving and poignant, "Child of the Rivers" typified the enigma Rani had faced as an adoptee – a journey through the emotional labyrinth of the adoption experience and the search for identity, the search for one's roots. In her poem, Rani describes her feelings about the birth mother, *where* she came from, and the *circumstances* of her birth. Rani's words reflect the extreme love she felt for mothers in general, her inner conflict regarding her birth, her trip to Bangladesh to rediscover herself, and the resulting peace she felt in Bangladesh during the process of coming to terms with her personal history. In the poem, she highlights her visit to the orphanage where she stayed as a newborn, where she met orphans with whom she could easily relate, and what it meant for her to see her name in the orphanage's register book.

In it, Rani succinctly states her sense of loss from her birth mother's absence. She refers to the people at the orphanage who first took care of her as "her first mothers" – implying that she was at peace with having many mothers. Her visit to the orphanage linked her present to her past through her mothers. Her visit to Bangladesh gave her hope in Canada by allowing her to appreciate the beauty of *her* country *where* she came from – the "most gorgeous" land she had ever seen full of "lush and green . . . with water all around."

PICKING UP THE PIECES

In Rani's writing, her parents in Canada were the parents who had nurtured her and continued to "keep" her "safe" in Canada where she lived. Unlike many adoptees that spend an exorbitant amount of psychic time in fantasizing about their birth parents, Rani rooted herself in the reality of her life in Canada. She went to Bangladesh with her (adoptive) parents to "discover" her origins. In that sense, for Rani, it was not a case of "genealogical bewilderment." She was mindful of what her adoptive parents had told her about her birth, abandonment, and adoption. In a strict sense, the poem epitomizes Rani's visceral sense of loss of her biological mother in the form of grieving. Rani seemed able to come to terms with herself in her early years. Geographically, Bangladesh is merely a tiny mass within the vast expanses of waters flowing through her and surrounding her shores – a child of the rivers. Rani, like Bangladesh, identified herself also as a child of the rivers.

Rani stands quite apart from the other war babies on the trip (Amina, Ryan, Lara, and Rajib) who were also exposed to similar information about their respective pasts. Having seen their names in the register book, none of the other war babies reacted the way Rani did, especially in terms of having continuing and lingering effects. While they were able to handle the past by essentially saying "let bygones be bygones," Rani needed to integrate into her life her "newly discovered" but "never-seen" birth mother who only existed in her mind. Her adoptive parents were devastated to see how Rani's journey into an arena of pain and loss at times brought her to tears at the thought of her birth mother. Rani needed to go beyond her past life, work through her feelings, and mend the present by filling in the "identity gap" that hitherto existed in her life. For Rani, the greatest challenge would be how to integrate her "never-seen" birth mother into her life in Canada.

As Rani saw it, it was ironic that she was unable to show her birth mother how well things had worked out for her in Canada. Unlike many adoptees that tend to believe that their parents had taken them from their birth mothers, a sense of being kidnapped, Rani had no such feelings of doubt. She understood *why* her birth mother had to abandon her at birth. Moreover, Rani neither held anything against her adoptive parents nor questioned their inordinate love for her. Looking back, Robin and Barbara maintain that the psychological journey into her past began at the time of that first visit to *Shishu Bhavan* where she was born. It was as though she took a spontaneous leap from one

MUSTAFA CHOWDHURY

level to another link in the process – to discover yet another dimension within her identity.

In 1990, Rani graduated with a grade 12 bilingual diploma and, later that year, moved to Kingston, Ontario, to enter the nursing program at Queen's University. She completed her first year of studies without much difficulty. However, as already mentioned in her parents' profile, in 1992 during her second year of studies, Rani had a nervous breakdown. At that time, Rani was exhibiting behavior similar to her earlier episodes as a teenager, recalled her parents. Her feelings interfered with her functioning in everyday life. Having abandoned her studies, she returned home to Saskatoon in a very disturbed state of mind. The summer of 1992 marked the end of Rani's studies and a renewal of a long battle with mental illness.

Back at home in Saskatoon, Rani again became despondent and isolated herself from others. She showed clear outward signs of illness but was unable to verbalize her state. With the intervention of mental health practitioners, Rani was sent to numerous specialists. They ran a battery of tests but could not come up with a definite diagnosis despite clear signs of melancholy, depression, and sadness. *What was the exact nature of Rani's illness?* Neither her parents nor her doctors could tell for certain *what* exactly was *happening* to Rani. However, the most likely diagnosis was that Rani suffered from a form bipolar disorder.

According to the family, Rani eventually came to recognize the gravity of her illness. However, neither she nor anyone else could attribute her condition to one single source or issue. *Was it a feeling of having been abandoned at birth?* Rani's father, Robin, feels that the cause of Rani's condition did not necessarily have anything to do with Rani's background per se because depression is a very common disease. However, Barbara believes that Rani's illness was complicated by her emotional needs and frustrations vis-à-vis Rani's search for her roots: the unusual circumstances surrounding her birth and abandonment. Both believe that the triggering event for Rani's subsequent descent into depression had to do with Rani's thinking about her birth mother whom she believed she "saw" in Bangladesh. Her parents believe that when she saw her *own* name in the register book at the orphanage, Rani felt, literally, the physical presence of her birth mother who, to use Rani's own words, had held her "tight."

The Morralls maintain that no words could ever describe Rani's feelings of depression. There was little that anyone could do or say to ease her pain and anguish. There were times when Rani used to sit up and weep, shedding tears mingled with deep regret. Obsessive thoughts plagued her mind, resulting in what might be called protean or extreme forms of variability of mind. Barbara believes that Rani needed someone reliable who could *understand* or *viscerally relate* to Rani's experience of feeling her birth mother was still physically with her in the face of the truth of her abandonment.

In the midst of her breakdown, the light of hope still burned in her. Rani, by nature, always maintained a compassionate and kind outlook on others. To Rani, her life was not about being good but, rather, to do good things. She wanted to remain vital to look upon others with dignity and respect, to move forward in life, and to make things "happen." When she was a student at Queen's, these feelings led her to volunteer her time at a home for people with disabilities where she was recognized through accolades and awards. By helping others, she found space in her heart to ponder about those who were mentally afflicted like her, who suffered the way she did.

Although Rani wrote a poem titled *Triumph Over Pain,* the irony of fate is that Rani herself was not able to triumph over her pain. The incredible anxiety that continually stalked her over the years made her into a ticking time bomb waiting to explode. In the final years of her life, Rani was in and out of hospitals, treatment centers, and institutions. Self-destructive behavior stemming from her feelings of abandonment, resentment, guilt, and confusion became the norm for her. She would take time out to regroup her psychic forces, but she could never steadfastly return to the calmer ways of life. She took her own life and died at 12:30 a.m. on June 7, 1999. She was twenty-seven years old.

In the book *Identity: Youth and Crisis,* the great psychologist Erick Erickson contends that an adoptee's identity must not be ignored, which in a psychological context relates to the individual's sense of genealogy through linkage between the past and the present. Erickson theorizes that ignorance or no knowledge about the important stages in one's past creates a mental discontinuity that complicates and makes it harder for an individual, especially in her/his adolescence, to come to terms with their past in adulthood.32[32] His contention fits well in the case of Rani but does not apply to the other four war babies who accompanied

Rani on that fateful trip to Dhaka. Rani had grieved for the loss of her biological mother whom she had never (nor ever could have) seen.

Rani's biological mother seemed so real to her, as demonstrated in Rani's dialogue with her through Rani's poetry. Rani longed to have (and perhaps believed she had) a spiritual relationship with an unknown, unseen biological mother. However, her most intimate real maternal relationship was with Barbara, her adoptive mother, or the rearing mother. This mental discontinuity between her biological origins and adoptive history, vis-à-vis her "mothers," plagued Rani throughout her adulthood.

Whatever issues Rani might have had prior to her visit to the orphanages in Dhaka, it is for certain that afterward, Rani was gripped by a particular type of melancholy that later developed into a deep depression. We have seen how Rani wrestled to integrate the facts of her life into a single narrative. We have discussed how the Morralls supported Rani with unconditional love, guidance, and protection throughout her life. It is difficult to say whether Rani had always suffered from depression or became depressed only after visiting her birthplace. However, the signs of the disquiet in her mind were evident to the Morralls, in hindsight, throughout Rani's adult life.

Dorothy and John Morris

Long before John and Dorothy got married back in 1968, when they were seeing each other, they recall talking about adoption among other things. Quite fortuitously, both had been equally interested not only in advancing the cause of adoption but also in having adopted children to make their own family. As far back the couple recalls, the whole situation regarding the plight of the war orphans was brought to the fore as a result of an article in the November 1971 issue of a journal called the *Weekend Magazine*. Interestingly enough it was the same article that influenced the Morralls we have just finished reading. John, the breadwinner of the family, had owned and operated a customs brokerage business in Brantford, Ontario, which he continued until his retirement in 1988. Dorothy, his wife, was primarily a stay-at-home mother who took care of the children and managed the household. The couple lived all their life in Brantford, Ontario.

Within a span of five years, between 1970 and 1975, the couple had a total of four children, three of whom were adopted from foreign countries. When Beth, their only biological child, was two, the couple picked Jorina, a war baby from Bangladesh. The couple also picked two other orphans from Vietnam, a boy and a girl, Aaron in January 1975 and Tuyet in April 1975. At the time of adoption, Jorina was nine months old. Aaron was thirteen months old when he came to the Morrises' home in 1975, although they were told about him by the authority when he was just a few days old. Between all the red tape and disruptions due to the ongoing fight, it took over a year to get him to Canada. He easily adjusted to the new environment much like the Bangladeshi war baby who was also an infant during her arrival in Canada.

The family, however, recalls the early days of Tuyet who was nine years old when she was adopted in 1975. She had a tough time adjusting to her life in Canada. She spoke very little English and had endured a great deal of hardships while in Vietnam, including contracting polio. In addition, these children also have stepsiblings from their father's previous marriage who live in Ontario and Alberta. The Morrises never made any distinction among their children whether born to the family or adopted. The couple had treated their children equally, having always maintained that all their children are *dear* to them for whom they provided a place of love, faith, and strength; and they have demonstrably maintained that they love them all unconditionally.

In choosing adoption as a means to expand their family, the couple believed that there were far too many babies around who needed a family. Their strong desire for adoption of orphans from the third world stemmed from their belief that they ought to give love and care to the orphans in need of permanent homes. They believed in their hearts' heart that by adopting them, they could at least do something concrete, even though it would mean very little given the number of orphans. It is this single realization alone that had motivated the couple even more deeply to look at adoption as a vehicle to create their own family by picking up orphans in need of love and care.

All through their active life, the couple was aware that there were many in Canada as well as outside of Canada who did not (and even to this day many do not) support interracial adoption, which they see as the destruction of one's ethnicity and identity. Awareness of such

MUSTAFA CHOWDHURY

prevailing sentiment on the part of many Canadians, however, did not discourage them from doing what they so passionately believed in. Turning a deaf ear to all the negative comments, an energetic and loving couple, both John and Dorothy did what they thought were the best for the orphans.

With a fervent commitment to orphans and children, the couple made humble contribution in cash and kind for orphanages in Bangladesh and Vietnam all through the years the children were growing up. They believed that this was the least they could do for the hapless orphans in need of a safe and secured home. For a number of years, the couple had also sponsored many children in Bangladesh. They enjoyed receiving their correspondence and knowing that their contributions were making a difference.

Jorina's arrival in their family in Brantford was a significant event for many reasons especially because, at that time, there were very few non-Caucasian families in the neighborhood. Naturally the baby's arrival in a "white" home was a kind of "gossipy" news in the community. The Morrises recall, within couple of years, however, the neighborhood started to change its faces as people of diverse backgrounds began to move in.

One unpleasant memory that the Morrises had to swallow was some conflicting news report surrounding the baby girl's birth story that came out in the newspaper and the follow-up queries from curious news reporters right at the airport on the day Jorina arrived. By and large, the news media was aware of the particular situation, that is, the *why* and the *how* of the war babies; and yet the Morrises' child was singled out with some more sensational news.

One version was that the said baby girl was born in an orphanage and that her birth mother gave her up at birth, something that was consistent with the stories surrounding the birth and abandonment of the rest of the war babies who came to Canada on the same day. Another slightly twisted version emanated from the Associated Press and Reuters news agencies was reported that the baby girl Jorina was found on a burned-out abandoned Pakistani (navy boat) warship from where she was rescued following the surrender of the Pakistani army in December 1971.

The couple was so excited to have their child in their arms that at that time, that they had no desire to meet the news reporter for clarification. The arrival of Jorina was a fulfillment of the couple's romantic desire to embrace a racially different orphan having endured a long wait. John and Dorothy were barraged with questions by the reporters right at the airport when they embraced the baby girl. Ignoring everything else, an excited couple, however, had continued to admire their precious little daughter from the minute they were handed over the child: "It does not matter. We don't care where she was born, she's ours," retorted a thrilled couple who could hardly wait to go home with the new baby (*Globe and Mail,* July 21, 1972).

When the couple was constantly badgered by the media, which maintained that "Jorina was recovered from an abandoned Pakistani navy boat last December," Dorothy's quick and standard reply was "We were told she was brought in an orphanage but it doesn't matter" (*Kitchener-Waterloo Record,* July 21, 1972). The last thing that the couple had in their mind was to verify *where* and under *what* circumstances the baby girl was born. When confronted by more reporters, and having been flagged again before they headed home, the Morrises said that they were already aware of these stories. John's polite but curt reply to the news reporters' query was that they would follow up with the orphanage authority to find out as much as they could, "because one day she'll want to know" too (*Kitchener-Waterloo Record,* July 21, 1972).

The couple's first priority was to focus on the baby's health to make the baby normal and healthy. Since Jorina was in real bad health during the time she was flown in to Canada, those in charge of the trip were pretty apprehensive, as they feared the little girl might not make it to Canada. The news media was also alerted to the fact that the health conditions of some of the war babies were not good, as most of them were underweight and prematurely born. As soon as the babies were brought in to the lounge, the news reporters started to make inquiries with the team members and escorts, asking all kinds of questions with regard to the latest health conditions of the babies.

The couple recalls how Dr. Robert Ferrie also took personal interest in the babies he had examined in Dhaka and brought to Canada. As a professional, Dr. Ferrie felt obliged to write a personal letter to them the day he returned to Canada with the war babies, giving his counsel with respect to baby Jorina's special needs to heal her boils and pain for which she was going through sleepless nights. He cautioned the couple as to what they *could* and *could not* do under the circumstances to ensure a healthy growth.

Having recommended certain medicine, Dr. Ferrie ended his handwritten note in the following manner: "I would call your own doctor but if you ever need me call any time at 637-9339. Enclosed is a prescription to tide you over until you can get him. If you need nursing help with bathing call the V.O.N. [Victorian Order of Nurses] or your public health nurse. We must get together and discuss it all soon, Yours for Jorina, Bob."[33] The Morrises remember how happy they were to hear from Dr. Ferrie who had just returned from Bangladesh with the war babies including Jorina. Despite exhaustion, he took the time to write to them. The couple quickly acted on the recommendation of Dr. Ferrie and did all they could with regard to the baby.

News reporters who made follow-up visits to the Morrises' house in the intervening months talked about them as an extraordinary couple. They were happy to see the progress the baby was making with a mixture of love, iron, and antibiotics. Looking back, the Morrises recall how miraculously, "within a matter of months, the frail little girl not only survived but also changed into a chubby, happy, gurgling baby who charmed everyone."[34] They remember those tension-filled days when they not only consulted the doctors but also prayed to Almighty for the scrawny pathetic puny waif they had brought home after months of delay for her good health and well-being.

Among other memories, the couple still has some bittersweet memories with regard to their hard fight to bring Jorina to Canada and their effort to complete the process of formal adoption after Jorina's arrival (outlined in the previous chapter). These, in particular, have remained in their memory lane, something that appears every now and then, although they would rather not rake up any such memory. As far as the Morrises are concerned, they had their share of wait and uncertainty during the period following their decision to adopt. The day the Morrises were informed by the Cappuccinos that a girl had been chosen for them, the Morrises instantly came to believe in their minds and hearts, having developed a mental picture of the baby, that the said baby was their *own*. From that day onward, this particular girl (daughter) was *theirs* as far as they were concerned.

According to Dorothy, in many ways, one might be inclined to compare the inordinate delays in having the baby over in their home in Canada from the Bangladesh orphanage and getting the formal adoption process completed, with the endurance of a pregnancy, which she had experienced prior to and immediately after the arrival of their baby from Bangladesh. The couple still recalls the various hoops that they had to go through in order to have their Bangladeshi child brought home.

To the Morrises' way of thinking, given the pathetic situation in which most orphans were housed, whether in Vietnam or Bangladesh, allowing them to be parented in Canada would, no doubt, be a better option. They were disappointed to see that often social workers did not understand that no matter what kind of life they have with the families, adoption in Canada or anywhere would be much better than anything they ever could have had in their country of birth.

With time when the baby turned into a charming girl and the couple was free to focus on other things, they shifted their attention to the inquiries of the reporters following Jorina's arrival with respect to *where* and *how* exactly she was found. From the newspaper clippings and other bits and pieces of papers that they had collected, they learned that Jorina was "recovered by Sister Margaret Mary in early February [1972] from the Meghna [river]."[35] Their daughter's birth certificate, produced by the Missionaries of Charity, states that she was born from an unknown mother on October 23, 1971, in Dhaka, Bangladesh.

In addition, the couple also wrote to Sr. Margaret Mary, then superior of the Missionaries of Charity, who was also the statutory guardian of the war babies in her orphanage. Thanking the couple for embracing the infant, Sr. Margaret Mary immediately wrote back. She informed the couple that by a stroke of luck, she had found the dying child by the ferry in late December 1971 when a visibly distraught man, claiming to be the infant's father, was about to throw the infant into the river. The man was relieved by the offer from the sister to keep her and handed over the said sickly infant to the sister who brought the same child to the orphanage. The baby weighed barely about three kilograms at the time and looked about three months old, having blood dysentery and covered with sores. Sr. Margaret Mary then named the baby girl Jorina and assigned an approximate date of birth based on her own guesstimation. She also informed the couple that Jorina was the first war baby that they brought to the orphanage *(Shishu Bhavan)*. This information is contained in a handwritten letter in an aerogram by

Sr. Margaret Mary to John and Dorothy Morris on January 28, 1973. The couple has treasured the letter among other items of interest and historical importance as primary source of their adoption.

Apparently, like many others, the Morrises knew that many war babies were brought to the orphanages secretly by the relatives of the birth mothers, saying that the infant's father or mother is dead and that the father or the mother who is alive is too poor to take care of the baby. This was a common story line that was followed pretty well by all those who brought such babies to the orphanage premises without categorizing or branding them as "war babies" because of the stigma surrounding their birth. Such babies were brought to the orphanage believing that a story line along the vein that "one parent dead and another parent unable to take care of the child" would perhaps be more acceptable socially than making a direct reference to the child as a "war baby."

The Morrises had no problem with any such stories even though the media made a bit of hoopla at the time, since they had been fully aware of the fact of sexual violence, enforced pregnancy, birth, and abandonment of the war babies in Bangladesh and Vietnam. The couple was already briefed by the Cappuccinos about the tragic circumstances surrounding the birth and relinquishment of such babies even before the war babies were picked out for adoption. An affectionate Dorothy made sure that the family had a short account of *how* they went about getting their daughter over in Canada, what roadblock they had to encounter and overcome before they were able to bring her home.. Dorothy presented that piece of history to her daughter later on when she grew up. We have seen the citation in chapter 4.

When the children were very young, the couple handled all their issues with kid gloves. However, as they began to grow, the parents treated them with deference, allowing them to use their own sense of judgment. As far as the couple was concerned, what is important to them is to love their children and instill in them, above all, the values of honesty and integrity. By and large, they left the children on their own, giving them enough freedom. With a ready smile and compassionate note, the couple had always found time for their children of various ages. The parents did not believe in killing their children with kindness. If and when they interfered, it was not because they mistrusted their own children; instead, they believed their intervention was needed to keep them safe from others who could not be trusted. The family, therefore, provided the basic essentials of life and taught all their children the quality of kindness, compassion, and generosity. Incorporating the varied racial and cultural backgrounds of their children, the Morrises have raised their children as well-rounded individuals, above all as "Canadian" in a multiracial and multicultural Canada.

Their children recognize with admiration their parents' enthusiasm and years of dedication in advancing the cause of adoption. They know their parents love them, took care of them, and have raised them in the way they thought to be the best for the varying needs of the children. Of course, just like any other family, there were highs and lows, ups and downs during the time children were growing up. They did their best to resolve the issues that had surfaced and continued to manage the family affairs using their parenting skills. It is indeed a stupendous achievement. One might say altruism is one of the defining features of the couple's lives.

The Morris family remains an illustration of a resilient family that embodies a sense of tradition and a spirit of flexibility in the way in which they functioned particularly when they were raising their children. Having worked hard, the couple successfully built a stable and secured place where all family members afforded, supported, trusted, and respected each other.

Beth is now a registered nurse, working in administration for Hamilton Health Sciences. The couple's second child, Tuyet, is now is married with two children and works as a data entry clerk for a customs brokerage company. The detail of Jorina, a war baby, is outlined below. Their last child, Aaron, is currently living in Toronto. Aaron is living somewhat of a transient lifestyle, working at various jobs and with intentions of continuing his education.

The Morrises lived together in Brantford until John died in May 2006. John's death was hard for the entire family, as the family members were close to each other in a strong bond that had tied them all together from the very beginning of the children's lives. Today Dorothy lives with Beth in the granny suite in her home in Brantford, Ontario, where she is visited by all her children. The Morrises remember how, years ago, they would jokingly refer to Beth as their only "home-made" child. The Morrises were quick to say that it was indeed their children who have enriched their lives.

The Morrises never craved for a plaque or any formal recognition, although everyone around admired them for their fervent commitment to children, recognizing the fact that they have done something in the Good Samaritan tradition. People in the neighborhood regarded the Morrises as "heroes" for their adoption of orphans all the way from Vietnam and Bangladesh. On many occasions, the couple was profiled in the news media locally and had received high praise for their selfless actions. The people of Brantford have not forgotten the Morrises who remain well known in the community as very generous and giving parents who had always done their best to provide for their family.

Jorina

Jorina was born reportedly in a village near Dhaka, Bangladesh, on October 23, 1971, and was brought to the orphanage, *Shishu Bhavan,* in December by Sr. Margret Mary. Naturally when Jorina arrived in Canada with the rest of the war babies in July 1972, she was already about nine months old but was very frail. During the formal registration, the couple did not drop the name the baby girl was given at the orphanage. They simply named her Lara (her first name) and kept the name Jorina as her middle name, although they changed the spelling from Jorina to Jarina and added the family's surname, Morris. The baby girl thus came to be called Lara Jarina Morris.

After completing high school at North Park Collegiate and Vocational School in Brantford, Ontario, Lara went to Georgian College in Barrie Ontario. She obtained an honor's diploma in tourism (business) management from Georgian College in 1993. While at Georgian College, Lara was part of a team that created an action plan that won the faculty award and a second-place award from the Travel and Tourism Research International Association of Canada. Over the years, Lara took many courses in a number of areas including an Ontario Management Development Program (OMDP) and Leadership Skills Certificate from Mohawk College in Hamilton, Ontario.

She then attained a human resources certificate from Mohawk College in 2010 and became a candidate for the certified human resources professional (CHRP) designation. Lara worked at a number of places, the longest period being at OLG Casino Brantford for over twelve years, originally as a table games inspector (supervisor). After many years of providing external customer service, she then moved to the HR department as a scheduling clerk for OLG Casino, Brantford, and then became the clerk/secretary for Brant Food For Thought (a local nonprofit organization). She volunteers her time for other local nonprofit organizations.

Lara has no recollection of her existence in Bangladesh. Lara has been told various stories about her life there in Bangladesh. One part of her story line is also along the vein that her birth mother and brother had passed away prior to her going to the orphanage, etc. Another part of her story line is what we have already noted – that she was recovered from an abandoned ship left by the Pakistani army personnel. Like her parents, it did not matter to Lara with regard to her exact story line, as she grew up believing the Morrises to be her *only parents* she is aware of. She also knows that her parents in Canada have limited knowledge of her birth history, which includes letters from the nuns at the orphanage. Her parents have never deterred her from wanting to find out more about her native country or her genetic history. Lara, however, has not made any attempt to "discover" her family roots, and, she believes, it is unlikely that she will do so in the future.

Her parents in Canada have given her an amazing life full of opportunities and experiences that would likely not have been possible had she remained in Bangladesh. "I can never thank them enough for that. I have also always felt extremely lucky and special for being 'chosen' over so many other orphaned children to be a part such an extraordinary family as mine,"[36] says a happy Lara. In fact, having been adopted by a loving family at such an early age, Lara has never considered to have been "abandoned at birth," and it has never bothered her that her parents are not her natural parents.

"I was loved and nurtured as if I were their natural child and therefore have never experienced any 'voids' in my upbringing and childhood," maintains a contended Lara (letter from Lara Morris to the author, cited in notes and references). She then continues, "My parents have never treated me differently from my other siblings (2 of which were adopted from Vietnam) and they provided all of us with everything we could ever need or want – a home, food, clothing, money, education, social activities, as well as love and a sense of family" (letter from Lara Morris to the author, cited in notes and references).

"Aside from typical sibling rivalry, there were never any issues of not fitting in with my family or being treated differently," recalled Lara. They grew up amid ups and downs, laughter and tears, just like any other family. Like the rest of the war babies in Canada, Lara is so well integrated that she does not see herself as a person of color. She, therefore, is not concerned with other people's perception of her. Given the fact that everyone in Canada came from somewhere else, Lara recalls she never had any problem in responding to her origin in a matter-of-fact way. Lara does not choose to associate or disassociate herself with other people based solely on their race, ethnicity, religion, or cultural background (letter from Lara Morris to the author). She sees "people as people"

Lara is one of the five war babies who went on a trip to Bangladesh back in 1989 when she was seventeen years old. We shall see the details of this in chapter 7 under the heading the "War babies' first visit to their country of birth." Lara claims she had the "once-in-a-lifetime opportunity to visit Bangladesh in 1989," and she would treasure the memory of this trip all her life (letter from Lara Morris to the author). "This trip gave me a glimpse of what my life would have been like had I not have been adopted," said an emotional Lara (letter from Lara Morris to the author).

"It was heart wrenching leaving the children behind – not knowing what their futures held, feeling that we could not help them enough," recalled Lara (letter from Lara Morris to the author). Even though Lara does not remember the first nine months of her life at the orphanage premises, for her, it was as though she had found her lost siblings from years past with whom she was reunited once again. "I only wish my parents [adoptive] were able to share this experience with me, because I still have difficulty describing the emotions I felt when I was at my orphanage," recalled Lara of her feelings of those joyous moments in Dhaka (letter from Lara Morris to the author). Important to note, since Lara neither has any memories of her life in Bangladesh nor has she ever established her roots there, she never felt what is generally referred to as the "severance of links" with birth mother or putative father. She did not face transitory crisis reaction either – something that is generally caused by the great environmental and cultural changes experienced by older children.

"Although it is not a plan in my immediate future, I do believe I will one day return to Bangladesh, perhaps to do charity work of some sort," says Lara (letter from Lara Morris to the author). Although twenty-five years have passed by since Lara had visited Bangladesh, she has not planned anything concrete in that regard. It is encouraging to know that to this day, she has not ruled out that possibility either.

Lara's life in Canada centers upon various activities in the community from the time she was growing up. Evidently, she has accomplished a great deal. She belonged to Drum and Bugle Corps and Winter Color Guard in Ontario and Quebec from 1981 to 1990 and has received various awards both for group and individual performances. She was featured in the *Brantford Expositor* a few times, as well as in the cover story of the *London Free Press* and other local papers during the teenager's first trip to Bangladesh.

A charming and witty Lara, who impresses everyone with her cheerful buoyancy, was also on *Romper Room*, a variety show called *Tiny Talent Time*, and in the Sesame Street movie *Follow That Bird* (with the Drum Corps). Also as a table games dealer at Casino Niagara and a table games inspector at OLG Casino Brantford, Lara has received various letters of praise for exemplary job performance.

Lara remains very close to her family even to this day. She considers John and Dorothy as her dad and mom with incredible heartwarming love and had never pictured in her mind anyone else as her father and mother. The family keeps in close contact with each other regularly. With the exception of her brother Aaron who lives in Toronto, they all live in Brantford, communicate regularly, and usually get together on holidays and weekends for family dinners and "games nights."

Ray and Elisabeth Mowling

Initially the Mowlings lived in the Toronto area in Ontario, until 1971, where they adopted their first daughter, Laura. They then moved to the west end of Montreal, Quebec. In Montreal they adopted Onil, Panou, and Katy. The couple then moved back to Ontario again in 1976. The Mowlings wanted to adopt orphans from around the world as their own children. Like other adoptive couples in the present group, they were also interested in creating their family through adoption. As they were told that they could not have children, they looked for adoption with a passion that made them look outside of Canada. The couple had also kept their eyes open for those deemed hard-to-place orphans.

While living in Montreal, the Mowlings were also involved in a number of initiatives, international adoption being one of them. In fact, immediately after their arrival in Montreal back in 1971, the couple had joined a group of families in the west end of Montreal. At that time, Elisabeth was general secretary of the Montreal branch of *Terre des Hommes (TDH)*, a Geneva-based adoption agency devoted to the well-being of children around the world. Among other initiatives, the TDH was deeply involved in the adoption of Vietnamese orphans in Canada in the 1970s.

Earlier the Mowlings had joined the Families For Children (FFC), which officially came into being in 1971, although as we have read in chapter 3, it had been in existence informally for some time prior to its formal establishment. The Mowlings had worked closely with Lloyd and Sandra Simpson, Fred and Bonnie Cappuccino, and Herb and Naomi Bronstein of Montreal, Quebec. By then, pretty well all of these couples had already adopted mixed-race children from Vietnam, Cambodia, and/or Korea and were planning to do more.

Between 1971 and 1975, the Mowlings adopted four children. "Our first adoption was a mixed racial child and that started the cycle,"[37] said Ray Mowling, referring to Laura, who is a Canadian-born child of Irish and West Indian (Trinidadian parents); Onil, a war baby, is from Bangladesh; third son, Panou, is from Haiti; and the fourth child, Katie, is from Vietnam. In outward appearances, the children are as different from one another as they are from their Caucasian parents. After having four children, the Mowlings did not wish to expand their family. Believing that additional children might make it harder for them to take proper care of all, they turned their attention to persuading others to adopt internationally.

In July 1972, when the FFC team went to Bangladesh to negotiate with the government and pick out a dozen or two war babies, Elisabeth volunteered to accompany the rest of the team members. She joined the Cappuccinos and the Ferries and became a part of the Canadian team, having provided her own money for the airfare. (We have seen the details of the team's preparation outlined in chapter 3.) Despite the passage of time, Elisabeth still remembers her preparations for the trip to Bangladesh. There were the last minute's errands she had to do, packing of all kinds of sundry items for the orphans in the orphanages as part of the team's donation that they had collected prior to their trip.

Generally speaking, it is hard for any couple to pick and choose a child, as everyone seems to look for a healthy best-looking child. Sr. Margaret Mary, then superior of the Missionaries of Charity and statutory guardian of the war babies, had reservations about the health of many newborns at the time. In particular, she was not very hopeful about some of the war babies' health conditions. Since Elisabeth was there with the team, she had a chance to pick out one boy for herself. It was Onil who, she recalled, "was one of the tiny ones, with beautiful deep, wise eyes."[38] At the very first sight, Elisabeth was struck by the boy's serene look, making her feel as though he was very special to her (his future mother). She did not seem to have any problem at all in choosing Onil as their son right there on the spot even though the boy was unbelievably frail.

Elisabeth does not remember exactly what other factors had attracted her to this particular boy among other babies. All she remembers is that the little boy was lying there with beautiful deep eyes. "He was scrawny, sick and had no hair, but it was those eyes that made him look like someone special."[39] Elisabeth considers herself lucky as she was at the orphanage premises. She had the advantage of instantly choosing her own child. As they already had a daughter, her natural preference was for a boy, although she was open to the idea. The team was told that the boy was awfully frail, and yet she picked him. For Elisabeth, it was a matter of instantly falling in love with the child. The minute she made up her mind to pick the frail little boy from among other infants, she felt connected with a feeling tremendously close to the boy as the boy's "instant mother."

Although years have rolled by, Elisabeth remembers the dilapidated orphanages and makeshift *Seva Sadan* in Dhaka City that were mind-boggling, to say the least. It was a pathetic scene to be around so many infants many of whom were unable to survive – some were stillborn, while some others had died shortly after their birth.

Upon their return to Canada, many in the Montreal area were touched by the newspaper coverage and became interested to hear from Elisabeth about the Bangladesh Project. Naturally, she became very emotional following her trip: "It was a shock, the whole scene in

MUSTAFA CHOWDHURY

the orphanage in Bangladesh. I had suddenly found out how the rest of the world lives. When I got home, it suddenly hit me. I couldn't feel that other people around me, with their wealth, really understood, or really wanted to understand what it was like over there. I guess I needed people to ask me how they lived, and what they could do" (Elisabeth said in an interview with Anne Redfearn that was published in the *Brampton Guardian,* August 19, 1976).

Elisabeth continued fund-raising for the orphans of Bangladesh. Ray recalls they had many positive responses from the people in the neighborhood. This was a success, as she was able to generate a great deal of interest and awareness among the people in and around the Montreal area. In one of the regular meetings of FFC, Elisabeth took great pride in reporting how heartwarming was the response of the local members of FFC when asked to dig into their pockets for Bengali families in need.[40] The couple continued to work hard. In fact, by mid-1970 a dynamic Elisabeth came to prominence through the highly publicized Operation Baby Lift from Vietnam and Cambodia in the spring of 1975.

Like other adoptive parents under discussion, the Mowlings too remember the long and unpleasant wait that they were subjected to before receiving their desired child from Bangladesh. The process of birthing and adopting for both sets of parents is a kind of joyous, dizzying, and psychedelic journey in which there were some common essential elements. In many ways, Elisabeth believes both birthing and adopting were similar especially in light of the fact that a certain amount of preparation and anxiety, such as considerable uncertainty like the expectant mothers surrounding the adoption plans that frequently inhibited them.

The Mowlings had tried to help their children in forming a comprehensive view of life that can best serve them in adulthood, and one that gave them a sense of identity and security through values of life. They were aware that many people believe that it might be easy for a family to forget the difference of race and culture of people and treat the child *as if the child were white.* The Mowlings saw this to be problematic, for they believed it would leave the child vulnerable. They worked hard to surround their children with positive people of the same racial and ethnic backgrounds as well as to expose them to settings where diversity is highly valued. They ensured that their children learn about the culture of the country of their birth.

When the children were from five to seven years of age, Elisabeth and Ray were separated in 1977 after eleven years of marriage and divorced in 1981. The couple believes they stayed together as long as they did because of the children. Elisabeth became a single parent of four young children and entered the busiest ten years of her life at the time. The children were not affected by the divorce as one might be quick to suspect. Instead, it was just the opposite. They remained committed to their children in maintaining a warm, loving attitude while taking care of all.

Both parents used to spend weekends with their children, sometimes taking two at one time. Despite their divorce, the prospect of financial burden never arose as the couple settled it in a manner that had helped the mother receive regular support from the father. The Mowling children grew up at Elisabeth's Mississauga house, where all four children lived with the mother. She also had a live-in nanny, Jacki from St. Vincent, to take care of the younger children, and do errands and chores. In fact, Elisabeth had nothing but praise for her. The Mowlings were profiled in the local newspapers on many occasions as a truly multiracial family.

As a matter of fact, the news media was also full of praise for the Mowlings who had adopted children all from four different countries, believing in their hearts that adoption of these orphans was the *best* alternative – that what needed to be done was done. One of the local newspapers described the Mowling residence at Meadowvale area as "a home brimming with joy and laughter, the laughter of four bright little children, all practically the same age but with different backgrounds."[41] Eight years later, seeing that the Mowling children were thriving in then single mom Elisabeth's house, another local newspaper accorded Elisabeth in a Mother's Day tribute, saying "the Village Mom [who] is a classic" who is "one of the most loving and lovely families in Meadowvale Village."[42]

Interesting to note, in many ways, Elisabeth's situation was quite different than other adoptive parents since she became a single mom. Between 1977 and 1986, Elisabeth single-handedly raised their children with the help of Jackie, the nanny whose name has just been mentioned. Even when Elisabeth was all by herself, she remained firm in what she believes: "it is obvious to me, as it must be to every parent, that a child needs a family in order to thrive," says Elisabeth (e-mail from Elisabeth Mowling to Mustafa Chowdhury, June 14, 2004). "Despite the best intentions and care in an orphanage, it is not possible to have the one-on-one-bonding, that a child should have with a mother and/or father in a family," argued Elisabeth (e-mail from Elisabeth Mowling to the author).

Elisabeth remembers those days when she enjoyed the cooking – large pots of spaghetti sauce and chili come to mind. Fortunately for the children, Jackie was well liked and became very popular with the children – one less thing for Elisabeth to worry about. Despite the usual stress and strain, Elisabeth recalls those years with fond memories: "At night, each child would hear their favorite song, and get tucked in, although I was often pretty tired. They all liked different songs, of course. Since there were only 18 months between the oldest and the youngest, anything that helped them define their personal space or preference was usually chosen" (e-mail from Elisabeth Mowling to the author). Opting to go back to work later on, she returned to teaching in a vocational high school. This was the time when Elisabeth recalled she used to come home at around the same time as the kids, involving a lot of driving – school, swimming classes, T ball, Brownies, martial arts, grocery shopping, buying clothing, etc.

One of Elisabeth's greatest skills was her particular way of parenting with openness with her children within a broad parameter that the children had to follow. The family used to have weekly family meetings when the kids would talk about *how* things were going and *what* they wanted to change. Elisabeth continued to raise the children this way until the kids were teenagers. In 1986 when her second husband, John, joined them, the family environment changed slightly – a change for the better. Needless to say, both John, the stepfather, and the children got along very well. He was a teacher at the high school where she taught, so teenagers did not scare him, she recalls. There was not any problem as is often the case with many teenagers. Ray too remarried in 1981 and had a son by his second wife. All got along very well, and the little boy, in turn, says Ray, had "adopted my older children as his brothers and sisters" (e-mail from Ray Mowling to the author). Shortly after that, Elisabeth left teaching and became a psychotherapist. This was her profession for twenty-four years, until her retirement in 2000.

Elisabeth's recollection with respect to Onil is still vivid. Around October 1971, they heard the news about the war babies who were being born in Bangladesh fathered by the Pakistani enemy soldiers. They also learned that these newborns would not have a good chance for a loving family or a good future in their country of birth. It only made sense to them to adopt such orphans who were seen as "unwanted" in their own country due to the stigma surrounding their birth. The Mowlings believed that these children would need loving families that were not available in Bangladesh. As they saw it, since Canada had no involvement in the two sides of the war, it did not matter to them who fathered such babies.

Elisabeth takes pride in her children whom she has raised, partly with her first husband, Ray, and partly with John, her current husband, although for ten years she was a single mom who managed the entire family all by herself. In recalling the resilience of the babies from overseas, there was something that had amazed the Mowlings right from the beginning when they started parenting. Their doctor would usually say something to the effect that their "child is too severely damaged and should never have been adopted" (e-mail from Elisabeth Mowling to the author). However, their experience was that, in every case, six months or a year later, the child would astound every witness with his progress. The Mowlings spoke confidently, saying that once the children knew they were emotionally safe and loved, they were played with, and, of course, physically looked after, they blossomed beyond their imaginations.

In talking about their family tradition, Elisabeth mentioned how they used to follow a tradition of their *own* that they had created while their children were growing up with regard to their children's birthdays. "We would celebrate 2 'birthdays' for each of the children. One was the actual date of their birth, celebrated with cake and presents, and usually a party; the second was the date of their arrival, which we celebrated with a cake" (e-mail from Elisabeth Mowling to the author). Not only that, but also they used to tell the children the stories of *how* they were chosen and of their travels from their country of birth. Elisabeth recalls, since Laura was adopted in Ontario, she would sometimes complain that the other kids all arrived on an airplane, but she merely arrived in a car.

Although the couple took their children to the local Unitarian Church on Sundays, both parents believed to remain open and flexible in terms of religion. They felt that the children needed to be exposed to the teachings of God, that they should be shown the principles of individual freedom of belief, the preservation of personal integrity, and the search for truth through critical integrity.

Another interesting aspect of the Mowling family is that, over the years, the Mowling children have bonded very deeply among all family members that has remained very strong even to this day. While raising their children, Elisabeth frequently had to deal with questions with respect to race, culture, and identity from different perspectives. Looking back, Elisabeth says that although she was not aware of the past lives of the children at the time of adopting their children, imagining children of different races or born in different parts of the world as her *own* was easy and appealing to her.

Naturally, the mother takes pride in observing how her children came to view themselves: "They did not see that they were of different races. They saw each other truly, and related as brothers and sisters – playing together at times or squabbling over toys, and splashing each other in the bathtub. Just as the shape of our brother or sister's nose is not important to us, so the shade of each other's skin color was not important to them" (e-mail from Elisabeth Mowling to the author). While raising their children, Elisabeth frequently had to deal with questions with respect to race, culture, and identity from different perspectives.

They remember the occasional outright glaring or curious stares at them at shopping malls or at the parks when they had their children of diverse backgrounds with them. Over the years, the Mowlings had heard one question over and over with regard to their children of different backgrounds: *How many are your own?* Naturally, Elisabeth became used to this particular question having heard endless times. Not surprisingly, a calm and courteous Elisabeth used to have a prompt and succinct retort: "These are all my own children."[43]

As a parent, Elisabeth believes that one of the most important points to remember is to be utterly frank with one's child regarding adoption: "The parents and the child must both feel good about it and discuss it. This can't be minimized for any multi-racial child. On the other hand, you've got to make him feel secure, that his home is permanent."[44] As far as the Mowlings are concerned, knowledge about one's own background, culture, and country of origin is critical in developing a positive self-esteem. "This makes it very difficult for a child to feel proud of her race. But it is important she be made to feel good about it deep down. The child's race, country, culture and the fact that she is adopted, are things the parents should feel good about too." (*Homemaker,* November 1975, p.12)

Today Laura is an artist and art teacher who is dealing with chronic fatigue and currently not able to work. She has a love of learning, which shows in her ability to deal with people. She has found her Trinidadian birth mother, full brother, and three cousins in the Toronto area, who all resemble her. All are unusually beautiful and handsome. Panou moved to Vancouver, British Columbia, to join the movie industry. He is a successful actor. He does not keep as much in touch with the family as the other three. He will phone Katy for her birthday; she touches everyone's heart. Katy, a slow learner, loves her work in a French bakery, where she has been for a great number of years. She is much appreciated there for her sensitive nature, friendliness, and willingness to work. Katy lives in her own apartment and receives some weekly support to help with grocery shopping, paying bills, activities such as line dancing and swimming, and going on outings.

Despite the fact that the Mowling children have moved out and are scattered around, the Mowlings are still bonded by the feelings of oneness with which they grew up. It is this strength that helps all their children to continue with life with all its ups and downs.

Onil

Born on May 23, 1972, at *Shishu Bhavan,* Dhaka, Bangladesh, the baby boy weighed three kilograms at birth. Like other war babies, he was also abandoned at birth by the birth mother who wished to remain anonymous. The orphanage authority named him Onil having given no other name. When Onil arrived in Canada at the age of less than eight weeks, he weighed little over 2.3 kg, having lost some weight since birth for malnutrition. One good thing about the frail boy was that even though he was underweight, he was not ill at all. In fact, he was a perfectly healthy boy otherwise.

Following his arrival in the Mowlings family in Canada, Onil used to scream a lot during the first few months, recalled the couple. It was only at a later time that the Mowlings had learned that Onil was allergic to the milk formula that the babies were given initially in the orphanage. They were relieved and delighted to see when the baby thrived on soya milk. Fortunately, within weeks, Onil began to gain weight.

The Mowlings retained the boy's name given at the orphanage as his middle name, having added the name Mark as his first name and Mowling as the family's surname during his formal adoption in Canada. Thus, Onil came to be known as Mark Onil Mowling.

Onil attended Meadowvale Public School in Meadowvale from 1977 to 1984. He went to J. A. Turner Secondary School in Brampton, Ontario, where he completed grade XIII in 1990. Following that, Onil also attended York University part time from 1995 to 2000. During his early years, he had continued his study of psychology at York University, Toronto. He also attended workshops and training courses in holistic healing techniques. Graciella Damewood of the Open Way Institute was one of Onil's teachers whom he remembers with deference. In fact, Damewood's perceptiveness had aided in Onil's emotional and spiritual journey and in enhancing his understanding particularly more about himself and others.

Onil does not remember the exact age when he came to understand the meaning of the word "adoption," although it had been a household word in the Mowling family in which all four children were adopted. He remembers his mother had been very open to him about his birth history. According to Elisabeth, it was important for her son to know the truth about the circumstances under which he was conceived, born, abandoned, and adopted. Looking back, Onil says his parents had ensured that every bit of information that was given to him was age appropriate. Naturally, with that in mind, they provided information to Onil and other children with caution. Initially, the parents were a bit nervous despite their cautious thinking about the pace of revelation and sharing of his "story." Looking back, Onil says he is happy with the ways in which he had learned about his birth history.

During the last several years, Onil had thought about trying a number of things with regard to his career. At one time, he thought about joining the police services. This had remained in his head for a while until his interest diminished to the point that he never acted on this. At another time, he became interested in and received training on tai chi to the instructor level, as well as in many other related courses. Over the years, Onil has changed jobs and has worked in many places. If and when he is unemployed, he continues to find another job and does not dawdle away his time.

Onil's people skills come in handy in preparing him for the workplace. By nature, Onil is optimistic even when he is faced with difficulties that tend to compound and exacerbate the situations, making one realize as though one is up the creek. One of Onil's greatest qualities is that he never abandons himself to despair. Given the pattern of chopping and changing on his part, one might be inclined to brand Onil as a typical Canadian who wants to enjoy his "freedom" first. No sooner had he started his studies than he began to feel that he needed to modify his plan. He would calmly say to himself that everyone makes mistakes and one cannot design a perfect mousetrap right at first shot. While doing psychotherapy in partnership with his mother, who is a psychotherapist by profession, he does not think for a minute that he is unrealistic or that he is pursuing something that is not achievable.

In fact, he uses the benefits of learning about and engaging in psychotherapy as a way to realize his own emotional contentment and nurture his own treasured heart. Being warm and spontaneous in his reaction, Onil's social skills have prepared him for the workplace of the future. Every time he changed his plan, he would say to himself he would worry about other things when they come to the crunch. Even when he was at the peak of his frustration, Onil never fell into despondency. As far as Onil is concerned, he is able to assess himself realistically, having taken into consideration his faults and follies along with his capabilities and potentials. He is rooted on the ground.

It is interesting to interject here that despite the usual parental worries and anxieties, his parents never interfered in their children's affairs, having provided them all the support they needed to make informed decisions. Even when Onil was chopping and changing his mind and work plan, they refrained from giving unsolicited advice and let him follow his bent. One important point that emerged from the parents' narratives is a sense of independence that they have tried to instill in their children's minds.

Onil knows, and confesses without any hesitation, that he had changed his career goals so many times that he cannot even keep track of it anymore. And yet Onil does not have any regret. Onil neither hankers after money nor does he have any great difficulty in finding employment to keep the pot boiling. Having worked at various places, Onil is presently working at Cadillac Fairview in the Toronto area and offers training courses for smaller security companies (Delta Security) in his spare time.

With his keen and comprehensive intellect and finely attuned perceptiveness regarding people and situation, Onil is quick to impress others as a smart man. Naturally, he is extremely warm and spontaneous in his interaction with the people who might come from a variety of backgrounds. Identity or self-respect had never been a question with Onil. In talking about identity crisis, which is pretty common with many adoptees especially when adopted in a racially different family, Onil feels that is he is a person with a sense of self-worth, having been clear about his own unified identity in Canada, the country he calls home. He is content with what he knows about his own background history.

He has no reason to be contemptuous of or mad at anyone in that regard. Development of a positive sense of identity and mental health is at risk when vital background and personal information are not available, argues Onil, who sees himself as an individual with a background quite different from most of the ethnic groups including Bangladeshis. Even during his teen years when adoptees generally tend to question everything, a coolheaded Onil confronted any and all questions with amazing calmness.

Onil emphasizes that he did not have to *unlearn* anything in Canada as is often the case with many older adoptees that come from different cultures and countries. The first six weeks of life in Bangladesh following his birth at a Dhaka orphanage had left no impression in his life at all. Bangladesh remains a distant country to Onil. As a matter of fact, according to Onil, when he "thinks of Bangladesh, he thinks of the tigers, the busy streets of Dhaka and the heat,"[45] that's all.

A determined Onil grew up knowing that he is a Canadian who was born in Bangladesh. In that sense, in a way, Onil did not seek a separate cultural identity having considered him a polyglot of races, languages, and religions. Instead, he was more comfortable in seeing himself to be a member of the world community. He never concerned himself as to how other people perceive him in Canada. Like other war babies we have looked at, Onil sees himself to be "different" from his (white) friend but a child of his (white) parents. Onil thus grew up considering him "Canadian" by all definition.

Therefore, as far as Onil is concerned, his past experiences have allowed him to make his own decisions and actions, and he finds it difficult to compare himself with other ethnic groups. Even though the question of his birth parents had existed in his mind during his adolescent years, there had never been a void in his life because of it. Unlike many adoptees that worry a lot about identity and birth history, Onil's main goal in his late teens was to find a better understanding of himself.

It was not until later years when he was in his late teens and early twenties that he had some serious questions about the *why* and the *how* of adoption from Bangladesh. He remembered learning from his mother about the circumstances surrounding his birth but did not want to dig into the story any further. He did some thinking along this vein and recognized and reconfirmed what he had thought about himself – that he is indeed different. He began to see more clearly that his skin was different than his parents and many of his friends at school.

This, however, was not a source of concern for a mature and coolheaded Onil. In that sense, Onil never felt, nor does he feel now, any urge to dig up his past to reflect on his birth history. He does not hesitate to say that he had been a nonsearcher all his life. A contended Onil is quite emphatic in saying that his survival and happiness had never been based on knowing *who* his birth parents *are,* or *were.*

Onil, however, recalls when he was growing up, he often wondered about the possibility of finding genetic information through his birth record, which might be needed sometime in the future. There were times when his speculations about certain hereditary diseases made him worry for a while. Some of his persistent thoughts had also turned into a persistent silent question about *who* he *looks* like. But after a while, he also recognized the impossibility of ever finding any information through his birth records, which contain no such information at all. He was able to give up the idea quite easily and move on with his life without further stress.

Again, Onil maintains that he had never experienced any feeling of isolation or alienation because of his adoption into a family where parents are white. At the same time, Onil is quick to point out that isolation is something he "had felt not because of being adopted but because of feeling and thinking different from others" (letter from Onil Mowling to the author, cited in notes and references). Onil espouses humanist values and sees himself as an individual without having to define himself in terms of a particular culture and ethnicity. *Is that a denial of social reality that surrounds him?* Or, *is this perhaps a denial of a person's own innermost feelings and thoughts?* One might say, perhaps yes, or perhaps no.

As far as Onil is concerned, having known exactly *who* he is, he himself provides the answer. One of the turning points in his life, says Onil, is the reading of a book titled *The Way of the Peaceful Warrior* by Dan Millman given to him by his mother. This was a timely gift by his mother: "This seemed to be necessary at the time. I think we all want to find a place in this world. I needed to identify with something" (letter from Onil Mowling to the author). Though still at his late teens, Onil read the book over and over again having found it extraordinarily interesting. He sees this as a turning point in his life because reading of this book had helped him develop his own perception of life and reality.

Onil does not have any longing to reunite with his birth mother. As a child, he used to dream a lot: "My dreams as a child were not about being rescued but returning home," recalls Onil (letter from Onil Mowling to the author, cited in notes and references). *What was that home like? Where was it?* In a particular recurrent dream that lasted for two long years, Onil recalls he was with five other children in a mall, "all waiting to be picked up from a place on Earth and brought back to our solar system of origin to meet with our families." Their mode of transportation was the ability to fly only at a certain time. It was as though someone would give them the ability to use this gift at some point while they were waiting for people at home to initiate contact.

Strange as it may sound, though, Onil does not recall ever dreaming about his birth parent, but in some way, this might be a representation of them. In his dreams, he used to think that he was an alien child from another planet. All this happened when he was a mere child. As he matured over the years, he became more of a practical man who, then on, knows the impossibility of it given the circumstances under which he was born and abandoned in Bangladesh. He deeply appreciated his parents' decision to adopt him by overcoming numerous barriers at a time when they could have easily adopted a child right from Canada.

During his early teen years, Onil had to deal with a number of issues that were typical of adolescent and were not necessarily connected with his past: "I found plenty of personal issues to come to terms with, without desiring the need to know my real parents. Only after I had dealt with my internal conflicts then I was ready to know about my parents," says Onil (letter from Onil Mowling to the author). Needless to say, for many adoptees, adolescence is generally turbulent and filled with low self-esteem and feelings of worthlessness. Fortunately, that was not the case with the other war babies also. Unlike many adoptees that move into adulthood under the cloud of anxiety, depression, low self-esteem, and chronic illness, they had moved on in their lives with no such baggage. Being utterly frank, Onil says, "I have not been interested in picturing my birth parents because I envision my mother in a Sari. So her face is not revealed. I have pictured my father in a military outfit, after I heard of the conditions of my conception" (letter from Onil Mowling to the author).

Thus, the theme of reunion, which is so common with adoptees in general, is absent in Onil's case. Having learned about the sexual violence of the Pakistani military personnel, Onil is always very respectful of his birth mother *whom* he sees as a victim. To Onil, she is neither a woman of disrepute nor selfish and uncaring. Naturally, he is very sensitive to and appreciative of his birth mother's predicament because of rape and subsequent social rejection in Bangladesh. As far as Onil is concerned, there is no need to punish the birth mother for relinquishing her child. Every time Onil thinks of his birth mother, he thanks her for trying her best. He thanks her again for giving him up when she knew that she could not have offered him what he needed as a child.

Onil understands and appreciates this without any reservation, although there are many adoptees that hold grudges against their birth mothers for abandonment, whatever might have been the circumstances or reasons. The way Onil sees it, a biological mother who is truly a victim of circumstances could well be affectionate and caring under normal circumstances. His birth mother had no choice, given her situation and the society's defined position on such matters. Put it succinctly, Onil has deep sympathy for his unknown and violated birth mother and, by extension, for all such victims.

Thus, apart from occasional dreams with regard to reunion with his birth family while as a mere child, he no longer had any disillusionment about such concept of reunion. Instead, to fulfill many of his desires, he spoke at great length with his mother (Elisabeth), the only mother he has known all his life. Onil credits his parents who have raised them since the time they were babies. Despite his parents' marriage breakdown in 1977 when he was only five years old, his family relationships have survived with no adverse impact on him or his siblings, maintains Onil.

As mentioned under the Mowlings, and now reinforced by Onil, one of the most important things that the Mowlings had ensured and agreed upon prior to their separation/divorce was the children's priorities, which were to be their priorities regardless of where the two parents live. Onil's remark makes it evident how amicably both parents had thought through parenting and made arrangements for the children to visit each parent on alternative weekends. Onil also touches on another important point – that adoptive parents, like birth parents, are not guaranteed to deal with teenage issues any better than the natural parents.

Onil had never visited Bangladesh ever since he came to Canada at the age of less than eight weeks. As far as he is concerned, this is not to say that he does not intend to visit Bangladesh at all. Although he has not planned any visit, he does not want to negate that possibility. In fact, Onil hopes that if opportunities present themselves, he would jump at them for sure. When in Bangladesh, he would like to do some voluntary work there, perhaps at the same orphanage where he was born. Onil acknowledges those who took care of him when he was born and remains humble in expressing his gratitude: "because I owe them my life and all the blessings that I have received, it would be a great honor to do my part in Bangladesh (letter from Onil Mowling to the author, cited in notes and references). However, since chances of going to Bangladesh seemed like a remote possibility in his early years, a practical Onil was quick to take a different approach to such desires.

He recognized early enough that his country of birth was far away from Canada and that he has been living in Canada all his life. Ever since he reached the age of majority, he had been involved in a number of areas that he had been pursuing. In his own words, "I have been working at providing my service and good will to those around me here in Canada," says Onil (letter from Onil Mowling to the author). He continues to add, "My path is to help protect and honor the relationships between women and men or men women and to help others do the same if they are ready. That is, I teach sexual assault prevention courses. And that is why I have identified myself with Nemesis" (letter from Onil Mowling to the author).

Having decided to get into martial arts as a way of doing something for the victims of sexual aggression, Onil feels that he has been doing something worthwhile. While on this very sensitive and important topic, Onil pointed out: "Long before I knew the meaning of my name or the past of birth parents, I took up the pursuit of the Martial Arts. I began to teach workshops on rape prevention. One of my greatest teachers Graciella Damewood and Dan Millman both said, 'what will be, will be.' I continue to respect them" (Letter from Onil Mowling to the author).

At the end of the day, when all is said and done, an apathetic Onil remains disinterested in Bangladesh and Bangladeshis, although he never denies his Bangladeshi roots. If he runs into anyone who happens to be a Bengali, it would be fine; again, if he does not come across any, it would not be the end of the world for him. The point he tries to make is that it really does not matter to him personally whether he meets or does not meet any Bengali or Pakistani.

There is something interesting, and somewhat enigmatic, with regard to Onil's reaction to the way in which people pronounce and/or misspell his name. Although, by and large, Onil is rather detached from Bangladesh and not terribly passionate about the country in which he was born, he is definitely angered when people do not call him Onil, the name that was given by the sisters in the orphanage following the language of his birth mother. A frank and candid Onil said that every time people misspell his name as "O'Neil," instead of "Onil," he gets turned off. In fact whenever people address him or write to him as O'Neil Mowling, he gets annoyed. It even bothers his parents who chose to retain the original Bengali name given by the orphanage authority in Bangladesh. Hearing or reading Onil's name differently had always been a source of annoyance to the Mowlings. Onil's resentment may be interpreted as a reflection of Onil's sentimental love and respect for the people who gave him a Bengali name. Nevertheless, despite his Bengali name and part Bengali and/or Pakistani heritage, Onil chooses to identify with Canada and Canadians. To quote Onil, "I still remain distant from celebrating Bengali customs or independence." (Letter from Onil Mowling to the author).

MUSTAFA CHOWDHURY

Recently Onil got married to Melissa Bartello who is Canadian with an Italian heritage. Born in Toronto and raised in Bolton, she became a registered nurse and works at hospital in the cancer care. Interesting to note, Mel and Onil met at a special bar one special night in the fall of 2012. Not only did they hit it off and become good friends, but also they soon started dating. "Knowing the fit with each other was right, we got married on February 1, in 2014," recalls Onil (e-mail from Onil to the author, June 30, 2014).

Onil lives in Toronto, while his parents are in Mississauga. For all practical purposes, Onil is only a phone call away from his parents. Needless to say, he is ever ready to show his indebtedness to his parents who have provided him and his siblings a wonderfully supportive and loving environment. Onil remains bonded to his siblings with whom he grew up feeling the same, as they share a similar story. He meets them every now and then and enjoys the best of time with his family members.

Roberto and Margo Ribeiro

Originally from Colombia, South America, Roberto and his wife, Margo, a French Canadian, both worked for the Canadian International Development Agency (CIDA) all through the late 1960s to 1990s. Like other adoptive couples under discussion, the Ribeiros too took deep interest in adopting racially different orphans in need of a safe home. Unlike the usual couples who make family through natural-born children, the Ribeiros took special interest in having children through adoption, something they simply saw as another means of constructing one's family.

This is where the Ribeiros stand apart from the usual fertile couples. Following the birth of their first child, Marie Helene, the Ribeiros decided to have another child. This was in late 1971 when they were quite aware of the political unrest in Pakistan. The couple was well abreast of the demands of the Bengalis, the tough and uncompromising position of the military dictator, and the Bengalis' struggle for independence. They were appalled to see the killings of unarmed civilians and torture by the Pakistani military personnel. At the same time, through his voluntary work with the Families For Children (FFC), Roberto had kept himself posted on the efforts of the organization and its proposed project to save the war babies of Bangladesh who were being born at the time.

Fortunately, Roberto, who was with the Nongovernment Organization (NGO) Division of CIDA at the time, was actively involved with a host of national and international organizations that were focused on issues facing the Indian subcontinent at the time. Specifically, in early 1972, CIDA was engaged in assisting the war-ravaged Bangladesh to rebuild the newly independent country. Personally both Roberto and Margo were aware of yet another social issue the government of Bangladesh was faced with at the time of birth and abandonment of the war babies. As head of NGO Division, Roberto wanted to "do something" about this issue. His personal awareness of the situation in Bangladesh and his voluntary work with FFC had thus triggered the family's interest even more for a Bangladeshi war baby. Without any delay, the couple made a formal request for a war baby through the FFC. The couple remains disinclined to talk about their experiences or their recollection of the time when the children were growing up.

The Ribeiro family consists of five children, four of whom were adopted from Bangladesh, Vietnam, Haiti, and Colombia. Naturally, with the adoption of their children from different countries, the family became multiracial, although French remained the spoken language in the family. As the Ribeiros had a chance to travel and live outside of Canada while at CIDA, the Ribeiro children were exposed to many cultures and languages at the same time. In raising their multiracial children, the Ribeiros emphasized the notion of "Canadianness" in the hope that they become truly Canadian. They purposefully de-emphasized the cultures of their children's country of birth, as they believed it is important for the children to grow up as "Canadian."

The Ribeiros have sweet memories of Shomor, whom they named Martin during his formal adoption in Canada. Right from the time Martin was picked out by Fred and Bonnie Cappuccino for the Ribeiros, their memories have remained embedded in their minds – feelings that grew into a quieter yearning for the baby. Comparing the restlessness of the time, Margo says "it was like having a labor pain," which she "would not like to talk about in public."[46] Although Roberto met and talked to the author, both remain tight-lipped and taciturn when it comes to sharing their experience of raising their multiracial children. They do not want to talk about stories of personal nature in public.

MUSTAFA CHOWDHURY

Because the family lived away from Canada for quite a number of years when the children were growing up, the Ribeiros did not get a chance to network with other adoptive families who were in touch with each other. There are a few records at the Cappuccinos' personal collection of the couple's correspondence. Evidently, Margo was in touch with both Bonnie Cappuccino and Sr. Margaret Mary in Bangladesh initially after the arrival of their son. Because the couple was out of the loop, having no interaction with the adoptive parents from the same bunch, Martin grew up with a lack of interest in his country of birth.

According to Roberto, initially Martin was an easygoing little boy with a big smile who used to readily make friends. Within a short period, the family, however, began to see complications in Martin. They thought Martin might need some extra time to get up to speed, and that's all. They remained under the impression that Martin had had a slight learning disability. This was something that they had recognized early on, which they naïvely thought they could handle themselves. They consulted their personal physician and worked closely with specialists, such as therapists, special educators, and counselors whom they were referred to in the early years. The Ribeiros were also advised by the psychologists that children with psychological symptoms are often likely to have problems of self-identity and difficulties in interpersonal relationships. While Martin was growing up, his parents were mindful of such precautionary remarks.

Appreciating the fact that children with a learning disability often need some additional help in working through their problems, the Ribeiros tried to explore various ways to deal with the issue. They worked closely with specialists who were assigned to Martin over the years when his learning disabilities had set him apart from experiences, relationships, and tasks that were appropriate to his age and his social environment.

For many years while Martin was growing up, the couple had reflected a great deal on things they had no control over – such as birth mother's poor diet and nutrition, trauma from neglect, prenatal care, or a lack of stimulation during the period before they became Martin's caregiver, etc., which they believe have affected Martin's intelligence. Much to their deep chagrin, they were informed that Martin is developmentally slow and that he needed to be treated as such to succeed in life. While dealing with Martin's mental issues, the

Ribeiros were advised by pretty well all, such as physicians, therapists, mental health professionals, and special educators, on *how* and *why* such conditions are caused in one's life.

Notwithstanding the fact that Martin's challenges were many, the family continued to seek advice and follow the instructions of the specialists by never giving up hope. In doing so, the family's first challenge was to shoulder additional responsibility of ensuring his acceptance within the family, especially the siblings.

In fact, this remained one of the important dimensions of the family relationships – demonstrations of love as they pertain to the Ribeiro children. The very way in which all children all are loved by and cared for equally where nobody is ever made to feel to be at the bottom of the family totem pole is a remarkable example of the Ribeiros' parenting skills. By sharing the care and treatment of Martin from an early age, the Ribeiros were able to be involved in a way that every member of the family became fully cognizant of what it meant to have a sibling with a "learning disability," thus creating a happy, harmonious, and gratifying home despite setbacks.

All through those tiring times, the family had demonstrated unwavering love and support of the absolute position as parents-in-charge. Despite the lapse of time, Martin's father maintains that having progressed in life, Martin was still developmentally behind what is considered the "norm" for his respective age. The Ribeiros prefer to remain private.

Shomor

Upon arriving Canada, Shomor's parents named him Martin Ribeiro, having dropped the original name Shomor. As was with most other war babies, Martin was underweight who was prematurely born on April 7, 1972, weighing only one kilogram at birth. At the time of his arrival, Martin was just over three months old and weighed less than two kilograms. His parents' first challenge, among other ones, was to pay extra attention to see that the baby gets nutritious food and gains adequate weight rapidly. Fortunately, as time went by, Martin began to gain weight and be active just like other normal child of his age.

As Martin began to grow, he attended the local elementary school in Hull, Quebec, like all other children of his age. It was at that time that his parents began to notice what may be called "abnormalities" or "irregularities," which made them anxious. This was a red flag that immediately made them worry about anticipated pedagogic challenges that Martin would likely face. The family began to notice signs of deterioration more and more, although he appeared to be quite normal otherwise. According to Roberto, they saw how Martin used to have difficulty taking in, sorting out, and connecting information from the world around him. As parents, they were distressed to see how quickly Martin's problems had already started to affect his behavior, his speech, his play, and his ability to understand and get along with others.

Learning about Martin being developmentally slow with a learning disability was heartbreaking but not heart-stopping for the courageous Ribeiros. Their first challenge was to attempt at understanding their own feelings toward the medically needy Martin who, by then, had created an early parenting experience for the Ribeiros far difficult from having ideal and healthy children they had dreamed earlier. Having been thrown in a situation of stress, in all practicality, they immediately immersed in understanding the issues, such as Martin's intellectual capacities and their implications vis-à-vis his siblings' attitudes and relationship of his siblings to the extent possible.

Consequently, they did not seem to find themselves in unchartered water when it came to parenting Martin despite being at a high risk for attachment problems. Their immediate reaction was to do a bit of homework – researching on learning disabilities to get some clues for narrowing the field of issues. Lack of oxygen to the brain is thought to have caused Martin's learning disability. The next step was to seek help and address the illness in the hope that it would make a positive difference. Having demystified their struggle as it related to Martin's illness, it was then a matter of reframing – changing perspectives so as not to be pessimistic but be able to develop coping strategies.

As the couple delved into the matter, both parents came to learn more about Martin's learning disabilities – that are due to a brain damage or inefficiency in the working of the brain. As well, they learned that there might have been other factors such as infection, problems during pregnancy, or genetic factors that could have contributed to affecting his intelligence. In the absence of any detailed medical history, Martin's parents had to rely on what medical diagnosis possible without going back to his birth history the details of which were missing. They accepted this fact with strength and courage. Having coped with their own feelings of shock and surprise, they moved on to face the challenges head-on.

Martin had always been fortunate to have parents and siblings around who were quick to adjust to the situations due to his particular type of illness. Commendably, everyone around recognized that there was a genetic predisposition toward some learning disabilities and some mental issues with Martin. The family, including its extended members, demonstrated an understanding of the situation Martin was placed in. No family members ever showed annoyance at any unsuccessful effort Martin made, nor did they consistently demand a level of performance of which he was not always capable.

As the Ribeiros recall, taking a look at both the external and internal forces that were acting on Martin had helped the family understand Martin's predicament better, allowing them all to move forward. It had not taken long to come to terms with the reality that Martin was indeed different. The family members firmly believed that being different did not mean being less and that Martin needed to be treated differently in order to achieve the same results.

Though emotionally arduous, they were able to adjust to Martin — *as is,* having faced squarely within the context of his abilities/disabilities vis-à-vis his intelligence. The Ribeiros maintain that there were symptoms that indicated that Martin had intrapsychic conflicts and stresses. Those who treated him observed that consequently such stress had slowed down his development on a cognitive, psychological, and social level. He was in need of constant therapeutic help, protection, and parental help. Naturally, his siblings gave him the necessary support, which helped Martin to have a strong determination to do well.

Fortunately, as time went by, Martin's situation had ameliorated to the point that he was able to make slight but tangible progress. Martin's parents also came to know *how* and *when* Martin needed to be commended for his efforts at studies, praised for his improvement, and be aware of *what* and *how* his limitations needed to be accepted by the rest of the family members including all siblings. Simply through nurturing and showing sensitivity to their son's unique needs, the parents created a good quality father-mother-son relationship and helped him attain his highest degree of self-independence. In doing so, the Ribeiros had demonstrated their filial love, and unusual parental skills and capacities.

Roberto is not sure whether due to his "learning disabilities," Martin was not interested in his country of birth or anything along that line. What he is sure of is that Martin has had a knowledge gap and that he had never expressed any interest in finding anything about his background, the country in which he was born and had lived for the first ninety days of his life. Simply put, Martin had never shown any interest in knowing anything about Bangladesh.

Whether Martin feels completely disjointed from his Bangladeshi heritage is hard to tell. What is true is that he grew up feeling little to no association with Bangladesh or anything to do with Bangladesh, the country he was born in, or Bangladeshi Diaspora of which he is a part. Adopted only at the age of three months and having been surrounded mostly by Caucasian friends and acquaintances, Martin never had an opportunity to interact with Canadians of the subcontinental background. Consequently, he never had to deal with a different identity or multiple identities, as is usually the case with many racially different minorities in Canada.

Nevertheless, his lack of interest, as mentioned by his father, is understandable given his early learning disabilities. Because of his mental state, they did not push him, fearing that this might raise his discomfort and distress, recalled Roberto. Although it was noticeable to both Dad and Mom in early years, they chose not to burden Martin additionally by highlighting historical facts about Bangladesh and the tragic story surrounding his birth, relinquishment, and adoption in Canada. Roberto believes that no one can ever tell *if* Martin is *ever* bothered by his inability to explain *who* he *is* or *where* he comes from originally. Having lived in Quebec since the age of three months, Bangladesh remains a faraway country in his mind, bearing no emotional relations on him as a person.

The Ribeiros don't think Martin would ever be interested in Bangladesh, as the emotions regarding Bangladesh and its people are always foreign to him. Given his lack of interest and the milieu in which he lives with his family, chances are he would never turn to Bangladesh even as a mere curiosity. The family recognizes that people with learning disabilities want to learn, but their neurological wiring often frustrates their efforts. An emotional dad wondered if the disconnection that had always been his safety net would ever transfer into a coming of age, giving him a feeling of a need to finally come to terms with his birth history, which had never raised in his mind even the slightest curiosity.

In fact, this is where Martin stands apart from the rest of the war babies who came to Canada with him. He never read even a guide book or history text on Bangladesh much unlike other ones who had read and learned quite a bit about their country of birth, being interested on their own. As a result, Martin remains unable even to have any imaginary connection with Bangladesh or the people of Bangladesh. He is rooted in Canada, the country he calls "home."

Despite Martin's limitations and pedagogic challenges that he has experienced from his early childhood, over the years, he has made good progress toward it. Overcoming setbacks, a disadvantaged Martin did not turn out to be the kind of boy to hide behind his mom's skirt. He has made definite strides in learning and developing life skills. Through sheer determination and with the family's help, he was able to attain his highest degree of self-independence.

The profiles of the Ribeiros and Martin are based on the bits and pieces of information that the author was able to collect through his informal meeting over coffee at the office premises, mainly through Roberto. What transpired out of his brief meetings over coffee is that at the end of the day, Martin had achieved emotional health and competence despite a history of adversity. His parents had remained determined to do all they could for Martin in the hope that while nature might be stranger than nurture, good nurturing and a positive environment could still make all the difference. Despite all odds, having encountered a series of barriers and stumbling blocks that appeared overwhelming, Martin overcame them to a great extent.

Having successfully handled many hurdles of complex nature and despite his limitations, Martin has made great strides. Though he did not pursue his high school studies, he had been successful in finding employment at a security company to make a decent living. Martin got married a few years ago and began to raise his family. In a sense, the self-entertaining and independent Martin had always been proud of his accomplishments. Unfortunately, and sadly to say the least, all of a sudden Martin had a massive heart attack in July 2013 and died instantly. The bereaved family did not wish to talk about Martin despite the author's effort to speak with his sister Marie Helene, who simply thanked the author for making the inquiry but was not interested to talk about her brother who had just passed away. On every occasion the author tried to speak with the Ribeiros, they had made it clear that adoption of Martin is a private matter and that it is not for public to pursue.

The news of Martin's sudden death brought tears to the author's eyes as he vividly recalled Martin, who coincidentally lived in the same neighborhood in Orleans. The author used to see him on the bus quite frequently. Since Martin's parents did not want the author to touch base with Martin, the author refrained from striking up a conversation with Martin, although often they happened to sit close to each other.

Phillipe Rochefort and Diane Rochefort

Presently living in Prince Edward Island, Phil and Diane Rochefort are a part of the fourteen adoptive parents who adopted one of the war babies, Rita (Rija) Ruphea, picked out by Fred and Bonnie Cappuccino from Dhaka on behalf of the couple.

The author had corresponded with the couple a few times over the years. They also had telephone conversations on several occasions, and the couple also sent a few family snapshots. However, the Rocheforts prefer not to be involved in the project. They wished the author good luck and responded to his initial questions on the understanding that there will be respect for privacy, which they prefer at this stage of their lives. The author agreed to do just that.

According to the already published and publicly available information, back in 1972, when the Rocheforts adopted Rija Ruphea, they were living in Espanola, Ontario. During that time, they were also in touch with other adoptive parents in especially the Toronto area.

The Rocheforts have raised six children out of which three are adopted and three are born to the family. Phil and Diane had considered adoption to be a personal statement of their commitment to raise multiracial children in Canada. They sure have done that to their satisfaction.

The family in the early years was involved with the adoptive family groups. However, with the passing of time and a move to rural eastern Canada, they quickly became involved in the community there, studying, making friends, and pursuing their lives as Canadians. At the same time, they continued to maintain multiracial contacts in their circle of friends and family. They are now spread over three different countries.

Rita (Rija) Ruphea

Born on February 15, 1972, at *Shishu Bhavan*, Dhaka, Bangladesh, the baby girl weighed two kilograms at birth. Official records in Bangladesh show her name as Rita (Rija) Ruphea. Her mother left her at the orphanage for adoption. The newspapers of the day that reported the arrival of the war babies in Canada on July 20, 1972, however, show her name as Rija. The Rocheforts had retained the name Rija Ruphea having added the family's surname. The baby girl came to be called Rija Ruphea Rochefort.

The author contacted Rija by e-mail to introduce himself and his project but met with no interest in response to his inquiry. As a result of this, and in deference to Rija, the author chose to respect her privacy and limit himself to information in the public domain.

According to the publicly available information through the Internet, Rija studied graphic design at college and has had a career in advertising. Having started as a production artist, she worked for both provincial and federal governments as well as for TD Bank, Royal Bank of Canada, and BMO (Bank of Montreal). Rija quickly moved up through the ladder. Today a Torontonian Rija is an experienced art director/designer with a background that includes clients and agency experience from design to digital direction.

Judging from the public information available, the author concludes that Rija has developed a number of innate skills and talents to forge a successful career for herself. These achievements are evidence of a successful transition to life in her adopted country, Canada.

Lloyd and Sandra Simpson

Lloyd, a construction estimator by profession, and Sandra, a social worker, have been living in Pointe Claire, Quebec, since they were married in 1965. The couple's commitment to the doctrine of adoption, especially with regard to racially different orphans, remains paramount to this day. Being appalled to see the plight of the children in Vietnam, ravaged by foreign troops, the couple joined hands with two other like-minded couples, Herb and Naomi Bronstein and Fred and Bonnie Cappuccino. Having seen the suffering and the dying of so many orphans of war, they collectively felt that they ought to "do something" for the thousands of mixed-race infants, resulted from sexual violence; many were rejected by their parents and society and were abandoned in the fields.

Working closely, the three couples continued to find ways to provide a protective environment for the children in turmoil. This was particularly so when the Vietnam War was coming to an end and the armies of North Vietnam were pushing into South Vietnam, leaving death and destruction in their work. They remained committed to what they strongly believed in – to step up to the plate. All through their lives, the Simpsons have been practicing what they have been preaching, that is, adoption of disadvantaged orphans from overseas. Those who know the Simpsons recognize them as a couple who had always remained ever ready not only to provide gratuitous care to orphans but also to direct assistance in their adoption in Canadian homes. In addition, they also embraced orphans of all ages, sexes, and racial backgrounds, many of whom are physically and mentally challenged.

With a view to saving the orphans of the war, each of the three above-noted couples established contact with Rosemary Taylor, an Australian who was working in Vietnam, Ho Chi Minh City, then Saigon, as director of operations. Each couple was determined to adopt at least one war orphan from Vietnam individually. As early as 1969, the Simpsons adopted their first child, Mai Lien, who was born in Vietnam and came to join them at the age of ten months through Friends for All Children. The Simpsons liaised with Taylor, who single-handedly assisted the orphanage staff and orphaned children of South Vietnam more than any other person during her stay in Vietnam. By then, through the efforts of Families For Children (FFC), officially founded in 1971 by the Simpsons, the Cappuccinos, and the Bronsteins, the issue of interracial adoption had already surfaced in the news media. It triggered a general interest among the members of the public especially during the imminent takeover of South Vietnam by North Vietnamese troops. The Simpsons and other key players had continued to work hard to achieve their objectives.

Since 1971, as a private nonprofit and nonsectarian agency, the FFC had expanded its role and had established homes in Guatemala, India, and Bangladesh. With offices in Toronto and Montreal, Sandra Simpson remains the president of FFC and arranges for sponsorship of children by North American "parents."

In July 1972 when Fred and Bonnie Cappuccino, the couple who also adopted a war baby, went to Bangladesh to negotiate and pick out a dozen or two war babies, the Simpsons were up to their eyes in work. Not only were they holding the fort of FFC but they were also looking after their own daughter, Mai Lien, who was having a major surgery. A truly optimist Sandra was seriously engaged at the same time in lobbying the Ontario government to expedite the incomplete home studies for the Ontario couples. Sandra worked closely with prospective applicants for adoption from Bangladesh and developed a strategy to deal with the impasse.

We have read this in chapter 3 about one of Sandra's grand schemes that was to line up a host of journalists by the strength of her personality. A large number of journalists and applicants for home studies for adoption immediately contacted the Office of the Minister of Community and Social Services as per Sandra's scheme all at the same time. They were successful in jamming the telephone line calling between 2:00 p.m. to 3:00 p.m. Everyone who was on the phone is known to have asked the minister the same question as to *when* and *how* soon would the government allow the home studies to be completed to enable the entry of the war babies in Canada for which both Canada and Bangladesh had already reached an agreement.

With occasional help from Trudy Hartt, whose profiles we have already looked at, Sandra liaised with all prospective adoptive parents and kept them abreast of what had been happening in Bangladesh where the Cappuccinos had gone to negotiate and firm up with the Bangladesh authority the exact handover of certain number of war babies to them. The Simpsons adopted Rajib, who was a part of the same bunch brought to Canada by the Cappuccinos in July 1972. The adoptive parents from the present bunch proudly recall Sandra's tough fight with Ontario government officials and their heartbreaking struggle with deep gratitude. Given Sandra's passion and dedication for the racially different orphans and her ongoing effort to save them from near death, she is seen as the Canadian version of Australian

Rosemary Taylor whose courageous risk made people look at her with great admiration.

In fact, all through 1970s and 1980s, Sandra found time to speak at meetings of organizations such as social service agencies, teachers, professionals, and many other advocacy and community groups working with children. More particularly, at that time Sandra used to attend meetings of the Open Door Society where she used to talk about adoption and acceptance of multiracial children in Canada. In dealing with prospective adoptive parents, the Simpsons recognized early on that those around them were not on the same wavelength in the process of understanding and embracing adoption – especially adoption of racially different children. Motivated by one single passion to help families arrange multiracial adoption in Canada through contacts in overseas, the Simpsons remain deeply committed to this day.

In continuing their work, the Simpsons were involved in several fronts. At the governmental level, they were involved in encouraging interprovincial cooperation; at an informal level, they were, and still are, an "official clearing house" to find homes for multiracial children for Canadians across the country.

Like the Cappuccinos, the Simpsons recall *how* and *why* they ended up with nineteen children. According to Lloyd, he had never planned on a large family, and yet as it turned out, they could never ignore an opportunity to place a child for whom they were able to provide a home. By the time they had nine children, they recall to have turned their attention to their ability to provide their children quality education, which seemed like an expensive proposition at the time. Being a bit apprehensive simply because of the cost involved in properly raising a child with education, they thought about not to adopt anymore. And yet both Lloyd and Sandra found ways to rationalize their desire to bring home more orphans. "What difference did it make to a child who wasn't going to get an education anyway?"[47] asked Sandra in an attempt to reinforce her desire for another child.

Interestingly enough, following the same line of argument, Lloyd also seemed to have changed his mind by then having already found another orphan who was going to be their tenth child. "Come on now, we have room for this one" (the *Canadian,* the *Weekend Citizen,* February 24, 1979), said a determined Lloyd, having already made up his mind for another addition but simply sought Sandra's support. It did not take them long to succumb to their innate desire to have more children. "I can't stand to see suffering" (the *Canadian,* the *Weekend Citizen,* February 24, 1979), said Sandra in one of her interviews with the news media back in the 1970s, frankly admitting her inability to bear the pains of suffering orphans.

Again, one of Sandra's common remarks relating to the orphan children is worth noting: that "they have experienced the worst, and they deserve the best" (the *Canadian,* the *Weekend Citizen,* February 24, 1979). With time, the couple repeated the same process and ended up having ten more children, one after another, totaling nineteen children within a span of couple of years, including Rajib, a war baby from Bangladesh. Of their nineteen children, only four are biological and the rest are all adopted from Ecuador, Vietnam, Cambodia, South Korea, India, Bangladesh, etc. Today they range from forty to fifty-seven years of age.

With nineteen children around, the Simpsons had followed a particular parenting style while the children were growing up. The couple knew that it would be easy to be overwhelmed with problems if they did not set any priority. In fact, they tackled those areas that were the most important to lessen the stress on the family, such as cutting down on the use of foul language by the children, discouraging verbal "put-downs," giving attention to all the children together, as well as giving some time alone with each child. They did this deliberately by scheduling private and personal times with each child, staggering bed and study times and taking along on errands in an attempt to remain abreast of personal issues of their children of varying ages.

Naturally, as a result, the children had always felt attached to the family. Not only that, but they also grew up feeling reassured especially knowing that they have caring parents who looked after their children's personal needs. In turn, the children also, recall the Simpsons, knew of what was expected of them as all the siblings bandied around together. Time and again, the children recall that while growing up, they had found their family to be one of the best places having had the good fortune of being under the care of loving affectionate parents around. It was important to them that they were always available to them. They grew up learning two key concepts with which they became familiar right from the beginning of their lives – "acceptance" and "reassurance."

The multiracial Simpson family drew the attention of the news media not only in Montreal but also all over the country.

When, for example, the two-year-old Damienne, another Vietnamese orphan, arrived at the Simpsons' home from Saigon in 1972, there were a series of news items not only on the Simpsons but also on the growing new trend on the adoption of racially different orphans by Caucasian Canadians. "The voice of one small, scared Vietnamese orphan will hardly be heard amid the clamor of 10 children," wrote one interviewer who visited the Simpsons back in the early 1970s when they had about ten children (*The Gazette*, October 13, 1972). The diversity within the Simpsons family, therefore, did not escape the notice of people around. In fact, the Simpsons' four-bedroom home was described as "a kaleidoscope of the world's trouble spot" from where orphans were picked up by the Simpsons (*The Gazette*, October 13, 1972). The news media was impressed with the highly nurturing environment in which the Simpsons had structured their family of nineteen children. Naturally, at that time, every now and then the Simpsons were portrayed in the news showcasing the new trend in Canada.

Having come from different countries of the world in an extraordinary way, the Simpson family stands out on its own as diverse and "Canadian" by all definition. In fact, the Simpson family, though headed by a Caucasian couple, is so diverse and multiracial that no one ever considers the Simpson family to be "a white family."[48] "It's because," says Sandra, "the white members are a minority in our family" (letter from Sandra Simpson to the author).

Diversity within the Simpson family is so strong that it had actually allowed the siblings to be close to each other. "The family tended to stay together since they enjoyed sports and made up a baseball team, and a hockey team," recalled Sandra (letter from Sandra Simpson to the author). This is what made the Simpson family atypical and yet very much Canadian of which Rajib, a war baby from Bangladesh feels to be a part of.

In her capacity as the president of FFC, Sandra traveled to India and Bangladesh every three months to supervise the operation of FFC homes there – three in India and one in Bangladesh. Between India and Bangladesh, the FFC houses over five hundred children including crippled victims of polio, the blind or half blind, and children born with congenital defects – cleft palates, hare lips, clubbed feet, and heart problems. A child advocate who is tirelessly devoted to orphans, Sandra is frequently called upon to share her experience with prospective individual families and organizations.

To the Simpsons, interracial adoption is an all-too-familiar scene that in reality, the racially different orphans with a disability are usually the least desirable candidates for adoption. Being in the field of adoption, the Simpsons truly believe that for placement of orphans, "just any old family isn't good enough" (*The Gazette,* October 13, 1972). To them what remain paramount are the family environment, filial love, and commitment of the adoptive parents from whom the adoptees "deserve the best" (*The Gazette,* October 13, 1972).

Perhaps the greatest achievement of the Simpsons is the impact they have brought on the minds of the people of Canada with respect to interracial adoption. Over the years, the Simpsons have developed a framework structure of their own to assist them and others in creating a complex maze of ingenuous channels of operation. Having extraordinary capacity for work, the Simpsons had been successful in making adoptive placements in Canada through their exemplary leadership. Many Canadians regard the couple as trailblazer in exemplifying adoption of racially different orphans as a means of creating or expanding one's family.

The Simpsons' deep commitment to the well-being of orphans has long been recognized by the governments of Ontario and Canada. They have earned people's respect for demonstration of an attitude of the highest professional competency together with a genuine concern for war orphans. In 1979, the Montreal Citizenship Council gave Sandra its Outstanding Citizen Award. Again, in 1983, Sandra received the Order of Canada for saving the abandoned, the sick, and the handicapped children in Asia. The same year, Sandra also won an award of the Ontario Medal. The couple's daughter, Kimberley, who ran the Dhaka orphanage in close consultation with Sandra, also received a Jaycees Award as one of Canada's five Outstanding Young Citizens of the Year. Again, describing the Simpsons as one of the most remarkable couples, Victoria Leach, adoption co-coordinator for the Ontario Ministry of Community and Social Services in the 1970s, had categorized them as committed and caring human beings. They have hearts as great as the outdoors.

The Simpsons are still incredibly close to their children – something that remains true even to this day at a time when the family is scattered across Canada and the USA. All family members still stick together and help one another, considering them to be a part of the great Simpson family – something that gives them a sense of pride. Mai Lien helps her mother with the sponsorship work from their home office in Toronto. Kimberley handles the FFC USA finances from her home in Arizona. The most satisfying experience of them centers on their children and grandchildren of diverse background – something that continues to give them more purpose to their own lives, keeping them engaged in tasks that are both enormous and breathtaking, to say the least.

Whenever the children and grandchildren come and stay with them, it is always like having a family reunion on a smaller scale. Everyone present enjoys the gathering even in the absence of all children. Today the Simpsons are considered the linchpin of FFC having nineteen children and ten grandchildren of their own.

Rajib

Rajib's arrival into the Simpson family is a sheer coincidence that the Simpsons would probably never forget. The Simpsons still remember the cable they received from the Office of the Canadian High Commissioner in New Delhi informing them that they were getting a boy by the name Rajib who was being substituted for Sunil. The cable also stated that Sunil could not pass the mandatory medical test conducted by Dr. Robert Ferrie. The Simpson also learned that Sunil, who was picked out earlier and who had to be hospitalized for isolation purposes, had died shortly after.

Rajib was born on July 1, 1972. He weighed three kilograms at birth when the Cappuccinos were already in Dhaka. He was chosen by Fred and Bonnie Cappuccino for the Simpsons, who stayed back in Canada. Rajib was picked out to be a part of the first contingent to join the Simpson family.[49] When the nineteen-day-old Rajib arrived in Canada, he did not seem to have gained any weight since his birth. During formal adoption, the couple kept his first name, added Cappuccino as his middle name and Simpson as the family's surname. The boy came to be called Rajib Cappuccino Simpson.

Rajib started to grow up like all other children and attended Brown Elementary School, Toronto, Ontario, successfully. He then went to Northern Secondary School (1988 to 1989) in the same neighborhood until he became seriously ill in 1989 with schizophrenia. As will be seen under the subheading the "War babies' first visit to their country of birth" in chapter 7, Rajib was one of the five war babies who went to Bangladesh for a weeklong visit organized by Canadopt back in 1989 when the war babies were sixteen years old. At the time, Rajib was a perfectly stable boy of sixteen but was already showing signs of becoming increasingly introverted. As it turned out, Rajib's visit to his country of birth had, in fact, made Rajib look at things quite differently than from the other war babies who accompanied him.

The Simpsons believe that because Rajib knew very little about Bangladesh, he had no clear idea about what he would see during his visit. It was as though Rajib was speechless when he saw how the poorest of the poor struggle daily simply to have two square meals, just to survive and continue to work hard into their old age. Such recognition or feelings of profound bewilderment must have made Rajib more resentful, remarked Sandra.

According to Sandra, having seen the level of incredible poverty first time in his life, he was visibly turned off by the indescribably miserable condition there. Seeing people living on the streets of Dhaka must have made Rajib feel that, had the circumstances not changed for him, he could have been one of them. He recognized how fortunate he must have been to not only escape the miseries of Bangladesh but also be adopted in Canada. According to the family, a mentally disturbed Rajib had continued to remain upset having seen the level of poverty and the presence of oppression, starvation, and human suffering in Bangladesh.

Sandra is also of the opinion that when Rajib went to Bangladesh while at his teens, he did not have any experience, not even a virtual one, about Bangladesh with its many facets and colors. Since Rajib did not speak the language (Bengali), he was not able to identify with the people there. She further added that Rajib "did not realize in 1989 the level of poverty until he actually saw it," and such sad spectacle must have made him instantly realize that "he was more Canadian than anything" (letter from Sandra Simpson to the author, cited in notes and references).

Sandra maintains that recognition of such a dimension of the economic life must have prompted Rajib more along the line to dissociate himself from his country of birth and associate more with Canada where he was being raised. His inability to integrate his two identities must have led to more confusion because of the vast difference between Canada where he grew up and Bangladesh where he was born. There is, however, no relation between Rajib's reaction to the knowledge of his adopted status and school/home adjustment and performance. As already mentioned, perhaps it had more to do with the *way* in which he was conceived and the circumstances surrounding his birth mother's gestation period.

It is possible that Rajib was not ready emotionally to accept easily what he saw in Bangladesh. He might have suffered a sudden blow at the time, maintains a concerned Sandra. His self-esteem as someone who came from that poverty-stricken country came to confront him at a time when he was not at all prepared to deal with that part of reality. Hitherto, Rajib never felt that he was caught between the two worlds, Canadian and Bangladeshi. His visit to the orphanage premises in Bangladesh must have shaken him up badly. In a sense, the trip resulted in a heightened awareness of his ethnicity — a true sense of *where* he came from.

The Simpsons also recognized that, in general, there is a desire in all adoptees to dig into their past to learn about their birth history in order to develop a good sense of *where* they came from and *who* their ancestors are. Noticeably, in Rajib's case, there was an exception right from the start. According to the family, from the start, Rajib, however, never took any interest in knowing about his country of birth or the story surrounding his birth and adoption. Rajib has had no desire at all to search for his root, nor did he ever show any interest to know *how* did it all happen and under *what* circumstances. Again, as Sandra recalls, though Rajib's path was strewn with uncertainty, Rajib never felt a compelling need to look into his past the way, for example, Ryan (another war baby from the same bunch about whom we have already read) did. As far as the mother is concerned, for Rajib, it was never a matter of a past that had to be found.

"There had been no deep-seated emotional issue relating to adoption that needed to be resolved either," observed Sandra with reference to Rajib's mental and behavioral changes (letter from Sandra Simpson to the author, cited in notes and references). Rajib grew up not knowing much about the Pakistani military atrocities in Occupied Bangladesh and the Bengalis' struggle for independence. As Sandra recalls, Rajib knew that he was adopted and that he was brought to Canada from a Bangladeshi orphanage. The Simpson, however, believed that all their adopted children deserve to know about their country of birth and origin, where life would have been very hard and that adoption of them was indeed a miracle.

Unfortunately, from 1990 on, Rajib has had major setback due to his prolonged illness. During his late teens, Rajib also lost his interest in school, finding it hard to concentrate on his studies and/or his hobbies. Up until the age of eighteen, Rajib was full of life and vitality. By nineteen, however, he broke down, resulting in nightmarish experience for the family members. Prior to that, he was "a bright, well-behaved, and easy-to-raise child until he was about eighteen or so," recalled Sandra (letter from Sandra Simpson to the author). According to Rajib's sister Melanie, a child born to the Simpsons, sometimes the most trivial incident used to cause sudden transformation, making Rajib agitated and combative (Melanie said this in a telephone interview with the author on August 10, 1998). In fact, as Melanie recalled, Rajib often used to be self-destructive with occasional histrionic outbursts that would render his conversation and verbalizations sometimes incomprehensible. Otherwise, maintains Melanie, Rajib always used to be a good-hearted person whose warmth could be felt by everyone around him.

By the time Rajib turned twenty, he needed constant supervision in order to control his behavior, which became even harder. In that sense, and with the passage of time, Rajib became more and more rebellious and difficult to handle even by those close to him. And yet the family had always tried to convey a message more along the line of love, friendship, and family solidarity. According to the Simpsons, nothing negative was found in Rajib's medical examination that was conducted in Bangladesh prior to the selection of the war babies. It was only in later years that the Simpsons realized the severity of Rajib's medical and psychological problems that came to present a far more serious challenge than one could anticipate.

The severity and scope of dysfunction displayed by Rajib had immediately made his parents recognize that their major thrusts must be the identification of mental disorders in the earliest stages of life. They also recognized that they must detect and treat malfunctions before it froze into severe disorder. This was a time when Rajib used to appear awfully tensed, uptight, and frightened. At this time, the family's main message to Rajib was that, regardless of what Rajib was doing and going through, he would remain lovable to all members of the family, and that Rajib should always trust his parents and siblings who would help him with his needs no matter what. Needless to mention, one of the greatest strengths of the Simpson is that the other children in the family did not feel neglected while the Simpsons dealt with one crisis after another.

During the stressful times, all family members recognized the strain of the situation and took their time to take care of each other. Taking small bits of progress and seeing them as a major success, the family continued to keep Rajib's situation from becoming worse. Behaviorally, "Rajib had been quite difficult, to say the least," said his sister Melanie Simpson (Melanie said this in a telephone interview with the author on August 10, 1998, cited in notes and references). Rajib often rebuffed his parents' emotional overtures, and yet the family was appreciative of the fact that Rajib could be behaving the same with any parent and that it was not a personal rejection on his part. This was clear in the Simpsons' minds about how Rajib looked at his family members at that time. Therefore, the parents believe that Rajib's illness had nothing to do with being adopted into the Simpson family.

By reminding the author that Rajib sees himself as "Canadian since he has known nothing else," Sandra reiterated her point further – that all through 1980s and 1990s, they were preoccupied with doubts and fears about further deterioration of Rajib's health and mind (letter from Sandra Simpson to the author). They remained busy trying to determine whether or not they ought to have tried something else – perhaps another hospital, another kind of treatment. And yet the Simpsons were confident that something would come of Rajib's treatment for the better. In his first hospitalization, Rajib was diagnosed as a schizophrenic in need of medical treatment. This is a peculiar kind of depersonalization and mounting anxiety. Being in a situation of stress, the entire family experienced the feelings of awe and strangeness with which Rajib used to appear all of a sudden and scare the rest of the family members.

While describing Rajib's health conditions, Sandra called him a "paranoid schizophrenic who is considered dangerous to himself and to members of the family when he had psychotic periods" (letter from Sandra Simpson to the author). Evidently the family had gone through terrible times all through the period Rajib was at home while under various types of treatment. After obtaining a formal diagnosis that Rajib is a schizophrenic with a matching treatment plan, the Simpsons prepared themselves to face the next round of challenges with courage and hope. Gradually for the entire family, Rajib's illness and challenges became another fact of their lives – balanced by love, affection, recreational activities, and education.

As parents who have raised nineteen children, the Simpsons knew on a gut level Rajib's problems and issues – that there was something wrong in his emotional development. Given Rajib's situation, they were never dismissive of Rajib's varying needs. As a matter of fact, having cared for their attachment to Rajib, they paid particular attention to help Rajib develop a more secure attachment for a head start in gaining positive self-control. Being the most sensitive, empathic, and effective parents who have a track record of secure attachments in all of their children, they never felt rejected and ineffective when they tried to get close to Rajib.

All through the crisis period, the Simpson family remained strong having demonstrated commendable family solidarity that is They stuck together through thick and thin for Rajib. They worked on the premises that love and affection must be demonstrated through the voice tones, gestures, and expressions, which contribute to the meaning of feelings toward one another. During the crisis, family members used to gather in a "circle," which became a common tradition with the Simpson family. Unfortunately, despite years of medication, there was no breakthrough, as Rajib remained the same – perhaps got worse with the passage of time.

In looking at Rajib, the man "as is" today, one can only remind oneself of the research findings on schizophrenia: that every person, whether raised through adoption or by his natural parents, is in his total personality a fusion of two universe; the endowment with which he is constituted by heredity and the environment in which he is raised that molds him.[50] According to the Simpsons, it is possible that a child feels, perceives, and even learns in vitro (i.e., in the uterus before birth), which could come from its undisturbed natural habitat. Again it is also recognized that a child who may turn out to be happy or sad, aggressive or meek would depend, in part, on the messages it gets about itself in the womb.

MUSTAFA CHOWDHURY

On the one hand, it is generally said that chronic anxiety or wrenching ambivalence about motherhood can leave a deep scar on an unborn baby's personality; on the other hand, such life-enhancing emotions such as joy, elation, and anticipation could contribute significantly to the emotional development of a healthy child. The brief profiles of each child, based on their own perception of themselves in relation to their family/environment in the present chapter, no doubt, give us an appreciation of the complex issue. In Rajib's case, we will perhaps never know how much of his different types of attitudes and personalities could be attributed to the ways in which he was conceived and had remained in his mother's womb during gestation, something that the birth mother had tried to hide from the rest of the people around.

When one considers the ongoing psychological stress of a birth mother during her pregnancy in Occupied Bangladesh, one is immediately reminded that such stress is likely to have produced negative outcomes for babies conceived under the most unwanted circumstances. As is maintained by medical experts, with pre- and perinatal psychology, many negative outcomes include low birth weight and ill temperament, the latter of which might be, in part, due to the fact that maternal stress could lead to abnormal brain development. Many of Rajib's illness, such as aggressiveness, obnoxious and demeaning behavior, mood swings, and paranoid psychotic schizophrenia, are attributed to the genetic predisposition, basic personality, and prenatal risk factors including the tempestuous period of gestation while he was in his mother's womb prior to his birth.

The ways in which many birth mothers had conceived their child in Occupied Bangladesh only reinforce what is generally maintained: that the mother's reaction to her pregnancy affects the child's mental development and future self-esteem. Given that Rajib was an "aborted infant" who "managed to live," he is a living example of resilience (*The Gazette,* October 13, 1972). He has enormous strength to survive although mentally unstable and seriously problematic. In layperson's term, one could say that the unusual circumstances surrounding Rajib's conception and gestation by his birth mother must have contributed to Rajib's mental well-being.

There are many who argue along the vein that a child is affected by psychological mood of the mother and those close to her. In that sense, Rajib will continue to bear the scars of war and violence that took place in Occupied Bangladesh throughout his lifetime no matter where he lives. Without blaming anyone, the Simpsons accepted the reality of Rajib, having learned that no one can control the particular arrangement of genes inherited by each human being. It meant understanding the challenges that Rajib was facing as a connection rather than something Rajib or they had caused.

It is safe to conclude that the present pessimistic world of Rajib is primarily a result of life characterized by a series of serious problems. As was the case, for days together, Rajib used to remain down in the dumps and would continue to erupt unpredictably. These problems had already caused unexpected conflicts in the family, which, by their nature, are not given to any resolution known to Rajib or his parents. His parents are aware that behaviorally, Rajib, like all other schizophrenics, had been quite difficult. Having seen Rajib's precarious situation, both parents and the siblings had always tried to make informed interpretation of Rajib's behavior and actions and construct focused strategies to deal with his particular situation.

At the end, given Rajib's fast-deteriorating situation, the parents recognized the need for Rajib to live away from home. They also recognized that this would involve specific risks, notably separation from the community in which he had lived and grown up thus far. There would be development of undue dependence on the treating institution and problems in reintegrating him into a more normal social situation. Having sought help from doctors, specialists, and counselors, the Simpsons agreed to do what was in the best interest of Rajib – to place him at an institution. Not surprisingly, seeing the rapid deterioration of Rajib's mental health, the family was forced to place Rajib at an institution for his own safety and the safety of the family members.

Rajib is now living in Whitby, Ontario, in an institution called the Ontario Shores Centre for Mental Health Sciences, generally referred to as the Ontario Shores. It is a public hospital providing a spectrum of specialized assessment and treatment services to those living with complex and serious mental illness. According to Mai Lein, though overwhelmed by frustration and anger, Rajib has adjusted well at the Ontario Shores where he has been living since January 2010.

According to the family, Rajib feels safe and is doing as well as can be expected. He even used to visit his sister Mai Lien at her office every now and then, although he does not come as frequently as he used to before. The family sends care packages as often as possible. He is kept heavily medicated, and what keeps the family going is the satisfaction of seeing Rajib being taken care of by professionals at the Ontario Shores – that this is not a case of having a marginal existence.

The family is still very much fond of Rajib. "Everyone misses him and yet no one can really do anything about his mental health and well-being," said Mai Lien (Mai Lien Simpson said this in a telephone interview with the author on March 10, 2011). The family continues to love Rajib, whom they know is living with a dejected mind through continuation and intensification of nightmarish days. Sandra sums up her son as someone who "is the nicest gentle person when well and exactly just the opposite when ill" (letter from Sandra Simpson to the author).

Del and Donna Wolsey

Del and Donna Wolsey, educators by profession, have been living in Komoka, Ontario, a small rural town near London, since the late 1960s. While teaching for the London Board of Education, they also attended the University of Western Ontario. Upon graduation in 1969, they took a two-year teaching assignment with the Canadian Department of National Defense in Germany, which gave them an opportunity to travel in Western and Eastern Europe (behind the iron curtain), the African continent, Middle East, and Southeast Asia.

The vision of forming a family by *choice* through *adoption* was solidified by the experiences of visiting cultures that heretofore had been only storybook fantasies, followed by the naïvety of thinking proximity to the need was advantageous – it was not (i.e., Germany is closer to Nepal, India, Bangladesh, etc.); and finally the harsh reality, after arriving back in Canada, that there was no easy route; and the bureaucratic, political, ideological struggle began with Canadian officials (municipal, provincial, and federal) and foreign (host countries) alike. There was "never a time we thought we might be venturing into something praiseworthy; different yes, but not commendable in any way. That would have indeed been strange motivation."[312] But it was, nevertheless, a time in Canada when adoption was not common and certainly not international or transracial. Because of their travels, they now had confirmation and support for their conviction that "all children had, at the very least, the right to a family and a safe home" (letter from Del and Donna Wolsey to Mustafa Chowdhury, February 10, 2012, cited in Notes & References).

As a young girl, Donna dreamed about running an orphanage or having a family of her own, with a house filled with a dozen children of varying nationalities. Reading the book *The Dutch Twins* (and many more in *The Twins Series*) by Lucy Fitch Perkins had inspired within Donna an emotional desire, a dream, centered on having a fulsome life filled with children whom she would hold, love, and raise together with her significant other. Fortunately, Donna found a lifelong partner, Del, who also felt the same way and shared her dreams and wishes. Following their wedding, the couple soon got into the "swing of things" and began to work toward realizing their cherished dream of having children of different races. An emotional Donna recalls quite vividly how, following their return to Canada in 1971, a heartbreaking newspaper picture, seen years ago, of helpless orphans spurred the couple to act and bring their dream to life.

Amina (a war baby from Bangladesh) was their first daughter brought to Canada from Bangladesh in July 1972. The next few years were busy. They recall seeing Amina thrive and being unable to hide their own feelings of being proud parents seeing how this racially different child became their "own child." In no time they decided to bring home more orphans to realize their dream of creating a multiracial family. Between 1972 and 1990, the Wolseys adopted three girls (Amina from Bangladesh [1972], Ju-lee from Korea [1974], and Sharina from India [1990]) and three boys (Jonathon from El Salvador [1986], Thilo from Vietnam [1974], and Dariq, a mixed racial baby born in Canada [1976]) and became a truly multiracial and multicultural family *by choice*.

Their six adoptive children, from six different countries, helped them learn the rewards of mastering necessary tasks and enrich their lives in some very unique ways. The couple's travel to different countries in Europe, the Middle East, South and East Africa, and many of the poverty-stricken Asian countries gave them a firsthand opportunity to reinforce the newspaper and TV images of deprived, war-torn children that continues to influence them even to this day. The couple has traveled, worked in orphanages, taught for nearly nine years in international schools, and consequently became more convinced that providing a family and a sense of home for these children was the right thing to do.

A strong-willed Donna followed her heart, knowing that her husband provided unconditional support for her initiatives. Believing that "there is always a place for everyone in the world,"[51] the couple dedicated their entire lives fulfilling this commitment. Whether it was through the support group that Donna had established, or through other channels, she remained active – always doing "something" to reach out to fill the needs of orphans. Always on her side like a shadow, Del too remained committed, having spent "his life dedicated to his family, the church, his job and helping others in need."[52]

Amina sees her dad as "one of those unique individuals who can walk into a room and make anyone feel at ease with his quiet, calming way" (Amina's research paper, p. 35). Del himself explained to Amina how he had recognized "the emphasis on family being one of 'function' and not of 'composition.' That was an important concept and we always emphasized with you kids: much the same idea as being a mom was mothering not just giving birth" (Amina's research paper, p. 16). In accordance with this basic philosophy, Donna and Del depended on each other and moved forward with their plan to create and sustain a diverse family.

Over the years, it seemed so appropriate for them to share their lives with other children who were less fortunate: "Adoption seemed an equally appropriate way of responding to their need for assistance. In our case, it was 'Let's adopt.' It seems to me that if someone else asks: what is the best gift for one of these little waifs lying in an orphanage in Bangladesh, the answer is a family," says an affectionate Del (Amina's research paper, p. 16). According to Amina:, My father had been the silent strength behind my mother's vision and quest to help orphan children" (Amina's research paper, p. 17). Del had been deeply influenced by his wife's "enlightened thoughts" and "yearning for international adoption." Naturally, he came to "see things" through the same lens as his wife.

Known as a trailblazer and having come to the attention of the news media, the Wolseys took the opportunity for others to see that "family" can take on many different configurations, theirs being a *family of choice* who developed strong kinship, respect, and bonds. This clearly demonstrated a new lifestyle worth pursuing. This attracted interest of many at a time when international adoption was still a rare occurrence in Canada.

Perhaps one of the most important legacies of the Wolseys is that as educators, whether it was at school or at a social event outside of the school environment, they remained resolved in integrating pluralism both in their profession as well as in personal lives. With the couple, "multiculturalism was a way of living, thinking and believing" (Amina's research paper, p. 13, cited in 17). One of the most valuable lessons Amina has learned from her parents is to respect each other's similarities and differences. The Wolsey children learned at an early age how each sibling should be encouraged to achieve one's full development on one's own. Today, all Wolsey children take great pride in what Amina sees as their mother's strong commitment to equity and diversity.

The Wolseys remember "Ami's first homecoming" and how they were thrust into "instant parenthood" – certainly a very different sort than the experience of biological parents. With no baby shower, no parenting classes for the expecting couple, or any other apparent markers of the couple, they went to the Toronto airport to pick up their daughter, coming from Bangladesh. Donna remembers the first thought that came across her mind was to inform her parents about their soon-to-arrive child from Bangladesh. They had not informed their own family of their plan to adopt, let alone an interracial adoption. To help her parents deal with their fears and reservations and to enable them to embrace their decision wholeheartedly, Donna needed to help them make the needed leap of faith into a whole new world. Donna felt that her parents had to be well informed and be given adequate time to understand what it was all about in order to react positively. This was not so much for her mother, but for her father. Donna believed he would need more time and opportunity to adjust. Just thinking about his anticipated reaction, Donna decided to broach the subject with him immediately. She did not want anyone in her family to be caught off guard when they bring home their dream child.

Amid her busy schedule, Donna juggled her time to take her dad to a local coffee shop to break the news that, within days, he was going to be a "grandpa." Immediately upon hearing the news and having seen no apparent sign of Donna's pregnancy, his mouth dropped and his throat tightened to the point that he could barely make a sound to respond. For some awkward minutes, he remained speechless, being dumbfounded by the suddenness of the news. After regaining his composure, he shot back with a typical Archie Bunker–type mind-set, asking *why* she was getting into trouble by taking a baby from a faraway country. Creating her family by bringing in someone else's child seemed neither natural nor desirable to him. A determined Donna, however, remained calm, without reacting to her dad's contrary views. As far as the Wolseys were concerned, the news of the arrival of their Bangladeshi war baby was shared with her dad for his *information only* and that she was not soliciting any advice or opinion. The decision to adopt internationally was made a long time ago and that the topic was not up for a family debate.

Moving forward, having brought Amina home, noticeably the couple became very happy to see how Donna's father came to love the little girl within weeks of her arrival. They were delighted and relieved that gone was the grandpa's fear of having a foreign baby of unknown origin. Fortunately for the family, in no time, the little baby girl, or as the family calls her "the little Ami," worked her way into Grandpa's heart as he put himself around this new family member. Over the years, he formed a particular growing nuclear relationship with all six adopted grandchildren. Grandpa began to feel so comfortable in the Wolsey house under the new and changed circumstance that he did not see the family to be any different than any other family. Everyone in the extended family was happy to see how the proud "grandpa" began to carry the photos of his grandchildren in his wallet to show off to his friends and acquaintances.

The Wolseys continued to pursue their lifelong ambition and to chase their two lifelong goals, of meeting people and trying to make the world a better place to live. During the time their children were growing up, Donna used to spend countless hours on the phone, encouraging and helping hopeful families adopt internationally and, at the same time, lobbying the authorities to simplify and facilitate the procedures surrounding international adoptions. It will be seen in the next chapter under the heading "Adoptive families' network and support group," immediately following the arrival of Amina, the Wolseys (Donna in particular) established Canadopt – a network of adoptive parents of racially different children. From the very beginning, the Wolseys strongly felt and believed that the adoptive families must meet and greet frequently to exchange information, share each other's experiences, and more particularly, learn from each other problems and issues associated with the raising of a racially different child in a predominantly monocultural environment. Donna remained busy in bringing adoptive families together through network and using whatever people resources she was able to gather.

The family was always in demand for conferences, different multicultural celebrations, and to meet and greet people in every walk of life. Such parental activities had been allowed for the children to gain a better understanding of the different cultures of the world. Back in the 1980s, the Wolsey family was branded as a family that was a "product of passion, patience and perseverance" (Amina's research paper, p. 2). In that sense, the Wolsey house is a reflection of their vision of life, which demonstrates fascinating stories and valuable experiences. In fact, working for Canadopt meant everything to Donna, who dedicated her life to realizing her only dream – the dream of a multiracial family consisting of the "forgotten children" of the world.

As true educators, the Wolseys had enriched their children with knowledge from many different facets of life and had empowered them with valuable life skills that are evident in their now grown-up children. They learned from an early age that they must do their best to help the helpless – those in need. The Wolseys' plan (now accomplished) was to have each child return to his or her native country and experience the life and culture one had left behind. With this goal in mind, they encouraged their children to visit their birth country and experience their unique cultures. Being in the field of education themselves, the Wolseys made sure that all their children lived a healthy life and received the best education possible within their means.

While growing up, the Wolsey house was a "haven for all kinds of people" (Amina's research paper, p. 28). As a result, there was always a "collage of people, stories, foods, and cultures," where people used to come and go. This gave them an opportunity to learn and respect people, and develop tolerance and understanding for other people's views and cultures. While the children were younger, the Wolseys identified their skills and met their needs by enrolling them in gymnastics, swimming, skating, tennis, diving, piano, flute, camps, etc. Ensuring that the siblings got along well, having respected each other for what they were or what they had to offer, was one noticeable aspect the Wolseys were particular in. Today all of their six children have grown into educated, confident, and well-rounded individuals.

The Wolseys' greatest achievement is the successful creation and care for interracial families at a time when the idea was not too common. Being passionate and resolute in their vision, action, and philosophy of life, they bore the trials and tribulations, and crossed numerous barriers, having broken the traditional boundaries through their eclectic family composition.

Currently retired from their full-time jobs and having returned from their last assignment (summer school ESL Taipa, China), the Wolseys are still continuing their work in encouraging international adoption especially of children of racially different origins. They came to be known as risk-takers in Canada at a time when interracial adoption was still an uncharted path in the early 1970s. In that sense, having broken the racial boundaries in Canada, the Wolseys have redefined the composition of a family that could be built *through adoption.*

Today, an ongoing activity of the couple is to organize gatherings for Canadopt community members: annual summer family picnics at Coldstream Conservation Area with normal attendance of seventy-five to one hundred adopted children and family members and friends. Eight or ten of the "original moms" continue to meet socially once a month to review old times and new challenges and blessings.

Amina

Born prematurely on April 3, 1972, at Mother Teresa's Home, Missionaries of Charity, at Dhaka, Bangladesh, Amina weighed two kilograms at birth. She arrived in Canada on July 20, 1972. However, slowly and steadily, a frail Amina improved but remained a source of concern for her parents for quite some time.

Amina grew up in her parents' home near Komoka, Ontario. She attended Parkview Elementary School in Komoka and Medway Secondary School in London. After completing secondary school, Amina attended the University of Western Ontario, London, Ontario, where she completed a bachelor of education. She then went to York University in Toronto where she completed another bachelor of education. Later on Amina completed a master's degree in education from the Ontario Institute of Studies in Education (OISE) of the University of Toronto.

After working for a few years as an elementary schoolteacher in the Toronto area, Amina left Canada for an overseas job in Singapore, followed by assignments in Chili, China, and Germany. Amina, however, left her job at the International School of Dusseldorf in June 2013. Now she teaches grade five in Dubai at Gems International School of Dubai - Al Khail. It is a brand-new school that was just built.

Amina recalls, it was always pretty evident to her from the start of her life that she was adopted. "There is no real disguising of that. I was very fortunate to have parents who knew that we needed to have a support system, so I grew up with a wide group of friends who had been adopted," maintains Amina (e-mail from Amina Wolsey to the author, cited in notes and references). "It was never really an issue that I was adopted, but I always have had a good sense of self," recalls Amina. Perhaps for this reason, Amina never seemed to have any difficulty in coming to terms with the fact that she was abandoned at birth and was adopted soon after. It never bothered her when growing up, nor does it bother her now as an adult. "It [adoption] was not really an issue. I figure I have been given a second chance in life. As a result, I am living the life to the fullest"[53]

Over the years, Amina had reflected at great length on her birth mother and the particular circumstances she was thrown into following her birth in Bangladesh. Today, as an adult, she sees the entire episode in the following light: "You have to understand the culture of the Bengali society in this particular time period. Many of these women who bore these children were raped by the enemy (the soldiers of West Pakistani military). In the Bengali society, if women bore a child out of wedlock, they were ostracized. They were cut off from their family, their community and their religion. They were tarnished and in some case banished for life. *What kind of future did these young women have, with limited funds, education and no support?* I think it was an extremely hard decision for these women to give up their children with the hope of having a better life for their child and for them" (e-mail from Amina Wolsey to the author).

While growing up, Amina had learned about her past in bits and pieces. As she advanced in age, she also learned about the sexual violence of the Pakistan army personnel, something that the news media had referred to as a pogrom, a kind of systemic rape; of being conceived as a result of this sexual violence, of her birth under these difficult circumstances, and of her adoption in Canada. She recognized all such historical anecdotes had made an impact on her life. But "this information does not define me," maintains Amina (e-mail from Amina Wolsey to the author). At the same time, Amina also does not really feel that a genealogical piece of information pertaining to her life is missing because she does not have the detailed information surrounding her birth. She sees herself in her own way, particularly the way in which she had been able to associate herself with the circumstances under which she grew up in her adoptive home, the only home she knows to be hers under her parents' love and care.

Amina asserts her identity by saying, "My life is full and I have defined *who* I am because of the experiences I have had. The past is the past." (e-mail from Amina Wolsey to the author). With age, of course, Amina had matured more and more. She also she recognizes "the tremendous struggle" that her parents had faced just to get her out of Bangladesh, including "many hours, numerous phone calls and letters to the local MPPs, MPs, visits to Ottawa, lawyers, government officials, Children's Aid Societies and Immigration Canada" (Amina's research paper, p. 21).

In retrospect, a frank and candid Amina did not seem to comprehend the gravity of her parents' dedication and commitment to the extent she feels today: "As a child, I never understood the sacrifices my parents made for me, nor have I ever taken the time to thank them for all the wonderful opportunities they gave us" (Amina's research paper, p. 26). She considers her parents are incredibly wonderful people simply because she knows "they are the one who nurtured and molded" her to be the way that she is today – a successful professional. "I am my parents' daughter and many of my beliefs and practices come directly from their modeling. Out of my life experiences, I take with me different pieces to guide me as an educator," says a proud Amina (Amina's research paper, p. 27). Naturally, she is forever grateful to her parents who have instilled in her the knowledge and skills she needed, not to mention the amount of time and money they have sacrificed.

As a professional adult, Amina is acutely aware of the hotly debated topic and the defining question behind the *nature vs. nurture* debate. Although Amina had no difficulty in coming to terms with the knowledge that she was adopted, she is aware of the situation of other members of her family and some of her siblings, who seemed to have a harder time accepting the fact that they were adopted. "My perspective is very different than my brother Thilo and my sister Sharina's perspectives," observes Amina, who shares her mother's strong will. Amina remembers how Thilo and Sharina had struggled throughout their childhood with the "skin that they were in," and with their sense of belonging in this society that always seemed to have taunted them. Fortunately, that was not the case with Amina, who had always felt to be an integral part of the family that was all along "very loving and supportive" (Amina's research paper, p. 10). Given the natural bond and strong ties with her parents and siblings and the natural bond that she feels was created in her, she believes in her family, which she came to regard "as a family unit it was pretty normal, except that it was a small representation of a mini nation" (Amina's research paper, p. 10). In elaborating the composition of her unique family, Amina believes perhaps the most natural thing in her life is the notion of pluralism and diversity.

Having moved from the small town of Komoka in Middlesex County to Toronto gave Amina a new lens through which to appreciate the richness of Canada's culture and diversity. While doing a practicum at York University, she found herself in awe of all of the celebrations, books, posters, guests, parents, etc., that educators included in their curriculum. In comparison with her monocultural public school experience in the small town of Komoka, the Toronto schools were a reflection of the ethnically rich society that encompassed Amina. The ties and bonds Amina had developed with her parents and siblings who were collected from six different countries from around the world remain as strong as ever: "As adults, having carved from their surroundings and experiences, each person's identity is (and was) as different as the country they came from. Visually we are quite different. However, I think, in a sense, it has been easier for each of us to be appreciated as an individual," said Amina (Amina's research paper, p. 25).

The family support network, Canadopt that her mom had established back in 1972 was not only like an extended family for them but also like an excellent platform to celebrate diversity and pluralism by the adoptive families and their children. Amina remembers Canadopt, which, according to her, contained the "ingredients of love, respect compassion, [and] support" that had "fused these multi-ethnic families together" (Amina's research paper, 16). "My family collectively represents a multicultural micro-society within the realm of a nuclear

MUSTAFA CHOWDHURY

family," says Amina, taking pride in her mother's initiative (Amina's research paper, p. 1).

Amina grew up reminding herself what her mother had told her and her siblings: "We did not want you to grow up thinking there was only one way to think or do things (the Canadian way or the Wolsey way). We wanted you to grow up seeing (in a natural way) that life, the way people did things, dressed, and thought were not always all the same. So we learned to cook food from different countries, ate in different ethnic restaurants, attended different cultural events and interacted, and socialized with people from many different countries. This was a natural interest for us and we wanted to expose you as well as to these many differences" (Amina's research paper, p. 9).

Amina fondly remembers how her parents tried to connect her with Farouk Chowdhury, then a PhD student at the University of Western Ontario, London, Ontario. Amina is still in contact with the Chowdhurys who now live in Dhaka, Bangladesh, and their daughter, Prima, who used to invite her over every now and then when they were growing up. "The Chowdhuries' apartment always smelled like spices and incense from a mystical land that one day I would have the opportunity to experience" (Amina's research paper, p. 9), says Amina about how she used to feel each time of her visits to the Chowdhury residence during her childhood. As far back as Amina remembers from age four, she was aware that she had a responsibility to help others. She learned this from her mother who, she remembers, had expressed that philosophy in one of her many interviews with the news media back in 1978 (Amina's research paper, p. 30).

As a child, and like other children of her age being busy with things at hand, Amina did not think much about Bangladesh. Nevertheless, Donna recalls, deep down she believed that someday Amina would go to Bangladesh: "She tells me she is going to take care of the people there and has always felt the need to go back and help the people in Bangladesh," says Donna about Amina in an interview with George Hutchison of the *London Free Press* (Amina's research paper, p. 30). Amina remembers about her childhood time as one of the key messages that her parents had inculcated in her and her siblings that "happiness is meant to be shared" (Amina's Research Paper, p. 30). Considering herself as one of the fortunate war babies, she grew up believing that she needed "to make the most, that life has to offer" because she is "living the dreams so many cannot" (Amina's research paper, p. 30).

Amina remembers her first visit to Bangladesh with fond memories. We shall see some of that in chapter 7 in regard to the homecoming of the Bangladeshi orphans in 1989 in which her mother played a key role in organizing the trip. While at the orphanage, suddenly it hit home that she and other fellow travelers could have been there. It was at this point when Amina recognized that one of those girls could have been her had she not been adopted. Needless to say, she truly felt blessed at that moment. "I think this was the point in my life where I also decided that not only am I going to live a good life and live it to the fullest, but I am living this dream for all of these girls that did not make it out and are living in sub-standard conditions," recalls Amina (Amina's research paper, 30).

Although a practical Amina knows she would never be able to track down her birth mother, she took delight and satisfaction in being a part of the reunion of one of her siblings, Jonathan, years later in 2005. Adopted from El Salvador, at an early age, Amina recalls Jonathan's actual reunion with a very touching first glimpse of his biological mother in her presence. Amina remembers this incident as an emotional experience. Amina cannot seem to forget what she had witnessed – how the frail and diminutive birth mother slowly approached Jon and embraced him with hugs and kisses, while tears were clouding her vision as she quietly whispered over and over again, "Please forgive me, I prayed to God every day that you went to a better place" (Amina's research paper, p. 30).

Amina treasures those moments that gave her an intense feeling as though she was having a vicarious reunion with her own birth mother at the time. This experience had reinforced in her mind the circumstances under which her birth mother had to abandon her in Bangladesh in secret, having no other choice in the newly independent but war-ravished country. Needless to point out, this experience also made her realize that women in developing countries who have had to give up their child or children live such difficult lives under situations no one can ever comprehend. A reflective Amina believes that the birth mothers' decision to give up their children is perhaps the only option for most of them, which, in many ways, is definitely a selfless act.

Following her parents' career, Amina also became an educator dedicating herself to teaching. Amina believes it is important for children to look beyond themselves and to find their place in the world as global citizen. "I believe by building self-awareness, educating students about the importance of their individual voice, giving them the skills to question, think critically and act on their beliefs will prepare them for the world at large," maintains Amina (Amina's research paper, p. 34). Her years of work with children of diverse backgrounds were both interesting and rewarding being fast paced with "all of the bells and whistles" (Amina's research paper, p. 34), which made it one of the leading schools in education.

Today, she conducts international workshops to educators and offers service training sessions on a wide variety of subjects to parents and fellow teachers. Having been placed internationally, Amina is truly able to take her experiences and help her students become the "best that they can be" (Amina's research paper, p. 34). In that sense, Amina has followed the footsteps of her parents, lifelong educators. Like her parents, Amina is a continuous learner always feeling that with her expertise, she has a lot to offer to the educational field. To quote Amina, "I am my parent's daughter, jet setting around the world and finding new places to explore, people to meet and stories to add to my repertoire of life experiences" (Amina's research paper, p. 34). Taking advantage of the opportunities of life, Amina, like her parents who have lived and traveled all over the world, feels "truly blessed to be able to have this amazing life," says Amina (Amina's research paper, p. 34). Today, for an educated and enlightened Amina, the winds of change have opened new doors.

Whether she is on the road having a conversation with a stranger or at a conference discussing ethnicity and identity, Amina is forthright in the way in which she sees herself. Time and again she says she defines her identity in a simple straightforward way without resorting to any pretension: "I have traveled all over the world and when someone asks me where I am from, I say that I am from Canada. I have received some interesting looks which always makes me giggle." To clarify further, Amina continues to say that her "parents are 'white folk' [from Canada]. I believe that parents are the people who spend the time to raise you, give you shelter and nurture you regardless of your blood relations." Having multiracial siblings at home and been grown up in a multicultural Canada that was envisioned by former prime minister of Canada, Pierre Elliott Trudeau, Amina proudly says, "Trudeau had a vision and I was a part of that vision" (Amina's research paper, p. 34).

In February 2010, Amina went to Bangladesh again for a short visit mainly to reconnect herself with the people in the orphanages that she has supported all along in many different ways over the years. Her expectation this time was that since she had already seen the hardships in Bangladesh, she would also like to "see some of its beauty as well" (e-mail from Amina Wolsey to the author). She was not totally disappointed. During her fifteen-day stay in Bangladesh, she had an opportunity to visit the orphanage from where she was adopted and the Children's Village in Sreepur, as well as the Chowdhurys (Farouk and Pauline) with whom she has remained in touch ever since she knew from her childhood.

Amina credits her family for her own accomplishments and feels incredibly lucky to have been adopted into a family that provided love to her and to all her brothers and sisters. She acknowledges her good fortune, with a twinge of sadness that she was chosen while many other war babies like her remained in the Bangladeshi orphanage whose whereabouts are not known.

In summing up her life, Amina believes the Wolsey children do have a guardian angel and have extremely good luck, for they were rescued from a life of uncertainty and poverty in their country of birth: "Our 'good Samaritans' were my parents. They chose to reach out and help a young stranger [a particular reference to her brother Jonathan who was adopted from El Salvador]. They did this without a second thought and we are the product of their care" (Amina's research paper, p. 24).

"As I glimpse through the worn photo album of my new life in Canada, I see myself as a happy and healthy child enjoying what life had to offer," said Amina proudly (Amina's research paper, p. 21).

Notes and References

[1] E-mail from Tony Boonstra to Mustafa Chowdhury, July 11, 2011. The Boonstras have reviewed their profile.
[2] Chris said this to the author during his interview at his parents' house in Ashton, Ontario, on June 10, 1997.

3   E-mail from Fred Cappuccino to Mustafa Chowdhury, February 20, 2013.
4   The Cappuccinos said this to reporter Kerry Diotte in an interview with the same reporter, published in the *Ottawa Journal,* December 12, 1979.
5   The Cappuccinos were interviewed by Sheila Arnopoulos of the *Montreal Star,* November 29, 1972.
6   Letter from Elizabeth Bissett, Head, Adoption Services, Children's Service Centre, addressed as TO WHOM IT MAY CONCERN, Re: Families For Children Incorporated, June 23, 1972. The Cappuccinos have given the author a photocopy of this letter. There is also a large bulk of documents that is still with Fred and Bonnie Cappuccino in their personal home library collection on *Bangladesh File.*
7   Families For Children. *Bangladesh Project.* Part E, Chapter 32, *Bangladesh Babies.* 1982. p. 275. Hereinafter referred to as the *Bangladesh Project.* The Cappuccinos have given the author a copy of the report. The Cappuccinos have reviewed their profile.
8   This was said by the Ferries to the author during an interview with the author at Dr. Robert Ferrie and Helke Ferrie's house in Alton, Ontario on May 20, 2000. The Ferries have reviewed their profile.
9   Letter from Helke Ferrie to Ontario couples, August 31, 1972. Helke Ferrie made a photocopy of this letter and presented it to the author. This letter and all other documents that have been cited in the book are in the Ferries' personal collection titled *Bangladesh Project* on *Bangladesh File.*
10 Letter from Dr. Robert Ferrie to Fred Cappuccino, Secretary, Families For Children, August 21, 1972, in the Cappuccinos' personal collection.
11 The name stems from ancient Chinese mythology. It is the name of the Chinese Buddhist Goddess of Mercy to Children.
12 This is from the letter of recommendation for a child to be adopted by the Ferries following a visit by the adoption coordinator. The letter is titled "Re: Dr. and Mrs. R. K. Ferrie," from Victoria Leach, Adoption Coordinator, Ministry of Community and Social Services, Government of Ontario, March 8, 1974, p. 2. This letter is in the Ferries' collection.

13   Letter from Doreen Good to Mustafa Chowdhury, March 11, 1997. Since then the author has been in constant touch with the couple and has been writing back and forth all through the research period. The Goods have reviewed their profile.

14   *Wentworth Marketplace,* September 6, 1972.

15   *Focus,* May 30, 1989.

16   *Mennonite Reporter,* April 14, 1975.

17   During his stay in Dhaka, Bangladesh, in 1997–1998, Ryan wrote to his parents on a regular basis and shared the same e-mails with his friends in Canada to keep them posted about his adventure in Bangladesh. Ryan has sent the author his entire e-mail trail that contains hundreds of e-mails he wrote to his parents. All references with regard to Ryan's activities in Bangladesh are from his voluminous e-mails. Hereinafter, referred to as *Ryan's e-mail.* The present e-mail is dated September 10, 1997.

18   The *Montreal Star,* October 12, 1972; also *Newsletter,* Families For Children, Vol. 11, No. 1V October 13, 1972, p. 2 makes reference to the said newspaper.

19   Letter from Trudy Hartt to Mustafa Chowdhury, November 1, 1998.

20   Letter from Trudy Hartt to Mustafa Chowdhury, *opt. cited;* As well, Trudy said this to the author when the family met with him at a downtown restaurant in Ottawa on June 23, 2000.

21   *Ibid.* In fact, this is how Trudy explained her position on this subject and explained to the author her personal take on it. She started her note to the author in this manner following a few phone calls in the early 1997.

22   Letter from Shama Hartt to Mustafa Chowdhury dated, July 17, 2000, in which she responded to a set of questionnaire. This was followed by a series of telephone calls.

23   Letter from Lise Bertrand to Mustafa Chowdhury dated June 2, 2002. Since then both Pierre and Lise have spoken to the author several times and have written back and forth to ensure accuracy. Both Pierre and Lise have reviewed their profile.

24   E-mail from Pierre Hogue to Mustafa Chowdhury, June 19, 2012.

25   Letter from Josée Hogue to Mustafa Chowdhury, June 18, 2002. Since then the author has been in touch with Josée as and when needed. All through the years, Josée had been very cooperative. The

author interviewed Josée on October 5, 2011, in Montreal, Quebec, for a TV program. Both Josée and the author have corresponded several times to ensure accuracy and appropriateness of sharing personal information with the readers. She has reviewed her profile.

26 *Weekend Magazine*, November 20, 1971, p. 18.

27 Letter from Barbara Morrall to Mustafa Chowdhury, September 23, 1996. The following year, on March 23, 1997, they met with the author at a hotel in Saskatoon where they had a lengthy discussion on their daughter. The couple gave the author photocopies of pertinent documents regarding adoption from Bangladesh. Since then they have been in touch with each other regularly.

28 Postcard from Bonnie Cappuccino, president, Families For Children, addressed to Robin and Barbara Morrall, written from Dhaka, Bangladesh, on July 11, 1972, while the team was in Dhaka, Bangladesh, to pick out a number of war babies for interested couples who wished to be adoptive parents in Canada. It is in the Morralls' family collection. The Morralls have given a photocopy of this letter to the author. The Morralls have reviewed their profile.

29 Letter from Barbara Morrall to Bonnie Cappuccino, President, Families For Children, dated August 30, 1972. The letter is with the Cappuccinos in their personal library collection on *Bangladesh File*.

30 This was read by Robin Morrall during service in remembrance of Rani Morrall, on June 11, 1999. The Morralls have sent this information to the author in 2001 following a telephone conversation with Barbara Morrall. The package contained other information on Rani and newspaper clippings on the passing away of Rani.

31 Following the return of the team to Canada, the teenagers made a big scrapbook that was sent to then president of Bangladesh, Hossain Muhammed Ershad, on behalf of the adoptees through Canadopt. As well, the poem was reprinted in several local Ontario newspapers.

32 For details, please see Erickson, E. *Identity: Youth and Crisis,* London, Faber & Faber, 1968.

33 Letter from Dr. Robert Ferrie to John and Dorothy Morris, July 19, 1972. It is with the Morrises' in their collection. The couple has given the author a photocopy of the letter. This letter and

other documents cited in the book with reference to Jorina and the Morrises are in their personal collection on *Bangladesh File.*

34 This was said by Dorothy Morris to the author during an interview with the Morrises in their home in Brantford, Ontario, on May 11, 1998, in the presence of their daughter Lara Morris. Both Dorothy and Lara have reviewed their profiles.

35 The couple was in receipt of a newspaper clipping of the *Bangladesh Observer,* July 20, 1972, which covered the departure of the war babies for Canada and contained this particular information.

36 Letter from Lara Morris to Mustafa Chowdhury, January 10, 2001. Since 1998, the author has been in touch with Lara and her parents. They have corresponded regularly. Lara also visited the author to his house in Ottawa in 2002.

37 E-mail Ray Mowling to Mustafa Chowdhury, July 19, 2012.

38 E-mail from Elisabeth Mowling to Mustafa Chowdhury, February 20, 2001. The same year the author also met Elisabeth and interviewed her at her home in Mississauga, Ontario, on June 9, 2001. Since then the author has been in regular touch with Elisabeth and both have been corresponding back and forth. Both Ray and Elisabeth have reviewed their profiles.

39 Elisabeth said in an interview with Anne Redfearn, published in the *Brampton Guardian,* August 19, 1976.

40 *Newsletter,* Families For Children, Vol.11, No. VII, January 20, 1973, p. 2.

41 *Community, the Mississauga News,* August 11, 1976, written by Anne Redfearn.

42 The *Meadowvale World,* Volume 11, No 8, May 1984, written by Evelyn Rea.

43 Elisabeth said in an interview with Anne Redfearn, which was published in the *Brampton Guardian,* August 19, 1976.

44 "The Long Wait" by Susan Carson, *Weekend Magazine* of the *Globe & Mail,* June 24, 1975, p. 21. In her interview with Susan Carson, Elisabeth said this to Susan.

45 Letter from Onil Mowling to Mustafa Chowdhury, June 10, 2001. Prior to this, author met Onil in Toronto on June 23, 1999, and on that day, Onil spent the entire afternoon with him followed by dinner at a local Bangladeshi restaurant. Since then the author has been in touch with Onil on a regular basis.

46 This was said to the author by Margo Carr-Ribeiro while having a coffee with her at Place du Portage, Hull, Quebec. At that time, Margo worked for CIDA, while the author worked for Human Resources Development Canada in the same premises. The date was August 10, 1997. Since then the author had tried to talk to the couple several times, but the couple had remained disinterested in talking about their personal life.

47 The *Canadian,* the *Weekend Citizen,* February 24, 1979.

48 Letter from Sandra Simpson, president, Families For Children, to Mustafa Chowdhury, July 16, 1998. Since then the author has spoken with Sandra Simpson on numerous occasions. As well, he has corresponded with Sandra and her daughter Mai Lien Simpson, who is in the Toronto office of the Families For Children. The couple has reviewed their profile.

49 Library and Archives Canada, Series: RG 76, vol. 1940, files 5020-1-710 pt.1.

50 For details see D. J. Beck's "Evaluating an individual's capacity for parenthood" in *A Study of Adoption Practice* by Michael Shapiro, Child Welfare League of America, Inc. Vol. 2, pp. 72 – 77.

51 Letter from Del and Donna Wolsey to Mustafa Chowdhury February 10, 2011. This was also expressed to the author by the Wolseys in an interview with the author way back on December 29, 2005, at the Wolseys' residence in Komoka, Ontario. The Wolseys have reviewed their profile.

52 Amina Wolsey, *Perspectives of Multicultural Family: An Education in Itself.* Research Paper for Masters of Education at Ontario Institute for Studies in Education, University of Toronto, 2002, p. 35. Hereinafter referred to as *Amina's Research Paper.*

53 E-mail from Amina Wolsey to Mustafa Chowdhury January 5, 2010.

CHAPTER SIX

Joys and Woes of the Adoptive Parents

T HIS CHAPTER DISCUSSES the adoption of the war babies from Bangladesh from the point of view of the adoptive parents. Our discussion is based on interviews by the author with the adoptive parents. These interviews represent some of the earliest research for this book, and our interviews with the parents were done in multiple sessions that spanned many years. Most adoptive parents in Canada wish to adopt a child that fits their *own* racial and ethnic origin. However, these parents chose to be *different.* They wanted children from different races and backgrounds to make their family more diverse and multiracial at a time when it was not very common in Canada. The courage and strong conviction needed to adopt and raise war babies stemmed from their deeply held views. They felt that modern nuclear families were breaking down. Communities around the world were failing to care for the neediest.

In poor countries, most of the orphans were likely to die as babies, and they felt that children, all children, equally deserved life. What emerges from our interviews is that our parents and their adoptive children were much like any other family. However, the circumstances around their respective families were unlike most families. Interracial adoption was an important element in defining parenthood for them. In that sense, the adoptive parents might be seen as atypical parents who were avant-garde in embracing a shift in values in adopting racially different children to make their *own* families. The adoptees were the "unwanted" babies of Bangladesh. Born of a violated mother, such babies were relinquished to orphanages where they were saved from imminent death by the adoptive parents in our book. The parents' fight with authorities to bring the children to Canada was a great victory for them. They have kept all pertinent information, or what may be called the "primary sources" in their possessions to date. They have treasured all of the correspondence on their struggle to get through the red tape and bureaucratic delays just to bring "home" a few of these war babies from Bangladesh.

Our interviews can be summarized in the following four broad questions: (1) *Why did they adopt and what had been their experiences?* (2) *How strong was their desire to adopt a war baby?* Or, *what motivated them to take the trouble of going through a tough fight for adoption of their choice?* (3) *How many of them had biological children before adoption?* (4) *What do they remember about the actual and potential stressful consequences of parenthood; or simply, what were some of the joys and woes of parenting?* Over the years, the adoptive parents were always frank, welcoming, and cooperative with the author.

The outline of this chapter is as follows. First, we discuss what led our parents to seek adoption in the first place. Next, we discuss their first challenge of caring for children who lacked even basic documented medical information. After that, we present how the parents describe their parent-child bonds with the adoptees. Then we explore how the different parents approached the problem of *when to tell* their adopted child about the child's history prior to adoption. Finally, our chapter ends with a discussion of how diversity and multiculturalism played an important part in defining parenthood to our erstwhile adoptive parents.

Motivation for adoption

There are a number of ways in which couples come together to form a family – through adoption, surrogacy, remarriage, or other combinations. The motives of people who adopt children are as varied as the backgrounds of the parents. "When John and I were going out together, we talked about having children, among other things. One of the things we were both in agreement with was adoption. We had both thought for a long time, way before we had met, that to be able to adopt children from other countries would be great and something we would really like to do,"[1] recalled Dorothy Morris who, together with her husband, John, adopted Jorina, one of the war babies. All of these adoptive parents of the war babies were adamant that they were neither "bleeding hearts" nor "do-gooders." Their desire for adoption grew out of happy marriages. For them, it was a genuine joy to have children of diverse backgrounds. For our couples, adoption is a lifelong interest.

Why the war babies of Bangladesh? Is it because of the diminishing number of infants available for adoption in Canada? Why were they interested in adopting abandoned and "unwanted" infants born as a result of rapes? Having asked these questions, I learned from the parents that they were greatly influenced by the ideals of the day – the 1960s in North America represented an era of uprisings to gain civil rights, ending discrimination in society, anti-Vietnam war protests, with people encouraged by the words of Kennedy from the White House and Martin Luther King from the streets of America. The parents recalled how they wanted to live up to the ideals of equality, justice, and the special responsibility to uplift rather than tear down. They were aware of the war babies through newspapers, magazines, and television programs. They recall seeing the pictures of Bangladeshi war babies on the evening news and being saddened by their plight. The brutality of the massacre in Occupied Bangladesh (March 1971–December 1971) drew their outrage. However, Bangladesh was just one place of many around the world where war babies were being born.

The parents wanted to adopt a child first. To them, in dealing with child poverty and orphans, in particular, children needed permanency, and permanency meant adoption. The origin of the child was a secondary consideration. To some of the parents, a Bangladeshi war baby was, in fact, *their* second choice. The thought of Bangladesh evoked in the parents bitter memories of Vietnam in terms of their concern over the plight of the children of the war-ravaged Republic of South Vietnam. Looking back, what had crystallized the idea of adoption of war orphans of Bangladesh was the precedent of the adoption of South Asian orphans who had made their way to Canada. Having seen how numerous families had opened their homes and hearts to the war orphans of a different race (especially from Vietnam in the late 1960s), the present bunch of adoptive parents believed that they too could provide a stable and loving environment for war babies.

It was a common theme in our interviews – the parents felt a keen, but humble, sense of "doing" something for the hapless babies by adopting them. The couples all wanted to adopt. In their estimation, the war babies were the neediest of orphans. Adopting a child from Bangladesh was seen by them as a humble attempt to "save" a child, a simple response to a life in crisis. Helke Ferrie, one of the adoptive mothers who adopted two war babies from Bangladesh, described it as a matter of "an unconditional giving of yourself to a child because he's hungry and he needs you."[2]

The primary interest of the adoptive parents was, first, to give the orphans a chance for life, and, second, a life without the social stigma of how they were conceived. The parents understood the risk that adopting a war baby meant that their child had a higher than normal risk of being afflicted, maimed, or diseased. The parents went ahead with the adoptions without the usual requisite background information that accompanies an adoption, such as the history of the biological parents, the medical history of the child, and the conditions under which a particular child was conceived and carried to term.

To the parents, the war babies lives were in jeopardy – *life vs. inevitable death*. They wanted to give these babies a chance to live. These to-be parents were all in one page with no reservation at all: that the Bangladeshi war babies deserved a chance, whether they are legitimate or illegitimate, healthy or diseased. Ray and Elisabeth Mowling, who adopted a war baby (Onil), recalled, "To us, the child [war baby] was not related to any enemy – it was just a child who needed a family so that the child could grow up healthy and happy. Aside from naturally feeling the joy of having a new baby in the family, there was the added feeling of contributing to some degree on a global level. We felt we were providing an opportunity for a positive future for a little human being who was born into such difficult circumstances."[3]

In getting their adopted children to Canada, all of the couples went through a lengthy and complex adoption process fraught with delay and uncertainty. However, for the Ontario couples, the process was made much more difficult by a provincial government administration that, behind closed doors, was insistent on the adoption of children from Canada first – especially those with disabilities. The insistence of the Ontario government that the parents *not* adopt according to each couple's *own choice* incensed and hardened the resolve of the adoptive Ontario parents. The Ontario couples' fight became a national fight engaging *all* of the prospective war baby adoptive parents. John and Dorothy Morris who fought to adopt Jorina understood the provincial government's position. "Most children in Ontario are housed, clothed, educated, fed, and medically treated. What they lack is the love and security of a home,"[4] argued John. "The little ones overseas, in most the cases, did not have even the chance to live, let alone a chance to get any of the advantages that Ontario children have. We felt we had to go where the need was the greatest,"[5] wrote John.

The Ontario government argued that adopting from overseas might *alienate* racially different children in having them grow up with racially different parents. The adoptive parents, however, believed that saving the children's lives far outweighed any of these types of concerns. Del and Donna Wolsey of Komoka, Ontario, who adopted Amina (a war baby), went ahead with their plan to adopt from Bangladesh recognizing well that it would involve extra commitments, energy, and acquisition of expertise on their part. They believed that orphans around the world are everyone's responsibility "whether here in Canada or globally. It is going to impact on us some time or another. [Canadians] should be on the leading, cutting edge of reaching out to children . . . wherever they are because they are the ones who need our support."[6] It should be noted that, according to this book, the parents were right.

To the adoptive parents, childlessness was not a strong factor in their decision to adopt interracially. Neither race nor gender of the child played any role in deciding to adopt. The adoptive parents largely held traditional values in regard to marriage and family life. They already had vibrant families. They were (and are) committed to their children and to each other. They felt anxiety and excitement with the prospect of adding a child to their family who had so many unknowns surrounding them. The parents remember *how* they fantasized about the arrival of their desired baby from Bangladesh – not knowing *what* the baby would look like; or *what* would be the needs of the baby born in Bangladesh; or even when, for certain, the baby would arrive "home." The wait for the babies to arrive seemed unbearable to the parents.

In a way, some saw the long waiting period while in the process as a period of "transacting" kinship with the war babies still in Bangladesh. Interesting to note, every couple seems to remember one thing in common – that at a time when they were preparing for a major change in their lives, such anticipatory anxieties were both painful and mind-boggling.

There was scarcity of news from Bangladesh even after the Canadian team had left for Dhaka to select the war babies. According to the couples, not knowing anything about the infants' progress in the orphanage, their feeding experiences, their sleeping patterns, and other associated habits, the would-be parents in Canada could not even build up mental images in their minds of the baby they were getting ready to embrace. Far too long, they were left hanging in the air with no news from Bangladesh.

In fact, they waited until the very last minute as to whether the government of Bangladesh *could* even process the war babies for immigration to Canada. They accepted the high risk of having to raise children with special needs in terms of medical and psychological problems. In the end, it was really the pathetic life-and-death struggle of the abandoned infants (usually death) that most swayed their decision. Canadian orphans who could not be adopted live in an institution in Canada. War babies who are not adopted often do not survive past early childhood. They were motivated by the knowledge that these infants' lives were in jeopardy and that they wanted to give these babies a chance to live.

Lack of documented medical information

One of the most significant problems that the parents faced was the lack of documented information with regard to the child and the child's birth parents. The documentation for each child included the name of the child, the child's gender, and the place and date of birth. A birth certificate for each child was produced by the Dhaka-based Missionaries of Charity. There was thus no falsification of certificates in the case of their adoptive parents' children in question. Instead, having made no attempt to amend their birth certificates, the adoptive parents had embraced them by making the war babies a *part* of their families without claiming to be their progenitors.

The register book at *Shishu Bhavan* is an "open" record for each child. No attempt was ever made to create an illusion of a biological relationship between birth mothers and putative fathers of the adoptees. No information about medical or the social condition of members of the biological family had ever been added since the time original files were created back in 1972 immediately upon the birth of the war babies some of whom were born in the premises or where some were brought to be housed for adoption. The *dossier* at the orphanage premises from where the babies were adopted, therefore, remained blank and devoid of some vital information that could be of further interest to both the adoptees and their adoptive parents.

Under normal circumstances, the case record on any baby anywhere generally includes data about pregnancy, length of labor, type of delivery, birth weights, measurements, condition of baby at birth, whether there had been any deformity, cyanosis, or jaundice, including general notes and responses to first feeding, etc. As well, generally, in an ideal situation, a pedigree chart drawn from the available family history is obtained that may enable one to detect the presence or absence of a hereditary pattern. The only concrete information that the parents had to go by was the weight of the children. A baby is considered premature if it weighs less than 2.5 kg at birth regardless of the length of pregnancy. It was, therefore, natural for the parents to be anxious about the survival or normalcy of the babies because many of them weighed less than 2.5 kg at birth.

Anticipating that there would be difficulties for parents and infants, the Children's Aid Society (CAS) workers had offered significant guidance to the would-be parents. They were cautioned to keep in mind that the newborns, even those carried to the full term, were not fully developed. Furthermore, they were cautioned that the examination of newborn infants, no matter how carefully done, is sometimes inadequate to detect serious defects. For that matter, they were advised that despite the close observation, a certain number of infants so observed may later turn up with conditions that were not noted and suspected previously.

The CAS workers' cautionary remarks were that, having contemplated and actually relinquished her child, the birth mother had, no doubt, serious difficulty in providing a positive physical and emotional prenatal environment for her baby in Occupied Bangladesh. By trying to keep her pregnancy secret, and likely attempting to induce abortion multiple times, the birth mother had most probably placed her baby at great risk. Doctors around the world, they were told, had found that pregnant women who are physically and/or sexually abused have a much greater probability of giving birth to children who have breathing difficulties and who have usually slower-than-average physical and mental development.

The parents' main concerns were whether there were problems associated to the infants' growth and development due to malnutrition, illness, and potential need for hospitalization in Canada. Within three months of the arrival of the first batch of war babies to Canada, the adoptive parents also learned in October 1972 about the firsthand experience of Dr. Wayne McKinney, then a pediatric resident at the Toronto-based Hospital for Sick Children who accompanied Helke Ferrie to Dhaka. Dr. McKinney's observations were that the war babies left behind in Bangladesh were found to "have big bellies," 100 percent of whom had worms, and that they were "all in less than optimal health."[7] However, Dr. Geoffrey Davis of the London-based International Planned Parenthood Federation (IPPF) in Dhaka, Bangladesh (the details are in chapter 1), who had worked with the doctors who treated the birth mothers and their "unwanted" babies when the babies were being born, surmised that the war babies who were born, after all, following many abortive attempts to terminate their lives, must be extremely resilient to have survived thus far to be born prematurely.

The parents were made to understand and appreciate the fact that, under the circumstance, accurate prediction of the future physical and mental potentialities of the child in question would be unreliable. The only dependable information that the parents would have would be their child's immediate health needs – the future could not be predicted. All the parents could really do was to nurture their children and let nature run its course.

The newly arrived babies from Bangladesh had different needs. Because of malnutrition and general illness, the frail babies required a lot of attention especially on a physical level. Some parents indicated that in worrying about the health and well-being of the malnourished war babies, they only needed to remind themselves of the events that took place in Bangladesh prior to the birth of the babies – sexual assault of their birth mothers who had conceived them under the most tragic circumstances and gave birth in secret. The lack of adequate medical information had thus contributed to the angst of the parents – the impossibility of determining *why* and *how* a child would be affected by a number of factors including genetic causes, illness or injury to the mother during pregnancy, trauma during birth, or environmental factors for viral infections before, during, and after birth of the babies.

The parents remembered how they were in touch with Sr. Margaret Mary, then superior of the Missionaries of Charity in Bangladesh, who was very anxious to hear more about the infants following their departure. Sr. Margaret Mary was seen as the *mother* of their

Bangladeshi-born war babies in the absence of the child's birth mother up until the child's arrival in Canada. The parents in Canada also continued to make humble contribution for *Shishu Bhavan* (from where the babies were brought to Canada) and other orphanages where war orphans were housed at the time. As far back the parents recall, they routinely continued this tradition for a long time. As mentioned already, some parents went ahead and adopted more orphans from Bangladesh and brought them to Canada in their homes, while with some others who had adopted Bangladeshi orphan also cared for the children who had remained in the orphanages in Bangladesh by assuming their financial responsibilities through donations from Canada.

Although the government of Bangladesh was not committed to adoption supervision, Sr. Margaret Mary wanted to help the adoptive parents in Canada through the difficult first few weeks when their children's lives were at great risk. The parents were appreciative of Sr. Margaret Mary's concerns, which she had expressed through frequent exchanges of letters. Initially, she wrote to Fred and Bonnie Cappuccino requesting that they circulate a note she had written to all of the adoptive parents about the health conditions of "her" babies whom they had adopted. The Cappuccinos helped coordinate with all adoptive parents to provide Sr. Margaret Mary with updates on the children from Bangladesh. She made every effort to track down medical information, such as shots or medical charts on the babies and birth mothers. In her correspondence with the parents, Sr. Margaret Mary did not perceive any problems in the parents' attitudes or in the babies' development or any signs of conflict, doubt, or rejection.

Within a relatively short time, and with unbelievable faith and courage, the parents eventually came to terms with these facts, recognizing once for all that no pertinent medical or genetic information would ever be available, although they had found it hard to continue their lives without certain misgivings. They remember rather being more concerned about having the war babies shipped out of Bangladesh to stable homes in Canada as early as possible. The consideration of heredity and the fear of associated risks were put on the back burner, so to say.

In the long run, the parents came to view the lack of documentation as part of their children's search for identity, which they tried to encourage and support. They did not believe that there was a need for perpetuation of anonymity over the lifetime of the child. In fact, the adoptive parents felt that they themselves were a part of the "search" *with* their children. Having no atavistic fear, the Wolseys, the Morralls, and the Goods even escorted their adolescent war babies to take a motherland tour in 1989. They still remember witnessing their children's exuberance in the same spirit and manner as the children themselves without an iota of atavistic fear that their children's thought of biological parents (though their whereabouts are not known) would one day take them away.

Parent-child bond

The war babies and their adoptive parents joined each other on July 20, 1972. The war babies were weeks or, at most, months old at the time of adoption. But they had already experienced significant trauma from both abandonment by their birth mothers and deprivation in the generally squalid conditions of orphanages in Bangladesh. This type of early trauma can be profoundly detrimental to the psychological growth of children. The parents were cautioned that the children might have significant problems bonding with their adoptive parents.

Since the babies had lived in *Shishu Bhavan* for a very short period, the parents believed that they were not disregarded or neglected from basic physical and emotional care, such as comfort, stimulation, and affection. But if the child had lacked initial attachment to caregivers while in Bangladesh, a possibility they could not rule out, then the child could well be at risk for being unable to adequately recognize and respond with pleasure to subsequent relationships with their adoptive parents. Sr. Margaret Mary assured the parents that the children had had good relationships with the caretakers at *Shishu Bhavan*. Both the parents and authorities in Canada were skeptical. However, Sr. Margaret Mary was vindicated because the war babies attached themselves to their adoptive mothers soon after arrival in Canada.

Looking back, the memories of July 20, 1972, the precise day on which they physically embraced the Bangladeshi war babies by "taking them as their own" have remained etched in their minds forever. One commonly expressed opinion was that each child is special in that there is no one right way to raise one's family or children, for every family has its own way to meet both its varied and unique needs. Each couple had followed one's own child-rearing practices. It was natural that they did not rely on a rigid schedule as their children encountered situations in which attention, encouragement, and reassurance were needed at various times at various levels under various circumstances. To them, being a parent is a continuing role and not just for a while until the enthusiasm lasts. This remains the basis of their understanding of parenting and parenthood.

Having been close to the adoptees from an early age, the parents believe their babies were able to engage themselves in various activities, something that must have stimulated attachment responses between parent and the child. A particular child and the same child's parents, in such cases, are said to have "fallen in love" with each other.

Traveling back in their minds to the earliest days, the parents recalled touching, stroking, hugging, gently rocking, bathing, cooing, and singing lullabies to their children. Most of the babies had problems with eating. Some babies simply refused to eat by spitting up his or her formula, or having an upset stomach, or having chronic diarrhea. The parents comforted their babies by rocking them in infant swings, patted them with powders, massaged them with lotions, and tickled them. These were very fragile babies.

Some parents remembered how they grinned and laughed at the babyish gestures; how, as the children began to grow, talked a baby's babble while playing peek-a-boo with the pillows; and how they used to spend hours together playing building blocks, rings, dolls, or toys. The odd times when the parents had to be away, they had used the services of housekeepers, nannies, babysitters, and *au pairs,* but each time it was done believing it to be in the best interest of the child.

The parents were not given a great deal of notice between when the babies had been selected and were en route to Canada. Dorothy Morris learned of their new daughter, Jorina (they later named Lara), only one week before her arrival. Dorothy wrote down her feelings for her soon-to-arrive daughter:

> Not flesh of my flesh
> Nor bone of my bone
> But still miraculously our own
> Never forget for a single minute
> You weren't born under my heart
> But in it.[8]

When Lara grew up, Dorothy presented this small poem to Lara. Strong bonds indeed.

The language of the parents in Canada (English or French) became the first language of the adoptees (that is to say, mother tongue). This is markedly different than many orphans whose speech and language abilities that should have developed, but unfortunately, do not do so due to learning disabilities borne from the trauma of their births and early childhood. In such cases, children are often not able to learn to speak the native language. Instead, they learn what may be called "institutional language," a "combination of gibberish and babbling." Much to the relief of the parents, fortunately, that was not the case with the war babies who came to Canada as mere infants. The acquisition of English and/or French language was not an issue at all.

Speaking from their own and varied experiences, the parents held the view that nurturing is a relationship between a parent and a child that accords the child a sense of security, stability, warmth, love, and filial affection. They also fondly remember their involvement with their children in various sports, recreational and educational activities, such as church choir, bowling leagues, parties, concerts, and so on, which used to bring immense pleasure to their lives. Some parents recalled the ongoing activities throughout their child's early adolescent years with groups, such as Scouts, Brownies, Girl Guides, religious youth groups, YMCA/YWCA, etc. Some also recalled the periods when the children were growing up, how they used to help them through the usual family and social activities that had greatly helped them mature and develop social skills.

The mother-child bond described by the parents is also consistent with the observations made by pediatricians all along: that throughout the years of growth and development of the children, who are on their way toward independence and self-sufficiency, must rely on the mother for a long time for much of their care and nourishment. In an attempt to expand this particular point, some mothers stated that it was very much a mutual and reciprocal affair in that during infancy, the mother and the child existed in a sort of symbiosis, each dependent upon the other for a favorable and healthy course of events. It became more pronounced with the war babies who were pitifully undernourished and underweight when they came to Canada.

Ray and Elisabeth Mowling are parents of four adopted children, including war baby Onil. According to Elisabeth, "despite the best intentions and care in an orphanage, it is not possible to have the one-on-one-bonding that a child has with a mother and/or father in a family."[9] "In order for a child to be successful in life," continues Elisabeth, "it needs only a minimum of one adult who takes a consistent and positive interest in its well-being."[10] Again, while describing her personal experiences, she was particularly emphatic in saying that "there are many studies which show that this kind of early bonding is extremely helpful in growing children, producing emotionally healthy and well-adjusted adults."[11]

Talking about the resilience and elasticity of their adopted children from Vietnam, Korea, India, or Bangladesh, etc., Elisabeth recalled how often doctors, at first glance, would say something like this: that the "child is so severely damaged and should never have been adopted."[12] And yet in every case, six months or a year later, the same child would astound everyone around with a smooth progress. As a mother of four adopted children, Elisabeth knew it all too well: "Once the children knew they were emotionally safe, and loved, and they were played with, and of course physically looked after, they blossomed beyond our imaginations."[13]

However, their two older children were withdrawn and not readily willing to accept the family's affection. They believe that this had something to do with regard to questions about their adoptions who suffer from adopted child syndrome (ACS).[14] By adolescence, to avoid the same of reaction from Onil, they did everything possible to raise his awareness of his adoption. In fact, for all of the parents, the adolescent years of the children marked important (and usually positive) changes in the parent-child bonds of the adoptive parents and the war babies.

Not so for Robin and Barbara Morrall, who adopted Rani. There is ample evidence to show that Rani's bond with her parents was very strong. However, Rani came to believe that because she had been abandoned at birth, she could well be abandoned again. Soon there begun to show a crack in her deep-rooted bond with her parents. She became depressed, thinking along the line that given the fact that because she was abandoned once, it might occur again in the future. In the height of depression, instead of risking the possibility of being left again, like many adoptees, Rani took it upon herself to do the leaving despite her strong bond with her parents. In other words, after years of struggling with mental illness, Rani committed suicide. At once pathetic and poignant, none of the other war babies had such extreme experiences. Only Rani seemed to have formed an imaginary bond with her unknown birth mother. We have seen some of this in chapter 5 under Rani's individual profile, and we shall explore this more deeply in the next chapter.

For Fred and Bonnie Cappuccino, the founders of the Bangladesh Project, which enabled them to bring the war babies to Canada, the parent-child bond is critical to the future success of an adoptee. The Cappuccinos recalled particularly how they had provided their children with the tools they would need to interact with people of numerous backgrounds. From the start of their lives, they had prepared their children for the vast society having developed well-rounded social skills and a sense of appropriateness. Emphasizing self-determination and meritocracy, they tried to put across their view that good talent rises to the top at its own accord and that excellence is always valued and rewarded fairly. Such actions had helped them develop strong bonds with their children which, to this day, remain unshakable.

Research has suggested that these bonds in adoptive parents are, in fact, different from biological bonds. Fred describes the difference as being that the experience of carrying a baby to term makes the baby central to the woman. For the man, he has nine months in which to prepare his life for fatherhood. It is argued that adoptive parents do not experience biological bonding, especially women. However, Fred argues that at least for the parents of the war babies, the greater-than-normal process, effort, and uncertainty surrounding the adoptions made the parents *feel* much closer to their adopted children than would normally be the case. They believe that having twenty-one children at home (out of which only two were biological) had allowed them to develop a special maternal/paternal bond that came through a process that consisted of a learning curve – to continue to love one's infant with all its ups and downs. In fact, whether it was the Cappuccinos or any other couple from the same bunch, adoption was a matter of making their children a complete member of their family – their *own* children in the present and in the past.

Another important element that emerged from the parents' narratives is to go through a period of practical step of nest building, creating physical and emotional space in their homes and in their lives as they grew to love their particular child. While raising their children, they kept into consideration each child's needs and focused on developing a healthy one-on-one relationship with all of their children, a relationship that was devoid of any conflict. The parents bragged about how they negotiated the basic parameters of their relationships with their children in one of the most natural ways – whether it was in terms of their closeness, commitment, intimacy, autonomy, and power, all of these elements had helped them create a lasting bond with their children.

The adoptive parents undertook a lifelong commitment to adoption largely with only one single consideration of saving as many babies from death as they could. In the midst of serious conversations, many facetiously remarked that it was as though they were in labor pain all along while the process was on; it was like going through the long waiting period. Furthermore, the waiting adopters went through a period of uncertainty fraught with significance and charged with emotion in expecting a child. Though not pregnant in the true sense of the word, in many ways, the adoptive mothers' mental predicaments of that uncertain period might be seen as the period of "getting ready" to take on an *all-new role* of that of a parent to a new child who was to arrive in their family.

The adoption literature reveals many studies that argue that one common characteristic of the adoptive parents is that they did not experience what is usually referred to as the "period of post-homecoming blues" upon arrival of their adopted child. In the present case, according to the adoptive parents, their attachment with their adopted child had begun to grow long before the actual arrival of the child in their homes. There is no denying of the fact that they had their fair share of pains and pleasures long before receiving their adopted child. "In many ways," said Doreen Good, the adoptive mother of Ryan (a war baby), "like childbirth itself, adoption was also achieved with pain that came in the form of disappointments, doubts, anxieties and quite a bit of self-questioning."[15] An affectionate Doreen sees motherhood as "cherishing and caring for children rather than the physical creation of a baby."[16] Again, while on this subject, to the Goods, it meant unqualified acceptance of a child about whom they knew next to nothing.

Although there was no preferential treatment of the children in the eyes of the parents, some war babies cherished the notion that they were branded as "special" by their parents. Recalling one of her conversations with Donna, Amina's adoptive mother, Amina remembers one day she told her mom on their way home in the car, "I'm very special because I was born in Bangladesh."[17] Donna responded, "No, you're very special because you're kind, thoughtful, sweet, and honest. That's what makes you special. It's what's inside you."[18]

With the passage of time, the couples continued to experience parent-children bonds that were created in a most natural way. They recalled how they were concerned about certain human phenomena generally noticeable at the onset of puberty – a mixture of defiance and dependence having felt more drawn to the child in question. They knew, like most parents, that the parents' genetic makeup, the mothers' health and nutrition during pregnancy, and what happens to mother during early pregnancy may exert considerable influence on the health and physical and mental status of the baby. Naturally, having such thoughts, they worried about the adolescent phase of their Bangladeshi child – especially about the child's ignorance or lack of adequate knowledge about his or her biological parents and about hereditary and transmission of unknown genetic factors. To the parents, bonding with their children was of the utmost importance for the success of the child.

Majority of the parents pointed out that they had the advantage of having had the opportunity for "hands-on" contact with either social service agency or adoption agency when their children were growing up. The continuing admonition they received earlier from their family physician and counselor on the phenomenon of abandonment, especially the kind of feelings the adoptees develop during their early adolescence, was very helpful. The parents, however, had adhered to their own values following their own child-rearing strategies in raising their children. All parents were aware of adoption statistics that paint a cautionary note: *children must never be subject to parental neglect of any kind*. Children who are reared without close and continuing ties to a responsible adult tend to have more-than-the-usual number of problems in their lives.

The bond that the parents talked about embodies the notion of love, affection, endearment, trust, frankness, and open communication. Most importantly, what it boils down to is the fact that these children had had the comfort, security, and loving parents and siblings with the belief that they were *wanted* for which their adoptive parents had provided them education and opportunities.

Given the racial difference, the question regarding *how* visible to make the adoptive status to the adoptee, as well as to the community, was *never* an issue at all. There was never any pretense that they were the biological parents of the child. They were all very frank to their children about their adoption status and history. In terms of being parents, they say that giving birth is one thing and parenting is altogether something else. According to Joyce Ladner, a researcher in the sociology of parenting, this differentiation is referred to as the distinction between biological and sociological parenthood where the latter is considered by family scholars as the more important factor.[19] The parents are aware of these studies.

The key point that the parents emphasized to their children was that to make the relationship stronger, the difference between the child and the parent must be emphasized in order not to have any confusion with respect to one's race and identity. All of them believed, and interacted on the premise, that each child must grow up with a good sense of self-esteem about *being adopted* and knowing about the child's own race. Looking back, the parents are convinced that such notion must have reinforced the parent-children bond at the end. We have already seen some of this in chapter 5 under profiles of the adopters and the adoptees. Also in the next chapter, we shall read the children's narratives. With no hesitation of any kind, the war babies talk about how grateful they are to their parents simply due to the fact that their parents in Canada had *embraced* them as their *own* children without ever denying the reality of the Pakistan-Bangladesh war, the sexual violence, and its aftermath.

As a social activist, Donna Wolsey put her heart and soul through her vision, action, and philosophy that broke the boundaries in Canada and redefined what a family could be at a time when interracial adoption was not yet too common in Canada. All of the adoptive parents spoke very warmly of their gift their children gave them love, respect, and, above all, familial bond. The strong bonds between the parents and the adoptees, and the success of most of the adoptees in integrating and flourishing in Canada, is a testament to the high-quality parenting provided by the adoptive parents.

Adoptive families' network and support group in Ontario

Within months of the arrival of the first contingent of the war babies in the summer of 1972, Donna and Del Wolsey formed a support group they named Canadopt. The Wolseys felt it a necessity for both the parents and the children. A key concern for the Wolseys was that the lack of experience with the racial background of the war babies could create challenges for the parents and extended family members. According to Donna, "the support group was formed with a view to banding together to know each other and to encourage interaction among them. As well, to battle government red tape that could hinder international adoption."[20] The core group consisted of seven families. In the first few years of the group, the Wolseys (Del and Donna), the Goods (Dale and Doreen), the Ferries (Robert and Helke), the Boonstras (Tony and Bonnie), the Morrises (John and Dorothy), the Rocheforts (Phil and Diane), all from Ontario, and the Morralls (Robin and Barbara), from Saskatchewan, remained in regular contact with each other. Canadopt grew to be much more.

It became a resource for couples across Canada, providing a meaningful support system for children adopted from overseas. As Donna saw it, because a child with a different physical characteristic from its parents makes the family look different to other families in their community, there is a need to know each other's social environments and problems. Originally, therefore, their goal had been to learn from each other in terms of handling the day-to-day challenges of raising a racially different child. Donna believed that they must work toward normalizing such attitude and behavior of the people around.

However, it eventually became a platform from which to lobby the government so that future couples would not be so hindered in international adoption. After only its first year, it began to help inform the public on international adoption: "Bangladesh[i] orphans thriving and happy in Ontario homes,"[21] wrote the local the *London Free Press*. Commending the Wolseys for their initiative, the local news media highlighted how it was essential to improve the cooperation between psychiatrists, physicians, educationalists, social workers, and adoptive parents to make international adoptions easier in Canada.

Collectively under Donna's stewardship, Canadopt grew into a close-knit group of families where at least one child was adopted from Bangladesh (though not necessarily a war baby). Some parents recall meeting informally every once in a while to exchange greetings, to catch up with each other, and to share individual experiences with the rest of the group members.

Typical activities offered through Canadopt included potluck dinners, get-togethers, informal discussions, parties, day camps, family camps, and a variety of recreational sports involving parents and their children. Other activities included bringing speakers and social workers for them to learn more about adoption, parenting, and motivating the children. One might say these were peer-led rather than professionally led support groups that had cared for each other with the ideas and techniques that helped them grow together having found a wealth of information on caring based on their unique experiences.

"This is a good place to come to watch families interact, the relationship between brothers and sisters, between moms and dads and their children and try to appreciate the incredible bonding and incredible relationship that has developed in the family,"[22] said Del. The network offered a safe and supportive place to raise questions, express uncertainty, vent frustrations, and share success stories.

As time went by, through formal and mostly informal reunions, the adoptive couples frequently banded together for the purpose of pooling individual experiences into a common force to help each other. As Canadopt volunteers got into the swing of things, Canadopt began to provide great opportunities to both adopters and adoptees to share realistic expectations and feelings.

Over the years, however, Canadopt's focus had changed as the adoptees became older. Doreen Good (Ryan's mother) recalled how in the early 1970s, the meetings and social gatherings were an important part of their lives. As time went by, their children gradually became less formally involved. "As parents it was helpful to have other parents to offer support, help and encouragement through the adoptive process and as a way of letting your children experience other families who were made up of multi-races, as a way of normalizing that,"[23] recalled Doreen.

Through Canadopt, the adoptive parents made excellent ongoing relationship with the like-minded people. Perhaps the two most tangible outcomes of Canadopt and other network groups were the creation of a sense of unity and awareness as well as provision of funds raised through a variety of activities, such as Christmas bazaars, car washes, dinners, etc. The idea of learning about each other's culture and to be sensitive to and open-minded in embracing other people's culture and cultural values was helpful as these allowed the participants to immerse in various cultures and experiences that had given them a worldly perspective of life. From a professional point of view, they were not only an "acknowledgment" but also an alternative to what is often referred to as the notion of the "rejection-of-difference," a notion that had emphasized family and group solidarity together.

The couples passionately treasure the news coverage. Commending the Wolseys for their initiative, the local newspapers tried to generate interest in adoption. Today, forty three years later, Canadopt still exists with over six hundred members across the country, still meeting each year for potlucks and helping hundreds of adoptees integrate into life in Canada. Not surprisingly, even to this day, Donna is actively involved with Canadopt, organizing yearly get-togethers and summer picnics for the members.

Apart from Canadopt, Helke Ferrie formed her own organization, Kuan-Yin Foundation, in Burlington, Ontario, which was active for a few years and then went out of existence. In Quebec, the Families For Children (FFC) included Lloyd and Sandra Simpson and Herb and Naomi Bronstein as key persons. Through frequent potluck dinners, the adoptive parents used to get together in addition to regular coffee and playtimes at the Lakeshore Unitarian Church for mothers and preschoolers. The group would regularly meet at the Lakeshore Unitarian Church in Montreal as a way for families with multiracial children to spend quality time together.

When to tell

Most adoption experts agree that children should be told at an early age that they have been adopted. In the past, the child who asked no question about his or her adoption was thought to be well adjusted, while the inquiring child was thought to have problems. This is an antiquated view, however; the topic still fosters significant anxiety with *how* and *when* to broach the subject with a child, at the same time, how not to overburden the child with the tragic story that typically accompanies the backdrop to an adoption story. Early awareness of the fact of adoption can alleviate the conflict that inevitably arises after a child first discovers that he or she is not being raised by his or her biological parents. For the adoptive parents of the war babies, it was particularly obvious because of the racial difference between the child and the parent. To the parents, it was doubly important to inform their children early before they might learn of their adoption from someone other than their parents.

Even though the challenge they had encountered in telling "someone else's child" unconditionally that he or she is *theirs*, they talked about the birth and origin of the child in plain truth. A general rule of thumb the adoptive parents had followed was that much trouble is saved if a child is told at an early age about being adopted and, conversely, that many troubles arise from delay in disclosing this information. Timely disclosures illustrate the value of the honest truth to a child, argued the parents.

Each adoptive parent had used their own sense of judgment and had delayed until one became convinced that a child's maturity had increased with age as well as their social world had widened to understand and appreciate the idea and necessity of adoption given the child's background history, love, and belonging. Having known that children are generally more emotional than intellectual, parents were also very particular on the use of phrases and terminologies. They were of the view that careless use of many commonly used terminologies would conjure up negative images in the child's mind. They recalled, never using the term "rejected" or "abandoned for adoption" whenever the topic adoption was broached in the family's conversation. They were doubly careful in ensuring that the child in question did not ever get to hear from them along the line such as the child was "rejected" by the child's biological mother/father and that the child was "chosen" by the adoptive parents.

An important element of the story that they all recall was the carefully crafted narrative to portray the birth mother in a compassionate way so that she was depicted so helpless that she had no choice but to give up the child in question. They were mindful of the fact that since the story of past could not be changed, they could not pretend to say about things that did not happen. They interacted with the children keeping

MUSTAFA CHOWDHURY

in mind the notion that denying the growing children what they needed to know would only result in creating negativity. In revealing their adoptive identity, the key message the parents had for their children was that *one should accept one's adoptive status and be proud of it.* In talking about the child who usually led them into talking about why the child was placed for adoption, implicit in the message they tried to communicate was the notion that the adopted child was not "bad from birth" as often thought of about adoptees. In doing that, they neither denigrated the birth mothers nor the country in which they were born.

This way, the parents believed, the children would be able to situate themselves better in comprehending *what* happened and *how* it happened. Needless to point out, the parents' recognition of the importance of adhering to historical truth had remained firm all through. Some remember during their early conversation with the war babies, they did not regale them with the squalid details of the terrible condition of the time. They held the view that it would be in the best interest of the child that these facts were faced squarely from the start by involving the child in that knowledge. Unlike the usual adoptive parents, many of whom remain in fear that with revelation of adoption history, "something would change forever," this particular group of adoptive parents did not seem to have any such fear at all. They had encouraged their growing children to understand the difference between *secrecy* and *privacy.* They based their logic on the understanding that as the child would grow in age, the child would begin to learn *how* to exercise good judgment about *what* to tell and to *whom.* The parents do not have any atavistic fear.

Fred and Bonnie Cappuccino, who adopted one Bangladeshi war baby and eighteen other war babies and orphans, believe that every child must be informed of all things as personal as *who* gave birth to them. However, that does not make it any easier to explain the "story" to the war babies: "unwanted" children of Bangladesh some of whom were sent away to Canada. Beyond the story of being unwanted, how does a parent explain the context of enforced pregnancy of Bengali women through sexual violence by Pakistani military personnel in Occupied Bangladesh? According to the Cappuccinos, it is a story that could be easy for any child to internalize in terms of the child being "undesirable" or "unloved." The parents feared potential consequences of such a situation.

In telling the story of adoption, the parents made sure that there were no conflicting stories about one's origin, nor was the knowledge of adoption ever a forbidden subject in their homes. The parents are aware of a fairy-tale dimension of adoption with some distortion and pretension that is often introduced along the vein of a "chosen" story line to make answers of origin more age appropriate or to avoid the issue altogether. None of the parents resorted to any kind of secrecy with a "chosen story line" that many adoptive parents tend follow, having twisted the original story with their own fabrication.

They were also aware of far too many adoptive parents who had tried to counteract feelings of abandonment, but that had only contributed further to the children's fear because the "chosen" child could be "unchosen" – that is, abandonment again for the second time. Consequently, being doubly cautious, they remained mindful of the latest round of counseling – that is, to tell the child as early as possible in order to make the adoption concept a natural part of family life. Their solution was to tell their child the plain truth.

In the adoption narrative, an adoptee is often led to regard the birth parent *as if dead,* if not literally, then at least symbolically. Adoptive parents generally make the story of adoption into a myth of family origin. There may be a "killing off" of biological parents or of a rescue operation on the part of the adoptive parents.

The present adoptive parents, being cognizant that they ought to be natural, explained to their (adopted) children that they were very special only in the sense that their biological parents were unable to raise them due to circumstances *beyond* their control. They believed in keeping the war babies in the historical loop. But they must not do that through a truncated narrative with a metaphorical truth as though birth parents and the child were to be *dead to each other.* The parents believed that the children must not remain in the dark and that there should be no mystery surrounding their birth and relinquishment in Bangladesh and adoption in Canada.

They believed in the notion that even though born as a result of rape, the child in question has a right to know his or her birth history – whatever little information there might be. Their goal in telling the plain truth was to take the chance that the child might internalize the story of his or her conception in the wrong way. To complete the narrative, though awfully inadequate in terms of vital information, they believed they should be transparent having no riddle in the minds of the adoptees in question. The truth, their parents believed, would avoid the danger of incurring the child's distrust. They were confident that as long as the child trusted them, then they, as a family, would be able to deal with any negative or disturbing emotions.

Most of the families, such as the Cappuccinos (Fred and Bonnie, who raised twenty-one children), the Ferries (Robert and Helke, who raised thirteen children), the Hartts (Joel and Trudy, who raised nine children), and the Simpsons (Lloyd and Sandra, who raised nineteen children), had multiple children – both adopted as well as born to the family. They were quite comfortable in that they had a good idea of *what* they and their children needed to know about *being adopted* and being *born to the family* and *when* they needed to know about each other. In that sense, it was a common phenomenon in the adoptive homes where there was an instant readiness on the part of the parents who were prepared to talk to their children about a range of associated topics at any given moment.

With that in mind, they strongly encouraged their children to be upfront in their interactions with family members – to say *what* they really thought and to express their innermost thoughts openly. According to the Simpsons, had they not spoken frankly to their children about their adoption, they would have begun a pattern of falseness in their relationship with their children, which would have allowed for future deceptions and traumatic moments of revelation at a later age, resulting in a feeling of children's feeling of not belonging with the adoptive family. In that sense, all adoptive parents tried through the years to bring the pieces of a complicated adoption puzzle in a systemic way into a lifelong development perspective and within the purview of their own family system. Accordingly, as time went by and the child began to mature year after year, they would talk about adoption using age-appropriate responses at the time to the best of their ability.

Some parents chose a quiet and relaxed moment to sit together and talk; some followed up on their children's queries, comments, and questions *as* and *when* raised; while some others used family photographs and newspaper clippings on their children's life story book or scrap book as a way of broaching the subject. Again, some parents recalled differently.

There was no particular "right time" to broach the subject of adoption, their children's birth, history, country of origin, and/or other pertinent information. It was a gradual and repeated process for children who were added one after another to the parents' families. The Goods (Dale and Doreen), who adopted Ryan, a war baby, and Rachona, a war orphan from Bangladesh, also acted and reacted on the premise that there ought to be an honest discourse in the family to avoid serious problems when adoptees reach adolescence.

The Boonstras (Tony and Bonnie) have raised seven children, five of whom were adopted orphans including Chris (a war baby). They told Chris when he was still very young during a "sit-down" with him and their other children. It was so obvious to all the children that they and their parents did not have the same biological line (because everyone has a different skin color). By and large, they were guided by their own sense of judgment on the "timing,"[24] recalled the Boonstras. They, as a family, found it relatively easy to explore their children's respective birth histories.

The Wolseys (Del and Donna) also recounted those days when their children, though little, were growing up and needed to understand the fact that they were both *born* and *adopted,* not one or the other. According to Donna, the key point is that it is not so much the timing of the disclosure but also the way in which the truth was presented was the issue. While the age of the child is important so that the child in question understands the gravity of the subject, it is also important to ensure that the parents' comfort level is natural and not stressed at the time of disclosure, observed Donna.

Early age-appropriate discussions were a kind of practice ground for the children, recalled John and Dorothy Morris. Adoption (within the multiracial families) was an obvious aspect of the adoptive families where the parents are Caucasian. Therefore, the racially different children were not surprised by the revelation of being adopted. However, the parents believed that searching for one's roots satisfies a *natural urge,* which is an emotional journey for *both* the adoptive parent and the adopted child.

Another ongoing challenge the parents had faced was to remain calm and sober when confronted with many social critics who tend to argue against removing children from their ethnic and cultural origin. The story of adoption of the war babies was publicly known because of the racial composition of the parents and their children who had often received more attention as a family when their multiracial children were younger – something that they attributed partly to the fact that people were, and are, generally curious about interracial families.

The Hartts (Joel and Trudy) recalled having discussions with their Bangladeshi daughter, Shama, about her birth mother. When the children were growing up, all adoptive parents discussed in the book had always displayed a strong generous impulse in finding more about the birth mothers in Bangladesh, though an errant impossibility. Technically speaking, the adoption of the war babies of Bangladesh was neither an "open" adoption (i.e., where the biological line can be known) nor a "closed" adoption (i.e., where the biological line is hidden or not legally allowed to be known), but a mixture of both. It is known to all about the circumstances under which birth mothers had conceived and given birth to such infants against their will; as well, everyone knows about the consequent abandonment and subsequent adoption of such babies, although nothing more is known in specific term.

However, not all of the adoptees took well to their status as adoptees. We have briefly mentioned Rani, who was the only adopted child in the Morrall family. Robin and Barbara Morrall had one biological son, John. The Morralls believed that Rani must be told the truth when she was old enough to "understand" the concept of adoption. They were careful in making sure that they have a "conversation" with her regarding her adoption. The couple, however, could not recall the exact time when the topic was first broached. Rani eventually became obsessed with her birth mother. We have already noted this in chapter 5. Whether this situation could have been avoided is not something we can answer here. However, we can say that the Morralls followed the same path as the other parents in terms of telling Rani at an early age, being open about not being her biological parents and helping Rani explore her birth country.

All adoptive parents acted on the assumption that it was all right to ask questions and be curious. Again, in responding to some pivotal questions, they paid extra attention to the child's temperament, experience, development, and environment to the extent possible. In a sense, it was a unique situation in which the parents made sure that if there was reticence on their part to talk about the past, it was not to be interpreted as unwillingness to be forthcoming with their child. In their own wisdom, the parents had recognized how their adopted child needed to be answered fully and must be encouraged to ask the right questions.

It will be seen in the children's narratives that never for a moment did they feel that the door to communication with their parents was closed. At the end, both parents and children were happy to see how early revelation had minimized any negative impact by assurance of demonstrated filial love and affection.

Diversity and multiculturalism

The war babies' adoptive families were all multiracial, for the most part multiethnic, and multicultural. This is unlike most Canadian families, whether adoptive or not. Transracial adoption was not yet in vogue in Canada in the early 1970s. However, both supporters and opponents of interracial adoption agree that the adopted racially different children have a right and a need to develop a sense of ethnic identity based on their birth heritage. In the late 1970s and early 1980s, many black American sociologists and social-work theorists argued, based on adoption outcomes in the USA, that transracial adoption was not the "best" solution – an assertion with which the adopters nor the adoptees in Canada disagree. Despite being racially different, neither the parents nor the adoptees had any such problems. The parents of the war babies believe that their multiracial families in the Canadian milieu of pluralism had helped them achieve better adoption outcomes.

According to the parents, the diversity in their respective families had allowed the adoptive *siblings* to develop a particular kind of sensitivity and tolerance, which the parents do not believe could have been acquired so easily in a typical monoracial family. They felt that it was incumbent on them to expose their children to the child's birth culture. To do this ably, the parents had to learn about *each* child's racial and cultural backgrounds. At the end, however, the parents believed that they ought to stress the need for the children to develop a "Canadian" multicultural identity – which meant being pluralistic and celebratory of whatever one calls one's own culture.

The parents remained mindful of the fact of their child's racial identity is not separate from but a part of his or her "Canadian" identity – since Canada consists of Canadians of many races, nationalities, and religions where diversity was, and is, an integral part. In their efforts to build a stable and secure place, all family members were affirmed and supported for *who* they are. Having a deep commitment to work together for a positive growth, the parents dug in for a long haul. As a result, despite the fact that each family member found the other to be different, each remained respectful of the other.

Not surprisingly, therefore, the parents who had large families *intentionally* fomented multiculturalism in their families. In 1971 Canada became the first country in the world to adopt a *multiculturalism policy. The Multiculturalism Act* embodies, in law, the principle of racial and cultural equality with the force of law. The policy was worked on the heels of the tumultuous 1960s – a time of great upheaval and protest in civil society in the Americas. The rapid social changes of the times greatly influenced the adoptive parents. The parents understood multiculturalism as something that would make strong efforts to create an inclusive society in which Canadians of all backgrounds can participate and meaningfully contribute to the ongoing evolution of a multicultural Canada. When their children were growing up, *the Multiculturalism Act* was already in place in Canada. The parents see it as a fundamental characteristic of the Canadian heritage and identity that ensures that all Canadians keep their identities, take pride in their ancestry, and have a sense of belonging.

Many of the parents referred to their eclectic family life in terms of instilling a Canadian sense of values toward democracy, freedom, human rights, and the rule of law. The key concepts that they emphasized were ethnic cohesion and cross-cultural understanding that encourages racial harmony. Diversity within their families immersed quite easily. Naturally, both parents and children paid attention to the ideal of celebrating and treasuring the differences among the family members.

Also emerged from the parents' narratives is their view of a broader concept of pluralism. Their greatest responsibilities were to observe *if* and *how* their transracially adopted children were likely to face issues that were not part of their biological children's reality, such as developing an identity, which linked upbringing, physical appearance, ethnocultural heritage dealing with racism and discrimination, as well as the social stigma of adoptive status. Some parents were of the opinion that given the fact that the children grew up in a diverse Canada, knowledge of such facts were necessary for them to be able to cope with prejudice, discrimination, and stereotypes. In other words, they believed that basic coping skills would give their children resistance, resourcefulness, self-confidence, and, most importantly, a point of reference in their lives.

Again, some parents talked about their encounters with strangers who would often stare at them while they are with their visibly different children with curiosity. The racial diversity of the family often became a source of amusement because much too often they used to be asked by people outside of their family questions like the following: where did you get him or her from? In such situations, the parents recalled often giving prompt and hilarious retorts like "through a mail-order catalogue." Though somewhat amusing, they said encounters of such nature had made them doubly careful, which, over the years, also made them more patient and less reactive. In retrospect, it was almost comedic to them to realize how much time they had spent practicing the answer to an innocuous question like *how* they ended up with a multiracial family. But they also cautioned that it was necessary to have *ready answers* for onlookers to avoid unsolicited and undesirable comments and remarks.

Some parents tried very hard to instill an appreciation for their child's cultural heritage through language, sports, arts, crafts, music, and religion. In doing so, they always encouraged their children to enrich their connection to those engaged in similar activities. The parents as a whole had acknowledged the difference of culture to emphasize to the point they believed it was necessary but did not overemphasize it. The parents also talked about what they have learned thus far in their efforts to become multiracial and multicultural cultural families – that ensuring equality, fostering fairness, and cultivating respect for different cultures are absolutely critical to building a better, stronger, and more prosperous Canada.

The parents wanted their children to be able to develop relationships with other children from the same country of origin. The adoptees would get exposure to culture through family activities, such as eating ethnic foods, watching movies, reading books, and attending cultural camps. However, there were also a few families that were less interested in engaging their children in nonmainstream cultural activities. To paraphrase their words, they "were mindful" that "racial difference" is a reality. The difference would affect the children throughout their lives. So it was important for their children to be Canadian first.

Perhaps for this reason, the multiracial aspect of the family, though a key concern for all of the parents, did not manifest itself in the same way for each of the couples discussed in the book. Some parents also used varying degrees of encouragement to their children to be interested in and proud of their origin. Bonnie believes that "the adoptive parents should try to learn about their multi-racial child's heritage and try to take pride in that heritage because it helps the child learn to appreciate his own heritage."[25] The Ferries (Helke and Robert) sent both of their Bangladeshi war babies to Indian boarding school to expose them to the subcontinental culture. According to Helke, "to have a Chinese face, a black face or a brown face with almond shaped eyes and a smile, to say 'I'm a Canadian' is perhaps the greatest compliment that can be paid to our country."[26]

The Wolsey's daughter, Amina, became good friends with Prima Chowdhury (Amina's parents knew Farouk and Pauline Chowdhury). Through the Chowdhury family, Amina regularly attended events hosted by the Bengali community in the Ontario's London area. The couple's commitment to expose Amina to the Bengali culture remained strong, as they believed that the birth culture of their daughter is truly a part of their transracially adoptive family. In 1989, Donna Wolsey organized a grand trip for Ontario adoptees from Bangladesh to visit Bangladesh. (For details, see chapter 7.)

Donna told Amina, "We did not want you to grow up thinking there was only one way to think or do things (the Canadian way or the Wolsey way). We wanted you to grow up seeing (in a natural way) that life, the way people did things, ate, dressed, and thought were not always all the same. So we learned to cook food from different countries, ate in different ethnic restaurants, attended different cultural events and interacted and socialized with people from many different countries. This was a natural interest for us and we wanted to expose you as well to these many differences,"[27] thus quoted Amina in her research paper while describing her own diverse family in which she grew up.

Amina also remembers having been exposed to a variety of different cultures in her own home when she was growing up: "As far as I can remember, my house has always been my parents' personal museum. The walls in our house map out their lives and adventures together. Pictures of the places they have been, paintings from France, Africa, Vietnam, Korea and Germany, as well as, numerous masks, hand carved wooden artifacts and a collection of unique musical instrument complement the walls. Eclectic foreign artifacts, each with its own story, are scattered throughout the house. As you enter the house, a cuckoo clock crafted in Switzerland greets you. As you turn into the 'family room' there are two glass showcases that house my mother's doll collection; each doll representing a country she has visited. The good silver is from the Middle East, the dinner plates from Africa, their bedroom set hand carved from Bolivia, Ju-lee's and my bedroom furniture from Bangladesh. Our home offered an education in itself."[28]

In contrast, the Ribeiros (Roberto and Margo-Carr), for example, did not encourage their Bangladeshi son, Martin, to dig for more information about his country of origin. According to Roberto, since Martin was developmentally slow from the beginning of his school years, they decided not to burden him with additional information that he might or might not be interested in. They left that search entirely up to the child (see chapter 5 under "Shomor"). The Ribeiros were of the opinion that their grown-up children would need to make their *own choices*. Their job, as the parents recounted, was to simply introduce their children to their background.[29]

Adopting a child from the war-torn Bangladesh in 1972 was a "natural" thing, said the Hartts (Joel and Trudy). "The war-babies of Bangladesh," said the Hartts, "needed the security and warmth of a stable relationship which they lacked in the premises where they were born or dropped off."[30] In fact, as will be seen, building on the diversity inherent within the family by adopting siblings of different countries had validated the functions of their family structure.

One of the common strategies of the adoptive parents was flexibility in child-rearing methods – whatever they needed to do, they did. Time and again, the parents said that whether it was then or now, loving their children is not about treating them equally or in the same manner. Instead, it is about loving them for *who they are* and supporting them according to their unique needs, which had often made them treat their children differently in order to be fair to all to achieve the same result. By this, the parents meant that some children needed more attention than others. We have not failed to notice in chapter 5 how the Morralls, the Simpsons, and the Ribeiros, for example, had to take a different approach for their Bangladeshi war baby than their other children, as the child in question needed to be treated differently for the child's unique type of illness.

From old dairies and notebooks in the attic, almost all of the parents kept a treasured scrapbook for each of their children. It might include newspaper clippings, school report cards, school activities, certificates, photos, awards, prizes, or a personal record describing what events took place. They all waited for when their children would be old enough to understand and appreciate it to show it to them.

Speaking from their own experiences, the parents maintain that one must be persistent. In a sense, each child in their families was a building block, a part of what is seen as Canadian mosaic. Having successfully "showcased" their families as "multiracial" and "multifaceted," they have demonstrated their ability to pull through thick and thin by following a *make-it-happen* strategy.

Table 4
Number of children in adoptive families

Name of the couple	Number of biological children	Number of adopted children	Total number of children
Dale and Doreen Good (Ontario)	0	2	2
Del and Dona Wolsey (Ontario)	0	6	6
Fred and Bonnie Cappuccino (Quebec)	2	1 9	21
Joel and Trudy Hart (Quebec)	1	8	9
John and Dorothy Morris (Ontario)	1	3	4
Kenneth and Mitzi McCullough (Nova Scotia)	Unknown	Unknown	Unknown

Lloyd and Sandra Simpson (Quebec)	4	15	19
Philippe and Diane Rochefort (Ontario)	3	3	6
Pierre and Lise Hogue (Quebec)	1	1	2
Ray and Elisabeth Mowling (Quebec)	0	4	4
Dr. Robert and Helke Ferrie (Ontario)	3	10	13
Roberto and Margo Carr-Ribeiro (Quebec)	1	4	5
Robin and Barbara Morrall (Saskatchewan)	1	1	2
Tony and Bonnie Boonstra (Ontario)	2	5	7

Source: Interviews and correspondences with the adoptive parents in Canada

Notes and References

[1] Letter from Dorothy Morris to Mustafa Chowdhury, November 23, 1999. The same letter also contains few pages of handwritten notes that Dorothy wrote following the arrival of Jorina. Dorothy meticulously recorded her own experiences and observations as the little girl began to grow. Dorothy presented the same notes to Jorina when she became an adult. Dorothy made a copy of that note for the author. The couple has kept all their correspondences with government officials in a file titled *Bangladesh File*. Hereinafter, referred to as *Dorothy's note*.

2   Letter from Helke Ferrie to Mustafa Chowdhury November 10, 1999. Helke also made the same statement to the author during the interview with her and husband, Dr. Robert Ferrie, which took place on May 20, 2000, at the Ferries' house in Alton, Ontario.

3   Elisabeth Mowling said this to the author during the interview on August 7, 1998, in her house in Mississauga, Ontario. Later on this was confirmed again by Elisabeth in writing in an e-mail to the author on February 2, 2002.

4   Letter from John and Dorothy Morris to William Davis, Premier of Ontario. There is no date in the letter. The couple claims that this letter was hand-delivered to the premier's office due to the urgency of the matter. The Morrises gave the author a copy of the letter. The couple has kept all their correspondences with government officials in a file titled *Bangladesh File.*

5   *Ibid.*

6   Amina Wolsey attributed this to her parents whom she interviewed for her research paper while at the University of Toronto. She quoted this in the document titled *Perspectives of Multicultural Family: An Education in Itself.* Research Paper for Masters of Education at Ontario Institute for Studies in Education, University of Toronto, 2002, p. 6. Hereinafter, referred to as *Amina's Research Paper.*

7   *The Gazette,* November 29, 1972.

8   *Dorothy's note,* p. 7 See also footnote 1.

9   E-mail from Elisabeth Mowling to Mustafa Chowdhury, February 2, 2002.

10   *Ibid.*

11   *Ibid.*

12   E-mail from Elisabeth Mowling to Mustafa Chowdhury, June 14, 1999.

13   *Ibid.*

14   None of the war babies suffered from what clinical psychologist David Kirschner had coined the term *adopted child syndrome (ACS)* – deviant behavior among adoptees supporting the notion that all adoptees suffer psychological damage because they were adopted. Kirschner estimates that about 10 percent of all adoptees manifest behaviors that could fall to the category broadly defined as ACS. Kirschner describes such behaviors as pathological lying, shallow or manipulative relationships, truancy, stealing, promiscuity, setting

fires, educational difficulties, and so on. He also observed that these adoptees may demonstrate low frustration tolerances, low self-images, and several other negative behavior patterns. American Adoption Congress, Boston, held on May 30, 1987, cited in *Intercountry Adoption: A Multicultural Perspective,* ed. by Howard Altstein and Rita J. Simon, Praeger, New York, 1991, p. 12.

[15] E-mail from Doreen Good to Mustafa Chowdhury, March 11, 2006. In addition, Doreen has also written to the author between 1998 and 2012 regarding their experiences in parenting. In her letter of May 12, 2012, Doreen has mentioned this again.

[16] *Ibid.*

[17] *Amina's Research Paper,* p. 25.

[18] *Ibid.*

[19] For more, see Joyce Ladner, *Mixed Families,* Anchor Press, Doubleday, N.Y., 1977, p. 75.

[20] Donna said this in an interview with Mustafa Chowdhury at her home in Komoka, Ontario, on December 29, 2005.

[21] The *London Free Press,* July 23, 1973.

[22] *Amina's Research Paper,* 2002, p. 16.

[23] Letter from Dale and Doreen Good to Mustafa Chowdhury, March 11, 1997.

[24] Tony Boonstra said this in an interview with Mustafa Chowdhury on May 14, 2004, in his house in Ashton, Ontario.

[25] Bonnie Cappuccino said this in an interview with Jane Finlayson, reporter with the *Citizen,* June 22, 1973.

[26] Helke Ferrie shared this with Mustafa Chowdhury from her voluminous notes that she has written on her fight for adoption of orphans of her choice. She had given the author a photocopy of her notes. This was discussed during the author's visit to her home at Alton, Ontario, on May 20, 2000.

[27] *Amina's Research Paper,* 2002, p. 9.

[28] *Ibid.,* 2002, p. 28.

[29] This was stated by Roberto Ribeiro to Mustafa Chowdhury on July 10, 2007, over a cup of coffee at Place du Portage, Gatineau, Quebec, work premises in which both were working at the time.

[30] Letter from Trudy Hartt to Mustafa Chowdhury, November 1, 1998.

CHAPTER SEVEN

War Babies through the Years

THE WAR BABIES were raised in homes where the dominant culture was mainstream Canadian and where their siblings often included other international adoptees. The multiracial milieu of their formative years gives us a starting point from which to understand the war babies' shared identity. The author conducted informal interviews with the adoptees to try to understand the war babies' experience of growing up in Canada and the interrelationships between their cultural identity and the place they call "home" in Canada.

The interviews comprised of a set questions: (1) *How well integrated did they feel within their family at adolescence? And, how do they feel now as adults? How do they relate to their (white) parents? (2) What is their view of racial and ethnic identification given that their parents are white and many siblings are multiracial? (3) If, and to what extent, have they experienced discrimination or racism because of their ethnic or racial background?* In addition, they were also asked, *How do they view their life history? Where do they think they belong, and where do they find their "home"?*

The interviews were conducted over a number of years and often required multiple meetings between the author and the adoptee. The adoptees roundly welcomed the interviews and engaged the author with interest and enthusiasm. The interviews were informal, sometimes with parents there and sometimes not. We present our findings from the interviews in six broad themes: (1) the early years of the adoptees' lives, (2) their desire to know about their past and country of birth, (3) their family relationship/bonding, (4) their first visit to their country of birth, (5) their racial and Canadian identities, and (6) their experience of racism in Canada.

Early years

The war babies had very similar experiences and emotions in their early years. They all learned about their respective adoptive family histories, customs, religions, values, and ethics, and assumed their individual place in their respective communities. Their adoptive parents gave them the guidance, courage, and emotional support to constructively incorporate the knowledge of their births in the Bangladesh's war of liberation into their lives in Canada.

The war babies appreciated how their (adoptive) parents had fought hard to bring *them* from Bangladesh in order to raise them. In their Canadian families, they were all taught to be respectful of each other, to appreciate *who* each person *is* without any reference to one's biological past. The war babies seemed to have very normal early years in their adopted families even though they were aware of their tragic origins. The war babies were precocious. In our interviews, the word "togetherness" was used to describe how they felt, as children, a very adult sense of being together with their adoptive families in terms of support, care, concern, intimacy, and love for each other within the family. They felt like they belonged, were loved, and were accepted. The war babies deeply appreciated growing up in families that had a mother, father, and children − the primal and inescapable "natural" human family.

Their memories of early life included seeking out friends and playmates at school and identifying themselves to peers as being part of eclectic, uncommon families. The adoptees shared common family practices (i.e., mainstream Canadian culture) and insisted on being open to friendships to all children, and in particular, they all strongly believed that color does not matter in fraternizing and befriending others. When the war babies reached the age of majority, their "blindness" to race helped them cope well with life in Canada.

Desire to know about their past and their country of birth

As far back as the adoptees could recall, they knew the word "adoption." It took a long time, however, for them to understand *what it meant to be adopted*. Most of the adoptive families had more than one racially different adopted child. Additionally, the adopted children were usually raised alongside biological children.

Consider the adoptee Chris Boonstra. Chris echoes the recollection of all of the war babies. He grew up in a small town in Quebec. His family consisted of seven children where five were adopted. He claims that he knew all along that he was adopted. He could not recall exactly when he became aware of what it actually meant to be adopted. During his early years, he had many questions regarding his personal history. His parents gave him a succinct historical narrative of the harsh truth of *how* he was conceived during the war of liberation in Occupied Bangladesh. He recalled numerous times when his parents found themselves in an awkward situation trying to explain him his origins. In particular, when he was very young, his parents tried their best to caution him that knowing about his birth history and birth parents would not necessarily result in inner peace or security.

As the war babies grew older and confronted the paradox of their complex identity, they felt that it was of utmost importance to know their past, to feel connected to the world both genetically and environmentally. They became aware of the paucity of documentation in their "official" records. They had been abandoned in *Shishu Bhavan*. There were no further records available. There was no documentary trail for them to trace their lineage before coming to Canada. As discussed in chapter 4, the dossiers recording their birth in the orphanage contained very basic tombstone data with no medical or genealogical information at all. They learned very early in their lives that there is not much information on their unique birth history.

They also learned at an early age that they were seen as "undesirable" and/or "disposable," hence the term "unwanted" children of Bangladesh. In fact, they had also learned that neither the "unwanted" babies nor their "disgraced" birth mothers were acceptable in Bangladesh. Both were seen as morally repugnant. What was even harder for the war babies was to come to terms with the fact that no pertinent information about them was available anywhere in order to learn more about their birth and adoption history.

By adolescence, having matured and contextualized the Liberation War of Bangladesh, the war babies constructed a story line of their births, which runs something like this: a victim of rape and sexual violence by the Pakistani military personnel in Occupied Bangladesh, a

Bengali birth mother gave birth in secret; the mother likely terminated her own life following the birth of a child steeped with social stigma and disgrace; however, if alive, the birth mother is likely living with a different identity to guard against discovery of a dark secret. The putative father, if alive, is probably somewhere in Pakistan having lived in India for about three years as a prisoner of war (POW) from where he was repatriated to Pakistan. Needless to say, their attitude toward their putative father is somewhat contemptuous. A reunion with the "adoption triangle," adoptees, adoptive parents, and birth parents, would never be possible. There was no one to be reunited with.

Search and reunion is something that tends to obsess many adoptees in adolescence. In Canada, an adoptee's record is kept secret until the child reaches the age of majority. However, our adoptive parents made no secret of the birth history. The parents welcomed the war babies to explore and learn about Bangladesh, its struggle for independence, and the sordid details surrounding their births. However, since there was neither genealogical nor medical information available about the biological parents, the war babies avoided the common fantasy that many adopted children have of one day reuniting with their biological parents. In fact, by adolescence, most of the war babies had no strong desire to revisit their births at all.

In 1989, Ryan, Lara, Rajib, Amina, and Rani went to Bangladesh where they confirmed what their adoptive parents had told them about their births. The details of their reactions are outlined below in the present chapter under the "War babies' first trip to their country of birth." They saw with their own eyes the conditions at the orphanage from where they were rescued and what they had left behind in Bangladesh. Despite their physical similarity to people in Bangladesh, there were vast cultural differences between them and Bangladeshis.

Lara grew up in Brampton, Ontario, in a family of four children where three were adopted. She feels connected to Bangladesh, but not to her biological roots. As the narrative goes, Lara is also aware of two versions of her birth story in the historical narrative – that she was rescued from a broken ship abandoned by the Pakistani soldiers and / or that her birth mother had died giving birth to her prematurely. A mature Lara does not reflect on the veracity of the two versions of her birth history having accepted both, that either she was abandoned at a naval ship or picked up by Sr. Margaret Mary of *Shishu Bhavan* when she was about to be thrown into the river. Sr. Margaret Mary had clarified *why* and *how* there were many "stories" surrounding the birth, abandonment, and rescue of the war babies in order to take away the stigma attached to them at the time. "It did not matter,"[1] said Lara, since the only parents she knows in her life are the parents she has in Canada.

"In all these years, I have never really wondered about my past, my parents or a family I may have left behind in Bangladesh and I have never made any attempt to try to find them,"[2] observed a candid Lara. She then went on to say, "To this day, I have not made any attempt to discover my family roots and it is unlikely that I will do so in the near future,"[3] observed Lara frankly.

"Even if it was possible to find my roots, I would not know where to begin,"[4] said an unprepared Lara. She fears she would have further worries down the road if it so happens: "I would like to learn the genetic history of my family, and from whom I have received my personality and character traits, however, I don't think I could maintain a relationship with my biological family at this stage in my life."[5]

Amina, who grew up in Komoka, close to London, Ontario, with six children all of whom were adopted, had been to Bangladesh twice, once in 1989 at the age of sixteen and again in 2010, sees her own situation from a different angle: "In retrospect, I knew very little about my heritage, language or culture as a young child, even though my parents attempted to educate me informally."[6] "My philosophy has been, the past is the past, and the present and future is where I choose to live,"[7] observed Amina. "Out of all those children [from the orphanage] why me? Why was I saved?"[8] asked a reflective Amina, who still remains puzzled as to how it all happened.

Years later, a mature Amina recalled what she had heard from her parents: "My beginnings were quite modest. I was conceived in war-torn Bangladesh during the War of Independence of 1971,"[9] said Amina in a matter-of-fact way and continued unhesitatingly, "Born in the Mother Teresa's Orphanage in 1972, the Punjabi name given to me was Amina Khartoum; Amina meaning precious jewel."[10] Maintaining that she knew very "little about the woman who gave birth" to her "other than she was probably very young,"[11] Amina remained firm and confident that demonstrated her full control over her emotions.

Ryan, who grew up in Exeter, Ontario, with another adopted sibling from Bangladesh, recalled events in the following manner: that many years ago in a place far from Bangladesh, he must have asked his mother a question, which might have gone something like "Mommy, why I am brown and you and Daddy are white?"[12] No doubt, answer to a seemingly straightforward question becoming of a child's mentality is, however, not as straightforward as it might seems. His mother at the time might have responded, Ryan recalled, by saying, "You were born in Bangladesh and Mommy and Daddy were born in Canada."[13] Probably sensing the obvious, his mother had brought out a picture book that she herself had already prepared, which is still on the bookshelves of his parents' home today.

Thus far, Ryan had been to Bangladesh three times. The first time he went at sixteen, in 1989, with several orphans and a few war babies through Canadopt's initiative. The second trip was in 1991, at nineteen, when he tried in vain to find his birth mother. (The details of Ryan's experience which we have read, are outlined under individual war baby in chapter 5.) In 1997, he went back again for a year. A reality check in his own mind convinced him of no possibility of ever finding his birth mother; searching for whom would be an excruciatingly painful journey leading to nowhere.

Of all the war babies discussed in the book, Ryan is the only one who delved more into the past. With maturity he learned and assessed his situation in the following manner: "My curiosity of my birth mother has changed. I now have a desire to know more and more about all the birth mothers – all 250,000 of them."[14] Again, he wrote, "As my understanding of war in general and the atrocities that occurred began to increase, so did my realization that I was a result of the Liberation War of Bangladesh. My birth mother was raped by a Pakistani soldier."[15] Though a distressing revelation, Ryan had remained firm in saying that "this realization did not produce any ill will or discontent"[16] in his mind. Having lived with his (adoptive) parents for as long as he remembers, he looks upon Dale and Doreen Good as *his parents,* whom he had known from the start of his life. "Emphatically, my conception of Parents was that of my adoptive Canadian parents. Any thoughts of my birth Parents were shielded by feelings of overall detachment,"[17] argued Ryan in favor of his position.

By deepening his understanding of the historical facts surrounding his birth, abandonment, adoption, and subsequent life in Canada, Ryan came to learn quite a bit about Bangladesh and Bangladeshis. But unfortunately, the more he lived in Bangladesh, the more detached he felt. With the passage of time, and following his return to Canada after staying Bangladesh for just over a year, Ryan lost his interest in Bangladesh as he became more involved in his life in Canada.

Rani, who grew up in Saskatoon, Saskatchewan, in a family of two children with one born-to-the-family child, stands apart from the rest of the war babies in terms of her desire to search for her roots. This goes as far as writing a poem in which she talks about how close she feels to her never-known birth mother when she visited Bangladesh with her adoptive parents. For a while, Rani's visit to the orphanage premises gave her a new sense of personal power that also gave her a high level of satisfaction. She felt more engaged, as her visit to her country of birth helped her link herself with her unknown birth mother.

Needless to emphasize, in many ways, these experiences of the adoptees were different. The Ferries' (Robert and Helke) daughter (we call her B, as she requested not to give her real name) grew up in Burlington (close to Toronto), Ontario, in a family of thirteen children where three children were biological and the rest international adoptees like herself. She is not conflicted in any way with her life situation. She is not interested in knowing any more about her Bengali birth mother and putative Pakistani father than what she was told by her parents. B never felt a need to reconcile her self-identification with two sets of parents. She was informed about her birth history and relinquishment appropriately, said the parents. This led her to believe that her birth parents could never be found. This single realization convinced her that her life is *what* she had been seeing all along in Canada. It simply consisted of the *family* members she had been living with. She only has *one set of parents,* the parents she knows from her childhood.

B's brother, whom we shall call A, is also a war baby adopted at the same time by the Ferries. He, like his sister, also did not want to be identified by his real name. A also learned the story of his birth mother and alleged father from his parents in Canada. He describes his biological father and mother as a "soldier" and as someone who "could have been a student."[18] There is another version of the story that his birth mother had "died following the delivery of the baby."[19] This is the extent of his knowledge of his birth parents that he had picked up from his parents. He remains "indifferent" with respect to his birth history. He is not interested to dig further.

Josée grew up in a francophone family in a small town in Quebec with her parents and a sibling who is the biological child of her parents. She knows the basic history of her birth and adoption: "I was born on November 24, 1971, in Dorenda, Bangladesh. Well that is what it says on my birth certificate and on my immigration documents. I was born during the war of independence and it is unknown as to who my biological parents are and what became of them."[20] Josée, to use an adoption terminology, is a "permanent nonsearcher." *Why does Josée not look for her birth mother, which could both be an enriching and energizing experience? Is she afraid of rejection? Is Josée afraid of her own life changing? Or, is Josée afraid of losing her Canadian identity with which she grew up?* Josée's frank and simple answer to all these questions is "None of the above."[21]

Having no bond with her biological mother and/or putative father, she is content with whatever little she knows about them. "Frankly, that's all I need to know about these people. To me it does not make sense to inquire about a man and a woman that have nothing in common with me except genes . . . If I meet them now, we would be total strangers; we would have different religion, different language, different values, etc. . . . My mother told me that if I want to go to Bangladesh she will go with me, and you know it is something I will look into."[22] She went to Bangladesh in 2004 alone and again in 2005 accompanied by her mother. Both visits were uneventful and dull, even though both the mother and the daughter were looking forward to having a good time. A disappointed Josée recalled feeling "strange." (The details of her experience and observations are outlined in chapter 5 under individual war baby.)

However, there is love in Josée's mind and heart for her birth country. "Don't get me wrong, I'm proud to say that I was born in Bangladesh,"[23] maintains Josée. Ever since she could talk, she remembers telling people that she was born in Bangladesh, that there was a war of independence from West Pakistan, and that is why she was adopted by a Canadian family back in 1972. It bothers her that most people ignorantly refer to India, Pakistan, and Bangladesh as one country – insinuating that they are all the same. A courteous Josée tries to enlighten others: "I remind these people by saying that Bangladesh is an independent country and that the people of Bangladesh had earned it the hard way."[24]

Shama grew up in Montreal, Quebec, in a family of nine children where eight were adopted. She recalls that she never took any serious interest in knowing about her biological mother until she was older. "I have always known about my biological roots, so there was no time of great discovery that sent me off spinning into urgency or panic. I do, however, remember watching a show on adopted children in search of their biological roots and what occurred to me and did cause much angst at the time was the need to know my medical history. This was when I was in university, so I was in my early 20's and not an adolescent,"[25] observed Shama. This led her to write to the orphanage authority in Bangladesh, although with no success in obtaining any new information. Shama was disappointed but not surprised.

"Knowing what I know about the circumstances of my conception and the time period, I have never felt the urge to meet or find my 'putative' father. I was told that given the war, it is most likely that he raped my birth mother. As for meeting or finding my birth mother, I've never felt an urgency to do so apart from [wanting to know about] my medical history,"[26] observed a calm Shama. On the surface, Shama has no emotional attachment to Bangladesh. Yet she thinks about Bangladesh: "There is part of me that would be interested in teaching ESL in Bangladesh, but there is a part of me that is also very conscious of what colonialism has done to the world, and in particular to underdeveloped countries like Bangladesh."[27] Shama has not ruled out the possibility of visiting her country of birth.

Shikha grew up in a small town close to Ottawa, Ontario, in a family of twenty-one children. Only two of the children are biological. As far as Shikha is concerned, her life began in Canada with her parents, Fred and Bonnie Cappuccino. Shikha never felt any doubt about whether her adoptive relationship is real or not. She remained content with the narrative she had heard from her parents. She has no desire whatsoever of needing to know more about her biological past.

Onil, who grew up in Mississauga, Ontario, in a family of four children, all of whom are adopted, also talked about his interest in visiting Bangladesh sometime. It is on his wish list. Speaking with discernible emotions, Onil said, "It would be nice to also have the opportunity to go back to the orphanage where I came from and provide my help."[28] "I would like to return to Bangladesh again and donate my time and/or money to help the orphanages,"[29] observed Onil who remains grateful to the orphanage authority that took care of him. "They took me in and nursed me to health," and "I owe them my life and all the blessings that I have received,"[30] said Onil.

Again, Onil also stands out as being interesting and entertaining at the same time different from his cohorts. "I am an extremist at times and at other times I am not. I don't particularly feel a need for an adopted triangle. In fact, if I were to meet my biological parents I don't think that I would feel a need to integrate them with my adoptive parents or come to terms with them,"[31] observed Onil with no hesitation of any kind. To date, in his life, "there has never been a void because of it."[32] "Happiness has never been based on knowing who they are, or were,"[33] said a straight-shooter Onil. While growing up, he had never experienced any "feeling of isolation or alienation" because of his adoption. Like other adoptees, Onil believes that the birth mother's wish for the child must have been that the child had the best of life. A contented Onil articulated his own feelings and the feelings of the other adoptees in the following vein: "Upon hearing of the tragedy I wish I could have found my mother and let her know how deeply sorry I was for her suffering and that something good came out of her sacrifice (victimization)."[34]

One of the most important points that came out through the adoptees' narratives is that they did not equate being "given up" with being "rejected" given the circumstances of the birth mothers. Whether they have a desire to visit Bangladesh or not, an important fact is that they do have a very good understanding of why a birth mother had to give up her child. Unlike many adoptees that become angry at their birth parents for relinquishing them, the present war babies did not hold anything against their birth mothers. They have learned that the victims of sexual violence in the war-ravaged Bangladesh had to pay a high price, which had caused untold devastations. By interpreting the word "abandonment" positively, they have successfully incorporated this harsh truth in their personal story line as part of the historical narrative surrounding their birth and adoption. In no way would these adoptees be willing to denigrate the mother who gave birth to them. One might say this is an instance of an invisible loyalty.

The adoptees' lack of interest to seek more information also point to another observation generally maintained by sociologists and social workers who work in the adoption field – that when the adoptees are troubled by certain issues, searching for their roots helps them bring them greater inner peace. It was not an issue of "psycho survival" for them as the children who grew up in loving homes – having been placed in adoptive homes, they knew *who* they were, *where* they came from, and *how* they were born in Bangladesh.

The jigsaw puzzle of identity is that the adoptees had accepted the fact that no further information is available to unravel. They grew up knowing that it was not a matter of suppressing any information. Having accepted this fact of their life, they were not left with any "genealogical bewilderment" or a nagging feeling for a lack of knowledge of their birth parents. The impossibility of finding ever their anonymous birth mother and the putative father meant that, from early on, the adoptees had recognized the nonexistence of two sets of parents.

Family relationships/bonding

The adoptees were quite straightforward while they fondly talked about their relationships with their parents, siblings, and extended family members. Having bonded with one's own family despite differences of race and ethnicity, each has a consistent story. According to the war babies, their parents have exercised great influence in their lives having set the stage for initiating and encouraging a positive home atmosphere, which gave the adoptees a sense satisfaction in *belonging together* despite many vicissitudes of life.

Having been raised in various cities and towns across Canada, they were exposed to certain common manifestations, such as supportive interaction, acceptance of others, patience, empathy, and cooperation. None of the adoptees had made any reference to any negative atmosphere in one's homes, such as put-downs, criticism of others, apathy, and blaming. They became aware of their "unrelatedness" through blood to their adoptive parents at an early age as the family members began to interact with them. As a result of their early positive experiences, they enjoyed the spontaneity, ease, and giddy pleasure in interacting with family members during their adolescent years. They recalled their parents' efforts to put across in their children's minds their view that for any adoptee, whether adopted within the same race or not, growing up in a family that loves and supports the child is of primordial importance.

In fact, openness and frankness of their parents were the key elements that had not only held them *together* but also helped them *minimize* any chance of having any misunderstanding surrounding their "story" of birth and adoption. Narratives related to their birth had actually helped them recognize that their parents in Canada are the only parents in the whole wide world who wanted to "have" them, unlike the people of the country in which they were born.

Three key concepts emerged from their narratives. They are "permanent home," "loving and caring parents," and the adoptees' sense of "gratitude" for their parents. The strength of their relationship with their parents is based on their own understanding of the fact that they came to learn from their parents' resolve to bring them to Canada, come hell or high water. They recognize they were not born to their parents and that they were simply picked out by their parents to raise them. They do not see any distinctions between *biological* and *adopted* children, all of whom are *loved* and *cared for* as children of their parents.

For the adoptees, their bond with their parents vis-à-vis their birth mothers is a simple arithmetic: they had been in their birth mothers' womb for nine months (or less in case of the premature ones, which was the case with most of the war babies) in Bangladesh before being born; whereas, having joined their adoptive families, they had been living in such families since the beginning of their lives as far back as they remember. Naturally, as they began to grow, their bond with their parents too grew stronger and stronger. It became more evident through many discourses with the adoptees whether it is Shikha, Lara, Chris, or any one, for that matter, all of them have comfortably brought their full identity to their adoption-adoptive mother interactions. Since they don't know their birth mothers personally, whether they are dead or alive, it seems as though it would not make any difference in their present lives. It was their understanding from their parents' action that one who can do something will do, and one who has the will to give, will give whatever it is that is required to pull through thick and thin.

Speaking at great length, a jovial Lara said how she has overlooked the genealogical difference, for she never felt a void in her life. "My adoptive family has always treated me as one of its own even though we are not genetically connected. I have never been made to feel 'alienated' or 'isolated' because I don't look like any members of my family, and they have never made me feel different" (e-mail from Lara Morris to Mustafa Chowdhury, May 8, 2000, cited in notes and references # 1).

The love that they had received from their racially different parents had embodied trust, obligation, and commitment in a troubled and anxious world rather than on blood tie. They don't know of any other persons to compare their parents' love and affection with. This single fact that no matter how morally repugnant they were seen in Bangladesh, they were "longed for" and "fought for" by their parents in Canada who made them feel valued. In one way or another, they echo each other in appreciating the fact that they were "chosen" by their adoptive parents – whether the parents preferred to use the word "chosen" or not.

A proud Lise (mother of Josée) recalled the first few weeks following their child's arrival from Bangladesh. Initially, Josée used to go to anyone, even to a stranger whom she had not seen. But soon, within a month after her arrival, the attachment grew to the point that when a neighbor wanted to take her, and Lise allowed her to do that, "Josée started to cry and did not want to leave" her mom's arms. At that instance, Lise recalled how happily she "felt so reassured," as her baby, by then, had already "recognized" her mother as *hers,* "as special."[35]

As far back as Josée remembers, she has stopped counting *how* many times she has been asked what it is like to be adopted, or if she considers her parents to be real parents or not. "No one else deserves that title but the ones who took care of me, loved me and prepared for the world ahead of me."[36] As far as Josée is concerned, her parents are irreplaceable for they are the rearing parents.

The same way, according to Shikha, one of the greatest characteristics of her family is the closeness of the family in which her parents were always there for each family member. Emphasizing her attachment to her parents, who were never self-righteous and preachy, she said the children picked up the values their parents hold most dear. She maintains that her parents had embedded in her a sense of possibility that transcended the artificial boundaries of race.

Again, a friendly Shama recounted her experiences along the same vein: "I see myself as being fortunate to be alive and with parents who wanted me, especially in light of the fact that there are many children out there who are with parents who don't want them."[37] As far as Shama is concerned, her (adoptive) mother is the "real" mother, as she knows no other mother other than the rearing mother in Canada whom she grew up knowing to be hers. The parents, brothers and sisters, uncles, aunts, grandparents, cousins, everyone seems so natural, so real that she had always felt to be an integral part of the Hartt family.

Since Onil was less than eight weeks old when he was shipped off to Canada, he did not experience the move from the Dhaka orphanage to his adoptive parents, observed Onil. To the war babies' way of looking at themselves, there is really no past that could be important to their lives, which began in their (adoptive) homes in Canada. This is reinforced by the traditional psychiatric opinion that children before two cannot think. This line of argument is also based on Sigmund Freud's contention that only with the acquisition of language do the children begin to use symbols and lay down memory engrams. Thus the war babies' assertion that the only parents they have known are their white parents in Canada is consistent with the current research on retention of memory on the part of the children. They were not disturbed by the fact of adoption.

For all practical purposes, their life began in Canada with their parents who happen to be their adoptive parents. Like the rest of the war babies, Onil considers his parents as his *only* parents. Not only that, but also his respect and *fondness* for his parents and siblings grew out of love and affection that he received at home. The attachment that Onil feels to his family members is one of the most fascinating facts of his family life – his wonderful relationships with parents and other siblings of diverse origin, as opposed to his unknown life in a country that did not "want" him.

Being utterly frank, Onil talked about the strangeness he feels with both of his unknown birth mother and putative father. If, by any chance, he comes across his birth mother, he would "simply say how sorry" he is "for her tragic circumstances."[38]

Similarly, Amina feels strongly bonded with her parents that she can never think of any other couple ever taking that place in her life. Her father is a person who had "spent his life dedicated to his family, the church, his job and helping others in need."[39] Over the years, her "father has enlightened and touched many with insight and actions, yet he continues to be unaware of the lives he has touched. He has been the silent strength behind my mother's vision and quest to help orphan."[40] "I would not trade them for million bucks," [41] said a contented Amina, taking pride in her parents. "I have known no other parents" is the standard response Amina puts forward no matter *how* the question is asked.

The same way, Chris sees his parents as his daily providers and caretakers fulfilling the role of parents as far back as he remembers. He acknowledges his unknown birth mother who gave birth to him under the most undesirable circumstances for which she had to abandon him. A nonsearcher by choice, he is appreciative of his birth mother's decision to abandon him. Like all other adoptees from the present bunch, he does not feel attached to his birth parents, nor does he care to know anything about them. He feels bonded with his parents and family members so strongly that there has never been any need to look elsewhere. By parents, Chris and all other adoptees meant the parents who have raised him, not the one who gave birth.

According to Ryan, his parents had started to love him from the minute he was picked out for adoption while he was still in the orphanage under uncertain circumstances. The strength of his bond with his parents became even more noticeable to him when he lived in Bangladesh in 1997 and 1998 and frequently became homesick. His e-mails to his parents and friends (outlined in chapter 5 under individual profile) describing his day to day activities in Bangladesh remain an illustration of his bond with his family and the country in which he was raised. In Bangladesh, Ryan found himself remembering events that took place in Canada where he grew up.

Being caught between Canada, the country he considers Canada as his "home," and Bangladesh, his country of birth, Ryan wrote, "I am distracted. I am drugged. I am disillusioned. It would seem that I am unhappy. It would seem that I am becoming unhappy even more. It would seem that I am thinking about home. It would seem that I am thinking more and more about home. *Where is home?*"[42] asks Ryan again and again, being placed between the devil and the deep blue sea. Ryan recognized how his love and excitement for his country of birth had turned out to be only a brief interlude. Ryan found himself utterly helpless, having experienced ongoing waves of discouragement. After an uncertain stay of a little over a year, a frustrated Ryan came to the conclusion that he was at a critical juncture in his life trajectory. Feeling wounded and deeply disappointed, and being on the cusp of burnout, Ryan terminated his quixotic quest for his country of birth and returned to his family in Canada in November 1998.

The adoptees see their attachment to the parents as a close *lifelong relationship* – a reinforcement of the fact that humans are made to desire close relationship. They recognize they are not the flesh of their parents' flesh, and yet they do feel to be a part of their parents, feelings of which have contributed toward familial integration. To paraphrase their own words, without a deep parent-child bonding, they would have had no proper framework for a healthy moral and emotional development. According to John Triseliotis, the most important thing in an adoptee's life is the quality of caring and relationship, which is paramount. Simply put, he argues, "Love itself can go a very long way to make up for other deficiencies."[43]

War babies' first visit to their country of birth

In January 1989 at the invitation of then president Hussain Muhammad Ershad (Ershad), a trip to Bangladesh was arranged for adoptees and their parents through the initiatives of Canadopt, which has been mentioned in chapter 5 under "Del and Donna Wolsey." This support group was active in coordinating the work in Canada under the stewardship of Donna Wolsey who had also adopted one of the war babies, Amina. Their visit was to coincide with the opening of a new orphanage, a $1.5 million community complex project in Sreepur constructed on a five-hectare (thirteen-acre) land, about seventy-two kilometers north of the capital city, Dhaka, funded by British Airways and the Montreal-based Families For Children (FFC), the same organization that brought the first batch of fifteen war babies in Canada in July 1972. President Ershad himself took personal interest in the well-being of Bangladeshi orphans, citing the initiative of the Children's Village as "an example in the field of childcare"[44] (*Toronto Star*, February 13, 1989) in Bangladesh.

Twenty-seven adoptees and some of their parents left Canada on January 27, 1989, for a whirlwind visit of seven days in Bangladesh. The trip included five war babies (Rani, Ryan, Lara, Rajib, and Amina); as well, Robin and Barbara (Rani's parents), Donna and (Amina's parents), and Dale and Doreen (Ryan's parents) were with the group. For the adoptees, the two-week trip to Asia, which included seven days in Dhaka, Bangladesh, was their first visit to their "homeland."

MUSTAFA CHOWDHURY

With the group were also reporters Dahlia Reich and Kathy Wallis and photographer and cameraman, Ed Heal and Wayne Jennings, of the *London Free Press* all of whom traveled together. Dr. Michael Allen, then a pediatric surgeon at Toronto East General Hospital, and Franck Jones (then life columnist, the *Toronto Star*) also went to Dhaka for part of the time while the group was in Bangladesh and wrote about the activities of the group.

Emile Gauvreau, then Canadian high commissioner to Bangladesh, provided the group a warm and festive welcome that was complete with banners, flags, and costume greetings to fit the occasion. Gauvreau's office provided the group with two buses that were at their disposal throughout their seven-day stay in Dhaka. The group stayed in Sunderban Hotel.

The first day, the group visited the new Sreepur-based Children's Village to see the FFC-initiated project. The emotionally charged teenagers were both excited and frightened at the same time; excited because their country of birth was to offer them an opportunity to connect in some way with their origin; frightened because, being jittery, they were not certain what they would see. The brand-new Children's Village included a dormitory, a mosque, a school, medical clinics, community hall, and a vocational training center and accommodated approximately seven hundred orphan children.

Once they went inside the orphanage, they saw many crippled children, some with no braces or crutches, some with rotting teeth, bloated stomachs, and open sores; as well, they saw a large number of malnourished children who were critically ill, some had seizures, some had numerous deformities. And yet the young Canadians recalled how they were struck by the discernible happiness in the face of the well-cared-for orphans in the orphanage compared to the sadness of the impoverished and uncared for children growing up on the streets.

Having seen so many orphans in one place, Amina recalled her strange feelings. The thought of "Oh my God, this could this could have been me,"[45] resonated not only in the mind of Amina but also in the minds of the rest of the orphans over and over again while they were with other children. In fact, this fear on their part that they could have been a part of the crowd had they not had an opportunity to be adopted in Canada had haunted them for days.

Having witnessed the stark reality of Bangladesh with their own eyes, the endless mass of people had simply overwhelmed the young Canadians. For the first time in their lives, they saw children roaming about and picking up scraps of discarded food and twigs. Everything was new to the teenagers, even the smell of the sprawling Dhaka City, the singing sound of the Bengali language, and the sights and sounds of the ever-present crowd and vendors.

Through this momentous trip, they were able to move to a new understanding and appreciation of both their country of birth and country of adoption. Instantly they began to feel very special and extremely lucky to have been adopted in Canada. Visit to the *Shishu Bhavan* premises, where the war babies were born or brought to, was perhaps the most unforgettable event. Ryan still treasures the memory of picking up a child and having gone straight to the rooftop a wonderful feeling: "All my heart and mind could see as I stood on the rooftop of my old orphanage was beauty. Beauty was everywhere. Beauty was in the poverty stricken cityscape that filled my eyes as far as I could see. And beauty was in the babies sleeping and the children playing throughout the rooms and courtyards of the building of love and hope,"[46] recalled Ryan.

Emotion reached a new height of intensity as they got their trembling hands on the register book. They were told it contains the names of the war babies. All five teenagers, Lara, Ryan, Ami, Rajib, and Rani, were courageously prepared to check out at the first opportunity a part of their documented birth history. It was pivotal to the teenagers to "see for themselves" the register book, which was as though a biological template that contains their identity and ancestry.

An excited Lara had reportedly screamed out loud when she spotted her name to be the first on the list. "Seeing it [my name] was just incredible. It was like seeing my past,"[47] wrote the news reporter about Lara's feelings of discovery. "I was crying, but I didn't know if I was happy or sad,"[48] recalled an emotionally charged Lara.

The same was the case with Rani, Amina, Ryan, and Rajib, who saw their names in the same book with their own eyes. Being imbued with a strangely intense feeling of profound joy and inordinate pleasure, they hugged each other ecstatically. Instantly, they constructed a picture out of facts they had known in Canada. Being overjoyed, they prided themselves on their powers of "discovery," which took on a momentum of its own as they flipped through the pages of the register book. There was no need for any more clues or information.

In their attempt to ferret out the true story of birth and relinquishment, the war babies, then only sixteen, had found an authentic narrative from that time onward. As soon as they searched and found their names/identification they looked for, they felt as though they are more worthwhile in the world. Finding the desired information was like filling in a gap that made them feel *where* they belong. Instantly, the young adults came to realize that their past history is no longer the history of "anonymous" children, as the "newly discovered" information had filled in an identity gap hitherto produced by nondisclosure.

It was an unforgettable moment to many local *ayas* (women who take care of the babies), some of whom were orphans themselves and very young at the time. Hafiza, who looked after many, including Amina, could not hold her tears, for it was like a reunion that caused a wave of emotion in their tender minds. The orphanage personnel's efforts to allay their fear of encountering a "denial of right," a reigning metaphor in the Canadian adoption vocabulary, remained evident all through the period the war babies were there.

After a hectic seven fun-filled days of stay in Dhaka, when the group left Bangladesh, sadness took hold, knowing it would be a long time if they would return again. Shattering their complacency, the teens returned home with a great sense of satisfaction, as the trip was truly a great eye-opener – having felt more informed and blended by images of happiness and warmheartedness of the people they met instead of misery and poverty about which they heard so much.

For the accompanying parents, too, this was one of the most significant journeys of discovery, which was an opportunity that gave their children a taste of their native country as well as a new appreciation for their adoptive home. The parents watched how their children, then in utter awe and wonder, had pulled together in an attempt to reassure and comfort each other while looking up the birth names in the register book. Looking for their "roots" was important to both the adoptees and their parents, who were there with them at the time, having witnessed the "truth" with their child as a part of that dramatic and defining moment.

One of the immediate and tangible outcomes of their visit to Bangladesh was a new sense of awareness that brought them even closer with a sense of *where* they came from. The Canadopt teens continued to remain active – they held meetings, organized car washes, designed T-shirts, sponsored children, did slide presentations, and participated more in their parents' fund-raising activities. They consider their commemorative flight to Bangladesh a very touching reunion even though it was not a reunion with their birth mothers or alleged fathers.

Whether we call it *homecoming,* as the news media termed it, or *motherland tour,* taken by the Bangladeshi adoptees, this is perhaps the most significant moment and focal point that illustrate an emphasis on self-fulfillment in the lives of these young Canadian adolescents, both war babies and other orphans. Years later, the adoptees became familiar with the dramatized presentation of Alex Hailey's *Roots* that had greatly touched both American and Canadian public. Having reached the age of majority and matured enough, they recognized one of the key messages – that ancestry is something sacred. It was reinforced in the adoption discourse saying that it is essential to one's identity.

Immediately upon their return to Canada, Cathy Walles of the *London Free Press* wrote a thirty-minute documentary titled *Children of Bangladesh* to show a glimpse of their past in their country of birth, which was aired first time on March 5, 1989, on CPPL-TV documenting the firsthand experience and observation of the now Canadian children adopted from Bangladesh.

Though sent away to foreign countries having considered them "disposable" and "unwanted," in a matter of sixteen years, the same children, however, became potential assets to be "showcased" as a success story. The children were now seen as "wanted" and, therefore, sought after: "It's ironic that we left the country as the unwanted outcasts of society and returned as almost celebrity figures with new names, new citizenships and a new outlook on life,"[49] observed Amina who noted a twist of fate in the entire episode.

All five war babies and other orphans returned to Canada with a warm feeling for Bangladesh. They felt an instant attachment to Bangladesh – an attachment that gave them a new *sense of belonging* to the point that they wanted to remain involved and interested. However, being among family members in Canada again, they realized that they are back to *their motherland,* Canada. Gradually their love and passion for their country of birth began to diminish as they got into the "swing of things" in Canada.

Racial and Canadian identity

The war babies described their views on what makes an identity, which, according to them, is composed of many aspects including the realities of birth that encompass race, gender, socioeconomic conditions of one's early years, as well as one's experience with or exposure to religion, together with the ever-increasing plethora and historical biogenetic information about oneself.

Ongoing discourse with the adoptees and the adoptive parents with respect to their own views and understanding of the notions of personal, social, and ethnic identity[50] reveals some of the fascinating aspects of their lives. In exploring whether they have a positive sense of ethnicity, which is generally manifested in pride in one's ethnic roots and appearance, the stark truth that emerged is their own understanding of their unique situation in relation to their families. Identity development is not unique to adopted children, they said this in unison. The complexity of adoption can, and often does, pose some additional challenges for adopted children and their families.

No one exhibited any feeling of confusion about one's own identity and self-image, which are usually reflected in low self-esteem and often in the development of behavioral problems. They neither disassociated from other visible minorities nor rejected their skin color. Instead, they simply formed an identity of their unique situation within the eclectic families in which they were raised. In that sense, they are much unlike many adoptees who have a devalued sense of self-esteem – not knowing *who* they *are* and having a low opinion of their own being placed in a state of "confused" identity.

Each had successfully found answer to the question: *Who am I?* Generally speaking, ethnicity is embedded in identity formation, the maintenance of which is based on an ethnic identification. In the case of the war babies, ethnicity did not get emphasized. We have noted in chapter 5 how it was rather downplayed by their parents. The origin of their birth and ethnicity, therefore, composed only a small part of them, primarily genetic. These are not the essence of *who* they are, and their ethnicity *does not* represent the families they belong to. As young adults, they had accepted formidable tasks, such as individuation, socialization, identity formation, and future orientation. An analysis of their views and comments would reveal that some war babies had taken interest in their racial background (for example, Ryan, Rani, Ami, Lara, etc.) following their visit to Bangladesh; while some others such as Chris, Onil, Shama, Josée, and war babies A and B had remained nonchalant, although not indifferent.

In the mid-1980s, when the word "visible minority" surfaced as a result of the government of Canada's special measure programs, the war babies were in their early teens. Gradually, as they grew, they came to understand the meaning of the term that refers those other than aboriginal people, who are non-Caucasian in race or nonwhite in color. They also learned *how* and *why* such term was (and is being) used to self-identify in order to ensure equity and fairness in employment. Some of the adult war babies are aware that although the issues of racial awareness and self-identification of the transracially adopted children have been studied at great length by many including Leon Chestang and Rita Simon, the result is still inconclusive.

To obtain a clear idea of the various stages of identity formation, the adoptees were asked the following two specific questions relating to past events and the accompanying feelings, which might have changed over time:

How do they perceive themselves? Do they have their own sense of identity and racial identification different from their parents?

Have their knowledge of and interest in Bangladesh influenced them one way or another in their identity formation?

The adoptees did not find themselves in a conflicted situation with respect to their racial background (which was not the same as their parents) or sociocultural heritage either at home or outside. The historical narratives of the adoptees based on truth had been very helpful to the children of diverse race. In negotiating their social status, while with friends or neighbors, they never felt that they belonged to a minority class or a disadvantaged group. This single phenomenon had allowed them to maximize socialization opportunity among people of diverse backgrounds.

The adoptees' identity is neither a single ethnic identity nor a double identity. In their own words, *they are Canadians born in Bangladesh.* In considering them to be Canadian, the most common argument they put forward is that they see Canada as their primal home where they grew up and not Bangladesh where they were born and from where they were shipped off when they were mere infants. According to the adoptees, they had never been in a sensitive situation in which they could feel to be different, often yearning to "belong" to or to "fit in," which is usually the case with older adoptees.

Even though they grew up "seeing" the color of their skins being different from their parents, all of them *identified* with their white parents. They learned to speak like their family members, having completely identified them with their parents in every way that gave them a natural feeling of *belonging*. In that sense, a foundation had been laid right at the beginning of their lives, which had enabled them to develop a strong sense of self-esteem. They immersed themselves in the dress, language, social networks, music, art, sports, food, and all of the expression of "Canadian" identities. They are nonwhite in a family headed by Caucasian parents where many siblings are both white and nonwhite. All of them are firm in asserting their identity as "Canadian" first in their perception of themselves, their self-image, and their relationships with other people. The very emphasis on their relationship with their "mom" and "dad" seemed so natural to them that it had reinforced their *own* perception of them as Canadian.

Put it in another way, never for a minute did they feel that being different meant being less. Instead, having considered Canada as their "home," they regard them as Canadian – that's all. This is consistent with and reflective of all of the war babies under discussion. Soon it emerged from various discussions that they also perceive themselves to be "white" in all but skin color. We have already noted they had no difficulty at all to identify themselves with their *white* parents even though they do not look like their parents. They were also aware of what Martin Luther King, James Baldwin, and Malcolm X had reminded the people that "whiteness is a state of mind." Since the war babies were merely infants when they were adopted, it is as though they never had any other parents, at least memory-wise. "I am not attached to Bangladesh at an emotional level. This can be explained most likely by my early departure from the country. Emotions are created by thoughts. And thoughts are sometimes the reflections produced by experience. In my case, I have no experience that I can recall about Bangladesh hence, there are no emotional responses available for me to create an attachment for a country I don't remember,"[51] said Onil.

Taking pride in their racial origin meant they had nothing to be ashamed of their background, an issue that they would have faced for certain had they remained in Bangladesh. In that sense, they never had to confront the complex question of *when* and to *what extent* they should stress the Pakistani/Bangladeshi part of the equation. Their sense of their ethnicity is, therefore, confined to what little they know about their background, having internalized while growing up, and their social and personal identities with a sense of belonging to the families that had adopted them.

However, during adolescence, which is the time when teenagers begin to break away from their families and establish their own independence, they had questions that were very complex and answers difficult to accept. Consequently, in early years, some had felt uncomfortable having a different ethnic background than their parents. However, they never said or described a situation in which they "wished to have been white" with the exception of Onil. When very young, he had wished he had the same color as his parents. Looking back as an adult, Onil does not see this as a rejection of his racial identity but perhaps a simple desire on the part of a young boy to be like his dad and mom. "When I was young, these comments [referring to the bullying by his fellow classmates] made me wish that I were Caucasian too."[52] Fortunately for them, such feelings did not last for long, as they were able to move on with their life: ". . . at some point I became comfortable with being different. And I enjoyed being me,"[53] recalled Onil.

"If I were to place an emotional attachment to any place it would be Canada. My home. For it was here that I was accepted and nurtured and loved. And that's what makes a home for me,"[54] argued Onil to whom "home" means Canada where he was raised and where he lives.

As the discourse progressed, a few more adoptees also recalled while still very young, sometimes they too had wished they were the same color as their parents. Some adoptees, however, do recall their earlier teen years when they had a sense of mystification that somehow became more complex because of the additional dimension of racial dislocation. As and when they were stared at on the streets, they only needed to look in the mirror to be reminded that they came from a place different from their parents. Again, a few adoptees also indicated that while still very young, when they saw themselves as being different, at least look-wise, they were confronted with questions along the following lines: *Who am I? Why was I adopted? Why was I not placed in Bangladesh? Why in Canada?*

"I am my parents' daughter and many of my beliefs and practices come directly from their modeling,"[55] said Amina. She sees herself to be a child of her (white) parents, the Wolseys, and identifies herself with the Wolsey family having no clash or conflict. Amina's recollection of an incident points to how natural she feels to be a part of the Wolsey family. "It was not until I met my friend Zehra in teacher's college who nicknamed me, 'brown on the outside but white as anything on the inside' when I realized that I have so much to learn about my culture. She took me to a mosque and introduced me to 'Pakistani' culture, (which is kind of ironic, since I am probably half Pakistani). I feel Canadian and that is my identity. However, I also feel like I am a citizen of the world. I am still learning and defining myself. In the end, I first see myself as a person not a color,"[56] said Amina.

While at York University, it dawned on Amina how *innately* she saw herself as "white": "It was the first time I realized I was assimilated into Canadian culture,"[57] wrote Amina. "Being a minority in my community did not bother me, as I had a good set of friends and such wonderful support at home. I saw myself as one of 'them' as opposed to a minority. I was Canadian, with my white parents, brown skin and different name (Amina) which I Canadianized to Ami in grade 5,"[58] said Amina without any genealogical bewilderment other than her physical appearances or visible minority look. Collectively speaking, mentally or otherwise, the war babies don't symbolize Bangladesh in any way.

One interesting and important point that emerged is that since their parents had both *emphasized* and *de-emphasized* the idea of racial identity, such a practice had helped them develop an all-encompassing Canadian identity, which is pluralistic and respectful of all others. Some adoptive parents, however, had remained open than others in exposing their children to their country of birth in order to help them develop a balanced identity. Some parents had established sustained social relationship with Indo-Canadians around their neighborhood. Again, as discussed in chapter 6, some parents did very little in this respect. We have already noted Amina's parents hooked her up her with

Farouk Chowdhury, then a PhD student at the University of Western Ontario, London, Ontario.

Robin and Barbara Morrall went out of their way to find, what they say the "people of Indian origin" for Rani, their child from Bangladesh. Again, some such as Roberto and Margo-Carr Ribeiro (parents of Martin) did nothing at all (the details are under the profile the Ribeiros in chapter 5).

However, as we have seen in the testimonies of the war babies, they chose to identify them more with their parents who represent mainstream Canadians. With no conflict or confusion, they had arrived at a mature sense of positive identity (within the meaning of a broader Canadian identity) having defied what the critics of transracial adoption have been saying all along: that the child will not know *who* he or she is. It is posited that they had passed through several stages of identification trajectory. As a result, they have a broader notion of themselves encompassing various nuances of feelings about Canada and Canadians of which they consider to be an integral part.

As the years went by, Shikha never noticed the difference in the color of her skin. She had no difficulty in establishing her identity as "Canadian," something that many racially different adoptees often find hard to come to terms with, since look-wise they appear to be different than their parents in the eyes of others. "There was never a moment in my life to suddenly realize that I'm different from the rest of my family,"[59] said a confident Shikha, who grew up with twenty-one children, nineteen of whom were adopted siblings who came from different parts of the world but all were known as the children of Fred and Bonnie Cappuccino. Though visibly different, her perception of herself with regard to race and color is that of a mainstream Canadian. Shikha, like the other war babies in the same group, sees herself as *a Canadian born in Bangladesh* without any qualms or nagging questions of any kind.

In early years, the war baby "A" (adopted by Dr. Robert and Helke Ferrie), who grew up in Burlington, Ontario, in a multiracial family of thirteen children where only three were biological, recalled having white friends at school with whom he played and chilled out. It was natural to him to see himself as one of "them" even though he did not look like them. He never considered himself to be a "minority" in spite of the fact that he had "brown" skin, and different birth history and genealogy. Never for a minute did he feel the need to reevaluate his sense of identity. If someone does not see him as "Canadian," A's curt response would be: "so be it."[60] It did not matter, nor does it now, how others perceive him. He did not spend much time in sorting out a new identity for himself to relate to other people. It behooves him to think of himself as Canadian without having any duality of character so common to many adoptees.

Again, A's sibling, B, another war baby, sees her family to be truly multiracial and, by all means and definitions, "Canadian." Her own knowledge of the country of her birth and the history surrounding her birth is so limited that she never delved into it with her parents. The cultural milieu of her childhood and growing years, like all other war babies who came to Canada, were and are "Canadian" even though she recognizes that she was born in Bangladesh. Both A and B chose not to identify at all with anything to do with Bangladesh except for the recognizing that they were born in Bangladesh. Though their sense of belonging is not devoid of their knowledge of their country of birth and birth history, there is no love lost in their case.

Shama, who grew up in Montreal, was quick to point out one of her experiences when asked by her anthropology professor to construct her identity. She faced enormous difficulties to write a monologue in which she was to disclose how her individual identity is constructed by the concepts of race, ethnicity, and culture. "The teachers and mentors I have had never identified me as different because of my color or ethnicity. Because of this, I have not identified ethnicity as an issue either. My goals are like anyone else's, Canadian or otherwise, and that is to make my life better." [61] This is how Shama tried to elaborate her point.

"I refuse to see myself so simplistically as well as refuse to allow others to put me into a 'box' so that they may feel more comfortable with themselves for having labelled me 'x.' I am Canadian because this is where I was raised and what I know. At the same time, I am of East Indian origin having been born in Bangladesh,"[62] observed Shama in an attempt to expand the theme. Shama feels positive about being able to claim her adoptive upbringing and heritage, but unable to value double inheritance.

Lara, who does not think that being "Canadian" and a "visible" and/ or an "ethnic minority" should be mutually exclusive"[63] determines her *identity* in the following manner: "When I evaluate myself, I regard myself as Canadian who was born in Bangladesh before I see myself as a person of color."[64] *What* she knows and *who* she is, is grounded on the simple fact that she was raised in Canada by a couple whom she knows as her *loving* parents. "Although who I am today is due to my upbringing in Canada, I do still recognize that my ethnic background is Bangladeshi and that can never be taken away,"[65] observed Lara. She is proud of her background, and she guards that background information as part of the historical narrative with respect to her identity though not in its entirety.

Again, there was a cluster of feelings with which Rani, who grew up in Saskatoon, Saskatchewan, had struggled in her teens to come to terms with her true identity through anger, fear, alienation, and emptiness. Rani alone had serious problem in situating herself between the past and the present unlike other war babies in the same group. The psychological journey into Rani's past was spontaneous until she visited the orphanage premises where she was born and saw her name in the register book, something that added a new dimension to the self. This is one place where Rani stands out quite apart from the rest of the bunch (Amina, Lara, Ryan, and Rajib) who were also exposed to the same information at the same time back in 1989 when they were sixteen years old.

Rani had struggled with her own self in order to situate herself between the mother she had known all her life in Canada and the mother who gave birth to her in Bangladesh. A desperate Rani struggled in shifting identities back and forth – between the Rani who grew up in Canada with Canadian parents and the Rani who was born in Bangladesh and conceived in the womb of an unknown mother who could not keep her baby. In seeking her identity, Rani was *torn apart*. She needed her past to work through her feelings and make the present by filling in the "identity gap" that had hitherto existed in her life.

Rani's pathetic situation and her inability to deal with the crisis reinforce Erick Erickson's pioneering clinical observation of identity development during adolescence in a psychological context as it relates to the individual's sense of genealogy. His argument that an adoptee's identity in a psychological context relates to the individual's sense of genealogy through linkage between the past and the present, which must not be ignored, seems readily applicable in Rani's case. Erickson's observation that ignorance or no knowledge about one's important stages in one's past creates discontinuity in one's life cycle, making it complicated and harder for an individual especially in her/his adolescent to move on with future, helps us understand Rani's struggle in her mind, although this was not the case with the rest of the war babies in the present bunch.[66]

Ryan, who gained an almost-celebrity status for being the first-ever-known war baby when he lived in Bangladesh for a year, illustrates one of the most important facts of the identification process – that the formative years greatly depend on environmental elements, such as physical, psychological, and sociocultural. Ryan knew from an early age that the color of his skin was obviously different than his parents, but he is inextricably connected with the respective family and the surrounding environments in which he was raised. Of all the war babies, Ryan is most pronounced in seeking his identity. He was candid in expressing and accepting the paradoxes and contradictions of his identity.

In Bangladesh, Ryan was still not totally "free of the jolts" of what he called the "strange and unusual culture" [67] of Bangladesh. Challenging his Canadian brain, Ryan had "tried to poke and prod" his "western upbringing all in a quest of awakening and discovering Bangladesh – the country of his ancestors and his ancestors' ancestors."[68]

He freely talked about two countries and two mothers – a Bengali mother who gave birth to his body and an adoptive mother who gave birth to his soul. "My name is Badol. I have two Mothers – one calls me Ryan, and the other calls me Badol. The one who calls me Ryan, I have known all my life. The one who calls me Badol, I have never met. I was born in Bangladesh to the Mother who calls me Badol. Three weeks later, I was born in Canada to the Mother who calls me Ryan. A Pakistani soldier raped the Mother who calls me Badal. I am a war-baby," [69] wrote Ryan in a matter-of-fact way, calling a spade a spade.

Ryan recognizes with pride that he belongs to both Bangladesh where he was born and Canada where he has been raised: "I was born on the sacred soil of a new country called Bangladesh. My blood is of here, and indeed, I feel proud to associate my birth with the birth of this nation. I have a deep and steadfast connection with this place despite the seemingly insurmountable afflictions. I am bound to feel love toward Bangladesh."[70] *Why?* To Ryan's way of thinking, one gave him life, while the other taught how to live it.

Nevertheless, Ryan is conflicted due to the fact that despite being in the midst of Bengali crowd in Dhaka, he felt lonely while walking into the anonymity of the crowd: "In the crowd I was no different than anyone else. Indeed, in Bangladesh, I am no different in appearance than the locals. The problem is that while my genes are Bengali, my brain is Canadian. I am barricaded against the Bengali and I am barricaded against the western. This fact is tough to bear,"[71] wrote an unhappy Ryan to his parents in Canada. There were times when Ryan became so nostalgic; especially when he used to get sick that for days he would miss Canada, his "home." "I started daydreaming and night dreaming about life in Canada. I became very turned off by rice. I craved for western food. So, I doled out the extra cash and I bought things like cheese and pasta and other stuff. This made me feel much better,"[72] thus wrote Ryan to his parents.

During his stay in Bangladesh in 1997–1998, Ryan could not allow his emotion to carry him away from the wonderful mom and dad he had left in Canada. He could neither identify himself with Bangladesh nor with the people of Bangladesh. And yet despite his Canadian upbringing and obvious difference in lifestyle, *he felt incredibly proud to claim himself a part of the Bangladeshi fabric.* Ryan voluntarily took out Bangladeshi citizenship at that time, something that was not required for him. Bangladeshi citizenship meant a great deal to Ryan personally – a decision that made him feel proud. To this day, this carries a tremendous significance to Ryan, who went for it for no other reason than "to solemnize" his "connection" with his country of birth.

At the end, however, Ryan remains a burning example of how childhood memories of where one is raised may override other memories and prepare one to identify oneself with, not where one is born but, instead, raised. Despite his demonstrably extraordinary and powerful mind in accepting the harsh reality of his birth and his life, Ryan chose to call himself "Canadian." Of all the war babies, Ryan articulates this in an exceptional way.

The present war babies are again much unlike the young Bengali Canadians who find their Bengali parents often struggling to embrace both "Canadian" and Bangladeshi values. Both Canadian-born children of Bangladeshi origin and their parents in Canada go through different levels of acculturation in an attempt to find an identity, a niche, which is balanced and workable in Canada. Bangladeshi Canadian parents

MUSTAFA CHOWDHURY

try to retain their mother tongue (Bengali) and traditional values, and follow a combined Bangladeshi Canadian lifestyle as well as child-rearing practices.

They also tend to emphasize norms of collectivist obligation to one's family and society. This may seem strikingly different than the mainstream Canadian society that tends to emphasize individualism and independence. The war babies raised in Canada, therefore, did not experience the need for any such cultural adjustments in their families. This is an interesting aspect of the difference that exists between the Bangladeshi war babies raised by white parents and children of Bangladeshi origin born and raised in Canada by Canadian parents of Bangladeshi origin in the 1970s and 1980s.

"It is always clear in my mind that I'm Canadian even if people don't know me and perceive me as not being Canadian because of my look,"[419] said a self-confident Josée. Her heritage is what her *parents* had taught her since she had been growing up: "The way I was raised plays a big part in defining me as Canadian or a Quebequois (which refers to my parents' French background)."[73] Having been raised in a small town in Quebec, Josée sees herself as a Quebecor: "I speak like a Quebecor, think like a Quebecor, therefore, I must be a Quebecor."[74]

When asked *where she is from,* a strong-willed Josée has a standard response – that she is from Canada. For those who remain persistent in asking about her origin, Josée's usually polite and curt response: "I was born in Bangladesh."[75] By and large, Josée would give no more answer. She wonders how appropriate it is for someone to actually question anyone along this line. *Why does Josée sometimes choose to ignore people who question her background or ethnicity?* Josée herself gives the answer: "Well, I find that my origins don't concern every person I meet in my life. In Canadian vocabulary one could easily say, 'It's none of your business,'"[76] states Josée. Nevertheless, a courteous Josée always stays calm and polite and takes her time in handling such inquisitiveness. "People in life don't introduce themselves by saying, 'hi my name is . . . I was born in Toronto, or Saskatoon. Why should I have to do that? Where I was born is a private matter and that I have the right to choose with whom I will share this,"[77] says Josée.

From the adoptees' narratives, it is clear that they do not have what might be considered a "group identity" perhaps due to the fact that they grew up in parts of the country under different social environments. Each family's notion of a "family" having "children of mixed backgrounds" had helped create a "bond" among family members that had overridden any kind of divisiveness or differences due to ethnicity.

We have seen in chapter 5 how the Ribeiros (parents of Martin), in particular, chose not to nourish a distinct ethnic identification, which they saw as problematic for integration and social cohesion for Martin, who was developmentally slow with a learning disability. According to the Ribeiros, even though Martin was not exposed to Bangladeshi culture and tradition, he neither felt disadvantaged nor did he suffer from innate insecurity because of his lack of knowledge about his country of birth. The same is the case with Rajib, who was diagnosed as schizophrenic around the time he was in his late teens. As a result, since his parents simply avoided the subject, he remains disinterested and somewhat indifferent to anything other than "Canadian."

Those who never went to Bangladesh seem to have much less emotional attachment to Bangladesh although they are not indifferent. This, however, does not mean that the latter group does not have a positive sense of ethnicity. They have a sense of ethnicity that Erickson refers to as something that influences one's ability to develop a "sense of wholeness recognized by acceptance of self."[78] Having known their birth history, they have a perspective of *who* they are. Not surprisingly, both groups, that is, the group that went to Bangladesh and the group that did not return to Bangladesh, candidly express their identity that embraces the values and heritage of their parents they have inherited in Canada without, of course, disregarding the historical fact of their birth in Bangladesh.

Being able to recognize the diversity within their own families at a micro level, they quickly learned through their parents' outlook how to value these and others in life. Over time, they have developed their own sense of values, that is, Canadian values, which they are both familiar and comfortable with.

Amina summed up the view of all of the war babies who are deeply attached through an unforgettable bond with their families: "As our parents celebrated humanity, equality for all people was believed, thought and practiced. With firsthand accounts of inclusion and mainstreaming, we are survivors of a road less traveled. Our trials and tribulations have made us who we are."[79] Speaking in unison about the notion of their identity, she said, "We had the visual appearance of minorities. However, we had been raised in Canadian households as infants. Assimilated into the Canadian culture, we were a new generation of Canadians creating new history."[80]

Experience of racism

This was an area in which all of them went back repeatedly to their earlier days from elementary school to college/university years and reflected on peer groups and personal relations with friends and acquaintances in the community. They freely talked about their experiences in schools and colleges and on the streets. As well, they spoke comfortably regarding job prospects and occupational mobility, which is often linked to immigrant status and nonwhite immigrants who are often known to be discriminated against. Some recall having experienced racism in different forms under different circumstances, while some could not recall ever experiencing any racist encounters at all.

With diverse family backgrounds, they did not have to go through a painful process of redefining themselves and understanding the multiracial order of the world around them. Having come to Canada at infancy and grown up with white parents, they did not have a home away from home. The adoptees recalled, having increasingly identified with the local white population of which their parents were a part, the war babies, nevertheless, knew that they themselves were not white per se.

They recalled how factors such as racial composition of the school and their neighborhoods, presence of other racially different siblings in the home, and the parents' perceptions and attitudes had all contributed to a fuller understanding and acceptance of their situation vis-à-vis the evolving Canadian society, which is still not a racist-free society.

When asked to recall any overt hostility or sneering or spitting at them by white children at school, or name-calling, none of them could recall any such incident. Happily enough, they don't recall ever being greeted by silence or nervous stares either. And yet what is also true is that, though very young, they seemed to have been quite conscious of their look, which was different from a white boy or a girl: "Mom, I saw another Chris at school,"[81] recalled Bonnie Boonstra, Chris' mother, hearing Chris say to her immediately upon return from school on the very first day. Bonnie soon figured out after asking Chris *what* exactly he meant by this. Using his own language and expression, the five-year-old Chris meant to say that there was another student in the class who looked like him (also a visible minority). Though only five or so, Chris was able to recognize the difference in the skin color – that there was another boy in the class who did not look like the rest of the children in the class but looked like him (and therefore, in Chris' own naïve way, he must be another Chris).

One of Amina's experiences dates back to early years when she was the only brown kid in the school in a small farming community outside of London, Ontario. When she was in grade one, there was a girl whom Amina recalled to have told all the other kids not to stand by her because she "was dirty,"[82] probably referring to the color of her skin. Naturally, Amina was hurt. She also remembers inviting her over to her house for dinner. This gesture on her part had actually helped her make this particular girl her new "friend" who, since then, never really bothered her, Amina recalled. Far from considering this as a negative experience, she now remembers it as rather an amusing experience that had caused mirth, to say the least.

While they were growing up, they had never felt isolated or alienated from the world around. Upon further probing along this line, however, some had indicated that there were times when they had experienced what might be called some sort of "strange behavior." When asked whether later on during their teen years they had any unpleasant experience at certain eateries, food courts, shopping malls, hotels, recreational clubs, etc., they could not recall any significant experience of overt prejudice with the exception of a few.

In seeking friends at school, they made no conscious effort to meet those who looked like them (meaning a visible minority student). When they were growing up, most of them were living in predominantly white areas having attended predominantly white schools. While it is true that the racial composition of the Canadian cities were rapidly changing during the 1970s, in the majority of the cities with the exception of Toronto, Montreal, and Vancouver, the number of nonwhite children was still very few especially in smaller towns. Neither the adoptees nor their parents saw that as a cultural mismatch even at that time. Instead, it was a natural process of developing friendship based on one's natural inclinations, liking and disliking, etc.

Again, the Boonstra family remembers the days when they used to take Chris out into the public, he was generally a novelty that would attract a great deal of attention of all those around him. Chris was about six or seven when the family moved to the Eastern Townships in Quebec where they do not recall ever seeing a person of color during their two-year stay. In those days, often they would cross the border into the United States for a Sunday afternoon drive to get into some English area. "There was always a negative attitude to having a person of a different race" [83] in their family, recalled the Boonstras. At that time, they also had Kara, another Bangladeshi girl they had adopted from Ottawa. "The border patrol would single out Chris and Kara, no questions were asked about the other four siblings because they were white. It really angered Bonnie but we did not discuss it with the kids, so I don't know if Chris picked up this prejudice at this early time,"[84] recalled Tony. When asked if they had experienced racist name-calling at school or in the neighborhood playgrounds, they do not remember any such incident with one or two exception.

However, Chris remembers his first unpleasant experience, which was with one of his managers at Bullwinke Family Food Restaurant in Edmonton where he worked for a couple of summers. Everything there was fine and hunky-dory, but at one point, and much to his surprise, he noticed that all visible minority busboys and waiters were working in the kitchen, while the frontline service was managed by white men and women only. Some of his colleagues used to go off to deep end because they knew something was amiss. They used to feel irritable having a myriad of complaints in their minds.

A debonair Chris, however, did not seem to think about it in the same vein as his coworkers. Naïve as he was at the time, he never bothered to get to the bottom of it, believing that it was not worth quibbling. It never dawned on him that it could be a case of predilection or preferential treatment based on the color of his skin. Chris was pretty young to understand what it really meant. He was not old enough to analyze such workplace arrangements in any meaningful way, as he had no knowledge of the concepts of "racism" and "discrimination" at the time. Having continued to work, Chris remained determined to move ahead. As and when he had ups and downs at work, Chris remained cheerful in adversity – something that he had faced with courage.

Upon further probing, some recollected how, on certain occasions, whether they were with their (white) parents or not, they were watched or stared at by curious onlookers and strangers around, or often they had to stand at counters waiting to be served. Some reported that on odd occasions while at the local ice cream parlor, the white man or woman behind the counter might have had served them last, although such rare experiences did not leave them with any thought of being treated differently. As a child, Lara, however, recalled how she had "encountered cruel and ignorant children" who had called her "names, such as 'dirty Paki' and 'brown cow.'"[85]

In a similar vein, Josée recalled how bad she used to feel seeing that her first name, Rajina, sounded different to everyone's ear. She believed it did not quite reflect *who* she *is,* as most of the people around were more familiar with English and French names. Though herself very young, she felt that people saw her "differently" simply because of her having a different type of name. "I was a part of soccer, softball and field hockey teams. And very often, the coaches would not even bother asking my name,"[86] recalled Josée. It perturbed her to see how they would simply look at her and would say, "You must be Rajina."[87] As far back as Josée remembers, this was something that used to get on her nerves. So Josée changed her middle name as her first name. "By the time I was 14 years old, my name became Josée,"[88] recalled Josée.

Again, Amina remembers one rather comical incident when she was around twenty, but she looked like she was fifteen or sixteen. Her little sister Sharina (who was adopted from India) decided that she was going to be creative when planting her beans in Sunday school. So she planted a bean up her nose, and it started to grow right away. When their mom rushed Sharina and Amina to the emergency, a nurse asked them lots of questions. Naturally, Donna (mother) felt very inclined to answer them. The nurse got more and more perturbed and grumpy as Donna was promptly responding to her questions. Finally, in exasperation, when she asked, "Excuse me! Who is the mother here anyway?" an anxious Donna took a breath and replied sweetly, "I am. I am actually the mother of both of them."[89] From that instant on, the nurse was much sweeter, recalled Amina. Though hilarious and somewhat an innocuous question, implicit in the nurse's mind was the clear picture that there was a difference between the two girls and the woman who brought them to the hospital with respect to their skin color. "Mom and Dad later joked. Was it the lack of pigment or the grey hair that threw her off?"[90] recalled Amina.

"There was one sad incident for Ryan when he was in Grade 1. If there was a disturbance on the school bus, the driver always made Ryan sit in the front seat. Other children told us about that and how unfair it was. We had to contact the bus company who dealt with the problem. That was the most overt incident of racism that we are aware of,"[91] recalled Doreen Good (mother of Ryan) who lived in Exeter, close to Toronto, Ontario.

"In my pre-teen years and in my teen years I experienced some events involving overt racism. It has always been in the form of name-calling. I always walked away. I found that simply avoiding a confrontation had worked the best and sometimes I joked with the verbal assailant and de-escalated their hostility,"[92] recalled Onil. Despite the passage of time, he remembers how he used to act and react: "When I was young, these comments made me wish that I were Caucasian too. I did not focus on the fact that I was different during these verbal assaults,"[93] recounted Onil with a distinct memory along with certain encounters of similar nature to a lesser extent.

Onil saw them as a learning experience that had always been both interesting and challenging. There were many friends who would come to his rescue: "Sometimes, I did nothing and the (Caucasian) people around me would defend me."[94] Again, there were occasions when Onil was completely at ease with the color of his skin: "At some point I became comfortable with being different. And I enjoyed being me,"[95] recounted Onil. Though still very young, Onil had a strategy to deal with such matters: "I didn't focus on the fact that I was different during these verbal assaults. I focused on the way it hurt me."[96] The reality on the ground was that even though he saw himself as being similar to his parents (despite the obvious fact that the color of his skin was different than his parents), there were occasions when perceptions of others were not the same.

Lara, whose example has already been cited, is much too familiar with *how* other people see her. "I often find that when I encounter people who have the same skin color as I do, they generally assume that we share the same race, ethnicity, religion, and/or cultural background,"[97] said Lara with reference to her experience at Casino Niagara where she was often approached by Indian, Pakistani, or mid-Eastern male customers who would start speaking to her in what they assume her native language. Not only do the condescending people take her as one of "their" people, but they also have a bit of unsolicited advice for her: "You shouldn't be taking the man's money (or out working), you should be at home raising children."[98] Lara recognizes harmless admonitions of such nature, which are based on their impression of Lara as someone who "shares the same cultural beliefs."[99]

Another experience with covert racism dates back to 1991 when Lara worked at a lodge in Alberta. She was hired over the phone, and when she met her employers for the first time in person, she immediately felt a barrier. As time went on, her relationship with her superior did not improve. Her employer maintained a positive working and personal relationship with all employees except her, despite Lara's constant efforts to be accepted and respected: "I was often blamed for others' mistakes, berated for my job performance, and rarely given encouragement or praise for a job well done,"[100] recalled Lara.

A badly jarred Lara felt as though her boss was breathing down her neck. In the end, Lara was accused of stealing food and was dismissed immediately, without hearing her side of the story. Lara was aggrieved to have experienced differential treatment, and yet she never found herself in a foul mood. She did not want to kick up a shindy. Turning a blind eye, a calm Lara continued to move on with her life, taking a forward-looking approach without causing any wave.

At school, especially during the early years, the war baby "A" (adopted son of Dr. Robert and Helke Ferrie) had no experience with racism. It was only when he moved to Toronto in the 1990s that he began to be aware racism as a social phenomenon that rears its ugly head every now and then. For the first time in life, he came to notice how some people perceive him "differently," although never in his life did he ever feel himself that way. While pursuing his studies at George Brown College, A had some unpleasant encounters, which were the first taste of what might have resulted from his being racially different from the rest of the students. Among twenty or so students in his class, he had a good relationship with pretty well everyone with the exception of one white class fellow whom A found to be different, almost indignant of him. This particular student, whose name A does not recall, saw A as a "foreigner." In any event, A made an effort not to have anything to do with him, having kept his cool in the hope that the same fellow would turn around and graduate to maturity in course of time. Unfortunately, even at the end of the session, he remained as bigoted as he was at the beginning. A's final opinion of his class fellow is that "some people never change for they are truly incorrigible."[101]

"Because we grew up in a multi-racial family, when I was faced with or observed racism, I could not grasp why people would be that way. I did not experience overt racism until I was in CEGEP [Collège d'enseignement géneral et professionelle] and university,"[102] observed Shama. The situations in which she had encountered racism had always taken her by surprise. Usually she finds them to be comments that are made by people who, unless it is pointed out to them as being racist, are not aware of what they have said or remarked.

One of Shama's most amusing experiences while at York University relates to *how* others, including her professor, might see her: "This does not mean that I am unaware of the fact that others don't see me as Canadian – having sat in a professor's office at York University only to have her ask me if English is my second language – the implication being that it probably is given the fact that I am not white. I've had many such experiences that remind me that others don't see me as 'Canadian' simply because my skin is not white – and with such experience I've had two typical responses – one, who cares what others think and two, what a great learning and teaching experience."[103] Needless to say, Shama's professor's assumption that English is not Shama's first language is primarily based on Shama's skin color even though she speaks flawless English just like any other born Canadian with no accent at all.

With a well-integrated and a fully developed Canadian identity, the war babies conclude that even the most loving family cannot be shielded from the harsh realities of prejudice and racism that still exist in Canadian society. In talking about people's perception, some of them again recalled being asked *if* and *when* they would be going home – "back to your country." Though a rather innocuous question arising not out of insular minds but of ignorance and one's perception of the other, queries along such veins did not or don't perturb them, as they have gotten used to them. As and when they encounter any behavior that might smack of racism, they try to rise above it and move forward, believing that for every one person that discriminates, there is one who does not. With that built-in mechanism, the adoptees were able to sustain racially motivated encounters with reason and calmness.

What emerged from their narratives is that whether they have experienced or not, they are aware that beneath the surface, many people harbor feelings that are mixed into myth and stereotype. Having lived in Canada all their lives, they are of the view that those who discriminate show a great lack of respect, compassion, and intelligence because they cannot see beyond the physical attributes of another person. They fail to understand that people are part of the human race.

Notes and References

1   Lara Morris said this to the author in an interview on May 11, 1998, at the Morrises' residence in Brantford, Ontario. The author also met the families again in 1998 and then followed up with the family while writing the manuscript. Later on Lara Morris who visited the author in Ottawa also wrote to him on May 8, 2000. Both are in touch with each other.

2   *Ibid.*

3   *Ibid.*

4   *Ibid.*

5   *Ibid.*

6   Amina Wolsey, *Perspectives of Multicultural Family: An Education in Itself.* Research Paper for Masters of Education at Ontario Institute for Studies in Education, University of Toronto, 2002, p. 29. Hereinafter, referred to as *Amina's Research Paper.*

7   *Ibid.*, p. 29.

8   *Ibid.*, p. 10.

9   *Ibid.*

10   *Ibid.*

11   *Ibid.*

12   During 1997 and 1998, Ryan Good lived in Bangladesh for a year. At that time, on a monthly basis, Ryan remained in touch with his family and friends in Canada with a view to keeping them posted on his activities. He forwarded all his e-mails to the author in 2000. The present citation is dated December 19, 1997. The author has used his e-mails extensively and followed up with Ryan as and when he needed any clarification. Hereinafter, referred to as *Ryan's e-mail.*

13   *Ryan's e-mail.* December 19, 1997.

14   *Ibid.*, p. 9.

15   *Ibid.*

16   *Ibid.*

17   *Ibid.*

18   War baby A said this to the author in a telephone interview on July 23, 1998, while living in Toronto.

19   *Ibid.*

20   Letter from Josée to Mustafa Chowdhury, June 18, 2002. Since then the author has met her in Montreal, Quebec; as well, he has corresponded with her several times. He is in constant touch with Josée.

21   *Ibid.*

22   *Ibid.*

23   *Ibid.*

24   *Ibid.*

25   E-mail from Shama Hartt to Mustafa Chowdhury on November 1, 1998. Following this, Shama came to Ottawa with her parents, Joel and Trudy Hartt, to meet with the author on June 23, 2000. Together, they met at a restaurant in downtown Ottawa and discussed the project over lunch. Following that, the author has been in touch with Shama and corresponded regularly. Shama Hartt is a Facebook friend of the author.

26   *Ibid.*

27   *Ibid.*

28   Onil Mowling said this to the author in an interview in Toronto at a downtown hotel on May 30, 2000. Since then the author has been in frequent touch with Onil. He has also confirmed this in an e-mail on January 11, 2004.

29   *Ibid.*

30   *Ibid.*

31   *Ibid.*

32   *Ibid.*

33   *Ibid.*

34   *Ibid.*

35   E-mail from Lise Bertrand to Mustafa Chowdhury, April 10, 2012. Over the years, author has corresponded with both Lise Bertrand and Pierre Hogue and talked to them separately over the phone on a regular basis. They took great interest in the project and provided feedback to the author especially with reference to chapters 5, 6, and 7.

36 Letter from Josée Hogue to Mustafa Chowdhury, September 20, 2001.

37 Same as # 25.

38 *Same as # 28.*

39 *Amina's Research Paper, p.13.*

40 *Ibid.*

41 *Ibid.*

42 *Ryan's e-mail,* September 20, 1997.

43 *Adoption: Essays in Social Policy, Law, and Sociology,* ed. by Philip Bean, Tavistock Publications, London, 1984. The article is titled "Obtaining Birth Certificates" by John Triseliotis, p. 40.

44 The idea was conceived by Pat Kerr, a former stewardess with British Airways, who financed the project. The invitation of the adoptees gave Bangladesh an opportunity to showcase the "story" of the adoption of Bangladeshi orphans (that included five war babies also) and to give the adoptees a chance to visit their country of birth while inaugurating the new village that was handed over by British Airways to Families For Children (FFC). Looking back, this concept in itself was a very new way of thinking in the 1980s. The Sreepur-based Children's Village was to amalgamate three homes in Bangladesh being run by FFC, which, since then, had adopted many children from around the world. When the Canadian team visited the new Children's Village, it housed close to seven hundred orphans.

45 *Amina's Research Paper,* p. 31

46 Ryan's e-mail, October 30, 1997.

47 The *Expositor,* February 27, 1989.

48 *Ibid.*

49 *Amina's Research Paper,* p. 70.

50 They are cognizant of the personal, social, and ethnic identity and associated terminologies. By personal identity, they meant the way in which a person defines himself in terms of his individuality and differences to others, such as gender, nationality, culture, religious affiliation, sexuality, etc. By social identity, they meant how an individual functions within many different social situations and relate to a range of other people. Social group may involve family, ethnic communities, cultural connections, values, and work. By ethnic identity, they meant a person's sense of belonging to an ethnic

group. It is drawn from the realization that a person's thoughts, perceptions, feelings, and behaviors are consistent with those of other members of the ethnic group.

51 E-mail from Onil Mowling to the author, January 7, 2001.
52 *Ibid.*
53 *Ibid.*
54 *Ibid.*
55 *Amina's Research Paper*, p. 35.
56 *Ibid., p. 17.*
57 *Ibid.*
58 *Ibid., p. 28.*
59 Shikha Cappuccino said this to the author in an interview on June 14, 2004. Since then, the author has been to Shikha's house in Ottawa on several occasions.
60 War baby A said this to the author in an interview.
61 E-mail from Shama Hartt to the author, January 10, 2000.
62 *Ibid.*
63 Letter from Lara Morris to the author, November 8, 2001.
64 *Ibid.*
65 *Ibid.*
66 For details please see, Erickson, Erick. *Identity.* London, Faber & Faber, 1968.
67 Ryan's e-mail to the author, October 10, 1997.
68 *Ibid.*
69 *Ibid.*
70 *Ibid.*
71 *Ibid.*
72 *Ibid.*
73 Letter from Josée Hogue to the author, September 20, 2001.
74 *Ibid.*
75 *Ibid.*
76 *Ibid.*
77 *Ibid.*
78 Eric Erickson, *Identity and the life cycle,* New York: Norton, 1980.
79 *Amina's Research Paper*, p. 67.
80 *Ibid.*
81 Bonnie Boonstra said this to the author during an interview at the Boonstra residence in Ashton, Ontario, on May 14, 2004.

[82] *Amina's Research Paper,* p. 31.

[83] Tony and Bonnie Boonstra said this to the author during an interview at the Boonstra residence in Ashton, Ontario, on May 14, 2004. Later on this was confirmed by Tony Boonstra in an e-mail to the author on April 20, 2012. Since the late 1990s, the author has been in touch with the couple and has corresponded regularly.

[84] *Ibid.*

[85] Lara Morris said this to the author in an interview on May 11, 1998, at the Morrises' residence in Brantford, Ontario. The author also met the families again in 1998 and then followed up with the family while writing the manuscript. Later on Lara Morris wrote to the author on May 8, 2000.

[86] Letter from Josée Hogue to the author, September 20, 2001.

[87] *Ibid.*

[88] *Ibid.*

[89] *Amina's Research Paper,* p. 25.

[90] *Ibid.*

[91] Letter from Doreen Good to the author, March 2010.

[92] Letter from Onil Mowling to the author, April 10, 2004.

[93] *Ibid.*

[94] *Ibid.*

[95] *Ibid.*

[96] *Ibid.*

[97] Letter from Lara Morris to the author, June 8, 2004.

[98] *Ibid.*

[99] *Ibid.*

[100] *Ibid.*

[101] Telephone Interview with the war baby A on February 10, 2007.

[102] Letter from Shama Hartt to the author, June 15, 2001.

[103] *Ibid.*

CHAPTER EIGHT

Cause Célèbre

THE SORDID STORY of the conception of the war babies, their birth, abandonment, and adoption of those who have survived in various countries in the world, though utterly absorbing, will remain incomplete perhaps forever. Given the fact that there is a dearth of primary sources to pursue their story, it is important for us to remind ourselves of Bina D'Costa's findings many years ago: that "there is no way of knowing the fate of all the adopted war-babies" ("Bangladesh's Erased Past," by Bina D'Costa *http://southasia.oneworld. net* opinioncomment.bangladesh's erased past).

Nevertheless, the life trajectory of the present bunch of fifteen war babies from Bangladesh and their life through the years in the homes of Canadian parents that we have looked at in the preceding chapters is based on primary sources. These war babies are a part of the historical narrative of the Bangladesh Project (1972) that has been well documented and may be traced through archival research, since they are a part of Canada's recorded social history.

Needless to mention, the great bulk of the evidence on adoption outcomes in Canada has come from the testimonies of the adoptive parents and the adoptees themselves. Having joined the adoptive families in Canada during their infancy, the fact of adoption became a natural part of the lives of the war babies. True, some of the war babies such as Onil or Chris, we have looked at, think very little about adoption; while with some others, such as Rani or Ryan, adoption became very critical in their growing years. Having suffered no emotional damage, and been placed in loving homes, the adoptees took advantage of the opportunity to proceed rapidly to develop a normal healthy life as they grew from adolescence to adulthood in Canada, the country they call "home."

If the Bangladesh government's measures with regard to the war babies seem heartless or inadequate, one must view them against the backdrop of the period immediately following the independence of

Bangladesh when such newborn infants were seen as "disposable" by Bangladeshis even though the newborns were in need of "rearing" and "mothering." Essentially, it was a moral question that the Mujib administration had to find an answer to: whether the parents through international adoption of the babies who did not have the same racial and cultural background of the orphans were morally acceptable. As there was no one to oppose the adoption of the war babies, neither there is a way to determine whether such adoption was seen as a "loss" of potential human resource, nor is there any documentary evidence to suggest that the intercountry adoption of Bangladeshi war babies was seen as riddance. What we know for certain is that the government of the day had spent a great deal of time reflecting on the notion of the "best interest of the child."

It is hard to tell whether by allowing foreign adoption of the war babies, the government of Bangladesh saw adoption as a way of making progress toward greater racial harmony, tolerance, or understanding of the universal values of welfare and charity or not. It is, however, possible to tell that the government had to take immediate measures to allow the adoption of those infants who were not "wanted" in their country of birth. Nevertheless, we have seen there were many outside of Bangladesh who saw them as "children of despair" and had readily embraced them. Despite many odds, the Mujib administration was able to rise to the challenge to bring ingenuity to solutions of problems as they arose with the birth and abandonment of these "unwanted" babies. Unfortunately, while there could be no argument about the fact that the adoption of the war babies fits within the Good Samaritan tradition of love and care, many who study transracial adoption question its outcome. Yanking off the babies from a foreign land and adopting them by parents of a different race and culture is not always seen in a positive light by many.

Historically speaking, all through the 1970s, due to politicization of race relations, the practice of transracial adoption came under serious scrutiny. In fact, by early 1970, the notion of adoption by parents of a child who is of different race to them became a controversial issue in the USA and the United Kingdom. In his groundbreaking research on adoption, Paul Sachdev had earlier raised the issue further by making reference to the report of Simon and Alstein where it was observed that transracial adoption had been on the decline. It was argued that many see it as a "cultural genocide" (edited by Paul Sachdev, Butterworth, Toronto, *Adoption: Current Issues and Trends,* p. 170) and the loss of the child's heritage and the risk of permanent marginality for children of one race being raised in families of another race. Interestingly enough, the changes in American adoption practice were supported by black social workers, who were engaged in persuading both family and child care departments to "eschew trans-racial adoption" (*ibid.,* p. 171).

In our present instance, the war babies' adoption is both intercountry adoption as well as transracial adoption, since the adoptive parents are of Caucasian background. In the adoption discourse, those who favor interracial and international adoption maintain that foreign adoptions allow adoptive parents save poverty-stricken children from starvation and/or life in the streets. Fortunately for the war babies, there were many families in Canada who wanted to embrace, love, and raise them. It is through adoption that the war babies' lives, which had started with a tragic and stark truth, had been changed and reshaped to a positive outcome by a group of ordinary Canadian parents.

We have learned at the outset that the Bangladesh Project was not an initiative of a group of childless parents in Canada and parentless children in Bangladesh. The arrival of the war babies is the culmination of the collective effort initiated by a group of enthusiastic and altruistic Canadian couples. Despite setback and difference of opinion about what steps needed to follow, the adoptive parents (then prospective applicants for adoption) stuck together as a solid group committed in their resolve to bring into their homes at least a few hapless orphans of Bangladesh. In that sense, their solidarity remains an example of how they had worked away adhering to the Quaker unanimity principle in making a decision – by hammering out the differences until reaching a consensus and then acting jointly and forcefully to reach their collective goals. We have seen in the preceding chapters how Fred and Bonnie Cappuccino had worked hard to achieve their goal.

Looking back, one might say, on the one hand, the Bangladesh Project was the Canadian version of the American Operation Baby Lift of 1975 by private agencies such as Holt International Agency and Friends for All Children that airlifted approximately 2,300 orphaned children, which is perhaps the greatest airlift of the previous century. On the other hand, the Bangladesh Project, due to its sheer insignificant number, was much unlike the Operations Baby Lift of 1975, which had many Vietnamese orphans who were older with significant issues related to relinquishment, attachment, emotional reaction, and attitudinal baggage to the overwhelming events of loss and change in their early years. In that sense, the Bangladesh Project does not have the same dimension of the Operation Baby Lift. Nevertheless, the arrival of the first contingent of fifteen war babies through the initiative of Families For Children (FFC) is a milestone in the history of interracial adoption in Canada. The rescue of the war babies of Bangladesh, whose racial background is different from that of their adoptive parents in Canada, remains a gripping human tale.

Their story is not typical; instead, it is an atypical story that separates the facts from the fiction having demystified and normalized adoption. In fact, the life story of this group of war babies demonstrates two significant points: first, the Mujib administration had the foresight to recognize that only interracial adoption outside of Bangladesh would give the "unwanted" war babies an opportunity for a new life, a new beginning based on some of the core Canadian values such as equality, justice, and fairness that are upheld under all circumstances.

Second, the government of Bangladesh frantically looked for expert advice and engaged International Social Service (ISS) to recommend steps to take with respect to the rape victims and their infants born as a result of rape. One of Mujib's immediate and unresolved dilemma was that, on the one hand, he had maintained that the children were a national asset, and the exporting of children for foreign adoption had implications that Bangladesh did not have the means or desire to care for her own children, something that would incur widespread reprobation; on the other hand, there were no plans in place to find homes for the newborns who were seen as "illegitimate" and, therefore, "unwanted" in Bangladesh. There were not any Bangladeshis to openly come forward to embrace them, ignoring the stigma attached to their birth.

To appreciate the story of the present war babies and their adoptive parents, it is important to bear in mind that the transracial adoption from Bangladesh was a response to the problem of the growing number of war babies with no homes. We have learned through the parents' testimonies that it was not a response to the needs of childless couples in Canada for whom white babies were no longer available. It is, therefore, not a story of the stereotypical couples who, after battling with infertility for years, turn to adoption to fulfill their dreams of having a family;

instead, it is a story of a group of Canadian couples genuinely interested in adoption from another race to offer a secure and loving home to an orphan. Through the adoptive parents' narratives, we have also seen how the couples had fought hard for adoption at a time when they had pretty well everything going on for them – contentment in marriage, emotional stability, and quality of relationship. Surely, they responded to the issue having felt an urge to "do something" for the "throwaway" babies who needed to be loved and cared for.

Whether the war babies grew up in Canada or anywhere else in the world, at the heart of the core issue of adoption is the deeper understanding of adoption as a way of making a family by embracing them as one's *own* children. Complex as it is, the phenomenon of adoption exists not in a vacuum but within social and cultural environments that changes over time and evolves with the passage of time. With the unfolding of their life story, there emerged an important point – that adoption begins as a lifelong intergenerational journey that touches the children, their siblings, and both biological and adoptive parents.

No doubt, when one considers the fact that this is a group of adoptive couples who chose *not to follow* the cherished philosophy of conventional adoption placement, which is generally oriented toward approximating biological parent, the present bunch strikes as extraordinary couples. They had gone to the hilt in their fight for their right to choose an orphan from a country of *their choice*. Recognizing that familial union through adoption is of utmost importance, these would-be-adoptive parents directed their efforts to bringing home at least a few of these war babies to fulfill their dreams. They did this having fully recognized the gravity of the problems faced by the newly formed government of Bangladesh. They took on the challenge to help change the lives of those they were allowed to bring to their homes in Canada. One would be inclined to say that these parents, who saw senseless abandonment of the war babies as the waste of so much human potential, are, in fact, heroes in disguise.

By receiving and accepting the war babies, the adoptive parents have debunked three commonly held myths of adoption. First, by bringing the abandoned babies to their homes, not only did the adoptive parents instantly become their *parents* but they have also deconstructed the myth that only infertile couples, who long for a child, choose to adopt; second, while it is true that interracial adoption is a controversial area, and the intensity of the controversy is reflected in the literature of social work and the allied professions, the outcome of the present adoption has debunked the myth that adoptive relations are fragile, unable to withstand biological relationship. Third, it has also demystified the commonly held myth that the children develop best when they live in families they can regard as their own – that is, of the same racial background. Evidently, when the adoptees came into the family of the racially different parents who were unswerving in their love for their children, they instantly embraced them with unconditional love creating a parent-child or child-parent bond that crossed racial boundary.

The parents' narratives in chapter 6 illustrate fascinating snippets of both psychological and biological parenthood. Having claimed a war baby with a resolved choice, they have successfully realigned their family relationships with both biological and nonbiological children. They not only have demonstrated their deep and unquenchable love and affection for their children, but have also given them a meaning of life, which would have been very different had they not been adopted. By embracing the "disposable" war babies as their *own* children, they were able to create life where there was none offering its own rewards creating joys of hope for the children. In solidifying their relationship with their adopted children, of course, the parents had to deal with the ramifications of genealogical discontinuity in the life of both the child and the family members. Frank and candid discussions with the adoptive parents reveal this important characteristic – the experience of bringing home their *chosen* child from Bangladesh and knowing that the same child *belonged* to them, which had been the greatest thrill of their lives.

According to the adoptees, their parents have proved that nurturing is an instinctive capacity that is not determined by woman's biology alone. Defying the myth that only through bearing children could a woman realize true happiness, the adoptive parents have demonstrated one of the facts of adoption and parenthood – that parenthood consists of both of bloodlines and lovelines. At the same time, the adoptees also recognize that although it is the adoptive mother who is often referred to in the literature as "unnatural" mother, as far as they are concerned, having been nurtured outside their biological family, it is the adoptive mothers who have raised the adoptees as "their" own children.

It also drives home an important point – their claim that theirs is not a fictive kinship but "real" relationship based not on blood but instead on a firm commitment, inordinate endurance, and complete acceptance on the part of the family. In that sense, both adoptees and their parents highlight a harmonious relationship that had yielded personal satisfactions on the part of the members of the family contributing to having a stable family as a group and the group's permanence with a strong attachment even though the adoptees are now grown up and are on their own. Important to note, some of the adoptees have their own families now.

If one considers the two most important elements of child development – the child's feeling of belonging and feeling of a secure home and a family, it behooves us to say that the intended objectives of adoption of the war babies have certainly been achieved. The present story symbolizes the strength of filial love and affection, which has demonstrably transcended the bureaucratic red tape of Canada and Bangladesh and the social negativity surrounding adoption. It highlights an extraordinary message of love, hope, and happy ending for those hapless orphans whose lives in their country of birth had no significant meaning of any kind.

The adoptees' narratives also reveal their appreciation of one of the facts of adoption – that it is only through adoption that they have been saved from lives of poverty, uncertainty, and disgrace. They recognize, had they not been adopted in Canada, their lives might have been typical of the experiences of most of the other war babies who have remained in Bangladesh in disguise without ever revealing their true identity. The constant accumulation of experience within their family lives and their own lives in their respective communities have continually shaped and reshaped their beliefs, personalities, and outlooks on life, leaving them to reflect with profound satisfaction – how, among other things, their parents' individual strengths and positive outlook toward life have contributed to the overall well-being of each family member. It also emerged from the adoptees own narratives that they were able to come to terms with one of the most important questions in their lives: *Who am I? Why and how does my diverse family belong together?*

Despite the varying emotional and attitudinal baggage with respect to one's level of identification, collectively speaking, the war babies do not have an ambivalent racial identity. We have not failed to notice how this realization had helped them move forward to building a solid relationship with each other, which remains strong to this day. They have grown up to be adults under healthy and positive conditions. Having been embraced in their infancy, they were nurtured and loved by loving parents who helped them develop a distinct identity with which they are very comfortable.

The war babies' story provides an interesting illustration of how children born in extremely difficult conditions are able to develop and adjust socially and psychologically under a completely different environment given a chance to survive. We have noticed how, having been raised in Canada, the adoptees were able to establish emotional reliability with families they were adopted into early in their lives. Not only do they acknowledge and recognize their visible minority looks but also they continue to retain family ties and social relations with their white parents, siblings, and friends of diverse backgrounds in a way that is natural and spontaneous. Their testimonies also reveal that there is no need to deny or avoid the distinguishing characteristics of people and the groups from which they came.

Our examination of the parent-child bond, based on the testimonies of the adopters and the adoptees, reveals how deeply both the children and the parents remain attached to each other having shown the strength of love by building a family for the long haul with unbelievable faith and courage. Their testimonies also reveal how their (adoptive) parents' love reconfirms the "realness" of their genuine bond. We did not fail to notice how both adopters and adoptees in their own words have found their greatest satisfaction in the parent-child or child-parent relationships. The adoptees have always identified their parents as *their parents* – no one used the word "adoptive" parents while referring to their parents.

Each adoptee spoke with confidence in stating that one's knowledge of one's genetic background is inconsequential in developing a sense of personal identity. "I have known no other parents" is the common response from them – something that we have noted in their testimonies. Never for a minute did the war babies fail to express their gratitude to their parents who have raised them with unconditional love and deep affection. They grew up knowing that they have a family; heir parents who love them would raise and care for them under all circumstances. Whether it is Amina, Ryan, or Chris or anyone else from the group, each and every one of them loves and cares for one's parents and families – a commitment for which the war babies would "never trade their parents for million bucks," expressed by Amina and echoed by all adoptees. The trust is such that, deep down, the adoptees know in their minds that their parents were, and still are, always there who would "step up to the plate" anytime they need them.

The testimonies of the war babies that we have read also sharply contrast the critics of many transracial adoptions who argue that a racially different child is likely to be seen as "not belonging to the family" especially by extended family members. Whether it is Lara, Shikha, Shama, Chris, or, for that matter, anyone else from the same bunch, we have seen in their own accounts how *close* they feel to their extended family members scattered across Canada. In that sense, having no conflict or confusion with such a positive identity, the war babies have defied what the critics of transracial adoption have been saying all along: that the child will not know *who* he or she is. True, while there might have been some confusion in early years, upon attaining maturity, there was no friction or confusion in their minds about their identity. Instead, they possessed a sense of wholeness, something that is evident in their initiatives. Many critics' fear that close and intimate family relations will not develop between the child and other family members seems baseless compared to the actual experiences of the war babies in the present context.

Again, the parent-child bond also demonstrates that their bond is real and strong. Each family had provided protection and safeguard that had not only ensured that the interests of the child were being protected but also guaranteed. Immediately upon their arrival in Canada, all of them became part of the large circle; in addition to having their parents, they had their grandparents, uncles, aunts, and a host of relatives. Far from having a feeling of a sense of personal isolation, as argued by those against by interracial adoption, the war babies grew up being embraced by all family members of diverse racial backgrounds.

While growing up, they believed that their sense of security had been built only on the foundation of basic trust and that their needs were best met through open, honest, warm, and stable family environment – something that all adoptees have talked about. Time and again, they have pointed out how a consistent and supportive family life had been built with a strong and safe emotional equilibrium from which they were able to develop confidence and pride. It is their early developed sense of security that had served as a dependable and durable protection for healthy and effective socialization that we have seen in the individual profile of each war baby.

Their parents embedded in them a sense of possibility that transcended the artificial boundaries of race. Their "stories" also reveal the interplay of ethnicity, integration, identity, and place in Canada. From childhood to adulthood, they had followed a similar trajectory of self-awareness and emerging consciousness about their lives in Canada in the adoptive families in which they grew up with multiple multiracial siblings. The grown-up adoptees have demonstrated their innate ability to establish friendships and relationship with a great number of people of diverse background, as well as their varying levels of desires to connect with Bangladesh.

At the end, each had found an answer to such questions. Each had also found a satisfying response to challenges in understanding *adoption* and *race* differently at different stages and levels of emotional and cognitive sophistication. They became content with the answer they had found early in their lives – that they are products of both biology and upbringing. Whether one finds oneself at one end of such a continuum or the other, or somewhere in the middle, *adoption* will be there as part of the fabric of what makes them *who they are* forever in Canada. No matter *where* and *how* they live, a core adoption truth of the Bangladeshi war babies in Canada is that they *really* and *truly* do have two families – the birth mother who gave birth and their putative father from whom they have received many physical, emotional, and intellectual characteristics and their genetic potentials; and their parents in Canada.

Most importantly, it boils down to this: that these war babies have had the comfort and security of loving and caring parents and siblings who provided them with a good home, education, and other opportunities; and belief and assurance that they were and, always are, "wanted" by their families. The content analyses of the adopters and the racially different adoptees' responses to interview questions and periodic conversations with both sets of parents and children reinforce Laurie and William Wishard's observations on adoption: that "both birth and adoptive parents can provide a child and parents a needed feeling of closeness and belonging" (Laurie Wishard and William Wishard

Adoption: The Grafted Tree, Cragmont Publications, San Francisco, 1979, p. 3).

Again, the present story of interracial adoption by *choice* by a group of fertile parents is also consistent with the findings of Alfred Kadushin who argues that the ideal, the principles, the values, and the assumptions underlie adoption practices: "Once adoption is legally finalized, adoptive parents take their place in the community of parents indistinguishable from biological parents" (Alfred Kadushin, "Principles, Values, and Assumptions Underlying Adoption Practice" in *Adoption: Current Issues and Trends,* ed. by Paul Sachdev, Butterworth, Toronto, 1984, p. 5). He further went on to say that "full acceptance by the community of the idea of adoption implies that the adoptive families are not perceived differently or accorded treatment different from that accorded other families" (*ibid.*).

What have contributed to the successful outcome of the Bangladesh Project is the fact that despite initial confusion, all of the adoptees were able to situate them quite well with regard to their past history and racial identity, which are different from their parents. In fact, for them, it was a matter of balancing the fact of being born in Bangladesh and raised in Canada without any maggot of fear and shame. Put it in another way, just as they would not trade their parents for a million bucks, they would never ever deny their Bangladeshi roots, their humble beginnings, and subsequent change through adoption in Canadian homes that were filled with positive and nurturing love and message of hope. Testimonies of the parents and their children make it clear.

We have seen in chapter 7 how excited and passionate were Rani, Amina, Rajib, Ryan, and Lara when they went to Bangladesh first time at sixteen. The feelings of joy that transpired from watching their name in the register book at the orphanage from where they were brought to Canada might be regarded as "ethnic rediscovery" of the racially different adoptees. Visit to their country of birth was a turning point in their lives.

Their knowledge of their birth history and ethnic background are, however, not entrenched in their psyche or ways of thinking. The fact that the families have respected each other's racial background and had de-emphasized a particular racial identity in order to develop an all-encompassing Canadian identity, which is pluralistic, the children grew up with a deeper appreciation of Canada's diversity and pluralism. We did not fail to notice how this had helped the adoptees develop a feeling that they are a part of Canada. Needless to point out, having defined their notion of identity, they look upon them as being Canadian. This point has been reinforced over and over again by the adoptees without ever ignoring the fact that they were born in Bangladesh. It is significant here to note that the warm and supportive family environment that they were exposed to was critically important and responsible for positive outcomes.

Another important fact we have noticed is that some of the war babies are interested in and keen on Bangladesh and remain proud, while some remain disinterested and somewhat indifferent to whom neither the name Bangladesh nor its people (Bangladeshi) spark any interest. With the latter, a sense of connection with one's origin did not come out as significant (and therefore, no manifestation of pride in their ethnic roots and appearance), although there was no denial or feelings of discomfort noticeable in them for events surrounding their birth.

Contrary to D'Costa's observation that nearly all war babies "have no intention to be found" ("Bangladesh's Erased Past" by Bina D'Costa *http://southasia.oneworld.net* opinioncomment.bangladesh's erased past), the present group of war babies has no fear or apathy at all. In fact, it is remarkable to notice the unhesitating manner in which they talked about the turbulent past they have known from early on in their lives: sexual violence on the part of the Pakistani military personnel, enforced pregnancies of their birth mothers, consequent birth and abandonment of the war babies in Bangladesh, and subsequent adoption in Canada. The majority of the war babies we have looked at remain interested in knowing more about their country of birth.

Considering the fact that the success of adoption cannot be assessed only on the basis of placement stability, one needs to identify other indicators of success (e.g., achievement of development outcome and satisfaction of the adoptees themselves). To do the assessment outcome of their adoption, one needs to see the subject in light of the degree to which the adoptees are now self-supporting adults and the like in Canada. Various accounts of the parents and the adoptees that we have read in chapters 6 and 7 collectively reveal the level of success the couples have achieved in parenting the war babies.

Having had the good fortune of being raised in a safe and secured home in Canada, the adoptees' social and psychological problems of personal identity and knowing their worth and direction have solidified their confidence and sense of security. In measuring the outcome, it is also important to look at each adoptee's adjustment in a number of different life sectors. While doing this, one needs to keep in mind the shame and indignity with which the people of Bangladesh had looked at their conception and birth, which had resulted in mass abandonment. As well, we need to keep in mind their potential future in Bangladesh had they remained there.

Our knowledge of the ultimate outcome of the adoption is, however, limited only to what have transpired out of the testimonies of the adopters and the adoptees, their poignant description of their own views, and their actual lives and families in Canada where they grew up and where they live. What we know for a fact is that Ryan has a successful business enterprise, Shama is a popular teacher, while Amina, stationed in Abu Dhabi, is involved in teaching and researching in the field of education, just to name a few.

Let us take a step back and ask some basic questions in order to compare the outcome: *What is known about the war babies who were left behind in Bangladesh? Where do they live in Bangladesh? Would the Bangladeshis ever be able find out the whereabouts of the war babies now in their early forties? How are they seen in Bangladesh in relation to the mainstream Bangladeshis?* The hard and cruel fact is that Bangladeshis are sadly unaware and uninformed about them, or to put it in another way, many Bangladeshis, allowing some exaggeration, are both misinformed about and disinterested in the war babies and their checkered lives. Or asked differently: *Do the Bangladeshis really care for the war babies?*

The answer might be both yes and no. We have seen the lives of the first batch of war babies adopted in Canada. There is, however, no record for other war babies that are in Bangladesh or in other countries. Availability of documentary evidence of the lives of the war babies in Bangladesh or in other countries would have allowed us to compare the success with those who were left behind in Bangladesh. Unfortunately, as it stands today, no one will ever know exactly what happened to those less fortunate war babies who were not placed through adoption and, as a result, had remained in Bangladesh without ever disclosing their true identity.

In the absence of any hard data, when we look back in an attempt speculate on the war babies that were left in Bangladesh, two important facts emerge about the orphanages where they were born or were brought to after their birth. First, factually speaking, because of the lack of adequate medical attention and proper nutrition in the orphanages, many of these foundlings had not survived to experience life. It was as though all these premises were veritable death traps where many had suffered very high percent mortality immediately following their birth; second, they must have grown up in an unforgiving society as neglected as a beggar on the street. Again, what we know for a fact is that they could not claim their right to live in their own country of birth, as they are too ashamed to self-identify at a time when the society views them as "undesirables." Upon reaching the age of majority, they simply took off and had begun to live *incognito.*

And yet interestingly enough, when Ryan self-identified as the first-ever-known war baby in Bangladesh, was highlighted as sensational news of the week. Such was the impact of his self-identification that he instantly gained an almost-celebrity status raising curiosities of Bangladeshis, not repugnance, which was shown at the birth of the same babies. Ryan's appearance as a war baby had caused a great wave in the people's mind more in a positive way than negative. Nevertheless, the sensation or curiosity and enthusiasm did not last that long. The initial zeal and fervor that Ryan generated during the first week of his appearance in 1997 frizzled out long before his departure from Bangladesh the following year. Not a single war baby (one would assume that there are many in Bangladesh) chose to come out of the closet following the publication of Ryan's story in the news media in 1997.

One would think that after reading or hearing about Ryan's appearance as the war baby of 1971, at least a few of the war babies would take some interest to come forward to follow suit. No, not a single war baby came out in public. Having lived for over forty years in their country of birth, they are still the "hidden" people of the Bangladeshi society. This is even though the International War Crimes Tribunal in its judgment of December 2014 had observed that the war babies and their birth mothers should be regarded as "heroes." Although six months have passed by since the judgement was rendered with commentaries like the above, not a single war baby has come out to self-identify yet. Instead, they continue to live in disguise with a false identity with no desire to ever come out in public to give their true identity despite the

MUSTAFA CHOWDHURY

assurance of respect and dignity that is expected to be accorded to them. Instead, the lives of the ubiquitous war babies in Bangladesh continue as "business as usual." *How many of the war babies had found their way into adoptive homes in Bangladesh and/or abroad?* This question also remains unanswered.

One could say easily it is truly anybody's guess. It was not until Prof. Yasmin Saikia came up with her highly acclaimed book titled *Women, War and the Making of Bangladesh: Remembering 1971* that we know a little bit about the war babies from firsthand sources. Through Saikia's investigative in-depth research work, she has "discovered" at least three war babies, two of whom did not want to be talked about at all although they spoke with Professor Saikia. The third war baby, a female named Beauty, spoke with Saikia at great length and insisted on using her real name (which is Beauty) and true identity much unlike her mother. Indeed, it is ironic that someone with a name like Beauty, having such an ugly birth history, grew up in an orphanage in Gaibandha, Rangpur, in northern Bangladesh where her mother left her to be taken care of. Beauty's mother, Nuri Begum (a *birangana*), uses a pseudonym from the start of "shameful life" in the newly independent Bangladesh.

As was the case, this happened just before Nuri Begum herself was placed in a mental hospital in Pabna, Bangladesh. The tragic story of Beauty and her mother is both calamitous and heartbreaking. Professor Saikia found out through Nuri Begum's own testimony that although she had publicly identified herself as a rape victim, she is now inclined to suppress the public memory of her victimization. By contrast, Beauty, however, wants "the world to know her story and, if possible, enable her to reconvene a human life as a person," wrote Saikia (Saikia, p. 82).

Through Saikia's findings, we have learned how "both [Nuri Begum and Beauty] have very difficult lives, not only socially and economically but because of the basic issue of their identity – what they can reveal and have to hide destabilizes and dislocates them" (Saikia, p. 83). Not surprisingly, both the "community and culture of Bangladesh refuse them admission and accommodation in their ranks" (Saikia, p. 83) even to this day. The once-married and now-divorced Beauty, a mother of two, could never forget her ex-husband's often repeated aggressive and unbearable comments: "Your mother is a whore, and you are one too." This remains a source of anger, pain, agony, and helplessness for the troubled Beauty who is a destitute today. "I don't have a human life even though I may look human" (Saikia, p. 83), says a distressed Beauty, who, though very much alive, is both seen and referred to by others, including herself, as a cadaver.

Such is Beauty's predicament that she cried out for help when she spoke with Professor Saikia: "I have no house, no family; I want to do some work, but I can't find a job. Where do I go at this time? What do I do for living? What do I do with my life, my time? I can't seem to find an answer. My mother doesn't want to see me, or spend time with me. She is afraid. She doesn't want to recognize me as her daughter. I have no identity" (Saikia, p.109). Her plight is such that even her biological mother now refuses to acknowledge her true identity for fear of societal opprobrium. And yet everyone around continues to humiliate her only to reduce her into a pariah. Beauty is not surprised at people's attitude toward her. She frequently falls into a deep funk being unable to brook the state of anguished mind she continues to be in. She is trying to learn to survive in spite of everything. At forty plus, she is still learning how to bear with denigrating comments, which are a part of her descriptive identity in her country of birth.

Given that people generally have a soft spot in their hearts for children without a home, ideally, there should not have been an exception for the war babies who ought to have been taken care of. However, unfortunately, the people of Bangladesh saw them as "illegitimate," and, therefore, they were treated as such as though they were "unwanted" or "throwaway." As mentioned, despite the positive ruling of the Tribunal, not a single war baby has chosen to self-identify. If the same trend continues, no one will ever know of any war baby in Bangladesh. Thus far, we only know about the circumstances of Beauty. Our knowledge of Beauty's present and past is confined to what Saikia has found and shared with us about the ubiquitous but invisible war babies living in Bangladesh.

It is understandable why the two war babies who talked to Professor Saikia wished to remain anonymous in a society that frowns upon them even forty three years later particularly for the ways in which they were conceived and born. The reality is so harsh that the much too neglected war babies have nothing to balance their lives while living in seclusion and anonymity in their own country of birth. Like Beauty, who remains public and open about her birth story, and unlike her mother, they must have been battling the ravages of poverty and feelings of guilt, shame, and embarrassment. Although the Tribunal has shown positive attitude towards the birth mothers and their babies, the society has not yet been convinced to embrace the war babies with dignity and honour. Since the Bangladeshi society has not yet shown a positive attitude toward acceptance of the war babies, they are not likely to "come out of the closet" even forty three years after their birth. Viewed from that angle, one may understand *why* there is still reluctance to self-identify.

Put it differently, one may also be inclined to say that having been grown up under punitive conditions, by no fault of their own; they may now be found among the ranks of the adult groups of hoodlums and goons. When one looks around, they are very likely to be found everywhere though incognito. While we cannot say with any degree of certainty as to what happened to those who remained in Bangladesh, one might observe that they are now a part of the masses of people who live under poverty on the fringes of the Bangladeshi society. What is also known for a fact is that there is no official record of them identifying them as the "war babies" of Bangladesh. Consequently, the successive governments of Bangladesh could not institute any program of financial/social provision to improve the lot of those usually referred to as the "disposable" children of Bangladesh.

In the absence of any documentary evidence, it is only known through hearsay evidence that some of the war babies were institutionalized (just as Beauty was) in various parts of Bangladesh at an early age. The reality on the ground is such that one cannot help but think that they must have grown up having spent the formative years of their lives in the deprieved environments of Bangladesh orphanages, as they were seen as the dregs of the Bangladeshi society, which did not accept them right from their birth. As the stories go, never having had an opportunity to experience the love and affection that an ordinary parent usually provides, they had run away as soon as they reached puberty.

They ran away because they did not want to subject themselves to embarrassment, shame, and stigma associated with their lives. They genuinely feared that due to a lack of parental identity, they would be subjected to whispers, indignation, and endless taunting remarks. For them, it was, therefore, a matter of finding their own niche perhaps in the seamier sides of life in Bangladesh. Many must have been forced to switch to the kind of lifestyle that is generally vulnerable to further self-destruction and victimization. Beauty's brief but powerful narration outlined by Professor Saikia only reinforces our initial suspicion that may well be sustained unless proved otherwise.

One may go on in circle with no answer. However, looking from a pragmatic angle, one may perhaps make another set of speculations from what is known about the Amerasians in Vietnam whose putative fathers were American soldiers. Had these fifteen war babies remained in Bangladesh like hundreds of other war babies, they would have been subject to the same indignation like the mixed-race Amerasians – fathered by the US servicemen in South Vietnam usually referred to as *bui doi,* meaning the *dust of life.* The Vietnamese society sees them as though they were living like dust – going wherever the wind was taking them, existing only from day to day.

It may be appropriate to remind us of what Jamil Majid, then third secretary at the Bangladesh High Commission in Ottawa, had thought about the future of the war babies in Bangladesh back in 1972. He feared that the war babies would be isolated in their country of birth where they would be denied even the very basic human rights. In fact, back then, Majid had nothing but praise for those who had initiated the Bangladesh Project, which he regarded as a "noble work" with a great deal of potential. Needless to mention, Majid's observation that "these children [the war babies] would have a difficult life" (the *Globe and Mail* September 12, 1972) in Bangladesh came true.

Our lack of knowledge of the war babies' whereabouts in Bangladesh, whether official or unofficial, only strengthens Majid's apprehension. Echoing the sentiment and official position of the government of Bangladesh, Majid predicted that the "unwanted" babies would have a much better family life in North America where the rights of the children and families are supported by child welfare and protection programs with certain unalienable rights, such as life, liberty, and pursuit of happiness.

Interesting to note, Majid's prophetic note or fear of the fate of the war babies back in 1972 was reinforced by concrete evidence of an invisible but distressing life of Beauty in Bangladesh that we have just alluded to. Continuing along the same vein, one might argue that those who have survived like Beauty are still around – homeless, destitute, and socially disadvantaged from the beginning of their lives. Like their birth mothers who had disappeared into the thin air, they too are not known to the people as to *who* they really *are.* The act of rejection of

MUSTAFA CHOWDHURY

them right at birth by the society as a whole must have wedged its way into the lowest level of poverty where no one really cared to accept them into their hearts: *Where do they stand in the social scheme of things?* One is likely to retort: obviously, the lowest rung on the social ladder had been reserved for them in their country of birth. In sociological sense, it usually means minority status, subordination, and powerlessness.

Based on common comments, one might also add, probably they grew up learning *how* to accept the disappointments in life, convincing them that such misfortunes were a part of their turbulent existence that had started with their birth in Bangladesh. The story of the dark shrapnel of war is forever embedded in the corners of the minds of those who were left behind in Bangladesh. They were deprived of adequate parental figures as models for their own development. Without homes of their own, they must have continued to live in danger of being cast adrift with a fear of a lack of an acceptable identity and social integration in Bangladesh.

Today a large bulk of the war babies in Bangladesh remains unaccounted for. Having known through smattering hearsay evidence, one may make a few more assumptions about those who had never found their way into adoptive homes. Unfortunately for us, there is no way of knowing anything about even the war babies who were fortunate enough to have been adopted or taken care of in Bangladesh. Whether we call them adoptive parents or guardians, they must have been dictated by the prevalent social values, as they chose not to share any such information with anyone. As a result, there is no statistics with respect to the war babies who might have been taken in by compassionate Bangladeshis to raise them.

If Beauty's life struggle is a reflection of the war babies who had remained and grown up in Bangladesh, it is truly a tragic ending of the drama that started with their birth in the war-ravaged Bangladesh. Nobody in Bangladesh will ever know the heartaches or even heartbreaks of the war babies who have long been denied the milk of human kindness.

On a positive note for the war babies who were left behind in Bangladesh, however, one may speculate along the line that some might have made a modest life for themselves with acceptable spouses and children who probably know absolutely nothing of the war babies' past.

In spite of all its pains, trials, and tribulations, one might argue that life is still worth living.

The war babies' secret and miserable life in Bangladesh brings us back to D'Costa's two observations that we have already alluded to: that "there is no way of knowing the fate of all war-babies," since we don't know *who* they are, and that "they have no intention of being found."

Let us now turn to the war babies who were a part of the same tragic birth but had the good fortune of being rescued through adoption in Canada by a group of ordinary Canadian parents. We may begin by saying that it is these parents who have changed the entire lives of the war babies by providing them a safe home and a proud identity in Canada. We do know not only their whereabouts but also the story of their lives through the years from their own narratives we have looked at in chapters 5, 6, and 7. Their lives are characterized by flexibility, sensitivity, and resourcefulness free from dogmatic or extraordinary ideological strains, a fact that transpired directly out of the narratives of the adopters and the adoptees.

Their adoption in Canada has not only legitimized them (by removing the inherent stigma) instantly as the children of the Canadian adoptive parents but also opened a wide window of opportunity. The removal of stigma attached to the war babies in the Bangladeshi society that continues to refer to them as the "illegitimate" children of 1971 is one of the greatest outcomes of their adoption in Canada. True, by the late 1960s, much unlike Bangladesh, the social stigma and the legal disadvantages of adopting an "illegitimate" child had already been removed in Canada.

Whether it is Josée, Onil, or Rija Ruphea, or anyone from the first bunch, all of them have a Canadian identity in their country of adoption where they are proudly living with human dignity. True, in the framework of search rhetoric, adoption is a "man-made" contract of kinship and not the one that begun by birth that evoke the transcendental laws of nature. Without entering into a debate about the right and wrong of interracial adoption, it may be safely observed that the war babies' adoption in Canada is a tangible example of a successful joint venture of the government of Bangladesh and the Families For Children (FFC).

The war babies, now in their forties, are Canadian citizens living a respectable life in Canada. What we can say for certain with regard to the present war babies is that, unlike those who were left behind, many of these adoptees have provided leadership in moving forward having emotionally and socially integrated their lives in multiracial and multicultural Canada. Today they not only are members of good standing but are also making substantial contribution in their country of adoption.

"I was humbled when I met one of the children [a war baby who came to Canada in July 1972] twenty years later and realized what a difference the intervention of these private Canadian citizens had made in his life," observed James Bartleman, then Canada's high commissioner to Bangladesh who assisted the Canadian team in bringing home the war babies to Canada (James Bartleman, *On Six Continents – A Life in Canada's Foreign Service, 1966–2002,* p. 64).

Little did Betty Graham, the Ontario director of child welfare who was opposed to adoption of the war babies, know that the overseas foreign-born children whom she believed were "diseased suffering from malnutrition and were louse ridden" would eventually grow up to be proud Canadians. Over time, they have successfully developed their own sense of values and negotiated their identities in multiracial Canada in a way that it became positive and enriching. Having no ambivalence about their identities in Canada where they came to live as infants, today they are not only proud of *who* they are but also proud of *their families* that gave them love and affection. They have acquired values that had helped them know the difference between "right" and "wrong."

They are leading a life that has been a beautiful gift of God, something that their parents have nourished and respected all through the years. The narratives of the Boonstras or the Goods, or others from the adoptive parents' bunch, reinforce their love and affection for their children, which demonstrably remain unconditional. Following a different path to parenthood, they have shown how to honor, admire, and celebrate the individual value of every child by embracing them as *theirs.* The Bangladesh Project may thus be seen as a promotion of racial understanding and harmony through the blending of the races in family makeup.

Seeing the actual life of the war babies in Canada, one might be inclined to say it is as though each child was exactly meant for each family that picked out the child with a miraculous hope for a new life, and that the Almighty God had a hand in bringing them together and driving them for integration in their respective families. In a way, this might also be a reinforcement of the myth of fate where the hapless war babies were seen not only as "chosen" but also as "fated" for the adoptive family of affectionate parents. It is an example of binding up the wounds of the hurting and the nurturing of the "unwelcome" children and of giving hope that had been a matter of joy and pride for both the adopters and the adoptees.

Having demonstrated their ability to grow and learn to become healthy, balanced, and productive persons, today the successful and integrated war babies brought to Canada in 1972 have countless opportunities beyond what Sr. Margaret Mary, then statutory guardian of the said infants, had ever imagined at the time of their placement in Canada. Though passed away, Sr. Margaret Mary was fortunate to see the positive outcome of their adoption. In chapter 3, we have seen the due diligence with which she had worked away to make the Bangladesh Project a success.

She was convinced that without "love" and "affection," a family of the same race may not necessarily ensure a perfect match or eventual attachment and bonding. For Sr. Margaret Mary, the war babies' adoption was not a matter of matching "like" parents with "like" children, since all prospective applicants for adoption that she had reviewed were couples of Caucasian backgrounds. Surely, her tireless efforts to find families for children's home and not children for families in screening and selecting adoptive parents for consideration of adoption as an unfaltering commitment did not go in vain. Since the parents had no emotional exploration of childlessness due to infertility, it was not an issue of exemplifying an extreme of the achieved parenthood by "rescuing" a war baby in dire need of a home. Nor did they selfishly take a child in order to create a family. Her belief that that "love" and "affection" of caring parents were more important than the parents' racial identity or nationality for placing a child turned out just the way she had expected and imagined in her mind.

The success of the present adoption initiative defies one of the moot points in the adoption discourse in North America – that, at best, the interracial adoption is a form of cultural genocide generally severing children permanently from their roots. We have seen how the "throwaway" babies, who were stashed aside fearing that they would face future rejection, having come to Canada, were able to change their entire life to a life of certainty. This is much unlike the native adoptees in Canada who are brought up with a consciousness of themselves as white. They have found themselves subject to the stereotyping and rejection experienced by the average. The war babies we have looked at did not claim to have experienced similar kinds of rejection or conflict. Nevertheless, with meager data, one cannot be absolutely conclusive about it. Additional research with a more representative sample of transracial adoptive families would be helpful in enhancing our understanding of the psychodynamics and outcome of the transracial adoption enterprise.

Though a very small sample, the outcome of the Bangladesh Project negates the commonly held view that the lack of physical similarity between parents and a racially different child further complicates a child's development. In fact, from the beginning, the news coverage and publicity of the arrival of the Bangladeshi war babies in the homes of Caucasian parents and the initiative of the FFC (described in chapter 3) had been very positive. It was not as though the war babies were yanked off from a foreign land to adopt them by parents of a different racial background. Instead, we have seen how the news media portrayed their arrival in Canada as a commendable initiative to rescue the hapless war babies. Perhaps because of sheer negligent number, interracial adoption compared to the state of biracial adoptions in the USA never became a serious issue in Canada even though by early 1970, there were a fair number of adoptions from Asian countries.

In a sense, the outcome of the Bangladesh Project also challenges the common thinking that being adopted can complicate the development of self-image and self-esteem especially when a child does not look like his or her parents. The outcome of the war babies' adoption that we have learned from their narratives seems to fall in perfect line with John Triseliotis' findings outlined in his often-quoted book titled *In Search of Origin*. The narratives of the adopters and the adoptees are consistent with Triseliotis' dismissal of the myth of the "blood-tie" having established the point that the people who matter to children are those who care for them, rather than those who give birth to them.

One might argue, the Cappuccinos' fight for adoption of *their* choice and the support by fellow Canadians demonstrate a quintessentially Canadian sentiment of love and compassion of the people of Canada, the majority of whom viewed the birth and abandonment of the war babies as tragic. Having gone to Bangladesh to rescue these babies, the Canadian team under Fred and Bonnie Cappuccino's stewardship is seen as avant-garde in creating a new phenomenon in the history of adoption, setting a new precedence that, to this day, remains unparalleled in Bangladesh's history. The support that the Cappuccinos had received at the time is incredible.

In that sense, it may not be an exaggeration to say that what began as a compassionate response to orphaned children in Vietnam became a social revolution with the arrival of the war babies from Bangladesh. Within a matter of thirty years, by 2000, intercountry (interracial) adoption became an accepted phenomenon in Canada just like the way it became an accepted global institution. Together, they illustrate one of the facts of the lives of the adopters and the adoptees: what makes a mother – the love and the care, which make a mother more than the child-bearing does.

At one level, the Canada-Bangladesh initiative may be seen as a way of expressing the commitment of the adoptive parents to solving some of the social problems of the war-ravaged Bangladesh, which its government could not resolve alone. At another level, as has been observed, the story of adoption of the racially different war babies also sets a living example that people can love each other and live together in harmony without any regard for racial differences.

We have seen through an examination of the archival records that, immediately following the departure of the team for Canada with the war babies, two key ministers of the Department of External Affairs and Manpower and Immigration were briefed by the Hong Kong–based Office of the High Commissioner for Canada, by the superintendent of Canadian Immigration in Hong Kong in the following manner: "Apparently the legalities of obtaining clearance for the orphans to leave the country were causing delays and it was only the personal intervention of the Prime Minister which enabled the party to leave on schedule. There is no question that the publicity given to the work of the Families For Children organization has raised Canada in the esteem of a large and important section of the Bangladesh population" (Library and Archives Canada. RG 76, Vol. 1237, File 5850-2-710).

The point may seem rhetorical, but it signaled a strong message of love and care on the part of the people of Canada and, more particularly, adoptive parents who left no stone unturned to bring some of these babies to their homes. The result of the enterprise, an inspirational true story of adoption and its outcome, gives grounds for optimism and offers no discouragement to those who are contemplating interracial adoption. And yet interracial adoptions have not received adequate research attention in Canada as they have in the United States.

The positive outcome of the Bangladesh Project proves another important point: that time is now ripe for a wider recognition by society, especially in Canada and Bangladesh, of the "human potential" of the adopted children and adoptive parents even though each might be racially different from the other. It is in that when one considers the fact that there was no "disrupted" adoption – a polite euphemism for failure. This is a great success. No one has/had any instances of onset of character disorder with the exception of three: Martin suffered from learning disability; Rajib from schizophrenia; and Rani, having developed bipolar disorder, had found peace in death. We have seen the details in their individual bios.

Despite the obvious success, one cannot be certain about the future of adoption in Bangladesh where it is still a hot-button issue/topic because it leads to numerous social conundrums. No matter what dramatic effect the Bangladesh Project might have had in Canada, it is only a small part of the ongoing intercountry/interracial movement and placement of orphans in Bangladesh. Many in Bangladesh seem almost obsessed and quick to make a distinction between parent by birth and parenthood delegated by law through adoption. As observed, the symbolism of blood continues to dominate the interpretation of kinship in both Islam and Bangladeshi culture and tradition subsuming references to sexual reproduction and biological ancestry that represents the unconditional love and enduring solidarity of a parent-child relationship.

Given the fact that in Bangladesh, the desirability of fostering a sense of ethnic identity and cultural heritage is axiomatic, one might ask whether interracial adoption be encouraged? Perhaps the question becomes more forceful especially when asked, *Should parental suitability based on their race be out of the question?* In other words, *Will the Bangladeshis, who inevitably equate motherhood primarily with biology and not nurturance, learn to appreciate an enlarged and altered understanding of motherhood and parenthood?* One might also ask, *Is it time to promote opportunities for the creation of rewarding personal relationship between adoptive parents and adopted children of racially different backgrounds?*

True, the data sample is much too meager to generalize an acceptable statement. Nevertheless, though inadequate, the weight of evidence should prompt serious dialogue among stakeholders and government representatives on the issue of interracial adoption. One might wonder whether such positive outcome could be linked to the broad policy question of whether Canada and Bangladesh should be involved in intercountry adoption, and if so, to what extent? The twists and turns of this argument will continue. At the end, one might ask, *How can adoption be internationalized in Bangladesh?*

In assessing the final outcome of the Bangladesh Project, let us refresh our memories by revisiting how a confident Amina sees her journey from the war-torn Bangladesh to Canada where she was destined to be raised in a milieu that was envisioned by Pierre Elliott Trudeau, then prime minister of Canada. "Trudeau had a vision and I was a part of that vision" (Amina Wolsey's e-mail to the author, October 2, 2009), said a proud Amina alluding to Trudeau's grand vision of Canada with its people of diverse race and culture.

Although Amina spoke about her own life and the life of her siblings of varied backgrounds who were raised, loved, and cared for by their parents, she might as well be seen to be speaking on behalf of all other war babies from the same bunch. Thus, in a sense, when Amina says "as we all continue our journey with the foundations our parents have given us, each one of us is closer to finding our true self, 'our liberation'" (Amina Wolsey's research paper, p. 68), she is speaking about the rest of the war babies who came to Canada in 1972.

In summary, this joint venture or the Bangladesh Project will go down in the annals of history as one of the most humanitarian efforts of our lifetime through the initiatives of a group ordinary but determined Canadian couples achieving extraordinary result by bringing home and raising a handful of war babies of *their* choice. Picking up a few of the war babies of Bangladesh from the brink of misery and a lifetime of homeless despair to the loving arms of Canadian families is, no doubt, an illustration of human values that can extend from families to nations, augmenting human hopes of living in a world that knows and practices love and understanding of the humankind.

MUSTAFA CHOWDHURY

The fact that they have been celebrating the differences among family members from the beginning of their family lives, the children grew up learning how they all are an inherent part of being human. The story remains an example of the greatness of the human spirit, which had allowed a group of couples' minds and hearts to embrace and love a child that was not wanted in the country in which the child was born. The heroic efforts of the FFC volunteers gave the phenomenon of adoption of racially different children a new dimension in the history of international and interracial adoption in Canada by becoming a permanent part of the Canadian adoption scene.

In Shakespearean term, "All's Well That Ends Well."

CHRONOLOGY OF EVENTS

March 25, 1971

Sudden surreptitious military attack on East Pakistan, then part of Pakistan; declaration of independence by Bengali rebels.

April 5, 1972

Rev. Fred and Bonnie Cappuccino met Prof. Muazzam Hussain of Universitté de Sherbrooke, Sherbrooke, Quebec, to discuss their proposed plan, which later came to be called the *Bangladesh Project* to bring in a number of war babies to Canada.

April 30, 1972

Board of directors of the Lakeshore Unitarian Church, Pointe Claire, Québec, unanimously approved the *Bangladesh Project* and granted leave of absence for Fred and Bonnie Cappuccino for an exploratory visit to Bangladesh.

May 12, 1972

Rev. Fred and Bonnie Cappuccino, accompanied by Prof. Muazzam Hussain, met Abdul Momin, high commissioner of Bangladesh in Ottawa, Ontario.

May 25, 1972

Rev. Fred and Bonnie Cappuccino met Fr. Benjamin Labbé, then executive director of the Dhaka-based Christian Organization for Relief and Rehabilitation (CORR), to discuss their plan with respect to the *Bangladesh Project* and seek his advice. Father Labbé was in Montreal, Québec, on a business trip.

June 3, 1972

Spearheaded by Sandra Simpson, herself an applicant for a war baby from Bangladesh through the *Bangladesh Project,* arranged for Ontario applicants (prospective adoptive parents) to jam the telephone line of the minister of Community and Social Services, government of Ontario. Various news reporters participated in the scheme and harassed ministry officials by asking pointed questions regarding the delay the government was making in conducting "home study" for the applicants.

June 19, 1972

Helke Ferrie, chairperson, Asian Adoptions, Ontario Branch, Families For Children (FFC), went on a hunger strike that lasted for three and a half days. The hunger strike was in protest of what Helke Ferrie claimed to be a deliberate delay by Betty Graham, director of Child Welfare Branch, Ministry of Community and Social Services, government of Ontario, in conducting them mandatory home study for the prospective applicants.

June 21, 1972

Helke Ferrie broke her fast after being publicly assured by René Brunelle, minister of Community and Social Services of his department's full cooperation in conducting the mandatory "home study" for the purpose of adoption.

June 25, 1972

Dr. Robert Ferrie and Helke Ferrie left Canada for Bangladesh en route to India.

June 28, 1972

Rev. Fred and Bonnie Cappuccino and Elisabeth Mowling left Canada for Bangladesh. They arrived in Dhaka, Bangladesh, the next day.

June 30, 1972

Rev. Fred and Bonnie Cappuccino and Elisabeth Mowling met Fr. Benjamin Labbé, then regional director of CORR (Christian Organization for Relief and Rehabilitation). He had spent many years working in Bangladesh, including the nine long months during the war of liberation. Father Labbé had a good relationship with the country's top officials.

July 1, 1972

Fred and Bonnie Cappuccino and Elisabeth Mowling met Zerina Rashid, a social worker, to discuss their plan in Dhaka and seek her assistance. They also met Zerina Rashid's husband, Abdur Rashid, then retired secretary, Department of Communication, government of Pakistan.

The same day the team also met Emile Baron of the Canadian International Development Agency who was stationed at the office of the Canadian High Commission in Dhaka. Baron gave the team a quick briefing on the state of affairs and offered every help they could provide.

July 3, 1972

Fred and Bonnie Cappuccino and Elisabeth Mowling met Kamal Hossain, then minister of Law and Parliamentary Affairs, to discuss the *Bangladesh Project* and seek the minister's personal intervention in expediting the matter.

The same day, they also met Abdur Rab Chaudhury, then coordinator of Relief and Rehabilitation, Prime Minister's Secretariat, government of the People's Republic of Bangladesh, and discussed the project proposal for international adoption.

July 4, 1972

Rev. Fred and Bonnie Cappuccino and Elisabeth Mowling met Abdul Awal, executive secretary of the National Board of Bangladesh Women's Rehabilitation Program, to discuss the *Bangladesh Project* with a view to expediting the process for section of the war babies who were being born and abandoned in large numbers.

July 15, 1972

Dr. Robert Ferrie conducted medical examination of the war babies and found fifteen war babies eligible to travel.

July 17, 1972

Government of Bangladesh issued travel permit/visa to the Canadian team to return to Canada with fifteen war babies for the purpose of adoption in Canadian homes.

July 19, 1972

Canadian team left Bangladesh with fifteen war babies via New Delhi and New York for Canada.

July 20, 1972

Canadian team returns home (Toronto and Montreal) with fifteen war babies of Bangladesh. The babies were handed over to the respective adoptive parents by the team leaders amid joy and delight.

October 25, 1972

Promulgation of the *Bangladesh Abandoned Children (Special Provisions) Order 1972* in the *Bangladesh Gazette Extraordinary,* Wednesday, October 25, 1972. It was, however, repealed through a proclamation of March 24, 1982.

February 5, 1989

Twenty-seven Bangladeshi adoptees (orphans), including five war babies, accompanied by some of their parents, visited Bangladesh for a week. It was coordinated by the Families For Children and Canadopt. They attended the opening of the Sreepur-based Children's Village. Under the stewardship of Donna Wolsey, the war babies, then sixteen, went to visit Mother Teresa's *Shishu Bhavan* where some of them were born and some were brought in and were taken care of until they were sent off to Canada for adoption. For the first time in their life, they had an opportunity to look up their name in the historic *Register Book*. Hussain Muhammad Ershad, then president of Bangladesh, took personal interest in proudly showcasing the war babies' adoption in Canada as a "success story" to the people of Bangladesh.

November 10, 1999

Ferdousi Priyobhashini came out in public to share her story of sexual violence in the hands of the Pakistani military personnel. Priyobhashini is considered the first rape victim to self-identify in public defying all the social stigmas attached to such occurrences.

ABBREVIATIONS

ACS (Adopted Child Syndrome)
BQS (Bangladesh Quaker Services)
CAS (Children's Aid Society)
COAC (Council on Adoptable Children)
FTC (Families For Children)
IPPF (International Planned Parenthood Federation)
ISS (International Social Service)
ODS (Open Door Society)
POW (Prisoner of War)
QPS (Quaker Peace Service)
TDS (Terre des Hommes)

GLOSSARY OF ACRONYMS AND NON-ENGLISH TERMS

Abandoned babies/children - in the context of the War of Liberation of Bangladesh, abandoned babies/children are those who were orphaned during the Bengalis' struggle for independence due to the death or disappearance of their parents. They are called abandoned because their parents are either dead; or, in some cases, they were left behind (orphaned) by their parents who were unable to take care of them due to physical injury, impoverishment, mental illness, or their inability to adequately to care for babies/children with disabilities, The term "abandoned babies/children" is often used interchangeably for "war babies" and/or "war orphans." Strictly speaking, "war babies" are quite different by definition. See below under "war babies."

Adoption - the process through which an infant or child is placed in a home with people other than the birth parents. These people are given parental rights over the child. They are responsible for his or her welfare.

Adoption agency - an organization that matches birth mothers or children available for adoption with adoptive families.

Adoption triad - a birth mother, adoptive parents, and an adoptee.

Adoptee - a person who is adopted.

Adoptism - a belief that forming a family by birth is superior to forming a family by adoption. In other words, a belief that keeping a child with his or her biological parents is inherently better than placing child for adoption.

Adoptive family - all the members of a family that was brought together by adoption.

Adoptive parents - people who adopt a child.

Al-Badr – a paramilitary wing of the West Pakistani army, which operated in East Pakistan against the Bengali nationalists during the Bangladesh Liberation War.

Al-Shams – a paramilitary wing of several Islamist parties in East Pakistan that, along with the Pakistani army, *Razakars* and the *Al-Badrs,* is held responsible for conducting a mass killing campaign against Bengali nationalists, civilians, and ethnic minorities during Bangladesh Liberation War.

Amerasian - a person whose parents are nationals of both America and one of the Asian/Pacific Island countries.

Aya - caregiver/caretaker.

Bangabondhu - refers to Sheikh Mujibur Rabman, who was given this title, in Bengali, meaning "friend of Bengal." A popular title now used to address him on formal occasions or even in private conversations, like Bung Karno for the late president Sukarno of Indonesia.

Biological siblings - sisters and brothers who have the same birth mother or father; they may be raised in different families.

Birangana - rape survivors of 1971, a title given by the Mujib administration in order to honor them as the nation's heroines by recognizing their sacrifice in the war of independence.

Birth mother - a woman who gives birth to a baby and places for adoption.

Birth parent - the noun "birth parent" was coined to refer to a parent who relinquishes a child for adoption. It is important to clarify that an individual becomes a birth parent at the time of relinquishment and is considered a parent until that moment.

Boydhobhumi - places of execution and slaughter in Occupied Bangladesh (March 1971–December 1971). Every now and then such slaughterhouses and premises are discovered in present-day Bangladesh with bones of people murdered by the Pakistani military personnel when found.

Closed records - birth records that are forbidden by law for adoptees to see.

Culture - describes what people develop to enable them to adapt to their world, such as language, gestures, tools to enable them to survive and prosper; customs and traditions that define values and organize social interactions, religious beliefs, and rituals; and dress, art, and music to make symbolic and aesthetic expressions.

Culture determines the practices and beliefs that become associated with an ethnic group and provides its distinctive identity.

Dai - Caregiver/caretaker; midwives who take care.

Eid-ul-Fitr - marks the end of the month of Holy Ramadan; festival of breaking the monthlong fast by Muslims. This day in Muslim world brings rejoicing and happiness.

Ethnicity - belonging to a group that shares the same characteristics, such as country of origin, language, religion, ancestry, and culture. Ethnicity is a matter of biological and historical fact and is not changed by the culture in which a person grows up.

Gono Unnayan Prochesta - a joint effort with Quaker Peace Service (QPS), an arm of the international Quaker movement, Quaker Services of Bangladesh.

Heritage - the traditions and customs of a person's original culture.

Hereditary disease - a disease passed from a parent to his or her child.

Identity - the qualities or traits that make up a person's personality; also classified as an individual's ethnic identity, personal identity, and social identity.

Ethnic identity refers to a person's sense of belonging to an ethnic group. Ethnic identity is drawn from the realization that a person's thoughts, perceptions, feelings, and behaviors are consistent with those of other members of the ethnic group. Ethnic identity recognizes that a person belongs to a particular group that shares not only ethnicity but also common cultural practices.

Personal identity is the way in which a person defines oneself in terms of one's individuality and difference to others. This might include factors such as age, gender, nationality, culture, religious affiliation, disability, sexuality, interests, talents, personality traits, and family and friendship networks. The way in which a person sees himself in relation to those around them and what makes them unique are all aspects of personal identity.

Part of our personal identity is given to us at birth, such as gender, nationality, and genetic history. Other aspects of our personal identity are formed during our early years of development and continue to develop during our life as we grow, mature, make choices, forge relationships, and build an evolving identity for ourselves.

Social identity is how we function within many different social situations and relate to a range of other people. Social groups may involve family, ethnic communities, cultural connections, nationality, friends, and work. They are an important and valued part of our daily life. How we see ourselves in relation to our social groupings defines our social identity.

In-racial adoption - refers to situation in which the adoptees and the adopting family are of the same race.

Jawan - foot soldiers

Joy Bangla – Victory to Bengal

Mukti Bahini - Liberation Army that fought for the independence of Bangladesh in 1971.

Muktijodhya – Freedom fighters who fought for the independence of Bangladesh in 1971.

Occupation Army Forces - refers to Pakistani Armed Forces in East Pakistan from March 1971 to December 1971 following the declaration of the independence of Bangladesh.

Occupied Bangladesh - refers to former East Pakistan when it was under the control of the Pakistani Armed Forces following the declaration of independence (March 1971–December 1971).

Open adoption - adoption agreement between adoptive parents and the birth parents that allows contact when adopted person grows up.

Open records - birth records that are available by law for adoptees to see.

Prejudice - An adverse judgment or opinion formed beforehand or without knowledge of the fact.

Razakar - Originating from Persian, literally means "volunteer." Within the context of the Bangladesh-Pakistan War, a *Razakar* is a loyalist who was in favor of one Pakistan. More specifically, *Razakars* were a special force created by the Pakistani army consisting of members of the Bengali, Bihari, and other communities loyal to Pakistan.

Saree/Sari – attire worn by Bengali women.

Seva Sadan - clinics and delivery centers that were set up by the Mujib administration to assist the 1971 rape victims as part of its rehabilitation program for women.

Shari'a - Islamic law derived from the Quran and Hadith.

Shishu Bhavan - established by Mother Teresa in December 1971, located at 23 Islampur Road, Dhaka, Bangladesh. It is a 350-year-old former Portuguese monastery, which was run by the nuns of the Missionaries of Charity. In 1972, the newly established *Shishu Bhavan* was used as a shelter for pregnant rape victims where many of them came in secret to give birth and leave the newborns behind for adoption.

Shonar Bangla - Golden Bengal

Terre des Hommes - a Geneva-based adoption agency devoted to the well-being of children around the world.

Thana - area of local police station authority.

Transracial adoption - adoption across nations and races.

Visible minority - the Canadian *Employment Equity Act* defines visible minorities as persons other than aboriginal people who are non-Caucasian in race or nonwhite in color. The visible minority population consists mainly of the following groups: Chinese, South Asians, black, Arab, West Asians, Filipino, South Asians, Latin American, Japanese, and Korean.

War babies - in the context of the War of Liberation of Bangladesh, the war babies are those babies conceived by Bengali women who were victims of rape committed by the Pakistani military personnel in Occupied Bangladesh (March 1971–December 1971). War babies may also be regarded as "war orphans" only in the sense that they were abandoned by their birth mothers upon birth at a time when their alleged or putative fathers (Pakistani military personnel) were not known. Nevertheless, all war orphans are not necessarily war babies. Only those who were conceived as a result of rape by the Pakistani military personnel in Occupied Bangladesh are known as "war babies."

War orphans - refer to Bangladeshi children orphaned during the Bengalis' struggle for independence due to the death or disappearance of their parents. They are called orphans because the war cost them their parents. In some cases, they were left behind (orphaned) by their parents who were unable to take care of them due to physical injury, impoverishment, mental illness, or inability to adequately to care for children with disabilities. They are also referred to as "abandoned children." War orphans are, therefore, not war babies, as they were not conceived in rape by the Pakistani military personnel.

SELECT BIBLIOGRAPHY

Primary sources

Archives of Ontario. Toronto.

Series: RG 29 -59, ACC 15296/2 TR 78-075, Box 6, File: *Bangladesh Infants* 1972–73.

Bangladesh. *The Bangladesh Abandoned Children (Special Provisions,) Order, 1972* (P.O. No. 124 of 1972), published in the *Bangladesh Gazette Extraordinary, 25 October, 1972.*

Canada. Department of External Affairs. Classified Information.

Series: 20 – F – Pak – 1-4.

Series: 38 – Il – II Bangla 001786.

Canadian Council on Social Development, *Press Release,* May 25, 1972.

Government of Ontario. Ministry of Community and Social Services, *Statement of Brunelle, Minister of Community & Social Services, Respecting Adoption of Foreign Children by Ontario Citizens, June 19, 1972.*

High Commission of the People's Republic of Bangladesh, Ottawa, Ontario, Canada, File No., EC/2/72 a.

International Social Service (American Branch), *Consultants' Reports, 1972,* Reference # 1115/Bangladesh asg.

–––. *Memorandum on Observations and Suggestions for Implementing Inter-Country Adoption* from Wells C. Klein, General Director, International Social Service, American Branch to M. Hassan-uz-Zarnan, Secretary of Labour and Social Welfare, Government of the People's Republic of Bangladesh, May 9, 1972.

–––. *Memorandum on Inter-country Adoption: A Solution for Some Children.* Prepared by Wells C. Klein, General Director, International Social Service, American Branch, March 27, 1 972.

–––. *Inter-Country Adoption in Bangladesh under the heading: Importance of Publicity and Public Information.* Prepared by Wells C. Klein,

General Director, International Social Service, American Branch, March 27, 1972.

Library and Archives Canada.

Manuscript Group (MG)

28 1 270, Vol. 18, *File:* CAPR.

O8 Vol. 297, Q 4-16575.

Record Group (RG)

26: Series 08, Vol. 275, *File* 2125, 1972.

RG 76 Vol. 1040, Box 141, *File:* 5020-1-606; *File:* 5020-1-710, pt. 1.

Missionaries of Charity, *Register Book, 1972,* Dhaka, Bangladesh.

———. Superior Sister Margaret Mary's Correspondences (from 1972 to 2000) with adoptive parents in Canada; also with Mustafa Chowdhury (author) while she was both in Dhaka, Bangladesh, and Kolkata, West Bengal, India.

Secondary sources

Books

Altstein, Howard, and Rita J. Simon, eds. *Inter Country Adoption: A Multicultural Perspective.* New York, Praeger, 1991.

Bean, Philip, ed. *Adoption: Essays in Social Policy, Law, and Sociology.* London, Tavistock Publications, London, 1984.

Chitnis, K. N. *Research Methodology in History.* New Delhi, Atlantic Publishers & Distributors, 1990.

D'Costa, Bina. *Nationbuilding, Gender and War Crimes in South Asia.* New York, Routledge Contemporary South Asia Series, 2011.

Elton, O. R. *The Practice of History.* London, Fontana Press, 1990.

Erickson, Erick. *Childhood and Society,* New York: W. W. Norton, 1963.

———. *Identity: Youth and Crisis.* London, Faber and Faber, 1968.

Joyce, Ladner. *Mixed Families.* New York, Anchor Press, 1977.

Kirk, H. D. *Shared fate: A theory and method of adoptive relationships.* Port Angeles: Ben-Simons Publications, 1984.

Kornitzer, Margaret. *Child Adoption in a Modern World.* London, Putnam, 1952.

March, Karen. *The Stranger Who Bore Me: Adoptee-Birth Mother Relationships.* Toronto, University of Toronto Press, 1995.

Sachdev, Paul, ed. *Adoption: Current Issues and Trends.* Toronto, Butterworth, 1984.

Saikia, Yasmin. *Women, War, and the Making of Bangladesh: Remembering 1971.* Durham, Duke University Press Books, 2011.

Triseliotis, J. *In Search of Origins: The Experiences of Adopted People.* London. Routledge, 1973.

Westhues, Anne, and Joyce Cohen. *Inter-country Adoption in Canada, Final Report.* Ottawa, Human Resources Development Canada, 1994.

Wishard Laurie arid Wishard William. *Adoption: The Grafted Tree.* San Francisco, Cragmont Publications, 1979.

Magazines, periodical articles, and reports

Bartholet, B. "International Adoption: Current Status and Future Prospects." *Future of Children,* 1993, vol. 30: 89–103.

Beck, D. J. "Evaluating an Individual's Capacity for Parenthood." *A Study of Adoption Practice by Michael Shapiro,* Child Welfare League of America, Inc., vol. 2: 72–77.

Bourgeis, Paulette. "Homes for Children of Despair." *Reader's Digest* (July 1, 1980): 52.

Brookfield, Tara. "Maverick Mothers and Mercy Flights: Canada's Controversial Introduction to International Adoption." *Journal of the Canadian Historical Association,* vol. 19, no. 1 (2008): 307–330.

Davis, Geoffrey. "The Changing Face of Genocide – Bangladesh." *Proceedings of the Medical Association for Prevention of War,* vol. 2, part 7 (June 1973).

Families For Children. "Bangladesh Babies," chapter 32, part E. *Bangladesh Project.* Maxville, Ontario, Families For Children: 254–284.

–––. *Newsletter* (1972–1973).

Haider, S. Jahangeer. "Women's Rehabilitation towards Emancipation: Practice, Prospects and Problems for Family Planning." *Proceedings of the Seminar on Family Planning,* November 21–25, 1972, Dhaka, Bangladesh: 535.

Homemakers, November 1975.

Kuan-Yin Foundation. *Bangladesh Project,* 1972 and 1973.

Madison, Bernice Q. and Michael Shapiro. "Black Adoption – Issues and Policies: Review of Literature." *Social Service Review,* XLVII, no. 4 (1973).

Mookheijee, Nayanika. "Muktir Gaan (songs of freedom), the Raped Woman and the Migrant Identities of the Bangladesh War." *Gender, conflict and migration. Women and migration in Asia,* 3, (2006), Sage, New Delhi.

–––. "Remembering to Forget: Public Secrecy and Memory of Sexual Violence in Bangladesh." *Journal of the Royal Anthropological Institute,* vol. 12, 2, (2006).

Simon, R. J., and H. Alstein. "The Case for Trans-racial Adoption." *Children and Youth Services Review,* vol. 18, (1996): 5–22.

Newspapers

Bangladesh Observer, July 20, 1972.

Burlington Gazette, vol. 7, no. 36, July 27, 1972.

Burlington Journal, July–December 1972.

Brampton Guardian, August 19, 1976.

Canadian – the Weekend Magazine, February 24, 1979.

Community – the Mississauga News, August 11, 1976.

Expositor (Brantford, Ontario), June 20, 1972; February 27, 1989.

Focus (Goderich, Ontario), May 30, 1989.

Gazette, July 21, 1972; October 13, 1972.

Globe and Mail, June 20, 1972; July 21, 1972; September 12, 1972; June 24, 1975.

International Herald Tribune, October 2, 1973.

le journal de Montreal, vol. IX, no. 38, 22 juillet, 1972.

Kitchener-Waterloo Record, July 21, 1972.

London Free Press, July 23, 1973; January 28, 1989.

Meadowvale World, vol. 11, no. 8, May 1984.

Mennonite Reporter, April 14, 1975.

Montreal Star, July 21, 1972; October 12, 1972; November 28, 1972.

Ottawa Citizen, July 21, 1972; March 26, 1990.

Ottawa Journal, July 21, 1972; December 12, 1979.

La Presse, 21 juillet, 1972.

Sarnia Observer, September 5, 1972.

Spectator (Hamilton, Ontario), June 19, 1972

Star-Phoenix, July 21, 1972; October 14, 1972.
Toronto Star, October 29, 1968; July 21, 1972; November 4, 1972; February 1, 1973.
Weekend Magazine, November 20, 1971.
Wentworth Marketplace, September 6, 1972.

APPENDIX

A. Documentary Evidence/479
B. Photo Gallery/509

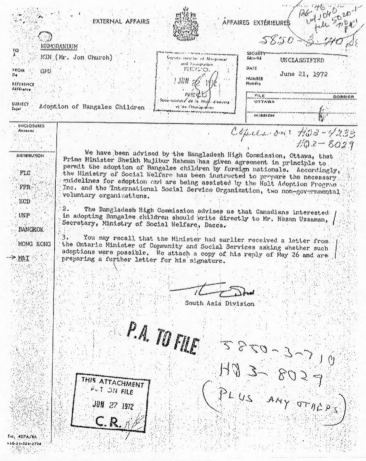

0218797   05267430   0622602   copper to 952 Rec

NNNNEEADGOTTO27
/20   LDNO48
TIM RR HOK
NDI

95059
5020- 1]

MANPOWER & IMMIGRATION
OTTAWA

JUL 70   8 42 AM '72   01731

UNCLASSIFIED
FM IMMIGDELHI 1874 JUL20/72
TO IMMIGOTT/CHIEF ADMISSIONS PRIORITY
INFO IMMIGHKONG TT IMFOR(BARR)CIC HAMILTON CIC MTL INNATL AIRPORT
CIC TOR INNATL AIRPORT DE IMMIGOTT
---BANGLADESH ADOPTIONS
15 INFANTS DEPARTED DELHI AS SCHEDULED 2115 JUL19 ACCOMPANIED
BY DR AND MRS FERRIE,MR AND MRS CAPPUCCINO AND MRS MOWLING.GROUP
WILL SPLIT UP IN NY WITH FERRIES TAKING 8 INFANTS DESTINED ONT
AND WEST TO TOR PER OURTEL JUL19 AND CAPPUCCINOS/MOWLING TAKING
7 INFANTS DESTINED QUE AND EAST TO MTL PER OURTEL JUL14.
2.INFANTS TRAVELLING ON UNNUMBERED JOINT TRAVEL DOCU IN LET FORM
RECOGNIZED AND STAMPED BY PASSPORT CENTRAL,DACCA AIRPORT,BANGLADESH.
THERE ARE PHOTOCOPIES OF TRAVEL DOCU LET FOR EACH CHILD WITH
PARTICULARS AND PHOTOGRAPH ATTACHED.THESE HAVE BEEN ENCLOSED
WITH FORMS 1000.THE PHOTOCOPIES DO NOT/NOT BEAR THE PASSPORT
CENTRAL VENDORSEMENT WHICH WAS STAMPED ON ORIGINAL JOINT DOCU
HELD BY CAPPUCCINOS.TDS OF CHILDREN ARRIVING TOR WITH FERRIES
WILL THEREFORE NOT/NOT SHOW ENDORSEMENT BY BANGLADESH PASSPORT
AUTHORITIES.FACSIMILE OF JOINT TD BEING AIRMAILED TODAY FOR
YOUR INFO.
3.72C VISAS ISSUED TO FERRIE CHILDREN ORUN AND SAVITRA DESTINED
BURLINGTON,ONT WERE STAMPED ON REVERSE OF THEIR PHOTOCOPY TD
WITH IMM595S ATTACHED.
              ...2

Source
RG 76
Vol.1040
file 5020-1 pt

PAGE TWO 1874 UNCLAS
4.DOCUMENTATION COMPLETED AND ASSISTANCE PROVIDED AT AIRPORT
PER OUR PREVIOUS TELS.GROUP PERSONALLY MET BY HIGHCOM AND MRS
JAMES GEORGE.
200540Z 280

2243 006

Ottawa,
K1A 0A2,
September 1, 1972.

Dear Mr. and Mrs. Cappuccino
and Mrs. Mowling:

   I was very pleased to receive your
August 27 letter with the report of your trip
to Bangladesh – a heart-warming odyssey indeed!
The success of your efforts to bring the babies
to Canadian families has brought much happiness
which we can all share in a measure.

   Your kind comments on the work of
Canadian officials are most gratifying. I will
certainly let Mr. Mackasey know how much his
personal interest was appreciated.

   May I take this opportunity to wish you
continued success with Families for Children and
may God Bless.

                              Sincerely,

                                    Original signé by.
                                    Original signé as
                                    P.E. TRUDEAU

                                    SEP - 7 1972

Mr. and Mrs. Fred Cappuccino
  and Mrs. Elizabeth Mowling,
   10 Bowling Green,
    Pointe Claire 720, Quebec.

     c.c: Minister of Manpower and Immigration,
           Att'n: Mr. Peter Connolly,
                   Executive Assistant *
PF/mh
           *For information.

Minister
Manpower
and Immigration

Ministre
Main-d'œuvre
et Immigration

Ottawa, Ontario
August 25, 1972

Mr. & Mrs. Fred Capucino
10 Bowling Green
Pointe Claire 720, Quebec

Dear Mr. & Mrs. Capucino:

Thank you very much for your thoughtfulness and that of the other families who have adopted the children recently arrived from Bangladesh, in sending me the beautiful arrangement of flowers.

I hope you will extend my gratitude for this gesture to the members of the other families as well. Thank you once again.

Yours sincerely,

Bryce Mackasey.

305 Rideau Street
Ottawa K1A 0J9

305, rue Rideau
Ottawa K1A 0J9

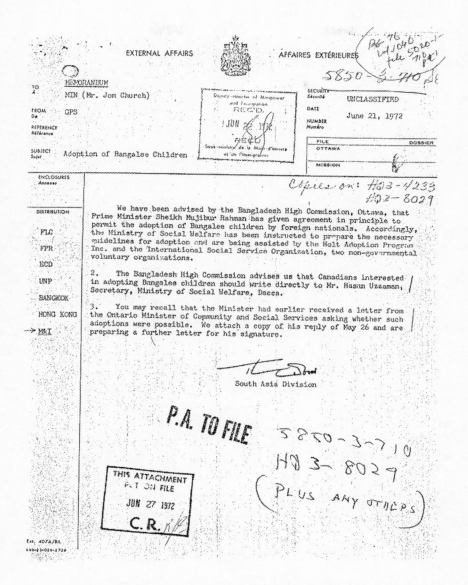

EXTERNAL AFFAIRS   AFFAIRES EXTÉRIEURES

5850-3-710

MEMORANDUM

TO À	MIN (Mr. Jon Church)
FROM De	GPS
REFERENCE Référence	
SUBJECT Sujet	Adoption of Bangalee Children

*Deputy minister of Manpower
and Immigration
REC'D.
1 JUN 26 1972
REC'D
Sous-ministre de la Main-d'œuvre
et de l'immigration*

SECURITY Sécurité	UNCLASSIFIED
DATE	June 21, 1972
NUMBER Numéro	

FILE OTTAWA	DOSSIER
MISSION	

ENCLOSURES
Annexes

DISTRIBUTION

FLC

FPR

ECD

UNP

BANGKOK

HONG KONG

→ M&I

Copies on: HQ3-4233
HQ2-8029

    We have been advised by the Bangladesh High Commission, Ottawa, that Prime Minister Sheikh Mujibur Rahman has given agreement in principle to permit the adoption of Bangalee children by foreign nationals. Accordingly, the Ministry of Social Welfare has been instructed to prepare the necessary guidelines for adoption and are being assisted by the Holt Adoption Program Inc. and the International Social Service Organization, two non-governmental voluntary organizations.

2.   The Bangladesh High Commission advises us that Canadians interested in adopting Bangalee children should write directly to Mr. Hasan Uzzaman, Secretary, Ministry of Social Welfare, Dacca.

3.   You may recall that the Minister had earlier received a letter from the Ontario Minister of Community and Social Services asking whether such adoptions were possible. We attach a copy of his reply of May 26 and are preparing a further letter for his signature.

South Asia Division

P.A. TO FILE   *5850-3-710*

HQ3-8029

(PLUS ANY OTHERS)

THIS ATTACHMENT
PUT ON FILE
JUN 27 1972
C.R.

Internal Memorandum from Head, South Asia Division, Department of External Affairs, to the Minister of External Affairs on the Adoption of Bangalee Children, June 21, 1972.

Source: Library and Archives Canada. RG 76 Vol. 1040, File:5020-1-710, pt. 1.

Box 69
Copetown, Ontario
June 6, 1972

To Honorable Pierre Trudeau,
Prime Minister of Canada,
Parliament Buildings,
Ottawa, Ontario

Dear Prime Minister Trudeau,

Dale and I are interested in adopting
a child from Bangladesh. We have been
working closely with Families for Children,
the Montreal Branch and the Ontario Branch.
We have had a homestudy completed by
a private social worker, Mrs Christine
Johnston and are waiting for this to be
approved by Miss Betty Graham, Head
of Child Welfare, Ontario. Enclosed you
will find a copy of the letter we have
just received from her.

We understand that Bangladesh has
released children to Canada for adoption.
If so, would you kindly advise us
and Miss Graham of this fact immediately.

Two couples from Families for Children
are leaving for Bangladesh on June 17, 1972
for the purpose of bringing back children

have been released for adoption. It is essential that we have provincial approval by then. The Federal Immigration authorities have assured Families for Children that they will do everything in their power to speed up entries into Canada for these children.

We ask that you give this your most urgent consideration and reply by return mail. Time is limited. It is essential that we work quickly for the welfare of these children.

Thank you for your time and co-operation.

Sincerely,
Dale and Doreen Good.

C-300

Letter from Dale and Doreen Good of Copetown, Ontario, to Prime Minister Pierre Elliott Trudeau, dated, June 6, 1972, urging him to intervene to expedite the process for adoption from Bangladesh.

Source: Library and Archives Canada. RG 76 Vol. 1040, File:5020-1-710, pt. 1.

No.   তারিখ ... The 17th July, 1972.

From : Mr. M. Sharafatullah,
   Deputy Secretary,
   Ministry of Labour & Social Welfare,
   Govt. of the People's Republic of Bangladesh,
   Bangladesh Secretariat, Dacca.

To : Mother Theresa,
   26, Islampur Road,
   Dacca, Bangladesh.

Dear Madam,

   Government have been pleased to allow Mr. & Mrs. Fred
Cappuccino, Mrs. Elizabeth Mowling and Dr. R.K. Ferrie to take
the 15 (fifteen) Babies (Particulars of whom are enclosed)
from your 'Home' to Canada for adoption under Canadian Law with
full rights of the Canadian citizenship in due course and with
no liability in regard to the children in future to the Government
of the People's Republic of Bangladesh.

   The above cases are expected to be duly covered by the
law that is proposed to be promulgated by the Government of the
People's Republic of Bangladesh very soon on Inter-Country adption.

   This has the concurrence of the Ministry of Law and
Parliamentry Affairs.

              Yours sincerely,

              Sd/-
            (M. Sharafatullah)
            Deputy Secretary,
         Ministry of Labour & Social
        Welfare, Govt. of the People's
        Republic of Bangladesh.

15 Children
DEPARTURE
Passport Control
Dacca Airport,
Bangladesh.

No. Lab/sgar/inqly/1171/13 Dated, Dacca the 17th July, 1972.

Copy forwarded to :-

1. Director, Social Services, Govt. of the People's Republic of
   Bangladesh for information and necessary action.

2. Director of Immigration and Passport, Govt. of the People's
   of Bangladesh with request to issue the necessary travel
   documents for the babies.

3. Mr. & Mrs. Fred Cappuccino, Mrs. Elizabeth Mowling and
   Dr. R.K. Ferrie for information.

              (M. Sharafatullah)
              Deputy Secretary.

Sex.	Child	Birthdate	Adopting Family.
F.	Rani	30.3.72	Mr. Robin and Mrs. Barbara Morrall 910 9th Kwe. N, Saskatoon, Sask.
M.	Orun	27.5.72	*MINISTER* Mr. Robert and Mrs. Helke Ferrie *PER 918* 3139 Princess Blvd, Burlington, Ontario
F.	████	8.7.72	*"* ████████████
M.	Omar	29.4.72	Mr. Tony and Mrs. Bonnie Boonstra 80 Baily Ave. St Thomas Ont.
F.	Ruphea Rita	15.2.72	Phillipe and Diane Rochefort 1807-623-8509, Box 1445, Espanola, Ont. or 263 Broke St. West Thunder Bay F. Ont.
M.	Bathol	27.6.72	Dale and Doreen Good Box 69, Copetown, Ont.
F.	Jorina	23.10.72	Mr. Mrs. John Morris 3 Acorn Lan, Brantford Ont.
	Amina.	3.4.72	Del and Donna Wolsay RR/3, Komoka, Ont.
M.	Prodip	25.3.72	Kenneth and Mitzi McCullough 3647 Windsor St. Halifax Nova Scotia.
F.	Shikha	12.3.72	Fred and Bonnie Cappuccino 1514-695-9827 10 Bowling Green Pointe Claire 720 Quebec.
M.	Rajib	1.7.72.	Lloyd and Sandra Simpson 1514-697-6494 5 Brunet, Pointe Claire 720 Que.
F.	Molly	4.5.72	Joel and Trudy Hartt 302 Acadia Dr. Beaconsfield, Que.
M.	Onil	23.5.72	Ray and Liz Mowling 191 Creswell Dr. Beaconsfield, Que.
F.	Regina(Rajina)	24.11.71	Pierre and Lise Hoque 653-6762 1254 Buiers St. St. Bruno. Que.
M.	Shomor	7.4.72.	Roberto and Margó Carr Ribeiro 68 Doucet, Hull, Quebec.

CHECKED DEPARTURE
Passport Control
Dacca Airport,
Bangladesh,

Letter of Approval addressed to Mother Teresa, Missionaries of Charity, by M. Sharafatullah, Deputy Secretary, Ministry of Labor & Social Welfare, People's Republic of Bangladesh, July 7, 1972.

This letter was also considered to be a travel permit for the war-babies to leave Bangladesh for Canada.

Source: Library and Archives Canada, RG 76, Vol. 1040, Box 141, *File:* 5020-1-710, Pt. 1.

Registered No. DA-1.

The
Bangladesh  Gazette

Extraordinary

Published by Authority

WEDNESDAY, OCTOBER 25, 1972

PART IIIA—Ordinances and Orders promulgated by the President of the People's Republic of Bangladesh.

GOVERNMENT OF THE PEOPLE'S REPUBLIC OF BANGLADESH

MINISTRY OF LAW AND PARLIAMENTARY AFFAIRS

(Law Division)

NOTIFICATION

No. 921-Pub.—24th October, 1972—The following Order made by the President, on the advice of the Prime Minister, of the People's Republic of Bangladesh on the 23rd October, 1972, is hereby published for general information:—

GOVERNMENT OF THE PEOPLE'S REPUBLIC OF BANGLADESH

MINISTRY OF LAW AND PARLIAMENTARY AFFAIRS

(Law Division)

President's Order No. 124 of 1972

THE BANGLADESH ABANDONED CHILDREN (SPECIAL PROVISIONS) ORDER, 1972.

WHEREAS it is expedient to provide for the special guardianship and adoption of abandoned children in Bangladesh and for matters ancillary thereto;

Now, THEREFORE, in pursuance of the Proclamation of Independence of Bangladesh, read with the Provisional Constitution of Bangladesh Order, 1972, and in exercise of all powers enabling him in that behalf, the President is pleased to make the following Order:—

1. (*1*) This Order may be called the Bangladesh Abandoned Children (Special Provisions) Order, 1972.

(*2*) It extends to the whole of Bangladesh.

2857

The *Bangladesh Abandoned Children (Special Provisions) Order, 1972* (P.O. No. 124 of 1972)

Source: Published in the *Bangladesh Gazette Extraordinary*, October 25, 1972.

(3) It shall come into force at once and shall be deemed to have taken effect on the 1st day of May, 1972.

2. In this Order, unless there is anything repugnant in the subject or context,—

(a) "adoption agency" means a person taking an abandoned child for adoption;

(b) "Director of Social Welfare" means Director of Social Welfare to the Government;

(c) "Government" means the Government of the People's Republic of Bangladesh;

(d) "abandoned child" means a child which, in the opinion of the Government, is deserted or unclaimed or born out of wedlock;

(e) "prescribed" means prescribed by rules made under this Order;

(f) "statutory guardian" means a person or authority appointed by the Government under this Order to have the care and custody of the person of an abandoned child.

3. The provisions of this Order and any rule made thereunder shall have effect notwithstanding anything inconsistent therewith contained in any other law for the time being in force.

4. (1) The guardianship of every abandoned child shall, on the commencement of this Order, stand vested in the Director of Social Welfare, who shall, by virtue of this provision, be its statutory guardian.

(2) The Government may appoint as statutory guardian any other person or authority in addition to or in place of the Director of Social Welfare.

5. The statutory guardian may make such arrangements as he deems fit for the care and welfare of the child and keep such child with such person or institution as he may specify:

Provided that if the mother or any other legal guardian of such child applies in writing to the statutory guardian for the care and custody of the child the statutory guardian may, in his discretion,

(a) temporarily deliver the child into the care and custody of the mother or the legal guardian; or

(b) divest himself of guardianship and deliver the child into the care and custody of the mother or legal guardian.

6. The statutory gurdian may deliver an abandoned child for the purpose of adoption to any adoption agency in or outside Bangladesh on such terms and conditions as may be prescribed and such delivery shall constitute a valid adoption.

The *Bangladesh Abandoned Children (Special Provisions) Order, 1972* (P.O. No. 124 of 1972)

Source: Published in the *Bangladesh Gazette Extraordinary*, October 25, 1972.

Inside

7. No Court shall call into question any action taken under this Order or any rules made thereunder.

8. No claim, suit, prosecution or other legal proceeding shall lie against the statutory guardian or any other person for anything which is in good faith done or intended or purported to be done under this Order or the rules made thereunder.

9. The Government may, by notification in the official Gazette, make rules for carrying out the purposes of this Order.

DACCA;
The 23rd October, 1972.

ABU SAYEED CHOWDHURY
President of the
People's Republic of Bangladesh.

NASIMUDDIN AHMAD
Joint Secretary.

Printed and Published by A. R. Siddiqui, Special Officer,
Bangladesh Government Press, Dacca.

The *Bangladesh Abandoned Children (Special Provisions) Order, 1972* (P.O. No. 124 of 1972)

Source: Published in the *Bangladesh Gazette Extraordinary,* October 25, 1972.

CANADA

PROVINCE OF QUEBEC

DISTRICT OF *Montreal.*

NO. *226/73*

SOCIAL WELFARE COURT

CERTIFICATE OF JUDGMENT OF ADOPTION

Judgment was rendered on the *twenty-first* day of February, one thousand nine hundred and seventy-three-------------

ordering the adoption by *Robert Rae Mowling, Personnel Director, and his wife, Elizabeth Koch,------*

domiciled at *the City of Beaconsfield, district of Montreal,*

Province of Québec, Canada of *Mark Onil Mowling-*

born on the *twenty-third day of May, one thousand nine hundred and seventy-two-*

at *Dacca, Bangladesh--*

and baptized (registered) on the *twenty-ninth day of May, one thousand nine hundred and seventy-two-*

by

(name of celebrant)

Godfather:

Godmother:

and ordering the transcription of this certificate in the duplicate register of *the Lakeshore Unitarian Church, Pointe Claire, Quebec, Canada.------------------*

SEAL

Deputy Clerk of the Social Welfare Court.

Paul Racine.

Formal Certificate of Judgement of Adoption of Mark Onil Mowling (war-baby) by Robert Ray Mowling and Elisabeth Koch at Social Welfare Court, District of Montreal, Province of Quebec, on February 21, 1973.

Source: It is in Elisabeth Koch's (Mowling) personal collection.

How I Got Here

In June 1972 you went to the capital city Dacca in Bengaldish, with some friends. This was going to be her second time to adopt a child. Laura was the first to be adopted

Like any other country Bengaldist had laws about adoption. But my mom had other ideas about adoption.

She was invited to supper at the Embassador's house. My mom talked about the laws of adoption. The one law that was standing in my mother's way was that only realatives could adopt the child. You were very lucky that the Embassador changed the law so my mom could adopt 16 kids for other familys that wanted children. You wanted to adopt me. But you knew that you should only adopt kid that were sick.

I call myself a lucky kid for two reasons.

Well one is that I was in one of Mother Teresa's orphanoge homes. And my future mom came back and saw I was sick So she adopted me right away. One the plane almost all the babies got sick. You know news travels very fast. Prime Minister Trudeau sent a letter saying congrat-ulations.

And thats how I got here. I think I'm pretty lucky to be adopted and brought to Canada. I got alot of choices and I know my mom loves me a lot

"Mother's Day" poem composed by Onil Mowling in May 1984, when he was 12 years old for his class introducing his own life "story."

Source: It is in Elisabeth Mowling's personal collection, a copy given to the author my Mrs. Mowling.

BIRTH CERTIFICATE.

(Duplicate copy should be sent to Municipality).

This is to certify that a ~~Male~~/Female child has been born from
Mrs........... Unknown........... on the day ...12.th...........
month.....May.......year...1972.......at...10.0.h. at the
Home called "~~SHISHU BHAVAN~~, ~~Dacca~~. National Board of Bengladesh
women's Rehabilitation Programme Dacca.

Signature:—

Sr. Margaret Mary M.C.

Dated:— 18/5/72
Place:— Dacca

Name: Shikha

Birth Certificate of Shikha, produced by Missionaries of Charity, *Shishu Bhavan*, Islampur, Dhaka, Bangladesh, signed by Sister Margaret Mary, Superior and statutory guardian of the war-babies born following the liberation of Bangladesh.

Source: It is in the Cappuccinos' personal collection.

This is ti certify that child. Shikha.
born on J2-5-1972 is an abandoned child,
and at present under our care at Shishu
Bhavan.
This child may be adopted by a suitable
bab family and I have no objection
as this will be best for the child's
futube development.

MISSIONARIES OF CHARITY

Margaret Mary

Superior.

Birth Certificate of Shikha, produced by Missionaries of Charity, *Shishu Bhavan,* Islampur, Dhaka, Bangladesh, signed by Sister Margaret Mary, Superior and statutory guardian of the war-babies born following the liberation of Bangladesh. This was produced to reiterate that Shikha was an abandoned baby and that she was found medically suitable to travel to Canada.

Source: It is in the Cappuccinos' personal collection.

Co-ordination Division
for External Assistance for
Relief and Rehabilitation,
Prime Minister's Secretariat,
525, Dhanmondi, Road No. 8
Dacca—5.

Cable: COEAR
Tele: 317181/9

DO. No. KMI-229   31st August, 1972

Dear Mr. Fred Cappuccino,

        Hope this will find you in good spirit
with your all babies and members of the family.
I am anxiously awaiting informations from you
about the babies you are nourishing with care,
love and sympathy. How the babies are? Are
they all happy? Are they living together still
in your residence? Please write few sentences
on them. Convey my best wishes to Mrs. Cappuccino
and Mrs. Mowling. How they are pulling on?

        We are all O.K. here including Mr. Rab
Chaudhury. We all in Bangladesh preserve good
amount of respect for people like you who have
come forward to help us rebuilding our devasted
country in different ways. I personally very
often remember you and my association though
for a short while, with your party during your
visit to Bangladesh.

        With regards,

                                Yours sincerely,

                                (K. M. Islam) 31.8.72

                                Asstt. Director.

Mr. Fred Cappuccino,
10, Bowling Green,
Pointe Claire -720,
Quebec, CANADA.

Arvida, August 26th. 1973

Dear friends,

　　Just a few words to tell you that we have moved to Arvida a few days ago. We tried to reach you, before leaving Montreal, without any success.

　　We would have liked to meet you and learn more about your trip to Bangladesh, but unfortunately Pierre was away all the time and it has been impossible. Perhaps at our next trip to Montreal...

　　Rajina is just marvellous; she seems to have adapted herself very easily; she is smiling all the time; she now stands up (with our help of course) but it is a great improvement since when she arrived she could hardly stay seated by herself for more than a few minutes. She eats and eats and eats. She now weights 18 pounds (4 pounds more than when she arrived), and she has 4 teeth.

　　She seems to be as happy with us as we are with her.

　　I hope everything is going as well with your little Shika.

Sincerely yours
Lise Hogue

Our new address:
894 Maxwell st.
Arvida
548-4441

OFFICER: / m m

CC:
DATE July 7/72
FILE   DESTROY

U N C L A S S I F I E D

FM IMMIGOTT LOG 439 JUL6/72

TO IMMIG DELHI   IMMED

FM R B BARR IMFOR

OUR 5020-1

REOURTEL JULY 5 CAPPUCCINO BANGLADISH ADOPTIONS.

CHILD WELFARE ONTARIO NOW ADVISE NOT PREPARED TO APPROVE INDIVIDUAL

CASES UNTIL IDENTITY OF CHILD KNOWN AND BANGLADESH AUTHORITIES CLEAR

FOR ADOPTION. CONSEQUENTLY INFORMATION ON IDENTITY INDIVIDUAL

CASES TO ONTARIO REQUIRED BEFORE 1009 WILL BE APPROVED. REQUEST YOU

PASS THIS INFORMATION TO DR. FERRIE. ALSO CAN YOU PROVIDE ANY

DETAILS OF POTENTIAL SPONSORS IN CANADA FOLLOWING DISCUSSIONS WITH

MRS. FERRIE AND MRS. CAPPUCCINO.

061945Z

DISTR FILE CIRC NUM

Families for Children   2243 006

lu Bowling Green
Pointe Claire 720, Quebec
August 27,1972

The Honorable Pierre Elliot Trudeau
Prime Minister of Canada
Parliment Buildings
Ottawa, Ontario

Dear Mr. Trudeau;

We are enclosing a report from our recent trip to Bangladesh in which
our adoptive parent's organization Families for Children was able to bring
back 15 babies to adoptive parents in Canada. The reason for sending you this
report is to let you know the high regard most people in Bangladesh have for
Canada and Canadians. We feel it was due to this regard that we were able to
suceed in bringing out these lovely babies.

We also feel very optimistic about the fight the people and Government in
Banglauesh are making to establish their new country. They are very dedicated.

The Canadians we met over there are people we can be proud to have
represent us; namely Emile and Rosemarie Baron and Mr. Glavin of the Canadian
High Commission, and Father Labbe of C.O.R.E.

We are sorry we did not write to sooner, but we were too exhausted when
we first got back.

Thank you and all the members of the Canadian Government who made it
possible for these babies to come in quickly. We and all the other parents
who were fortunate enough to adoptone of these babies are very grateful that
we live in Canada with such a humane and understanding Government.

Very sincerely yours;

Fred, Bonnie + Liz
Fred and bonnie Cappuccino and Eliz. Mowling

PHONE: 236-0138

HIGH COMMISSION
OF
THE PEOPLE'S REPUBLIC OF BANGLADESH Embassy Hotel,
25 Cartier Street,
Suite No. 209

No. EC/2/72   OTTAWA   June, 7, 1972

Dear Mr. Cappuccino,

      I thank you for your letter of June 1, 1972.

      I have just received a letter from Mr. Abdur
Rob Choudhury, Secretary, Co-ordination Division
for External Assistance for Relief and Rehabilitation,
Prime Minister's Secretariat, Government of
Bangladesh, stating that our Prime Minister has
approved the principle of inter-country adoption
for some of the babies you have in mind. However,
the Ministry of Social Welfare is right now working
on the details of rules and procedures for this
purpose. Some international social welfare agencies
like International Social Services, Holt Adoption
Programme etc., are also helping them.

      I will be happy to issue a visa on your
U.S. passport.

Yours sincerely,

(Abdul Momin)
High Commissioner

MA/rr

Mr. Fred Cappuccino,
10-Bowling Green,
Pointe Claire 720, Quebec,
Canada.

Letter from Abdul Momin, High Commissioner of Bangladesh in Canada to Reverend Fred Cappuccino, Secretary, Families For
Children informing of the Government of Bangladesh's intention to allow adoption of the war-babies, June, 7, 1972.

Source: It is in the Cappuccinos' personal collection.

Dear Bonnie and Fred —

Just a note to tell you how pleased we are with our new son. If we had selected him ourselves we couldn't have chosen better. I had been hoping that he would be passably good-looking, but knew that if he was healthy I really didn't have the right to ask for much more, so had been trying to prepare myself for a somewhat homely child. And what a pleasant shock — he's beautiful! He's also extremely good-natured and very sociable. He's also a very nice size — I don't feel nearly as cautious with him as I think I might with a smaller little person. Ken and he took to each other right off as well. The kind of person he is has very much eased the transition from being two to three for us. Our social worker has asked for any background information you might have on him — I don't think it's terribly important, so don't put yourself out to get it to us if you have it. We may be able to keep up with your activities through Trudy (if we both have time to write!) If not, best wishes to you in your continued work. Once again, thanks.

Maji and Ken

Wow! He's really fantastic!!

NATIONAL BOARD OF BANGLADESH WOMEN'S REHABILITATION PROGRAMME

TREC , 16/B, Road No.7, Dhanmondi R/A, Dacca-5,
Phone: 312412, 311210 & 314386 , TREC Post Box No.177, Ramna, Dacca,

April 4, 1972

TO WHOM IT MIGHT CONCERN

Re: Babies delivered by Seva Sadan, Dacca to Mother Theresa.

These babies were all delivered in absolutely normal
confinements without interference of any kind.

Because of the nutritional status and extreme youth
of the mothers, the chance of survival of any of these
children is virtually small or nil. It is to be expected
that most if not all babies born to malnourished teen age
children in this country at this time have little or no
chance of survival. Even with the best perinatal and
paediatric care available in the world they would still
not survive.

Dr.G.L.R.Davis
MB,BS,(Syd.)
Whitby Road
Milford-on-Sea
Hants.

GRAMS: BANGLADOOT
OTTAWA

PHONE: 236-0138

HIGH COMMISSION
OF
THE PEOPLE'S REPUBLIC OF BANGLADESH

C/O Embassy Hotel, Suite No. 209, 25-Cartier Street.
OTTAWA

No. EC/2/72   31st July, 1972,

Dear Mr. Cappuccino,

Although the newspapers had reported the arrival of orphan babies from Bangladesh for adoption in this country, none mentioned that you and Mrs. Cappuccino were also back. Of course, Dr. Hussain had telephoned to tell me that the babies were coming but, unfortunately as I had an important engagement that evening I could not come down to Montreal to welcome them. All the same my congratulations to you on the successful conclusion of your project.

2.   May be, one day we will be able to see to some of these babies. Meanwhile, if we could have the particulars of the adoptive parents (unless they wish to remain anonymous),we could send out congratulatory messages to them.

3.   When we meet next I would be interested to talk to you about your experiences in Bangladesh.

With regards to both of you,

Yours sincerely,

(A. Momin)
High Commissioner.

Mr. Fred Cappuccino,
I0-Bowling Green,
Pointe Claire 720, Quebec,
Canada

P.S. It is likely that next week-end and also on Monday the 7th August I will be in Montreal. That may give me one opportunity of seeing you soon. I could get in touch with you while in Montreal.

Source: From Fred and Bonnie Cappuccinos' personal collection.

Arvida, August 26th, 1972

Dear friends,

Just a few words to tell you that we have moved to Arvida a few days ago. We tried to reach you, before leaving Montreal, without any success.

We would have liked to meet you and learn more about your trip to Bangladesh, but unfortunately Pierre was away all the time and it has been impossible. Perhaps at our next trip to Montreal...

Rajina is just marvellous; she seems to have adapted herself very easily; she is smiling all the time; she now stands up (with our help of course) but it is a great improvement since when she arrived she could hardly stay seated by herself for more than a few minutes. She eats and eats and eats. She now weights 18 pounds (4 pounds more than when she arrived), and she has 4 teeth.

She seems to be as happy with us as we are with her.

I hope everything is going as well with your little Shikha.

Sincerely yours
Lise Hogue

Our new address:
894 Maxwell st.
Arvida
548-4441

Letter written on August 26, 1972 by Mrs. Lise Hogue (now Bertrand) to Reverend Fred and Bonnie Cappuccino to be sent to all adoptive parents of the first contingent of war-babies; as well, to Sister Margaret Mary in *Shishu Bhavan,* Missionaries of Charity, Islampur, Dhaka, Bangladesh, who was the statutory guardian of the war-babies, as an update on her baby, Rajina (later called Josée).

Source: The letter is in the Cappuccinos' personal collection.

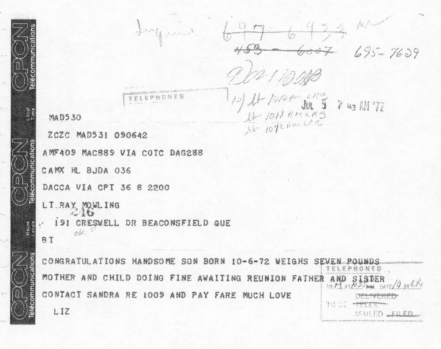

```
MAD530
    ZCZC MAD531 090642
    AMF409 MACS89 VIA CGTC DAG288
    CAMX HL BJDA 036
    DACCA VIA CPT 36 8 2200
    LT RAY MOWLING
      191 CRESWELL DR BEACONSFIELD QUE
    BT

    CONGRATULATIONS HANDSOME SON BORN 10-6-72 WEIGHS SEVEN POUNDS
    MOTHER AND CHILD DOING FINE AWAITING REUNION FATHER AND SISTER
    CONTACT SANDRA RE 1009 AND PAY FARE MUCH LOVE
      LIZ
```

Telegram sent by Elisabeth Mowling from Dhaka, Bangladesh, to her husband Ray Mowling in Montreal following the birth of a war-baby at *Shishu Bhavan* from where she picked the same boy mentioned in her telegram for adoption.

Source: It is in Fred Cappuccinos' personal collection.

MISSIONARIES OF CHARITY

This is to certify that child. Jorina
born on.23.19.74 is an unclaimed child,
and at present under our care at SHISHU
BHAVAN.

This child may be adopted by a suitable
family and I have no bbjection as this
will be best for the child's fututre
development.

MISSIONARIES OF CHARITY

Sr. Margaret Mary m.c.

Superior.

Source: Missionaries of Charity, Dhaka, Bangladesh

MISSONARIES OF CHARITY,
"SHISHU BHAVAN"
DACCA.

BIRTH CERTIFICATE.

(Duplicate copy should be sent to Municipality).

This is to certify that a ~~Male~~/Female child has been born from
Mrs..... Unknown................ on the day ..2.3rd..............
month..October.......year..1971........at........... at the
Home called "SHISHU BHAVAN", Dacca.

Signature:- *Sheangarab ken ene*
MISSIONARIES OF CHARITY
" SHISHU BHAVAN "
76, ISLAMPUR ROAD.
DACCA-1

Dated:- 29/10/71
Place:- Dacca

Name: Jorina ....

PHOTO GALLERY

This rare photo of 21 war-babies was taken during the second week of July 1972 at Mother Teresa's *Shishu Bhavan,* 26 Islampur Road, Dhaka Bangladesh. Out of 21 babies, 15 were allowed for adoption in Canadian homes. Six other prematurely-born frail babies were found medically unsuitable to sustain an overseas trip. Some had died within days.

Source: Missionaries of Charity gave each adoptive family a copy of this picture.

War babies leave for new homes

Devote to task of national reconstruction

ZILLUR RAHMAN URGES PEOPLE

Gowon says
Simla accord
a crowning
success

Kissinger holds
talks with Hanoi
negotiators

War babies

Stranded Bengalis
Particulars of
armed forces
personnel sought

Source: *The Bangladesh Observer*
July 22, 1972

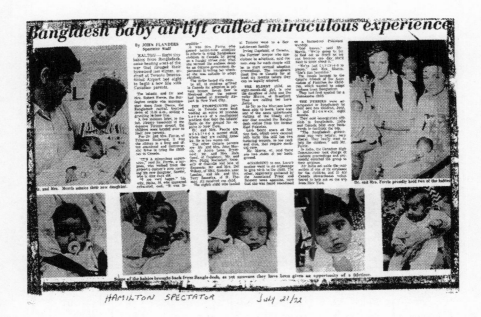

Newspaper coverage of the arrival of the war-babies in Toronto, Ontario on July 20, 1972.

Source: *Hamilton Spectator*, July 21, 1972

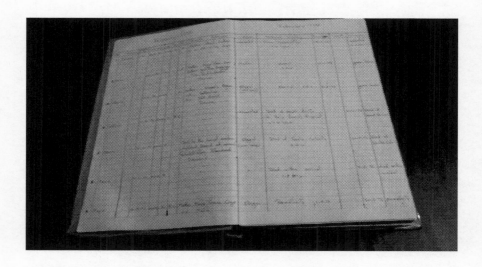

Register Book, Missionaries of Charity, *Shishu Bhavan,* Islampur, Dhaka, Bangladesh 1972. This highly confidential historic log book contains the names of the war-babies that were born in the orphanage premises as well as those war-babies who were brought to the orphanage authority to be housed for adoption.

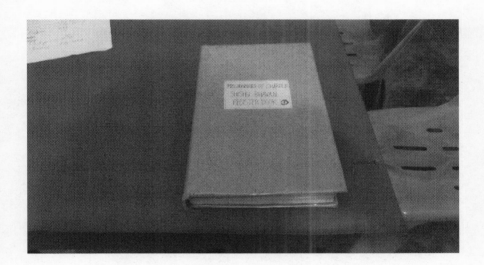

Register Book, Missionaries of Charity, *Shishu Bhavan,* Islampur, Dhaka, Bangladesh 1972. This highly confidential historic log book contains the names of the war-babies that were born in the orphanage premises as well as those war-babies who were brought to the orphanage authority to be housed for adoption.

Source: Missionaries of Charity's *Shishu Bhavan*, 26 Islampur Road, Dhaka, Bangladesh.

Staff Photos by George Bird
Rev. and Mrs. Fred Cappuccino and their newly-arrived Bangladesh baby, Shikha.

Mrs. Mitzi McCullough signs for son, held by immigration department official.

Newspaper coverage of the arrival of the war-babies in Montreal on July 20, 1972

Source: *The Montreal Star,* July 21, 1972

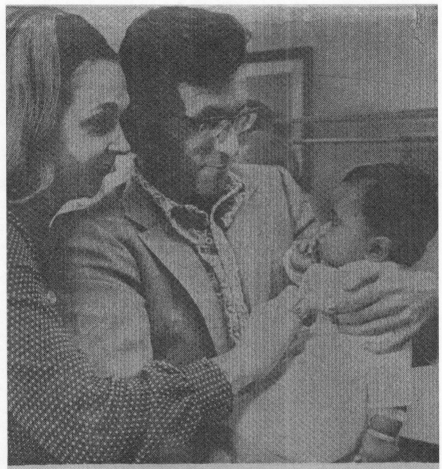

Mr. and Mrs. Pierre Hogue of St. Bruno, with little eight-month-old Rajina.

Newspaper coverage of the arrival of the war-babies in Montreal on July 20, 1972

Source: *The Montreal Star,* July 21, 1972

Bienvenue chez nous!

Ray and Elisabeth Mowling with their newly-arrived son Onil
(war-baby) and daughter Laura.

Source: *le journal Montreal,* Vol. IX, no. 38, juillet 22, 1972.

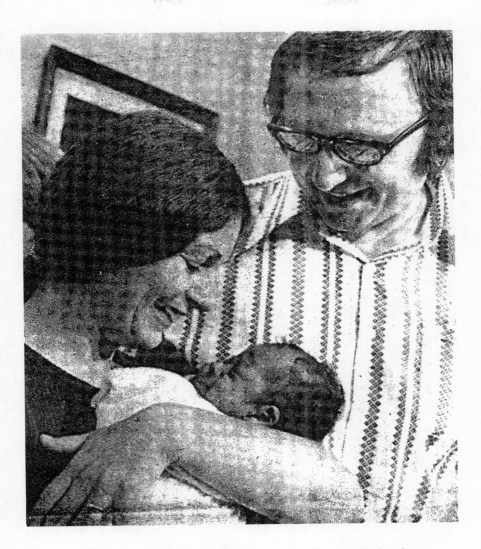

Joel and Trudy Hartt holding their newly-arrived daughter, Shama (war baby).

Source: *le journal Montreal*, Vol. IX, no. 38, juillet 22, 1972.

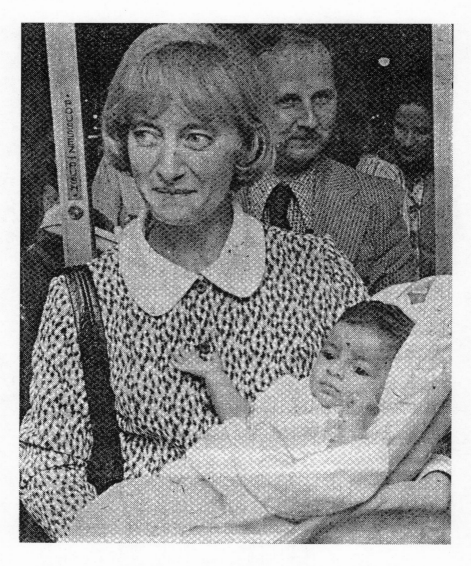

Mrs. Sandra Simpson with her newly-arrived son Rajib (war baby).

Source: *la presse,* Montreal, 21 juillet 1972.

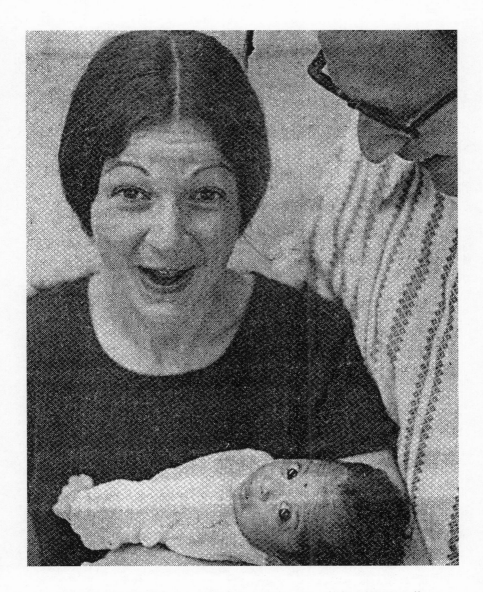

Trudy and Joel Hartt with their newly-arrived daughter Molly
(later changed to Shama).

Source: *la presse,* Montreal, 21 juillet 1972.

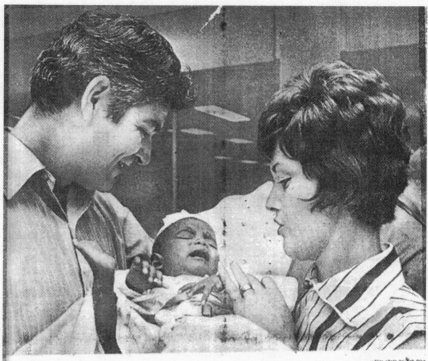

A BANGLADESH ORPHAN gets a smiling welcome from her new adoptive parents, John and Dorothy Morris of Brantford, last night at Toronto International Airport. They'll name her Lara and keep her Bengali name, Jorina, as a middle name. Seven other babies orphaned or abandoned in the aftermath of last winter's war of independence in Bangladesh arrived on same flight last night.

15 babies arrive from Bangladesh

Eight babies orphaned or abandoned after the Bangladesh war of independence met their new parents at Toronto International Airport last night.

The children, and seven more on a separate flight to Montreal, are the first Asian war orphans brought to Canada by the Families for Children Association.

The babies' ages range from nine days to eight months, and Irving Copeland, the association's lawyer, said last night it first tried to arrange adoptions for South Vietnamese children, but was thwarted by that country's law, which requires adoption by proxy there before a child can leave.

Robert Ferrie, a Burlington surgeon, and his wife, Helke, went to Bangladesh to arrange adoptions after federal and pro-

vincial government paperwork was completed at the end of June.

Earlier last month, Mrs. Ferrie went on a 3½-day hunger strike to protest what she called d

See BABIES, page 4

Source: *The Toronto Star*, July 21, 1972.

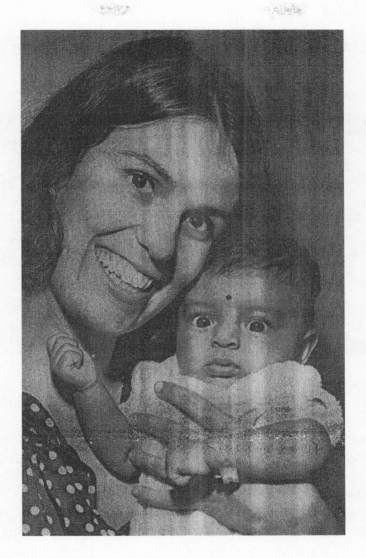

Mitzi McCullough gazes upon Prodip (now called Matthew), her son from Bangladesh.

Source: The Gazette, Montreal, July 21, 1972

Dr. Robert Ferrie and his wife Helke Ferrie of Burlington, Ontario, who went to Bangladesh in July 1972 as part of the team headed by Reverend Fred and Bonnie Cappuccino on behalf of the Families For Children. Earlier in June 1972, Helke went on a hunger-strike to protest what she claimed a deliberate stalling on the part of the Director of Child Welfare, Ontario Ministry of Community and Social Services. In Dhaka, Dr. Ferrie conducted the medical examination for the first contingent of war babies who were adopted in Canada. Of the 15 babies, the Ferries adopted two in July 1972 that they picked out and brought them along. Photo taken by the author at the Ferries' residence in Alton, Ontario in 2000.

Rani Morrall (war-baby) with an orphan at Children's Village in Sreepur, Bangladesh during the first week of February 1989. This was her first and last visit to Bangladesh through Canadopt that organized the trip with a group of adoptees from Bangladesh, accompanied by her parents.

Source: This photo is in the Morrall's personal collection.

Amina Wolsey (war-baby) is being interviewed by Mustafa Chowdhury (author) in her apartment in Toronto in July 1998.

Source: This photo was taken by Nazrul Islam Mintu, publisher of the Bengali weekly *Deshé Bideshé* who accompanied the author to Amina's apartment.

February 11, 1989 — The London Free Press

Bangladesh

RETURN FROM B

...mob scene a day before the official opening of the Sripur children's village as Ami Wolsey, 16, of Komoka is hugged ...ida, who cared for several of the London teens when they were abandoned as infants.

News coverage of the adoptees' (orphans and a group of war-babies) visit to Bangladesh

Source: *The London Free Press*, February 11, 1989.

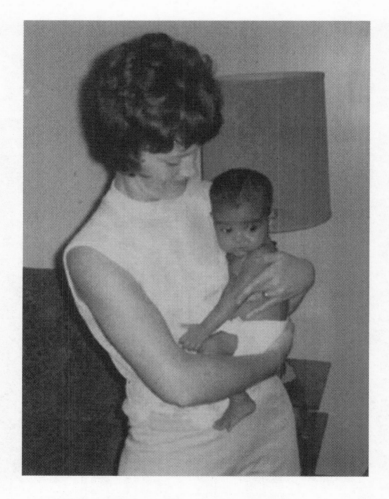

Dorothy Morris with Lara Jarina Morris (war-baby) shortly after her arrival in the Morris' family in Canada in July 1972.

Source: This picture is in the Morris' personal collection.

It doesn't take much encouragement for children to dig into their desserts as Ray Mowling finds out as he serves seconds to Panou, 6, O'Neil, 4, Laura, 5½, and Katie, 5, as Liz Mowling laughs at a joke. (Photo by George Beshiri, Brampton Guardian)

Source*: Community: The Mississauga News*, August 11, 1976.

Del and Donna Wolsey with their six children in the early 1990's.

Source: This picture is in the Wolseys' personal collection.

Lara Jarina Morris (war-baby) in her early teens in 1980's
holding a photo album with a picture of her own with her sister,
Beth Morris.

Source: This picture is in the Morris' personal collection.

Reverend Fred and Bonnie Cappuccino at author's house in Ottawa, Ontario, Canada in June 2008.

Source: This picture was taken by the author in June 2008. It is in the author's personal collection.

Onil Mowling (war-baby) with Mustafa Chowdhury at a downtown Hotel Toronto in 1999.

Source: This photo was taken by a Hotel Staff. It is in the author's personal collection.

Christopher Boonstra (war-baby) with his parents, Reverend Tony and Bonnie Boonstra in Richmond, near Ottawa, in the late 1990's.

Source: This photo was taken by the author. It is in the author's personal collection.

Lloyd and Sandra Simpson of Montreal with their 19 children out of which 4 are born to the family.

Source: *The Toronto Star*, December 24, 1981.

Reverend Fred and Bonnie Cappuccino pose with 19 of their 21 children in this 1990 family snapshot. Front row from left: Kalidas, Tibiki, Fred, Pierre, Lakshmi, Annie Laurie. Middle: William Tell, Shikha, Mei-lin, Kailash, Tulsidas, Bonnie, Mahleka, Vodinh, Tran. Back: Mohan, Kahlil, Robin Hood, Michael Scott, Ashok, Shan. Missing: Machiko and Kimchi.

Source: *The Citizen's Weekly*, July 6, 2003

Shikha Cappuccino (war-baby) in her apartment in Ottawa, Canada in 2004.

Source: This photo taken by the author in February 2004. It is in the author's personal collection.

Mustafa Chowdhury, Joel Hartt, Shama Hartt (war-baby) in Ottawa, Canada 2000.

Source: This photo taken by Mrs. Trudy Hartt. It is in the author's personal collection.

Mrs. Barbara Morrall and Rani Morrall (war-baby), surrounded by staff at Children's Village, Sreepur, near Dhaka, Bangladesh, during the first week of February 1989. Many of the staff in the picture remembered Rani when they took care of her in 1972 when they worked at *Shishu Bhavan* where Rani was born.

Source: This photo was taken by Dr. Robin Morrall. It is in the Morralls' personal collection.

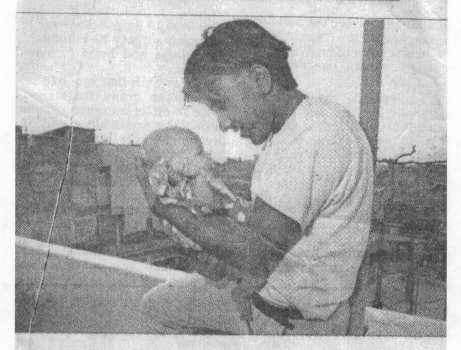

A last glimpse of Bangladesh

Ryan Good, 16, of Exeter, one of a group of London area teenagers and their parents who visited Bangladesh, holds a baby at Mother Theresa's orphanage in Dhaka where he was a child. Reporter Dahlia Reich and photographer Ed Heal of The London Free Press report on a journey that "bombarded the senses." **Pages C6-7**

Source: *The London Free Press*, February 11, 1989.

Rani Morrall dressed in Bangladeshi costume for a dance in the mid-1980.

Source: The picture is in the Morralls' personal collection.

Dorothy and John Morris with their daughter Lara Jarina Morris
(war-baby) at their home in Brantford, Ontario in 1998.

Source: This photo taken by the author. It is in the author's
personal collection.

Author, Shikha Cappuccino (war-baby) her daughter Karma, her father Reverend Fred Cappuccino and her daughter Katarina at the Ottawa-based Canada-Bangladesh Muslim Community's Annual *Iftar Mahfeel* in August 2012.

Source: This photo was taken by a volunteer at the *Iftar Mahfeel*. It is in the author's personal collection.

Shikha Cappuccino (war-baby) her daughters Katarina and Karma at the Ottawa-based Canada-Bangladesh Muslim Community's Annual *Iftar Mahfeel* in August 2012.

Source: This photo was taken by a volunteer at the *Iftar Mahfeel*. It is in the author's personal collection.

Rani Morrall with a group of orphans at Children's Village, Sreepur, near Dhaka, Bangladesh, during the first week of February 1989.

Source: This photo was taken by Dr. Robin Morrall. It is in the Morralls' personal collection.

Rajib Cappuccino Simpson (war-baby) in his early teen.

Source: This photo is in the Simpson's personal collection.

Rajib Simpson (war-baby) with an orphan in the Children's Village in Sreepur, near Dhaka, Bangladesh in 1989.

Source: This photo is in the Simpson's personal collection.

Ryan Good (war-baby) vacationing in Jamaica with his wife Martine and children, Calin and Cadelle in the summer of 2012.

Source: This photo was given to the author by Ryan Good to share with people.

Josée Hogue(war-baby) and her father Pierre Hogue in 2000.

Source: This photo is in Josée's personal collection.

Josée Hogue (war-baby) when she was ten years old.

Source: This photo is in Josée's personal collection.

Shama Hartt (war-baby) with her daughter Savannah in 2012.

Source: This photo is in Shama Hartt's personal collection.

Larra Morris (war-baby) in 2012

Source: This photo is in Lara Morris' personal collection.

Quotations from the war babies

"My life is full and I have defined *who* I am because of the experiences I have had. The past is the past" **(Amina Lynn Wolsey).**

"My parents are the one who nurtured and molded me to be the way that I am today" **(Amina Lynn Wolsey).**

"I am my parents' daughter and many of my beliefs and practices come directly from their modeling. Out of my life experiences, I take with me different pieces to guide me as an educator" **(Amina Lynn Wolsey).**

"As our parents celebrated humanity, equality for all people was believed, thought and practiced. With firsthand accounts of inclusion and mainstreaming, we are survivors of a road less travelled. Our trials and tribulations have made us who we are. We had the visual appearance of minorities. However, we had been raised in Canadian households as infants. Assimilated into the Canadian culture, we were a new generation of Canadians creating new history" **(Amina Lynn Wolsey).**

"In all these years, I have never really wondered about my past, my parents or a family I may have left behind in Bangladesh and I have never made any attempt to try to find them" **(Lara Jarina Morris).**

"I consider John and Dorothy as my dad and mom with incredible heartwarming love and had never pictured in my mind anyone else as my father and mother" **(Lara Jarina Morris).**

"Even if it was possible to find my roots, I would not know where to begin. I would like to learn the genetic history of my family, and from whom I have received my personality and character traits, however, I don't think I could maintain a

relationship with my biological family at this stage in my life"
(Lara Jarina Morris).

"My family has always treated me as one of its own even though
we are not genetically connected. I have never been made to feel
'alienated' or 'isolated' because I don't look like any members of
my family, and they have never made me feel different" **(Lara
Jarina Morris).**

"As my understanding of war in general and the atrocities that
occurred began to increase, so did my realization that I was a
result of the Liberation War of Bangladesh. My birth mother was
raped by a Pakistani soldier. This realization did not produce any
ill will or discontent" **(Ryan Badol Good).**

"Emphatically, my conception of parents was that of my
adoptive Canadian parents. Any thoughts of my birth parents
were shielded by feelings of overall detachment" **(Ryan Badol
Good).**

"Bangladesh, we were both born of blood. We are both babies of
a very tragic but important war. Out of this ferocious bath, you
and I were born" **(Ryan Badol Good).**

"My name is Badol. I have two mothers – one calls me Ryan,
and the other calls me Badol. The one who calls me Ryan,
I have known all my life. The one who calls me Badol, I have
never met. I was born in Bangladesh to the mother who calls me
Badol. Three weeks later, I was born in Canada to the mother
who calls me Ryan. A Pakistani soldier raped the mother who
calls me Badol. I am a war baby" **(Ryan Badol Good).**

"In the crowd I was no different than anyone else. Indeed, in
Bangladesh, I am no different in appearance than the locals.
The problem is that while my genes are Bengali, my brain
is Canadian. I am barricaded against the Bengali and I am
barricaded against the western. This fact is tough to bear" **(Ryan
Badol Good).**

MUSTAFA CHOWDHURY

"Knowing what I know about the circumstances of my conception and the time period, I have never felt the urge to meet or find my 'putative' father. I was told that given the war, it is most likely that he raped my birth mother. As for meeting or finding my birth mother, I've never felt urgency" (**Shama Jameela Mollie Hartt**).

"There is part of me that would be interested in teaching ESL in Bangladesh, but there is a part of me that is also very conscious of what colonialism has done to the world, and in particular to underdeveloped countries like Bangladesh" (**Shama Jameela Mollie Hartt**).

"If I were to meet my biological parents I don't think that I would feel a need to integrate them with my adoptive parents or come to terms with them. To date, there has never been a void because of it. Happiness has never been based on knowing who they are, or were" (**Onil Mark Mowling**).

"While growing up, I had never experienced any feeling of isolation or alienation because of my adoption" (**Onil Mark Mowling**).

"Upon hearing of the tragedy I wish I could have found my birth mother and let her know how deeply sorry I was for her suffering and that something good came out of her sacrifice (victimization)" (**Onil Mark Mowling**).

"My birth mother is neither a woman of disrepute nor selfish and uncaring. There is no need to punish the birth mother for relinquishing her child. Every time I think of my birth mother, I thank her for trying her best. I thank her again for giving me up when she knew that she could not have offered me what I needed as a child" (**Onil Mark Mowling**).

"I am not attached to Bangladesh at an emotional level. This can be explained most likely by my early departure from the country. Emotions are created by thoughts. And thoughts are sometimes the reflections produced by experience. In my case, I have no experience that I can recall about Bangladesh, hence there are no emotional responses available for me to create an attachment for a country I don't remember" **(Onil Mark Mowling).**

"If I were to place an emotional attachment to any place it would be Canada. My home. For it was here I was accepted and nurtured and loved. And that's what makes a home for me" **(Onil Mark Mowling).**

INDEX

A

abandonment, xvi, xviii, xxxi, xlii–xliii, xlvii, 3–4, 14–15, 19–20, 22, 41–42, 276–78, 372, 389–90, 429–30, 440–41

abortion, xxxi–xxxii, 3–4, 8, 12–16, 18–19, 29, 32, 37, 43, 53, 99, 356

ACS (adopted child syndrome), lii, 362, 383, 461

adopted children, xxviii, xxxvi, li, 28, 52, 57, 59, 77, 80, 180, 362–64, 374–75, 387–88, 405–6, 453–54

adoption
  in-country, 150–51
  informal, xlvii, 26–27
  Islamic concept of, 28
  legal, 27, 56, 100, 151
  legality of, 55
  mixed-race, 53
  private, 51
  provision of, 51
  trans-cultural, 43

adoption agencies, 48–49, 66, 91, 188, 365, 463

adoption applications, 85, 92–93

Adoption: Current Issues and Trends (Sachdev), 431, 439

adoption decree, 159, 163

Adoption: The Grafted Tree (Wishard), 439

adoption laws, 55, 58, 76

adoption plans, 37, 293

adoption statistics, 51, 365

adoption triad, 27, 463

agencies, child welfare, 30

agreement, 24, 51, 57, 73, 318, 351

Air Canada, 111, 120–21, 128, 135–36

Air India, 92, 120, 124

Akhter, Halima Hanum, 13

Alexander, Lincoln, 87, 106, 114

Algonquin College of Applied Arts and Technology, 185

Allen, Michael, 401

Anglican Church of Canada, 68, 144, 148, 160, 168, 170

anxiety, li, 129, 135, 154, 192, 199, 217, 231, 268, 278, 293, 300, 304, 327, 329

Askewith, Gordon, 90

Awal, Abdul, xlii, 40–41, 154, 157, 169, 459

ayas (midwives), 99, 122–23, 211, 262, 403, 464

B

Baldwin, James, 407

Bangladesh, Occupied, vii, xv, xxvii, xxx–xxxi, xl, xlvi, 1, 5–9, 22, 34–35, 62–63, 176, 230, 329–30, 387

Bangladesh Abandoned Children (Special Provisions) Order, 1972, xlix–l, 46, 58, 100, 151, 154, 460, 469

Bangladesh Project, 66–70, 75, 91–92, 112–13, 115–16, 118–19, 165, 167–68,

215, 339, 356
CCSD (Canadian Council on Social Development), 69–70, 76, 113, 145, 469
CEGEP (Collège d'enseignement general et professionnel), 242, 253, 423
Chaudhury, Abdur Rab, xlii, 40, 66, 96, 459
childbirth, 12, 364
child care, 41, 43
Child Haven International, 191, 198, 202
childlessness, xxxvi, 354, 450
"Child of the Rivers" (Rani), 274–76
children, xxxiv–xxxix, 51–55, 79–91, 112–18, 167–72, 175–83, 188–98, 207–12, 216–20, 234–43, 285–87, 293–99, 315–21, 345–81, 431–34
    abandoned, xvi, xviii, li, 28, 43, 46, 49–50, 54, 61, 151–52, 467
    biological, 77, 191, 207, 210, 351, 381, 387
    homeless, 62
    home-made, 196
    illegitimate, xv, 42, 448
    multiracial, 204, 308, 315, 319, 369, 375
    natural-born, 189, 307
    orphaned, 28, 30, 79, 288, 317, 431, 452
    unwelcome, xv, 17, 31, 50, 76, 371, 387, 450
Children of Bangladesh (Walles), 404
Children's Service Centre, 116, 345
Children's Village, 344, 400, 517, 531, 537, 539

child's right, 25
Child Welfare, 31, 52, 59, 70–71, 73, 88, 90–91, 113, 115–17, 161, 170, 204, 446, 516
Child Welfare Act, 51
Child Welfare League of America, 349, 471
child welfare professionals, 70, 172
Chowdhury, Farouk, 341, 410
Chowdhury, Mustafa, iii–iv, ix, xxvi, 115, 140, 164–67, 174, 188, 204, 295, 332, 344–49, 382–84, 397, 425–26
Chowdhury, Pauline, 379
CHRP (certified human resources professional), 287
CIC (Citizenship and Immigration Canada), xxix, 52, 186
CIDA (Canadian International Development Agency), 63, 67, 94, 111–12, 166, 307–8, 349, 459
Citizen Adoption Coalition, 236
citizenship, 50, 52, 159, 181, 186
COAC (Council on Adoptable Children), 54, 461
Concordia University, 236, 242
Cook County Hospital, 188
Copeland, Irving, 93, 159
CORR (Christian Organization for Relief and Rehabilitation), xxx, 16–17, 33, 86, 94, 98, 153, 169, 457–58
CUSO (Canadian University Services Overseas), 93

D

Davis, Geoffrey, xxxii, xlii, 5, 14, 23–24, 357
Davis, William, 87, 161, 170, 383

M

Mackasey, Bryce, 76–78, 106, 114, 121, 135, 146, 167
MacKrell, Vivian, 88
Malcolm X, 407
Mary, Margaret, xxxi, 14–15, 17, 49–50, 98–99, 101–5, 151–52, 154–59, 169, 198–99, 248, 252, 284–85, 357–59, 450
Maxville Elementary School, 199
McConnell, Ron, 270–71
McCullough, Mathew, 174, 259
McCullough, Mitzi, 135, 138, 141, 259, 381, 515
McDermott, Marvin, 81
Mcdonell Memorial Hospital, 190, 194
McGill University, 178
McKinney, Wayne, 357
McLellan, Gordon, 58, 88, 113
McNie, Jack, 87
Meadowvale Public School, 299
medical practitioners, 13
Medway Secondary School, 337
Mennonite Reporters, 144
Millman, Dan, 303, 306
Missionaries of Charity, 14–15, 32, 49, 98, 151, 165, 169, 173, 181, 221, 241, 284, 292, 337, 355
Moen, Ken, 271
Mohawk College, 287
Momin, Abdul, 64, 66, 96, 146, 150, 457
Montreal Star, 143–44, 166–67, 192–93, 345–46, 472, 508–9
Morrall, Barbara, 80, 129, 133, 140, 144, 166, 260–62, 265, 347, 362, 375, 382, 410, 531

Morrall, Kim, 270
Morrall, Robin, 80, 114, 133–34, 140, 144, 166, 260, 262–64, 266, 268, 270–71, 276–77, 347, 362, 367
Morris, Dorothy, 81, 115, 129, 132, 141, 161, 166, 170, 279, 281–83, 285–86, 290, 347–48, 360–61, 381–83
Morris, John, 81–82, 115, 129, 132–33, 141, 170, 262–63, 270–72, 279, 281–82, 285–86, 295–96, 351, 353–54, 374–75
Morris, Lara, 288–90, 348, 397, 424, 427–28, 544
Mowling, Elisabeth, lvii, 24, 67, 80, 92–93, 96, 102, 109, 115, 121, 124, 128, 295–97, 382–83, 458–59
Mowling, Onil, 136, 141, 164, 174, 290–92, 296, 298–307, 348, 362, 393–94, 398, 408, 421, 425, 427–29
Mowling, Ray, 135–36, 166, 291, 295
Muhammad, Prophet, 28
Mujib administration, xvi, xxxii, xlii, xlvii–xlix, lvii, 13, 15, 33–35, 38, 61–62, 93–96, 146, 150, 209, 430
Multiculturalism Act, 377
Munro, John, 120, 129
murder, xxvii, xxx, xliii, xlv, 3–4, 7–9, 22
Muslim Family Ordinance of 1911, 26
Muslims, 26, 28, 30, 57, 203, 225, 242, 465

N

Nari Punarbashan Board, 16, 18, 45
newborns, xvii, xlviii, 2, 15–17,
     19–21, 32, 34–35, 37, 40, 42,
     44–45, 99, 104–5, 108, 122
New Delhi, xxiii, 21, 24, 106–7,
     110, 124–26, 128, 470, 472
Newsletter, 59, 64, 66–67, 112–13,
     165, 346, 348, 471
NGOs (Nongovernment Organi-
     zation), xxix, 13, 42, 61–63,
     308
North American Council on Adop-
     tive Children, 197
Northern Secondary School, 324
North Park Collegiate and Vocation-
     al School, 287

O

ODS (Open Door Society), 53,
     236, 319
OISE (Ontario Institute of Studies
     in Education), 337
OMDP (Ontario Management De-
     velopment Program), 287
Ontario Federation of South Asian
     Studies, 197
Ontario Medal for Good Citizen-
     ship, 197
Orangeville Secondary School, 213
Order of Canada, x, 197, 322
orphanages, xl–xli, 15–19, 21,
     32–33, 95–99, 104–8, 158–
     61, 198–99, 211, 272–75,
     281–82, 284–85, 287–89,
     393–94, 398–403
orphans, xvi, 25–28, 30, 34, 39–41,
     81–82, 150–52, 195–98,
     204–6, 208–9, 260–61,
     280–82, 316–22, 352–54,

403–4
     adoption of, 198, 260, 280, 287,
     384
OSAP (Ontario Students Assistance
     Program), 214
Ottawa, xxvi, 64, 71–72, 74–75,
     77–78, 80, 86, 89, 91, 94,
     177, 179, 185, 424–25,
     529–30
Ottawa Christian School, 177
Ottawa Citizen, 143, 192–93, 472
Ottawa Journal, 143–44, 194, 345,
     472

P

pain, xxi, liv, 7, 197, 217, 274–76,
     278, 282, 320, 364, 443, 448
Pakistan, xv, xix–xx, xxiii, xlvi, 23,
     26, 55–56, 59, 69, 95, 144,
     254, 307, 388, 466
parentage, mixed, 43, 190
parenthood, lvii, 27, 29, 49–50,
     171–72, 260, 349, 351, 360,
     434, 449, 453, 471
parenting, ix, xlviii, liii, 103, 172,
     197, 266, 295, 305, 351,
     360, 366, 368, 384, 440
parents, biological, 27–28, 50, 171,
     181, 334, 353, 359, 365–66,
     370, 372, 375, 388, 392,
     394, 439
Parksville Elementary School, 183
Parksville Middle School, 183
Parkview Elementary School, 337
Partie Quebecois, 181
passports, 107–9
Pelletier, Jean, 93
Penal Code of 1860, 13
Perkins, Lucy Fitch, 332
Peron, Monique, 85
pluralism, 179, 334, 340, 376–77, 439

104, 292, 466

sexual assault, 1–3, 357

sexual violence, xvii, xix–xxi, xxv, xxx, xxxvii, xli, xliii, xlvi, lii, 1, 3, 5, 10–11, 257, 338

shame, xlvi, 8–9, 18, 45, 94, 274, 439, 441, 444–45

Shank, Bill, 270–71

Sharp, Mitchell, 65, 73, 112–13, 145, 165

Shishu Bhavan, xxxi, xxxiii–xxxiv, xl, 15–18, 32, 45–46, 104, 107–8, 152–53, 158, 165, 198–99, 220–21, 262, 358–59

Shoultz, Odert von, 14

Simon, Rita, 406, 430

Simpson, Lloyd, lvii, 84, 111, 135, 138, 141, 291, 316, 319, 369, 373, 382, 527

Simpson, Sandra, lvii, 81, 84, 100, 110–11, 121, 135, 138–39, 141, 177, 265, 316, 318–22, 324–27, 349

Sir George College, 236

skin color, 212, 252–53, 297, 374, 405, 407, 418, 420–21

Sobhan, K. M., 6, 14, 22, 24

soldiers, xlvi, 2, 7, 11, 18, 35, 40, 44, 52, 54, 144–45, 149, 188, 257, 296

American, xlvi, 54, 188, 446

Pakistani, 7, 18, 35, 40, 43, 144–45, 149, 229, 388, 390, 413, 546

songwriting, 269, 274

South Asian of the Year Award, 197

South Huron District High School, 220

South Perth Centennial School, 220

South Vietnam, 145, 317, 352

Star-Phoenix, 145, 262–63, 473

St. Columbia Presbyterian Church, 178

stillborn babies, 17, 292

St. Joseph's Hospital, 215

suicide, xlvi, 3–4, 7–9, 11, 33, 266, 270, 363

Sunderban Hotel, 401

T

Talisman, Sidney, 39

Taylor, Rosemary, 62, 190, 317

TD Bank, 316

TDH (Terre des Hommes), 54, 62, 98, 291, 461, 467

Teresa, Mother, xvii, 16–17, 32–33, 46, 109, 118, 141, 159, 181, 198, 202, 220, 241, 271, 337

Tiny Talent Time, 290

Toronto, 22, 66, 73, 83, 87, 111, 120–21, 128, 133, 263, 307, 323–24, 421–22, 425, 469–71

Toronto East General Hospital, 401

Toronto Star, 23, 111, 143, 147, 168, 207, 400–401, 473, 514, 527

transracial adoption, 43, 47, 52, 172, 190, 239, 376, 430–32, 437, 467

Triseliotis, John, 400, 426, 451, 471

Trudeau, Pierre Elliott, 62, 73, 86, 115–16, 135–36, 146, 168, 344, 454

truth, xix, xxv, xxxix–xl, 8, 183, 228, 232, 240, 267, 278, 297, 299, 373–75, 403, 406

Turner, Mary Jane, 80

Y

yateem (orphan), 28
York University, 242, 244, 299, 337,
    340, 409, 423
Young, Dorothy, 132

Z

Zaman, Hasan uz, 74

Mustafa Chowdhury's narrative impressively details the lives of the war-babies through the years, with anecdotes of their rearing, nurturing, and becoming adults. We know of no other book with the depth of purpose, scope, and revelation of heretofore ignored historical facts. His work is an invaluable contribution to the story of adoption in Bangladesh and Canada. It is a fascinating book for anyone interested in inter-racial adoption. Chowdhury investigated a wide range of topics including the importance of family and of tender loving care for each member of the family. We see both the adopters and the adoptees talk about their different experiences of courage, perseverance, and love, each from their own perspective.

Reverend Fred and Bonnie Cappuccino

As parents of one of the 15 Bangladeshi adoptees that Mustafa Chowdhury writes about, we greatly appreciate his effort to document their stories with sensitivity and compassion. His hard work has resulted in a book that is a "must-read" for people interested in interracial adoption and the early history of Bangladesh. Bravo and thank you, Mustafa for this labour of love.

Barb and Robin Morrall

Bangladesh won its independence from Pakistan in 1971. It left many dead, victims scarred for life and others simply forgotten. Many of those dead and scarred and forgotten were commonly referred to as "war babies." Many were adopted internationally. But where is their story? What does silence of the plight of the babies of war mean? What happened to those adopted? Where did they go? How have they fared? Mustafa Chowdhury's book, born out of commitment and perseverance, is their story; they are now mature, successful, talented members of society and can speak for themselves. His book inspires and helps us begin the discussion and invites us to honour their lives.

Del and Donna Wolsey

Printed in the United States
By Bookmasters